The Handbook of
Technical Analysis

The Wiley Trading series features books by traders who have survived the market's ever changing temperament and have prospered—some by reinventing systems, others by getting back to basics. Whether a novice trader, professional or somewhere in-between, these books will provide the advice and strategies needed to prosper today and well into the future. For more on this series, visit our Web site at www.WileyTrading.com.

Founded in 1807, John Wiley & Sons is the oldest independent publishing company in the United States. With offices in North America, Europe, Australia and Asia, Wiley is globally committed to developing and marketing print and electronic products and services for our customers' professional and personal knowledge and understanding.

The Handbook of Technical Analysis

The Practitioner's Comprehensive Guide to Technical Analysis

MARK ANDREW LIM

Other Wiley Editorial Offices
John Wiley & Sons, 111 River Street, Hoboken, NJ 07030, USA
John Wiley & Sons, The Atrium, Southern Gate, Chichester, West Sussex, P019 8SQ, United Kingdom
John Wiley & Sons (Canada) Ltd., 5353 Dundas Street West, Suite 400, Toronto, Ontario, M9B 6HB, Canada
John Wiley & Sons Australia Ltd., 42 McDougall Street, Milton, Queensland 4064, Australia
Wiley-VCH, Boschstrasse 12, D-69469 Weinheim, Germany

ISBN 978-1-118-49891-0 (Paperback)
ISBN 978-1-118-49893-4 (ePDF)
ISBN 978-1-118-49892-7 (ePub)

Typeset in 11/14 pt. Sabon LT Std Roman by Aptara Inc., New Delhi, India
Printed in Singapore by Markono Print Media Pte. Ltd.

10 9 8 7 6 5 4 3 2 1

I dedicate this work to my family, for their unconditional support and encouragement through thick and thin.

Contents

Foreword

I sincerely believe that this handbook is a feast for serious technical traders as well as for hardcore technical analysis practitioners. This handbook is especially meant for beginner professionals looking to improve their trading performance, and in the process, trying to avoid some of the more painful collisions with complex charting theories. I wish I had this book years ago. That said, I enjoy reading it today, finding Mark's pearls of wisdom an aid to improve my technical trading.

Mark is one of Malaysia's distinguished technical analysis gurus whose dazzling mind produces more fresh ideas in a book than most other experts in an entire lifetime. Since knowing him back in 2002, he has been an influential mentor and a respectable trader, becoming well known from 2002 to 2007 as being one of Malaysia's finest traders. Most of his trading techniques and theories in the handbook are now included in most of my trading programs.

There are a lot of books on technical analysis. Most of them concentrate on very specific items, exploring a particular concept in great depth. A long and detailed handbook covering a broad range of topics with practical value such as this is much more difficult to find. Mark gives his readers diverse market indicators to identify positive investment climates, backing them up with in-depth theoretical explanations and real-world chart examples. He exposes powerful technical signals and uncovers some of the most obscure concepts in technical analysis, reducing them to a set of very clear and lucid rules.

I believe that this handbook provides an excellent starting point, as well as a comprehensive reference text for technically orientated practitioners. It outlines the primary principles of technical analysis and provides a solid foundation for moving forward into more advanced and cutting-edge concepts. For the experienced trader, this book will also serve as a reliable refresher, reinforcing good technical trading practices that are both enduring and effective. It explains technical trading in a clear and easily understandable format, examining entire concepts, from start to finish. All techniques discussed are succinctly illustrated with clear chart examples.

Mark's handbook points the way for readers interested in the master chartist approach. He distils his vast market expertise into a simple set of technical guidelines and rules. As an example, Mark explains why he believes the markets respond in specific behavioral manner to phenomena such as volume divergence and breakaway gaps. His chapter on volume and volatility also makes it clear why market tops react in a certain manner before the 'storm' and why market bottoms tend to 'storm' before the rebound. These simple but yet profound concepts will change the way many readers approach trading and investing in the markets.

I congratulate Mark on his hard work in producing this profound handbook. It is a big achievement for the technical analysis community and we are proud of his contribution. Finally, I believe that the only thing readers need to do after reading this handbook is to make a commitment to apply his work, with the appropriate mind-set to become successful traders and investors.

I wish all readers and technical analysis fans lots of success, happy learning, and trading with technical analysis!

–Dr. Nazri Khan,

MSTA, CFTe, President, Malaysian Association of Technical Analyst (MATA); Vice President, Affin Investment Bank Malaysia

Preface

The Handbook of Technical Analysis provides a unique and comprehensive reference for serious traders, analysts, and practitioners of technical analysis. This book explains the definitions, concepts, applications, integration, and execution of many technical-based trading tools and approaches, with detailed coverage of various technical and advanced money management issues. It also exposes the many strengths and weaknesses of various popular technical approaches and offers effective solutions wherever possible. Innovative techniques for pinpointing and handling potential market breakouts and reversals are also discussed throughout the handbook. A dedicated chapter on advanced money management helps complete the trader's education.

This handbook will prove indispensable to foreign exchange, bond, stock, commodity futures, CFD, and option traders, especially if they are looking for a fast and comprehensive route to mastering some of the most powerful tools and techniques available for analyzing price and market behavior. It is replete with hundreds of illustrations, tables, and charts, giving the trader and investor an instant visual understanding of the underlying principles and concepts discussed. Markets analyzed include bonds, commodity, equities, and foreign exchange.

With extensive content and coverage, *The Handbook of Technical Analysis* also provides the perfect self-contained, self-study exam preparatory guide for students intending to sit for examinations in financial technical analysis. This book helps prepare students to sit for various professional examinations in financial technical analysis, such as the International Federation of Technical Analysts CFTe Levels I and II (USA), STA Diploma (UK), Dip TA (AUS), as well as the Market Technicians Association CMT Levels I, II, and III (USA) examinations in financial technical analysis. This handbook is organized in an accessible manner that allows the students to readily identify the topics and concepts that they will need to know for the exam. It covers the most important topics, as well as incorporating the latest technical developments in the markets so as to give the students a real-world appreciation of the topics learned. The student will find important learning outcomes at the beginning of each chapter.

The Handbook of Technical Analysis aims to be as visual as possible. Most of the charts and illustrations in this handbook were created with the objective that they would provide a rapid and efficient review of all the concepts and applications upon the second or third reading. This makes it the perfect tool for students reviewing for an examination.

OVERVIEW OF THE BOOK CONTENTS

Chapter 1 (Introduction to the Art and Science of Technical Analysis) introduces the reader to the general assumptions, approaches, and classifications associated with the application of technical analysis. It introduces the concept of the self-fulfilling prophecy and information discounting and deals with the issue of subjectivity in technical analysis.

Chapter 2 (Introduction to Dow Theory) introduces the basic concept of Dow Theory and its various tenets. It also deals with the current challenges and applicability of Dow Theory. Much of modern classical technical analysis is derived on the original assumptions of Dow Theory, and as such represents an important chapter.

Chapter 3 (Mechanics and Dynamics of Charting) describes the mechanics of chart construction and how price is quantized and filtered into OHLC data. The significance of OHLC data is dealt with in detail, including four different definitions of gaps. Charts are classified in terms of five different constant measures and how they are affected by the type of chart scaling employed. There is also a detailed discussion about how trade performance and reward to risk ratios are affected by the bid-ask spread, with respect to long and short entry and exit orders. Finally, various types of futures contracts are covered, focusing on rollover premiums and discounts, backwardation, contango, and back-adjusted and unadjusted futures charts.

Chapter 4 (Market Phase Analysis) deals specifically with market phase, describing the various phases via numerous technical approaches. It analyzes and interprets market phase in terms of volume and open interest action, chart patterns, moving averages, divergence, price momentum, sentiment, cyclic action, Elliott waves, and Sakata's method. This helps the practitioner better anticipate and forecast potential phases in the market with more consistency.

Chapter 5 (Trend Analysis) deals with the various definitional issues associated with trend action. It also introduces the reader to the concept of wave degrees or cycles. It points out that the inability to identify wave degrees may very well result in ineffective technical analysis and trade performance. The chapter then covers the 16 important price action characteristics that will greatly improve the forecastibility of potential reversal and continuation in the markets. The *bar stochastic ratio oscillator* is also introduced. Price filters are discussed in detail and classified into three main categories. This is followed by the description of the various types of trade orders and their functions. The chapter also covers stoplosses and their relationship with proportional sizing. Trendlines, channel construction, fan lines, trend retracements, price gaps, trend reversal forecasts, and continuations are also covered in detail.

Chapter 6 (Volume and Open Interest) deals with volume and open interest action and defines volume divergence with respect to price-based and non-price-based volume indicators. VWAP, volume filters, volume cycles, and various volume oscillators are also discussed, pinpointing some of their weaknesses and possible solutions.

Chapter 7 (Bar Chart Analysis) covers bar chart analysis. It presents the reader various generic reversal and continuation setups with respect to single, double, triple, and multiple price bar formations. It also describes the significance of the 16 price action characteristics and how they can be employed to forecast potential price bar reversals and continuations in the market. Finally, various popular price bar formations are discussed via numerous chart examples.

Chapter 8 (Window Oscillators and Overlay Indicators) classifies indicators into window oscillators and price overlay indicators. Overlay indicators are further subdivided into numerical, geometrical, horizontal, and algorithmic indicators. The differences between static and dynamic indicators are also explained. The practitioner is then introduced to the seven main approaches to analyzing oscillators. Cycle tuned oscillators, multiple timeframe oscillator analysis, and various popular oscillators and indicators are described in detail.

Chapter 9 (Divergence Analysis) describes the application of divergence in technical analysis. Detailed coverage of the definitional issues helps clarify the confusion surrounding the topic. The practitioner is introduced to bullish, bearish, standard, and reverse divergence. Various explanations are also presented with respect to the functioning of reverse divergence. The concepts of double divergence, detrending, and signal alternation are also covered in detail. The chapter concludes with numerous chart examples illustrating the various forms of divergence in equities and commodities.

Chapter 10 (Fibonacci Number and Ratio Analysis) introduces the practitioner to Fibonacci ratio and number analysis. It covers Fibonacci retracements, extensions, expansions, and projections with numerous chart examples. All Fibonacci calculations are clearly explained and illustrated. The differences between numerically and geometrically based Fibonacci operations are also discussed. Guidelines for drawing Fibonacci retracements in single, double, and multiple leg retracements are covered in detail. Fibonacci price and time ratio analysis of Elliot waves are also explored. Various popular Fibonacci applications such as fan lines, channel expansions, and arc projections are illustrated via real-world charts.

Chapter 11 (Moving Averages) analyzes various moving averages, such as exponential, simple, and weighted moving averages. The practitioner is shown how to calculate various averages. The chapter extensively covers the seven main components and nine main applications of moving averages. Moving averages functioning as signals and triggers are also discussed.

Chapter 12 (Envelopes and Methods of Price Containment) covers price bands or envelopes and their various modes of price containment. The practitioner is introduced to the six main functions of a price envelope. The different forms of central value that may be adopted by an envelope and the construction of the upper and lower bands are also analyzed in detail. The practitioner is then shown how to tune the bands with respect to the dominant cycles in the markets. The five main forms of price containment are illustrated with suggestions for effective entry and exit of the bands.

Chapter 13 (Chart Pattern Analysis) discusses the application of chart pattern analysis. A detailed breakdown of the classification of chart patterns is presented with specific examples. There is extensive coverage of the minimum measuring objective, conditions for pattern completion, and alternative price targets. The chapter concludes with the extensive treatment of many popular reversal and continuation chart patterns.

Chapter 14 (Japanese Candlestick Analysis) introduces the practitioner to Japanese candlestick analysis. Many of the most popular Japanese candlestick formations are presented and covered in detail. Japanese candlestick formations should be read within the context of the market, and this is achieved with reference to the 16 price action characteristics discussed extensively in this chapter. The practitioner is then shown how to integrate Japanese candlestick analysis with other forms of technical analysis, such as cycles, chart patterns, oscillators, Ichimoku Kinko Hyu charting, Fibonacci levels, volume action, and moving averages.

Chapter 15 (Point-and-Figure Charting) covers Point-and-Figure charting, focusing on the minimum continuation and reversal box size, vertical and horizontal counts, box filtering, and the effects of chart scaling, as well as coverage of the most popular point and figure formations.

Chapter 16 (Ichimoku Charting and Analysis) presents a powerful set of price overlay indicators, collectively referred to as Ichimoku Kinko Hyu charting. The chapter focuses on the construction, analysis, and application of the various overlays with special attention to the time displacement and lookback periods. Methods of trend identification, potential reversals, and continuations are also discussed with respect to the various Ichimoku overlays.

Chapter 17 (Market Profile) covers market profile charting. There is detailed treatment of the value area calculation, determination of the Point of Control via Time Price Opportunity (TPO) count and volume, as well as coverage of the various popular TPO distributions.

Chapter 18 (Basic Elliott Wave Analysis) introduces Elliott wave analysis with special focus on wave construction, alternation, truncations, impulsive and corrective wave formations, as well as the application of Fibonacci ratio and number analysis to the Elliott wave structure. The significance of pattern, time, and ratio is also discussed.

Chapter 19 (Basics of Gann Analysis) covers some of the most popular Gann techniques for forecasting potential price reversals, which includes the squaring of price and range, squaring of the high and low, the square of nine time and price projections, Gann lines, Gann retracements, and Gann grids.

Chapter 20 (Cycle Analysis) covers the basic elements of cycle analysis. The principle of summation, harmonicity, proportional commonality, nominality, variation, and synchronicity are covered in detail. Cycle inversions, translations, and the tuning of oscillators to the dominant cycle are illustrated clearly on various charts. The practitioner is also presented with five basic approaches to identifying cycles.

Chapter 21 (Volatility Analysis) discusses the five measures of market and price volatility. There is also coverage of the concept of normal and standard deviation, mean deviation, skewness, kurtosis, average true range, and stock beta. Plus there is discussion of the volatility indices and their application.

Chapter 22 (Market Breadth) covers the elements and factors that affect the reliability and consistency of market breadth analysis. Market fields and components such as its nine breadth data fields and eleven data operations are discussed in detail. Various popular market breadth indicators and their applications are then illustrated via numerous equity and commodity charts.

Chapter 23 (Sentiment Indicators and Contrary Opinion) introduces the topic of sentiment analysis and analyzes the behavior and psychology of the market participants. The chapter covers contrary opinion, irrationality, and necessary conditions for the reliability of sentiment indicators. Various popular sentiment indicators are examined with the appropriate charts.

Chapter 24 (Relative Strength Analysis) is about measuring the relative strength of one market against another. The directional implications and definitions such underperformance and outperformance are explained with various examples. The application of technical analysis to RS lines is examined and illustrated via numerous charts.

Chapter 25 (Investor Psychology) covers the basic elements of investor psychology. The chapter discusses how trends, consolidations, and market reversals develop with respect to various psychological and emotional biases. It also describes the underlying forces that create chart patterns in terms of the biases of investors and traders. Topics relating to cognitive dissonance and positive feedback loops are covered in detail.

Chapter 26 (Trader Risk Profiling and Position Analysis) introduces the practitioner to trader profiling. The practitioner is exposed to the concept of risk capacity and is shown that most market participants are usually both risk averse and risk seeking at the same time, with respect to price, time, and risk size. Trade orders based on behavioral profile are also discussed in detail. The collection of bullish and bearish indications across multiple timeframes is discussed in terms of the long, medium, and shorter term trader and investor.

Chapter 27 (Integrated Technical Analysis) introduces the concept of integrated technical analysis. It shows the practitioner how to effectively combine various technical tools to achieve better forecasts and trade decisions. It stresses the importance of identifying significant bullish and bearish clustering and oscillator signal agreements in order to locate high probability trades. Multiple timeframe analysis and multicollinearity are also discussed in detail.

Chapter 28 (Money Management) covers the elements of money management for traders. It classifies money management into passive and dynamic exposures. The four stochastic exit mechanisms are introduced and explained in detail. The concept of linear and geometric expectancy, asymmetric leverage, minimum winning percentage, and win-loss distribution are discussed from the perspective of improving trade performance. Familiarity with the concepts and disciplined application of passive and dynamic components of money management are essential skills for the long-term survivability as a trader.

Chapter 29 (Technical Trading Systems) introduces the practitioner to the basic elements of constructing, testing, and optimizing technical trading systems. It covers system conceptualization, system components, and performance measurement specifications.

Appendix A (Basic Investment Decision Making Based on Chart Analysis) illustrates how charts are employed to make trading and investment decisions. The practitioner is shown how to describe both the stock and the climate or environment in which the stock is trading in bullish and bearish terms and how to identify various participatory options available in the stock with respect to the client risk capacity and expectation.

Appendix B (Official IFTA CFTe, STA Diploma (UK), and MTA CMT Exam Reading Lists) provides a list the official IFTA CFTe, STA Diploma (UK), and MTA CMT exam reading requirements.

This book also includes an overview of the companion website and test bank.

ONLINE MATERIALS

This book also includes access to a companion website (www.wiley.com/go/limta) that includes:

- An online test bank based on the topics outlined in the official syllabuses for both the MTA and IFTA professional examinations
- Answers to the end-of-chapter questions in the book
- Excel spreadsheets that help illustrate the mathematics underlying various technical and money management concepts within the handbook
- Updated charts
- Additional content on new topics added to the exams

For instructions on accessing the test bank, please refer to the About the Test Bank and Website at the end of this book.

Acknowledgments

I would like to express my deepest appreciation and gratitude to Nick Wallwork, Emilie Herman, Chris Gage, and everyone at Wiley for their amazing work and inspiration, without which the creation of this book would not be at all possible.

I am especially indebted to Emilie Herman for her phenomenal contribution and expertise in helping me put this book together. I thank Emilie for her constant encouragement and guidance and for putting up with all the delays during the difficult and very challenging writing process. I would also like to convey my heartfelt appreciation to Chris Gage for his amazing work on the manuscripts.

Finally, I truly thank all my past and current graduates for their amazing participation, patience, and dedication. It is through their constant feedback, criticisms, and fervent participation that much of the technical analysis in this book have been refined and crystallized into its current form. A special word of thanks also goes out to Mr. Eric Lee at MetaQuotes (Singapore) for his very kind assistance.

The charts in this book are sourced, with kind permission, from Stockcharts .com and MetaQuotes Software Corp. Note that MetaTrader is a trademark of MetaQuotes Software Corp.

About the Author

Mark Lim graduated from King's College London in Special Physics. He was awarded the Bronwen Wood Memorial Prize in financial technical analysis by the Society of Technical Analysis (UK) in 2007. He holds both the MSTA (UK) and the International Federation of Technical Analysts CFTe designations and is a full member of the Society of Technical Analysis (UK). Mark's expertise includes stock, CFDs, commodity futures, and options trading. He is currently involved with mathematics and physics at the postgraduate level.

Mark is the author of *The Profitable Art and Science of Vibratrading* (Wiley, 2011). He is also a contributing author of *The Wiley Trading Guide Volume II*. He conducts a range of technical analysis and trading Masterclasses via online webinars and on-site seminars, covering intermediate to advanced profit extraction methodologies for directional and nondirectional trading.

Mark can be reached at www.tradermasterclass.com.

CHAPTER 1

Introduction to the Art and Science of Technical Analysis

Technical analysis is a fascinating field of study. It is as much science as it is art. Its main strength is that a lot of it is visual, giving practitioners a better feel of the underlying dynamics of the markets. We shall also be looking at the various challenges to technical analysis, their resolution, and how technical analysis affects trading in general. The classification of technical approaches, market participants, and various markets will also be discussed in detail.

1.1 MAIN OBJECTIVE OF TECHNICAL ANALYSIS

It is generally accepted that human beings are born with certain instincts, tempered and molded by evolution via the passing of time. Every human being strives and seeks to fulfill these powerful instinctive forces.

The three main motivational instincts are:

1. The instinct to survive
2. The instinct for comfort
3. The instinct to propagate

The instinct to survive is probably the strongest and most overpowering. Survival almost always precedes the need for comfort or to propagate the species. The instinct to survive includes:

- The instinct to stay alive
- The instinct to satisfy hunger
- The instinct to seek safety, that is, being in a group/herd
- The instinct to avoid danger (by having natural fears like the fear of fire, loud sounds, heights, etc.)

This powerful instinct to survive is the main driving force in life for striving to make a profit. But in order to make a profit to ensure continued survival, there must be a positive change in the actual or perceived value of something that we own. This change in value of some variable may be anything that will allow us to profit from change. *One very popular and convenient variable of change is price.* We can participate in this price change by satisfying a very simple mechanical rule that will ensure profitability every single time, which is to always buy when prices are low and sell when they are higher, popularly referred to as the *buy low, sell high* principle. See Figure 1.1.

Unfortunately, in order to satisfy this simple rule of guaranteed profitability, we need to be able to do more of one thing, which is to be able to determine the direction of price ahead of time in order to know exactly *when* to buy low and subsequently sell higher. Hence, it is not only the mechanical action of buying low and selling high that counts, but also the *timing* of the action itself that is critical. This

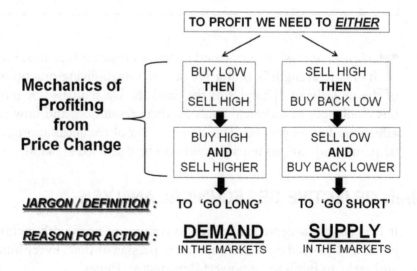

FIGURE 1.1 The Mechanics of Profiting from a Change.

introduces an element of chance or probability into an otherwise fairly straightforward mechanical venture. Profitability therefore requires effective and efficient action in two dimensions, that is, price and time. Traders and analysts keep track of this action using a two-dimensional visualization tool, that is, a price-time chart, which tracks price on the vertical axis and time on horizontal axis.

In short, the ability to forecast or predict price or market action in a reasonably accurate fashion represents one of the skills that may be critical for longer-term success as a professional trader or analyst.

1.2 DUAL FUNCTION OF TECHNICAL ANALYSIS

Technical analysis essentially serves *two* main functions:

1. *For Identification:* It identifies and describes past and present price action. It serves as a historical record of what has transpired in the markets. It provides a descriptive representation of market action. This allows the market practitioner to observe how the market has performed in the past, which includes its average volatility over a specified period; its highest and lowest historical price extremes; the common areas of consolidation, average duration, and price excursion of trends; the amount of liquidity and participation in the markets; the average degree and frequency of price gapping; the impact of various monetary economic announcements on price, and so on. This information is especially critical prior to any investment or trading decision.
2. *For Forecasting:* Once a particular price or market action is identified, the practitioner may now use this information to interpret what the data actually means before inferring future price action. This inference about potential price action is wholly based on the assumption that price patterns are repetitive to some reasonable degree and therefore may be used as a basis for price predictions.

1.3 FORECASTING PRICE AND MARKET ACTION

There are three main approaches to predicting potential future price action or behavior, namely via:

1. Fundamental Analysis
2. Technical Analysis
3. Information Analysis

See Figure 1.2.

Forecasting Stock Prices Using Fundamental Analysis

One way to gauge the potential price of a stock is by analyzing the company's performance via its financial statements and accounts in order to determine its *intrinsic value* or the worth of the security in light of all its holdings, debt, earnings, dividends, income and balance sheet activity, cash flow, and so on. This accounting information is nor-

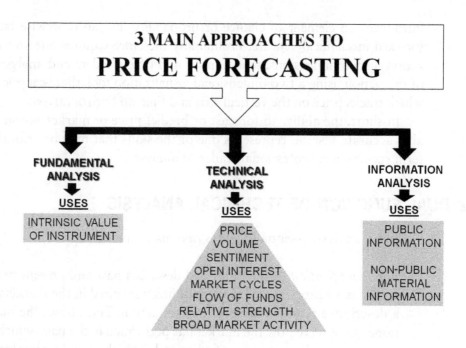

FIGURE 1.2 Three Approaches to Price Forecasting.

mally represented in ratio form, as in price to earnings (P/E), price to earnings growth (PEG), price to book, price to sales, and debt to equity ratios, to name but a few.

The logic is that a strongly performing company *should continue to perform well into the future* and garner more demand from investors excited to participate in the expected capital gains derived from the stock's price and appreciating dividend yields. The price of a stock is expected to rise if there are sufficient buyers, signifying a *demand* for it. Conversely, the price of a stock is expected to decline if there are sufficient sellers, signifying an *oversupply* in the stock. Demand is potentially generated if the current stock price is below its estimated intrinsic value, that is, it is currently *undervalued* or *underpriced*, whereas supply is created if the current stock price is above its estimated intrinsic value, that is, it is currently *overvalued* or *overpriced*. See Figures 1.3 and 1.4 for illustrations of using intrinsic value to forecast potential stock price movements.

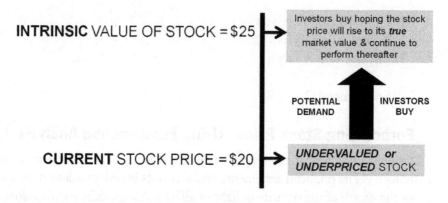

FIGURE 1.3 Price Forecasting Based on Intrinsic Value of a Stock.

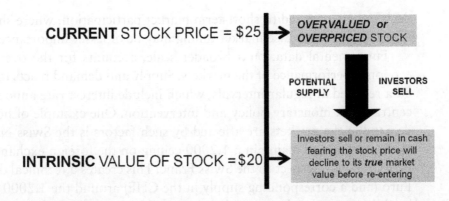

FIGURE 1.4 Price Forecasting Based on Intrinsic Value of a Stock.

There are various ways to determine the degree of over- or undervaluation in a stock, some of which include comparing P/E and earnings per share (EPS) ratios or investigating to what extent a stock is trading at a premium or discount in relation to its net current asset value, debt, and other fundamentals. Fundamental analysis helps provide indications as to which stocks to buy based on prior company performance, that is, over the last accounting period. Some investors resort to more active asset-allocation methods to try to time the market for a suitable stock to buy into or get out of, rather than just relying on the traditional buy-and-hold strategy. They resort to studying broad market factors and sector-rotation models in order to buy into the best fundamentally performing stocks within a strengthening industry or sector. This method is popularly termed the *top-down approach* to investing. A *bottom-up approach* relies more on a specific company's fundamental performance. A buy-and-hold strategy in today's volatile markets may not represent the most effective way of maximizing returns while minimizing potential risks. As a result, many fundamentalists frequently look to various asset pricing and modern portfolio models like the Capital Asset Pricing Model (CAPM) to try to achieve the best *balance between risk and expected returns* over a risk-free rate (along what is called the *efficient frontier*).

One of the problems with fundamental analysis is the credibility, reliability, and accuracy of the accounting practices and financial reporting, which is susceptible to manipulation and false or fraudulent reporting. There are various unscrupulous ways to dress up a poorly performing company or financial institution. A simple Internet search will reveal numerous past and ongoing investigations related to such practices. The other problem is the delay in the financial reporting of a company's current financial state in the market. By the time the next audited report is completed and published, the information is already outdated. It does not furnish timely information to act upon, especially in volatile market environments, and, as a result, does not directly account or adjust for current or sudden developments in the market environment. Nevertheless, fundamental analysis does give valuable information about specific securities and their performances. Its main weakness is its inability to provide clear and specific short-term price levels for traders to act on. Therefore, fundamental information is better suited to longer-term investment decisions, as opposed to short-term market participation, where short-term price fluctuations and precise market timing may be of lesser importance.

Fundamental data, on a broader scale, accounts for the overall underlying economic performance of the markets. Supply and demand reacts to the economic data released at regular intervals, which include interest rate announcements and central bank monetary policy and intervention. One example of how supply and demand in the markets are affected by such factors is the Swiss National Bank's (SNB) decision to maintain a 1.2000 ceiling on the foreign exchanges rate of the EURCHF, with respect to the Swiss Franc. This creates a technical demand for the Euro (and a corresponding supply in the CHF) around the 1.2000 exchange-rate level. Many traders have acted and are still acting on this policy decision to their advantage, *buying every time the rate approaches 1.2000,* with stops placed at a reasonable distance below this threshold. The integrity of this artificial ceiling remains intact as long as the SNB stands steadfast by their policy decision to uphold the ceiling at all costs. See Figure 1.5.

It behooves the analyst and investor to examine the actual decision-making process involved with investing in a stock based on intrinsic value. While it does provide an indication, with all else being equal, of the integrity of a certain stock relative to the universe of stocks available, there is a disruptive behavioral component that affects this process. It is not just the calculated or estimated intrinsic value that is an important element but also the general perception or future expectation of this value that plays an arguably greater and more significant role in determining the actual share price of a stock. This may explain why shares prices do not always reflect the actual value of a stock. This disagreement between price and value is the result of divergence between the actual intrinsic value and perceived or projected value.

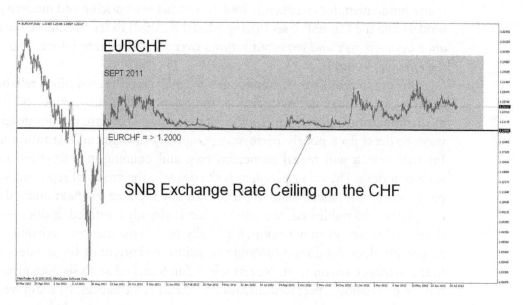

FIGURE 1.5 SNB Policy Impacting on the Value of the CHF.
Source: MetaTrader 4

Forecasting Stock Prices Using Information

Generally, information may be gleaned from various public sources such as newspaper reports, magazines, online bulletins, and so on, upon which market participants may then formulate an opinion about the market, making their own predictions about potential market action. Unfortunately, such publicly available information usually has little merit when used for forecasting purposes, as those more privy to non-public material information would have already moved the markets substantially, leaving only an inconsequential amount of action for latecomers to profit from, at the very most. This is where technical analysts have the unfair advantage of observing the markets moving on the charts and immediately taking action, regardless of the cause or reasons why such action exists. They are only interested in the effects such activity has on price. Technical analysts typically do not wait for news to be public knowledge prior to taking action or making a forecast based on a significant price breakout.

The use of non-public material information potentially affords insiders substantial financial gain from such knowledge, as the release of critical or highly sensitive company information may cause a substantial change in the company's stock price. Hence it is no great feat to be able to forecast potential market direction based on such prior knowledge, especially if the non-public material information is highly significant or headline worthy. Needless to say, insider trading is illegal in the equity markets. But the possibility will always exist that it can occur and in fact has on many occasions. Unfortunately, in unregulated over-the-counter (OTC) markets, nothing stops brokers from front running large client orders, which is just another form of insider trading.

Forecasting Stock Prices Using Technical Analysis

Technical analysis is essentially the identification and forecasting of potential market behavior based largely on the action and dynamics of the market itself. The action and dynamics of the market is best captured via price, volume, and open interest action. The charts provide a visual description of what has transpired in the markets and technical analysts use this past information to infer potential future price action, based on the assumption that price patterns tend to repeat or behave in a reasonably reliable and predictable manner. Let us turn our attention to some popular definitions of technical analysis.

The following definition of technical analysis tells us that *charting* is the main tool used to forecast potential future price action.

Technical analysis is the study of market action, primarily through the use of charts, for the purpose of forecasting future price trends.

John Murphy, ***Technical Analysis of the Financial Markets***
(NYIF, 1999)

The next definition of technical analysis tells us that the charting of *past information* is used to forecast future price action.

Technical analysis is the science of recording, usually in graphic form, the actual history of trading… then deducing from that pictured history the probable future trend.

Edwards and Magee, *Technical Analysis of Stock Trends*
(AMACOM, 2007)

Notice that the last two definitions specifically refer to the forecasting of *trend* action.

It is interesting at this point to draw a parallel here with information used in fundamental analysis. Technical analysis is often criticized for the use of past information as a basis for forecasting future price action, relying on the notion that certain price behaviors tend to repeat. Unfortunately virtually all forms of forecasting are based on the use of prior or past information, which certainly includes statistical-, fundamental-, and behavior-based forecasting. Companies employ accounting data from the most recent and even past quarters as a basis for gauging the current value of a stock. In statistics, regression-line analysis requires the sampling of past data in order to predict probable future values. Even in behavioral finance, the quantitative measure of the market participant's past actions form the basis for predicting future behavior.

The following definition of technical analysis tells us that it is the study of pure *market action* and not the fundamentals of the instrument itself.

It refers to the study of the action of the market itself as opposed to the study of the goods in which the market deals.

Edwards and Magee, *Technical Analysis of Stock Trends*
(AMACOM, 2007)

This next definition of technical analysis tells us that it is a form of *art,* and its purpose is to identify a trend reversal as early as possible.

The art of technical analysis, for it is an art, is to identify a trend reversal at a relatively early stage and ride on that trend until the weight of the evidence shows or proves that the trend has reversed.

Martin Pring, *Technical Analysis Explained, 4th Edition*
(McGraw-Hill, 2002)

The following definition is most relevant in the formulation of trading strategies. It reminds the market participants that *nothing is certain* and we must weigh our risk and returns.

Technical analysis deals in probabilities, never in certainties.

Martin Pring, *Technical Analysis Explained, 4th Edition*
(McGraw-Hill, 2002)

The next statement gives a behavioral reason as to *why* technical analysis works.

Technical analysis is based on the assumption that people will continue to make the same mistakes they have made in the past.

Martin Pring, *Technical Analysis Explained, 4th Edition*
(McGraw-Hill, 2002)

This definition by Pring stresses and underscores the point that there is a real reason and explanation as to why past price patterns tend to repeat. The tendency of price to repeat past patterns is mainly attributed to market participants repeating the same behavior. Although it is not impossible with sufficient and continuous conscious effort and strength of will, human beings rarely change their basic behavior, temperament, and deep-rooted biases, especially in relation to their emotional response to fear, greed, hope, anger, and regret when participating in the markets.

The following statement about technical analysis explains its effectiveness in *timing* early entries and exits.

Market price tends to lead the known fundamentals.... Market price acts as a leading indicator of the fundamentals.

John Murphy, *Technical Analysis of the Financial Markets*
(NYIF, 1999)

This definition by Murphy highlights a very important assumption in technical analysis, which is that price is a reflection of all known information acted upon in the markets. It is the sum of all market participants' trading and investment actions and decisions, including current and future expectations of market action. It also reflects the overall psychology, biases, and beliefs of all market participants. Therefore, the technical analysts believe that the charts tell the whole story and that everything that can or is expected to impact price has already been discounted. This assumption forms the very basis of technical analysis, and without it, technical analysis would be rendered completely pointless.

Fundamental versus Technically Based Market Timing

Before proceeding any further, it is best to briefly explain the meaning of a few commonly used terms in trading and technical analysis:

- To go *long* means to buy to open a new position
- To *liquidate* means to sell to close a position previously held
- To go *short* means to sell to open a new position
- To *cover* means to buy to close a position previously shorted

Both fundamental and technically based market timing aim to satisfy the same basic principle of *buying low and selling high*. There are four basic scenarios where this may occur:

1. Long at a low price and liquidate at a higher price
2. Long at a relatively high price and liquidate at an even higher price

3. Short at a high price and cover at a lower price

4. Short at a relatively low price and cover at an even lower price

Listed below are the some of the strengths of each approach with respect to timing the markets.

Technically Based Market Timing **offers the ability to**
- Provide precise entry and exit prices
- Provide the precise time of entry and exit
- Provide real-time bullish and bearish signals
- Provide real-time entry and exit price triggers
- Scale in and out based on significant price levels
- Time entries and exits based on volatility behavior of the underlying
- Exit extended trends at technically significant price-reversal levels
- Time entries and exits based on market order flow
- Define percent risk in terms of significant price levels
- Use volume and open interest analysis to gauge strength of an underlying move in order to time entries and exits
- Use market breadth and broad market sentiment to gauge the strength of an underlying move in order to time entries and exits
- Forecast potential peaks (for shorting or liquidating positions) as well as potential troughs (for getting long and covering positions) via the use of cycle and seasonality analysis

Fundamentally Based Market Timing **offers the ability to:**
- Gauge undervalued stocks with a potential to appreciate in value, but lacking information regarding the precise price or time to get long or to cover
- Gauge overvalued stocks with a risk of depreciating in value, but lacking information regarding the precise price or time to get short or to liquidate
- Screen and participate in fundamentally strong stocks in a sector or industry as part of an active asset allocation or rotation strategy, but lacking information regarding the precise price or time to get long

The Fundamentalist versus Technical Analysts

Listed below are some characteristics of the fundamentalist and technical analyst:

The Fundamentalist:
- Is mainly concerned with intrinsic value
- Strives to understand the underlying *causes* for potential market moves
- Is focused on which company to participate in
- Can tell you which company to invest in, but cannot tell you the most advantageous moment to start participating in that stock

The Technical Analyst:
- Is mainly concerned with structure and dynamics of market and price action
- Is more concerned with the *effects* of potential market moves rather than the cause of them

- Cannot usually determine what the intrinsic value of an asset is or whether it is under-or overvalued, but is able to determine precisely when to start participating, purely from the perspective of price performance
- Is not concerned with the underlying factors that led to the rise in price; this is irrelevant for all practical purposes as they believe that price is a *reflection of all information available in the markets* and therefore that is all that really matters

In short, from what we have covered so far, we know that technical analysis:

- Uses past information
- Uses charts
- Identifies past and current price action
- Forecasts potential future price action based on historical price behavior (especially the start of a new trend)

Technical Data and Information

Technical analysts study market action. Market action itself is mainly comprised of the study of:

- Price action
- Volume action
- Open interest action
- Sentiment
- Market breadth
- Flow of funds

Of all the data that technical analysts employ, price is the most important, followed closely by volume action. Price itself is comprised of an opening, high, low, and closing price, normally referred to as *OHLC data*. OHLC data normally refers to the daily opening, high, low, and closing prices, but it may be used to denote the OHLC of any bar interval, from 1-minute bars right up to the monthly and yearly bars.

1.4 CLASSIFYING TECHNICAL ANALYSIS

Technical analysis may be categorized into four distinct branches, that is, classical, statistical, sentiment, and behavioral analysis. Regardless of which branch is employed, all analysis is eventually interpreted via the various behavioral traits, filters, and biases unique to each analyst. Behavioral traits include both the psychological and emotional elements. See Figure 1.6.

Classical technical analysis involves the use of the conventional bar, chart, and Japanese candlestick patterns, oscillator and overlay indicators, as well as market breadth, relative strength, and cycle analysis. Statistical analysis is more quantitative, as opposed to the more qualitative nature of classical technical analysis. It

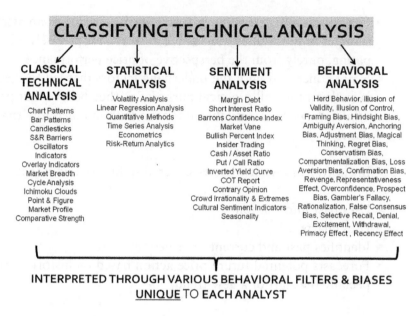

FIGURE 1.6 The Four Branches of Technical Analysis.

studies the dispersion, central tendencies, skewness, volatility, regression analysis, hypothesis testing, correlation, covariance, and so on. Sentiment analysis is concerned with the psychology of market participants, which includes their emotions and level of optimism or pessimism in the markets. It studies professional and public opinion via polls and questionnaires, trading and investment decisions via flow of funds in the markets, as well as the positions taken by large institutions and hedgers. Finally, behavioral analysis studies the way market participants react to news, profit and losses, the actions of other market participants, and with their own psychological and emotional biases, preferences, and expectations.

Mean Reverting versus Non–Mean Reverting Approach

The type of technical studies employed also depends on the approach taken by traders and analysts with respect to their personal preferences and biases regarding the action of price in the markets. Basically, traders either adopt a *contrarian* or a *momentum-seeking* type approach. Being more contrarian in their approach implies that they do not usually expect the price to traverse large distances. In fact they are constantly on the lookout for impending reversals in the markets. In essence, they expect price to be more *mean reverting*, returning to an average price or balance between supply and demand. Those that adopt the mean-reverting approach prefer to employ technical studies that help pinpoint levels of overbought and oversold activity, which includes divergence analysis, regression analysis, moving average bands, and Bollinger bands. They prefer to trade consolidations rather than trend action. They normally buy at support and short at resistance. Limit entry orders are their preferred mode of order entry. Conversely, being more momentum seeking in their approach implies that they usually expect the price to traverse large distances and for trends to continue to remain intact. They are constantly on the lookout for continuation type breakouts in the markets. In short,

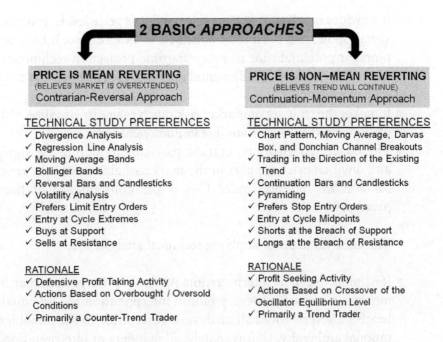

FIGURE 1.7 Mean Reverting versus Non–Mean Reverting Approaches.

they expect price to be more *non–mean reverting*, where demand creates further demand and supply creates further supply, both driven by a powerful positive-feedback cycle. Those that adopt the non–mean reverting approach prefer to employ technical studies that help pinpoint breakout or trend continuation activity, which includes chart pattern breakouts, moving average breakouts, Darvas Box breakouts, and Donchian channel breakouts. They prefer to trade trends rather than ranging action. They normally short at the breach of support and long at breach of resistance. Stop entry orders are their preferred mode of entry into the markets. See Figure 1.7.

Advantages and Disadvantages of Technical Analysis

The advantages of applying technical analysis to the markets are:

- It is applicable across all markets, instruments, and timeframes, where price patterns, oscillators, and overlay indicators are all treated in exactly the same manner. No new learning is required in order to trade new markets or timeframes, unlike in fundamental analysis where the analyst must be conversant with the specifics of each stock or market.
- There is no need to study the fundamentals of the markets traded or analyzed in order to apply technical analysis, since technical analysts believe that all information that impacts or potentially may impact the stock or market is already reflected in the price on the charts.
- Technical analysis provides a clear visual representation of the behavior of the markets, unlike in fundamental analysis where most of the data is in numerical form.

■ It provides timely and precise entry and exit price levels, preceded by technical signals indicating potential bullishness or bearishness. It has the ability to also pinpoint potential time of entry via time projection techniques not available to fundamentalists. Fundamental analysis does not provide the exact price or time of entry.

■ It makes the gauging of market risk much easier to visualize. Volatility is more obvious on the charts than it is in numerical form.

■ The concerted effort of market participants acting on significantly clear and obvious price triggers in the markets helps create the reaction required for a more reliable trade. This is the consequence of the self-fulfilling prophecy.

The disadvantages of applying technical analysis are:

■ It is subjective in its interpretation. A certain price pattern may be perceived in numerous ways. Since every bullish interpretation has an equal and opposite bearish interpretation, all analysis is susceptible to the possibility of interpretational ambiguity. Unfortunately, all manners of interpretation, regardless of the underlying analysis employed—be it fundamental, statistical, or behavioral—are equally subjective in content and form.

■ A basic assumption of technical analysis is that price behavior tends to repeat, making it possible to forecast potential future price action. Unfortunately this tendency to repeat may be disrupted by unexpected volatility in the markets caused by geopolitical, economic, or other factors. Popular price patterns may also be distorted by new forms of trade execution that may impact market action, like automated, algorithmic, or high-frequency program trading where trades are initiated in the markets based on non-classical patterns. This interferes with the repeatability of classic chart patterns.

■ Charts provide a historical record of price action. It takes practice and experience to be able to identify classical patterns in price. Though this skill can be mastered with enough practice, the art of inferring or forecasting future price action based on past prices is much more difficult to master. The practitioner needs to be intimately familiar with the behavior of price at various timeframes and in different markets. Although classical patterns may be applied equally across all markets and timeframes equally, there is still an element of uniqueness associated with each market action and timeframe.

■ It is argued that all market action is essentially a *random walk process,* and as such applying technical analysis is pointless as all chart patterns arise out of pure chance and are of no significance in the markets. One must remember that if this is the case, then all forms of analysis are ineffective, whether fundamental, statistical, or behavioral. Since the market is primarily driven by perception, we know that the random-walk process is not a true representation of market action, since market participants react in very specific and predictable ways. Though there is always some element of randomness in the markets caused by the uncoordinated actions of a large number of market participants, one can always observe the uncanny accuracy with which price tests and reacts at a psychologically significant barriers or prices. It is hard to believe that price action is the result of random acts of buying and selling by market participants where the participants are totally unencumbered by cost, biases, psychology, or emotion.

- The strong form of the *Efficient Market Hypothesis* (EMH) argues that since the markets discount all information, price would have already adjusted to the new information and any attempt to profit from such information would be futile. This would render the technical analysis of price action pointless, with the only form of market participation being passive investment. But such efficiency would require that all market participants react instantaneously to all new information in a rational manner. This in itself presents an insurmountable challenge to EMH. *The truth is that no system comprising disparate parts in physical reality reacts instantaneously with perfect coordination.* Hence it is fairly safe to assume that although absolute market efficiency is not attainable, the market does continually adjust to new information, but at a much lower and less-efficient rate of data discounting. Therefore, technical analysis remains a valid form of market investigation until the markets attain a state of absolute and perfect efficiency.

- Another argument against technical analysis is the idea of the *Self-Fulfilling Prophecy* (SFP). Proponents of the concept contend that prices react to technical signals not because the signals themselves are important or significant, but rather because of the concerted effort of market participants acting on those signals that make it work. This may in fact be advantageous to the market participants. The trick is in knowing which technical signals would be supported by a large concerted action. The logical answer would be to select only the most *significantly clear and obvious* technical signals and triggers. Of course, one can further argue that such signals, if they appear to be reliable indicators of support and resistance, would begin to attract an increasing number of traders as time passes. This would eventually lead to traders vying with each other for the best and most cost-effective fills. What seems initially like the concerted action of all market participants now turns into competition with each other. Getting late fills would be costly as well as reduce or wipe out any potential for profit. *This naturally results in traders attempting to preempt each other for the best fills.* Traders start vying for progressively earlier entries as price approaches the targeted entry levels, leading finally to entries that are too distant from the original entry levels, increasing risk and reducing any potential profits. This disruptive feedback cycle eventually erodes the reliability of the signals, as price fails to react at the expected technical levels. Price finally begins to react reliably again at the expected technical levels as traders stop preempting each other and abandon or disregard the strategy that produced the signals. The process repeats. Therefore, SFP may result in technical signals evolving in a kind of six-stage *duty cycle*, where the effects of SFP may be advantageous and desirable to traders in the early stages but eventually result in forcing traders into untenable positions. See Figure 1.8.

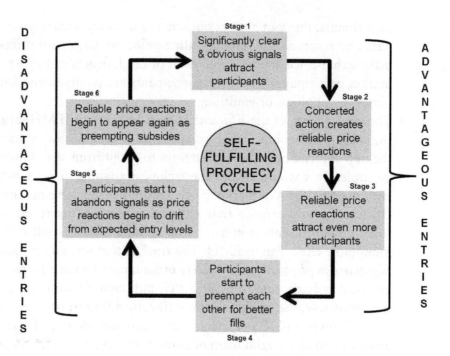

FIGURE 1.8 The Idealized Six-Stage Self-Fulfilling Prophecy Cycle.

1.5 SUBJECTIVITY IN TECHNICAL ANALYSIS

As with most forms of analysis, technical analysis has both objective and subjective aspects associated with its application. It is objective insofar as the charts represent a historical record of price and market action. But it is subjective when the technical analyst attempts to *analyze* the data.

Analyzing price and market action consists of three main activities, namely:

1. Identifying price and indicator patterns
2. Interpreting the data
3. Inferring potential future price behavior

Analyzing price and market action is ultimately subjective because all analysis is interpreted through various behavioral traits, filters, and biases *unique to each analyst or observer*. Behavioral traits include both the psychological and emotional elements. As a consequence, each analyst will possess a slightly different perception of the market and its possible future behavior.

Subjectivity in the Choice of Analysis and Technical Studies

The sheer number of ways to analyze an individual chart contributes to the overall level of subjectivity associated with each forecast. The problem is twofold:

- What is the most appropriate form of technical analysis that should be applied to a particular chart?
- What is the most appropriate choice of indicators to apply to a particular chart?

FIGURE 1.9 A Simple Price Chart.
Source: MetaTrader 4

These are the usual questions that plague novices. The following charts depict the various popular forms of analysis that can be applied to a basic chart of price action. The following examples are by no means exhaustive. Figure 1.9 starts off with a plain chart devoid of any form of analysis.

The next chart, Figure 1.10, shows the application of basic *trendline analysis* on the same chart, tracking the flow of price action in the market.

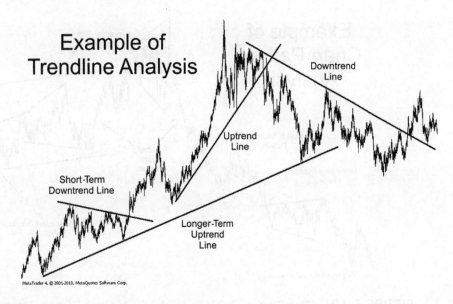

FIGURE 1.10 Trendline Analysis on the Same Chart.
Source: MetaTrader 4

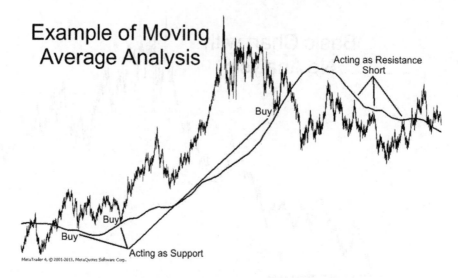

FIGURE 1.11 Moving Average Analysis on the Same Chart.
Source: MetaTrader 4

In Figure 1.11, *moving average analysis* is now employed to track the same flow of price action and to provide potential points of entry as the market rises and falls.

Figure 1.12 depicts the application of *chart pattern analysis* to track and forecast the shorter-term bullish and bearish movements in price.

Figure 1.13 is an example of applying two forms of technical analysis, that is, *linear regression analysis* and *divergence analysis* to track and forecast potential market tops and bottoms. Notice that the market top coincided perfectly with the upper band of the linear regression line, with an early bearish signal seen in the form of standard bearish divergence on the commodity channel index (CCI) indicator.

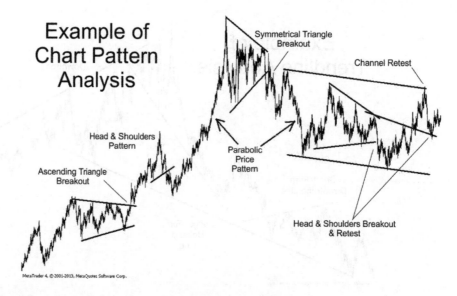

FIGURE 1.12 Chart Pattern Analysis on the Same Chart.
Source: MetaTrader 4

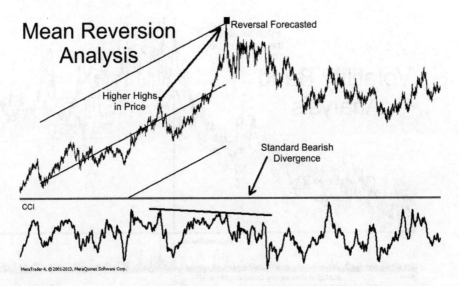

FIGURE 1.13 Linear Regression and Divergence Analysis on the Same Chart.
Source: MetaTrader 4

Figure 1.14 is an example of applying a couple of additional forms of analysis to the basic linear regression band. In this chart, *price action analysis* is used in conjunction with *volume analysis* to forecast a potential top in the market, evidenced by the preceding parabolic move in price that is coupled by a blow-off.

In Figure 1.15, volatility band, volume, and overextension analysis are all employed to seek out potential reversals in the market. We observe that price exceeds the upper volatility band, which may potentially be an early indication of price exhaustion, especially since it is accompanied by a significant volume spike. The moving average convergence-divergence (MACD) indicator is also seen to be residing at historically overbought levels, which is another potentially bearish indication.

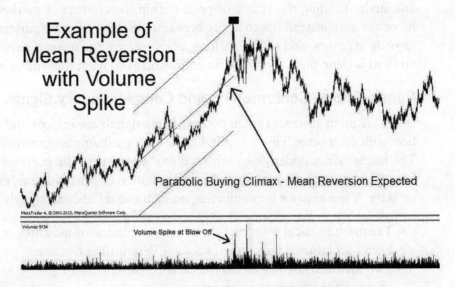

FIGURE 1.14 Linear Regression and Volume Analysis on the Same Chart.
Source: MetaTrader 4

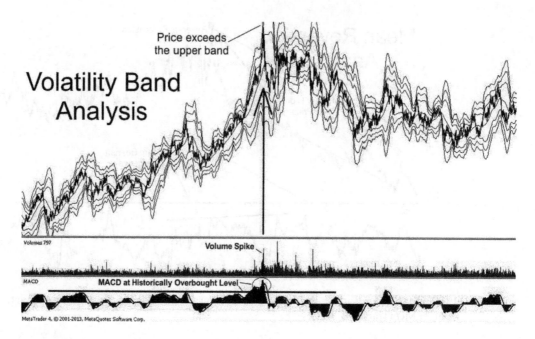

FIGURE 1.15 Volatility Band, Volume, and Overextension Analysis on the Same Chart. Source: MetaTrader 4

As we can see from just a few forms of analysis presented in the preceding charts, there are many ways to view the action of the markets, depending on the *context* of the analysis employed. For example, if the analyst is more interested in viewing and understanding the action of price within the context of over-reaction or price exhaustion in the markets, he or she may opt to apply technical studies that track levels or areas of potential over-reaction or price exhaustion. Technical studies that tract such behavior include linear regression bands, Bollinger bands, moving average percentage bands, Keltner and Starc bands, areas of prior support and resistance, and so on. Alternatively, if the analyst is more interested in viewing and understanding the action of price within the context of market momentum, he or she may instead opt to apply breakout analysis of chart patterns, trendlines, moving averages, and so on. As long as the reason for using a particular form of analysis is clear, there should be no confusion as to what the studies are indicating.

Contradictory, Confirmatory, and Complementary Signals

There are many instances when two oscillator signals are in clear and direct opposition with each other. This is inevitable, as each oscillator is constructed differently. The mathematics underlying each oscillator varies with the purpose it is designed for, and in most cases, it involves the manipulation of price, volume, and open interest data. A few reasons for conflicting oscillator and indicator signals are:

- The mathematical construction of each oscillator or indicator is different.
- Each oscillator or indicator tracks a different time horizon.
- Two identical oscillators may issue inconsistent readings due to missing data on one of the charting platforms.
- Two identical oscillators may also issue inconsistent readings due to variations in the accuracy, quality, and type of data available on different charting platforms.

For example, applying an oscillator that uses price, volume, and open interest as part of its calculation will yield inconsistent readings should one of the data be unavailable on the charting platform. The analysts may not be aware of the missing data and struggle to make sense of the inconsistency. The accuracy of the data is also of paramount importance for effective analysis of price and market action. Dropouts in the data as well as the inclusion or exclusion of non-trading days will cause inconsistent readings between charting platforms. There may also be variations in the oscillator readings should volume be replaced with tick volume, sometime also referred to as transaction volume. Tick volume tracks the number of transactions over a specified time interval, irrespective of the size of the transactions.

It is also important to note that conflicting signals may not always be in fact conflicting. As pointed out, the time horizons over which each signal is applied may be different. In Figure 1.16 we observe that the CCI readings over the range of prices are markedly different. The 20-period CCI indicates a slightly overbought market whereas the 100-period CCI suggests that prices are slightly oversold. There is in fact no real conflict between the two apparently opposing signals. The indicators are merely pointing out that prices are slightly overbought or overextended in the short term, but over the longer term, prices are in fact slightly oversold, that is, relatively cheap. Therefore, instead of viewing the signals as opposing or contradictory, the astute trader immediately realizes that the most advantageous point for initiating a long entry would be when prices are cheap both in the long *and* short term. This is easily identified on the charts by looking for oversold readings on both the 20- and

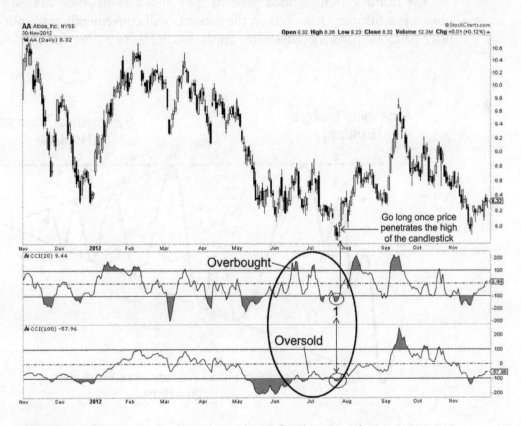

FIGURE 1.16 Conflicting Signals on the Daily Alcoa Inc Chart.
Courtesy of Stockcharts.com

100-period CCI within the area of consolidation, as indicated at Point 1. Therefore, the trader may decide to go long once price penetrates the high of the candlestick indicated on the chart. In this example, we see conflicting signals actually complementing each other and affording the trader an advantageous entry at relatively low prices.

The important point to remember is that any form of analysis may be employed, as long as the analyst is intimately familiar with the peculiarities associated with each form of analysis. It is better to be conversant with one form of analysis than to employ a slew of technical approaches without fully grasping the intricacies of each approach. This leads to confusion and ineffective analysis. It must be noted that combining technical studies will frequently result in both confirmatory and contradictory signals as we have seen, with many of the signals being also complementary as well. Only add studies once the first form of analysis is fully mastered. The practitioner must always remember that no form of analysis is always perfectly representative of the market, and it is inevitable that different forms of analysis will many times lead to conflicting signals.

Subjectivity in Pattern Identification

As mentioned, interpretation and inference of potential future price action based on historical price behavior is essentially an exercise in subjectivity. Each analyst will interpret and infer future price action according to his or her own experience, knowledge, objectives, beliefs, expectations, predilections, emotional makeup, psychological biases, and interests.

The identification of price patterns may also present some challenge to the novice practitioner. Occasionally, the markets will conveniently trace out various price patterns that may cause some confusion. Refer to Figure 1.17.

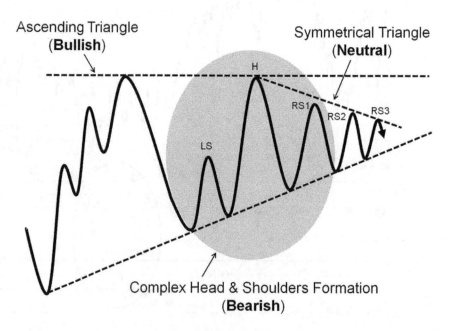

FIGURE 1.17 Conflicting Chart Pattern Signals.

In this example, we see two chart patterns indicating potentially contradictory signals. The ascending triangle is regarded as a bullish indication, while the complex head and shoulders formation is potentially bearish. Therefore, as price starts to contract, forming a symmetrical triangle, an analyst may be somewhat perplexed at the conflicting signals, being unable to provide or issue a clear forecast as to whether the market is indeed potentially bullish or bearish.

One way to resolve this apparent conflict is to first identify the size of each pattern. *The sentiment associated with larger patterns or formations will take precedence over that of smaller formations.* These larger formations are more representative of the longer-term sentiment whereas the smaller formations are more indicative of short-term sentiment. Hence in our example, the bullish sentiment associated with the ascending triangle takes precedence over the bearish sentiment associated with the complex head and shoulders formation. Therefore, until price breaches the complex head and shoulders neckline, the entire formation may be regarded as a potentially bullish pattern. Following this simple rule helps reduce some of the subjectivity involved in reading price and chart formations.

Figure 1.18 depicts an idealized scenario where all the chart formations are potentially bearish. There is no conflict in sentiment between these formations as they are all in perfect agreement. The smaller formations act as additional evidence and add to the overall bearish sentiment. There is also a lesser amount of subjectivity involved when reading the sentiment associated with formations that are in perfect agreement. Nevertheless, it should be noted that although such formations may appear somewhat more straightforward with respect to

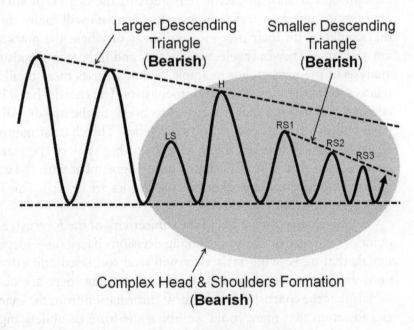

FIGURE 1.18 Chart Pattern with Complementary Signals.

inferring potential future price direction, any upside breakout of the larger descending triangle may well precipitate a vigorous and rapid rally in prices due to the unexpected nature of such a move. Traders must exercise caution especially when shorting such a formation as prices can quickly explode to the upside, caused by an avalanche of *short covering*.

Interpretational and Inferential Subjectivity

This element of subjectivity with respect to interpretation and inference is not merely confined to applications in technical analysis. In fact, *every form* of analysis involves a certain amount of subjectivity and arbitrariness when it comes to its interpretation. For example, let us assume that the price of oil has risen significantly. This event in itself can be interpreted in two different ways. One fundamentalist may strongly believe that this rise in oil prices will impact the markets adversely as it will raise the underlying cost of commodities, whereas another fundamentalist may strongly believe that the rise in oil prices is a direct result of market demand, a bullish scenario indicating a healthy and growing economy. In another example, a technical analyst may strongly believe that an overbought oscillator reading is a clear indication that the trend is strong with further continuation expected in price, whereas another technical analyst may strongly believe that the overbought signal is a clear indication that the market may be already overextended and therefore expects a reversal in trend. The beginner quickly realizes, after some reflection, that *for every bullish interpretation, there exists an equal and opposite bearish interpretation*. This is one of the main reasons why forecasting is regarded as largely subjective.

Subjectivity and Selective Perception

Human bias is another factor that adds to the degree of subjectivity when attempting to interpret technical signals. Chartists will many times ignore signals that conflict with their preconceived ideas of where the markets ought to be at any one time. They only select oscillators and indicator signals that support their analysis of the market. For example, a chartist uses three oscillators, the MACD, relative strength index (RSI), and stochastics. The chartist has a bullish view of the markets and believes that it is about to break to the upside. All of the oscillators have bullish readings except for stochastics. The chartist ignores the stochastics signal because it does not agree with his or her view of the markets. On a subsequent occasion, it is MACD that is not in agreement with the chartist's view, and only the signals from the other two oscillators are heeded. This is known as selective perception. See Figure 1.19.

Selective perception adds to the subjectivity of the forecast, as there is no fixed point of reference or basis for making decisions based on evidence. Choosing only signals that agree with one's view will lead to biased and erroneous interpretations and unfounded forecasts. In fact, it is when there are discrepancies in the signals that the chartist gains the most information from the markets, as it may be an indication that there could well be some form of underlying weakness in the markets.

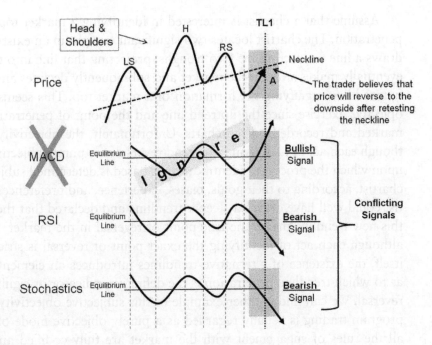

FIGURE 1.19 Selective Perception and Conflicting Oscillator Signals.

Subjectivity in Determining an Event: The Point of Entry

Identifying, interpreting, and inferring market action are not the only areas where subjectivity plays a significant role. The determination of the exact points of entry to and exit from the market is also subjective at the most fundamental level of observation. What appears to be essentially objective is also built on a foundation of subjectivity. An example will help illustrate the point. Refer to Figure 1.20.

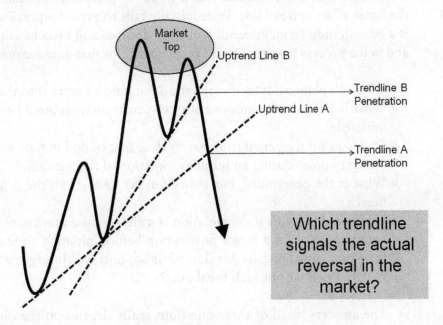

FIGURE 1.20 Example of Subjective Objectivity.

Assume that a chartist is interested in identifying a market top via a trendline penetration. The chartist locates two significant troughs in an existing uptrend and draws a line connecting the two troughs, projecting that line into the future. Price eventually makes a top in the market and subsequently declines and penetrates the uptrend line, signifying the formation of a market top. This seems to be a *totally* objective exercise since the uptrend line and the point of penetration were clearly marked and recorded on the charts. Unfortunately, the objectivity ends here. Although each act of identifying the trend reversal was purely objective, the *variables* upon which the process of identification is based is determined subjectively by each chartist, according to their goals, biases, experience, and preferences. Another chartist could well have drawn a steeper trendline and declared that the penetration of this new trendline marks the true point of reversal in the market. As you can see, although each act of identifying the exact point of reversal is strictly objective in itself, the existence of alternative trendlines introduces an element of subjectivity as to which trendline penetration is the definitive indicator or signifier of the trend reversal. We can find another example of this subjective objectivity. Automated or program trading is usually regarded as a purely objective mode of trading where all the rules of engagement with the market are fully codified and mechanically executed. This removes all subjectivity with respect to the entries and exits. Just as in our previous example, the point of penetration of each trendline was also purely objective. However, should the automated trading software allow for some parameter adjustments, this instantly introduces an element of subjectivity as to which parameter adjustments are the definitive settings for a profitable trading campaign. Therefore, no matter how objective each individual act is, once the possibility of alternative acts exists, the issue of subjectivity arises. In a sense, each determination is individually objective, but collectively subjective.

The very act of determining the exact entry point to initiate a trade is somewhat subjective. Let us assume that a trader is interested in initiating an entry at the break of an uptrend line. Price initially fails to exceed a previous peak, which is a bearish indication. Price subsequently declines and breaches the uptrend line, and in the process triggers a trade. Some questions that a trader may now ask are:

- At which point after the breakout do I initiate an entry into the market?
- What is a reasonable amount of price penetration required before an entry is initiated?
- Do I wait for the penetration bar to close first or do I initiate an entry at some arbitrary point during an intraday violation of the trendline?
- What if the penetration bar closes too far away from the original trendline breach?
- How would I know if the violation is merely a false breakout?
- Should I allow for a larger penetration before initiating an entry in order to filter out potential false breakouts? If so, how much larger a penetration is required to filter out such breakouts?

The answers to all of these questions really depend on the objectives of the trader and what he or she is attempting to achieve. There are essentially two ways

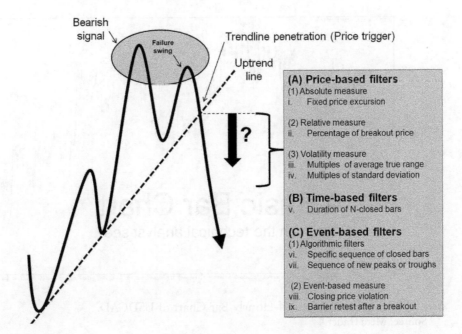

FIGURE 1.21 Subjectivity in the Rules of Engagement.

of initiating an entry at the breakout of some price barrier. The first is to initiate an entry at some arbitrary point just after a breakout. The other is to initiate a trade based on some fixed rules of entry and exits. See Figure 1.21.

Subjectivity arises not because the rules of engagement are unclear, but rather because of the number of choices available. Hence, each trader will select the rules of entry and exit that suit their personality, risk capacity, or familiarity with a certain mode of engagement. A trader could initiate a trade once price moves a certain distance away from the breakout, or once the penetration bar closes. Traders may even choose to enter the market after a certain amount of time has elapsed from a breakout. Figure 1.21 lists three main types of filters that traders frequently use to initiate an entry. Price, time, and algorithmic filters will be discussed in more detail in Chapter 5.

Summarizing, even if the rules for identification, interpretation, and inference are rigidly codified, the very fact that we have choice renders the entire analysis subjective from the ground up. Hence the argument that technical analysis is subjective in fact represents a general comment on all forms of analysis. It is not unique to technical analysis!

Here is a little exercise in subjectivity associated with pattern recognition. See Figure 1.22. Without looking at Figure 1.23, try to see if you can figure out the trend changes by drawing simple trendlines. After you have finished, refer to Figure 1.23 to see if you have drawn the same trendlines as indicated on the chart.

There will most likely be a difference in the points chosen in drawing the trendlines. The very fact that you can draw alternate trendlines introduces an element of subjectivity in identification, interpretation, and forecasting.

FIGURE 1.22   A Basic 4-Hourly Bar Chart of USDCAD.
Source: MetaTrader 4

Now go back to Figure 1.22 and try to identify some chart patterns (if you know some). After you have finished, turn to Figure 1.24 to see if you have drawn the same patterns.

Were there differences in the chart patterns drawn? Do not worry if there are differences. It is merely a consequence of subjectivity.

Subjectivity in Pattern Recognition Diminishes with Practice

Here is another example based on the same USDCAD chart. Were you aware of the subtle angular symmetries in the USDCAD? See Figure 1.25. Analysts also pay

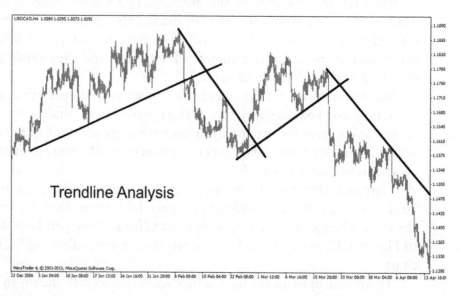

FIGURE 1.23   Trendline Analysis on the 4-Hourly USDCAD Bar Chart.
Source: MetaTrader 4

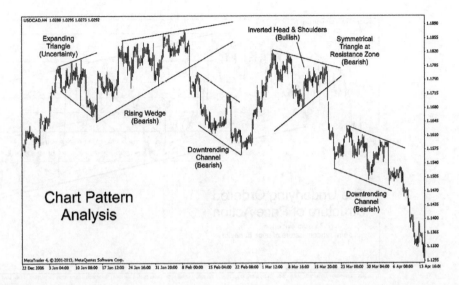

FIGURE 1.24 Chart Pattern Analysis on the 4-Hourly USDCAD Bar Chart.
Source: MetaTrader 4

attention to the angles of ascent and descent in the markets. A novice may not be able to clearly identify chart patterns, trendlines, or angular patterns at the very beginning. But with enough practice, the pattern-recognition abilities will gradually improve, becoming more obvious as the skill in reading charts improves. As a consequence, the amount of subjectivity associated with identifying patterns will gradually diminish.

Refer to Figure 1.26. Here is the same chart of the USDCAD again. But this time, we see the underlying beauty and symmetry of price, tempered and forged by the expectation, psychology, biases, and emotions of all market participants. To a trained eye, a simple chart of price action is as beautiful as any work of art. For technical analysis is, in itself, an art.

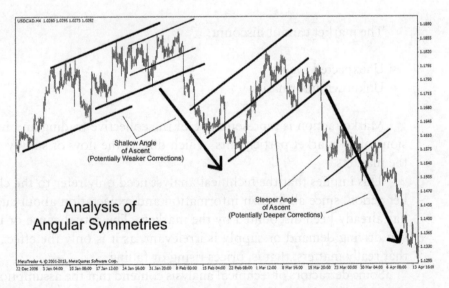

FIGURE 1.25 Angular Symmetries on the 4-Hourly USDCAD Bar Chart.
Source: MetaTrader 4

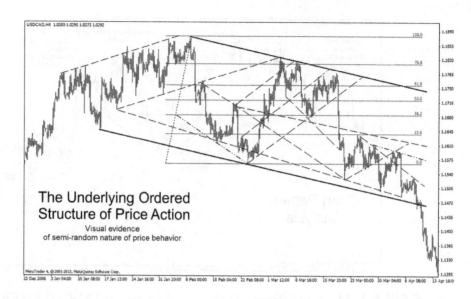

FIGURE 1.26   Underlying Market Symmetry on the 4-Hourly USDCAD Bar Chart.
Source: MetaTrader 4

1.6 BASIC ASSUMPTIONS OF TECHNICAL ANALYSIS

Technical analysis is based on a few fundamental assumptions. *The first assumption is that market action, which includes price action, reflects all known information in the markets.* The market discounts everything except acts of God.

This means that the markets can only discount:

- Known information
- Expectations about known information
- Expectations about potential events

The market cannot discount:

- Unexpected events
- Unknown information

Market action is representative of the collective trading and investment decisions of all market participants, which directs the flow of supply and demand in the markets.

This implies that the technical analyst need only refer to the charting of market action, since all known information and expectation about such information has already been discounted by the markets. The actual cause or underlying reason driving demand or supply is irrelevant, as it is only the effect of such action that really matters, that is, prices rising or falling.

Some detractors of technical analysis contend that the assumption that all information is absorbed or discounted by the market is flawed. They argue that, with the exception of illegal insider trading, price cannot possibly discount an unexpectedly large block purchase of shares in the market before it occurs. The detractors are in fact perfectly correct in their contention, except for the fact that the markets do not actually discount unknown information or unexpected events. The market can only react to what is known or expected, which includes insider activity. It does not react to what is unknown or unexpected. Although insider information is nonpublic, it is still considered to be known information, since the action of insider buying and selling impacts market action and as such represents information in the markets.

It may be more realistic to think of the market as in a *continuous process of assimilating and adjusting to new market information*, rather than an unrealistic full-blown discounting of all information instantaneously.

What Are the Markets Really Discounting?

It is not merely news, economic releases, or corporate data that the markets are discounting. The assumption is that it discounts *everything*. This includes:

- Information about actual events
- Expectation about actual events
- Information about expected events
- Expectation about expected events
- Expectation about the possibility of unexpected events

Some also argue that there are many other forms of discounting like *buying the rumor and selling on the fact*. They are curious as to what the expectation should be in such a case. Should the expectation be that prices will appreciate once the good news is released or should the expectation be that prices will fall once the good news is public knowledge (since everyone is in fact selling on good news)? How would we know if the market is discounting the:

- Rumor itself
- Expectations about the rumor
- Expected good or bad news
- Actual news

In reality, *the market discounts all of the above*. Regardless of what the markets are discounting, be it quantifiable or otherwise, the end result is that price and markets action will ultimately reflect the *collective expectation* of all participants.

Market Discounting versus EMH

Efficient Market Hypothesis (EMH) states that for a market to efficiently discount and reflect all information perfectly, all of its participants must act on all information in the same rational manner instantaneously. Does this definition of EMH also apply the basic assumption in technical analysis that the market discounts everything?

Detractors of EMH contend that the act of discounting everything is not realistic or is largely impossible. They argue that the problem lies in the action taken by the participants. Not all participants will react to the same event or information in the same way, and in fact, some participants may act on it in a contrary fashion, that is, shorting the market rather than going long. They also argue that not all of the participants will react at the same time. Some will take preemptive action or act in anticipation of the event while other participants will act during the actual receipt of the information. There will also be participants who may react long after the information is released. Hence, trying to achieve a certain level of coordinated action for efficient discounting will be virtually impossible.

The detractors of EMH also contend that for the markets to discount all information effectively, *all participants must have access to that information and must act on it*. The market will otherwise be unable to discount or reflect all information effectively. This requirement itself presents a difficult challenge. They argue that it is virtually impossible to get all of its participants to act on all of the information. It is also unrealistic to expect all participants to have access to that information, and even if they do, we cannot expect the participants to be standing by at all times in readiness to act on such information. They further argue that information is never free. It is unrealistic to expect that all participants are able to afford the information, let alone *all* information.

There is a very subtle difference between efficient discounting in EMH and basic market discounting in technical analysis. As far as market discounting in technical analysis is concerned, there is no requirement of perfect efficiency except for the requirement that it discounts everything that becomes known to it, which includes the *sum total of all actions taken by its participants*, be it in a timely or untimely, rational or irrational fashion. Market action itself represents the ultimate truth and is a *direct consequence* of the market discounting all information known to it, regardless of whether the information is perfectly efficient or otherwise. The market continues to discount *all information* and expectations of such information as and when it unfolds and becomes known to the market. The term efficiency therefore, as far it applies to the basic assumption in technical analysis, refers to very act of discounting all information as it becomes known to the market, regardless of the type, quality, or speed at which it receives the information. For the technical analyst, price is (always) king and represents the ultimate truth in the market. The markets are never wrong. All market action is considered perfect and efficient under the basic premises of technical analysis. Hence, we see that the term efficient does not carry the same meaning or implications as in the case of EMH. In EMH, *efficient* has a very specific meaning.

The premises upon which EMH are constructed require that all new information be discounted *immediately* and *rationally* in order for the market to be perfectly efficient. Efficient under EMH means that the market participants must react:

1. *Instantaneously* to all market information
2. *Rationally* to all market information

EMH requires new information in order for prices to change. Bullish news will cause prices to rise and bearish news will drive prices down. Acting rationally means that all participants will make the same logical decision based on the new

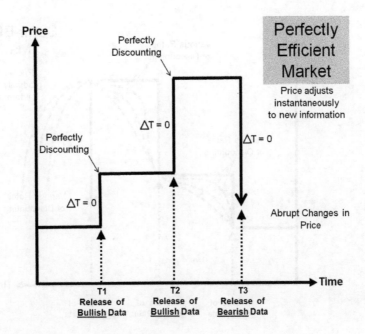

FIGURE 1.27   Efficient Market Adjusting to New Information.

information received. Instantaneously means acting or responding immediately to new information. Therefore, for the market to efficiently discount or reflect all information, all of its participants must act on all of the information in the same manner instantaneously. See Figure 1.27.

EMH contends that since the markets are efficient, there is no point in employing technical analysis, as prices would have already adjusted to the new information and the analyst would have no way of forecasting future action without such information. The reality is that there is discounting in the markets, but it is in no way perfectly efficient. In other words, the markets are at best *semi efficient*. This is because it is impossible to have all market participants acting instantaneously and rationally. It is a physical and logistical impossibility in the physical world. A simple "handclap" test will prove the point. If a large group of participants was asked to clap in response to a specific single event like the ring of a bell, we would find that there is little chance of observing a perfectly coordinated handclap across the group once such an event occurred.

As we have already discussed earlier, not all participants in the real world would react in exactly the same manner or arrive at the same logical decision based on the new information. Some market participants may have a different view of the markets and view the new information as inconsequential with minor impact on the markets, and may even trade against the new information. Also, there are a large number of strategies that one can employ to trade the markets based on the same information. As a result, when new bullish information is released, participants may:

- Enter a long position immediately
- Enter a short position based on an average-up scale-trading strategy

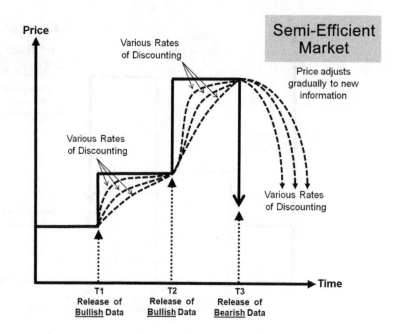

FIGURE 1.28   A Semi-Efficient Market Gradually Adjusting to New Information.

■ Scale in more positions as the market rises
■ Scale out positions that may have already been in profit
■ Wait for prices to become overextended before fading the breakout

Even if the market participants were to act rationally and all make the same logical decisions based on the new information, they may not be able to act on the information instantaneously. They may have received delayed information or were not standing by in readiness to act on the information when it arrived. They may also find it physically impossible to act on all information, especially when information streams in continuously in very quick succession. They may also be unable to afford the cost of such information. As such, the discounting of new information will take place at a slower rate, with a semi-efficient market adjusting gradually to the new information as market participants compete with each other for the best fills. See Figure 1.28.

Figure 1.29 is a 5-min chart of the EURUSD depicting the markets adjusting to new information, in this case the nonfarm payroll and unemployment report. Notice how prices swing back and forth as traders compete with each other in light of the new information. Price finally makes a top at the 61.8 percent Fibonacci projection (projecting AB from Point C) level and begins consolidating.

Nevertheless, EMH assumes three basic levels of information discounting:

1. The Weak Form: The weak form of EMH suggests that all current *prices* have already been fully discounted and, as such, reflect all past price information. Therefore, they cannot impact future prices. The application of technical analysis is therefore pointless and meaningless.

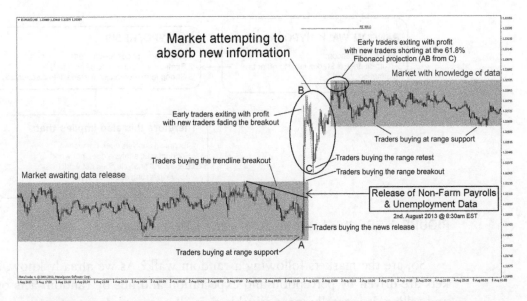

FIGURE 1.29 A Semi-Efficient Market Gradually Adjusting to New Information.
Source: MetaTrader 4

2. **The Semi-Strong Form:** The semi-strong form of EMH suggests that all information, once public, is of little use as price would have already adjusted to the new information making the use of such information unprofitable and pointless. Market participants would have little opportunity to take advantage of such information. This implies that even fundamental analysis is pointless and meaningless.

3. **The Strong Form:** The strong form of EMH suggests that all information, regardless of whether public or private, would have been already fully reflected in the current price. Consequently, all forms of analysis and forecasting are pointless and meaningless.

Random Walk

Closely related to the EMH is the concept of Random Walk. Random walk suggests that prices move in a purely random manner and that:

- Past prices do not have any influence on current price
- Current price has no influence on future price (Markovian condition)

All information is already incorporated into the current price. This would mean that there is no way whatsoever to forecast future action, and prices are as likely to go up as they are to go down. This renders all form of analysis and forecasting pointless and meaningless. Random walk is in a way related to EMH, insofar as current price represents the current state of all information. In random walk, prices do not adjust to any new information, unlike in EMH. Its motion is purely random or *stochastic*.

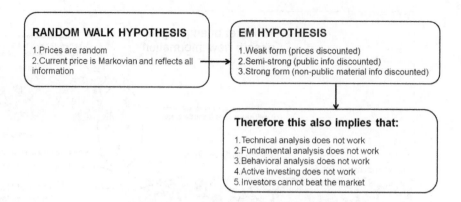

FIGURE 1.30 Random Walk, EMH, and Their Implications.

So, are the markets following a random walk? As we already know, the markets are driven by perception and expectation and not by random acts of buying and selling. It is totally inconceivable that all participants invest in the markets in a purely random fashion, completely unencumbered by cost, emotions, psychology, and biases. As we already know, market participants tend to react in a highly predictable manner time and time again. It is the author's opinion that random walk is simply not a true representation of everyday market action. See Figure 1.30.

Real-World Discounting

In the real world, markets overreact and there is insider activity. With insiders buying and selling, prices adjust to reflect this information. See Figure 1.31. Once the new bullish or bearish information is released, the insiders would in fact be liquidating positions in profit, selling off the shares to the public.

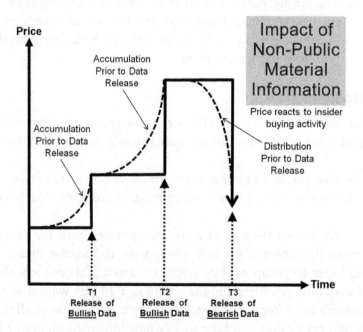

FIGURE 1.31 Insider Activity Impacting Market Action.

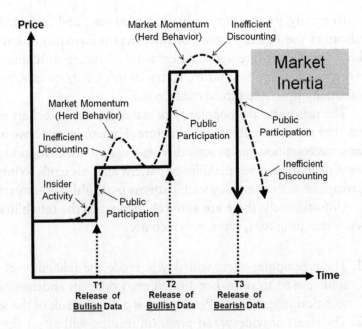

FIGURE 1.32 Markets Overreacting to New Information.

Figure 1.32 shows the market overreacting to new information. We see the insiders accumulating shares prior to the release of the new information. The public joins in after the information is published. Public participation begins to increase as more participants join in the now obvious rally in prices. This contributes to the herding behavior that finally causes the market to overreact to the new information. This is exactly what the insiders are hoping for, in order to extract the greatest amount of profit. Eventually a top is formed as the market runs out of buyers and/or money to invest. The activity subsides only to repeat again.

Price versus Value

One interesting question that many novices ask is whether the market is discounting price or value. In fact, a more fundamental question to ask would be whether price represents value. If it does, then how do we explain a stock valued at $10 rising to a price of $30 in the absence of any significant changes in its fundamentals?

In reality, market action is merely the collective expectations of all its participants. What we are really trading is expectation. It has not very much to do with absolute intrinsic value, but rather its *expected* value. In short, current *price is the result of expectations about future price and value.*

Market Behavior Repeats Itself

The second assumption or premise of technical analysis is that market behavior has a tendency to repeat itself. This means that past price and chart patterns will provide a reasonable basis for forecasting potential future behavior. The underlying explanation for the repeatability of price and market behavior lies in the fact that market behavior is driven by human psychology, which seldom changes over time. The uses of past patterns to predict futures moves are grounded in the *reliability and consistency of human behavior.*

Ironically, most equity valuation modeling and standard economic statistical indicators are based on past or historical information as well. How else are we able to make an intelligent assessment of future outcome without reference to past data? It is human nature to try to infer, extrapolate, generalize, and predict potentially probable future outcomes.

The reason for the popularity of classical price and chart patterns lies in the fact that they are essentially visual in nature. Human beings have an innate tendency for pattern recognition and as such there is a natural inclination to gravitate toward such forms of analysis. The reliability of pattern analysis tends to improve as more market participants start to employ such patterns in their day-to-day trading and forecasting.

Unfortunately, there are some challenges to the reliability of using past action as a forecasting tool, some of which are:

1. The preempting effect will slowly erode the reliability of historical patterns as traders start to outbid or outsell each other in anticipation of the approaching technical trigger levels. Preempting is a direct result of the self-fulfilling prophecy.
2. The effect of widespread program trading will affect the reliability of historical pattern trading as programs are able to trade in ways not easily replicated by manual or human trading.
3. The ever-changing influx of new participants into the markets will slowly affect the reliability of chart and price patterns unfolding in the expected manner. Although human psychology remains largely predictable over the longer-term horizon, short-term patterns are sometimes impacted by new participants who have a slightly different approach than the usual participants in that market.

The Market Tends to Move in Trends

Lastly, from the definitions given of technical analysis, it is generally accepted that the market has a tendency to move in trends. This explains the popularity of trend-based methodologies. Of course, it is not hard to understand the basis for the popularity of trend trading, since trend action affords market participants the greatest profit over the shortest possible duration in the markets.

But if we analyze this statement more closely, we understand that the term trend is inconclusive. What is actually is a trend? When is a trend a trend and when does it cease to be one? There have been many attempts to define what a trend is objectively. Successively higher or lower peaks and troughs is one widely accepted method, and is by far the preferred mode of identifying a trend. But then this begs the next question, which is: what constitutes a peak or a trough? Significant containment of price below or above a trendline or sloping moving average may also be deemed a valid way of defining a trend. We shall delve into the specifics of defining trends, consolidations, and other formations in Chapter 5.

Although trend following is popular, there are some challenges to using it, some of which are:

- Inefficient trade sizing in volatile markets
- Inefficient profit capture during trends

- Inefficient performance in ranging markets
- Inefficient adaptation to more volatile trend action
- Inability to identify trend changes efficiently
- Possibility of negative slippage in fast-moving markets
- Possibility of large drawdowns due to the low winning percentages
- Reduced performance caused by whipsaw action during consolidations
- Influx of trend-capturing systems produces inefficient fills
- Ineffective back and forward testing

Finally, it is important to note that a trend in one timeframe may be a sideways market in another.

1.7 FOUR BASIC ASSUMPTIONS IN THE APPLICATION OF TECHNICAL ANALYSIS

There are four underlying premises associated with the application of technical analysis, namely:

1. Price behavior is expected to persist until there is evidence to the contrary.
2. For every bullish indication or interpretation, there exists an equal and opposite bearish indication or interpretation for the same price behavior or phenomena.
3. Extreme bullishness is potentially bearish (and extreme bearishness is potentially bullish).
4. A technical tool or indicator has no real significance except for that attributed to it by market participants.

The first premise is about preserving the status quo. It should be noted that most technical analysis is based on a set of assumptions. Most assumptions derive from one grand underlying premise, that being the preservation the prevailing price behavior. For example, a trend is expected to persist until there is evidence to the contrary. Hence a state of persistence is assumed to be the status quo. If a cycle is identified, it is assumed to persist until cyclic failure is clear and obvious. If the market is in consolidation, it is expected to continue to range until a breakout is identified.

The second premise is also a fairly obvious, not only in relation to technical analysis but also with much of life. For example, an analyst may make a case for rising oil prices as the reason for a rise in the Dow Jones index since it is indicative of increasing demand, representing evidence of a recovering economy. The same analyst may also make a case for rising oil prices as the reason for a decline in the Dow Jones index due to the widely held perception of increasing cost, and hence bearish for the economy in general. Another example would be to find the stochastics at an oversold level and conclude that the current uptrend is strong since it is potentially or implicitly bullish. Alternatively, the stochastics could be at an overbought level, leading to the conclusion that the current uptrend is strong since an overbought level is regarded as explicitly bullish.

The third premise above is obvious when using oscillators such as stochastics, RSI, and MACD. A reading of 100 percent on the stochastics is extremely and explicitly bullish but it is also regarded as a potentially or implicitly bearish condition since it is at a level where price may generally be regarded as being overextended or exhausted. There is an underlying expectation or assumption that a reversion to the means would eventually take place (note that this may not always be true, for example, in the case of cumulative type indicators). A breakout above a rising channel is also explicitly bullish but it is also regarded as implicitly bearish since it also represents a state of overextension or exhaustion in price, with respect to the rising channel formation.

The fourth premise is specifically about the effects of the self-fulfilling prophecy. It is easy to understand why a largely concerted wave of buying or selling at various points on a price chart may cause a significant reaction in price. This concerted wave of buying or selling will generally be more pronounced if these points are significantly clear and obvious to most market participants using technical analysis. Hence we generally notice a larger than average penetration bar during trendline breakouts, especially if the trendline is significantly clear and obvious to most traders. This also implies that should an indicator be essentially faulty or illogical in its design, if enough participants risk actual capital based on its signals, it would begin to exhibit a greater level of reliability.

The Efficacy of Technical Analysis at Various Timeframes

Technical analysis generally works more efficiently at timeframes where there are fewer forms of analyses available. For example, on higher timeframes like the daily, weekly, monthly, or yearly charts, fundamental analysis plays a very important role in helping to forecast potential market action. But at very low timeframes like the one-minute charts, fundamental analysis may not be as useful, especially if the stopsize is very small. In essence, the smaller the stopsize, the more important will be the role of applying technical analysis when trying to forecast very short term movements in price. This is the main reason why technical analysis is generally more reliable at lower timeframes.

1.8 MARKET PARTICIPANTS

Market participants comprise the average investors and traders, financial institutions, commercial and central banks, hedgers, arbitrageurs, brokers, hedge funds, mutual and pension funds, and so on. Here are the eight main categories of market participants:

1. Retail
2. Institutional
3. Speculator
4. Supply Side
5. Demand Side
6. Professional
7. Investor
8. Novice

FIGURE 1.33 Market Participants by Way of Time Spent in the Markets.

Market participants may also be categorized as:

- Discretionary Traders
- Nondiscretionary Traders

But there are many other ways of categorizing market participants. We can categorize them by the amount of time they spend in the markets or by the methodology that they employ when trading or investing in the markets. Figure 1.33 lists the five main groups of market participants by the amount of time they spend in the markets.

Figure 1.34 lists the same five groups of market participants by way of the methodology that they employ when trading or investing in the markets.

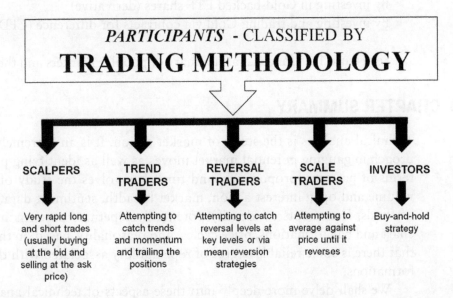

FIGURE 1.34 Market Participants by Way of Trading and Investing Methodology.

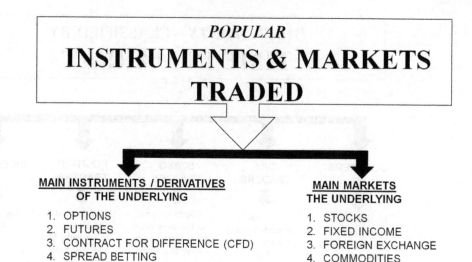

FIGURE 1.35 Popular Markets and Instruments.

Popular Markets and Instruments

Market participants may trade and invest in either the main *markets* or *instruments* that allow access to these markets. These instruments are also referred to as derivatives, since they are derived from the main underlying markets. For example, a market participant may participate in gold in several ways:

- By buying the physical Gold itself (main market)
- By buying or selling a futures contract on Gold (derivative)
- By buying or selling an options contract on Gold (derivative)
- By investing in Gold-backed ETF shares (derivative)
- By investing and trading Gold via contracts for difference (CFD) (derivative)

See Figure 1.35 for a visual summary of popular markets and their derivatives.

1.9 CHAPTER SUMMARY

Technical analysis is the study of market action. It is an extremely popular approach in gauging potential market moves as well as identifying past activity in terms of patterns, proportions, and time. It involves the study of price action, volume and open interest action, market breadth, sentiment data, and the flow of funds. It attempts to identify potentially repetitive patterns in the form of chart and bar formations, price cycles, and seasonality, based on the assumption that there is some reliable degree of repeatability associated with these technical formations.

We shall delve more deeply into these aspects of technical analysis over the rest of this handbook.

CHAPTER 1 REVIEW QUESTIONS

1. What are the challenges to technical analysis?
2. A basic assumption in technical analysis is that the market discounts everything. EMH also requires the discounting of all information. In what ways are they different?
3. Describe how an analyst may resolve conflicting signals or chart patterns.
4. Explain why identifying a trend change is largely a subjective exercise.
5. Is random walk a true reflection of the markets?
6. Describe the three levels of discounting new information under EMH.
7. What is a good definition of technical analysis?
8. List as many advantages and disadvantages of using technical analysis as you can.

REFERENCES

Edwards, Robert D., and John Magee. 2007. *Technical Analysis of Stock Trends*. New York: AMACOM).

Kirkpatrick, Charles, and Julie Dahlquist. 2007. *Technical Analysis: The Complete Resource for Financial Market Technicians*. Upper Saddle River, NJ: Pearson Education Inc.

Murphy, John. 1999. *Technical Analysis of the Financial Markets*. (New York: New York Institute of Finance (NYIF).

Pring, Martin J. 2002. *Technical Analysis Explained: The Successful Investor's Guide to Spotting Investment Trends and Turning Points*. 4th ed. New York: McGraw-Hill.

CHAPTER 2

Introduction to Dow Theory

LEARNING OBJECTIVES

After studying this chapter, you should be able to:

- Understand the basic concepts and assumptions of Dow Theory
- Apply the concepts of Dow Theory to forecast potential entry and exit points in the market
- Identify the strengths and weaknesses of applying Dow Theory
- Explain the importance of price and volume confirmation as a basis for determining potential market action
- Highlight the current challenges to Dow Theory

Dow Theory lays the basic foundation for modern day technical analysis. Its premises underpin the very study of market action analysis and have withstood the test of time. In this chapter, we shall be discussing the basic assumptions of Dow Theory and its relevance in today's markets.

2.1 ORIGINS AND PROPONENTS OF DOW THEORY

Charles H. Dow is credited for much of the early work that led to what is known today as *Dow Theory*. Dow's successor, William P. Hamilton, carried on developing and organizing much of Dow's original early writings, which included the *Wall Street Journal* editorials that were published around the beginning of the twentieth century. Hamilton's work culminated in his book *The Stock Market Barometer*. A close acquaintance of Dow's, S. A. Nelson, published a book about Dow's work entitled *The ABC of Stock Speculation* and was the first person to refer to Dow's concepts and ideas as the "Dow Theory."

Robert Rhea, a student of Hamilton, was later responsible for much of the categorizing, refining, and formal codification of Dow's basic premises, which were laid out in Rhea's book *The Dow Theory*. It was Robert Rhea's work that really developed Dow's Theory and laid the basic foundation with three important assumptions. The first is that the primary trend is not susceptible to manipulation, although there is a possibility that it could occur over the shorter term. Rhea's second assumption was that the averages discounted everything and that price is a reflection of all information. Finally Rhea proposed that Dow Theory itself is not perfect and that investing according to its principles will not guarantee profitability. At most, it should be regarded as a set of guidelines for investing.

Dow published, in 1884, a stock market average of 11 stocks that he later developed into a 12-stock Industrial Index and a 20-stock Railroad Average. Dow wanted to create an index of stocks to better reflect the general action of the markets instead of trying to gauge market behavior via individual stock action, which was at the time fairly erratic and open to manipulation. The index was meant to average out or smooth these erratic price movements. The action of the averages was meant to act as a barometer of the current market environment.

Since then, the 12-stock Industrial Index has gradually evolved into 30 stocks and is known today as the Dow Jones Industrial Average. The Railroad Average is known as the Dow Jones Transportation Average.

2.2 BASIC ASSUMPTIONS OF DOW THEORY

There are six basic tenets of Dow Theory, namely:

1. The averages discount everything.
2. The market has three trends.
3. Primary trends have three phases.
4. A trend persists until its reversal is indicated.
5. The averages must confirm one another.
6. Volume must confirm the trend.

In addition to the six basic tenets, only closing prices are recognized in Dow Theory.

The Averages Discount Everything (Pricing in Information)

It is believed that the markets discount everything, except acts of God. This means that the market is the end result of all participatory action, which represents all *information* that may be known to the markets. The mechanism by which information is known to the market is that of actual participation via capital injection. Although the market cannot discount unexpected events, that is, acts of God or unknown information, it can absorb, react, and adjust to market shocks fairly rapidly. The pricing of all known information need not be instantaneous or be driven by rational participants. There is also no requirement that all participants always act on all information all of the time, or that they react in the same manner.

Figure 2.1 depicts prices declining before September 11, 2001. Is the market trying to discount information that is not as yet known or is it merely coincidental?

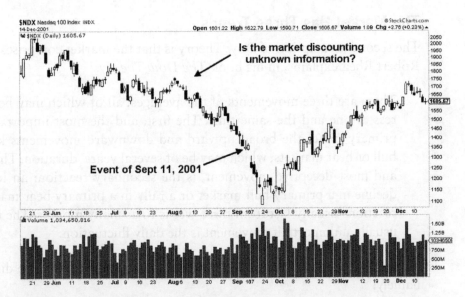

FIGURE 2.1   Is the Market Discounting Unknown Information?
Courtesy of Stockcharts.com

Figure 2.2 shows the gold market *adjusting very rapidly* to information about the same event. The market is attempting to discount all information once the information is made known to it.

In short, the market action is the sum of all participatory activity, based on the aggregate of the participants' beliefs, biases, personal predilections, as well as *future* expectations. Price is the ultimate reflection and embodiment of everything that is knowable. As such, the technical analysts need not concern themselves with the causes or circumstances giving rise to various market action, but only with the effects of the underlying causes.

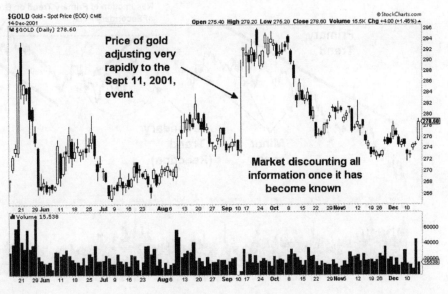

FIGURE 2.2   Gold Adjusting Rapidly to New Information.
Courtesy of Stockcharts.com

The Market Has Three Trends

The second assumption of Dow Theory is that the market comprises three trends. Robert Rhea explains, in his book *The Dow Theory*:

> There are three movements of the averages, all of which may be in progress at one and the same time. The first, and the most important, is the primary trend: the broad upward and downward movements known as bull or bear markets, which may be of several years' duration. The second, and most deceptive movement, is the secondary reaction: an important decline in a primary bull market or a rally in a primary bear market. The reactions usually last from three weeks to as many months. The third and usually unimportant movement is the daily fluctuation.

> Summarizing, the market is believed to express itself as three distinct trends, namely:

1. Primary trend (major trend)—lasting from months to years (long term)
2. Secondary reaction (intermediate trend)—lasting from weeks to months (medium term)
3. Minor trend—lasting from days to weeks (short term)

See Figure 2.3.

(1) The Primary Trend The largest trend is by far the primary trend, which is normally expected to last from months to years. Rhea hypothesized that primary trends are not susceptible to manipulation and therefore represent a more reliable

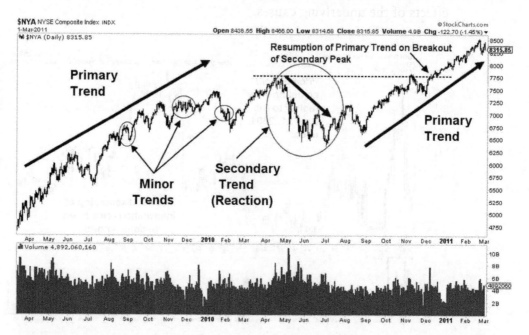

FIGURE 2.3 All Three Trends in the NYSE Composite Index.
Courtesy of Stockcharts.com

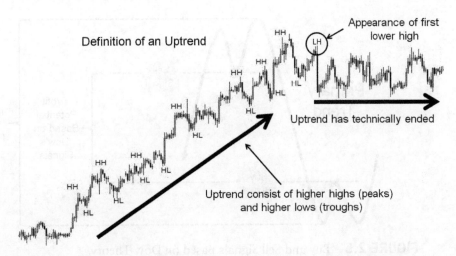

FIGURE 2.4   An Uptrend in Terms of Successively Higher Highs and Lows.

barometer for investment decisions. It is sometimes referred to as the *tides* of the oceans. Although the primary trend usually lasts from months to years, Rhea commented that is it very difficult to forecast the extent or duration of a primary trend.

There are two types of primary trends, namely:

1. Primary *bull* trend (bull market)
2. Primary *bear* trend (bear market)

In Dow Theory, an uptrend is defined primarily as successively *higher* peaks and troughs. A downtrend is defined as successively *lower* peaks and troughs. Notice in Figure 2.4 that the appearance of a lower high in an uptrend may represent an early indication that the uptrend may be coming to an end.

In Dow Theory, an indication of a trend continuation or reversal is signaled by the penetration of a previous peak or trough. As such, one of the main criticisms of Dow Theory is that buy and sell signals arrive too late, usually missing out on one-third or more of the entire trend. According to Dow, it is more important to participate in a primary bull or bear trend once it has been confirmed or once it proves that it has the strength to penetrate old peaks or troughs. Dow believes that losing out on some potential profit for the added safety of participating in a confirmed trend is well worth the sacrifice. It should also be noted that all investment and trading decisions are based strictly on the primary trend alone, with the exception of trading lines that may form from the daily price fluctuations. See Figure 2.5.

Figure 2.6 depicts a primary bull trend in gold that lasted approximately 12 years.

Figure 2.7 depicts a primary bear trend in the 30-year Treasury bond yield that lasted approximately 23 years.

It should be noted that if trends are defined via trendline violations rather than by the successive sequence of rising or falling peaks and troughs, there may be some discrepancies between exactly when a change in trend actually occurs, especially when different chart scaling is employed. Logarithmically

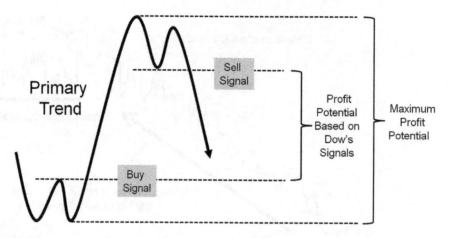

FIGURE 2.5 Buy and Sell Signals Based on Dow Theory.

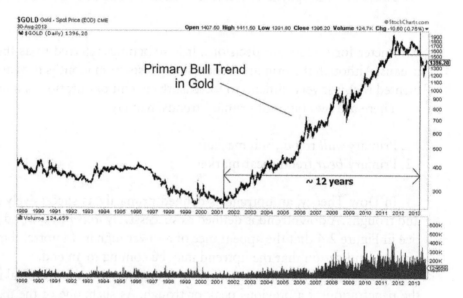

FIGURE 2.6 A Primary Bull Trend in Gold.
Courtesy of Stockcharts.com

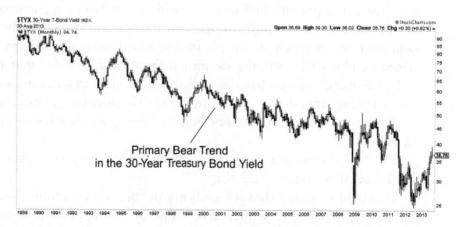

FIGURE 2.7 A Primary Bear Trend in the 30-Year Treasury bond Yield.
Courtesy of Stockcharts.com

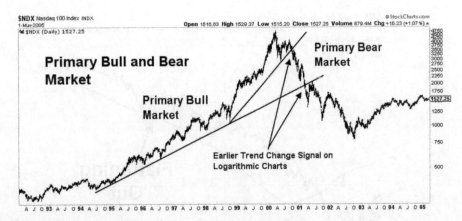

FIGURE 2.8 Bull Market Turning into a Bear Market with Early Trend Change Signals on a Logarithmically Scaled Chart of the Nasdaq 100 Index.
Courtesy of Stockcharts.com

scaled charts tend to give earlier trend change signals since uptrend lines are violated sooner. Conversely, arithmetically scaled charts tend to give slower trend change signals as uptrend lines are violated much later. See Figures 2.8 and 2.9.

Sometimes it may be hard to decide which scaling to use in order to apply technical overlays in a manner that would provide consistent signals. If an analyst has been using logarithmically scaled charts on a regular basis, his or her interpretation of the price action may differ from an analyst who regularly uses arithmetically scaled charts. Figures 2.10 and 2.11 show Apple Inc. displaying a more bearish flattening-out-type behavior on a logarithmically scaled chart, whereas the arithmetically scaled charts depict a stronger and steadier uptrend for the same stock over the same period.

(2) The Secondary Trend or Reaction The secondary trend is also referred to as the secondary reaction because it moves or reacts in the opposite direction

FIGURE 2.9 Bull Market Turning into a Bear Market with Late Trend Change Signals on a Arithmetically Scaled Chart of the Nasdaq 100 Index.
Courtesy of Stockcharts.com

51

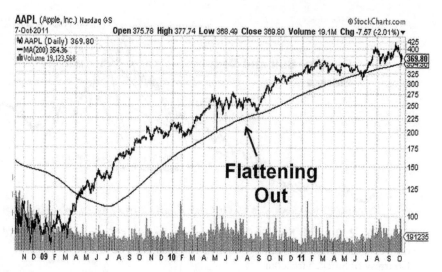

FIGURE 2.10 Bearish Flattening Type Action on Apple Inc.
Courtesy of Stockcharts.com

of the existing primary trend. It usually lasts from weeks to approximately three months, and frequently slightly longer. It is sometimes referred to as the *waves* on the tides. The secondary reaction usually retraces from one- to two-thirds of the primary trend's range. Any retracement or correction beyond two-thirds *on high volume* usually signifies that the secondary reaction may in fact be a new primary bear market. It is important to note that Dow Theory also stresses the importance and psychological significance of the 50 percent retracement level, a view shared by another prominent technician, W. D. Gann.

A primary bull trend resumes its uptrend once price breaches the highest peak formed by the secondary reaction, while a primary bear trend resumes its downtrend once price breaches the lowest trough formed by the secondary reaction.

FIGURE 2.11 Non Flattening Type Action on Apple Inc.
Courtesy of Stockcharts.com

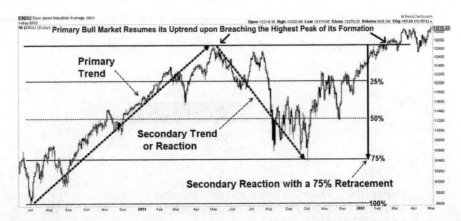

FIGURE 2.12 Primary Bull Market Resuming Its Uptrend after Breaching the Highest Peak of the Secondary Reaction on the Dow Jones Industrial Average.
Courtesy of Stockcharts.com

Figure 2.3 showed the NYSE Composite Index resuming its primary bull market around the beginning of 2011 after breaching the peak formed during the formation of the secondary reaction. Figure 2.12 depicts a 75 percent secondary reaction on the Dow Jones Industrial Average. The primary bull market resumes its uptrend upon breaching the highest peak formed during the secondary reaction.

Figure 2.13 depicts various secondary reaction retracements in the EURUSD.

(3) The Minor Trend   The minor trends are not regarded as important in Dow Theory. In fact, Hamilton commented in his book, *The Stock Market Barometer,* that "The stock market is not logical in its movements from day to day."

Minor trends usually last from days to weeks. They are sometimes referred to as the *ripples* on the waves.

Under Dow Theory, the day's erratic fluctuations represent market noise and no investment decision should be based on such erratic activity, with the exception

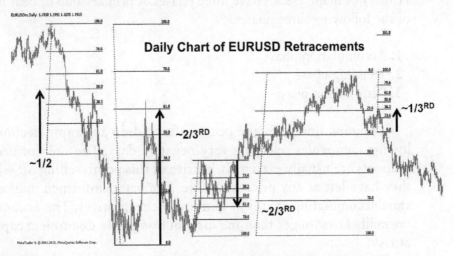

FIGURE 2.13   Secondary Reactions on the EURUSD Daily Chart.
Source: MetaTrader 4

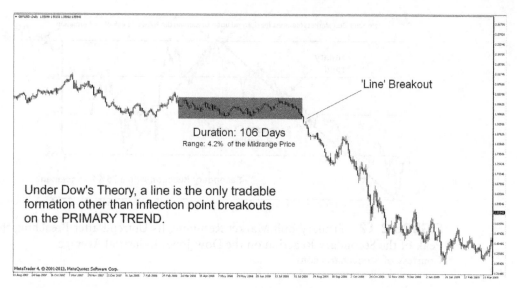

FIGURE 2.14 Example of a Line on the Daily Chart of the GBPUSD.
Source: MetaTrader 4

of lines being formed. Lines are simply narrow horizontal ranging formations on the daily chart. They are usually formed in anticipation of some significant news or economic announcement. These narrow consolidations usually result in strong breakouts. Dow Theory recognizes lines as potentially profitable formations, even though they are essentially regarded as minor trends. A line is the only tradable formation under Dow Theory other than inflection point breakouts in the primary trend. See Figure 2.14.

We see that each of the three trends is defined by its *duration* and *extent*. We shall now look at primary trends in a little more detail.

Primary Trends Have Three Phases

Primary or major trends have three phases. A primary bull or bear market consists of the following three phases:

1. Accumulation phase
2. Trending phase
3. Distribution phase

Accumulation normally occurs after a deep and rapid decline in prices following companies releasing very negative data. The uninformed market participants are usually extremely bearish at this point, selling off whatever shares they have left at any price available. The better informed market participants start accumulating shares at extremely cheap prices. The accumulation phase normally lasts longer than the distribution phase due to less capital and profit at risk.

The trend phase consists of the uptrend and downtrend phase. The uptrend phase is driven by market participants expecting higher prices after an accumulation.

The initial general sentiment tends to be slightly less bearish. The public begins to participate as rising prices becomes more obvious and as more bullish news is reported. At higher prices, margin debt starts to increase as the public scrambles to invest in the rapidly rising market. The uptrend phase tends to last longer than the downtrend phase due to less capital and unrealized profit at risk, at lower prices.

The downtrend phase normally starts to accelerate as more companies start to report increasingly bearish news. The uninformed traders and investors begin to unload positions. As prices begin to fall unexpectedly, the public begins to liquidate positions. Bearish sentiment continues to intensify as prices sink to new depths. The downtrend phase tends to be shorter lived than the uptrend phase, due to the larger amounts of capital and unrealized profit at risk, at higher prices.

Distribution normally occurs after a prolonged and rapid rise in prices. Companies tend to outperform and most media and news headlines are extremely bullish. The uninformed market participants tend to be extremely optimistic, buying up whatever shares are available in the market at any price, normally referred to as being in a state of *irrational exuberance*. Margin debt is at extreme levels. The smart investors continue to liquidate shares in a very gradual manner during the distribution process, again careful not to drive down prices too rapidly so that they may continue to sell at the higher prices. The distribution phase is normally shorter in duration than the accumulation phase, due to the larger amount of capital and unrealized profit at risk at higher prices, at the top of the market. See Figure 2.15.

Also, the longer the accumulation or distribution lasts, the greater will be its subsequent breakout move. See Figure 2.16.

A Trend Persists until Its Reversal Is Indicated

In Dow Theory, a trend is assumed to persist until there is evidence to the contrary. Trend changes are identified by a penetration of a previous significant peak or trough. Therefore, unless a prior support or resistance level is breached, the trend is assumed to be still intact. See Figure 2.17.

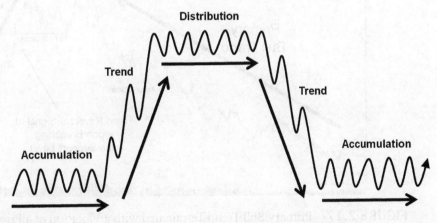

FIGURE 2.15   The Idealized Three Phases of a Primary Bull Trend.

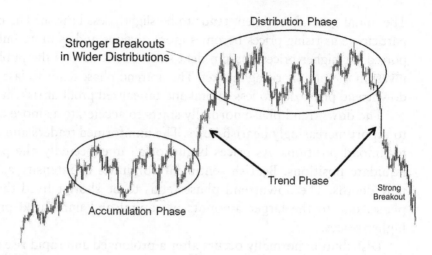

FIGURE 2.16 A Real World Example of the Three Phases of a Primary Bull Trend.

There are basically three types of reversal formations that will signal a change in the direction of the existing or predominant trend, namely:

1. Failure swings
2. Non-failure swings
3. Double tops/bottoms

The term *failure swing* was first used by Welles Wilder in his book, *New Concepts in Technical Trading Systems*, when describing the oscillator swings on the relative strength index (RSI) indicator. The three basic *top reversal* formations are illustrated in Figure 2.18. A breach of a prior support signals a

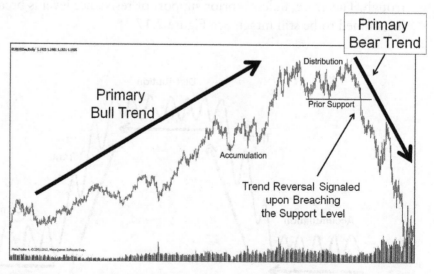

FIGURE 2.17 Primary Bull Trend Terminated with a Violation of a Prior Support Level.
Source: MetaTrader 4

THREE BASIC VARIATIONS OF A TOP REVERSAL

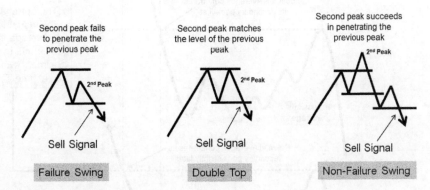

FIGURE 2.18 Top Reversal Patterns.

potential change in the direction of the trend. It also represents a technical sell signal. Note that the non-failure swing formation provides a more conclusive sell signal at the penetration of the second or lower support level, rather than at the first higher support level. This is because the formation was still in the process of making a higher peak, so more evidence is required to ascertain that a potential trend change is indeed on the way. Nevertheless, many traders use the first higher support level to scale in or out of some positions, with the remainder of the position scaled in or out at the breach of the second lower support level.

The three basic *bottom reversal* formations are illustrated in Figure 2.19. The same rationale applies except in reverse.

The Averages Must Confirm One Another

In Dow Theory, there is a requirement that both the Industrials Average and the Railroad Average must extend beyond their secondary peaks in order for a trend to be established, that is, the trend in one average must be *confirmed* by the other

THREE BASIC VARIATIONS OF A BOTTOM REVERSAL

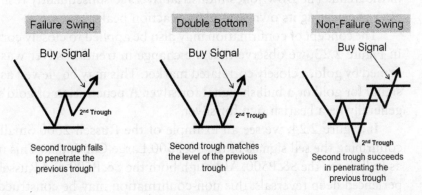

FIGURE 2.19 Bottom Reversal Patterns.

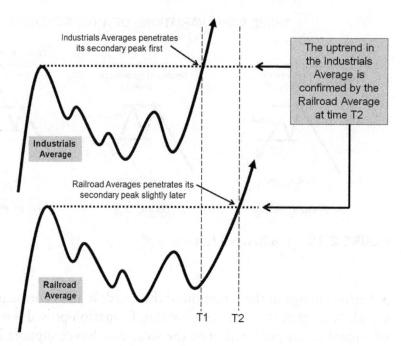

Industrials Averages penetrates
its secondary peak first

The uptrend in
the Industrials
Average is
confirmed by the
Railroad Average
at time T2

Industrials
Average

Railroad Averages penetrates its
secondary peak slightly later

Railroad
Average

T1   T2

FIGURE 2.20   Confirmation of the Averages.

average. In Figure 2.20, we observe that the Industrials Average penetrated its secondary peak at T1 while the Railroad Average penetrated its own secondary peak a little later at T2. Hence the uptrend was only confirmed at time T2. As far as Dow Theory is concerned, the uptrend was not confirmed until the Railroad Average penetrated its own secondary peak at T2.

In Figure 2.21, we observe that the Dow Jones Industrial Average breached its own secondary peak at T1, which was confirmed later by the Dow Jones Transportation Average breaching its own secondary peak at T2. It is at T2 that the uptrend in the markets was finally confirmed, according to the tenets of Dow Theory.

In Figure 2.22, we observe that the Dow Jones Industrial Average experienced a weak non-failure swing sell signal, signifying a change in the trend. The bearish signal was not confirmed by the Dow Jones Transportation Average and this was therefore regarded as a bullish indication. There is non-confirmation of a reversal in the trend. The Dow Jones Industrial Average subsequently resumed its uptrend after penetrating its own secondary reaction peak.

The concept of confirmation may also be applied to closely correlated markets. In Figure 2.23, we observe that the change in trend in silver was not as yet confirmed by gold, a closely correlated market. This may be viewed as either a bearish signal for gold or a bullish signal for silver. A penetration of gold's support would generally be a bearish sign for silver.

In Figure 2.24, we see an example of the Russell 2000 Small Cap Index not confirming the sell signals in the S&P500 Large Cap Index. This may be regarded as bullish for the S&P500. Although both the S&P500 and Russell 2000 have experienced deep reversals, this non-confirmation may be construed as an *oversold indication* on the S&P500.

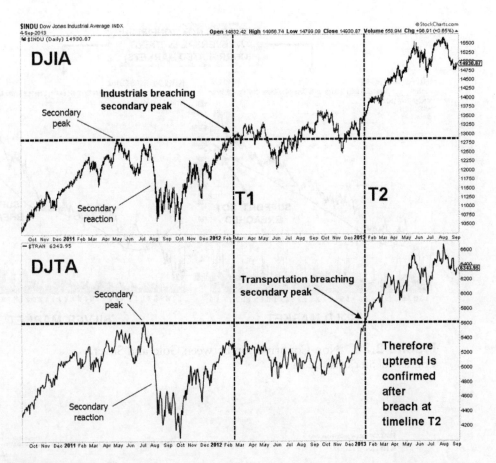

FIGURE 2.21 Confirmation of Trend Continuation Based on Dow Theory.
Courtesy of Stockcharts.com

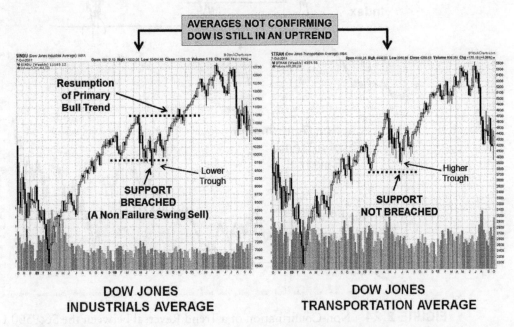

FIGURE 2.22 Non-Confirmation of Reversal in Trend on the Dow Jones Industrial Average.
Courtesy of Stockcharts.com

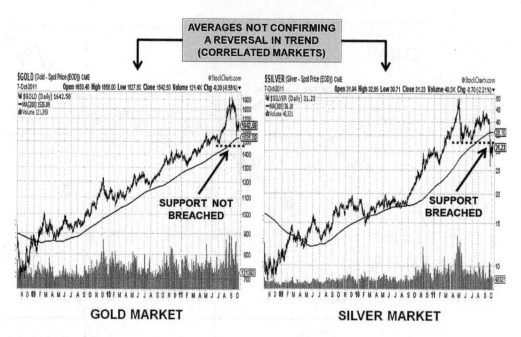

FIGURE 2.23 Non-Confirmation Between Gold and Silver.
Courtesy of Stockcharts.com

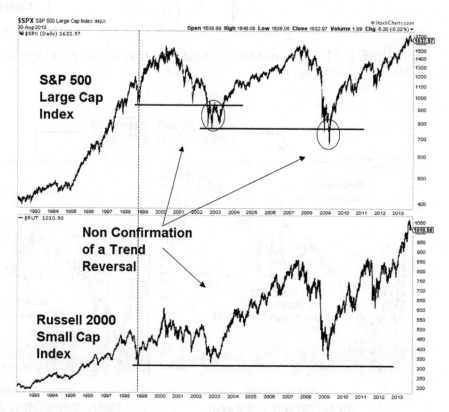

FIGURE 2.24 Non-Confirmation of a Trend Reversal between the S&P500 Large Cap Index and Russell Small Cap Index.
Courtesy of Stockcharts.com

Volume Must Confirm the Trend

In Dow Theory, volume has to increase or expand *in the direction of the existing trend*, that is, volume has to confirm the trend. If volume does not expand in the direction of the existing trend, then this is seen as a sign of weakness in the trend and may potentially lead to a weakening or reversal of the existing trend. It should be noted also that volume is considered to be a secondary indicator.

Expanding in the direction of the existing trend means that:

1. In an uptrend, volume should be increasing.
2. In an uptrend, volume should be decreasing during a downside retracement.
3. In a downtrend, volume should be increasing.
4. In a downtrend, volume should be decreasing during an upside retracement.

If any of the four conditions listed above is not met, the existing trend may be potentially weaker than expected and may lead to a reversal in the existing trend. In Figure 2.25, we see volume, in area A on the chart, expanding in the direction of the existing primary bull trend in gold. Notice that on average, volume has declined during the retracement phase, as seen in area B on the chart. This is essentially a bullish indication for gold. We therefore expect more upside moves in gold over the longer term.

Figure 2.26 illustrates the volume action associated with the primary bull trend between 2006 and 2010 in the GLD SPDR Gold Trust Shares. We see volume expanding in the direction of the trend in period 1, 3, 7, and 9. For periods 2, 4, 6, 8,

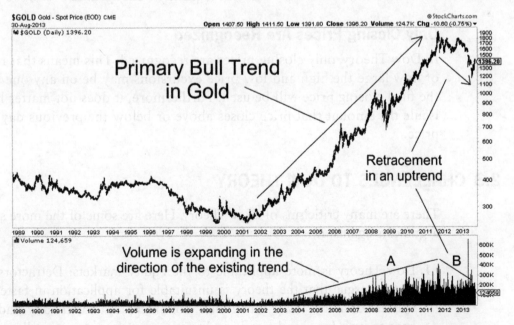

FIGURE 2.25 Volume Expanding in the Direction of the Existing Primary Bull Trend in Gold.
Courtesy of Stockcharts.com

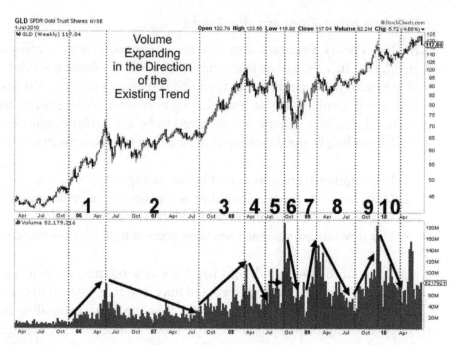

FIGURE 2.26 Volume Expanding in the Direction of the Existing Primary Bull Trend in GLD SPDR Gold Trust Shares.
Courtesy of Stockcharts.com

and 10 we see volume declining whenever there is a correction or retracement in the GLD ETF, which is bullish. This all fits in perfectly with the assumption that GLD was in a primary bull market between 2006 and 2010 and is an extremely bullish indication for GLD. GLD subsequently went north to over $180 per share.

Only Closing Prices Are Recognized

In Dow Theory, only closing prices are recognized. This means that regardless of how large the high and low price excursions may be on any one day, only the final closing price will be used. Furthermore, it does not matter how miniscule the amount that price closes above or below the previous day's closing price.

2.3 CHALLENGES TO DOW THEORY

There are many criticisms of Dow Theory. Here are some of the more significant arguments against it:

1. Dow Theory is more applicable to the equity markets: Detractors of Dow Theory argue that the theory is unsuitable for application in faster moving markets or across lower timeframes. For example, a commodity trader would have to wait for months and maybe even years for a buy or sell signal based on the penetration of a previous peak or trough in the primary bull or bear trend. Hedgers would have few or no counterparties to take the other side of

the trade. Furthermore, the capital risk would be astronomically high if the trader is expected to place a stop loss order based on the motion of the primary trend.

2. The primary trend is susceptible to manipulation: Monetary policy such as near-zero interest rates set by central banks over extended periods combined with colossal stimulus packages and quantitative-easing (QE)-to-infinity-type operations impact the longer-term action of the markets by creating an artificially super bullish environment where even its participants have little or no fear of anything untoward happening to the markets. Collective energy market rigging and the latest Libor scandal are further evidence that markets have and will always be susceptible to manipulation. Hence, Dow's main reason for trading the primary trend is questionable in today's highly impacted markets.

3. The averages are not a true reflection and barometer of the market environment: Unfortunately, in today's markets, the majority of indices are themselves tradable and are therefore open to manipulation. For example, the VIX was meant to reflect the level of fear in the markets. It main objective is somewhat thwarted by the large amount of speculative trading impacting the VIX. Physical gold prices are also at the mercy of heavy shorting in its corresponding ETFs, like the GLD, or via its futures and options contracts. Such products never existed in Dow's time.

4. Only closing prices are recognized: Recognizing only the closing price ignores potentially large intraday ranges that may occur during the day's trading session. These important price rejection levels are totally disregarded. Furthermore, there seems to be some conceptual conflict between recognizing the smallest amount required to close higher or lower while at the same time discounting potentially large and significant day to day fluctuations, regarding them as merely noise.

5. The buy and sell signals based on the primary trend are safer: This may or may not be true, but detractors of Dow Theory argue that such signals usually occur late in the trend and miss a large part of it.

6. The identification of a new primary trend: Due to the difficulty in establishing whether a retracement is part of a secondary reaction or the inception of a new primary trend in the opposite direction, investments based on the belief that the retracement is merely a secondary reaction will run a higher risk of losing capital should the market unfold contrary to what was expected.

7. The averages must confirm each other: The rationale behind this logic is that in a healthy economy, the goods produced by industry are in great demand and this is evidenced by the amount of transport activity generated in trying to ship these goods to the consumers. Therefore, underperformance in either the industrial or transportation averages leading to non-confirmation would logically signal potential trouble in the economy. Unfortunately, the Dow Jones Industrial Average today is composed of many stocks that do not produce any physical product that requires shipping or transport, in general. Many of today's companies are more involved in financial products, telecommunications, and insurance. This severely diminishes the effectiveness of confirmation between the industrials and the transports. Many practitioners today prefer

to look for confirmation between large cap and smaller cap indices like the S&P500 and Russell 2000 as a more reliable barometer of market action.

2.4 CHAPTER SUMMARY

As we have seen, Dow Theory forms the basis for much of technical analysis in the twenty-first century. Although technical analysis has evolved significantly since Dow's time, many practitioners still regard the basic application of Dow Theory as one of the most reliable approaches in determining and confirming the existence of a trend. The incorporation of the concept of market phases and volume confirmation within Dow Theory has also significantly impacted the way investors and traders participate in the market, more than a century after its introduction.

CHAPTER 2 REVIEW QUESTIONS

1. Describe the basic tenets of Dow Theory.
2. Give examples of the primary trend being manipulated.
3. Is Dow Theory still relevant in today's market?
4. Describe the main weaknesses of Dow Theory.
5. Explain why volume should expand in the direction of the existing trend.
6. In what ways is accumulation similar to distribution?
7. Why is the secondary reaction more problematic than the primary trend?
8. What are the main differences between Dow's and Ralph N. Elliott's determination of a trend?

REFERENCES

W. P Hamilton. 2006. *The Stock Market Barometer.* New York: Cosimo Classics.

S. A. Nelson. 2007. *The ABC of Stock Speculation.* Marketplace Books.

Robert Rhea. 1994. *The Dow Theory.* Flint Hill, VA: Fraser Publishing Co.

Richard Schabacker. 1997. *Technical Analysis and Stock Market Profits.* Upper Saddle River, NJ: FT Press.

Jack Schannep. 2008. *Dow Theory for the 21st Century: Technical Indicators for Improving Your Investment Results.* Hoboken, NJ: John Wiley & Sons.

CHAPTER 3

Mechanics and Dynamics of Charting

Traditional charting is a two-dimensional matrix upon which technical data or information is viewed. It affords the practitioner a means of tracking technical data in a meaningful way, revealing various repetitive price pattern behavioral traits and market volatility. In addition, charting also clearly reveals price distortions and illiquidity in the market. It allows for the application of technical analysis such as the drawing of trendlines, channels, envelopes, and chart patterns on price, helping to uncover important price reaction levels, which are driven by the consistent underlying psychology and perception of all market participants. In this chapter, we shall cover the basics of chart construction and how technical data is displayed.

3.1 THE MECHANICS AND DYNAMICS OF CHARTING

There are many ways that a technical analyst can analyze and display market data. Data may be displayed either in a numerical or graphical form. All numerical data may be displayed graphically, if required. Analysts using numerical information to study market action may also resort to various quantitative and statistical techniques in an attempt to predict future price direction and volatility. These quantitative analysts and statisticians employ various forms of time series and stochastic analysis and conduct back and forward testing on technical data. They also try to identify price anomalies and arbitrage opportunities using sophisticated software programs and high-speed data connectivity.

More traditional analysts prefer to work using only a graphical representation of technical data, which comes in the usual form of a price-time chart, where the vertical axis tracks the movement of price and the horizontal axis tracks the motion of time. The price axis may be scaled in an arithmetic (linear) or logarithmic (ratio) fashion. On some charts, the time axis may not always be plotted in equal increments or units of time, but rather acting more as a *counter for new blocks of data* rather than an explicit representation of the passing of time. On such charts, time is regarded as implicit along the *x* axis.

Traditional analysts study classical chart patterns, trendlines, window oscillators, overlay indicators, and various other price formations. Analysts who use charts to study technical data are called chartists. Note that quantitative analysts and statisticians also tend to use charts to display numerical data, although it is optional.

Technical Data

Some of the more common technical data or information employed to construct charts include:

- Price Data:
  - Open (O)
  - High (H)
  - Low (L)
  - Close (C)
- Transaction-Related Data:
  - Volume (V)
  - Open Interest (OI)
- Market-Breadth Data:
  - Advances (A)
  - Declines (D)
  - Total Issues (T)
  - Up Volume/Down Volume (UV, DV)
  - New Highs/New Lows (NH, NL)
  - Bullish Percent Data
- Sentiment Data:
  - Put/Call Ratio
  - Short Interest Ratio
  - Specialist/Public Ratio
  - Cash/Asset Ratio
  - Investor and Advisor Poll Data
  - Margin Debt
  - Implied Volatility (VIX)

The majority of charts are simple price-time charts, using the basic open, high, low, and close information, popularly referred to as OHLC data. Let us now turn our attention to how OHLC data is created.

Quantization of Price

In order to create OHLC data, we first need to specify the time interval over which price activity occurs. For example, let us assume that we are interested in identifying the opening, high, low, and closing prices over five-minute intervals. We therefore need to separate or *quantize* price activity with respect to time, for each successive 5-min interval, or *period*. An interval or period may be of any duration, but the most popular intervals are 1-min, 5-min, 15-min, 1-hour, 4-hour, daily, weekly, monthly, and yearly. In our example, the price at the beginning and end of any 5-min interval represents the Opening (O) and Closing (C) price respectively, while the highest and lowest price within that period represents the High (H) and Low (L) prices. In most cases, the closing price will also represent the opening price of the next 5-min interval, unless there is a gap in price. Figure 3.1 depicts price activity within a 5-min period. Price is quantized into 5-min intervals and is summarized into four pieces of information, namely the OHLC data. Note that OHLC data is also used to construct *other representations of price activity* like bar charts, Gann bars, and Japanese candlesticks.

The range of a bar or candlestick is simply the absolute difference between the high and low price, that is, range = |H − L|.

Refer to Figure 3.2. To create OHLC data for bars and candlesticks over longer periods, simply identify the:

1. Opening price of the first period (O)
2. Closing price of the last period (C)
3. Highest price between the opening and closing price (H)
4. Lowest price between the opening and closing price (L)

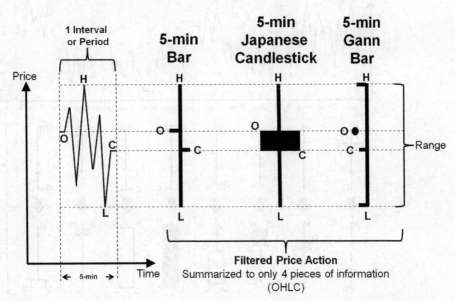

FIGURE 3.1   Filtering Price Action into Four Pieces of Information (OHLC).

67

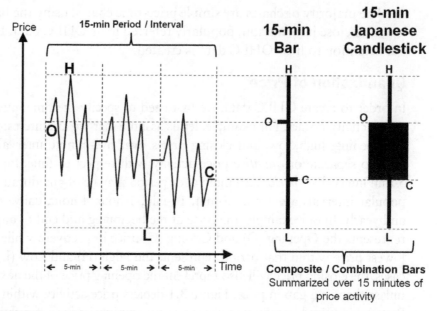

FIGURE 3.2 Higher Timeframe Price Action Represented by Composite/Combination Bars (OHLC).

We observe the creation of a 15-minute bar and candlestick in Figure 3.2 via such a process. This method may be used over any duration to create bars and candlesticks of longer or multiple periods, normally referred to as *higher timeframe* bars and candlesticks. Hence, a 15-minute bar represents a bar that is associated with a higher timeframe, unlike 5- or 10-minute bars.

Figure 3.3 shows a series of OHLC based bars and its equivalent candlesticks being formed by the quantization of price into 5-minute intervals or periods.

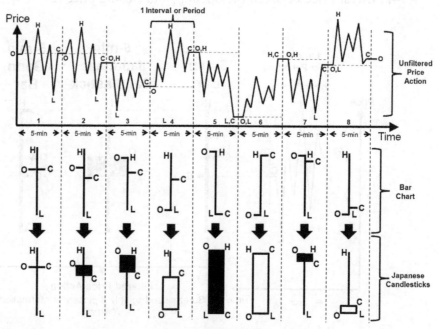

FIGURE 3.3 The Quantization (Filtering) of Price Action.

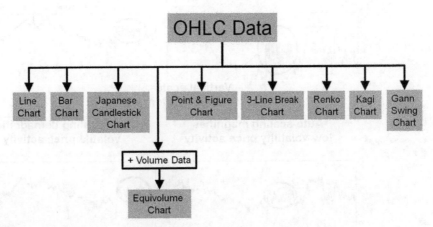

FIGURE 3.4 OHLC as the Basis of Most Chart Constructions.

OHLC data is therefore simply a summary of price activity within a certain interval or period. The longer the duration of the interval or period of the resulting OHLC data, the higher will be the timeframe associated with such bars and candlesticks. As can be seen in Figure 3.4, most charts are created from basic OHLC data, with the exception of the equivolume chart, which requires additional information on volume in order to construct its bars. In short, equivolume bars require OHLCV data, with V representing volume.

Figure 3.5 illustrates three different representations of the same sequence of OHLC data in the form a line, bar, and candlestick chart.

When viewing charts, it is always best to turn off the auto-scaling feature. Auto-scaling attempts to fill the entire screen with price activity. As such, the heights of bars and candlesticks constantly change, depending on whether price is ranging or trending. If prices are flat or ranging, it will expand all price activity and attempt to stretch it across the entire screen, making low-volatility activity seem more volatile by increasing the height of all the bars and candlesticks on the screen. Conversely, when prices are trending, auto-scaling will shorten the height of all bars on the

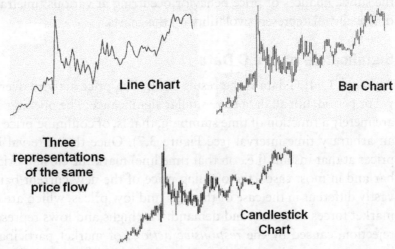

FIGURE 3.5 Examples of Various OHLC-Based Charts.
Source: MetaTrader 4

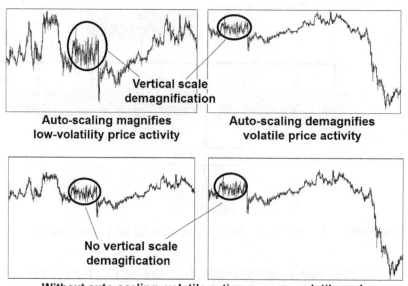

Vertical scale
demagnification

Auto-scaling magnifies
low-volatility price activity

Auto-scaling demagnifies
volatile price activity

No vertical scale
demagification

Without auto-scaling, volatile action appears volatile and
low volatility price activity appears less volatile
(price retains its true visual representation)

FIGURE 3.6   Example of Auto-Scaling Misrepresenting Volatility.
Source: MetaTrader 4

screen in order to fit in the trend action, making volatile price activity look less volatile. In short, the vertical scaling is not preserved or constant. *Switching off the auto-scaling function normalizes volatility on the charts, allowing for more accurate price visualization.* Referring to the top two charts in Figure 3.6, we observe a certain region of price activity (encircled) being portrayed as more volatile than it really is, by virtue of increasing the height of all its bars when prices across the screen are ranging or flattish. We see the encircled area of activity suddenly shrink in the top right chart once auto-scaling fits in a subsequent trend. In the bottom two charts, we see prices maintaining the bar heights in spite of a subsequent trend appearing on the screen. In short, auto-scaling makes it very difficult to gain familiarity with the subtle nuances of price behavior occurring at various timeframes of activity. It drastically misrepresents volatility on the charts.

Significance of OHLC Data

Although OHLC data is the result of filtering price activity over a specified interval or period, not all data have similar significance. The opening and closing prices are merely a function of time stamping, that is, of confining price activity to within an arbitrary time interval (see Figure 3.7). Once that interval is completed, the prices at that instant (i.e., on that time line) mark the closing price of the previous bar and in most cases, the opening price of the new current bar. The situation is vastly different in the case of the high and low prices, which are created by actual market forces of supply and demand. The highs and lows represent areas of price rejection, caused by the *responsive actions* of market participants. Traders and investors are reacting to high and low prices by risking capital in the markets. This makes the high and low prices more significant when compared to opening and

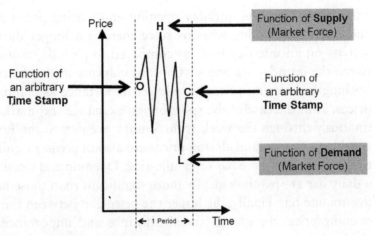

FIGURE 3.7 Significance of OHLC Data.

closing prices. It should be noted that the longer the interval or period, the more significant will be the high and low prices formed.

Nevertheless, opening and closing prices begin to gain more importance and attention from market participants, making such prices more reliable and actionable, if:

- The durations *between* active trading sessions are longer.
- The opening and closing prices are created over a longer interval (i.e., belonging to a higher-timeframe bar or candlestick).

There are larger price gaps between the previous closing and new opening prices. (See Figure 3.8.) Longer durations *between* active trading sessions increase the psychological importance and significance of opening and closing prices. As such, daily opening and closing prices are generally of greater interest to market

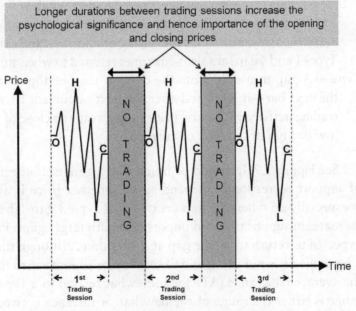

FIGURE 3.8 Significance of Opening and Closing Prices.

participants than the intraday opening and closing prices between the morning and afternoon trading sessions since there is a longer duration of non-trading activity on an interday basis as compared to periods of non-trading activity between the intraday trading sessions. In markets where the trading is continuous, opening and closing prices have lesser importance as compared to high and low prices, as in the case of the spot foreign exchange (fx) market, which trades continuously through the week from Sunday evening to the Friday close. Generally speaking, opening and closing prices are also of greater significance if they belong to a higher-timeframe bar or candlestick. Opening and closing prices belonging to a daily bar are psychologically more significant than those belonging to a one- or five-minute bar. Finally, the larger the price gap between the last closing and new opening price, the greater the significance and importance of the opening and closing prices.

3.2 GAP ACTION: FOUR TYPES OF GAPS

There are essentially four ways to define a gap, which is represented by a range of prices where *no trading activity* takes place:

Type 1: A gap measured from the close of the previous bar to the open of the next or current bar—it is created instantaneously at the open. There is an instant jump in prices—either up or down—with no trading activity taking place between the two prices.

Type 2: A gap measured from the high or low of the previous bar to the open of the next or current bar—it is created instantaneously at the open. There is no trading activity within that price range.

Type 3: A gap measured from the highs or lows of the previous bar to the highs or lows of the next or current bar—it is created only after the next or current bar has closed. This is the gap usually referred to as a window in Japanese candlestick or bar charts. It is also the type of gap referred to frequently when studying breakaway, runaway (also called measuring or midway), and exhaustion gaps (although Types 1 and 4 gaps are also sometimes referred to when studying such formations).

Type 4: A gap measured from the close of the previous bar to the high or low of the next bar—it is created after the next or current bar has closed. There is no trading activity within the price range from the close of the previous bar to the low or high of the next or current bar.

See Figure 3.9. It should be noted that a gap itself normally represents an area of support or resistance, depending on whether price is above or below it. This is especially so when the gap created is a Type 3 gap. The gap or price window increases in significance and importance with larger gaps. Prices are also generally expected to return to fill the gap at a later date, although there are many instances where this does not occur. Finally, it may be of interest to the reader to know that the average true range (ATR) is somewhat related to a Type 4 gap, where the true range is either the range of the new bar or distance between the close of the last bar and the high or low of the new bar, depending on whichever is greater.

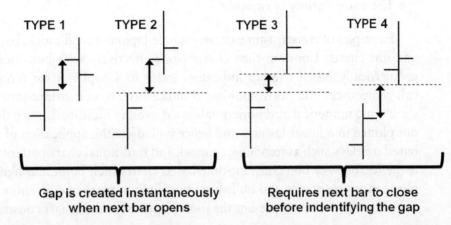

Four Definitions of a Gap

FIGURE 3.9 Four Types of Gapping Action Representing Areas of Non-Trading Activity.

We shall be covering gaps in more detail in Chapter 5, where we will be analyzing gaps in relation to market phase. The four main types of gap covered are:

1. Common gaps
2. Breakaway gaps
3. Runaway/Continuation/Midway gaps
4. Exhaustion Gaps

3.3 CONSTANT CHART MEASURES

There are five types of constant measure charts, namely:

1. Constant Time Charts—bar closes when a specified time interval is met, for example, Candlestick Charts, Bar Charts, Equivolume Charts
2. Constant Range Charts—bar closes when a specified excursion in price is met, for example, Point-and-Figure Charts and Renko Charts
3. Constant Volume Charts—bar closes when a specified volume is met
4. Constant Transaction (Tick) Charts—bar closes when a specified number of transactions (trades) is met
5. Constant Volatility Charts—bar closes when a specified amount of standard deviation or ATR is met

Constant-Time Charts

Constant-time charts quantize price activity into units of time, or intervals. Each bar is complete once a specified amount of time has elapsed. Hence, such charts are also referred to as *interval charts*. Below are the characteristics associated with constant time charts:

- The bar range is variable
- The bar duration is constant

- The bar volume is variable
- The transactions per bar is variable
- The bar volatility is variable

Examples of constant-time charts include Japanese candlestick, bar, equivolume, and line charts. Constant-time charts work effectively with both numerically and geometrically based overlay indicators (refer to Chapter 8 for more on numerical, geometrical and horizontal-based indicators). Non constant-time based charts should use numerical and horizontal-based overlay indicators, since the time axis is not plotted in a linear fashion and hence will affect the application of geometrically based overlays such as trendline, channel, and traditional chart-pattern analysis. This is the reason why non constant-time based charts such point and figure charts employ bearish resistance and bullish support lines in place of conventional trendlines. Constant-time charts represent the most popular form of chart construction.

Bar Charts As seen in Figure 3.1, a bar chart is easily created via the quantization of price into specified time intervals or periods. Bar charts clearly depict levels of supply and demand in the market. Unfortunately, opening and closing prices are harder to read from a distance as the open and close markers may be too indistinct when the chart is populated with a large number of bars.

Line Charts Line charts are created by connecting all of the closing prices. Each time interval creates a new closing price. Line charts do not provide much information about potential levels of supply and demand since they ignore high and low prices, which are the true indicators of market force. Nevertheless, because line charts filter out all information except closing prices, they are usually employed as a trend identifier or simple summary of price activity.

Japanese Candlestick Charts Japanese candlesticks are created in essentially the same manner as standard price bars, as seen in Figures 3.1 to 3.3. The only difference is that the space between the opening and closing price is boxed up and is referred to as the *real body*. Real bodies may be filled or hollow depending on the configuration or relative position of the opening price to the closing price. Real bodies may also be represented as black or white candlesticks.

Candlestick formations may be classified as follows:

1. Bullish or bearish
2. Reversal or continuation
3. Simple, double, or multiple

We shall be delving more deeply into candlestick formations in Chapter 14. For now, refer to Figure 3.10. As with price bars, it is not possible to determine whether the high or low prices were created first, since most of the intrabar price information has been filtered out.

Equivolume Charts Equivolume charts are based on constant-time based bars, incorporating volume over a specified time interval and displaying it visually on

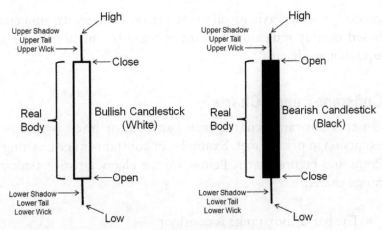

FIGURE 3.10 Bullish and Bearish Japanese Candlesticks.

the charts in terms of bar width, rather than height. Equivolume bars are constructed using high and low prices. Open and close prices are disregarded. Larger volume over a particular interval or period will result in a wider bar. Because of the variable bar width, the horizontal or time axis is not plotted in a linear fashion, even though equivolume bars represent constant-time based bars. As such, geometrically based overlay indicators such as trendlines, channels, and chart patterns are somewhat affected or distorted when applied to such charts. Figure 3.11 clearly depicts the non-linear increments along the horizontal or time axis on the daily equivolume chart of Apple Inc. Notice that the trendlines intersect the

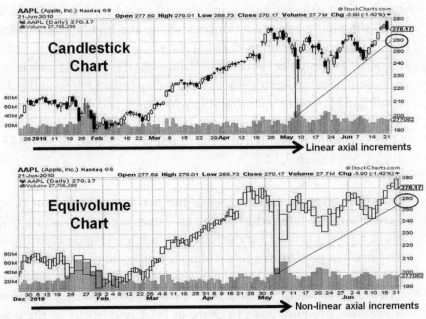

FIGURE 3.11 Comparing a Japanese Candlestick to an Equivolume Chart.
Courtesy of Stockcharts.com

vertical or price axis at different prices. Conversely, numerical and horizontal-based overlay indicators are not affected by the non-linear axial increments on equivolume charts,

Constant-Range Charts

On constant-range charts, each bar, box, or brick is complete once a specified excursion in price is met. Examples of constant-range charting include Renko and Point and Figure charts. Below are the characteristics associated with constant-range charts:

- The bar or box range is constant
- The bar or box duration is variable
- The bar or box volume is variable
- The transactions per bar is variable
- The bar or box volatility is constant

Point and Figure Charts Point and Figure charts represent the most popular form of constant-range charting. Once a specified amount of price excursion is recorded or detected, a new bar is plotted. These bars are referred to as *boxes*. Point and Figure charts are populated by continuation and reversal boxes. A continuation box specifies the minimum price excursion required for a new box to be plotted in the direction of the existing trend. The reversal size consists of a specified number of boxes required for a reversal to be plotted on the charts. The size of the boxes is arbitrarily chosen. For example, a $1-box size requires price to move at least $1 before a new box is plotted, and if the reversal size is 3 boxes, price will be required to move at least (3 × $1) = $3, before a reversal may be plotted on the chart. Closing prices are normally used to determine the completion of a box, although many practitioners also use the high and low prices. Rising prices are indicated by a column of rising Xs, whereas declining prices are indicated by a column of falling Os. As constant-range charts, the time axis is non-linear and as a consequence, geometrically based overlay indicators would exhibit inconsistent readings. This is the main reason why Point and Figure charting uses a unique form of trendlines which are not based on drawing a line between two points. Only one point is required and the trendlines rise and fall along 45 and −45 degree angles. See Figure 3.12.

Renko Charts Renko charts are another form of constant-range charting. The Renko bars are referred to as bricks. There are bullish white bricks and bearish black bricks. They are very similar to Point and Figure charting except that each new brick is plotted in a new column. A new brick is plotted once the minimum price excursion required for a new brick to be created is met. Since the creation of a new brick is not time dependent, the time axis is plotted in a non-linear fashion. All reversals require price to move at least two bricks in the opposite direction. Hence, Renko charts are essentially two-brick reversal charts. Again, the size of the brick is arbitrarily chosen. See Figure 3.13.

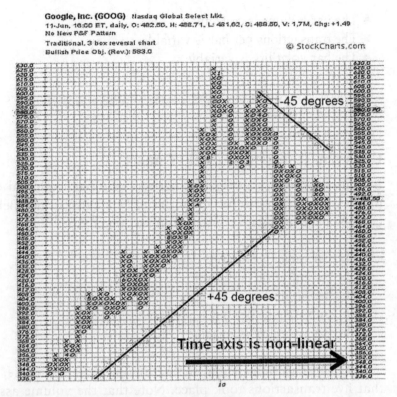

FIGURE 3.12   A Point and Figure Chart of Google Inc.
Courtesy of Stockcharts.com

Constant-Volume Charts

In constant-volume charts, a new bar is plotted once the minimum volume traded is met. Below are the characteristics associated with constant-volume charts:

- The bar range is variable
- The bar duration is variable

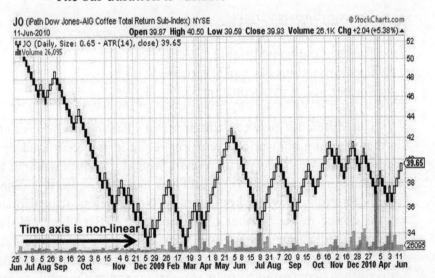

FIGURE 3.13   A Renko Chart of iPath Dow Jones-AIG Coffee Total Return Sub-Index.
Courtesy of Stockcharts.com

- The bar volume is constant
- The transactions per bar is variable
- The bar volatility is variable

Since the creation of a new bar is not time dependent, the time axis is plotted in a non-linear fashion.

Constant-Transaction (Tick) Charts

In constant-transaction or tick charts, a new bar is plotted once the minimum number of transactions for a new bar to be created is met. Below are the characteristics associated with constant-transaction charts:

- The bar range is variable
- The bar duration is variable
- The bar volume is variable
- The transactions per bar is constant
- The bar volatility is variable

Each transaction is represented by one tick. Therefore, five ticks indicate that five transactions took place. Note that the volume associated with each transaction is unspecified, though it may be inferred, depending on the market traded. The time axis for constant-transaction charts is plotted in a non-linear fashion.

Constant-Volatility Charts

In constant-volatility charting, each new bar is plotted once the minimum price excursion for the creation of new bar is met. Below are the characteristics associated with constant-volatility charts:

- The bar range is variable
- The bar duration is variable
- The bar volume is variable
- The transactions per bar is variable
- The bar volatility is constant

This difference between this form of charting and constant-range charting is that the minimum price excursion required is determined by price volatility. For example, we could set up a chart whereby each new bar is plotted once the minimum price excursion of 2 × ATR is met. In a sense it is objective, as the bar size is determined by market volatility. Nevertheless, it is also subjective insofar as the choice in the number of multiples of ATR to be employed is concerned. Figure 3.14 illustrates the use of a Point and Figure chart where the box size is set to 1 × ATR. Notice its use of constant-volatility charting to identify trends more effectively as compared to regular constant-range charting, as seen on the right-hand side of the illustration.

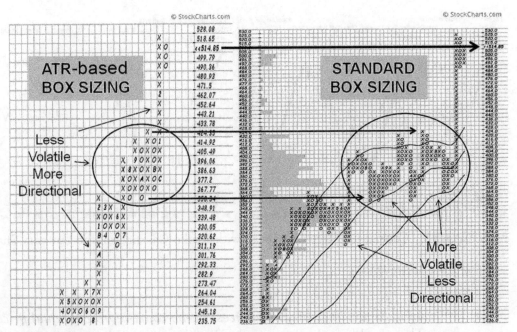

FIGURE 3.14 Comparing Constant-Volatility to Constant-Range Charting.
Courtesy of Stockcharts.com

Chart Constructs with No Measures of Constancy

There exist certain chart constructs where there exist no measures of constancy. This implies that the range, duration, volume, number of transactions, and volatility of each bar is variable.

Three-Line Break Charts *Three-line break charts are unique in that they possess no measures of constancy.* Once price closes above the previous high or below a previous low, a new line is created. Once three successive lines are created, a reversal may only be plotted if price meets or exceeds the low (or high, in an upside reversal) of the last three periods in a downside reversal. There are bullish white lines and bearish black lines. See Figure 3.15 for a comparison between three-line break and Renko charting for the Currency Shares Euro Trust.

Chart Scaling   There are three basic types of scaling employed when creating price charts, namely the:

1. Linear or Arithmetic Scale
2. Ratio or Logarithmic Scale
3. Square Root Scale

The most common scalings used are the linear and ratio scalings. The square root scale lies somewhere between the linear and ratio scales with respect to its scale increments. It is not commonly used on most platforms.

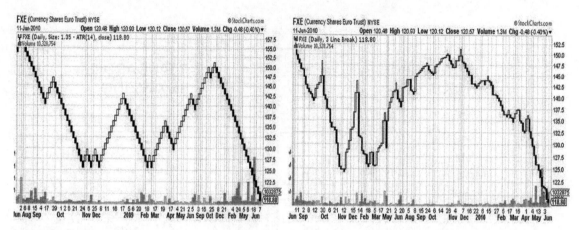

FIGURE 3.15 Comparing Three-Line Break with Renko Charting on the Currency Shares Euro Trust.
Courtesy of Stockcharts.com

In linear scaling, equal distances on the chart represent equal price changes. This would imply that equal price changes at higher prices would result in lower percentage changes. For example, a price change from $10 to $20 would represent a $10 change in price and a 100 percent change in price, that is, ($20–$10)/$10 × 100 percent. A price change from $90 to $100 would also represent a change of $10 in price but at this higher price level, its percentage change is merely ($100–$90)/$90 × 100 percent = 11.1 percent. Hence, for linear scaling, *the percentage change is not preserved for equal units of price change.*

If P_N represents the Nth price, then linear scaling simply means that:

$$(P_N - P_{N-1})$$

is a constant for every equal distance move on the chart. See Figure 3.16.

In ratio scaling, equal distances on the chart represent equal price percentage changes. This would imply that equal percentage changes at higher prices would result in larger price changes. For example, an equal percentage change of 100 percent based on a price change from $10 to $20 would require a price change of $90 at the $90 price level, that is, the price difference between the $180 and $90 price level. Hence for ratio scaling, *the price change is not preserved per equal units of percentage change.* This also means that equal distances on the chart does not equate to equal percentage changes.

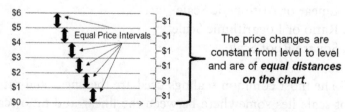

FIGURE 3.16 Linear Scaling.

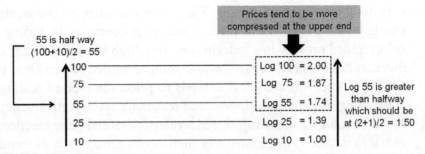

FIGURE 3.17 Ratio Scaling.

If P_N represents the Nth price, then ratio scaling simply means that:

$$(P_N - P_{N-1})/P_{N-1}$$

is a constant for every equal distance move on the chart. Figures 3.17 and 3.18 show how the percentage increments need to rise to account for an equal price change. This formula represents what is also referred to as *stock returns*.

The ratio scale tends to *compress price action at higher prices and expand it at lower prices*, whereas linear scaling represents price evenly across the entire price range. Consequently, for very large price differences, linear scaling will not represent price activity clearly at lower prices due to the ever-increasing price range that is made to fit on one chart. But it would reveal upper price activity with better clarity when compared to ratio scaling, which tends to compress upper price action, making it relatively more difficult to observe price patterns and volatility behavior. But a log scale would reveal lower price action with more clarity. In short:

- Linear scaling provides better upper end definition and visualization of prices, but relatively poorer clarity at lower prices.
- Ratio scaling provides better lower-end definition and visualization of prices, but relatively poorer clarity at higher prices.

As a general guideline, use linear charts when the price range under observation is relatively small. For stock price ranges exceeding $100, it may be more appropriate to use ratio charting. It is also best to employ ratio charts for viewing

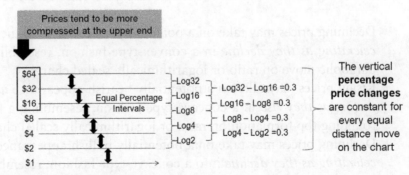

FIGURE 3.18 Ratio Scaling.

very long-term market action. This mainly applies to the equity markets. For charts based on futures or foreign exchange contracts, including any instrument being traded on very low margin (i.e., very high leverage), linear charts would be more suitable, as ratio charts would compress price too much at higher prices.

When applying technical analysis to price, the type of scaling may affect the forecasting of potential support and resistance levels, introducing inconsistencies and discrepancies in the forecasted levels of potential price reaction. This affects all overlays that rely on geometry in their construction such as trendlines, channels, and chart patterns. Consequently, if the scaling changes, the angles of all trend-lines will also change accordingly, indicating different levels of potential support and resistance. Scaling does not affect overlays that are constructed numerically like moving averages and price envelopes. It also does not affect overlay indicators that indicate *horizontal* levels of support and resistance, like:

- Prior support and resistance levels
- Fibonacci extensions, retracements, projections, and expansions
- Gann one-eighth and one-third price retracements
- Gann Square of Nine price projections

It should be noted that if square root scaling is employed, it will indicate an uptrend line penetration that is later than that for ratio scaling but earlier than an uptrend line penetration based on a linear scale. This is rather disconcerting, as the majority of traders will react to violations of the uptrend line based on either linear or ratio scaling. Hence, a trader utilizing square root scale charting will find him- or herself initiating entries and exits either too early or too late with respect to important and significant price reaction levels in the market.

Insofar as drawing uptrend and downtrend lines using linear and ratio scaling, it behooves the practitioner to note the following:

- Uptrend lines are penetrated sooner while downtrend lines are penetrated later on ratio or logarithmically scaled charts
- Uptrend lines are penetrated later while downtrend lines are penetrated sooner on linear or arithmetically scaled charts

See Figures 3.19 and 3.20.

Switching between linear and ratio scaling may also result in the following:

- Declining prices may take on a potentially bearish appearance *with prices accelerating as they decline* in a convex-type fashion, resembling a downward parabolic move on ratio or logarithmically scaled charts
- Rising prices may take on a potentially bearish appearance *with prices decelerating as they rise* in a concave-type fashion, resembling a flattening out or rounding top formation on ratio or logarithmically scaled charts
- Declining prices may take on a potentially bullish appearance *with prices decelerating as they decline* into a concave-type fashion, resembling a flattening out or rounding bottom formation on linear or arithmetically scaled charts

FIGURE 3.19 Comparing Uptrend Line Penetrations on Linear and Ratio Charts on the SPDR Dow Jones Industrial Average.
Courtesy of Stockcharts.com

- Rising prices may take on a potentially bullish appearance *with prices accelerating as they rise (or rising evenly)* in a convex-type fashion, resembling an upward parabolic move (or steadily rising prices) on linear or arithmetically scaled charts

See Figures 3.21 and 3.22.

Figure 3.23 highlights the discrepancies between linear- and ratio-scaled charting when drawing price channels based on identical price inflection points. Geometrically based barrier overlays give rise to inconsistencies when compared using

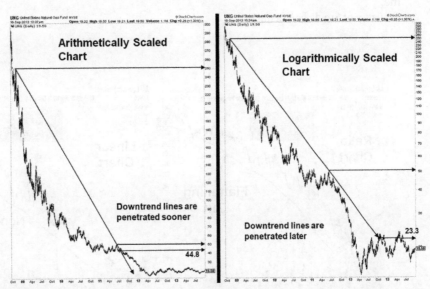

FIGURE 3.20 Comparing Downtrend Line Penetrations on Linear and Ratio Charts on the U.S. Natural Gas Fund.
Courtesy of Stockcharts.com

FIGURE 3.21 Comparing Linear and Ratio Scaling on the Daily Chart of A123 Systems Inc.
Courtesy of Stockcharts.com

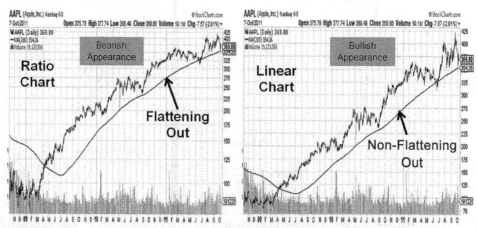

FIGURE 3.22 Comparing Linear and Ratio Scaling on the Daily Chart of Apple Inc.
Courtesy of Stockcharts.com

FIGURE 3.23 Comparing Channels on Linear and Ratio Scaling on the Daily Chart of
Energy Services of America Corp.
Courtesy of Stockcharts.com

different chart scaling. Note that numerically based barrier overlays like moving averages are not affected by chart scaling and display no discrepancies in their readings.

The Bid-Based Chart and Bid-Ask Spread   Charts are typically drawn based
on bid prices, although many charting platforms also allow for the display of
price action based on ask and mid-prices. The use of bid-based price charts has a
significant effect on trading chart patterns, pullbacks, and breakouts, by virtue of
the spread between the bid and ask prices. It is also dependent on whether we are:

- Buying at the ask
- Buying at the bid
- Selling at the ask
- Selling at the bid

In general, trade performance is generally adversely affected when initiating
long entries and executing long exits on bid-based charts. It does not specifically
affect short entries or short exits. Nevertheless, since a trade consists of a buy and
a sell, the bid-ask spread affects all trades.

Initiating short entries on bid-based charts allows the trader to enter at the
precise price level intended. For example, assume that we want to short at a prior
resistance level of $10. Assume that the bid-ask spread, that is, the price difference

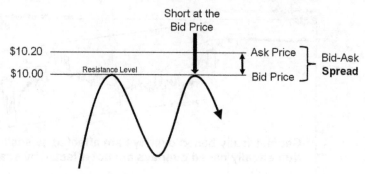

FIGURE 3.24 Shorting Resistance at the Bid.

between the bid and ask price, is $0.20. The moment we see price on the bid-based chart test the $10 level, we enter a market order to short at $10. Ignoring the possibility of negative slippage for now, we are filled at $10. There seems to be no difficultly in establishing a short at the intended price. The outcome is similar to using a pending order to initiate a short entry. If we placed a sell limit order at $10, we should also be filled at that intended price or better. Even if the short represented an exit such as a stop loss or profit target, we would still be able to exit at the intended price. This is because we are shorting (i.e., selling to open or close a position) at the bid (i.e., sell) price. There seem to be no difficulties associated with initiating short entries or exits at the intended price on a bid-based chart. See Figure 3.24.

Now let us turn our attention to long entries. Let us assume that we intend to go long on an upside breakout, initiating an entry $0.05 above the $10 breakout level. We see prices test the $10.05 level and we immediately initiate a market order. We then find out that we had actually entered at $10.25, instead of $10.05. This is because when we enter an order to buy, we need to accept the ask price, which is $0.20 above the bid price. Hence, even though we have initiated a long position at precisely the right time of entry based on a bid-priced chart, we nevertheless bought in at a higher price that we had intended. This is referred to as the problem of the *expensive longs*. See Figure 3.25.

Assume now that we initiate the same entry, but this time using a pending order in the form of a buystop entry order. We place a buystop order to go long at $10.05, just as before. We later find that we were filled at exactly $10.05. Unfortunately, when the buystop order was filled at the ask price of $10.05, the bid price was still below the $10 breakout level, being $0.20 below the ask price at $9.85. This essentially means that we have bought into a position before the breakout, based on the resistance level on bid-priced chart! This is referred to as the problem of the *early longs*. Traders therefore have no choice but to buy in at a relatively higher price, which reduces the profit potential, or to buy in too early at the exact intended price. Either way, the bid-ask spread adversely affects both long instantaneous and pending order entries. Let us now look at how the bid-ask spread affects long entries in declining markets.

Let us now imagine that we intend to buy at the prior support level of $10. We see price test the $10 level and we immediately enter a market order to go long.

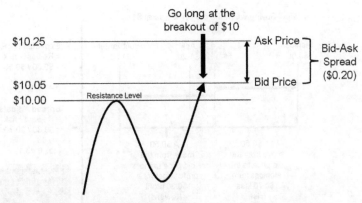

FIGURE 3.25 Going Long at the Breakout.

We soon find out that we bought in at $10.20, that is, at the ask price. Again, we encountered the problem of the expensive longs. This occurred because the very moment the market order was filled, the ask price was $0.20 above the support level as viewed on a bid-priced chart.

Assume now that we placed a pending order to buy in at $10. We soon find out that we were filled at exactly $10, that is, at the ask price that we had originally intended to be filled at in the market. Unfortunately, when we were filled at $10, the bid price was already below the support level, at $9.80, as viewed on the bid-priced chart. This means that we bought into a support level after it was already breached! This is referred to as the problem of the *late longs*. See Figure 3.26.

The bid-ask spread also affects the reward-to-risk ratios. The spread:

- Increases the probability of exiting at the stoploss (loss promoting)
- Reduces the probability of exiting at the profit (profit restricting)

With market orders, the spread is deducted from the profit and added to the loss, which is *reflected in the trading account*. In Figure 3.27, a trader buys when the bid price was at $1. Since the bid-ask spread was $0.20, the trader went long at $1.20. With a profit target at $1.50, the maximum profit would be $0.30, instead of $0.50. But for a stopsize of $0.50, the maximum would be $0.70, instead of $0.50. Hence the actual spread-adjusted reward to risk ratio (R/r ratio) is

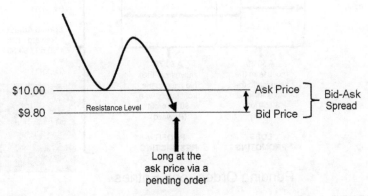

FIGURE 3.26 Going Long at Support.

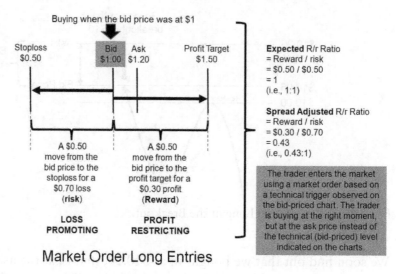

FIGURE 3.27 Buying Based on Bid Prices on the Charts.

0.43, and not 1. Hence the spread adversely affects the R/r ratio for instantaneous long market order entries executed based on bid prices.

With pending orders, the spread is not deducted from the profit or added to the loss and is *not reflected in the trading account*. The spread cost is hidden within the dynamics of the pending order setup, such that to make a profit price has to traverse a greater distance, whereas for a loss price has only to move a relatively shortly distance. As such, for long entry pending orders, the spread does not alter expected the R/r ratio, but it does adversely affect the probability of securing a successful trade by virtue of the amount of work that the market has to do in order to generate profit and the ease of being stopped out. See Figure 3.28.

To mitigate the adverse effects of the spread on the reward-to-risk ratio for instantaneous long entries based on bid prices on the chart, the trader needs to

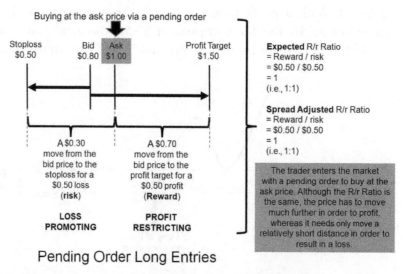

FIGURE 3.28 Buying Based on Ask Prices via Pending Orders.

increase the ratio of target size and stopsize over the spread. The most obvious way to accomplish this is to trade at a higher timeframe or on a larger wave cycle. The larger the absolute size of the profit target and stoploss, the less will be the relative cost of trading against the spread. The spread affects the short-term trader the most, especially scalpers, and that is why they need to *buy at the bid* and *sell at the ask price* in order to reduce the cost of trading. A standard level-one (L1) trading platform will not allow traders to buy at the bid or sell at the ask price.

3.4 FUTURES CONTRACTS

Futures contracts were originally created to allow commodity producers a means of hedging against falling prices, and hence they are essentially a bearish mechanism. By shorting an equal amount in the futures market, producers need not worry about falling prices during harvest time. They have already locked in production costs and any potential profit, irrespective of future prices rising or declining. Depending on when the goods are ready for sale, producers may choose nearby or further-out futures contracts to hedge their costs and lock in any profit.

Unlike equity markets, in the futures market all contracts eventually *expire*, requiring the trader who intends to hold on to a position to *roll over* into the next available contract. Contracts are available at various expiration months, but usually every quarter in March, June, September, and December, extending out beyond a year in many cases.

A futures contract is normally fairly illiquid through its lifespan until the last three to six months before expiry. Volume and open interest are greatest around two to three months before expiry. As it approaches expiry, volume subsides as traders begin rolling over into the next available contract. It should be noted that this decline in volume toward the expiry of a contract may cause some confusion and may even lead an analyst to believe that any trend present is potentially weak due to the decreasing volume and open interest. A quick peek at the next nearby contract will normally show that volume is in fact increasing over the same period as traders pile into the next contract. Hence, to gauge the true volume and open interest action across rollover points, a continuous chart should be employed. See Figure 3.29.

Figure 3.30 shows the volume over the same period using a continuous contract. We observe that we are now able to visualize continuity in volume action across multiple contracts, rather than isolated instances of volume action within each separate futures contract.

When trying to decide on the most appropriate contract to trade, look for the contract with the largest volume and open interest. This may not always be the nearby contract. It is also best to roll over slightly before expiry in order to avoid the volatility caused by traders exiting at the very last stages of the contract.

The contract with the closest expiry is referred to as the *nearby, nearest,* or *front-month* contract. The next available contract further out is referred to as

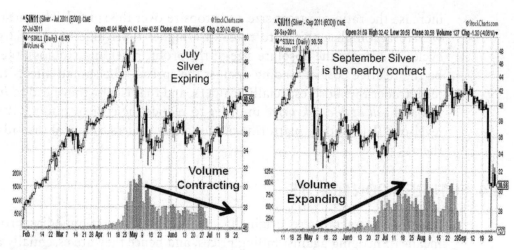

FIGURE 3.29 Comparing Volume Action on the Daily Chart of Silver July and September 2011 Futures.
Courtesy of Stockcharts.com

the *next contract*. It is the second further-out contract with an expiry closest to the nearby contract. Contracts further out are also referred to as *back-month* contracts. Traders may choose to continue rolling over into the next nearby or front-month contract. They may also choose to only roll over into the next month contract, that is, two contracts further out, instead of rolling over into the next nearby contract. Once liquidity starts to subside, traders will normally start to roll over into the next nearby contract. Sometimes traders may also enter into two

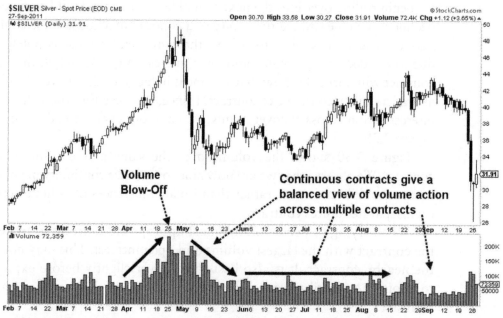

FIGURE 3.30 Volume Action on the Continuous Daily Chart of Silver.
Courtesy of Stockcharts.com

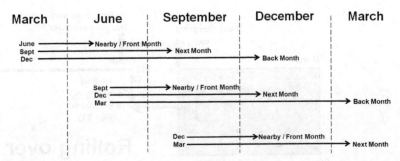

FIGURE 3.31 Identifying the Front-, Next-, and Back-Month Futures Contracts.

futures contracts, one closer and another further out, to create a calendar spread or for other hedging purposes.

The nearby or front-month contract has a few distinguishing characteristics such as:

- An expiration date closest to the current date
- The narrowest bid-ask spread
- The narrowest spread with respect to the spot price
- The most liquid contract

Figure 3.31 shows quarterly contract months expiring over a 12 month period. Assume that we are currently in the month of March and that the March contract has already expired. We may now choose to participate in the June contract, which represents the nearby or front-month contract. We may instead choose to participate in the next month or next nearby contract, that is, the September contract. We may even consider, depending on the trading strategy, to participate in a far-out or back-month contract like the December or following March contract.

Futures contract-delivery months are given a letter of the alphabet for identification purposes, namely: F for January, G for February, H for March, J for April, K for May, M for June, N for July, Q for August, U for September, V for October, X for November, and Z for December.

When a futures contract approaches expiry, traders begin to roll over into the next nearest contract with the next closest expiry. The new contract may not be trading at the same price as the nearby expiring contract. It may be trading at a higher price, requiring the trader to pay a premium in order to participate in the new contract. In such cases, we say that the new contract is *trading at a premium to the previous contract*. Traders are required to roll over at a premium and this will adversely affect the potential profitability of the trading campaign. It is not uncommon for successive new contracts to roll over at a premium, resulting in accumulated losses, diminishing profits along the way. Hence it is actually possible to lose money by being long in a rising or sideways market if the rollover premiums are large enough. Rolling over at a premium causes the trader to experience *negative roll yields*. See Figure 3.32.

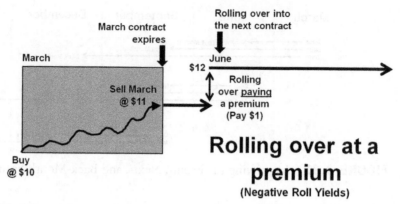

FIGURE 3.32 Losses from Negative Roll Yields.

Sometimes, the next contract may be trading at a lower price, in which case the trader rolling over into the new contract will receive a payment. In such cases, we say that the new contract is *trading at a discount to the previous contract*. It is not uncommon for successive new contracts to roll over at a discount, resulting in accumulated gains, boosting profits along the way. It is therefore actually possible to make a profit by being long in a declining or sideways market if the rollover discounts are large enough. Rolling over at a discount causes the trader to experience *positive roll yields*. See Figure 3.33.

Another interesting characteristic of futures contracts is that further-out contracts may be trading a successively lower or higher prices compared to the nearby contract or spot price. When further-out contracts are trading at successively higher prices when compared to the *expected spot price at expiry*, we say that the market is in *normal contango*. Conversely, if further-out contracts are trading at successively lower prices when compared to the expected spot price at expiry, we say that the market is in *normal backwardation*. Sometimes, the terms contango and backwardation (especially when the term normal is dropped) may also be used loosely to mean that further-out contracts may be trading at successively lower or higher prices compared to the nearby contract or *current spot price*. This

FIGURE 3.33 Profiting from Positive Roll Yields.

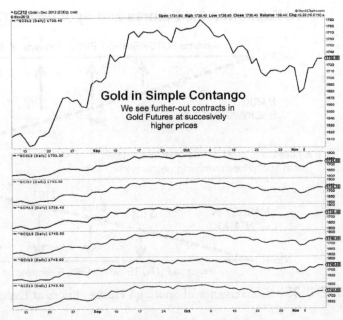

FIGURE 3.34 Simple Contango Observed on the Daily Chart of 2012 Gold Futures. Courtesy of Stockcharts.com

is of course an informal use of the terms, but nevertheless, it is common practice among futures traders. See Figure 3.34 for an example of this popular definition of simple contango.

We observe the further-out gold contracts trading at successively higher prices when compared to the nearby December contract. Although we observe simple contango, the contracts may or may not be in normal contango, which requires some knowledge of the expected or estimated spot price at expiry, in order to determine if normal contango actually exists.

One important aspect about futures contracts is that *futures prices always converge to the spot price at expiry*. Hence, if a contract is in contango, and assuming that the spot price remains constant, it will eventually decline in price, experiencing negative yields as it converges toward the lower spot price at expiry or maturity. Conversely, if a contract is in backwardation, it will eventually rise in price, experiencing positive yields as it converges toward the higher spot price at expiry or maturity. Hence, in certain situations, especially with some mispricing, it may be possible to long a far out backwardated contract and simultaneously short a nearby contract, gaining from the convergence as expiry approaches, irrespective of the future direction of price. In short, a gain is locked in without any directional risk involved. Again, profitability depends on the spread and aggregate trading costs accumulated over the period of convergence, toward expiry. See Figure 3.35.

Figure 3.36 is an example of contango eroding returns in the Natural Gas market during 2009. Natural gas experienced a tremendous rally throughout 2009, which was not matched by the U.S. Natural Gas Fund which tracks natural gas prices via futures contracts. Although the market was rising, rolling over at relatively large

At Expiration the Futures and Spot Prices <u>Converge</u>

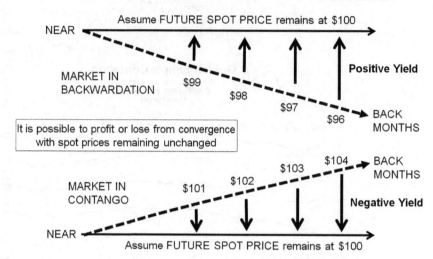

FIGURE 3.35 Convergence of Spot and Futures Prices at Expiration.

premiums actually resulted in a loss if traders rolled over continuously. We see the U.S. Natural Gas Fund experiencing excessive negative roll yield as it seriously underperforms gas prices. It should be noted that very short-term traders who trade individual contracts without having to roll over positions are not affected by negative roll yields, nor do they profit from positive roll yields.

Figure 3.37 clearly shows the underperformance of the U.S. Natural Gas Fund with respect to prices in the natural gas market.

As we have already seen, there may be a premium or discount gap between the nearby and the next contract. As far as traders are concerned, this only requires a payment or receipt of payment with respect to the price difference and number of contracts held at rollover. But for the chartist, the challenge is to find a way to preserve the continuity of prices across such price gaps. There are many ways to

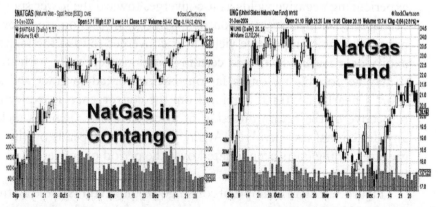

FIGURE 3.36 Comparing Performance on the Continuous Daily Chart of Natural Gas and the U.S. Natural Gas Fund.
Courtesy of Stockcharts.com

94

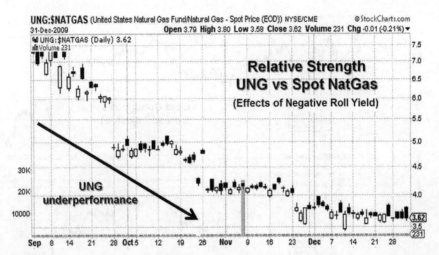

FIGURE 3.37 Relative Strength Chart of the Continuous Daily Chart of Natural Gas against the U.S. Natural Gas Fund.
Courtesy of Stockcharts.com

represent disjointed data in a more meaningful manner. Here are some popular approaches:

- Unadjusted nearest-futures contracts
- Back (or Spread) Adjusted continuous contracts
- Perpetual contracts

This simplest way to use charts of individual futures contracts is to just connect the nearest contracts without accounting for the gap, that is, unadjusted with respect to the price difference or *spread* between any two contracts. This approach preserves the actual sequence of nearby contract prices. It also serves as an accurate record of historical prices. Even so, it is not possible to apply technical analysis in a meaningful way to such concatenations of disjointed contract prices. It also makes back and forward testing impossible due to the gaps between prices, which are not representative of the actual price flow. See Figure 3.38.

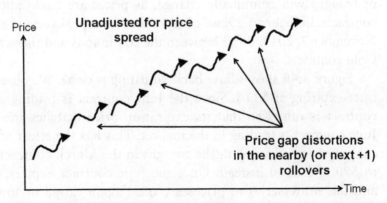

FIGURE 3.38 Unadjusted Nearest Futures Chart.

FIGURE 3.39 Identifying Price Discrepancies between the Continuous Daily Chart of Gold and the December 2013 Gold Contract.
Courtesy of Stockcharts.com

Another way to use concatenate charts of individual futures contracts is to raise or lower the previous contract price at expiry (or at a certain N number of days before expiry) to match the new contract price. This is referred to as back-adjusting, and it essentially removes the price difference or spread between contracts, creating a *continuous flow of prices* between the individual contracts. It is advantageous insofar as it allows for the proper and meaningful application of technical analysis. In addition, back-adjusted continuous charts always display the current price in the market and may therefore be used for trading purposes. It is also conducive to back and forward testing of trading strategies. Unfortunately, as a result of back adjusting, past prices do not reflect the actual traded contract prices during those periods. As such, past prices associated with significant peaks or troughs will continually change, as prices are back adjusted to match new contracts. In Figure 3.39, we observe that price peaks and the OHLC readings for November 7, 2011, differ between the continuous and the actual December 2013 Gold contracts.

Figure 3.40 shows how back adjusting is done. We observe the March contract expiring at $110. Since the June contract is trading at $120, the March contract is raised so that its expiration price matches the new price that the June contract is trading in the market. This has the effect of raising the historical prices associated with the troughs in the March contract from $80 and $90 to $90 and $100 instead. Once the June contract expires, the process repeats and the entire series of prices are once again raised or lowered, according to the price that the September contract is trading at in the market. If the entire

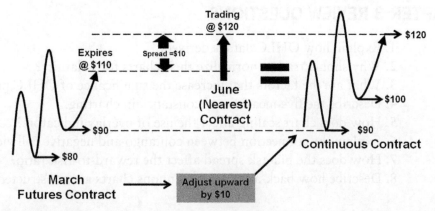

FIGURE 3.40 Back Adjusting in Continuous Charts.

series is raised by another $10 due to the September contract trading at a $10 premium, the historical prices associated with the troughs in the March contract will now be raised again from $90 and $100 to $100 and $110 instead. As can be seen, historical prices continue to undergo change and are adjusted to the *net accumulated spread.*

Another disadvantage is that due to back adjusting, there is a possibility that past prices may become negative, especially if newer contracts are continually trading at a discount.

This continual shifting of historical prices in back-adjusted continuous charts diminishes their use in relative strength analysis. Relative or comparative strength charts will not display accurate ratio relationships if past prices on continuous charts keep varying every time data is back adjusted. In such cases, it would be better to use *perpetual contracts,* as prices are not back shifted with each new front-month contract. Unfortunately, perpetual contracts do not display the current market price, but rather an *estimated* price, which is useless for trading purposes. It estimates the new or further-out rollover contract price by means of a weighting factor, interpolating the contract price between expiration dates. Nevertheless, perpetual contracts are useful when used as a basis for constructing relative strength charts. It does not introduce as much distortion in the ratio relationship, unlike continuous charts.

3.5 CHAPTER SUMMARY

In this chapter we learned how prices are filtered and used to construct various types of charts. We also observed how the bid-ask spread affects trading and R/r ratios as well as how linear and ratio chart scaling affects geometrically based overlay barriers such as trendlines and channels. The discussion on futures contracts highlighted the challenges that chartists face when trying to make sense of a sequence of individual futures contracts and how backwardation and contango affected profitability. The various chart constructs mentioned in this chapter will be analyzed in greater detail in subsequent chapters.

CHAPTER 3 REVIEW QUESTIONS

1. Explain how OHLC data is derived.
2. Why should traders normalize their charts for volatility?
3. What are the factors that increase the significance of OHLC prices?
4. Describe the five measures of constancy in charting.
5. How does chart scaling affect the use of overlay indicators?
6. Explain the connection between contango and negative roll yields.
7. How does the bid-ask spread affect the reward-to-risk ratio?
8. Describe how back-adjusted continuous charts are constructed.

REFERENCES

Murphy, John. 1999. *Technical Analysis of the Financial Markets*. New York: New York Institute of Finance (NYIF).

Nison, Steve. 1994. *Beyond Candlesticks*. New York: John Wiley & Sons.

Nison, Steve. 2001. *Japanese Candlestick Charting Techniques*. New York: New York Institute of Finance (NYIF).

Schwager, Jack D. 1996. *Schwager on Futures*. New York: John Wiley & Sons.

CHAPTER 4

Market Phase Analysis

Markets move in phases. Not being able to recognize market phases and their transitions will greatly disadvantage the practitioner. Market phase analysis can be applied across all time frames, deciphering long as well as very short-term market behavior. Via the application of multiple time frames, market participants will be able to clearly identify macro phase behavior and its impact on more diminutive micro phase action. In this chapter, we shall learn to interpret market phase via a multitude of technical approaches, both Eastern and Western.

4.1 DOW THEORY OF MARKET PHASE

As we have learned from Dow Theory in Chapter 2, a *primary* bull or bear trend consists of three phases, specifically:

1. Accumulation phase
2. Trending phase
3. Distribution phase

This description of how markets rise and fall in various phases is now generally regarded as the basic underlying characteristic of market action.

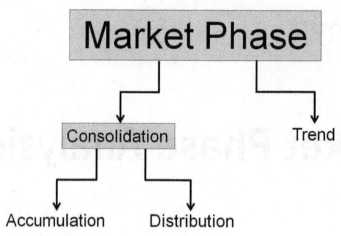

FIGURE 4.1 Components of Market Phase.

According to Dow Theory, a primary trend typically spans from months to years in the equity markets. Due to the high leverage that is afforded traders in the futures markets, primary trends in the commodity futures markets tend to span relatively shorter durations. High leverage tends to induce greater volatility in the markets. This is an important point to bear in mind when attempting to gauge the average duration and extent of market phase behavior in such markets. Although Dow Theory's original description of market phase relates primarily to the equity markets, the existence of these phases is found across all markets.

In essence, there are only two basic phases, that is, the *consolidation* phase and the *trending* phase. The consolidation phase may be further subdivided into the *accumulation* and *distribution* phases. See Figure 4.1.

Whether consolidation represents accumulation or distribution is only ascertained *after the fact*. That is, if the market rises after consolidating, we say that the consolidation represents accumulation (buying activity). Conversely, if the market declines after consolidating, we say that the consolidation represents distribution (selling activity). One of the objectives of technical analysis is to try to look for evidence to suggest whether accumulation or distribution is taking place *during* a consolidation. For example, it is observed that volume normally declines gradually during a consolidation. Very low levels of volume are usually a strong prognostication that the consolidation may potentially be coming to an end with a subsequent transition to a trend up or trend down phase. On a daily chart, consolidations normally lasts about three to six months, sometimes longer. See Figure 4.2.

These phases are also evident on the lower, *sub-hourly* timeframes. In Figure 4.3, we see micro phase action on the 15-min EURUSD chart.

Market Phase Sentiment and Participatory Behavior

The psychological and participatory aspects associated with each market phase are briefly described as follows.

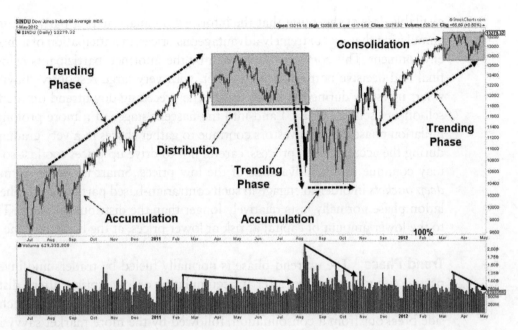

FIGURE 4.2 The Three Phases in a Primary Bull Trend on the Daily Chart of the Dow Jones Industrial Average Index.
Courtesy of Stockcharts.com

Accumulation Phase Accumulation normally occurs after a deep and rapid decline in prices. Companies tend to underperform with the release of very negative data, exacerbated by extremely bearish media headlines and news. The unsophisticated or uninformed market participants are usually extremely bearish at this point, desperately and frantically selling off all shares in the market at whatever price is

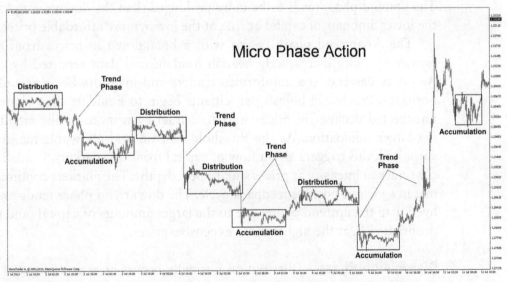

FIGURE 4.3 The Three Phases on the 15-Min EURUSD Chart.
Source: MetaTrader 4

101

available. It is at this point that the informed or smart market participants start accumulating shares at extremely advantageous prices, in anticipation of a more bullish environment. This *contrarian* approach by the informed participants helps create a final and decisive bottom in the market, with very large responsive buying by the smart investors during the last stages of the preceding downtrend (in the form of a sell-off or "selling climax") and into the nascent stages of a more prolonged accumulation phase. Smart investors continue to gather shares in a very gradual manner during the accumulation process, careful not to drive up prices too fast so that they may continue to take advantage of the low prices. Smart investors normally have *deep pockets* in order to engage in such contrarian-based participation. The accumulation phase normally lasts relatively longer than the distribution phase. This is due to the lower amount of capital at risk at lower prices, at the bottom of the market.

Trend Phase   The uptrend phase is normally fueled by traders and investors expecting either higher prices after an accumulation or lower prices after a distribution. Technical traders tend to get in much earlier, especially during a clear technical upside breakout from a consolidation, followed by the more market savvy investors. Media and news headlines also tend to be more upbeat at the early stages of an uptrend. As the uptrend progresses and starts to become more obvious, the general public begins to become aware and attracted to the rising prices. Previously bearish participants are also beginning to cover their short positions. With increasingly bullish fundamental data released or reported by companies, public participation begins to increase rapidly. Regret bias is felt by increasingly more participants as prices rise higher, inviting those who miss out on the earlier prices to buy at every dip on the way up. Participants who sold off positions too early are also now regretting their decision and are similarly trying to get back in at any opportunity. At even higher prices, the mass of public participation, that is, the *herd*, starts to use more margin, to the extent of even borrowing funds in order to invest in the rapidly rising market. The markets continue to spiral to new heights in a vicious positive feedback cycle. The uptrend phase tends to be more prolonged than the downtrend phase, due to the lower amounts of capital at risk, at the lower, more affordable prices.

The downtrend phase begins with a breakdown in prices from a distribution range, with increasingly bearish fundamental data reported by companies. As prices descend, the uninformed traders and investors begin to unload some positions. Previously bullish participants begin to liquidate their shares. Further unexpected declines in prices start to attract even more public attention, causing larger liquidation. As the threshold of pain and allowable margin limits is surpassed, this triggers an outflow of capital from the markets. Bearish sentiment continues to intensify as prices sink to new depths. The markets continue to plummet in a vicious positive feedback cycle. The downtrend phase tends to be shorter lived than the uptrend phase, due to the larger amounts of capital (and unrealized profit) at risk, at the higher more expensive prices.

Distribution Phase   Distribution normally occurs after a strong and rapid rise in prices. Companies tend to outperform with the release of very positive data, accompanied by the most bullish media headlines and news. The unsophisticated or uninformed market participants tend to be extremely bullish at this point as they get caught up in a buying frenzy, buying up all shares in the market at whatever price available, popularly referred to as being in a state of *irrational exuberance*. Margin debt is skyrocketing. The informed or smart market participants start their campaign of selling off shares at these extremely advantageous prices, in anticipation of a more bearish action. As before, this contrarian approach by the informed participants helps create a final and decisive top in the market, with very large responsive selling by the smart investors during the last stages of the preceding uptrend (in the form of a blow-off or buying climax) and subsequently selling over a distribution phase. Smart investors continue to liquidate shares in a very gradual manner during the distribution process, again, careful not to drive down prices too rapidly so that they may continue to take advantage of the higher prices. The distribution phase normally lasts a relatively shorter time than the accumulation phase. This is due to the larger amount of capital (and unrealized profit) at risk at higher prices, at the top of the market.

Technical Aspects of Consolidations

Accumulation tends to have the following characteristics:

- It generally occurs at the end of a relatively rapid decline in prices and ideally in the proximity of a historical or significant prior bottom in the market.
- There is no evidence of lower troughs being formed.
- It represents the start of either a new primary bull market on a longer-term horizon (or a new shorter-term uptrend if based on lower timeframes).
- Accumulations tend to last longer than distributions.
- Volume begins to subside as a potential upside breakout approaches.
- The longer the accumulation process, the more powerful the subsequent breakout will be to either side of the range, typically accompanied by a surge in volume.
- Accumulations tend to experience lower volatility in contrast to distributions due to the lower prices and consequently lower capital at risk.

Distribution tends to have the following characteristics:

- It generally occurs at the end of a prolonged uptrend in prices and ideally in the proximity of a historical or significant prior top in the market. Signs of market exhaustion begin to manifest.
- There is no evidence of higher peaks being formed.
- It represents the start of either a new primary bear market on a longer-term horizon (or a new shorter-term downtrend if based on lower timeframes).
- Distributions tend to last for a relatively shorter period than accumulations.
- Volume begins to subside as a potential downside breakout approaches.
- The longer the distribution process, the more powerful the subsequent breakout will be to either side of the range, typically accompanied by a surge in volume.
- Distributions tend to experience much greater volatility in contrast to accumulation due to the higher prices and consequently greater capital (an unrealized profit) at risk.

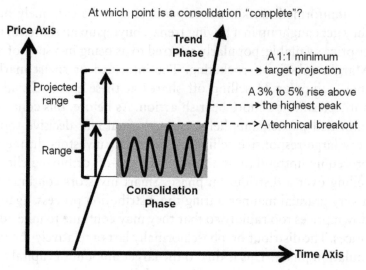

FIGURE 4.4 Most Popular Technical Levels Signaling the Completion of a Consolidation.

Completion of a Consolidation Phase

When attempting to identify points between phases, the issue of subjectivity arises yet again, as it does fairly frequently in technical analysis. The question a trader or analyst would always ask is "At which point does the consolidation actually end?" There is no absolute consensus or measure to determine the exact point in time or price at which a consolidation ends. It really depends on the approach and objectives of the trader or analyst.

For example, some market practitioners look for a 3 percent to 5 percent rise above the highest peak from a consolidation range as evidence of completion, whereas others look for the minimum *measuring objective* (i.e., expected minimum price target) to be met before completion is confirmed, which is usually a price excursion equal to the range or height of the consolidation. But more popularly, most traders and analysts look for a clear and simple technical breakout from a consolidation range as potential evidence that the consolidation has completed. Even so, the price at which the breakout itself occurs depends largely on the type and degree of price filtering employed. See Figure 4.4.

Logically, once a consolidation is complete, it also implies that a trend may already be in effect.

4.2 CHART PATTERN INTERPRETATION OF MARKET PHASE

Market phase can also be potentially identified by the type of chart patterns that manifest themselves at each stage of the three phases. Basically, most chart patterns belong to one of two groups, that is, reversal or continuation. Both the accumulation and distribution phases tend to be populated by reversal patterns. Interestingly, *the majority of reversal and continuation chart patterns are usually also regarded as consolidation patterns*, with the exception of V tops and V bottoms. The reason is obvious. The market, when expressing indecision, rest, or exhaustion, usually consolidates either by ranging or making relatively small corrective moves before resuming the existing trend or making a full-blown reversal. Therefore, a chart pattern is usually regarded as a consolidation pattern if it:

- Unfolds within a relatively confined and well defined price range
- Lacks any significant trend component

Although V tops and V bottoms are reversal patterns that occur more frequently during distributions than accumulations, both of these patterns are not normally regarded as consolidation since they do not unfold within a relatively confined and well-defined price range nor do they lack any significant trend component.

As we will see in Chapter 13, chart patterns have both *intrinsic* and *extrinsic* bullish and bearish bias. Extrinsic bias may also be referred to as location-based sentiment. Intrinsic bias is the inherent bullish or bearish sentiment associated with a chart pattern that is independent of location and where sentiment is strictly based on the nature of the pattern. When extrinsic and intrinsic biases are in alignment, distributions and accumulations have a greater potential for reversals, making more reliable tops and bottoms in the market respectively. As for trends, when intrinsic bias is in alignment with the directionality of the trend, i.e., the trend sentiment, the potential for a continuation is usually greater.

For example, an ascending triangle is intrinsically bullish, that is, it has a bullish bias. Regardless of where this pattern occurs with respect to past price action, it will always be inherently a bullish indication. If this bullish pattern is found at the price level of some historically significant market top, we say that it is extrinsically bearish, that is, the pattern is located at a significant resistance. However, if this pattern occurs at the price level of a historically significant market bottom, we say that this pattern is both intrinsically *and* extrinsically bullish. When the intrinsic and extrinsic biases are in agreement or aligned, the tendency for a reversal is potentially greater. If the ascending triangle occurs during an uptrend, and is not in proximity to any significant top or bottom in the market, the chances for a continuation are also greater as the intrinsic bias is in agreement with the directionality of price, that is, a bullish pattern occurring in a bullish trend.

Some chart patterns, like symmetrical triangles and horizontal channels, are essentially intrinsically neutral chart patterns with no obvious bias in sentiment. Some authors and practitioners classify them as continuation patterns whereas others refer to them as reversal patterns. The only determining factor as to whether these patterns represent reversals or continuations must therefore lie beyond the pattern itself, that is, sentiment that is dependent on factors that are *external* or extrinsic to the pattern, like the:

- Direction of the preceding trend
- Location with respect to historical extremes in price
- Location with respect to the phase of an underlying market cycle
- Location with respect to other supportive and resistive overlay barriers to price
- Bullish or bearish divergent formations

When attempting to determine the *reliability* of potential reversals during the accumulation and distribution phases, or continuations during the trend phase, it is important to look for *agreement* between the intrinsic and extrinsic biases. Any disagreement is seen as an indication that a reversal or continuation may be inherently weak. Here is a summary of some common chart patterns and their associated intrinsic and extrinsic biases.

Intrinsically Bullish Patterns:
- Bullish Pennants
- Bullish Flags
- Ascending Triangles
- Inverted Head and Shoulders
- Rounding Bottoms
- Cup and Handles
- Falling Wedges
- Double, Triple, and Multiple Bottoms

Intrinsically Bearish Patterns:
- Bearish Pennants
- Bearish Flags
- Descending Triangles
- Standard Head and Shoulders
- Rounding Tops
- Rising Wedges
- Double, Triple, and Multiple Tops

Intrinsically Neutral Patterns:
- Symmetrical Triangles
- Horizontal Channels

Intrinsically Bullish Patterns with Respect to Trend Sentiment:
- Bullish Pennants occurring in an uptrend
- Bullish Flags occurring in an uptrend
- Ascending Triangles occurring in an uptrend
- Inverted Head and Shoulders occurring in an uptrend
- Rounding Bottoms occurring in an uptrend
- Cup and Handles occurring in an uptrend
- Falling Wedges occurring in an uptrend
- Symmetrical Triangles occurring in an uptrend
- Horizontal Channels occurring in an uptrend
- Broadening Formations occurring in an uptrend

Intrinsically Bearish Patterns with Respect to Trend Sentiment:
- Bearish Pennants occurring in a downtrend
- Bearish Flags occurring in a downtrend
- Descending Triangles occurring in a downtrend
- Standard Head and Shoulders occurring in a downtrend

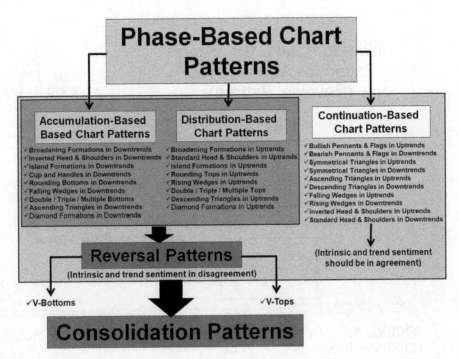

FIGURE 4.5 Phase-Based Charts Patterns.

- Rising Wedges occurring in a downtrend
- Symmetrical Triangles occurring in a downtrend
- Horizontal Channels occurring in a downtrend
- Broadening Formations occurring in a downtrend

As a general guide, intrinsic bias and trend sentiment are in disagreement with each other for reversal patterns. Conversely, intrinsic bias and trend sentiment should be in agreement with each other for continuation patterns. For intrinsically neutral formations, their extrinsic bias or sentiment is derived from the trend sentiment. For example, a symmetrical triangle will adopt an extrinsically bullish bias in an uptrend and an extrinsically bearish bias in a downtrend. It is important to note that although broadening, diamond, and island formations are essentially intrinsically neutral, they are regarded as reversal formations. As such, their extrinsic sentiment or bias will be in disagreement with any prevailing or preexisting trend sentiment. See Figure 4.5 for a visual summary of the various chart patterns normally associated with each phase, with reference to their intrinsic and extrinsic biases or sentiment.

In Figure 4.6 we observe an inverted head and shoulders pattern as accumulation on the EURUSD chart. Though we can state that the inverted pattern is intrinsically bullish, there is no evidence on the chart to indicate that it is also extrinsically bullish, as there is no information regarding the historical lower extremes in price, or its location with respect to the phase of an underlying market cycle or other overlay barriers. Notice the trend phase kicking in after the upside breakout.

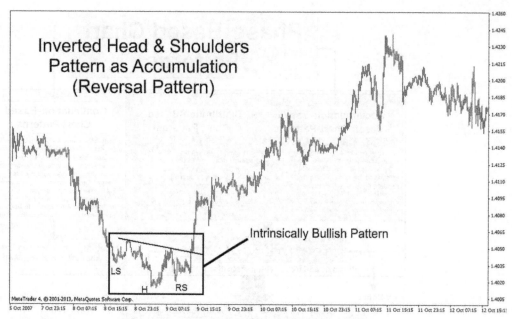

FIGURE 4.6 An Inverted Head and Shoulders Formation as Accumulation on the EURUSD Chart.
Source: MetaTrader 4

In Figure 4.7 we observe a standard head and shoulders pattern as distribution on the 15-min EURUSD chart. Notice the pattern forming a potentially new consolidation after reaching its minimum price objective, that is, a 1:1 ratio projection of the height of the pattern, as measured from the neckline breakout.

FIGURE 4.7 Head and Shoulders Formation as Distribution on the 15-min EURUSD Chart.
Source: MetaTrader 4

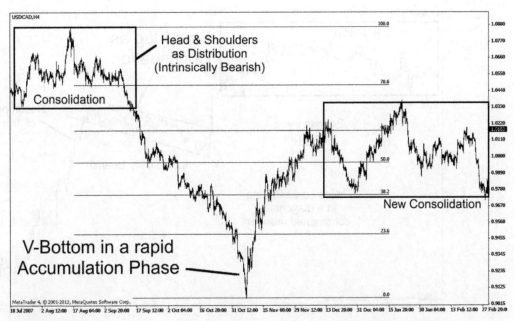

FIGURE 4.8 V-Bottom Formation as Accumulation on the 4-Hour USDCAD Chart.
Source: MetaTrader 4

In Figure 4.8 we observe a very rapid accumulation phase in a V bottom formation, which was preceded by an intrinsically bearish head and shoulders distribution phase on the 4-hour USDCAD chart. Of all the reversal patterns, the V-type reversals are the hardest to forecast and anticipate due to their rapid action. They are normally only identified in hindsight.

In Figure 4.9 we observe a symmetrical triangle as continuation within a trend phase. Although symmetrical triangles are intrinsically neutral, the existence

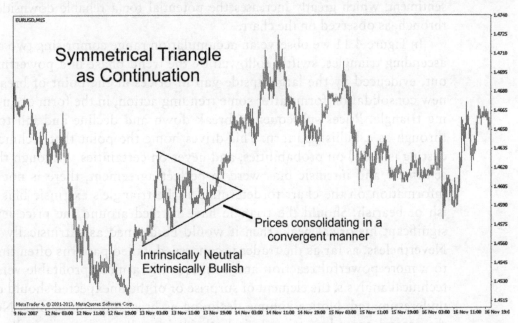

FIGURE 4.9 Symmetrical Triangle as Continuation in a Trend Phase on the EURUSD Chart.
Source: MetaTrader 4

FIGURE 4.10 Bear Flag Formation as Distribution on the Sub-Hourly EURUSD Chart.
Source: MetaTrader 4

of the preexisting uptrend imbues the formation with an element of extrinsic bullishness.

In Figure 4.10 we observe a bear flag formation triangle as continuation within a trend phase. The bear flag consolidation is confirmed once price violates the pattern. Notice the preceding distribution phase leading to a strong downside breakout. Note that the flag's intrinsic bias is in agreement with the bearish trend sentiment, which greatly increases the potential for a reliable downside follow through, as observed on the chart.

In Figure 4.11 we observe an accumulation range comprising two adjacent ascending triangles, swiftly followed by the trend phase in a powerful breakout, evidenced by the large upside gap in prices at the point of breakout. A new consolidation forms after some trending action, in the form of an ascending triangle. Prices subsequently break down and decline and fail to follow through as a bullish pattern. This drives home the point that technical forecasting is based on probabilities, and never on certainties. Although the trend sentiment and intrinsic bias were in perfect agreement, there is not enough information on the chart to determine if the triangle's extrinsic bias is bullish or bearish. Should the triangle have formed around the price level of a significant historical peak, then it would be deemed as extrinsically bearish. Nevertheless, as far as the trader is concerned, failed patterns often times lead to a more powerful reaction and consequently a more profitable venture. In technical analysis, the element of surprise or of the unexpected should never be underestimated. Notice volume declining as breakout approaches. Note that the second ascending triangle is both intrinsically and extrinsically bullish, since it is forming within a clear and obvious support area in the market, as evidenced by the first ascending triangle.

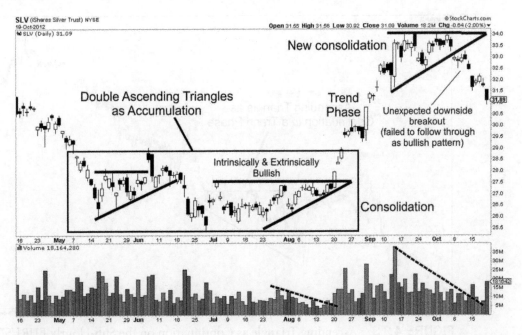

FIGURE 4.11 Ascending Triangles as Accumulation on the Daily iShares Silver Trust (SLV) Chart.
Courtesy of Stockcharts.com

In Figure 4.12 we observe a symmetrical triangle acting as accumulation within a larger consolidation zone on the daily chart of Gold. Although the symmetrical triangle is intrinsically neutral in sentiment, it is very clear that the symmetrical triangle pattern has bullish extrinsic bias, as it is located at a very well established accumulation zone that has been tested by multiple bottoms. In proximity also lies additional barrier support in the form of a downtrend line. Notice the trend phase that ensues after a short return move to the triangle breakout barrier.

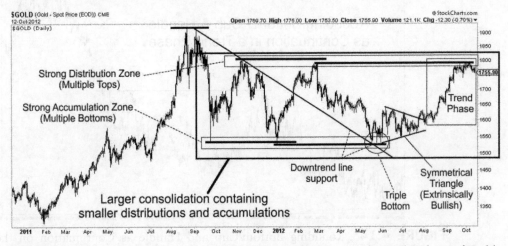

FIGURE 4.12 Nested Accumulations and Consolidations on the Daily Chart of Gold.
Courtesy of Stockcharts.com

111

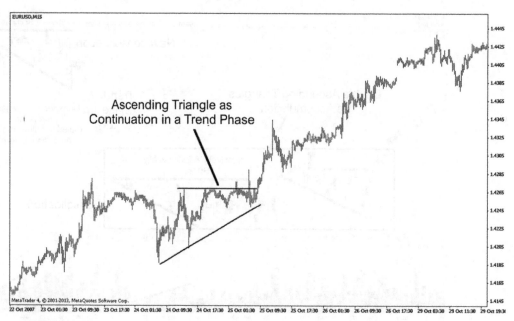

FIGURE 4.13 Ascending Triangle as Continuation on the Sub-Hourly EURUSD Chart.
Source: MetaTrader 4

In Figures 4.13 and 4.14, we observe an ascending triangle and a rounding bottom acting as continuation in trend phases.

4.3 VOLUME AND OPEN INTEREST INTERPRETATION OF MARKET PHASE

Market phase can also be potentially identified by the type of volume action that manifests itself at each stage of the three phases. Figure 4.15 depicts a typical sequence of volume action as the market progresses to the next phase. Notice that

FIGURE 4.14 Rounding Bottom/Cup and Handle as Continuation on the 4-Hour EURUSD Chart.
Source: MetaTrader 4

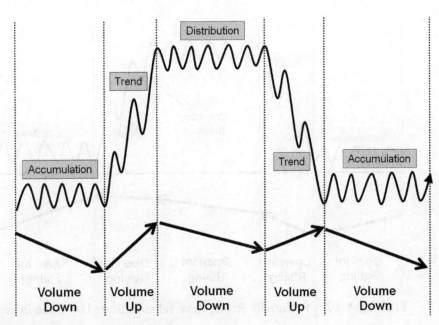

FIGURE 4.15   Phase Related Volume Action.

volume tends to decline to relatively low levels just prior to a phase transition. Hence, we may use volume as a *timing indicator* for forecasting potential phase transitions.

Should an uptrend or downtrend be inherently weak, then this is normally indicated by a fall-off in volume *during* the trend phase. This is a sign of trend exhaustion and it signals a potentially earlier onset of a distribution or accumulation phase. See Figure 4.16.

Besides phase related volume action, open interest may also reveal potential phase behavior. For the most part, open interest action tends to correlate fairly

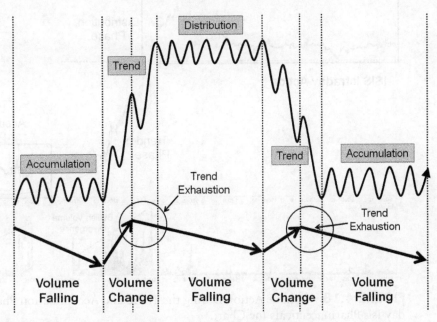

FIGURE 4.16   Trend Exhaustion as Indicated by Volume Action.

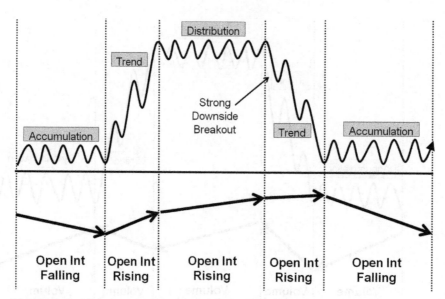

FIGURE 4.17 Potentially Strong Reversal as Indicated by Open Interest Action.

closely to volume action. It is when they disagree or diverge significantly that additional evidence is obtained about potential future market action. If open interest increases during a consolidation instead of decreasing, the breakout move and subsequent trend tends to be much more rapid and extended. See Figure 4.17.

Figure 4.18 is an intraday chart of Isis Pharmaceuticals Inc. We see the extended distribution phase being violated by a downside gap in prices, accompanied by high volume. The trend phase than ensues with bullish volume divergence and subsequently transits into an accumulation phase. Note how volume gradually

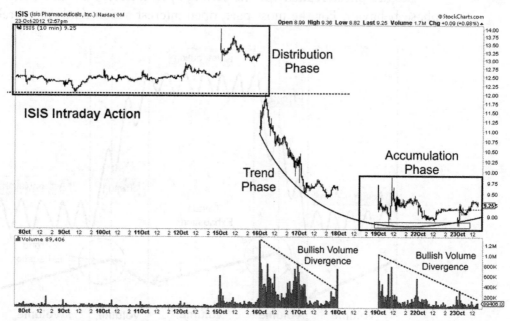

FIGURE 4.18 Volume Action During the Trend and Accumulation Phases on the Intraday Isis Pharmaceuticals Inc Chart.
Courtesy of Stockcharts.com

114

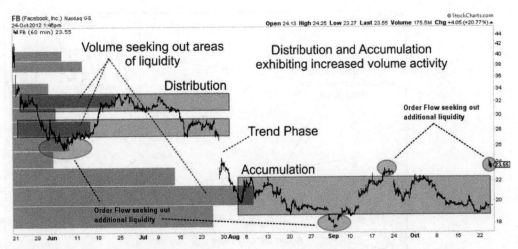

FIGURE 4.19 Price-Based Volume Action on the Hourly Facebook Inc Chart.
Courtesy of Stockcharts.com

decreases as the accumulation progresses, signaling a potentially imminent break-out, be it to the upside or downside.

Besides volume action acting as a timing indicator for potential breakouts, higher than normal volume at the *initial* stages of an accumulation or distribution is a strong indication that a bottom or top in the market has been formed. Figure 4.19 is an hourly chart of Facebook Inc. Notice how relatively large *price-based* volume, as opposed to the traditional *interval* or *time-based* volume, coincides with the distribution and accumulation zones, with the market testing the consolidation boundaries for additional liquidity. Hence, price levels associated with historically high volumes of activity represent potential levels of accumulation or distribution.

4.4 MOVING AVERAGE INTERPRETATION OF MARKET PHASE

Market phase can also be potentially identified by the behavior of moving averages at each stage of the three phases. Figure 4.20 displays a simple moving average as it encounters the trend and consolidation phases.

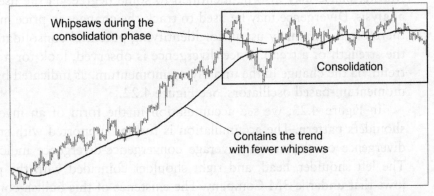

FIGURE 4.20 Moving Average Action during the Trend and Consolidation Phases.

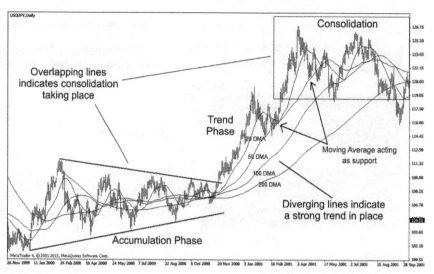

FIGURE 4.21 Moving Average Action during the Trend and Consolidation Phases on the Daily EURUSD Chart.
Source: MetaTrader 4

By applying popular multiple moving average lines, the behavior of moving averages with respect to trends and consolidations becomes more evident. Refer to Figure 4.21. When a trend is in effect, we observe that the multiple moving average lines start to diverge from each other. The greater the divergence, the stronger will be the ensuing trend. Therefore, when multiple moving average lines begin to converge, this represents an early indication of a potential consolidation.

During trending phases, the moving average displays the minimum incidences of whipsaws, but during any consolidation phases it will exhibit a significant increase in whipsaw action due to the flattening-out effect of averages in a sideways or ranging market.

4.5 DIVERGENCE AND MOMENTUM INTERPRETATION OF MARKET PHASE

Market phase may also be identified to some degree via the use of divergence analysis. Divergence may be used to track the changes in price momentum, and therefore is extremely useful for identifying potential consolidations as well as the strength of a trend. Once divergence is observed, look for a slowing of the trend via the change in the underlying momentum, as indicated by the diverging momentum-based oscillators. See Figure 4.22.

In Figure 4.23, we see accumulation in the form of an inverted head and shoulders pattern. The accumulation is further supported with standard bullish divergence on the moving average convergence-divergence indicator (MACD). The left shoulder, head, and right shoulder coincided with the projected cycle lows that underlie 3M Company. The existence of this bullish confluence within the accumulation greatly increases the probability for a strong upside move.

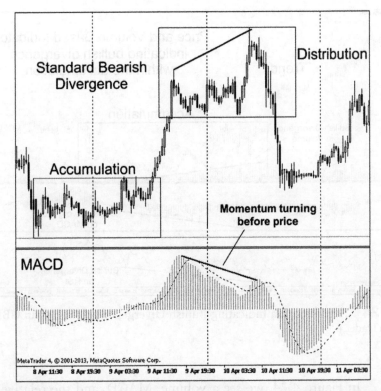

FIGURE 4.22 Distribution Indicating Bearish Divergence on the Hourly EURUSD Chart.
Source: MetaTrader 4

FIGURE 4.23 Accumulation Indicating Bullish Divergence on the Daily 3M Co. Chart.
Courtesy of Stockcharts.com

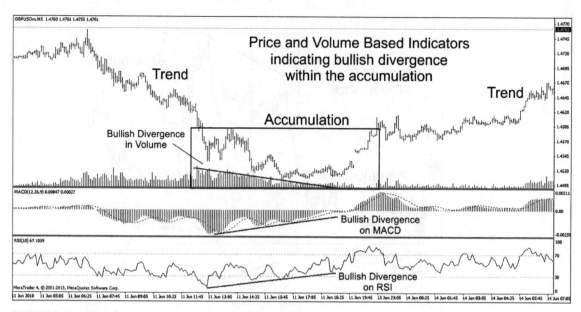

FIGURE 4.24 Accumulation Indicating Bullish Divergence on the 5-Min GBPUSD Chart.
Source: MetaTrader 4

In Figure 4.24, we see a volume, MACD, and the relative strength indicator (RSI) all indicating bullish divergence with the price within the accumulation. Both the MACD and RSI are momentum-based indicators. We see momentum turning before price. This is particularly useful, especially at the tail end of a trend where a clear indication that a consolidation may be forming could help the trader anticipate an early entry. Note that for bullish divergence in volume, falling prices must be accompanied by decreasing volume.

4.6 SENTIMENT INTERPRETATION OF MARKET PHASE

Accumulations and distributions are associated with various sentiment indications, resulting from the behavior of market participants as they respond to market news, price action, rumors, other participants' behaviors, brokers, and so on. As they swing back and forth between fear, greed, and hope in the markets, various identifiable patterns start to emerge that are repeated fairly consistently, especially when markets move to extremes. *Sentiment indicators* track these behavioral patterns via the aggregate sentiment, emotions, and psychology of market participants. It is at market extremes that these indicators are most accurate and reflective of the underlying mood of optimism or pessimism. Examples of some sentiment indicators are:

- Put-Call Ratios
- Arm's Index
- Odd Lot Sales
- Margin Debt
- Cot Report
- VIX

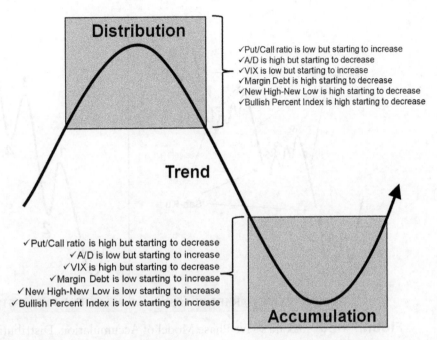

Distribution

✓Put/Call ratio is low but starting to increase
✓A/D is high but starting to decrease
✓VIX is low but starting to increase
✓Margin Debt is high starting to decrease
✓New High-New Low is high starting to decrease
✓Bullish Percent Index is high starting to decrease

Trend

✓Put/Call ratio is high but starting to decrease
✓A/D is low but starting to increase
✓VIX is high but starting to decrease
✓Margin Debt is low starting to increase
✓New High-New Low is low starting to increase
✓Bullish Percent Index is low starting to increase

Accumulation

FIGURE 4.25 Sentiment Indicator Behavior at Accumulation and Distribution.

- Short Interest Ratio
- Cash Asset Ratio
- Advance-Decline Line
- New Highs–New Lows
- Up Volume–Down Volume
- Market Vane Reports
- Bullish Sentiment Index

Figure 4.25 is a simple visual guide of how some sentiment indicators vary as the market swings between tops (distribution) and bottoms (accumulation). For a more detailed discussion of sentiment indicators, refer to Chapter 23.

4.7 SAKATA'S INTERPRETATION OF MARKET PHASE

Sakata's Five Methods is a unique Japanese approach for interpreting and understanding the markets, which originated with Munehisa Honma. Under Sakata's approach, the market is divided into five distinct phases, as opposed to the conventional three-phase model by Dow. The five distinct phases are:

1. San Zan—*Three Mountains*. This is equivalent to the Western triple top formation which represents the distribution phase.
2. San Sen—*Three Rivers*. This is equivalent to the Western triple bottom formation which represents the accumulation phase.
3. San Ku—*Three Gaps*. This is equivalent to the Western triple gap formation which occurs during the trending phase, popularly known as the breakaway, runaway, and exhaustion gaps.

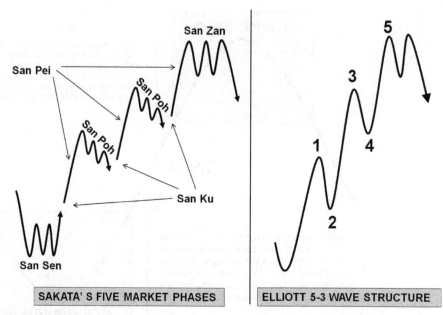

FIGURE 4.26 Sakata's Five Phase Model of Accumulation, Distribution, and Trend.

4. San Pei—*Three Thrusts*. This represents the three trending phases between accumulation and distribution. This closely resembles Elliott's three impulsive numbered waves 1, 3, and 5.

5. San Poh—*Three Methods*. This represents the three corrections after each thrust. This somewhat resemble Elliott's three corrective waves lettered as a, b, and c in upcoming Figure 4.28.

Sakata's five market phases are illustrated in Figure 4.26. We see that it is very similar in appearance to Elliott's. Elliott waves have specific rules and guidelines with respect to wave construction, whereas Sakata's five-phase model is less rigid.

Although Dow's three-phase model of market phase may seem initially to be inconsistent with Sakata's five-phase and Elliott's motive wave model, it can be shown, using simple chart patterns, that the two models need not necessarily be viewed as distinct from each other. Figure 4.27 depicts Sakata's five-phase model operating within Dow's three-phase market. It offers a plausible resolution between Eastern and Western approaches to market phase analysis.

4.8 ELLIOTT'S INTERPRETATION OF MARKET PHASE

Elliott described the markets as moving in an *impulsive* five-wave up followed by a *corrective* three-wave down motion. The trending phase is represented by impulse waves 1, 3, and 5. The accumulation phase is represented by the corrective waves 2 and 4, and in most cases including the entire abc correction itself. Distribution is usually represented by the abc correction. See Figure 4.28.

Figure 4.29 depicts an Elliott wave count for Gold from 2000 to 2012. Notice that volume gradually decreases over the span of each significant consolidation, as seen at points 1, 2, and 3. We observe that primary waves 1 and 2 occur

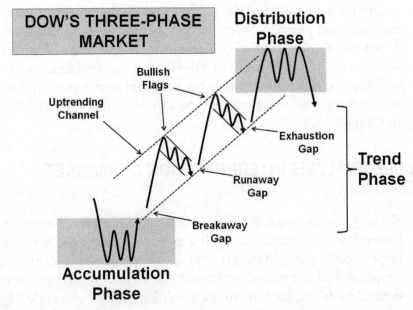

FIGURE 4.27   Sakata's Five-Phase Model Operating within Dow's Three-Phase Market.

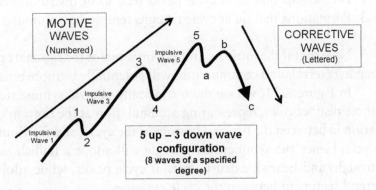

FIGURE 4.28   Elliott Wave Structure.

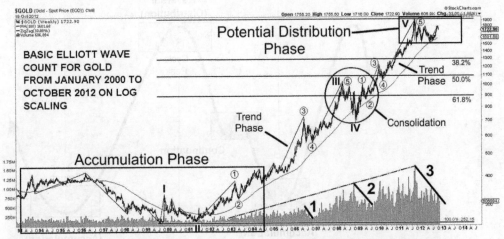

FIGURE 4.29   The Elliott Wave Phase Model on the Weekly Gold Chart.
Courtesy of Stockcharts.com

within the accumulation phase, followed by the powerful wave 3 move during the first trend phase. Notice also that volume peaks out around the top of wave 5, within the new area of consolidation, in the form of an inverted head and shoulders pattern. The use of Fibonacci price and time projection techniques will help the practitioner gauge the potential termination and start of each wave within the 5-3 wave structure. (For a detailed discussion of Elliott Waves, refer to Chapter 18.)

4.9 CYCLE ANALYSIS INTERPRETATION OF MARKET PHASE

We may also use market cycles to determine if a price formation is potentially a reversal or a continuation. It all depends on where the formation unfolds with respect to the phase of the cycle. Once a cycle period is identified, it will be fairly simple to find out where the formations lie with respect to the cycle phase. As a general guideline, for formations unfolding on the same cycle degree:

1. Formations that lie in between cycle extremes tend to be continuations
2. Formations that lie at cycle peaks tend to be distributions
3. Formations that lie at cycle troughs tend to be accumulations

Note that if the intrinsic and extrinsic biases for the chart patterns are in agreement, reversals and continuations will potentially be more reliable. See Figure 4.30.

In Figure 4.31, we see the intrinsically neutral symmetrical triangle adopting three distinct roles, representing accumulation at the bottom of the cycle, continuation in between the top and bottom of the cycle, and distribution at the top of the cycle. Hence the symmetrical triangle will adopt a bullish extrinsic bias at cycle troughs and bearish extrinsic bias at cycle peaks, while adopting the preexisting trend sentiment between the cycle extremes.

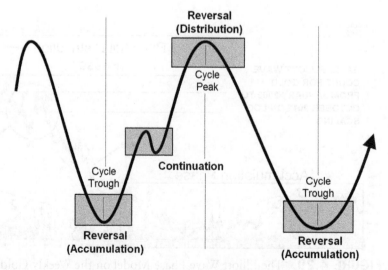

FIGURE 4.30 Using Cycles to Determine Market Phase.

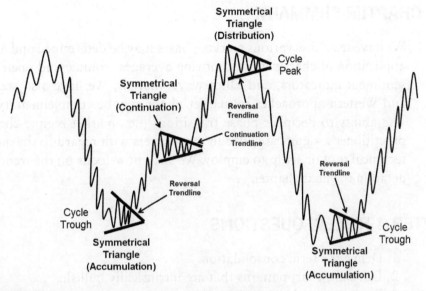

FIGURE 4.31 Using Cycles to Determine Market Phase.

In a similar fashion, we see the symmetrical triangle, in Figure 4.32, adopting three distinct roles, representing accumulation at the bottom of the uptrending channel, continuation in between the top and bottom of the channel, and distribution at the top of the uptrending channel. Had the pattern been an inverted head and shoulders pattern instead, the probability of a reversal at the bottom of the channel or a continuation in the middle of it would be potentially greater. Resistive and supportive confluences, comprising other overlay barriers such as Fibonacci levels and so on, help to yield more reliable forecasts of potential price reaction levels in the market.

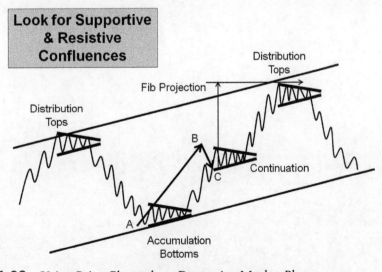

FIGURE 4.32 Using Price Channels to Determine Market Phase.

4.10 CHAPTER SUMMARY

We have seen how various market phases may be determined and identified via the application of chart patterns, moving averages, volume and open interest, cycles, sentiment indicators, and Elliot wave analysis. We have also seen how Eastern and Western approaches to market phase may be complementary to each other. The ability to decipher phase transitions (i.e., market regime changes) gives the practitioner a significant edge in the markets with regard to the most appropriate technical tool or setup to employ. We shall now focus on the trend phase in more detail in the next chapter.

CHAPTER 4 REVIEW QUESTIONS

1. Define the term consolidation.
2. List eight chart patterns that are intrinsically bullish.
3. Explain why the majority of chart patterns are consolidation patterns.
4. Describe how you would determine if accumulation is taking place.
5. Which sentiment indicators best describe distributions?
6. How would you use moving averages to gauge market phase?
7. Explain how you would use a cycle to determine market phase.
8. How do you use divergence to identify potential consolidations?

REFERENCES

Frost, A. J., and Robert R. Prechter. 1999. *Elliott Wave Principle*. New York: John Wiley & Sons.

Morris, Gregory. 2006. *Candlestick Charting Explained*. New York: McGraw-Hill.

Murphy, John. 1999. *Technical Analysis of the Financial Markets*. New York: New York Institute of Finance (NYIF).

Trend Analysis

Trend trading has transfixed traders for decades with the promise of rapid profits. Countless books have been written expounding the virtues and advantages of such an approach. In this chapter, we shall attempt to unveil the underlying characteristics of trend action and how to decipher pure price action to better understand the behavior of the market. We will also discuss price filtering and the effective application of tradesizing and stopsizing to with respect to technical trade setups.

5.1 DEFINITIONS OF A TREND

Classification of a Trend According to Dow Theory

In Dow Theory, trends are classified and defined by their duration and extent:

- Primary or major trends are longer term and span from months to years
- Secondary trends or reactions are medium term and span from weeks to months
- Minor trends are shorter term and span from days to weeks

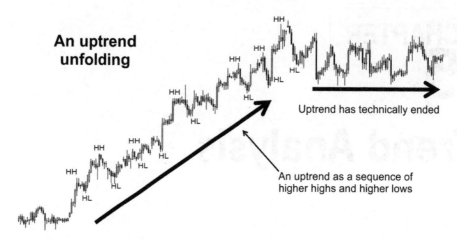

FIGURE 5.1 Peak and Trough Representation of an Uptrend.

In Dow Theory, an uptrend is defined using *peak and trough analysis*. An uptrend is represented by a series of successively higher highs (peaks) and lows (troughs), while a downtrend is represented by a series of successively lower highs and lows. This is the most popular definition of a trend. See Figures 5.1 and 5.2.

Definition versus Absolute Measure of a Trend

The problem with definitions is that if price action does not unfold in a manner required under its definition, no trend would be recognized or even acknowledged. In addition, if price action was inordinately erratic or chaotic, the identification of a trend using peak and trough analysis may prove extremely challenging, if not impossible in some situations. All definitions impose limitations, which may lead to situations where an actual trend may not be acknowledged or recognized.

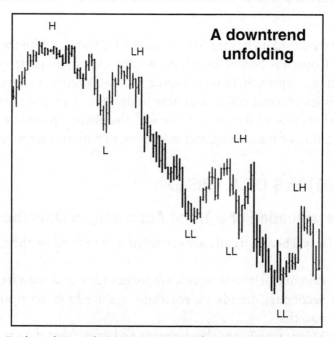

FIGURE 5.2 Peak and Trough Representation of a Downtrend.

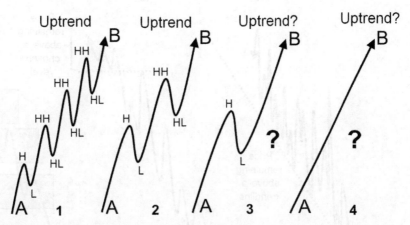

FIGURE 5.3 Limitation of Dow's Peak and Trough Definition of a Trend.

See Figure 5.3. Under peak and trough analysis, trend actions in scenarios 1 and 2 satisfy the conditions for being classified as uptrends, because they exhibit a series of higher highs and lows. But what about trend actions in scenarios 3 and 4? There are no higher highs or lows in scenario 3, and no highs or lows whatsoever in scenario 4. Do we classify them as uptrends? Under Dow's peak and trough definition, they do not classify as uptrends. Nevertheless, in all four scenarios, price traversed from Point A to Point B. Do we then deny that trends existed in scenarios 3 and 4? Many practitioners believe that it may be better to define a trend by an *absolute measure* of distance traversed rather than by the behavior of price during a trend.

To avoid the dependence on a particular price behavior as a means of identifying a trend, many practitioners choose to use other means of trend identification, such as:

- Price remaining above or below an overlay indicator
- Price remaining above or below an arbitrarily chosen price level
- The absence of a reversal of a specified amount during a trend

One popular example of price remaining above or below an overlay indicator in order to qualify as a trend is best illustrated via the use of trendlines and moving averages. As long as *price activity remains above a trendline in an uptrend*, the uptrend is considered to be still intact. The converse applies for downtrends. This would obviate the need to inspect price behavior during a trend. In similar fashion, as long as price remains above a certain moving average, an uptrend is considered to still be intact. With respect to other price overlays, the trend is considered to still be intact if:

- Price remains above the Bollinger, linear regression, and moving average *lower band* in an uptrend (the converse for downtrends)
- Price remains above the *lower boundary* of a chart pattern in an uptrend (the converse for downtrends)

127

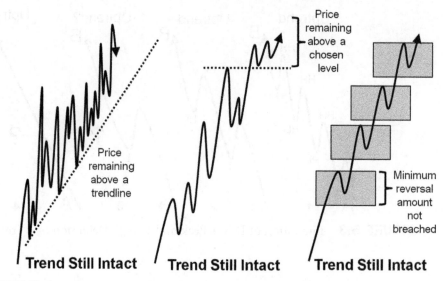

FIGURE 5.4 Alternative Definitions of an Uptrend in Effect.

Some practitioners also define a trend by its ability to *remain above or below some arbitrarily chosen price level*. As long as price remains above a chosen support level, an uptrend is considered to still be intact. Similarly, as long as price remains below a chosen resistance level, a downtrend is considered to still be intact. This chosen price level may represent some historically significant support level in an uptrend—or resistance in a downtrend—the violation of which would imply a very high probability of the trend reversing.

A third method of identifying an ongoing trend is via the *absence of a reversal* of a specified amount during a trend. This third approach is employed on constant-range charts such as Point and Figure and Renko charts. As long as the reversal size is not breached, the trend is still intact. See Figure 5.4.

Describing Consolidation and Trends via Wave Cycles and Degrees

It is also important to be able to describe and identify trends and consolidations in terms of wave cycles or degrees. We may describe any trend or consolidation in terms of *wave cycles*, which exist at various wave *degrees*. Below are the terms associated with a wave cycle comprising three degrees:

- Higher Wave Cycle (HWC)—highest wave degree relative to the MWC and LWC
- Medium Wave Cycle (MWC)—a subwave of HWC and is of a lower degree than the HWC
- Lower Wave Cycle (LWC)—a subwave of both the HWC and MWC and is at the lowest wave degree

Note that the *minimum* number of wave degrees in any trend is two. Figure 5.5 depicts a wave of three degrees.

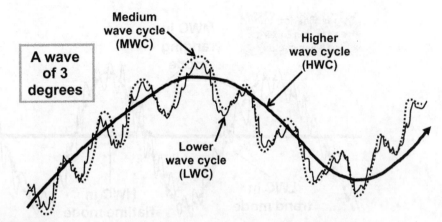

FIGURE 5.5 Trend Action in Terms of Wave Cycles and Degrees.

The MWC and LWC are both subwaves of the HWC and are regarded as wave cycles of lower degrees. It is critical that a trader be able to visualize price cycles on the chart. Without knowing which wave cycle is being traded, any of the following scenarios may result:

- Inability to select consistent breakout levels
- Inability to select effective stoploss levels
- Inability to apply effective stopsizing
- Inability to distinguish between trend and consolidation mode
- Inability to determine the direction of the predominant trend

Elliott waves are studied in terms of wave cycles and wave degrees. Figure 5.6 depicts an Elliott wave count in terms of wave cycles and wave degrees. Refer to Chapter 18 for a detailed discussion of Elliott waves and the 5-3 fractal trend structure.

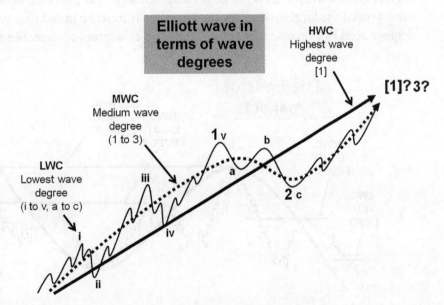

FIGURE 5.6 Elliott Wave in Terms of Wave Cycles and Degrees.

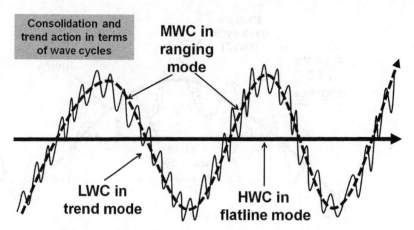

FIGURE 5.7   Consolidation and Trend Action in Terms of Wave Cycles and Degrees.

As seen in the Figure 5.7, a market may be both in trend and consolidation modes at the same time, *depending on the wave cycle being observed.*

We may also define breakouts via the degree of the wave cycles. Figure 5.8 illustrates breakouts in terms of the wave degree being traded. Hence, we have breakouts based on waves of lower, medium, and higher degrees. In other words, the breakout level will depend on the wave degree being traded. Being aware of the wave degree being traded will allow the trader to *size the stoploss* effectively, according to the average wave amplitude and volatility associated with that particular wave degree. *Volatility at one wave degree may not manifest at a higher or lower wave degree.*

Significance of Higher Wave Degree Reversals

There is a reason why turning points of larger wave cycles (or trends) are more significant than those of smaller wave cycles. It all has to do with wave-degree convergence. *When a large wave cycle (or trend) reverses, all the wave cycles of lower degrees reverse in sync with the larger wave cycle.* It is at the point of reversal that all subwaves of the largest wave reverse together. It must be noted that waves of higher degrees need not reverse when waves of a lower degrees reverse. See Figure 5.9.

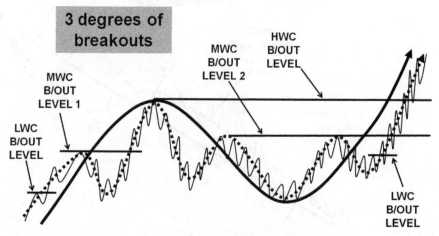

FIGURE 5.8   Breakouts in Terms of Wave Cycles and Degrees.

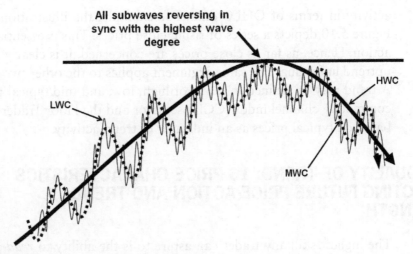

FIGURE 5.9 Reversal of All Subwaves.

Reversals, Corrections, and Retracements

Reversals and retracements imply a turnaround in prices, and may be of any amount or degree. Corrections and pullbacks tend to imply a more shallow reversal or retracement, usually no more than a few percent.

Trends in Terms of OHLC Data

Trend may also be defined in terms of individual open, high, low, and close (OHLC) data. Figure 5.10 depicts various trend activity with respect to the high, low, close, and mid/typical prices. Although we see that the market is flat in terms of peak and trough analysis, that is, there is no evidence of successively higher or lower peaks and troughs, we cannot deny the presence of some form of trending

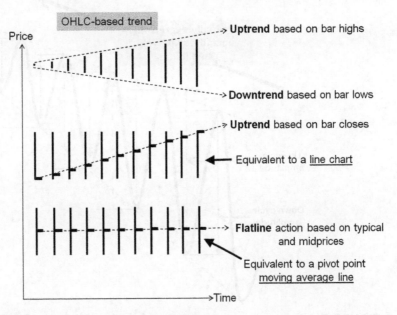

FIGURE 5.10 Trend Based on OHLC Data.

activity in terms of OHLC data. For example, the illustration in the middle of Figure 5.10 depicts a series of rising close prices. This is essentially a *line chart* in action. Hence, as far as close prices are concerned, it is clearly an example of an uptrend unfolding. The same argument applies to the other two examples as well. A trend may be defined in terms of high, low, and mid/typical prices. In fact, the commodity channel index (CCI) oscillator and the Floor Trader's Pivot Points are based on typical prices as an indicator of trend activity.

5.2 QUALITY OF TREND: 16 PRICE CHARACTERISTICS IMPACTING FUTURE PRICE ACTION AND TREND STRENGTH

The highest skill any trader can aspire to is the ability to *read pure price action*. This is an important skill because price is regarded as the most important indicator of potential future price action. When attempting to decipher the possible future action of price, we need to be familiar with 16 critical price characteristics that may potentially impact future price activity, namely variations in:

1. **Cycle Amplitude:** Look for decreasing cycle amplitude in uptrends and downtrends. A decrease in cycle amplitude in an uptrend is an early indication that there may potentially be underlying weakness in the uptrend (see Figure 5.11). In similar fashion, a decrease in cycle amplitude in a downtrend is regarded as a bullish indication. Note that the up cycle amplitudes must, on average, be larger than the down cycle amplitudes for an uptrend to take place. Conversely, for a downtrend, the up cycle amplitudes must, on average, be smaller than the down cycle amplitudes. Nevertheless, it is the *change* in the successive up and down cycle amplitudes that are the most important characteristic for deciphering future price activity.

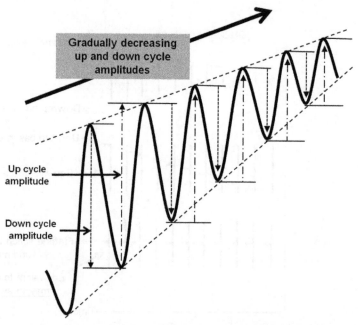

FIGURE 5.11 Decreasing Cycle Amplitudes in an Uptrend Is Bearish.

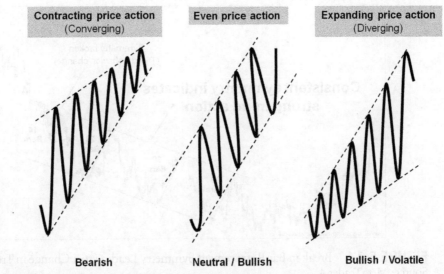

FIGURE 5.12 Decreasing Cycle Amplitudes in an Uptrend.

Figure 5.12 illustrates three idealized examples of changing cycle amplitudes. Contracting formations are bearish in an uptrend and bullish in a downtrend. Expanding formations (where both upper and lower boundary trendlines are pointing in an upwardly direction) are generally bullish in an uptrend. The converse applies to downtrends. The trend with steady and consistent cycle amplitude is regarded as bullish in an uptrend and bearish in a downtrend, and is generally regarded as the most reliable trend in terms of extent and duration.

2. Cycle Period: Decreasing cycle periods are also an early indication of potential weakness in a trend. A gradual reduction in the cycle period during an uptrend is an early indication that there may potentially be underlying weakness in the uptrend. In similar fashion, a gradual reduction in the cycle period during a downtrend is a bullish indication. See Figure 5.13.

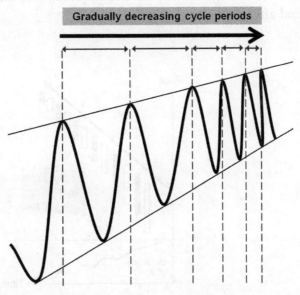

FIGURE 5.13 Decreasing Cycle Periods in an Uptrend.

133

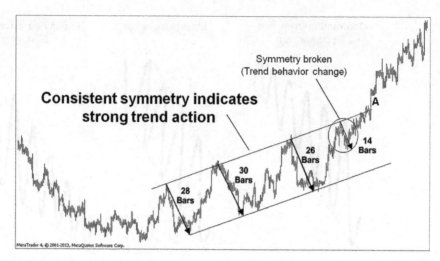

FIGURE 5.14 Break in Bar Retracement Symmetry Leading to a Change in Trend Behavior. Source: MetaTrader 4

3. Bar Retracement Symmetry: A change in the number of bars in a retracement is also an early indication of a potential change in trend behavior. Figure 5.14 shows a change in the bar retracement symmetry leading to a strong upside move.

4. Average Bar Range: A decrease in the average bar range in an uptrend is an early indication of potential weakness in an uptrend. In a similar fashion, a decrease in the average bar range in a downtrend is a bullish indication. See Figure 5.15. We can track the bar range using the average true range (ATR) oscillator. Unlike average bar range, the ATR oscillator will account for gaps between the bars as well.

Figure 5.16 shows a declining ATR during a steady uptrend in the GLD SPDR Gold Trust Shares. Although volume is bullish, the ATR is indicating otherwise. A large bearish candlestick completes the bearish picture. Price declined after the volume climax.

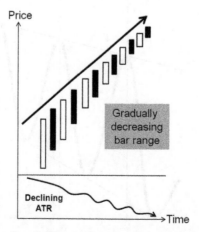

FIGURE 5.15 Decreasing Bar Range Indicating Potential Trend Weakness.

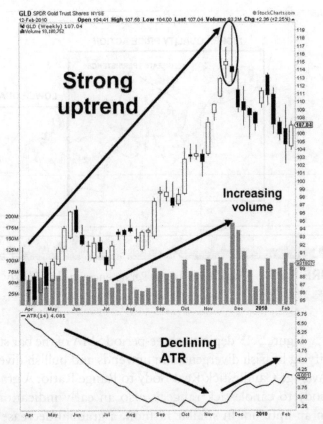

FIGURE 5.16 Decreasing Bar Range/ATR Indicating Potential Trend Weakness on the Weekly Chart of the GLD SPDR Trust Shares.
Courtesy of Stockcharts.com

5. Price Persistence (continuity of trend action): Prices tend to persist for longer periods when price is of high quality. High quality prices have:
   - Relatively small bar ranges
   - Approximately equal bar ranges

   When these two qualities are present, price tends to move in a predictable manner. The trends and reversals are clear and decisive, making the tracking of price action much easier for the trend trader. In this mode, prices exhibit relatively low levels of volatility. See Figure 5.17.

6. The Average Bar Stochastic Ratio (closing price compared to bar range): A gradual decline in close prices with respect to the bar itself is also an early indication of potential weakness in an uptrend. In a similar fashion, a gradual increase in close prices with respect to the bar itself is also an early indication of potential bullishness in a downtrend. We measure this increase or decline in close prices with respect to the bar itself as a ratio, and it is referred to as the *bar stochastic*. Unlike the standard stochastic oscillator which compares the relative position of the closing price over the last N periods, the bar stochastic measures the relative position of the closing price within the bar itself. It is essentially a one-period %K. A simple moving average of the bar stochastic ratio is used to monitor this price action behavior. See Figure 5.18.

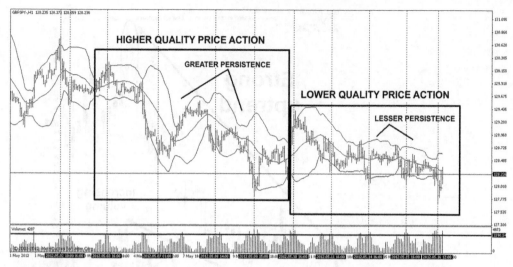

FIGURE 5.17 Variation in Trend Persistence on the Hourly Chart of GBPJPY.
Source: MetaTrader 4

Figure 5.19 depicts a three-period SMA of the bar stochastic accurately identifying bearish divergences in uptrends and bullish divergences in downtrends.

7. Average Candlestick Real Body to Range Ratio: A gradual decrease in the real body to candlestick range is also an early indication of potential weakness in an uptrend. In similar fashion, a gradual decrease in real body to candlestick range is a bullish indicator in a downtrend. A simple moving average of the real body to candlestick range ratio is used to monitor this price action behavior. See Figure 5.20.

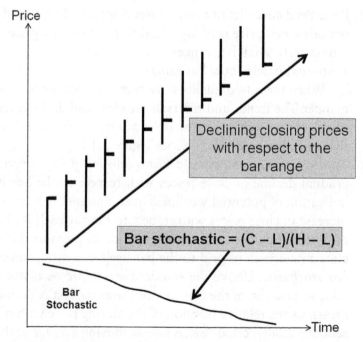

FIGURE 5.18 Declining Bar Stochastic Ratio Indicating Trend Weakness.

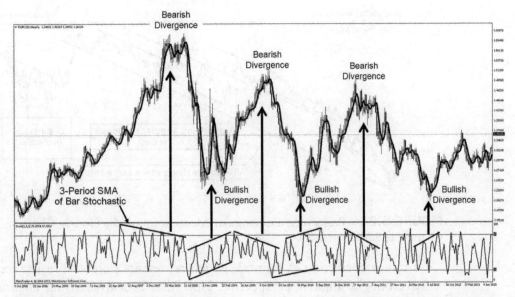

FIGURE 5.19 A 3-Period SMA of Bar Stochastic Indicating Bullish and Bearish Divergences on the Weekly Chart of EURUSD.
Source: MetaTrader 4

8. Angular Symmetry and Momentum: Any change in the angular symmetry is also an early indication of potential bullishness or bearishness in the markets. In Figure 5.21, 3M Co. is displaying consistent angular symmetry over a period of three years. Generally speaking, an increase in the angle of ascent is bullish for the stock, while a decrease is bearish. Trendlines 1 and 2 are also parallel, which is a strong prognosticator of potential bullishness. This is because trendline 1 was subsequently followed by a steady rise in share price and we tend to expect this to also unfold in a very bullish manner after

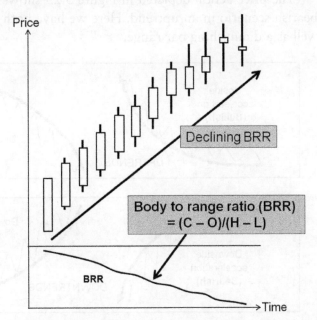

FIGURE 5.20 Declining Average Real Body to Candlestick Range Ratio Indicating Trend Weakness.

FIGURE 5.21 Preservation of Angular Momentum on the Hourly Chart of 3M Co.
Courtesy of Stockcharts.com

a minor correction at point 3, which represents potential resistance from an overbought angular perspective. Note that a bearish rising channel is seen developing above trendline 2, helping to strengthen the case that a minor correction is highly probable. In fact, 3M Co. went on to rise above $140 after correcting at point 3 (not shown on the charts).

In Figure 5.22, an upside acceleration in price is bullish whereas an upside deceleration in price is bearish. Similarly, a downside acceleration in price is bearish whereas a downside deceleration in price is bullish. Upside and downside acceleration is normally parabolic in nature. It should be noted that although an upside acceleration in price is bullish, the uptrend may not be self-sustaining if the rate of ascent was excessive. Such rapid increases in price usually end in a blow-off or buying climax with prices subsequently collapsing. Similarly, downside acceleration in prices may also end in a selling climax.

The price action depicted in Figure 5.23 shows an even more potentially bearish scenario in an uptrend. Here we have both a deceleration in price as well as a diminishing bar range.

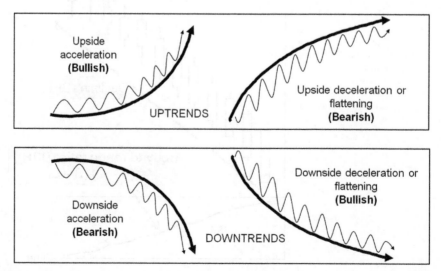

FIGURE 5.22 Acceleration and Deceleration in Trend Momentum and the Associated Sentiment.

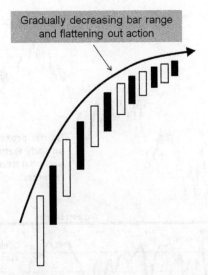

FIGURE 5.23 Diminishing Angular Momentum Is an Indication of Potential Weakening of a Trend.

In Figure 5.24, we see Gold with a consistent trend rate of approximately $3.30 per day. Notice that once the trend rate changes, the behavior of the market also switches to a new regime, displaying greater volatility and larger swings in price. Again, the new trend rate of $10.30 may be unsustainable over the longer term. Gold prices in fact declined rapidly thereafter (not shown on the chart).

9. Barrier Proximity: There is always a high probability that a trend may reverse as it approaches a strong and significant price barrier. In Figure 5.25, we observe the price for iShares MSCI Emerging Markets Fund rebounding after testing a strong and significant support level. We also notice the cycle-tuned stochastic indicating an oversold condition at the point of reversal.

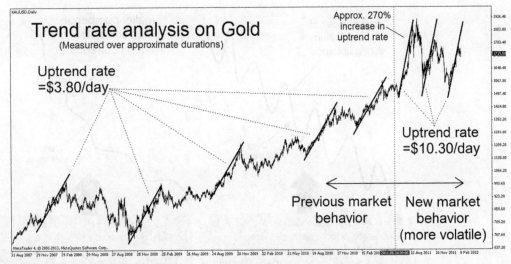

FIGURE 5.24 Oversold Barrier Proximity Leading to a Reversal on the Daily Chart of iShares MSCI Emerging Markets.
Courtesy of Stockcharts.com

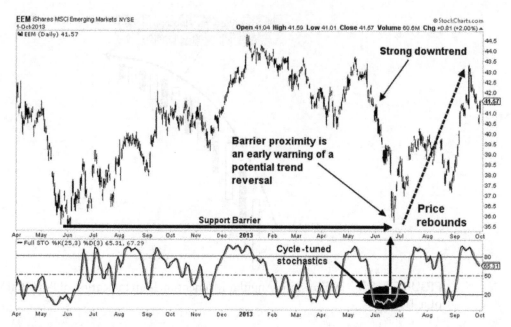

FIGURE 5.25 Oversold Barrier Proximity Leading to a Reversal on the Daily Chart of iShares MSCI Emerging Markets.
Courtesy of Stockcharts.com

10. Frequency and Depth of Trend-Based Oscillations: An uptrend is considered to be more reliable if it displays a reasonable number of oscillations. Oscillations should be fairly frequent and not too shallow or too deep. Such a trend is indicative of healthy profit-taking activity. With some profit taken off the table as the trend unfolds, traders and investors tend not to react as emotionally and irrationally at higher prices where the risk of losing pent-up and unrealized profit is greater. In Figure 5.26, the uptrend illustrated on the right-hand side displays relatively little profit-taking activity. With a relatively larger amount

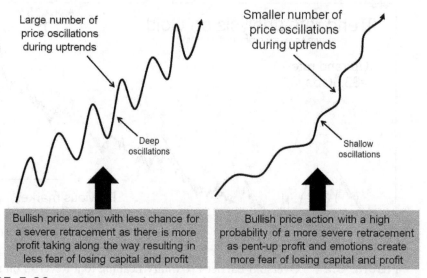

FIGURE 5.26 Frequency and Depth of Trend-Based Oscillations Impacting on the Persistence of Existing Trends.

FIGURE 5.27 Quality of Trend-Based Oscillations Impacting on the Persistence of Existing Trends on the Daily Chart of Apple Inc.
Courtesy of Stockcharts.com

of pent-up and unrealized profit at risk, there is a high probability that traders and investors will rapidly exit the market at the slightest hint of bearishness. This makes such a trend potentially more bearish at higher prices.

In Figure 5.27, we see Apple Inc. prices oscillating in a steady, rising channel. This was subsequently followed by rapidly rising price with the minimum of oscillations. As prices rise the second time toward the historical high in Apple, they do so in a similar uptrend rate with relatively little profit taking. Between time lines 1 and 2, we see the ATR declining as prices rise. This is a bearish indication. We see Apple prices decline substantially thereafter. Note that profit-taking activity in the form of price oscillations also occurs at various wave degrees within a trend.

11. Relative Measure of Consolidation Size and Duration: Trend interruptions are more significant if:
  - Price formations are of greater magnitude (taller chart patterns).
  - Price formations develop over a longer period (wider chart patterns).

  Larger trend interruptions normally tend to lead to a greater probability of a reversal. In a strong uptrend, a larger head and shoulders formation would be deemed more bearish than a smaller formation. Similarly, a larger rounding bottom formation would be more bullish than a smaller one in a downtrend. In short, *size takes precedence over form*. Moreover, the longer it takes for a consolidation to unfold, the greater will be its disruptive power with respect to the trend, should a reversal occur.

12. Third Gap Exhaustion: The appearance of a third gap in a trend is also an indication of potential trend exhaustion and a possible reversal. In Figure 5.28, we observe the prices of the SPDR Industrial Average ETF making a top after

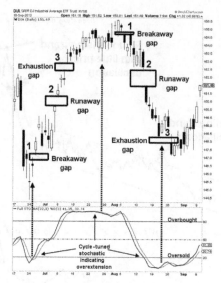

FIGURE 5.28   Third Gap Indicating Potential Exhaustion in a Trend on the Daily Chart of SPDR DJ Industrial Average.
Courtesy of Stockcharts.com

the appearance of a third gap in the uptrend. This also coincided with overbought conditions on the cycle-tuned stochastic. Prices finally bottomed after the appearance of another third gap in the subsequent downtrend, which again coincided perfectly with the cycle-tuned stochastic at oversold.

13. Completion of the Average Period Range: One of the most reliable characteristics of price activity lies with its average period range, with the period being any chosen duration of observation. For example, let us assume that the average daily range of a certain FOREX pair is 120 pips per day. This would essentially mean that any price activity beyond this average range in either direction prior to the completion of the trading day will be regarded as a potential sign of exhaustion and a reversal may be expected. It is important to note that these averages period ranges may also be associated with underlying wave cycles in the market. Once the average range is breached prematurely, the practitioner begins to look for various signs of a reversal, paying special attention to supportive and resistive confluences. The average period range may be obtained via either of the following approaches:

- The use of the average true range indicator (ATR) set to a reasonable lookback period on an interval chart of interest.
- By finding the 2 standard deviation value of bar range over a certain number of periods.

   The practitioner should conduct a simple backtest to find the most reliable lookback period for each of the above approaches. Note that with the latter approach, ninety percent of the period ranges will remain below the calculated value, the breach of which represents a greater degree of overextension or exhaustion.

14. Overextended Price Action with Respect to an Overlay Barrier: Any price penetration above an uptrending line is generally regarded as a potential sign of

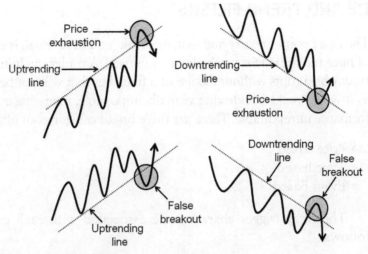

FIGURE 5.29 Price Exhaustion.

exhaustion, with a reversal expected. Similarly, a reversal is expected for any price penetration below a downtrending line. It should also be noted that any short term penetrations below an uptrending line or above a downtrending line are usually regarded as false breakouts rather than being specifically categorized as overextended. See Figure 5.29.

15. Volume Spread Action: The relationship between volume and price is most significant when price and volume exhibit extreme behavior. There are basically 4 scenarios where this relationship is of interest:
    ■ Very large bar range accompanied by very large volume: This is normally regarded as trend promoting, being a potentially bullish sign when the bar closes at or very near the high. In an uptrend, this would suggest a strong continuation of any existing uptrend, and reversal of any exiting downtrend. If the close was near or at the bottom of the range, then it would be regarded as potentially very bearish, suggesting a potentially strong continuation of any existing downtrend and reversal of any existing uptrend.
    ■ Very large bar range accompanied by very low volume: This is normally regarded as trend inhibiting, although not necessarily as an indication of a potential reversal. It implies a lack of commitment underlying the price move.
    ■ Very small bar range accompanied by very large volume: This is also normally regarded as trend inhibiting and is regarded as a significantly stronger indication of a potential reversal. It shows that even with such a large commitment in capital, there was no further extension in price, implying a strong opposition to the existing trend. This is popularly referred to as a "squat bar."
    ■ Very small bar range accompanied by very low volume: This is normally regarded as trend inhibiting although not necessarily leading to a potential reversal.

16. Volume and Oscillator Divergence: The appearance of standard or reverse divergence between price and volume, or with any oscillators, may give an early indication of potential reversals or continuations in the market. (Please refer to Chapter 9 for more on divergence analysis.)

5.3 PRICE AND TREND FILTERS

The exact point of entry and exit, or breakout and reversal, is determined by the type of filter and the extent to which it is employed. A trader can initiate trades based on intraday breakouts without the use of a filter, but that will not be an effective approach as it would make backtesting virtually impossible, rendering a profitable trading performance unrepeatable. There are three broad categories of filters, namely:

- Price based
- Time based
- Event based

The entry trigger characteristic associated with each category of filter is as follows:

- Price-based filters indicate the exact price of entry but do not indicate when an entry will be initiated.
- Time-based filters indicate the exact time of entry but do not indicate the price at which an entry will be initiated.
- Event-based filters do not indicate the exact price or time of entry until an event has occurred.

Within each broad category of filters, there are subcategories, namely:

1. Price-Based Filters
   i. Absolute Measure
      - Fixed price excursion
   ii. Relative Measure
      - Percentage of breakout price
   iii. Volatility Measure
      - Multiples of average true range
      - Multiples of standard deviation
2. Time-Based Filters
   i. Duration of N-closed bars
3. Event-Based Filters
   i. Algorithmic Filters
      - Specific sequence of closed bars
      - Sequence of new highs or lows
   ii. Event-Based Measure
      - Closing price violation
      - Barrier retest after a confirmed breakout

See Figure 5.30.

There may be scenarios where two-stage filtering may be required in order to contain and limit the maximum risk allowable per any single trade, under the rules of money management. Without controlling the maximum risk allowable per any single trade, the trading system may eventually experience risk of ruin. This is why price-based filters are the preferred mode of filtering.

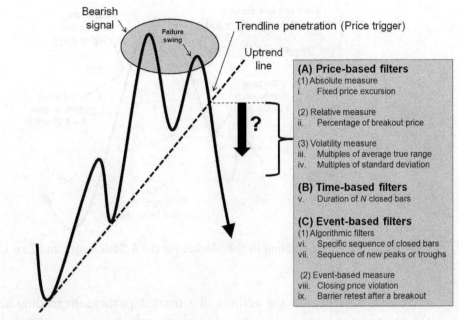

FIGURE 5.30 The Three Modes of Filtering.

As an example, let us assume that a trader has decided to use a closing violation as the trigger for entry. The problem with closing violations is that prices may close too far beyond the entry level. To prevent this, an additional price-based filter is used to limit entry to within a specified distance. In essence, the trader is primarily employing the closing violation as an entry trigger, but is depending on the price-based filter to limit risk should the violation be overextended. In short, *double filtering is especially useful when employing time- or event-based filters*, since these filters do not specify the exact price of entry, making the controlling of risk ineffective and inefficient, if not impossible.

5.4 TREND PARTICIPATION

Participating in the Market

There are four basic ways of entering and exiting the markets, namely:

- To go long—buying to open a new position
- To go short—selling to open a new position
- To liquidate—selling to close an old long position
- To cover—buying to close an old short position

If a trader holds no open positions in the market, the trader is said to be in *cash*. To square a position is to exit it. Traders may also reduce or neutralize all directional risk by *hedging* their positions with equal and opposite positions in the market. Buying at the current price is also referred to as buying at the market.

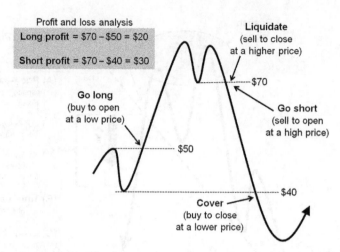

FIGURE 5.31 Participating in the Market via the 4 Basic Entry and Exit Orders.

Figure 5.31 depicts the actions of a market participant trading according to the principle of buying low and selling high, which involves any of the four following scenarios:

- Buying low and selling high
- Buying high and selling higher
- Selling high and buying back lower
- Selling low and buying back even lower

Orders for Entering and Exiting a Position

There are two basic types of orders that will allow traders to participate in the market:

- Stop Entry and Stop Exit Orders: Essentially, *stop orders* are instructions to enter or exit a market immediately, at any price. A stop order cannot guarantee that an order will be executed, or *filled* at the specified price, but it can guarantee execution. When entering the market at the current price, we use a *market order*. Stop entry and stop exit orders may be placed in the market as pending or working orders. Once triggered, all stop entry and stop exit orders turn into market orders. Orders can also be placed instantaneously as market orders. For entry, either a buystop or sellstop order may be placed. For exiting if price moves adversely against a position, a stop exit order may be employed, normally referred to as a *stoploss* order. Pending stop entry orders are usually placed when a continuation in price is expected. Stoploss orders may experience additional loss under gapping price action due to negative slippage. Slippage is the difference between the specified order price and the actual filled price.
- Limit Entry and Limit Exit Orders: *Limit orders* are instructions to enter or exit a market at a specified price, or better. If the broker cannot fill the order at the specified price or better, the order will not be executed. Hence, limit

orders can guarantee that an order will be filled at the intended price or better, but they cannot guarantee that an order will be executed. Limit orders can only be placed in the market as pending or working orders. They cannot be placed instantaneously like stop or market orders. For entry, either a buy limit or sell limit entry order may be placed. For exiting, if price moves favorably with respect to a position, a limit exit order may be employed, normally referred to as a *take profit* order. Limit entry orders are usually placed when a reversal in price is expected. Profit-take orders can potentially exit with greater profit under gapping price action. Only positive slippage is possible with limit orders.

In order to enter or exit the markets, orders are placed with the brokers, giving them instructions on how to execute entries and exits:

1. Entries above the Market: For entries above the market, a trader may place a *buystop entry* order if the trader believes that prices will rise higher. Conversely, if a trader believes that prices will reverse at a certain level above the market, a trader may place a *sell limit* order at that price level. Being a limit order, entry is not guaranteed unless the broker can execute the order at the specified entry price, or better, that is, higher. To short above the market using a stop order, a trader may use a *Market if Touched* (MIT) sell order.

2. Exits above the Market: For profit taking above the market, a trader may place a *sell limit* to exit, normally referred to as a profit-take order. Being a limit order, exit is not guaranteed unless the broker can execute the order at the specified exit price or better, that is, higher. Conversely, for cutting loss above the market, a trader may place a *buystop* order to exit, normally referred to as a stoploss order. Being a stop order, exit is guaranteed but the exact exit price is unknown.

3. Entries below the Market: For entries below the market, a trader may place a *sellstop entry* order if the trader believes that prices will continue to decline. Conversely, if a trader believes that prices will reverse at a certain price below the market, a trader may place a *buy limit* order at that price level. Being a limit order, entry is not guaranteed unless the broker can execute the order at the specified exit price or better, that is, higher. To long below the market using a stop order, a trader may use a *Market if Touched* (MIT) buy order.

4. Exits below the Market: For profit taking below the market, a trader may place a *buy limit* to exit, normally referred to as a profit-take order. Being a limit order, exit is not guaranteed unless the broker can execute the order at the specified exit price or better, that is, higher. Conversely, for cutting losses below the market, a trader may place a *sellstop* order to exit, normally referred to as a stoploss order. Being a stop order, exit is guaranteed but the exact exit price is unknown.

5. Entries and Exits at the Market: For entry at the current price, a market order is used. The entry is instantaneous, but there is no guarantee of being filled

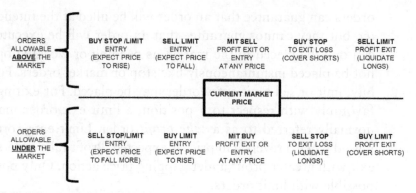

FIGURE 5.32 Entry and Exit Orders.

at the indicated prices on the quote screen. Negative slippage may sometimes occur when placing market orders. Exit at the current market price is also executed via a market order. Being a stop order, exit is guaranteed but the exact exit price is unknown.

Other orders include:

- Day Orders instruct the brokers to keep an order pending only until the end of the trading day.
- Good till Cancelled orders instruct the brokers to keep an order active until further notice.
- Market on Close orders to buy or sell are executed during the last minutes of the trading day, at or near the closing price.
- Contingent Orders are orders that are executed once another order is filled or triggered; examples include one cancel other (OCO) and one trigger other (OTO) orders.

Refer to Figure 5.32 for a summary of entry and exit orders, above, below, and at the market.

5.5 PRICE INFLECTION POINTS

The Four Modes of Initiating Trend Capture

There are four simple ways of initiating or establishing an entry in the market, namely via:

- Overlay Breakout Entries: An entry may be initiated on an upside or downside breakout of a price overlay that may or may not be in the direction of the predominant trend.
- Overlay Barrier Entries: A barrier entry may be initiated at an overlay boundary that may or may not be in the direction of the predominant trend. *A barrier entry means buying at a barrier support and shorting at a barrier resistance.* Barrier entries also include buying or shorting at a retest of a barrier.

- Failed Breakout Entries: An entry may be initiated in the opposite direction after a failed breakout, which may or may not be in the direction of the predominant trend.
- Random Entries: An entry may also be initiated in a random fashion.
- Pattern /Sequence-Based Entries: Entries that are initiated after a particular sequence of bars have unfolded (algorithmic) or after a pattern is completed, for example, DeMark Sequential and Japanese candlestick entries.

General Scenarios for Market Tops and Bottoms

As we learned in Chapter 4, there are basically three variations of a market top and bottom. See Figure 5.33. Examples of a more complex top or bottom would be a head and shoulders formation, a broadening formation, an island, a diamond formation and a rounding top or bottom.

Swing Points and Barrier Strength

An inflection point such as a peak that is flanked by a larger number of bars on either side of the bar with the highest price is generally regarded as a more significant peak. As such, the resistance level associated with such a peak will be regarded as a significant and strong barrier to price. The resistance and support levels associated with peaks and troughs that are flanked by a smaller number of

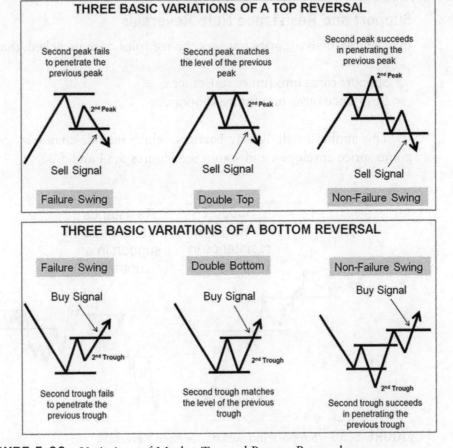

FIGURE 5.33 Variations of Market Top and Bottom Reversals.

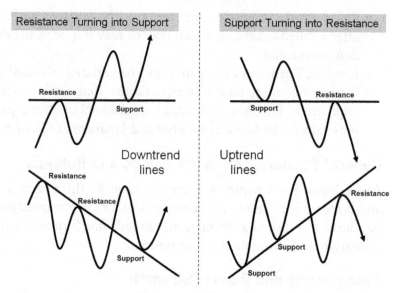

FIGURE 5.34 Support and Resistance Role Reversals.

bars on either side of the highest or lowest bar are considered to be less significant and reliable. *N* bars on either side of the highest peak or lowest trough is referred to as an inflection point of strength *N*.

Support and Resistance Role Reversals

In technical analysis, price barriers change roles once breached, that is:

- Support turns into future resistance.
- Resistance turns into future support.

This applies to all overlay barriers, which include channels, trendlines, pivot points, price envelopes, and so on. See Figures 5.34 and 5.35.

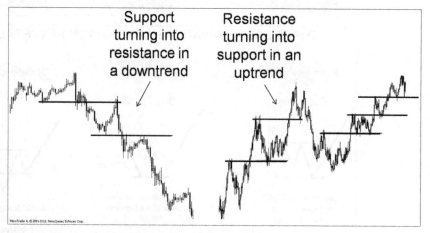

FIGURE 5.35 Support and Resistance Role Reversals.
Source: MetaTrader 4

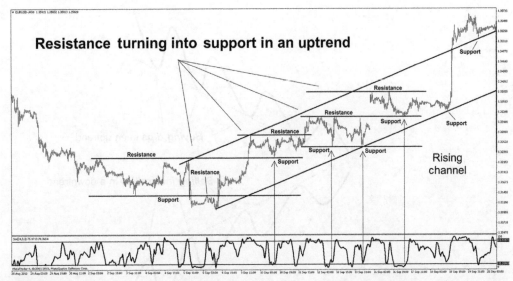

FIGURE 5.36 Support and Resistance Role Reversals on the 30-Min Chart of the EURUSD.
Source: MetaTrader 4

Figure 5.36 shows price finding support and resistance at prior peaks and troughs, as well on the rising channel on the 30-min chart of the EURUSD. Notice the cycle-tuned stochastic oscillator providing additional confirmation at the support and resistance levels, being overbought at resistance and oversold at support.

Trading in the Direction of the Trend

To trade or initiate positions in the direction of the existing trend means to buy in an uptrend and short in a downtrend. It is generally easier and safer to trade in the direction of the existing trend for a variety of reasons, some being:

- Buying dips in an uptrend and selling rallies in a downtrend gets the trader into positions where positions are initiated at the most advantageous prices with the smallest stopsizes possible.
- The trader is able to hold onto positions initiated in the direction of the existing trend and as a consequence extract greater profit from the markets.

Buying on a dip and selling into a rally are examples of *retracement entries* taken in the direction of the existing trend. Figure 5.37 illustrates buying on dips in an uptrend and selling into *bear rallies* in a downtrend. A trader may use simple up and down trendlines or channels to time the retracement entries. The use of a cycle-tuned oscillator will also help fine-tune the entries.

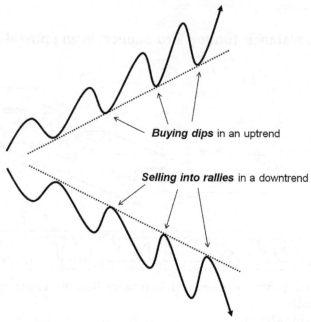

Buying dips in an uptrend

Selling into rallies in a downtrend

FIGURE 5.37 Buying Dips and Selling Rallies.

Trend Filters

A trend filter helps to identify a trend amidst the market noise and price volatility. Below are three popular trend filters used to achieve such an objective (which is by no means exhaustive):

- Via a double moving average crossover, with the shorter crossing above the longer moving average signifying the start of a potential uptrend and the shorter crossing below the longer moving average signifying the start of a potential downtrend
- Via longer-term oscillator signal line crossovers, with the oscillators crossing above its signal lines signifying potential longer-term bullishness and oscillators crossing below its signal lines signifying potential longer-term bearishness
- Via the containment of prices above or below overlay barriers such as moving averages or trendlines, with price staying above the moving average or trendline signifying that an uptrend is still intact and price staying below the moving average or trendline signifying that a downtrend is still intact

One popular approach is to use the oscillator signal line crossovers in an uptrend or downtrend to time entries, with the use of either an MACD signal (or zero line) crossover or a double moving average crossover as a trend filter. Figure 5.38 illustrates an MACD-filtered stochastic crossover trigger to time entries into the market. Long entries are initiated every time the stochastic crosses above its signal line with the MACD above its zero line. Short entries are initiated every time the stochastic crosses below its signal line with the MACD below its zero line. The stop is placed just above the previous peak in a short position and

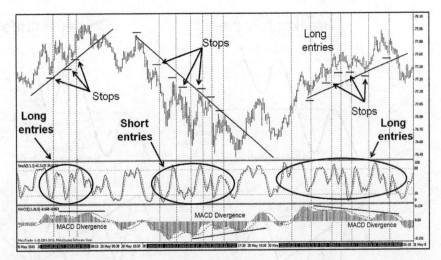

FIGURE 5.38 MACD-Filtered Stochastic Signal Line Crossover Entries on the EURUSD.
Source: MetaTrader 4

just below the previous trough in a long position. The stops are set to trail price by advancing to the next lower peak in a downtrend or to the next higher trough in an uptrend. Note that the divergence in the MACD helps to warn the trader of a potential reversal.

Stopsizing Issues Related to Stop Placement

A stop is usually placed just below significant troughs for long positions in an uptrend and just above significant peaks for short positions in a downtrend. For entries too far from a significant peak or trough, a stop may be placed at some multiple of ATR or standard deviations away from the entry.

Stopsizes associated with *barrier entries* will always be approximately the same size, as the significant peak or trough is usually the point of entry itself. The stoplosses will therefore be placed just behind the barrier, depending on the extent of price filtering employed.

Stopsizes associated with *breakout entries* present a completely different scenario. Stopsizes for breakouts will vary with each entry, since the significant peak or trough associated with each entry may vary in distance from the entry. See Figure 5.39.

This presents a significant problem to traders risking a fixed percentage or fixed unit size per trade. The varying tradesize associated with the changing stopsize for breakout entries will affect the performance of the system, especially if:

- A fixed percentage of *current* capital is exposed per trade and narrow stops are taken out frequently, causing significant loss.
- A fixed percentage of *original* capital is exposed per trade and wide stops are taken out frequently, causing significant loss.

To resolve this issue, we use *proportional stopsizing*, which was first introduced by the author in *The Wiley Trading Guide Volume II*. Proportional stopsiz-

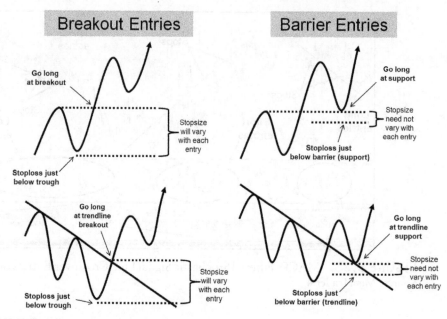

FIGURE 5.39 Stopsizing Dependent on Breakout or Barrier Type Entries.

ing limits the losses in either scenario by allocating a fixed percentage of original capital to narrow stops and a fixed percentage of current capital for stopsizes that exceed a fixed threshold size. The procedure for determining the proportional tradesize is as follows:

1. Do a backtest to find the *average stopsize* for at least 300 to 500 trades (if possible).
2. Calculate the two standard deviation value based on all the stopsizes in the sample.
3. Add this two-standard deviation value to the average stopsize (this represents the *proportional stopsize*).
4. Determine the maximum percentage of current capital to risk for each trade and calculate its corresponding dollar value risk per trade.
5. Divide this dollar value risk per trade by the proportional stopsize (this represents your *proportional tradesize*).

Therefore, the trader would initiate trades based on the proportional trade-size for all trades where the stopsize is at or below the proportional stopsize. For *stopsizes that exceed the proportional stopsize*, calculate the tradesize by simply dividing the maximum dollar value risk per trade by the stopsize. The term proportional refers to the percentage risk allocated per trade that is initiated for entries with stopsizes at or below the proportional stopsize. For such entries, the percentage of risk will vary proportionally with the stopsize, where the maximum risk will always be capped at the maximum percentage risk per trade. For a more detailed description of the tradesizing issues that plague traders, refer to Chapter 28.

5.6 TRENDLINES, CHANNELS, AND FAN LINES

Provisionary (Tentative) and Confirmed (Valid) Trendlines

A trendline is created by projecting a line forward into the future drawn from two significant inflection points. For uptrends, a line is drawn between two significant troughs and projected into the future, whereas for downtrends a line is drawn between two significant peaks and projected into the future. When drawing trendlines, lines must not cut through any price action at any point along the line. A trendline is said to be only *provisionary* or *tentative* until it is tested for the first time, that is, at the third point of price contact on the trendline. Once tested, it is then regarded as a *confirmed* or *valid* trendline. All trendlines are drawn between two inflection points except for bullish support lines and bearish resistance lines in Point and Figure charting, where only one reference point is used. Fan lines use two inflection points but only one point is located at a peak or trough, while the other is along a predetermined vertical axis. Note that the term tentative or valid is only applicable to conventional trendlines and not to fan lines.

Short-, Medium-, and Long-Term Trendlines

A trendline may be defined as short-, medium-, or longer-term depending on the amount of price activity it contains above or below it. Longer-term uptrend lines contain more price activity above them than shorter-term uptrend lines. The converse is true for downtrend lines. See Figure 5.40.

Trendline Support and Resistance: The Behavioral Component

As mentioned in an earlier section, all price overlays, including trendlines, represent barriers to price action. As barriers, they provide support and resistance to price. Price approaching a trendline from above will potentially experience support

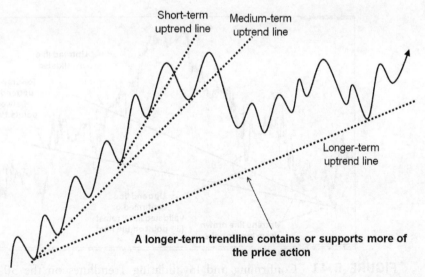

FIGURE 5.40 Short-, Medium-, and Longer-Term Trendlines Defined by the Amount of Price Activity They Support.

at the trendline, while price approaching a trendline from below will potentially experience resistance. This occurs because most market participants will usually place buy orders above a barrier and short orders below it. Hence, when price approaches the barrier from above, the initial triggering of buy orders will cause an upside reaction, creating temporary support. When price approaches the barrier from below, the initial triggering of sell orders will cause a downside reaction, creating temporary resistance. As such, support and resistance are regarded as behavioral consequences of human psychology, biases, and emotions.

Invalidating and Redrawing Trendlines

A trendline is *invalidated* once it is breached. This does not mean that it is thereafter unusable or ineffective. A head and shoulders neckline is a popular example of a trendline being invalidated when the formation is confirmed, that is, when the neckline is breached. Price very frequently retests the neckline after being breached. See Figure 5.41 for an example of an invalidated trendline and the redrawing of a new trendline. The new trendline is drawn between the new significant trough and the original lower trough in an uptrend. For downtrends, the new trendline is drawn between the new significant peak and the original higher peak. Once a trendline is invalidated, it is thereafter referred to as an *internal* line.

So what actually constitutes a valid trendline penetration? The answer depends on the type and extent of filtering employed. If the trader were to apply the closing filter rule, then a valid trendline penetration would only be acknowledged once price closes beyond it. But what if price made a very significant intraday downside penetration but eventually closed back above an uptrend line? In such a situation, the penetration is usually regarded as significant but nevertheless invalid, based on the filter rule employed. As we can see, the implications can be

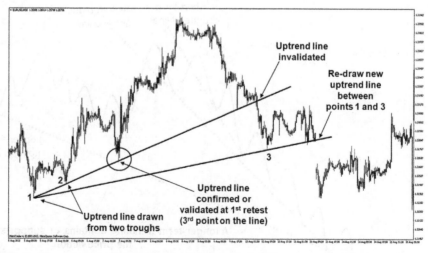

FIGURE 5.41 Confirming and Invalidating Trendlines on the 30-min Chart of the EURUSD.
Source: MetaTrader 4

rather interesting. We yet again observe the problems with defining price action. The best way to resolve this dilemma is as follows:

- Use only price-based filters and avoid time- and event-based filtering. This would allow the trader to decide exactly how much price excursion is required to represent a valid penetration of a trendline, or for that matter, any price barrier. Even if the amount of price excursion fails to be recognized as a valid penetration, this does not mean that a new trendline cannot be drawn. The trader will monitor price reactions at both the original and newly drawn trendlines.
- Use double-stage filtering when employing time- or event-based filters to gauge valid trendline or price barrier penetrations. *As long as the second filter is price based*, the trader would be able to identify a valid penetration once the price exceeds a specified price. As before, this does not preclude the drawing of a new trendline, even if the intraday or intra-period penetration has not exceeded the second filter's validation price.

Elements of Trendline Reliability

What constitutes a reliable trendline? Quite simply, *a reliable trendline may be defined as a trendline that provides consistent support and resistance to price action.* A trendline that experiences a lot of whipsaws is considered unreliable.

Factors influencing trendline reliability include:

- Angle of trendline: A steep uptrend, that is, above 45 degrees, is usually regarded as less stable and may not be able to sustain itself over the longer term. Any trendline associated with such a trend is therefore deemed less reliable. A weak trend with a very shallow angle of ascent is also regarded as less stable and any trendline associated with such a trend is also deemed less reliable. The most reliable uptrend line is one where it the angle of ascent is approximately 35 to 45 degrees.
- Duration of trendline: Longer-term trendlines are generally regarded as more reliable than shorter-term trendlines. A longer-term trendline would have been in the market for a much longer period of time and would be more obvious to all market participants, be they short-, medium-, or longer-term traders. As such, a longer-term trendline will attract a larger number of buy orders above it and sell orders below it, and in the process transform into a stronger and more significant barrier to price. This makes longer-term trendlines more reliable. Longer-term trendlines also attract the institutional players, resulting in larger orders placed at the trendline, giving rise to a stronger inhibiting effect with respect to price.
- Number of price retests: The greater the number of retests a trendline experiences, the more indicative it is that traders are aware and paying attention to a trendline. Such a trendline will normally attract more orders around it as traders realize that it is rejecting price in a consistent manner.
- The clarity of the price retests: The more precise the retest, the more indicative it is that the market participants are aware of such a trendline. As before, this will attract more orders around the trendline, making it a more formidable barrier to price.

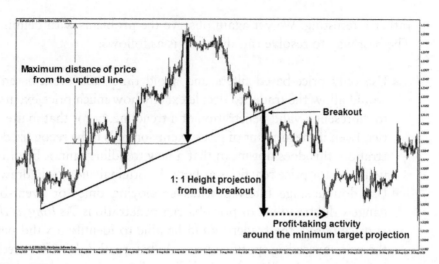

FIGURE 5.42 Trendline Minimum Price Target Projection on the 30-min Chart of the EURUSD.
Source: MetaTrader 4

- Confluence with other indicators: The more confluence or convergence there is with other bullish or bearish indicators at the point of contact on the trendline, the stronger will be the rejection of price at the trendline.
- Preceding action: The contraction of cycle amplitude, cycle period, bar range, and body-to-range ratio are indications of a potentially weak uptrend and a potentially bullish downtrend. As such, this makes any trendline associated with such trends also suspect and unreliable over the longer term.

Trendline Measuring Objectives

To forecast the minimum price target for a trendline, simply apply a one-to-one projection of the distance that *price has moved farthest from the trendline* from the breakout point. Figure 5.42 shows a typical one-to-one price projection from the breakout point. We see that prices bottomed very close to the minimum projected target.

Strengths and Weaknesses of Trendline Analysis

Strengths
- Trendlines, being straight lines, will catch any trend changes effectively.
- Trendlines are able to identify trends without the need to identify specific price patterns and formations.
- It is simple to construct and may be applied across all timeframes and markets with equal ease.
- A trendline is viewable across all timeframes

Weaknesses
- Trendlines, just like moving averages, are also subject to whipsaws and are less effective in erratic, volatile, or ranging markets.
- Because trendlines are geometrically based overlays, they are affected by the type of scaling used, that is, ratio or linear.

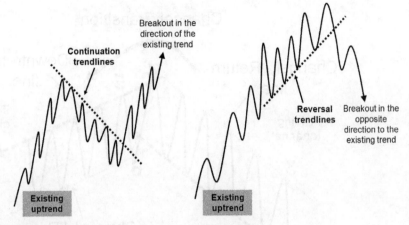

FIGURE 5.43 Continuation and Reversal Trendlines.

- Consolidation may cause a trendline to be breached at some point in time, in the absence of a legitimate trend reversal.

Continuation & Reversal Trendline Entries

We may also classify trendlines as reversal or continuation in the following manner:

- Trendlines that allow breakout in the direction of the existing trend are referred to as *continuation* trendlines.
- Trendlines that allow breakout in the opposite direction to the existing trend are referred to as *reversal* trendlines (see Figure 5.43).

As such, the practitioner must ascertain which wave degree is being observed in order to determine whether a trendline breach is a continuation or reversal of the existing trend.

Channel Construction

Channels may also be created by projecting a trendline from a significant peak or trough that is parallel to the uptrend or downtrend line. Channels are useful in that they indicate potential:

- Entry levels
- Profit-taking levels
- Future price targets
- Stoploss levels

Figure 5.44 illustrates the construction of a rising channel. First, draw an uptrend line based on two significant troughs, indicated at Points 1 and 2. Then locate a significant peak above the trendline, which in this case would be the peak at Point 3. Draw a line parallel to the uptrend line from the peak at Point 3 and project it upward. This projected line is called the *channel* or *return* line. This

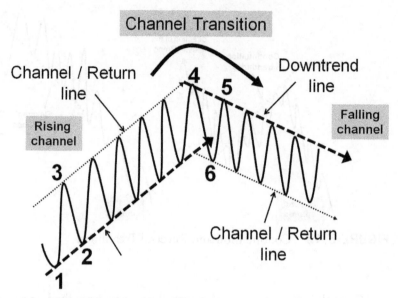

FIGURE 5.44 Channels and Channel Transitions.

formation constitutes a *rising channel*. To draw a falling or declining channel, we first draw a downtrend line based on two significant peaks, indicated at Points 4 and 5. We then draw a line parallel to the downtrend line from a significant trough, indicated at Point 6, and project it downward. Notice that the trough at Point 6 has violated the uptrend line, which may be an early indication of a potential trend change. We see the rising channel *transitioning* into a falling channel. (Please refer to Chapter 13 for alternative approaches to constructing a price channel.)

Nested Channels

Figure 5.45 shows Silver price transitions within a larger falling channel. We say that the smaller channels are contained or *nested* within the larger channel. Channel nesting can occur at multiple levels, with large channels comprised of ever-decreasing channel sizes. In essence, channel nesting has fractal-like properties.

Figure 5.46 depicts nested channeling on a chart of the USDCAD. Notice the channels reacting at the Fibonacci retracements levels.

Price Target Projection

Channels are extremely useful for projecting potential price targets. Figure 5.47 illustrates the use of the return line as a possible price target, providing resistance to the motion of price. The price targets at Points 5 and 6 were forecasted accurately via channel projection.

Anticipating Channel Breakouts

It also should be noted that if the subsequent price action fails to test either one of the channel boundaries, it may be an early indication of a possible channel breakout in the opposite direction of the failed price retest. A failure to test a channel bottom in an

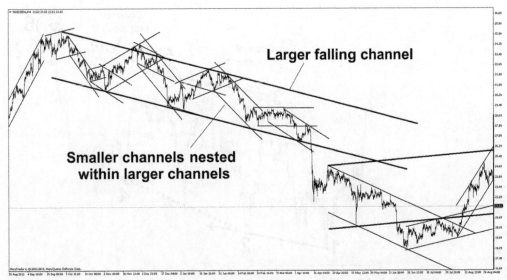

FIGURE 5.45 Nested Channel Transitions on the 4-Hour Chart of Silver.
Source: MetaTrader 4

uptrend and a channel top in a downtrend represent even stronger evidence of a potential continuation of the existing trend. This is especially so if the channel breakout bar is accompanied by large volume. Refer to Figure 5.14. Notice that price failed to test the lower channel boundary, which was followed by a strong continuation of the existing uptrend. Note also the large channel breakout bar at point A.

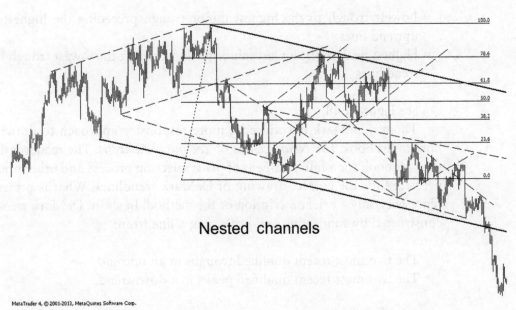

FIGURE 5.46 Nested Channel Transitions on the 4-Hour Chart of Silver.
Source: MetaTrader 4

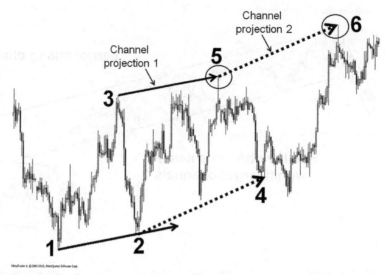

FIGURE 5.47 Channel Projections on the EURUSD Chart.
Source: MetaTrader 4

Sperandeo and DeMark Trendlines

Victor Sperandeo introduced a powerful way of drawing trendlines in his book *Trader Vic: Methods of a Wall Street Master*. For more details about his approach, the reader is advised to read his book. There is no way the author can do justice here to Sperandeo's superb approach. In short, Sperandeo trendlines are constructed by connecting and projecting a line from a:

- Lowest trough to the highest minor trough preceding the highest peak for uptrend lines
- Highest peak to the lowest minor peak preceding the lowest trough for downtrend lines

See Figure 5.48.

Thomas DeMark introduced a more responsive approach to drawing trendlines in his book *The New Science of Technical Analysis*. The reader is advised to read his book for a full treatment of pivot selection process and other prerequisites necessary for the correct drawing of DeMark trendlines. What is presented here represents only a brief description of the method. In short, DeMark trendlines are constructed by connecting and projecting a line from:

- The two most recent qualified troughs in an uptrend
- The two most recent qualified peaks in a downtrend

See Figure 5.49. The trendline that is drawn using the two most recent troughs represents the correct approach to creating DeMark trendlines.

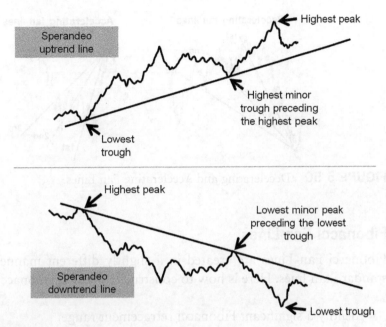

FIGURE 5.48 Sperandeo Up trend and Downtrend Lines.

Standard Fan Lines

Standard fan lines indicate *a change in trend*. They may be either accelerating or decelerating. The violation of the third fan line represents strong confirmation of a trend change. As with all types of fan lines, *they provide support and resistance to price action*. When support is breached, it turns into resistance, and vice versa. They are traded in a manner representative of any trendline. To construct accelerating fan lines, locate a significant higher peak and draw a downtrend line connecting this significant peak to gradually rising lower peaks. Only draw three downtrend lines. To construct decelerating fan lines, locate a significant lower trough and draw an uptrend line connecting this significant lower trough to gradually declining higher troughs. Only draw three uptrend lines. See Figure 5.50.

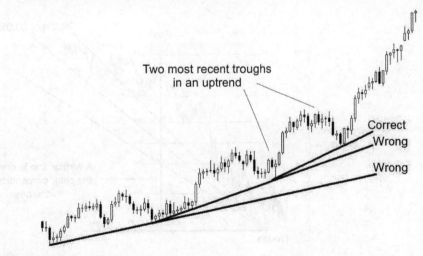

FIGURE 5.49 DeMark Uptrend Lines.

163

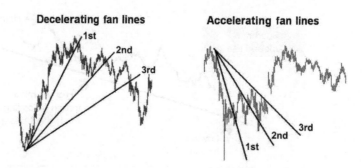

FIGURE 5.50 Decelerating and Accelerating Fan Lines.

Fibonacci Fan Lines

Fibonacci Fan Lines are created in a slightly different manner as compared to standard fan lines. Here is how to construct a *bearish* Fibonacci fan line:

- Identify a significant Fibonacci retracement range.
- Draw a vertical line from the peak of the retracement range to the trough's price level.
- Divide the vertical line into 38.2, 50, and 61.8 percent levels.
- Project three lines from the trough, intercepting the three retracement levels located on the vertical line.

See Figure 5.51.

Speed Lines

Edson Gould's speed lines also track the progress of a trend as it attempts to bottom or top. Speed lines are created in exactly the same way Fibonacci fan lines except that the retracement ratios are one-third and two-thirds. See Figure 5.52.

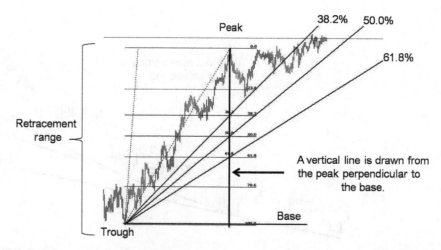

FIGURE 5.51 Bearish Fibonacci Fan Lines.

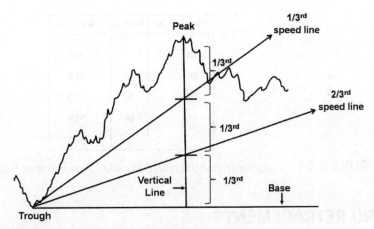

FIGURE 5.52   One-Third Decelerating Speed Lines.

Other Types of Trend Overlay Indicators: Andrew's Pitchfork

Andrew's Pitchfork is a geometrically based price-overlay indicator. The projected lines provide support and resistance to price action. The middle line is called the median. To construct a *bearish* Andrew's Pitchfork, we need to:

- Find a significant peak.
- Identify a subsequent upside retracement back up to the peak (but not exceeding it).
- Find the midpoint between the retracement trough and the retracement peak.
- Draw and project a line from the significant peak through this midpoint (referred to as the median line).
- Project lines parallel to this median line from the retracement peak and retracement trough.

The converse applies to bullish pitchforks. Figure 5.53 depicts daily Silver prices finding support at the median line and upper band in a downtrend.

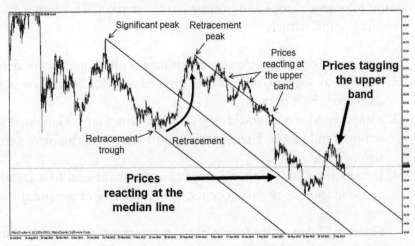

FIGURE 5.53   Price Reacting to the Andrew's Pitchfork on the Daily Chart of Silver.
Source: MetaTrader 4

165

Fibonacci (%)	Dow (%)	Gann (%)
23.6		12.5 25.0
38.2	33	37.5
(50)	50	50.0
61.8 78.6	66	62.5 75.0 87.5

FIGURE 5.54 Comparative Analysis of Popular Retracement Ratios.

5.7 TREND RETRACEMENTS

Retracements: Dow, Fibonacci, and Gann One-Thirds and One-Eighths

There are various approaches to measuring trend retracements. Fibonacci retracements are based on various ratios related to the Fibonacci Phi (Φ) ratio. Dow paid particular attention to the one-third and two-thirds retracements, while Gann employed one-third and one-eighth retracement ranges. Probably the most important retracement percentage of all is the 50 percent retracement level. Both Gann and Dow regarded 50 percent as the most significant retracement percentage, with most major tops and bottoms forming around this retracement level. These retracement approaches will be dealt with in more detail in a subsequent chapter. For now see Figure 5.54 for a table comparing the various retracement percentages used in the Fibonacci, Dow, and Gann approaches to trend retracement. We see strong convergence of retracement percentages around specific retracement ranges, especially the between the 33 to 38.2 percent, 50 percent, and 61.8 to 66 percent ranges.

5.8 GAPS AND TRENDS

Gaps help to define various stages within a trend, which helps to provide an indication of potential tops and bottoms in the market. There are basically four types of market gaps, namely:

1. Common Gaps: Gaps that occur within a trading range (considered insignificant)
2. Breakaway Gaps: Gaps that are created as price breaks away from a consolidation or chart pattern.
3. Runaway/Measuring/Midway/Continuation Gaps: Gaps that are created in a strong trend phase. There may be more than one runaway gap appearing in a strong trend.
4. Exhaustion Gaps: Gaps that are created at the end of a trend, after which a consolidation or reversal occurs. It is indicative of potential trend exhaustion.

Figure 5.55 depicts the four types of market gaps on a weekly chart of Wheat. We see common gaps within the consolidation phase followed by the trend-related gaps. We see prices top after the third gap, which represents potential trend exhaustion.

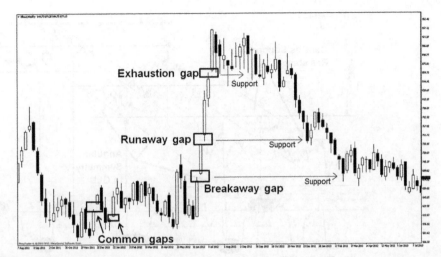

FIGURE 5.55 Gaps Defining the Three Phases of a Trend on the Weekly Chart of Wheat.
Source: MetaTrader 4

In Figure 5.56, we see the same trend exhaustion occurring at a significant resistance level created by a strong price rejection at the high of a very bearish shooting star pattern. We also notice how the gaps help define the various phases of the market.

It must also be noted that gaps tend to create areas of potential support and resistance. In Figure 5.55, we observe the gaps giving rise to subsequent levels of support in wheat. In Figure 5.57, we also observe gaps giving rise to areas of support and resistance on the 15-min chart of SPDF Gold Trust Shares (GLD).

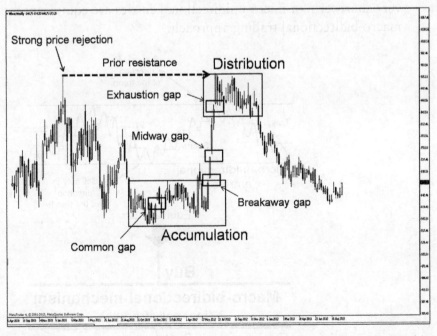

FIGURE 5.56 Forecasting Trend Exhaustion Using Gap Analysis on the Weekly Chart of Wheat.
Source: MetaTrader 4

167

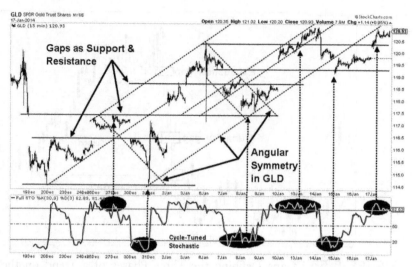

FIGURE 5.57 Forecasting Potential Areas of Support and Resistance via Gaps on the 15-min Chart of GLD.
Courtesy of Stockcharts.com

Notice how the cycle-tuned stochastic helps to corroborate the levels of support and resistance by being overbought at resistance and oversold at support.

5.9 TREND DIRECTIONALITY

A *unidirectional* entry is a trade taken only in the direction of the existing trend, be it to the upside or downside. A *bidirectional* entry is a trade taken in either direction, depending on which way the breakout occurs. Figure 5.58 illustrates how very short-term or micro-unidirectional entries are equivalent to a longer-term or macro-bidirectional trading approach.

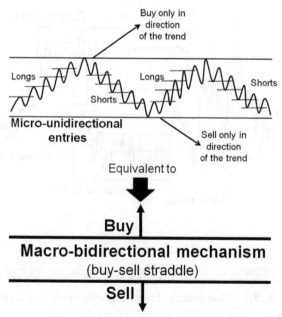

FIGURE 5.58 Micro-Unidirectionality as a Basis for Macro-Bidirectionality.

Assume that a trader only initiates a breakout in the direction of the existing trend. The trader would be initiating long position in an uptrend and short positions in a downtrend. Over the long term this would be equivalent to a longer-term bidirectional trader entering the market on a breakout. Hence we see that even though a trader only trades in one direction at any one time (being unidirectional), over the longer term this would essentially result is trading bidirectionally in the market as the trend moves up and down. The only condition that would disrupt this equivalence would be if the unidirectional trader did not take every qualified trade.

5.10 DRUMMOND GEOMETRY

Drummond Geometry was developed by Charles Drummond over a long period of time. Drummond geometry helps keep the trader on the right side of the markets. It basically consists of:

- A short-term moving average referred to as the PLdot line
- Inter-bar trend lines

The reader is advised to refer to *The Ultimate Trading Guide* by John Hill, George Pruitt, and Lundy Hill for a detailed look at Drummond geometry. The PLdot line is represented by a simple three-period moving average of typical price. This moving average may be forward shifted by one period to provide an early prognostication of market sentiment. To be very brief, when price is above the PLdot the market is regarded as bullish, and when price is below the PLdot the market is expected to be bearish. Another approach that some practitioners take is to buy when the PLdot line turns up and sell when it turns down. Note that inter-bar trendlines connecting the highs and lows are also used to forecast potential support and resistance. See Figure 5.59.

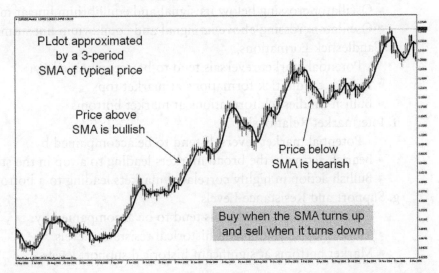

FIGURE 5.59 PLdot Line Indicating Potential Future Direction on the Weekly Chart of the EURUSD.
Source: MetaTrader 4

5.11 FORECASTING TREND REVERSALS

The following is a summary of characteristics associated with forecasting reversals via various forms of technical analysis. For detailed analysis of each approach, refer to the relevant chapters within this handbook.

a. Volume Divergence

Potential market reversals tend to be accompanied by:

- Diminishing volume in an uptrend or downtrend (indicating potential weakness in the trend)
- Extreme volume in the form of buying or selling climaxes (indicative of market tops and bottoms)

b. Chart Patterns

Potential market reversals tend to be accompanied by:

- Bearish chart patterns occurring after a strong and prolonged uptrend
- Bullish chart patterns occurring after a strong and prolonged downtrend
- The appearance of a large broadening, diamond, or island formation

c. Cycle Analysis

Potential market reversals tend to be accompanied by:

- Cycle peaks at market tops
- Cycle troughs at market bottoms
- Decreasing cycle amplitude during a trend
- Decreasing cycle period during a trend

d. Oscillator Analysis

Potential market reversals tend to be accompanied by:

- Overbought signals at market tops
- Oversold signals at market bottoms
- Bearish divergence with price at market tops
- Bullish divergence with price at market bottoms
- Oscillator crossing below its signal and equilibrium line at market tops
- Oscillator crossing above its signal and equilibrium line at market bottoms

e. Candlestick Formations

Potential market reversals tend to be accompanied by:

- Bearish candlestick formations at market tops
- Bullish candlestick formations at market bottoms

f. Intermarket Relationship

Potential market reversals tend to be accompanied by:

- Bearish action in the broad markets leading to a top in the stock
- Bullish action in highly correlated markets leading to a bottom in the stock

g. Support and Resistance Levels

Potential market reversals tend to be accompanied by:

- Market tops at significant historical resistance levels
- Market bottoms at significant historical support levels

5.12 CHAPTER SUMMARY

In this chapter, we dealt with issues concerning the definition and identification of a trend. We have also discussed various powerful trend indicators that helped identify the early onset of a trend. The practitioner is advised to pay particular attention to the 16 characteristics that may significantly impact the future of price action and potential strength of a trend.

CHAPTER 5 REVIEW QUESTIONS

1. What is a trend?
2. Explain the disadvantages of defining market and price action.
3. What are the early indications of a potential reversal?
4. Briefly describe the 12 ways in which price action may be understood.
5. How can channel analysis help pinpoint potential reversals and continuations?
6. What are the factors that impact trendline reliability?
7. Explain the advantages of using proportional sizing.
8. In what ways are price-based filters more useful than time and algorithmic filters?

REFERENCES

Covel, Michael W. 2009. *Trend Following*. Upper Saddle River, NJ: FT Press.

DeMark, Thomas. 1994. *The New Science of Technical Analysis*. New York: John Wiley and Sons.

Hill, John, George Pruitt, and Lundy Hill. 2000. *The Ultimate Trading Guide*. New York: John Wiley and Sons.

Sperandeo, Victor. 1991. *Trader Vic: Methods of a Wall Street Master*. New York: John Wiley and Sons.

CHAPTER 6

Volume and Open Interest

LEARNING OBJECTIVES

After studying this chapter, you should be able to:

- Understand the significance of volume action and its implications for market action
- Recognize the early indications of potential trend weakness via volume and open interest divergence
- Identify bullish and bearish signals on volume and open interest indicators
- Forecast potential reversals and corrections in the market via volume cycles
- Set up effective volume filtering for more efficient timing of entries and exits
- Read volume across successive contract months in the futures markets

Although price is regarded as the best indicator of potential future price behavior, volume and open interest offer additional evidence to corroborate bullish or bearish setups. Volume and open interest can indicate potential underlying weakness and also function as timing indicators for potential breakouts. Many novices misread declining volume as a weakness in a consolidation. The relationship between volume with bar range also offers critical insights into the actions of buyers and sellers, especially when extremely low or high volume is accompanied by unusually large or narrow bar ranges, respectively. Mastery over the interpretation of volume and open interest action is of paramount importance to the art and science of forecasting potential price activity in the markets.

6.1 THE MECHANICS OF VOLUME ACTION

Dow Theory of Volume Confirmation

We learned in Chapter 2 that under the tenets of Dow Theory, volume is expected to *confirm the trend*, that is, it should expand in the direction of the preexisting or predominant trend. Volume is regarded as a supporting or secondary indicator of potential future price action. To confirm the trend:

- Volume should increase as price rises and decrease in any downside retracements in a preexisting uptrend (bullish volume action).
- Volume should increase as price declines and decrease on any upside retracements in a preexisting downtrend (bearish volume action).

Any volume action contrary to the above is an indication that an uptrend may potentially be bearish and a downtrend bullish. *Volume is an indication of market participation.* It is the total number of shares or contracts traded over a specific time interval. When studying volume, the practitioner should always remember two basic principles, which are:

1. A rise in volume indicates that market participants are interested in seeing the price go higher in an uptrend or lower in a downtrend and are willing to buy higher in an uptrend or sell lower in a downtrend in order to participate in the unfolding market action.
2. A decline in volume indicates that market participants are losing interest in seeing the price go higher in an uptrend or lower in a downtrend and are more willing to buy lower in an uptrend and sell higher in a downtrend, if not exiting positions in the market.

Notice that, in Figure 6.1, both rising and declining volume are regarded as *bullish* volume if both volume and price rise and decline together in a preexisting uptrend. Conversely, both rising and declining volume are regarded as *bearish* volume if volume and price move in opposite directions to each other in a preexisting

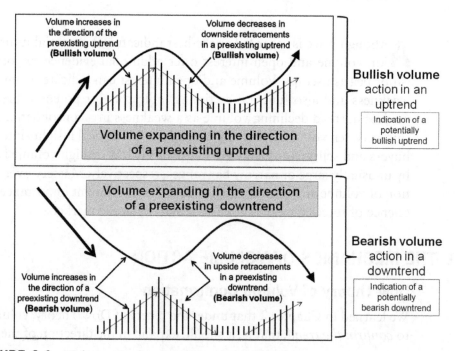

FIGURE 6.1 Volume Confirming a Preexisting Trend.

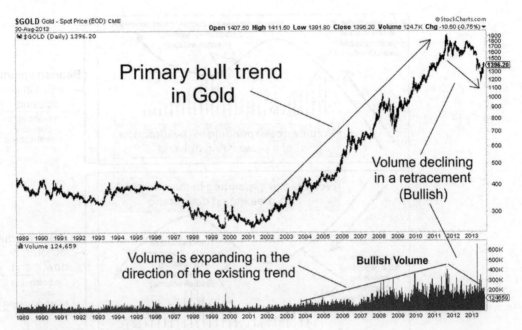

FIGURE 6.2 Bullish Volume Expanding in the Direction of the Preexisting Trend on the Continuous Daily Chart of Gold.
Courtesy of Stockcharts.com

downtrend. This shows that declining volume does not necessarily imply bearishness and similarly, rising volume does not imply bullishness. This is a simple mistake that many novices make when trying to interpret volume action. *The bullish or bearish sentiment associated with volume action depends on the direction of the price.*

In Figure 6.2, we observe volume expanding in the direction of the primary bull trend in gold, in which volume declines during a retracement, as expected.

In Figure 6.3, we observe volume action that is not confirming the preexisting trends. Here we see that both rising and declining volume are regarded as *bearish* volume if both volume and price move in opposite directions to each other in a preexisting uptrend. This is an indication of a potentially weak or bearish uptrend. Conversely, both rising and declining volume are regarded as *bullish* volume if both volume and price rise and decline together in a preexisting downtrend. This is an indication of a potentially bullish downtrend.

Volume Confirmation and Divergence

This leads us naturally to the concept of volume *confirmation* and *divergence*. Simply put:

- Volume divergence occurs whenever volume declines, irrespective of the direction of price.
- Volume *convergence* or *confirmation* occurs whenever volume rises, irrespective of the direction of price.

Volume divergence implies that market participants are not interested in seeing prices rise or decline further. As prices rise and volume subsides, traders and investors indicate that they are less interested in participating in the upside move.

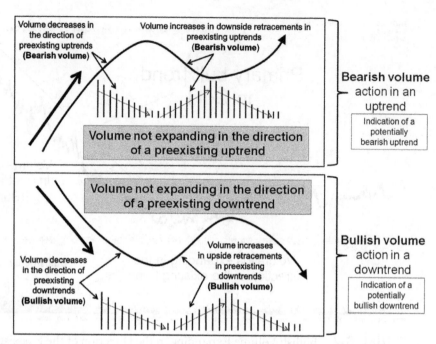

FIGURE 6.3 Volume Not Confirming a Preexisting Trend.

This is bearish for an uptrend. Similarly, as prices fall and volume subsides, traders and investors indicate that they are less interested in participating in the downside move. This is bullish for a downtrend.

When both volume and price rise together, traders and investors indicate that they are interested in participating in the upside move. We say that there is a convergence between price and volume, or that volume confirms price. This is bullish for an uptrend. When volume rises and prices decline, traders and investors indicate that they are interested in participating in the downside move. This is bearish for a downtrend. In short:

- Volume convergence, that is, volume increasing, is an early indication of a potential continuation of the existing trend.
- Volume divergence, that is, volume decreasing, is an early indication of a potential reversal of the existing trend.

It is important to note that, unlike for standard price based oscillators, the direction of price is irrelevant in the determination of volume divergence. Although the existence of divergence is not dependent on the direction of price, we still require knowledge of it in order to determine whether the divergence is *bullish* or *bearish*. It should also be noted that there is no *reverse* divergence classification associated with volume (refer to Chapter 9 for a detailed treatment on the classification of divergence). Volume divergence *always* indicates potential weakness in an existing trend, whereas volume confirmation always indicates potential strength in an existing trend. In short:

- Bullish divergence can only occur in a *downtrend*, indicating a possibility of a potential upside reversal in the trend.

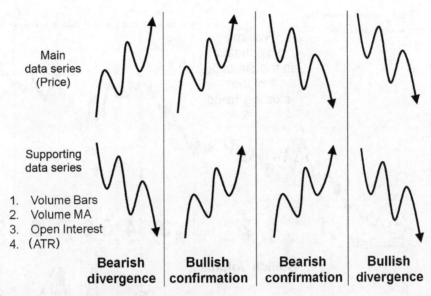

FIGURE 6.4 Volume Divergence and Confirmation.

- Bearish divergence can only occur in an *uptrend,* indicating a possibility of a potential downside reversal in the trend.

See Figure 6.4.

In Figure 6.5, we observe bullish volume divergence as Isis Pharmaceuticals traces out a bullish rounding bottom. This is an example of divergence providing additional evidence of a bullish chart formation.

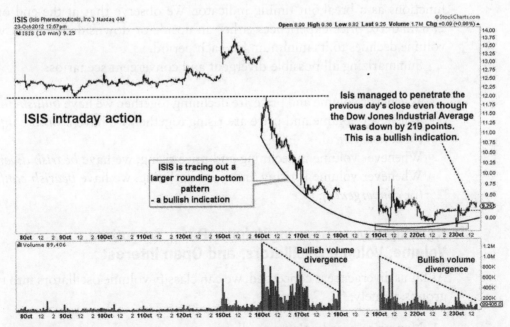

FIGURE 6.5 Bullish Volume Divergence on the Daily Chart of Isis Pharmaceuticals Inc.
Courtesy of Stockcharts.com

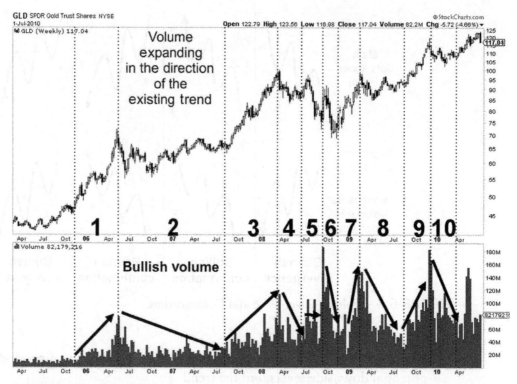

FIGURE 6.6 Bullish Volume on the Daily Chart of SPDR Gold Trust Shares.
Courtesy of Stockcharts.com

In Figure 6.6, we observe bullish volume in periods 1 to 10, except in period 5, where the volume action was somewhat flat. Periods 1, 3, 7, and 9 display bullish confirmation, while periods 4 and 6 display bullish divergence. Periods 2, 8, and 10 display volume declining during a consolidation. In a consolidation, volume functions as a breakout timing indicator. We observe that at the end of periods 2, 8, and 10, price experiences either an upside or downside breakout whenever volume declines to its minimum for each period.

Summarizing all possible divergent and convergent scenarios:

- Whenever volume and price are declining together, we have *bullish divergence*.
- Whenever volume and price are rising together, we have *bullish confirmation* (or *convergence*).
- Whenever volume is declining and price rising, we have *bearish divergence*.
- Whenever volume is rising and price declining, we have *bearish confirmation* (or *convergence*).

Reading Divergence for Volume Bars, Smoothed Volume, Volume Oscillators, and Open Interest

As far as divergence is concerned, we can classify volume oscillators into two main groups, namely:

1. Non-price-based volume oscillators
2. Price-based volume oscillators

Price-based volume oscillators *incorporate price data* in their construction, whereas non-price-based volume oscillators only incorporate volume data in their construction. It should be noted that reading price-based volume oscillator divergence differs from reading non-price-based volume oscillator divergence. Some popular price-based volume oscillators include:

- On Balance Volume (OBV)
- Accumulation/Distribution Line (ADL)
- Chaikin Money Flow
- Chaikin Oscillator
- Demand Index
- Herrick Payoff Index

Some non-price-based volume oscillators include:

- Standard Volume Bars
- Smoothed Volume
- Detrended Volume
- Rate of Change of Volume (ROC Volume)
- Percentage Volume Oscillator (PVO)

Figure 6.7 summarizes the way divergence is read for each classification. The main difference between the two classifications is how bullish divergence and bearish confirmation are observed on the charts. Bearish divergence and bullish confirmation are read the same way for both classifications.

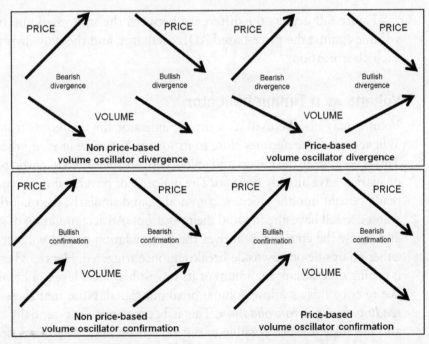

FIGURE 6.7 Reading Volume Divergence on Non-Price-Based versus Price-Based Volume Oscillators.

FIGURE 6.8 Reading Volume Divergence on Price-Based versus Non-Price-Based Volume Oscillators on the Daily Chart of the Currency Shares Euro Trust.
Courtesy of Stockcharts.com

Figure 6.8 depicts the difference between the smoothed and detrended (PVO) volume against the price-based ADL oscillator, and the way divergence is read for each classification.

Volume as a Timing Indicator

Volume may also be used as a timing indicator for breakouts from consolidations. *Whenever volume declines close to its lowest historical level, a breakout is expected.* This is because all the buyers and sellers who are interested in participating in the stock or market have already done so. The majority of buyers who wanted to buy have already bought into the stock or commodity, and similarly, the majority of sellers who wanted to sell have already sold their positions. An accumulation of stop orders above and below the consolidation over the consolidation period will act as a catalyst for either an upside or downside breakout, once triggered. Hence, whenever the volume is testing a significant minimum or its lowest historical levels, a breakout is expected. We refer to this as a low volume breakout signal. Note that *there is no divergence reading during a consolidation.* This is because price is essentially moving sideways and therefore it is not possible to distinguish between divergence or convergence, let alone bullish or bearish divergence. It should also be noted that there is a tendency for price to reverse when volume is at its minimum or lowest historical levels. We refer to

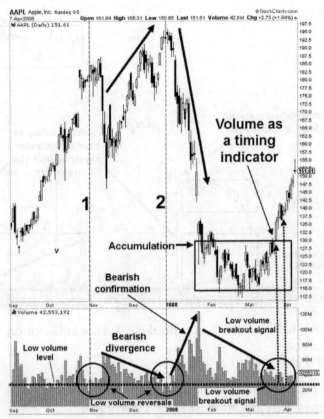

FIGURE 6.9 Volume as a Reversal and Breakout Timing Indicator on the Daily Chart of Apple Inc.
Courtesy of Stockcharts.com

such reversals as *low volume reversals*. In Figure 6.9, we observe price breaking out from an accumulation after volume declined to its lowest level. We also observe two low volume reversals just prior to the consolidation, at time lines 1 and 2.

In Figure 6.10, we observe three consolidation breakouts occurring whenever the lowest or minimum volume level is tested. Notice an increase in volume on the breakout bars, as seen on bars 1, 2, and 3 in the chart.

Volume-Weighted Average Price/Moving Average (VWMA)

A volume-weighted moving average (VWMA) may also be created to track overvalued and undervalued stock in the market. Typically, price is considered potentially bullish when it is above the VWMA, and bearish when below it. For a detailed calculation of the VWMA, refer to Chapter 11. In Figure 6.11, we notice price rising decisively every time it crosses above the VWMA and declining in a similar manner when it crosses below it. We also notice that the crossovers occur at the daily volume cycle peaks.

It should be noted that the stock is regarded as undervalued if it lies below the VWMA and overvalued if it is above it. Hence many institutional traders deem it advantageous to only look for buy signals for a particular stock or market when it is undervalued with respect to the VWMA, and sell signals when it is above it.

181

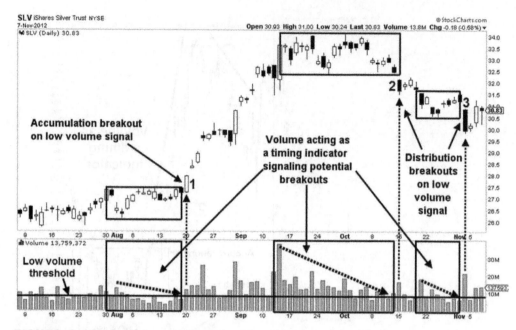

FIGURE 6.10 Volume as a Breakout Timing Indicator on the Daily Chart of iShares Silver Trust.
Courtesy of Stockcharts.com

Volume Buying and Selling Climaxes

A market top or bottom is usually accompanied by either:

- Relatively large or extreme volume
- Relatively low or minimal volume

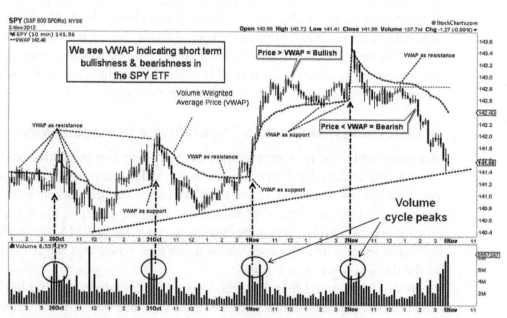

FIGURE 6.11 VWMA on the Daily Chart of S&P500 SPDRs.
Courtesy of Stockcharts.com

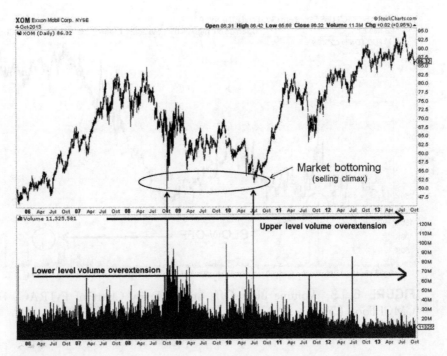

FIGURE 6.12 Selling Climaxes Signaled by the Volume Overbought Level on the Daily Chart of Exxon Mobile Corp.
Courtesy of Stockcharts.com

Here are the four possible scenarios for a top and bottom with respect to volume:

1. A market top associated with extreme volume is called a *blow-off* or *buying climax*.
2. A market bottom associated with extreme volume is called a *sell-off* or *selling climax*.
3. A market top associated with extremely low or minimal volume is called a *low volume top*.
4. A market bottom associated with extremely low volume is called a *low volume bottom*.

In Figure 6.12, we observe a market bottom being created by a couple of selling climaxes on the daily chart of Exxon Mobile Corp. We notice the extreme volume associated with each selling climax. We identify this extreme volume level as the upper overextended volume level. This upper volume level will serve as a signal for predicting potential market bottoms or tops. Notice that we have also identified a lower overextended volume level for forecasting less significant market corrections.

In Figure 6.13, we observe a couple of blow-offs or buying climaxes at relatively high volume on the Daily Chart of E-TRACS UBS Bloomberg CMCI Food ETN.

In Figure 6.14, we observe overextended volume levels in the SPDR Gold Trust Shares. The volume overextension level is identified by visual inspection and set at a level where only the most significant tops or bottoms are found in the SPDR Gold Trust Shares. Setting it at a lower level tends to result in more frequent signaling of less significant tops or bottoms. Notice the downside breakout of a

FIGURE 6.13 Volume Blow-Offs on the Daily Chart of E-TRACS UBS Bloomberg CMCI Food ETN.
Courtesy of Stockcharts.com

significant support level at extreme volume. Note also that the overextended volume spikes are all above the rolling 100-day 2-sigma level.

In Figure 6.15, we used a Bollinger Bandwidth oscillator to time volatility in the Silver market. Notice the volatility spikes coinciding with volume overextensions, signaling market tops and bottoms. Many practitioners also filter out volatility below a certain threshold and regard it as noise.

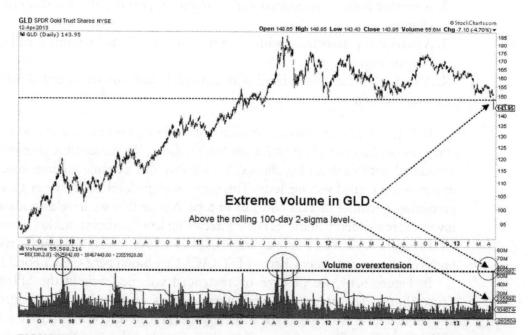

FIGURE 6.14 Volume Overextensions on the Daily Chart of SPDR Gold Trust Shares.
Courtesy of Stockcharts.com

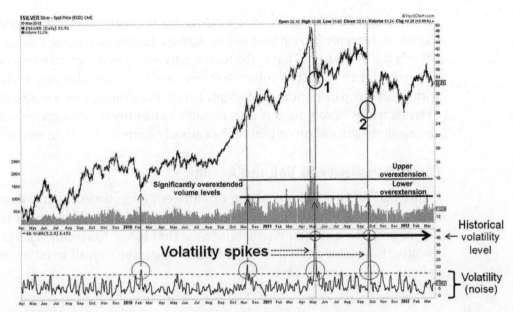

FIGURE 6.15 (Volatility Filtered) Selling Climaxes on the Continuous Daily Chart of Silver.
Courtesy of Stockcharts.com

Tops and bottoms can also be formed on very low volume. Figure 6.16 depicts a series of low volume reversals consisting of both low volume tops and bottoms. We notice that a low volume top or bottom is formed in the market whenever a lower volume threshold is tested, indicated by the time lines located at the circles shown on the daily chart of Apple Inc.

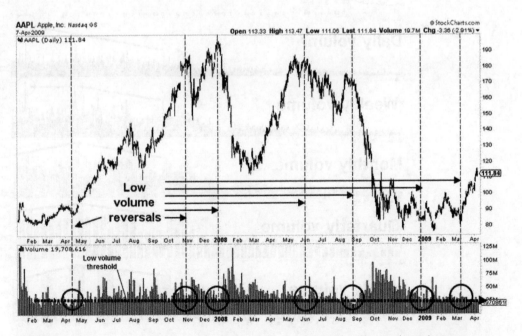

FIGURE 6.16 Low Volume–Based Reversals on the Daily Chart of Apple Inc.
Courtesy of Stockcharts.com

It is important to note that *overextensions in volume can signal either a top or a bottom*. Extreme buying and selling activity generates volume and can result in either a top or bottom. That is the reason why we cannot use the terms overbought or oversold with respect to volume extremes unless we are able to associate volume with either a top or bottom formation. Therefore, although we are able to pinpoint overextensions in volume, it is only possible to identify overbought or oversold levels in volume after a top or bottom has already formed, that is, in retrospect.

Chart Sensitivity to Volume Action

Figure 6.17 depicts volume action on different timeframes. Notice that the daily and weekly volume action peaks in 2013, whereas the volume peaks in 2011 on higher timeframe charts. We therefore see that lower timeframe charts are more sensitive to volume action. At higher timeframes, the overall trend or behavior of volume action is more obvious.

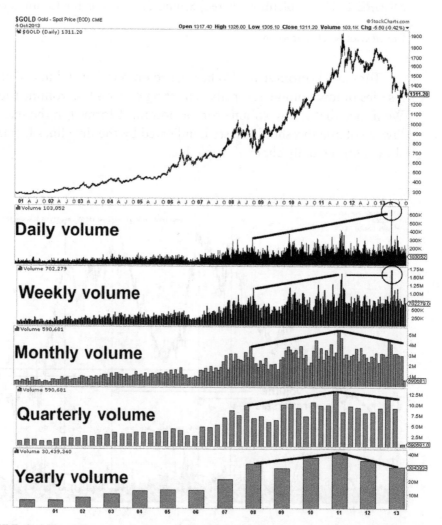

FIGURE 6.17 Volume Action on the Continuous Multiple Timeframe Chart of Gold.
Courtesy of Stockcharts.com

Volume Action and the Strength of a Price Barrier

An indication as to the potential strength and reliability of a price barrier may also be gauged from the action of volume at or across the point of support or resistance. Figure 6.18 shows two scenarios for resistance and support. Support and resistance formed at a volume peak are generally regarded as the most reliable and provide the strongest barrier to future retests. This is because even with the large surge in volume, price was still unable to penetrate the barrier. This gives traders confidence that the price barrier should hold up on future retests. Since expectation is everything in the market, this goes a long way to garner confidence in the barrier. Support and resistance formed across a volume dip or trough is considered less reliable since the reason for price not being able to penetrate the barrier is mainly due to a lack of interest or participation at the price barrier. Traders were not interested in taking price through the barrier. Hence the barrier only held up due to a lack of buying or selling pressure.

In fact, there are five possible scenarios of volume action associated with support and resistance, which are:

1. Volume increasing across support or resistance
2. Volume decreasing across support or resistance
3. Volume peaking at support or resistance
4. Volume bottoming at support or resistance
5. Volume flatlining across support or resistance

Volume increasing or decreasing across a barrier signifies a change in sentiment at the barrier (see Figure 6.19). Increasing volume as price approaches the barrier gives the impression that there may be sufficient market force to drive price through it. But

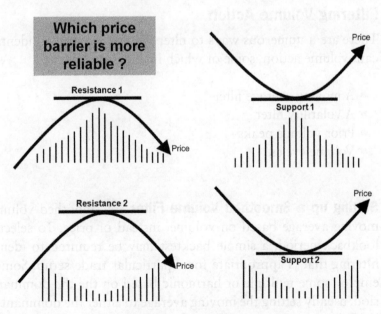

FIGURE 6.18 Price Barrier Strength and Reliability.

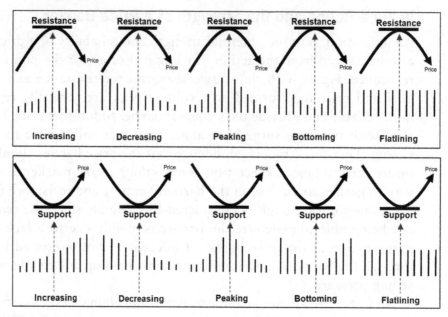

FIGURE 6.19   Volume Action Associated with Support and Resistance.

as prices start to reverse at the barrier volume picks up, driving price away from it with either bearish or bullish confirmation. Conversely, decreasing volume as price approaches the barrier gives the impression that there may be insufficient market force to drive price through it. But as prices starts to reverse at the barrier, volume declines even further. Decreasing volume across support and resistance tends to see a retest of the barrier, and in more extreme circumstances, may even see price return to penetrate the barrier. Finally, flatlining volume across support and resistance does not provide enough information about potential future action of price with respect to the barrier.

Filtering Volume Action

There are a numerous ways to filter volume in order to identify the most significant volume action, some of which include employing:

- A moving average filter
- A volatility filter
- Prior volume peaks
- Volume cycles

Setting up a Smoothed Volume Filter   A smoothed volume filter is simply a moving average based on volume, instead of price. To select the most effective lookback period, a simple backtest may be required to identify the amount of filtering that is appropriate for a particular trade setup. Some practitioners also employ some multiple or harmonic based on the the dominant trading cycle period, usually setting the moving average to either the dominant cycle period or one half of it. In either case, whenever volume spikes above this overextended moving

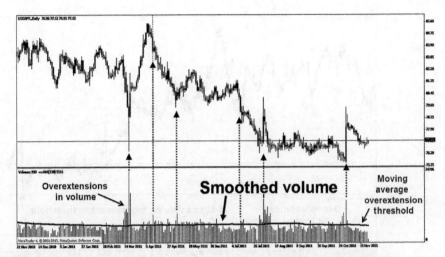

FIGURE 6.20 A Smoothed Volume Filter on the Daily Chart of USDJPY.
Source: MetaTrader 4

average line, it is considered to be significant and may potentially lead to a top or bottom forming in the stock or market. See Figure 6.20.

Setting up a Two- or Three-Sigma Volume Filter   Alternatively, we may also filter out all volume except for the most significant surges using a two- or three-standard deviation (i.e., sigma) filter, also called a volatility filter. This is easily constructed by applying either a two- or three-standard deviation Bollinger Band on volume, also referred to as a two- or three-*Sigma filter*. It should be noted that only the Bollinger upper band is used. A standard deviation oscillator may also be used, but it is less useful as it does not provide the overlay by which an overextension can easily be identified as it crosses over the threshold. Figure 6.21 depicts a three-Sigma volume filter signaling the most significant volume surges, which tend to result in the most significant tops and bottoms in the market.

Volume Filtered Inflection Points

Many practitioners also use volume as a means of filtering out price inflection points. They only use peaks and troughs that are considered significant, that is, those that are associated with above average volume, to construct trendlines and channels. In Figure 6.22, we shall use tick volume (transaction volume) as a basis for selecting significant inflection points. We draw a simple tick volume overextension level or threshold via visual inspection, making sure that only the most significant peaks in tick volume appear at or above the threshold. Inflection Points 1, 2, and 3 are associated with overextended tick volume and so are used to construct a channel. A trendline is drawn from Point 1 to Point 2. A parallel line is then projected from Point 3. Notice that price reacts to the channel at Point X, which represented a short-term buying opportunity before the market reversed downward, violating the rising channel.

In Figure 6.23, we use the same daily chart of USDJPY to construct an alternative price channel. This time we construct a trendline from Points 1 and 2 and project a parallel line from Point 3. We immediately notice a large bearish

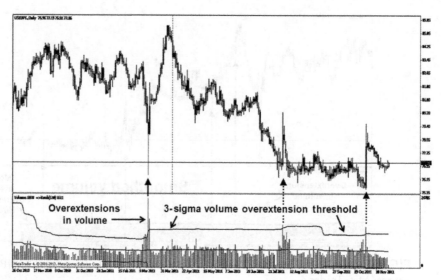

FIGURE 6.21   A Three-Sigma Volume Filter on the Daily Chart of USDJPY.
Source: MetaTrader 4

candlestick breaching this parallel uptrend line. If we project another parallel line from Point 4, and retrace it back in time, we see that it coincides perfectly with the trough that was formed at Point X around the end of January 2011. Although this was done retrospectively, it is nevertheless now part of a valid rising channel. If we continue to project another two parallel lines from Points 5 and 6, we notice that the new channel also contains price effectively, providing resistance and support at the channel top and bottom, respectively. This chart depicts the near perfect underlying angular symmetry in the Silver market. This again shows the importance of constructing chart patterns based on significant inflection points.

Relative and Absolute Volume   Absolute volume is not as important as relative volume in technical analysis. It is the *change in volume* that provides the

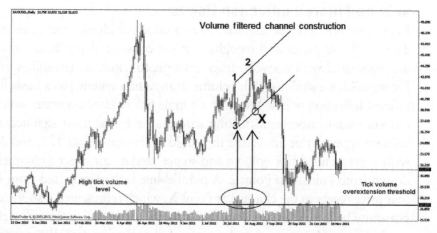

FIGURE 6.22   Channel Based on Tick Volume Filtered Inflection Points on the Daily Chart of Silver.
Source: MetaTrader 4

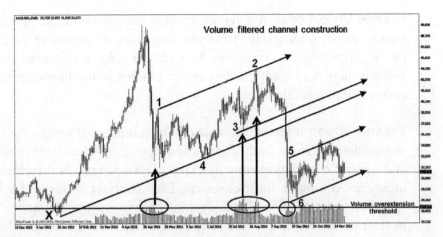

FIGURE 6.23 Channels Based on Tick Volume Filtered Inflection on the Daily Chart of Silver.
Source: MetaTrader 4

most information about potential price action in the markets. Rising and declining volume provide useful information about the level of interest or participation at various prices and indicate whether an ongoing trend is bearish or bullish. In contrast, historical or significant volume peaks and troughs (i.e., volume overextensions) provide a future reference level for signaling potential tops or bottoms in the market.

It should also be noted that a change in volume is not an absolute requirement for a trend to develop or unfold. A trend can persist over prolonged periods on flat volume. The other interesting characteristic about studying relative levels in volume is that of bull versus bear market volume. Bull market volume tends to outweigh bear market volume for a variety of reasons, a few being:

- Many investors prefer to hold on to losing positions in a falling market in the hope that the positions will eventually rebound to breakeven or profitability. These participants are displaying what is called loss aversion bias. Many investors believe that unrealized losses are not real losses and so are willing to hold on to losing positions. This willingness to hold on does not contribute to the overall trading activity in a bear market.
- Investors and traders have the ability to use *house money* or profit to further fund new positions in a rising bull market.
- More investment funds start to market their services in a bull market, attracting more potential investors to participate in the market

Absolute volume is useful for identifying potential price rejection levels based on significant or historical prices. It is also useful when comparing the amount of participation across different stocks, sectors, industries, or commodities in the search for greater liquidity especially when trying to gauge the total volume turnover with respect to the total number of outstanding shares in a stock. This will provide information about the absolute level of participation in a stock.

Volume Distortions   A surge in activities such as arbitrage, program trading, and high frequency trading (HFT) may also distort and misrepresent the traditional meaning or representation of volume. As such, the volume information that traders use and rely on to read market action may not in fact be totally indicative of true volume action in the classical sense.

Volume—Open Interest Interplay   Open interest is simply the total amount of outstanding contracts in the futures and options markets. Unlike stocks, all futures and options contracts eventually expire. Open interest is therefore the number of unliquidated long or short contracts. Each contract consists of a long and corresponding short position. These contracts are in a sense still active, or *open*. Open interest increases when *a new long and corresponding short position are initiated*, and decreases when both the long and corresponding short position are exited. Open interest remains unchanged when either the long or short position is *replaced by a new position*, but not both at the same time.

Generally speaking, open interest is interpreted the same way as volume. It is indicative of the level of interest or participation in seeing price rise or fall. Open interest divergence is therefore read in the same way as non-price-based volume oscillators. When prices, volume, and open interest are all rising, this is indicative of a bullish market, predominantly driven by buying pressure. Conversely, when prices are rising but both volume and open interest are declining, this is indicative of a bearish market, predominantly driven by shorts covering their positions and longs leaving the market. For declining markets, rising volume and open interest is bearish and is predominantly driven by short selling. Falling volume and open interest is bullish in a declining market, mainly due to the diminishing number of long positions being liquidated and short positions being initiated. It shows that the market participants are less interested in seeing the market decline further.

As far as trading is concerned a trader should look for appropriate buy signals when price, open interest, and volume are all rising. Conversely, a trader should look for a suitable exit in order to liquidate long positions if rising prices are accompanied by declining open interest and volume. In a declining market, traders should look for appropriate signals to go short if both the open interest and volume are rising, and rapidly seek to cover all short positions when both the open interest and volume start to decline together. In Figure 6.24, we observe a bullish confirmation between volume and Silver prices with volume peaking at Point 1, at the highest price. But we notice bearish divergence between open interest and price. This is an early indication that many longs are liquidating as prices rise. We subsequently see Silver prices retrace significantly.

It should be noted that the level of open interest may be indicative of the nature of a potential reversal or breakout. For example, if open interest is very high, the ensuing reversal may be significantly more rapid, due to the large amount of open contracts liquidating and covering.

Volume versus Tick (Transaction) Volume   In the over the counter (OTC) foreign exchange (fx) market, many brokers offer *tick volume* instead of actual volume.

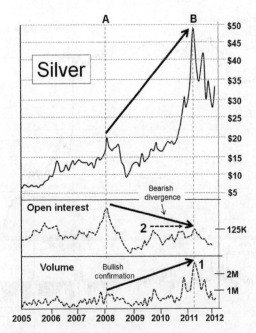

FIGURE 6.24 Open Interest Indicating Bearish Divergence on the Continuous Daily Chart of Silver.

One tick represents one trade. Tick volume therefore represents *transaction volume*. One transaction can be comprised of 1 contract or 1000 contracts. Although tick volume does not represent actual volume, there still exists a very strong correlation between actual volume and tick volume, and tick volume may be used as a proxy for actual volume, as far as comparing relative levels of overbought and oversold.

Breadth Volume and the Arms Index The Arms Index, or TRIN, incorporates breadth volume, advances, and declines. It is simply the ratio of:

$$TRIN = (advances/declines)/(Up\ Volume/Down\ Volume)$$

In short, a rising but not overbought tick and a falling but not oversold TRIN represent a bullish signal where the trader looks for an appropriate long entry. Conversely, a falling but not oversold tick and a rising but not overbought TRIN represent a bearish signal where the trader looks for an appropriate short entry. For longer-term trading, when tick is oversold (i.e., above its two-sigma level on a weekly chart), and TRIN is overbought (i.e., near or above the 3.0 level on the daily charts), this signals a bullish scenario and the trader looks for an appropriate long entry. Conversely, if the tick is overbought and the TRIN is oversold, this signals a bearish scenario and the trader looks for an appropriate short entry.

In Figure 6.25, we observe both the tick and TRIN at oversold levels. This indicates short-term bullishness on the 1-min chart of the S&P500 Large Cap Index. We subsequently see the index rising.

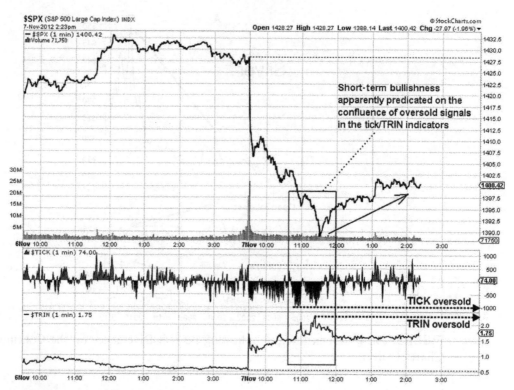

FIGURE 6.25 Tick/TRIN Interplay Indicating Bullishness on the Daily Chart of the S&P500 Large Cap Index.
Courtesy of Stockcharts.com

In Figure 6.26, we see a short-term downtrend in the S&P500 accompanied by a bearish rising TRIN. We also notice that the tick is largely absent of activity between 1:45 p.m. and 2:45 p.m. This represents a short-term bearish signal.

Two-Dimensional Volume Analysis We may also analyze volume two dimensionally, via:

- Volume by price
- Volume by time

Volume by time represents the total volume traded over a specified time interval or period. *Volume by price identifies the total volume traded at each price level.* Figure 6.27 depicts a large volume turnover around the $17 price level in SLV. This level therefore represents a significant support. Notice that this volume information is not obvious from conventional volume bar action.

In Figure 6.28, we see a lot of volume turnover between $77 and $86 on the daily chart of 3M Co. This price range represents the most traded range, with some resistance coming in at the $90 to $92 level. These price ranges represent potential future support and resistance levels in 3M Co.

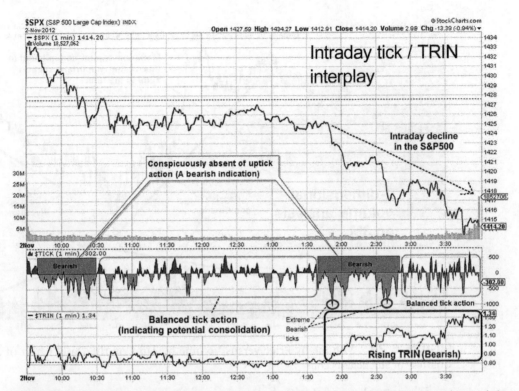

FIGURE 6.26 TICK/TRIN Interplay Indicating Bearishness on the Daily Chart of the
S&P500 Large Cap Index.
Courtesy of Stockcharts.com

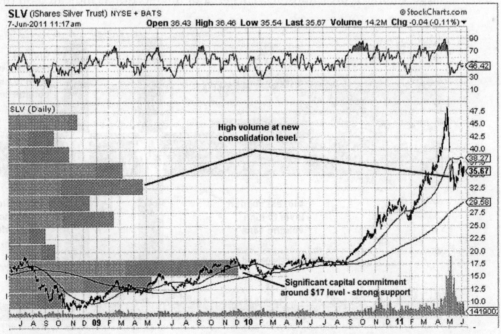

FIGURE 6.27 Volume by Price Identifying Strong Support on the Daily Chart of iShares
Silver Trust (SLV).
Courtesy of Stockcharts.com

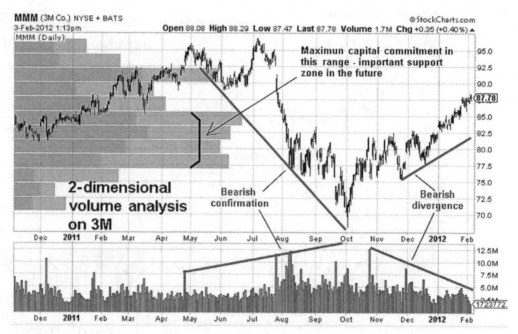

FIGURE 6.28 Volume by Price versus Volume by Time on the Daily Chart of 3M Co.
Courtesy of Stockcharts.com

We may also use this two-dimensional form of volume analysis to locate the
most significant support and resistance levels in the market. To do this, we first
locate the largest volume by price range. In Figure 6.29, we selected the $74 to
$80 range as the range with the most significant volume by price. We then locate
the largest volume by time intervals. We find the area of intersection of these two
large-volume representations. This area of intersection is indicated on the chart as

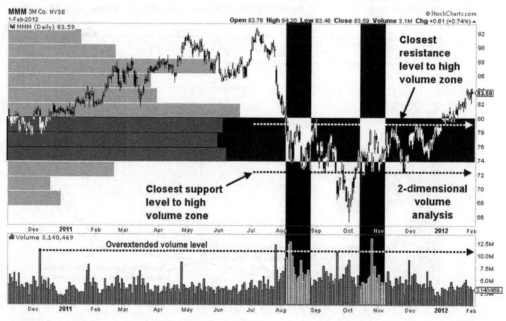

FIGURE 6.29 Locating Significant Support and Resistance using Two-Dimensional
Volume Analysis on the Daily Chart of 3M Co.
Courtesy of Stockcharts.com

two white boxes. The last step is to locate the closest peak or peaks above the area of intersection. This will potentially represent the most significant and reliable resistance level within the price formation. To locate the most significant support level, we locate the closest trough or troughs below the area of intersection. This will potentially represent the most significant and reliable support level within the price formation. We see both significant support and resistance levels acting as effective barriers to price action on the daily chart of 3M Co.

Volume to Bar Range (Spread) Relationship The relationship between bar range (spread) and volume may also be used to forecast potential breakouts and reversals.

The four basic combinations of bar range and volume are:

1. **Narrow range on low volume (Low Volume Rest Bar):** Indicates a potential for reversal especially during a *strong* and rapid up or downtrend. For weak to average trends, it tends to indicate a point of rest. It reflects a lack of participation. See Example 1 in Figure 6.30.
2. **Narrow range on high volume (High Volume Reversal Bar):** Indicates a strong potential for a reversal. In an uptrend, price remains confined to a narrow range on very large volume. If the volume represented buying pressure, the range would be much wider. Hence, this is indicative of sellers attempting to take control. It is a bearish signal. The converse applies for downtrends. See Example 2 in Figure 6.30.
3. **Wide range on low volume (Low Volume Reversal Bar):** Indicates a potential for reversal as the large price move was backed or supported by a relatively low amount of participation. It reflects a lack of interest. The longer the price bar on low volume, the more bearish it is in an uptrend and bullish in a downtrend. See Example 3 in Figure 6.30.
4. **Wide range on high volume (High Volume Continuation Bar):** Indicates a potential for continuation as the large price move was backed and supported by a very large amount of participation, that is, interest in seeing price continue. It is bullish in an uptrend and bearish in a downtrend. See Example 4 in Figure 6.30.

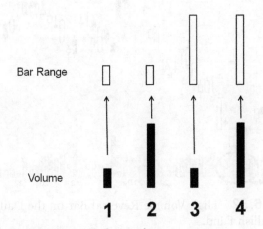

FIGURE 6.30 Volume-Bar Range Relationship.

FIGURE 6.31 High Volume Reversal Bars on the Daily Chart of PowerShares DB U.S. Dollar Bullish Fund.
Courtesy of Stockcharts.com

In Figure 6.31, we observe two narrow range candlesticks on high volume at Points 1 and 2. Notice how price subsequently reverses rapidly in the opposite direction after the formation of these high volume reversal bars. We also see a low volume breakout signal near the apex of the descending triangle formation during the month of August. Notice the large volume surge on breakout.

In Figure 6.32, we observe a narrow range candlestick on high volume around the beginning of November which led to a significant rebound in price in the U.S. Dollar Index Bullish Fund.

FIGURE 6.32 High Volume Reversal Bar on the Daily Chart of PowerShares DB U.S. Dollar Bullish Fund.
Courtesy of Stockcharts.com

FIGURE 6.33 High Volume Reversal Bar on the Daily Chart of PowerShares DB U.S. Dollar Bullish Fund.
Courtesy of Stockcharts.com

In Figure 6.33, we see another example of a high volume reversal bar occurring around May 23, 2011. Notice the bearish divergence in volume and on the MACD leading up to the high volume reversal bar. This is a bearish scenario, and is regarded as potentially more reliable since the bearish reversal bar occurred within a larger downtrend. We see prices decline after its formation. We also see a high volume continuation bar indicated at Point X. Similarly, high volume continuation bars are regarded as potentially more reliable if they occur in the direction of the predominant trend.

In Figure 6.34, we see a high volume reversal bar occurring around the end of October 2011. This reversal bar also occurred at a historically overextended volume level, as indicated on the chart.

Constant Volume Charts Constant volume charts are especially useful for pinpointing reversal bars on high or low volume. Since the volume is fixed for each bar, it will be relatively easy to identify potential reversal bars by *just referring to the bar range alone and its height in relation to the rest of the bars*. In Figure 6.35, we see two types of reversals bars. The narrow range bar is bearish and is indicative of sellers taking control, while the wider range bar is indicative of a lack of interest in the price rise.

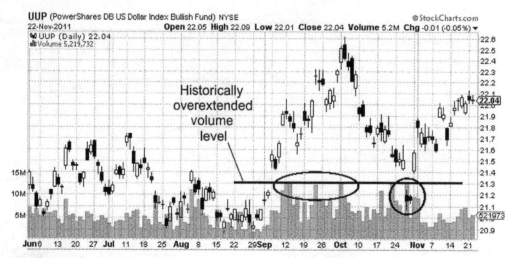

FIGURE 6.34 High Volume Reversal Bars on the Daily Chart of PowerShares DB U.S. Dollar Bullish Fund.
Courtesy of Stockcharts.com

Volume Leading Price versus Price Leading Volume Does volume lead price? Most practitioners will agree that without participation, that is, volume, price will be unable to move in a significant manner. Nevertheless, technical buy and sell signals need not require much volume for them to appear on the charts. For example, a small breakout of a very significant trendline may precipitate a larger breakout, inviting tremendous volume as the penetration becomes more obvious. In such cases, price may be seen leading volume. With the widespread use of technical analysis today, there may be a greater tendency for price to lead volume more frequently.

Volume Cycles in the Financial Markets We may anticipate potential price action using volume peak cycles that occur on an intraday basis in the markets. The intraday volume cycle normally peaks around 1:30 p.m. to 2:30 p.m. GMT. At these volume peaks, price will either reverse or continue, but very rarely remain unchanged. We see this occurring on the 30-min EURUSD chart as seen

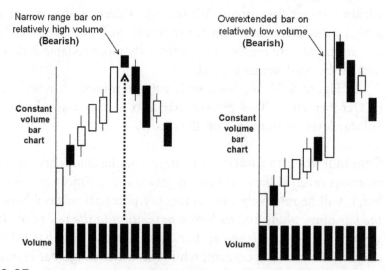

FIGURE 6.35 Constant Volume Charts Indicating Bearish Reversal Bars.

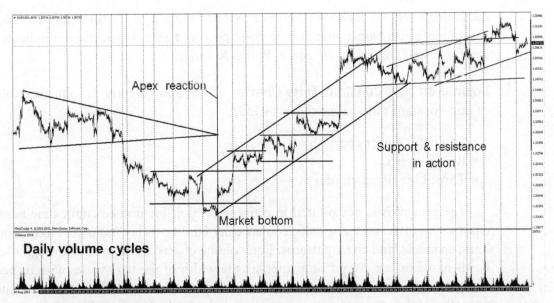

FIGURE 6.36 Volume Cycle Peak Reactions at Support and Resistance on the 30-Min Chart of EURUSD.
Source: MetaTrader 4

in Figure 6.36. Almost every price reversal on the EURUSD occurs at an intraday tick volume peak. *This is especially useful if price is retesting a previous support or resistance level.* Many practitioners also prefer to employ a bidirectional or straddle entry, catching price whichever way it traverses during a volume peak, since price rarely remains unchanged after a cycle peak.

In Figure 6.37, we observe price successfully rebounding off trendline retests at Points 1, 4, and 5, which all occurred during a tick volume cycle peak. These support levels were further corroborated by a cycle-tuned stochastic oscillator

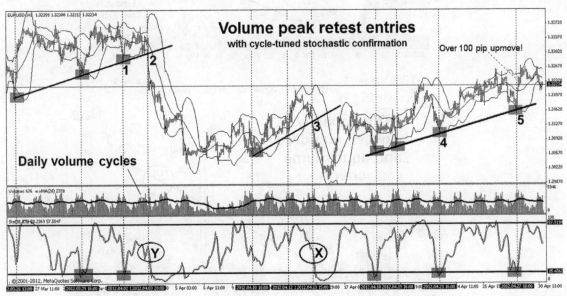

FIGURE 6.37 (Stochastic Filtered) Tick Volume Cycle Peak Reversals on the Hourly Chart of EURUSD.
Source: MetaTrader 4

indicating oversold conditions. Notice that at Points 2 and 3 the trendline failed to support price. Notice that at both these points, the stochastic did not indicate a clear oversold condition, as seen at Points X and Y.

Volume on Non-Constant Time Charts   As seen in Chapter 3, some examples of non-constant time-based charts include:

- Point and Figure charts
- Renko charts
- Three Line Break charts

The time axis is not plotted in a linear fashion for non-constant time-based charts. This affects the angle of geometrically based overlay indicators like trendlines, channels, and chart patterns. Equivolume charts are unique. Although each bar is based on a constant time interval, the width of the bars varies with respect to volume. This results in the time axis being plotted in a non-linear fashion, just as in the case for non-constant time-based charts. In Figure 6.38, we observe a discrepancy in the violation of the trendlines between both types of charting.

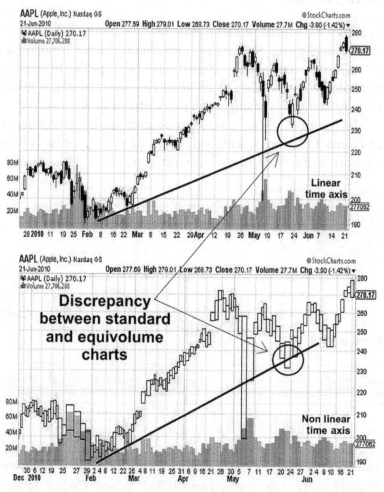

FIGURE 6.38   Discrepancy in Trendline Penetrations on the Daily Chart of Apple Inc.
Courtesy of Stockcharts.com

6.2 VOLUME OSCILLATORS

There are numerous volume-based oscillators and indicators, with some of the more popular ones being:

- Volume Weighted Moving Average (VWMA)
- Accumulation Distribution Line (ADL)
- On Balance Volume (OBV)
- Chaikin Money Flow
- Chaikin Oscillator
- Demand Index
- Herrick Payoff Index
- NYSE Up/Down Volume Line

We analyze oscillators for bullish and bearish signals using the eight standard methods of observation (refer to Chapter 8 for more on oscillator analysis):

1. OBOS Overextended Levels
2. Equilibrium and Zero Line Crossovers
3. Signal Line Crossovers
4. Price-Oscillator Divergence
5. Geometrically Based Oscillator Pattern Analysis
6. Numerically Based Oscillator Pattern Analysis
7. Horizontally Based Oscillator Pattern Analysis
8. Oscillator-on-Oscillator Analysis

Price-Based Volume Indicators: The OBV and A/D Line

The On Balance Volume (OBV) oscillator is simply a cumulative or running total of each period's volume added or subtracted from a running total depending on whether the current period's close is higher or lower than the preceding period's close price. If the current period's close is higher than the preceding period's close price, the current period's volume is added to the running total. If it is less than the preceding period's close price, the current period's volume is subtracted from the previous running total. If the closing price remains unchanged, no volume is added or subtracted from the running total. The disadvantage of using the OBV is that its absolute value or reading is dependent on the start date. Nevertheless, *this does not affect the changes in the relative value of the OBV line*. As such, all eight oscillator analysis methods may still be employed to determine bullish and bearish signals. One major weakness of the OBV oscillator is that the current period's volume is added or subtracted from the cumulative total regardless of the current period's price behavior. For example, assume that the current period's bar closes just below the previous period's close price. This would mean that the current period's volume would be subtracted from the running total regardless of the fact that the current bar may have made a new significant high, way above the previous bar's high. To redress this issue, many practitioners prefer to use the ADL, Chaikin Money Flow (CMF), or the

FIGURE 6.39 OBV Indicating Bullish Divergence on the Daily Chart of Citigroup Inc.
Courtesy of Stockcharts.com

Chaikin Oscillator. In Figure 6.39, we see the OBV indicating bullish divergence on the daily chart of Citigroup Inc. Prices rebound strongly thereafter.

In Figure 6.40 we observe the OBV indicating bearish divergence on the daily chart of Copper. Prices fell strongly thereafter.

Price-Based Volume Indicators: The Accumulation Distribution Line (ADL)

The accumulation distribution line, or ADL, is calculated as follows. Simply calculate the value of the multiplying factor $[[(C – L) – (H – C)]/(H – L) \times$ current

FIGURE 6.40 OBV Indicating Bearish Divergence on the Daily Chart of Copper.
Courtesy of Stockcharts.com

period's volume] and add this value to its running total. This running total represents the ADL. Notice that if (C – L) = (H – C), then:

$$C - L = H - C$$
$$2C = H + L$$
$$C = (H + L)/2$$

This means that when the current bar closes at its midpoint, no volume is added or subtracted from the running ADL. The further up price closes from the midpoint, the more volume is added to the running total. Similarly, the further down price closes from the midpoint, the more volume is subtracted from the running total, since the expression [(C – L) – (H – C)] turns negative. This redresses the insensitivity of the OBV in responding to price behavior when adding or subtracting volume. The ADL accounts for the current bar's price action when incorporating volume. It should be noted that no matter how wide the range is for the current bar, the maximum volume added will always be the day's total volume, and not some multiple of it. This is clearly seen by replacing the close price with the high in the expression [(C – L) – (H – C)]/(H – L) giving [(H – L) – (H – H)]/(H – L) = 1. Hence the day's total volume is the maximum volume that can be added or subtracted from the cumulative ADL. In Figure 6.41, we observe the ADL indicating bullish confirmation, whereas the volume bars are indicating bearish divergence. The volume bars are indicating an underlying weakness in the uptrend. The trader should wait for price confirmation of a reversal before participating in the market.

In Figure 6.42, we observe that when the OBV and ADL are rising or falling together, the price will trend in a decisive manner, and whenever the two oscillators are moving in opposite directions, there is a tendency for price to range

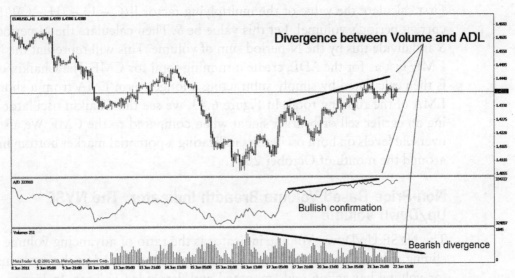

FIGURE 6.41 The ADL Oscillator Indicating Confirmation on the Hourly Chart of EURUSD.
Source: MetaTrader 4

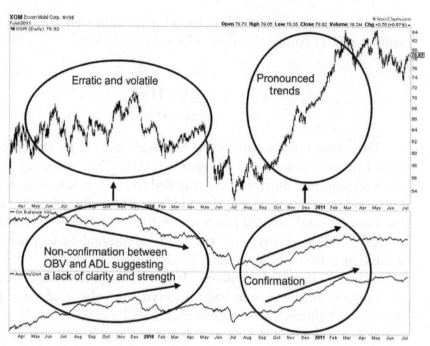

FIGURE 6.42 OBV and ADL Signaling Trend and Range Mode on the Daily Chart of Exxon Mobile Corp.
Courtesy of Stockcharts.com

or consolidate. This is useful for gauging behavioral or regime changes in the market. It may be potentially helpful for traders deciding whether to employ a trend-following or range-bound strategy.

Price-Based Volume Indicators: The Chaikin Money Flow and Chaikin Oscillator

The Chaikin Money Flow (CMF) is calculated in a manner similar to the ADL. First calculate the value of the multiplying factor $[[(C - L) - (H - C)]/(H - L) \times$ current period's volume]. Let this value be S. Then calculate the N-period sum of S and divide this by the N-period sum of volume. This will represent the N-period CMF. Just as for the ADL, create a running total for CMF. The Chaikin oscillator is then calculated by simply subtracting a longer-term EMA from a shorter-term EMA of the running total. In Figure 6.43, we see the Chaikin oscillator generating an earlier sell or bearish signal when compared to the CMF. We also see the oversold levels on both oscillators indicating a potential market bottom in Copper around the month of October 2011.

Non-Price-Based Volume Breadth Indicator: The NYSE Up/Down Volume

The NYSE Up/Down Volume indicator is the ratio of advancing volume over declining volume. Being non-price-based, divergence is read in the same manner as for volume bar action and smoothed and detrended volume. In Figure 6.44, we observe the NYSE U/D indicator signaling an early bearish signal that was later confirmed by the NYSE Composite Index.

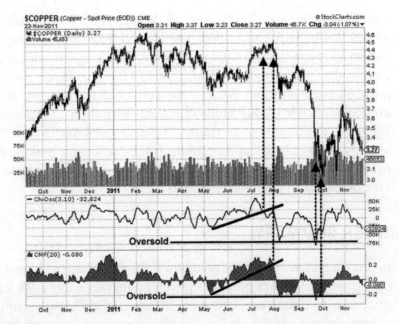

FIGURE 6.43 The Chaikin Money Flow and Chaikin Oscillator Signaling a Potential Reversal on the Daily Chart of Copper.
Courtesy of Stockcharts.com

Open Interest Indicators: The COT Report and Herrick Payoff Index

The Herrick Payoff Index uses open interest in its calculations. As such, it may only be used with futures and options. It incorporates price in its calculations and as such divergence readings should be observed in the same manner as all other price-based volume oscillators. As with all volume oscillators, bearish signals are

FIGURE 6.44 NYSE Up/Down Volume Line Generating an Early Bearish Signal.
Courtesy of Stockcharts.com

indicative of money flowing out of the market whereas bullish signals suggest money flowing into the market. The Herrick Payoff Index may be scrutinized for bullish and bearish signals using any or all of the eight modes of oscillator analysis. Finally, the Commitment of Trader, or COT, report is released every Friday. It reports all open positions held by the commercials (hedgers, non-cash positions), non-commercials (hedge funds, financial institutions, large traders), and for the aggregate position of small traders. Traders and investors use the COT report to identify potential tops and bottoms in the market by looking for changes in the net commercial or non-commercial open positions, as well for a test of any significant or historical open interest levels.

6.3 CHAPTER SUMMARY

In this chapter, we have observed how volume and open interest play a critical role in helping to decipher potential price and market action. We have also seen how price-based volume oscillators are interpreted differently from non-price-based volume indicators. We shall be applying most of what we have learned in this chapter, with particular emphasis on volume divergence and filtering volume action, throughout the rest of this Handbook.

CHAPTER 6 REVIEW QUESTIONS

1. What is the difference between volume and tick volume?
2. Describe bearish and bullish volume.
3. How is volume divergence distinct from standard oscillator divergence?
4. How would you use volume as a timing indicator?
5. Describe the various modes of volume filtering.
6. Describe the relationship between volume, open interest, and price.
7. Which is more useful, absolute or relative volume?
8. How are volume cycles useful and where would you normally find them?

REFERENCES

Archelis, Steven B. 2001. *Technical Analysis from A to Z*. New York: McGraw-Hill.

Arms, Richard W., Jr. 1989. *The Arms Index*. Homewood, IL: Dow Jones-Irwin.

Colby, Robert W. 2003. *The Encyclopedia of Technical Market Indicators*. New York: McGraw-Hill.

Morris, Greg. 2006. *The Complete Guide to Market Breadth Indicators*. New York: McGraw-Hill.

CHAPTER 7

Bar Chart Analysis

> **LEARNING OBJECTIVES**
>
> After studying this chapter, you should be able to:
>
> - Understand the significance of bar chart analysis and its use in forecasting potential tops and bottoms in the market
> - Recognize the early indications of potential trend change via commonly used bar chart patterns
> - Identify buy and sell signals via single, double, triple, and multiple bullish and bearish bar formations
> - Read bar action behavior more effectively via the 16 price and volume reversal characteristics

The study of bar chart patterns forms the basis of pure price action analysis. It represents the most fundamental skill that every technician should possess in order to be adept in technical analysis. In this chapter we shall cover various single, double, triple, and multiple bullish and bearish price bar patterns commonly used by practitioners of technical analysis.

7.1 PRICE BAR PATTERN CHARACTERISTICS

Construction of a Price Bar

A standard price bar comprises an open (O), high (H), low (L), and close (C) price, normally referred to by its acronym, OHLC. Price activity may be quantized over a specified duration or time interval and summarized into OHLC data. For example, Figure 7.1 depicts five minutes of price activity, which may be represented by a bar. The range of the bar is simply the absolute distance between the high to low, |H − L|.

To summarize price activity over longer durations, comprising multiple intervals, simply use the opening price of the first interval, closing price of the last interval, and the highest and lowest prices over the entire duration observed. See Figure 7.2.

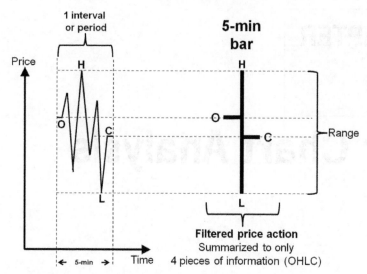

FIGURE 7.1 Construction of a Price Bar.

In Figure 7.3, we observe price activity over a series of 5-minute intervals and the corresponding graphical representation of OHLC price bars for each interval represented below.

Classification of Price Bar Formations

There are three basic ways to classify price bar formations, namely via:

1. The number of bars that make up the formation:
   - Single bar formations
   - Double bar formations
   - Triple bar formations
   - Multiple bar formations

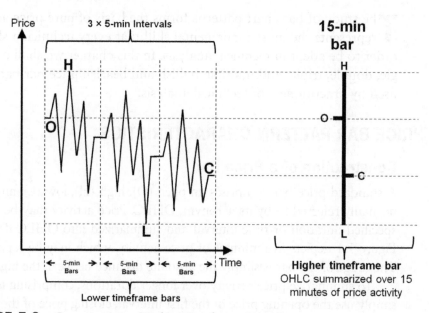

FIGURE 7.2 Constructing a Higher Timeframe Price Bar.

2. The intrinsic bias or sentiment associated with the price bar formation:
   - Bullish formations
   - Bearish formations
3. The directional expectations of the formation:
   - Continuation formations
   - Reversal formations

7.2 PRICE BAR PATTERN CHARACTERISTICS

Bar reversals and continuations may be classified in single, double, triple, and multiple bullish and bearish patterns. A bullish pattern in an uptrend and a bearish pattern in a downtrend are considered to be *continuations* patterns. Similarly, a bearish pattern in an uptrend and a bullish pattern in a downtrend are considered *reversal* patterns. In short, whenever the:

- Intrinsic and trend sentiments agree, the pattern is considered a continuation pattern
- Intrinsic and trend sentiments disagree, the pattern is considered a reversal pattern

We say that the trend sentiment is bullish for uptrends and bearish for downtrends. Intrinsic sentiment is the inherent bullish or bearish bias that is associated with a particular pattern. For example, the intrinsic sentiment is bearish for a standard head and shoulders pattern and bullish for an inverted head and shoulders pattern. Hence, an inverted head and shoulders pattern in an uptrend is considered a continuation pattern since the trend and intrinsic sentiment are both in agreement, that is, they are *both* bullish. For more on intrinsic sentiment bias, refer to Chapter 4.

We shall now look at various generic bullish and bearish formations of single, double, triple, and multiple bar reversal patterns. For bearish patterns, we assume

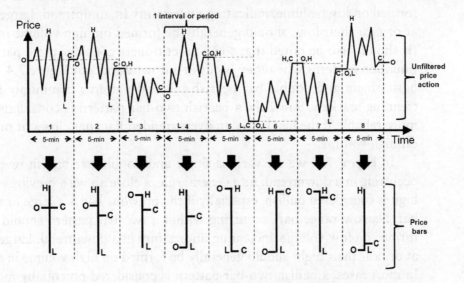

FIGURE 7.3 A Series of Price Bars Representing Each Period's Price Activity.

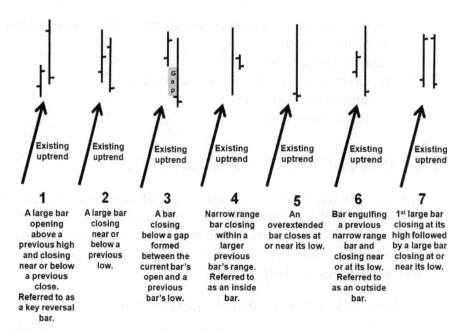

FIGURE 7.4 Seven Basic Single and Double Bar Bearish Reversal Patterns.

that the existing trend is up, with the reverse for bearish patterns. This is because in order to be classified as a reversal pattern, trend sentiment must be in disagreement with the pattern's intrinsic sentiment or bias.

Seven Generic Single and Double Bar Bullish and Bearish Reversal Formations

In Figure 7.4, we see various single and double bar bearish reversal patterns occurring in an uptrend. As a general rule, *a close below a previous bar's close or low is considered bearish, especially if the previous bar is a large or wide ranging bar*. Narrow range bars occurring within a two bar pattern should generally be formed on low volume, indicating uncertainty in an uptrend. Large bars closing at or near their lows should generally be formed on high volume in an uptrend. (It should also be noted that some practitioners consider these patterns as continuation patterns when they occur in a downtrend.) In Figure 7.4 are the seven basic single and double bar bearish reversal patterns commonly found in uptrending markets. Similarly, a bearish two-bar pattern is considered potentially more reliable if the last bar is an overextended bar that closes at or near its low on high volume.

In Figure 7.5, we see various single and double bar bullish reversal patterns occurring in a downtrend. As a general rule, a close above a previous bar's close or high is considered bullish, especially if the previous bar is a large or wide-ranging bar. Narrow range bars occurring within a two-bar pattern should generally be formed on low volume, indicating uncertainty in a downtrend. Large bars closing at or near their highs should generally be formed on high volume in a downtrend. In most cases, a bullish two-bar pattern is considered potentially more reliable if the last bar is an overextended bar that closes at or near its high on high volume.

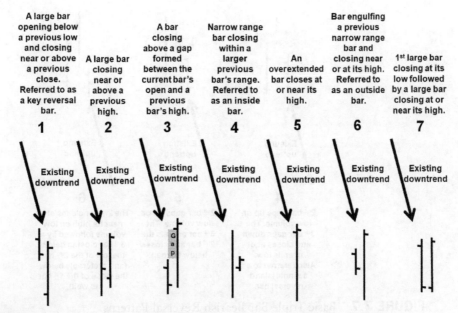

FIGURE 7.5 Seven Basic Single and Double Bar Bullish Reversal Patterns.

Six Generic Triple Price Bar Reversal Formations

In Figures 7.6 and 7.7, we see six basic triple bar bearish reversal patterns occurring in an uptrend. As a general rule, the larger the gaps, the more bearish will be the pattern upon completion. Also, the larger the range of the first and third bars, the more reliable will be the reversal pattern. For most triple bar patterns, the middle bar usually occurs on low volume, except possibly for pattern 1 where larger volume is also considered more bearish. This is because the buyers failed to keep the closing price near or above the midpoint of the bar and instead allowed the sellers to drive price to close at or near the low of the bar. A bearish three-bar pattern is generally considered more reliable if the last bar is an overextended bar that closes at or near its low on high

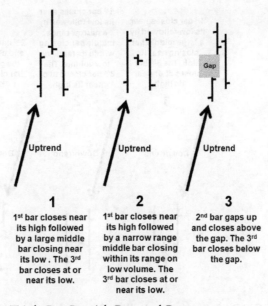

FIGURE 7.6 Basic Triple Bar Bearish Reversal Patterns.

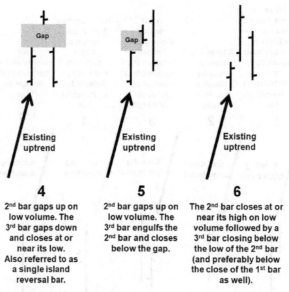

FIGURE 7.7 Basic Triple Bar Bearish Reversal Patterns.

volume. Similarly, a bullish three-bar pattern is considered potentially more reliable if the last bar is an overextended bar that closes at or near its high on high volume.

In Figures 7.8 and 7.9, we see six basic triple bar bullish reversal patterns occurring in a downtrend.

Four Generic Multiple Price Bar Reversal Formations

In Figure 7.10, we see four basic multiple bar bearish reversal patterns occurring in an uptrend. As a general rule, the larger the gaps the more bearish will be the reversal pattern. Also, the numerous bars between the first and last bars should generally occur on low volume, except possibly for Pattern 2 where high volume is also indicative of

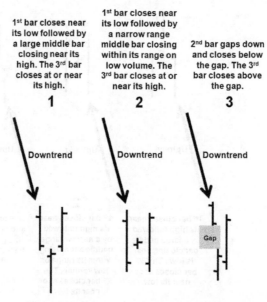

FIGURE 7.8 Basic Triple Bar Bullish Reversal Patterns.

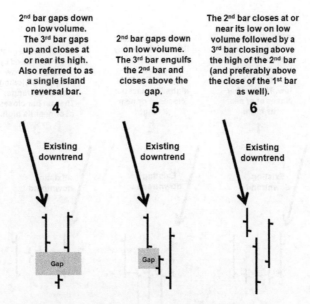

FIGURE 7.9 Basic Triple Bar Bullish Reversal Patterns.

sellers attempting to keep the closing prices at or near the low of each wide-ranging bar. Normally, low volume on the numerous bars between the first and last bar in pattern 2 indicates that the wide-ranging bars are not supported by sufficient demand and hence bearish. In short, extremely high or low volume occurring on the numerous wide-ranging bars between the first and last bar indicates bearishness in an uptrend. A bearish pattern is considered potentially more reliable if the last bar in a multiple bar pattern is an overextended bar that closes near or at its low on high volume.

In Figure 7.11, we see four basic multiple bar bullish reversal patterns occurring in a downtrend. As before, wide-ranging bars between the first and last bar in

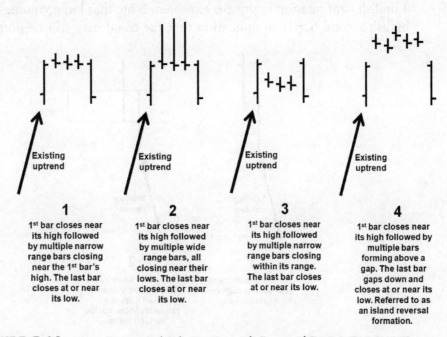

FIGURE 7.10 Four Basic Multiple Bar Bearish Reversal Patterns.

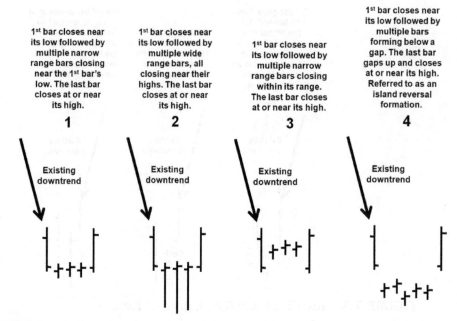

FIGURE 7.11 Four Basic Multiple Bar Bullish Reversal Patterns.

pattern 2 can also occur on high or above average volume, indicating bullishness. Narrow-ranging bars between the first and last bar on low volume is also indicative of potential bullishness. A bullish pattern is considered potentially more reliable if the last bar in a multiple bar pattern is an overextended bar that closes near or at its high on high volume.

Two Simple Continuation Bars

As far as continuation bars are concerned, Figure 7.12 depicts two patterns where a bullish continuation in price is expected. Note that large volume occurring on a bullish second bar is an indication that the trend may still be potentially strong.

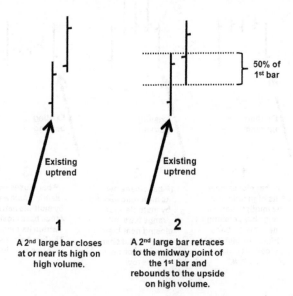

FIGURE 7.12 Two Basic Continuation Bar Patterns.

In pattern 1, the second bar breaches the high of the previous bar on high volume. In pattern 2, price retraces to the 50 percent level of the previous bar and subsequently rebounds on high volume, breaching the previous bar's high. The reverse applies for bearish continuation bar patterns.

Sixteen Main Price and Volume Action Reversal Characteristics

Besides studying the individual price behavior associated with each bar pattern, the practitioner should also be aware of the 16 basic price and volume action characteristics that are indicative of a potential reversal, namely:

1. Decrease in price cycle amplitude
2. Decrease in price cycle period
3. Change in bar retracement symmetry
4. Decrease in average bar range
5. Lack of the quality of price persistence
6. Decrease in average bar stochastic ratio
7. Decrease in average candlestick real body to range ratio
8. Changes in angular symmetry and momentum
9. Proximity to a price barrier
10. Reduction in frequency and decrease in depth of trend-based oscillations
11. Appearance of relatively larger and longer lasting consolidations
12. Appearance of an exhaustion gap
13. Completion of the average range for the period under observation
14. Overextended price action with respect to a price barrier
15. Price accompanied by extremely high or low volume
16. Standard divergences between price, volume, and oscillators

These reversal indications above apply equally to Japanese candlestick analysis. The trader and analyst should always be wary of any a price bar formation that is accompanied or preceded by any of the 16 price action characteristics listed above. These characteristics are strong indications of a potential change in trend or price retracement. Please refer to Chapter 5 for a detailed discussion of these reversal characteristics.

One of the most important price reversal characteristics is that of barrier proximity (listed as item (9) on the list). *Reversal patterns are most reliable at significant price barriers*. For example, a bearish key reversal day is more reliable when it occurs at a significant resistance level. Similarly a bullish exhaustion bar is more reliable at a significant support level.

Figure 7.13 will help illustrate some of these price reversal characteristics. The daily chart of the National Bank of Greece is an example of price action characteristic (14) depicting an overextended or overbought price bar with respect to a volatility barrier, namely the Bollinger upper band. This will be potentially even more bearish if the overbought price bar was associated with an extreme reading in volume. The overextended price bar is further preceded by an exponential rise in price, which is an indication of a rapid change in angular momentum, as described

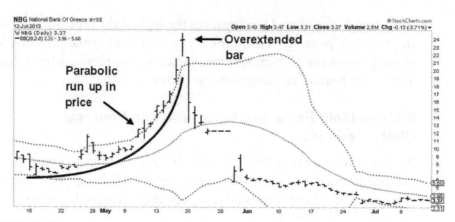

FIGURE 7.13 Overextension Preceded by an Exponential Rise in Price.

in price action characteristic (8). Such increases in price are usually unsustainable and are therefore potentially bearish. Price also depicts a lack of oscillations during the rapid run-up. This is a potentially bearish indication as there is a lack of healthy profit-taking activity, as described by price action characteristic (10).

Hence it is always best to gauge the degree of bearishness or bullishness associated with any price bar formation with respect to the 16 price and volume reversal behavior characteristics. All price bar formations should be read in the context of these 16 price and volume reversal characteristics. This will afford the trader and analyst a more accurate and consistent assessment of the overall likelihood for potential price reaction or reversal.

7.3 POPULAR BAR REVERSAL PATTERNS

Key Reversal Bar

A bearish *key reversal bar* forms a higher high than the previous bar and closes near or below the close of the previous bar. Price may open with a large gap up in the direction of the uptrend and close on high volume. The wider the key reversal bar, the more reliable will be the bearish follow-through action to the downside. The appearance of any of the 16 price and volume reversal characteristics only strengthens the degree of bearishness associated with the pattern. The exact converse applies to bullish key reversal bars in a downtrend.

In Figure 7.14, we observe a bullish key reversal bar occurring on high volume. Price subsequently rebounded in rapid fashion.

In Figure 7.15, we observe a bearish key reversal bar occurring on above average volume on the daily chart of Apple Inc. The bearish key reversal bar opens above the high of the previous bar, forms a new high, and subsequently closes below the previous bar's close. Note that in many cases, a rapid follow-through to the downside may not always unfold. The market occasionally consolidates or hovers slightly below or around a bearish key reversal bar before declining. We see this occurring between the 16th and 23rd of July on the chart.

In Figure 7.16, we observe a bullish key reversal bar occurring on high volume on the daily chart of ITC Holdings Corp. We observe some of the 16 price reversal

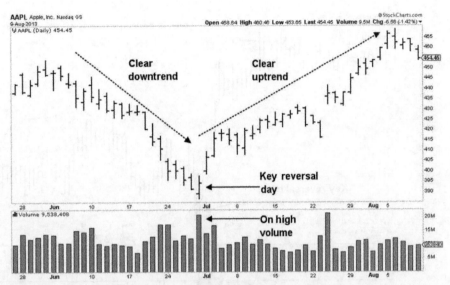

FIGURE 7.14 Bullish Key Reversal Day on the Daily Chart of Apple Inc.
Courtesy of Stockcharts.com

characteristics occurring with the pattern. The bullish key reversal bar forms below the lower Bollinger band, indicating an overextended or oversold condition
with respect to volatility. We also see the StochRSI at oversold. Both of these conditions indicate a greater potential for a bullish reversal. Note also that the key
reversal bar closed near its high on extreme volume, indicative of a selling climax.

Two Bar Reversals

In Figure 7.17, we observe a typical two bar bearish reversal on the daily chart
of the TSX Composite Index. The first bar closes near its high while the second
closes near its low. It would be preferable if the two bars had wider ranges. We

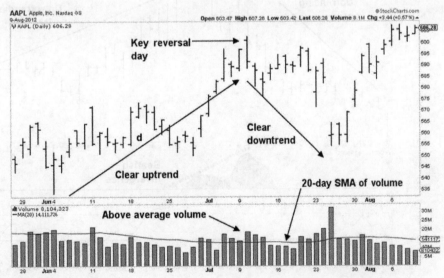

FIGURE 7.15 Bearish Key Reversal Day on the Daily Chart of Apple Inc.
Courtesy of Stockcharts.com

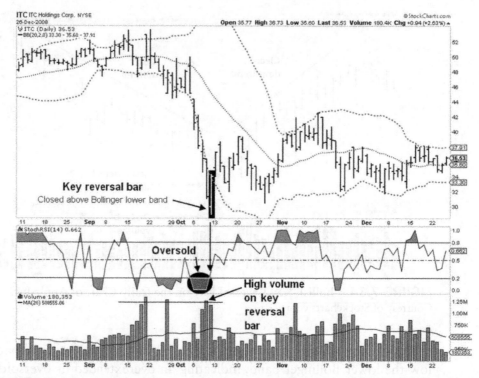

FIGURE 7.16 Bullish Key Reversal Day on the Daily Chart of ITC Holdings Corp.
Courtesy of Stockcharts.com

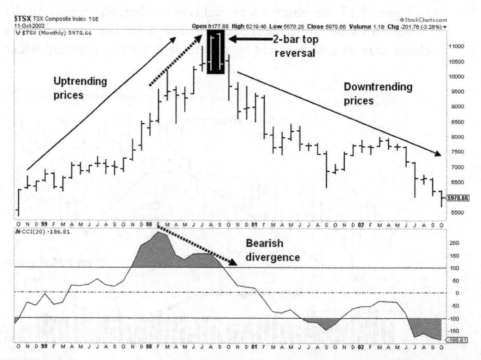

FIGURE 7.17 Bearish Two-Day Reversal on the Daily Chart of TSX Composite Index.
Courtesy of Stockcharts.com

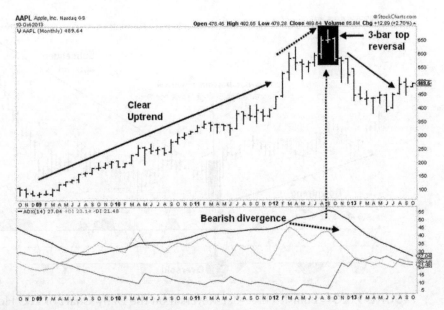

FIGURE 7.18 Bearish Three-Bar Reversal on the Daily Chart of Apple Inc.
Courtesy of Stockcharts.com

also see bearish divergence with the commodity channel index (CCI) oscillator. Price subsequently declined in rapid fashion.

Triple Bar Reversals

In Figure 7.18, we observe a three bar bearish reversal occurring in a clear and strong uptrend on the daily chart of Apple Inc. The first bar closes near its high while the third closes near its low. There is also bearish divergence with the +DM oscillator.

In Figure 7.19, we observe a three bar bullish reversal occurring on the daily chart of ITC Holdings Corp. Notice that the middle bar occurs on below-average volume while the first and third bars close on high volume.

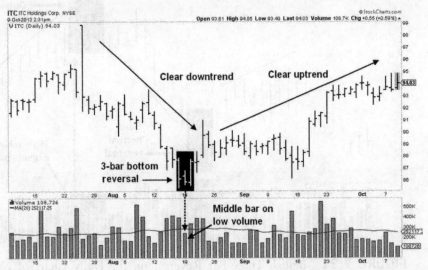

FIGURE 7.19 Bullish Three-Bar Reversal on the Daily Chart of ITC Holdings Corp.
Courtesy of Stockcharts.com

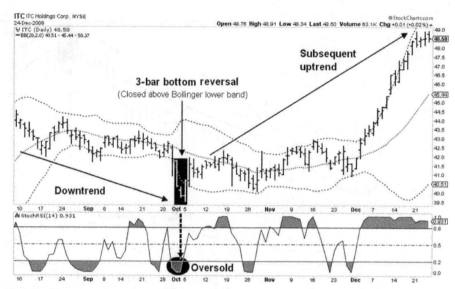

FIGURE 7.20 Bullish Three-Bar Reversal on the Daily Chart of ITC Holdings Corp.
Courtesy of Stockcharts.com

In Figure 7.20, we observe a three bar bullish reversal occurring on the daily chart of ITC Holdings Corp. The entire pattern occurs on an oversold condition on the StochRSI. Note that the last bar closes between the Bollinger bands, which is bullish. This pattern corresponds to pattern 5 in Figure 7.9.

In Figure 7.21, we observe a three bar bullish reversal occurring on the daily chart of Newmont Mining Corp. Notice that the middle bar occurs on below average volume while the first and third bars close on high volume. The large third bar closing near its high is an indication of added bullishness. This is followed by a bearish outside day formation with the outside bar closing near its low on high volume. Notice that the outside day formation engulfs four previous bars.

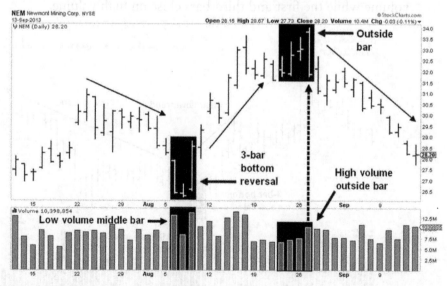

FIGURE 7.21 Bullish Three-Bar Reversal on the Daily Chart of Newmont Mining Corp.
Courtesy of Stockcharts.com

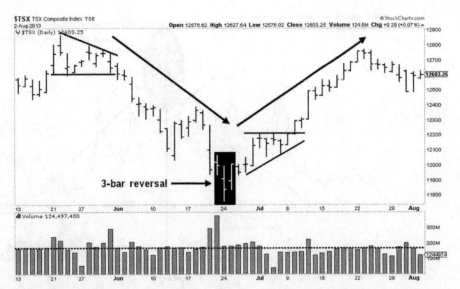

FIGURE 7.22 Bullish Three-Bar Reversal on the Daily Chart of TSX Composite Index. Courtesy of Stockcharts.com

In Figure 7.22, we observe a three bar bullish reversal occurring on the daily chart of TSX Composite Index. Notice the large middle bar occurs on lower volume as compared to the first bar, which is bullish. This pattern corresponds to pattern 6 in Figure 7.9.

Multiple Bar Island Reversals

In Figure 7.23, we see a bearish island formation occurring on overbought conditions on the stochastic oscillator, on the daily chart of Direxion Daily Gold Miners 3X Shares. Notice that the entire formation occurs on low volume, indicating a lack of conviction by the market participants. The gap up is followed by a gap down, isolating the formation.

Outside Bars

Outside bars are bars that engulf one or more preceding bars. The preceding bars are contained within the range of the outside bar. This pattern is generally considered a reversal pattern. The larger the outside bar, the more bullish or bearish will be the signal for a reversal. Many practitioners also consider the outside bar as a continuation pattern if the outside bar closes near or at the high, in the direction of the existing uptrend. The larger the number of preceding bars that are contained or encompassed within the range of the outside bar, the greater will be the tendency for producing stronger breakouts. Outside bars should close at or near their high or low for a more reliable reversal or continuation. The outside bar should also close on high volume. This pattern is similar to engulfing patterns in Japanese candlestick analysis. In Figure 7.24, we see a large bearish (a close in the opposite direction of the uptrend) outside bar encompassing 11 preceding bars on the daily chart of ITC Holdings Corp. An uptrend line violation coinciding with a bearish breakout of an outside bar should provide a reliable signal for a short entry.

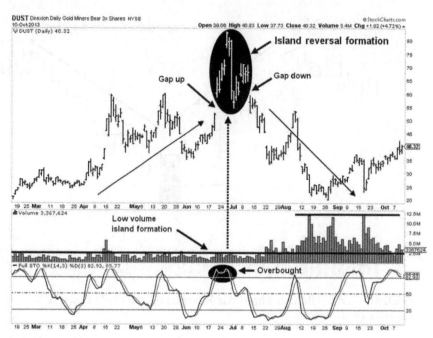

FIGURE 7.23 Bearish Island Reversal on the Daily Chart of Direxion Daily Gold Miners Bear 3X Shares.
Courtesy of Stockcharts.com

Inside Bars

Inside bars are considered reversal bars. For a more reliable reversal pattern, the first bar should be as wide as possible, occurring on high volume, whereas the second bar should be as narrow as possible, occurring on very low volume. In Figure 7.25, we see two inside bars forming and testing the same resistance level. The high of both inside bars 1 and 2 exceeded the upper Bollinger band, but systematically closed below it, which is usually regarded as an indication of price

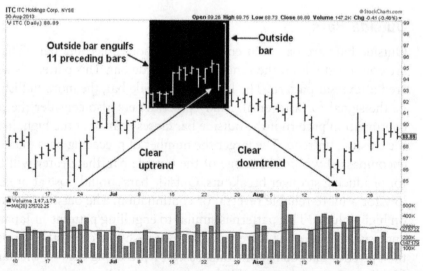

FIGURE 7.24 Bearish Inside Day Reversal on the Daily Chart of ITC Holdings Corp.
Courtesy of Stockcharts.com

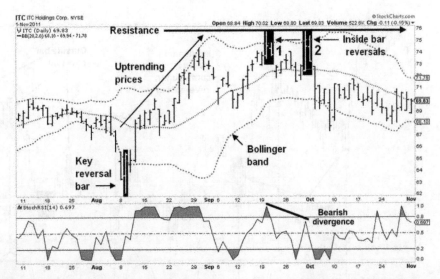

FIGURE 7.25 Bearish Inside Day Reversals on the Daily Chart of ITC Holdings Corp.
Courtesy of Stockcharts.com

exhaustion. We also see bearish divergence occurring between the StochRSI and the inside bar at Point 2.

In Figure 7.26, we see three successively lower inside bar formations occurring on the daily chart of Silver Wheaton Corporation. Each inside bar formation was formed below the Bollinger band, indicating potential price exhaustion, and especially so if the declines were also accompanied by bearish volume. We also see a bearish outside bar forming in late August 2013, after which prices declined.

Figure 7.27 depicts inside and outside bars occurring on the daily chart of Alacer Gold Corp. Notice that the bullish and bearish patterns line up perfectly with the stochastic oscillator overbought and oversold indications.

Inside bars are somewhat related to their Japanese candlestick equivalent, namely the Harami pattern. All outside bars may be regarded as Japanese candlestick engulfing patterns but not all inside bars are regarded as Harami patterns. It is a question of internal proportions. A Harami requires that the

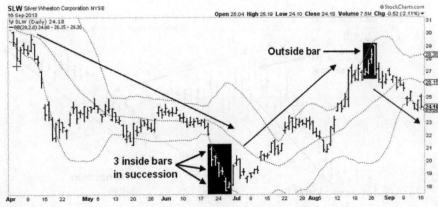

FIGURE 7.26 Inside Day Bullish Reversals and Outside Day Bearish Reversal on the Daily Chart of Silver Wheaton Corporation.
Courtesy of Stockcharts.com

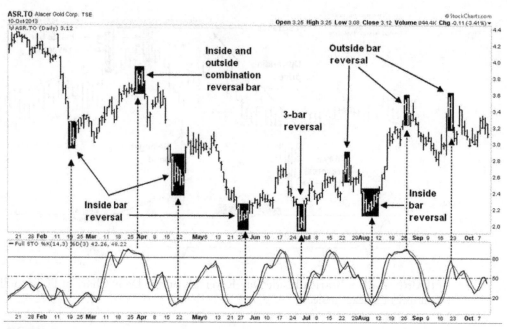

FIGURE 7.27 Various Inside Day, Outside Day, and Three-Bar Reversals on the Daily Chart of Alacer Gold Corp.
Courtesy of Stockcharts.com

narrow range candlestick be no more than one-fourth to one-third the range of the larger preceding candlestick. But an inside bar has no such restrictions.

Exhaustion Bars

Exhaustion bars are regarded as reversal bars. In an uptrend, they open above the previous bar's high. The larger the bar, the more bearish it will be within the context of an uptrend. There is no gap between the exhaustion bar and the subsequent bar, unlike in single bar island formations. The exhaustion bar should close at or near its low in an uptrend. The reverse is true for bullish exhaustion bars in a downtrend. In Figure 7.28, we see a bullish exhaustion bar forming a bottom on the daily chart of J.P. Morgan Chase & Co.

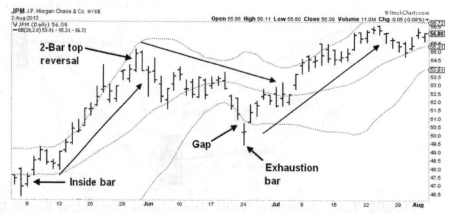

FIGURE 7.28 Bullish Exhaustion Bar on the Daily Chart of J.P. Morgan Chase & Co.
Courtesy of Stockcharts.com

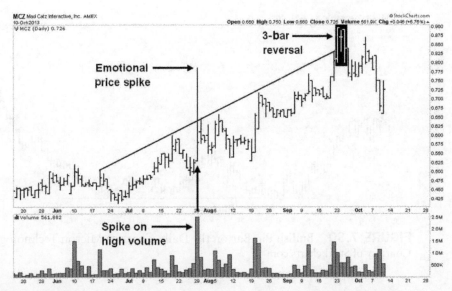

FIGURE 7.29 Emotion Spike Bar on the Daily Chart of Mad Catz Interactive Inc.
Courtesy of Stockcharts.com

Price Spikes

In emotional markets, price often produces a spike as a result of increased volatility. These bars are usually wide-ranging bars accompanied by high volume. In Figure 7.29, we see a large emotional price spike on high volume on the daily chart of Mad Catz Interactive Inc. We also notice a typical three bar bearish reversal forming a top in the stock.

Pin Bars

Pinocchio bars or *Pin* bars, are single bar misrepresentations of market strength or weakness. It is an intra-period price penetration of some barrier, suggesting a potential breakout. Price rapidly retraces back below resistance or back above support. A upside pin bar breakout gives traders a false impression of bullishness in a downtrend, whereas a downside breakout gives traders a false impression of bearishness in an uptrend. Pin bars normally breach the following common price barriers:

- Moving averages
- Levels of resistance or support
- Trendlines

Pin bars differ from exhaustion bars. Exhaustion bars do not usually provide a false impression of price penetrating a barrier. Pin bars may also be an artifact of specialists running stops.

In Figure 7.30, we observe a pin bar breaching support on the daily chart of Micron Technology Inc. Many traders would have been fooled into initiating a short position upon seeing the breach of support. *Pin bars are usually breakouts that form on low volume.*

227

FIGURE 7.30 Bullish Pin Bar on the Daily Chart of Micron Technology Inc.
Courtesy of Stockcharts.com

Failed Support- and Resistance-Based Breakout Entries

Pin bars are single bar breakouts of any price barrier. A more general form of price bar patterns providing false impression of strength and weakness are basic false breakouts based on the violation of support and resistance, which may be based on single or multiple bars. A false breakout of support or resistance occurs when there is a non-failure swing. In Figure 7.31, we observe a false upside breakout of a prior resistance level. A short is initiated once price retraces back below the resistance level with a stoploss placed just above the high of the breakout. Victor Sperandeo referred to this as a 2B entry in his book *Trader Vic: Methods of a Wall Street Master*.

In Figure 7.32, we observe numerous false upside and downside breakout entries on the daily chart of Silver. A long or short is normally initiated at a close below resistance in a false upside breakout or a close above support in a false downside breakout.

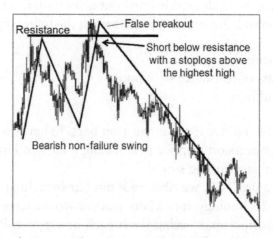

FIGURE 7.31 Bearish (Non-Failure Swing) False Breakout Short Entry.

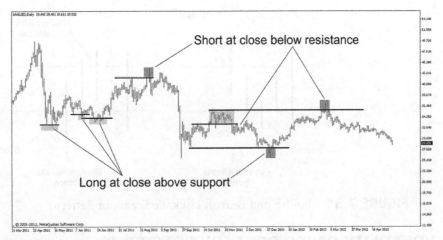

FIGURE 7.32 False Support and Resistance Breakouts on the Daily Chart of Silver.
Courtesy of Stockcharts.com

DiNapoli Double Repo Pattern

In Figure 7.33, we observe a bearish *Double Repo* reversal pattern. This pattern was introduced by Joe DiNapoli in his book *Trading with DiNapoli Levels*. The reader is advised to consult the original text for a detailed and complete discussion of the Double Repo pattern. In short, the Double Repo pattern generates a sell signal in an uptrend once it closes above and below a three-day SMA twice. The three-day SMA is forward shifted by three days. According to Joe DiNapoli, the patterns must be preceded by at least eight to ten days of bullish price action. The topping formation should not exceed eight to ten bars. In Figure 7.33, we observe a bearish double repo pattern preceding a rapid decline in the continuous daily chart of sugar prices. The reverse applies in a downtrend.

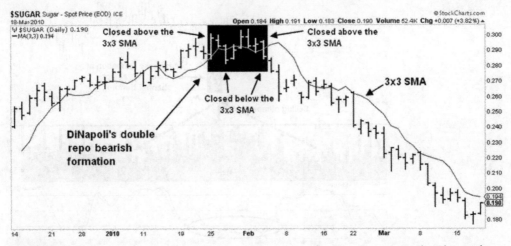

FIGURE 7.33 DiNapoli's Double Repo Pattern on the Continuous Daily Chart of Sugar.
Courtesy of Stockcharts.com

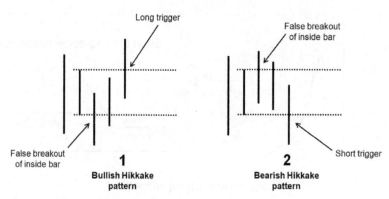

FIGURE 7.34   Bullish and Bearish Hikkake Breakout Pattern.

7.4 VOLATILITY-BASED BREAKOUT PATTERNS

Hikkake Pattern: The Failed Breakout Reversal Entry

The Hikkake pattern is characterized by an entry initiated after an initial failed breakout of an inside bar. Figure 7.34 is an illustration of a bullish Hikkake pattern where a false breakout inside bar was followed by an upside breakout. In this pattern, we only take the re-entry in the opposite direction of the failed breakout. Similarly, we see a bearish Hikkake pattern with an initial false upside breakout. The short entry was later initiated once price reversed and violated the low of the inside bar. The breakout should occur within three bars of the initial failed breakout. Hikkake means to *trap or ensnare*.

Figure 7.35 depicts a bullish Hikkake pattern forming a bottom on the daily chart of the iShares Emerging Market Fund, which is seen coinciding with the

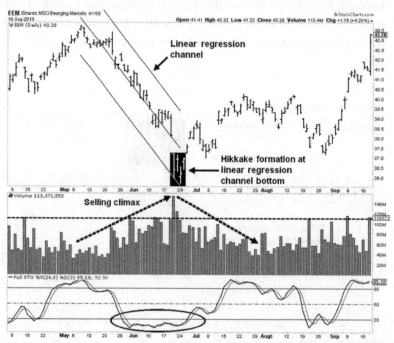

FIGURE 7.35   Bullish Hikkake Pattern on the Daily Chart of iShares Emerging Markets Fund.
Courtesy of Stockcharts.com

230

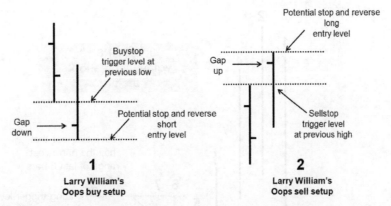

FIGURE 7.36 Bullish and Bearish William's Oops Entry Pattern.

linear regression lower band support. We see the Hikkake pattern forming on high volume, representing a selling climax in the stock. Note that stochastics is also in an oversold condition.

William's Oops Entry

Figure 7.36 depicts an example of Larry William's *Oops* Entry approach consisting of a bar opening beyond the range of the previous bar. A sellstop entry order is placed at the high of the previous bar if the new bar opens above the previous bar's high. A stoploss is placed at the new bar's high. Similarly, a buystop entry order is placed at the low of the previous bar if the new bar opens below the previous bar's low. A stoploss is placed at the new bar's low. In both cases, if price reverses, a stop and reverse order is initiated at the stoploss levels. We may also look to Japanese candlestick morning and evening start formations, including the piercing line and dark cloud cover candlestick patterns, to find patterns conducive to Larry William's Oops setup. *It is best to look for a bullish Oops pattern in an uptrend and a bearish Oops pattern in a downtrend.* Refer to Larry's book *How I Made One Million Dollars Trading Commodities* for more details.

In Figure 7.37, we see a bearish Oops pattern on the daily chart of Dynegy Inc.

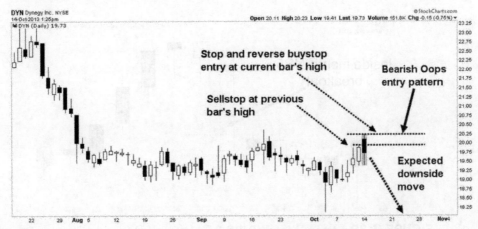

FIGURE 7.37 Bearish Oops Entry Pattern on the Daily Chart of Dynegy Inc.
Courtesy of Stockcharts.com

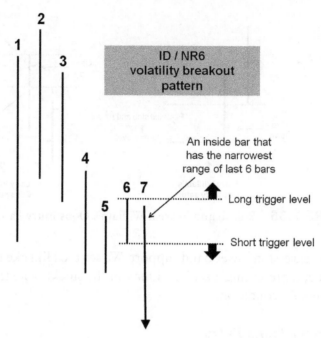

FIGURE 7.38 ID/NR6 Pattern.

ID/NR4-7 Breakouts

The *Inside Day Narrow Range* pattern or ID/NR pattern is a volatility breakout pattern. An ID/NR *n* pattern denotes an inside day breakout from the narrowest bar over the last *n* days. In Figure 7.38 we observe an ID/NR6 pattern where we see an inside bar breakout. The last bar is the narrowest bar of the last six days. This pattern has no bearish or bullish sentiment associated with it. The breakout can occur in either direction.

In Figure 7.39 we observe an Inside Month/NR5 pattern breakout where we see an inside bar breaking out to the upside on the monthly chart of Dynegy Inc.

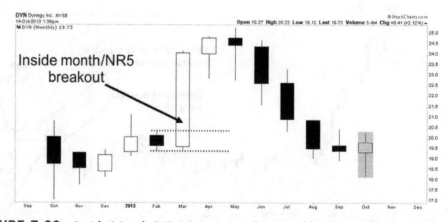

FIGURE 7.39 Inside Month /NR5 Pattern on the Monthly Chart of Dynegy Inc.
Courtesy of Stockcharts.com

7. 5 CHAPTER SUMMARY

In this chapter we discussed the dynamics of bar action and how it is potentially indicative of future price activity, especially when accompanied by significant indicator and volume action. We also looked at various breakout patterns that may prove effective in catching continuations or reversals in the market.

CHAPTER 7 REVIEW QUESTIONS

1. What is the difference between exhaustion bars and pin bars?
2. Why is the ID/NR7 pattern referred to as a volatility breakout pattern?
3. What are the main characteristics of a key reversal day?
4. Describe the 16 price and volume reversal characteristics.
5. Explain how volume impacts bar chart pattern analysis.
6. Describe two triple bar bearish patterns and how you would trade them.
7. Describe the ideal conditions for an inside bar reversal.
8. Describe how you would use oscillators to help gauge the degree of bearishness or bullishness of various bar reversal patterns.

REFERENCES

Bollinger, J. A. 2001. *Bollinger on Bollinger Bands*. New York: McGraw-Hill.

DeMark, Thomas. 1994. *The New Science of Technical Analysis*. New York: John Wiley and Sons.

DiNapoli, Joe.1969. *Trading with DiNapoli Levels*. Sarasota, FL: Coast Investment Software, Inc.

Kirkpatrick, Charles, and Julie Dahlquist. 2007. *Technical Analysis: The Complete Resource for Financial Market Technicians*. Upper Saddle River, NJ: Pearson Education.

Pring, Martin J. 2002. *Technical Analysis Explained: The Successful Investor's Guide to Spotting Investment Trends and Turning Points*. 4th ed. New York: McGraw-Hill.

Sperandeo, Victor. 1991. *Trader Vic: Methods of a Wall Street Master*. New York: John Wiley and Sons.

Williams, Larry. 1979. *How I Made One Million Dollars Trading Commodities*. New York: Windsor Books.

Window Oscillators and Overlay Indicators

O scillators and indicators have fascinated traders and analysts since the first average was created. Oscillators and indicators can help reveal underlying strengths and weaknesses of price action, which would not have been obvious otherwise. In this chapter we will learn about the construction and proper application of oscillators and various overlay indicators to help better forecast potential reversals and breakouts in the markets.

8.1 DEFINING INDICATORS AND OSCILLATORS

Classification of Oscillators and Indicators

Indicators are subdivided into two categories:

1. Overlay indicators: Overlay indicators are plotted on the same chart as price action, as well as window oscillator action. They represent *barriers* to price or window oscillator action, that is, they provide support and resistance at various price and oscillator levels. It should be noted that window oscillator

action plotted on the price chart *does not represent a valid or meaningful overlay indicator*, and as such does not provide support and resistance. For example, a standard moving average convergence-divergence (MACD) or relative strength index (RSI) oscillator plotted on the price chart itself will not interact with price in any meaningful way. Conversely, overlay indicators plotted on window oscillator action *do represent a valid and meaningful overlay indicator*, and as such provide a valid barrier to oscillator action. For example, an overlay indicator such as a Bollinger band plotted on an RSI window-based oscillator would indicate levels of overbought and oversold in the RSI. Finally, there are four types of overlay indicators, namely:

A. Numerically based overlays: These overlays forecast future price barrier levels mathematically. For example, a Fibonacci upside price target based on 161.8 percent expansion of the range AB from C is calculated as C + (1.618 × AB).

B. Horizontally based overlays: These overlays forecast future price barrier levels based on prior resistance and support levels. Forecasts are therefore *independent* of time, that is, they do not vary with the passing of time. Price gaps (rising and falling windows) are also a horizontal overly indicator of potential future support and resistance. Although such forecasted reaction price levels do not vary with time, it is important to note that such reaction levels may still be invalidated, especially when breached a significant number of times. (It should be noted that some numerically based indicators such as Fibonacci ratio and Gann's Square of Nine price projections may also be classified as horizontally based overlays, unlike numerically based indicators such as moving averages and Bollinger bands.)

C. Geometrically based overlays: These overlays forecast future price barrier levels via the drawing of *diagonal* trendlines or lines that are projected from particular peaks and troughs, also referred to as price *inflection points*. Since they are diagonal, forecasts of potential barrier levels based on these overlays will vary over time, and the forecast of potential barrier levels will depend on *when* price tests these overlays. In other words, the forecasts of potential future price barrier levels depend on the geometry of the barrier created.

D. Algorithmically based overlays: These overlays forecast future price barrier or breakout levels based on a specific sequence of bar or candlestick action. Some examples include two-bar breakouts, Guppy's count back line, and DeMark's TD sequential indicator.

2. Window oscillators: These are mathematically derived indicators that are normally based on open high low close (OHLC) data, volume, and open interest. There are two types of window oscillators, namely:

A. Bounded oscillators: Values or readings of window oscillators that range from 0 to 100 percent (we say that the oscillator has been *normalized*). The advantage of using a bounded oscillator is that it provides a meaningful way of *comparing relative levels of overextension*, that is, relative levels of overbought and oversold, between different stocks or markets over the same number of periods. The main disadvantage is that during strong trend action, the values or readings tend to remain at overbought or oversold for extended periods, and as such provide little useful information other than that a strong trend is in effect.

B. Unbounded oscillators: The values or readings of unbounded window oscillators have *no upper or lower limit*. Note that although unbounded window oscillators have no theoretical upper or lower limit, some unbounded window oscillators do have a lower limit of zero, such as volume, ADX, Bollinger Bandwidth, and average true range (ATR). These window oscillators are therefore referred to as being semi-bounded. The main advantage of employing an unbounded oscillator is that it provides *historical levels* of overbought and oversold. These historical levels of overbought and oversold are specific to a particular stock or market at a selected timeframe, and care should be taken when used to compare the degree of overextension between different stocks or markets. An unbounded window oscillator may sometimes be converted into a bounded window oscillator via normalization, confining the range of window oscillator action between 0 and 100 percent. Normalization will always convert a point-based oscillator (e.g., MACD, momentum, CCI, ATR, ADX, etc.) into a percentage scaled oscillator, ranging between 0 and 100 percent. It should be noted that some practitioners refer to unbounded oscillators as *window indicators*, rather than oscillators. This is mainly due to the fact that an unbounded oscillator *need not actually revert back to its central or equilibrium value*. Values can rise or fall indefinitely with no indication of whether they will revert to equilibrium levels. As such, many practitioners prefer to use the term *indicator* as many unbounded oscillators tend to not *oscillate* around their equilibrium levels but rather trend in one or the other direction. Unbounded oscillators that tend to trend include those that employ a *net running or cumulative total* of all past values, such as the Net Advance Decline Line, OBV, and so on.

See Figure 8.1 for comparisons between bounded and unbounded window oscillators. Notice that overlays may be applied to window oscillators as well.

See Figure 8.2 for a flow chart summary of indicator classification.

Chart Scale Sensitivity and Invariance

Chart scaling only affects indicators that are geometrically based. As such, it does not affect window oscillators, as the values of all window oscillators are numerically determined, that is, mathematically calculated. It also does not affect overlays that are numerically and algorithmically determined. For example, a simple moving average represents the average of N period closing prices, irrespective of whether the chart was scaled arithmetically (linear based) or logarithmically (ratio based). The average price of N period closing prices is *scale invariant*, that is, it does not change with scaling. Another example of scale invariance involves algorithmically determined overlays. Assume that we wanted to buy at the breach of a five-day high. Once we have identified such a pattern, we would initiate a long position once price breaches the five-day high. Again, we see that such sequence bar patterns are unaffected by scaling. The high prices will still have the same

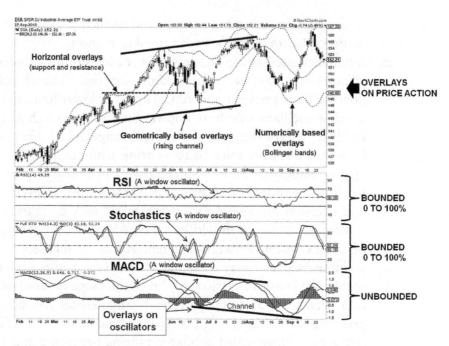

FIGURE 8.1 Overlay, Bounded, and Unbounded Technical Indicators.
Courtesy of Stockcharts.com

values, irrespective of the scaling employed. *Horizontally based indicators* like support and resistance are also scale invariant. Horizontal overlays are indicators where the forecasted price depends only on the price axis. Time is not an element in its forecast.

Unlike support and resistance, trendline forecasts of potential future barrier levels are *time dependent*. The potential support provided by an uptrend line depends

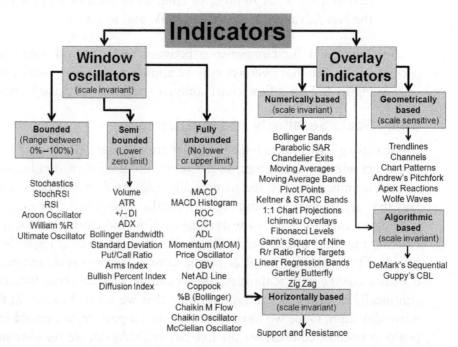

FIGURE 8.2 Classification of Technical Indicators.

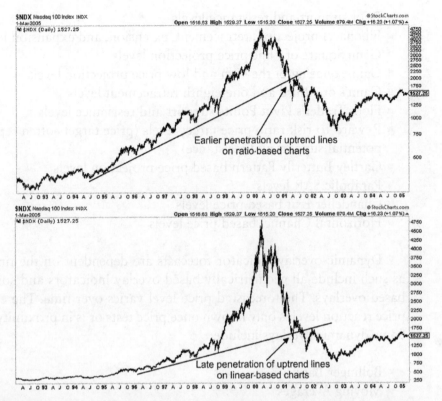

FIGURE 8.3 Geometrically Based Overlays Displaying Non-Scale Invariance.
Courtesy of Stockcharts.com

on when price tests it. The more time has elapsed, the higher will be the trendline support level when tested by price. Trendlines are a form of geometrically based overlay indicators. Unfortunately, *geometrically based overlays are the only group of indicators that are not scale invariant*. Forecasted prices vary with the scaling employed. For example, two trendlines based on different scaling would forecast different future support and resistance levels.

In Figure 8.3, we see that for uptrend lines, ratio scaling produces earlier penetrations as compared to linear scaling. The compression that occurs at higher prices on ratio-scaled charts affects the angle of all trendlines, which are based on the geometrical relationship between inflection points.

In short, scaling does not impact the forecasts of potential future price barrier levels if the overlay indicator is numerically, horizontally, or algorithmically based.

Static and Dynamic Overlay Indicators

Finally a distinction has to be made between *static* and *dynamic* overlay indicators and their relationship with numerically, horizontally, geometrically, and algorithmically based overlay indicators. Static overlay indicator forecasts are not dependent on the time element, and as such include all horizontally and algorithmically based overlays, as well as many numerically based overlays. The forecasted price reaction level does not change over time, unless it is invalidated and a new forecast is required. Hence all horizontal overlay indicators like support and resistance are clearly static overlay indicators. Static overlays include:

- Prior support and resistance levels
- Fibonacci projection, retracement, extension, and expansion levels
- Gann Square of Nine price projection levels
- Gann squaring of the high and low price projection levels
- Gann's one-third and one-eighth retracement levels
- Floor Trader's Pivot Points support and resistance levels
- Reward-to-risk ratio price target levels (price targets often represent levels of potential support and resistance)
- Gartley Butterfly Pattern based price projection levels
- Parabolic SAR levels
- Chandelier Exit based price levels
- Horizontal Channel based price levels

Dynamic overlay indicator forecasts are dependent on the time element and as such include all geometrically based overlay indicators and some numerically based overlays. The forecasted price level varies over time. The exact forecasted price reaction level is only known once price tests or is in proximity to the overlay. Some dynamic overlays include:

- Bollinger Bands
- Moving Averages
- Moving Average Bands
- Keltner Bands
- STARC Bands
- Ichimoku Overlays
- Linear Regression Bands
- Andrew's Pitchfork
- Trendlines
- Rising and Falling Channels
- Chart Patterns
- Wolfe Waves

8.2 EIGHT WAYS TO ANALYZE AN OSCILLATOR

There are eight basic ways to use a window oscillator to indicate potential buy (bullish) and sell (bearish) signals, namely:

1. OBOS Overextensions
2. Equilibrium and Zero Line Crossovers
3. Signal Line Crossovers
4. Price-Oscillator and Oscillator-Oscillator Divergence
5. Geometrically Based Oscillator Pattern Analysis
6. Numerically Based Oscillator Pattern Analysis
7. Horizontally Based Oscillator Pattern Analysis
8. Oscillator-on-Oscillator Analysis

It should be noted that many practitioners require that buy and sell reversal signals based on window oscillators require *price confirmation*, that is, *price is required to breach an overlay indicator*. Just because an indicator issues a bearish or bullish reversal signal does not necessarily mean that prices have reversed or broken through a barrier. The signals may be based on oscillator action, but the trigger for entry or exit must always be based on price action. Oscillator values breaching overlays do not represent price confirmation but are regarded as merely a signal of potential bullishness or bearishness.

For a valid price confirmation, price may breach any of the following overlays:

- Numerically based overlays
- Horizontally based overlays
- Geometrically based overlays

Nevertheless, the most reliable and popular overlays used for price confirmation are prior support and resistance levels, simple trendlines, moving averages, and chart pattern breakouts or reactions.

OBOS Overextended Levels

Overbought and oversold (OBOS) levels are indicative of overextensions in price, where a potential reversal in price is expected. It should be noted that an overbought signal is first and foremost an indication of a strong uptrend in effect, with a high probability of a potential bearish reversal. Similarly, an oversold signal is first and foremost an indication of a strong downtrend in effect, with a high probability of a potential bullish reversal. As such, price confirmation is required when trying to identify reversals. These overextensions may occur at expected percentage levels or may be formed at levels specific to the stock or market itself. Overextensions may be identified as follows:

1. For Bounded Oscillators:
   - Overbought is represented as relatively high percentage readings, usually at or above 70 or 80 percent (depending on the oscillator employed)
   - Oversold is represented as relatively low percentage readings, usually at or below 20 or 30 percent (depending on the oscillator employed)
2. For Unbounded Oscillators:
   - Overbought is represented as historical or significant peaks in the oscillator
   - Oversold is represented as historical or significant troughs in the oscillator

The overbought (OB) and oversold (OS) levels for two popular bounded oscillators are defaulted at:

- Stochastics: OB (80 percent) OS (20 percent)—note that many practitioners up shift these OBOS levels to OB (90 percent) OS (30 percent) to account for the upside bias in certain markets or during strong and prolonged uptrends.
- RSI: OB (70 percent) OS (30 percent)

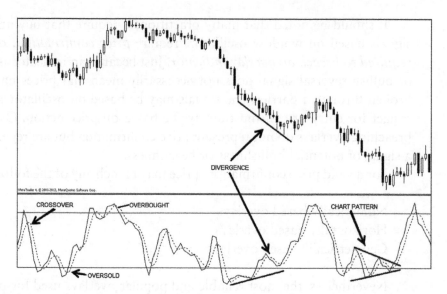

FIGURE 8.4 Various Buy (Bullish) and Sell (Bearish) Signals Generated by Divergence, Signal Crossovers, Chart Patterns, and Overextensions.
Source: MetaTrader 4

The OB and OS levels for unbounded oscillators are:

- CCI Oscillator: OB (+100) OS (−100)—note that these values are measures of volatility. This oscillator coincides well with the Bollinger band 1 standard deviation values. The ± 200 levels also match the Bollinger band ± 2 standard deviation (or sigma) bands.
- Standard Deviation Oscillator: OB (+1 or +2 Sigma) OS (−1 or −2 Sigma)
- Most unbounded oscillators do not have widely accepted levels of overextension. This is because such levels are specific to a particular stock or market historical oscillator action.

Figure 8.4 depicts various signals being generated by oscillator divergence, chart patterns, overextensions, and signal crossovers.

Figure 8.5 depicts a historically significant overbought level on the MACD unbounded oscillator, on the daily chart of Amazon.com Inc. Notice that every time the MACD tests or exceeds the overbought level, this is was followed by a reversal or correction in price, as seen at time lines 1 to 6. These overextension levels are best determined via visual inspection.

Figure 8.6 depicts overbought and oversold levels on the cycle-tuned bounded stochastic oscillator. Notice that the oversold levels coincided perfectly with bottoms in the Silver markets, as indicated by all of the up arrows. Note that although the stochastics and RSI have default values for the overbought and oversold levels, our example used the historically significant overbought and oversold levels, which were determined via visual inspection (in lieu of the conventional 80 and 20 percent OB and OS levels respectively).

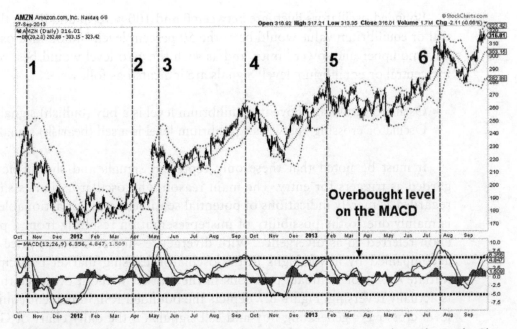

FIGURE 8.5 Overbought at Historically Significant MACD Levels on the Daily Chart of Amazon.com Inc.
Courtesy of Stockcharts.com

Equilibrium and Zero Line Crossovers

Another way a window oscillator can indicate buy or sell signals is via the crossing of the equilibrium value, which is represented by any of the following penetrations:

- Fifty percent level crossing in bounded oscillators
- Zero line crossing in unbounded oscillators

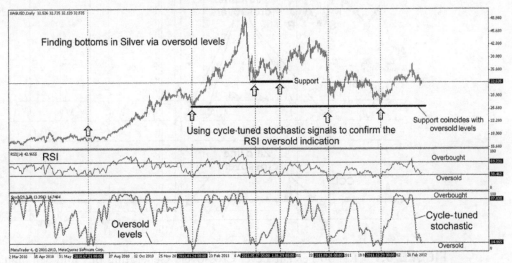

FIGURE 8.6 Oversold on the Stochastic Oscillator on the Daily Chart of Silver.
Source: MetaTrader 4

Bounded oscillators fluctuate between 0 and 100 percent and hence their central or equilibrium value would be at the 50 percent level. Unbounded oscillators have no upper and lower limits, and as such the zero level would best represent the central or equilibrium level. Signals are indicated as follows:

- Oscillator crossing above its equilibrium level is a buy (bullish) signal
- Oscillator crossing below its equilibrium level is a sell (bearish) signal

It must be noted that these only represent signals and should not be regarded as triggers for entry. The main reason why oscillator signals should be regarded as merely indications of potential sentiment and not actionable signals is mainly due to the possibility of misrepresentation resulting from a phenomenon referred to as divergence. With divergence, higher highs in price may be accompanied by lower highs in the oscillator, causing market participants to initiate shorts or liquidate positions in the market without evidence that price is actually reversing. Figure 8.7 depicts the bounded RSI 50 percent equilibrium level crossovers generating buy and sell signals on the daily chart of Goldman Sachs Group Inc. Notice that, using the defaulted lookback periods for the RSI and the commodity channel index (CCI), the buy and sell signals generated by both oscillators are nearly identical. The unbounded CCI generated signals via its zero level crossings.

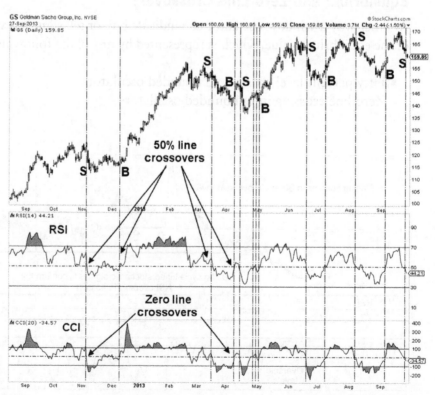

FIGURE 8.7 RSI 50 Percent Level Crossovers Generating Buy and Sell Signals on the Daily Chart of Goldman Sachs Group Inc.
Courtesy of Stockcharts.com

In fact, this coincidence of buy and sell signals by both oscillators in the chart example in Figure 8.7 above creates false consensus and may lead the trader into a false sense of confidence. Many oscillators will tend to give the same buy and sell signals because they are highly correlated, being constructed using the same underlying price data. This similarity between oscillators is referred to as multicollinearity. In this case, the RSI is collinear with respect to the CCI. To mitigate the adverse effects of multicollinearity, it is best to use oscillators that are derived from data other than price alone. For example, a combination of stochastics, Chaikin's money flow index (which incorporates volume), and some other sentiment or market-breadth oscillators like the McClellan Oscillator or Put/Call ratio will yield significantly less collinearity. Many novice traders make the mistake of putting on a combination of price-based momentum oscillators CCI, stochastics, ROC (rate of change), the MACD, and the MOM (momentum) oscillators all at the same time. This produces an uncanny agreement between all these oscillator signals in generating buy and sell signals which overwhelms the novice trader and leads him or her into a false sense of confidence, believing that this agreement represents a strong signal. In short, collinearity provides redundant information. In Figure 8.8, we observe the effects of multicollinearity across the RSI, MACD, and ROC, all of which are displaying similar divergences and crossover signals.

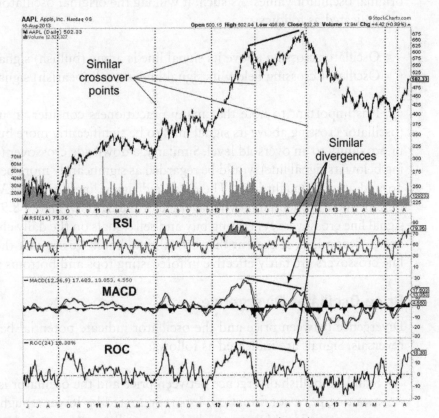

FIGURE 8.8 Multicollinearity on the Daily Chart of Apple Inc.
Courtesy of Stockcharts.com

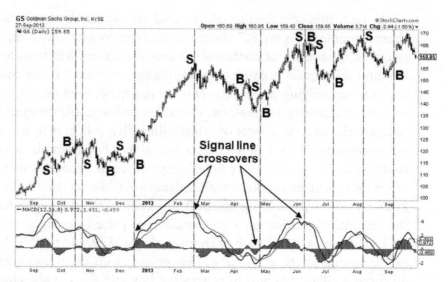

FIGURE 8.9 MACD Signal Line Crossovers Generating Buy and Sell Signals on the Daily Chart of Goldman Sachs Group Inc.
Courtesy of Stockcharts.com

Signal Line Crossovers

Buy and sell signals may also be generated via signal line crossovers. A signal line is a smoothed version of the original oscillator, that is, it is a moving average of the original oscillator values. As such, it will lag the original oscillator action. Signals are indicated as follows:

- Oscillator crossing above its signal line is a buy (bullish) signal
- Oscillator crossing below its signal line is a sell (bearish) signal

It is important to note that many practitioners consider an upside crossover (oscillator crossing above its signal line) to be significantly more bullish if it occurs in proximity to an oversold level. Similarly, a downside crossover (oscillator crossing below its signal line) would be regarded as significantly more bearish if it occurs around an overbought level. The defaulted signal line for the MACD is usually a nine-period exponential moving average of the MACD. Figure 8.9 depicts MACD signal line crossovers generating buy and sell signals on the daily chart of Goldman Sachs Group Inc., as seen at the vertical time lines. We see that the MACD signal line crossovers are fairly effective in forecasting tops and bottoms in the stock.

Price-Oscillator Divergence

Divergence between price and the oscillator indicate potential bearish or bullish reversals. Signals are indicated as follows:

- Standard bullish divergence between price and the oscillator is a bullish setup awaiting price confirmation. It is represented by lower troughs in price being accompanied by higher troughs in the oscillator. A potential upside reversal is expected.

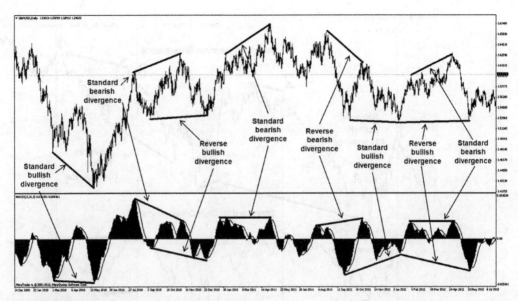

FIGURE 8.10 Bullish and Bearish Divergences Accurately Forecasting Reversal on the Daily Chart of GBPUSD.
Source: MetaTrader 4

- Standard bearish divergence between price and the oscillator is a bearish setup awaiting price confirmation. It is represented by higher peaks in price being accompanied by lower peaks in the oscillator. A potential downside reversal is expected.
- Reverse bullish divergence between price and the oscillator is a bullish setup awaiting price confirmation. It is represented by higher troughs in price being accompanied by lower troughs in the oscillator. A potential upside continuation is expected.
- Reverse bearish divergence between price and the oscillator is a bearish setup awaiting price confirmation. It is represented by lower peaks in price being accompanied by higher peaks in the oscillator. A potential downside continuation is expected.

(For George Lane's Bull and Bear setups, refer to Chapter 9.) In Figure 8.10, we observe bullish and bearish divergences forecasting potential reversals with uncanny accuracy on the daily GBPUSD chart. Please refer to Chapter 9 for more on divergence. Note that although divergence can also be indentified between oscillators, it is the divergence between price and an oscillator that is regarded as more pertinent.

Figure 8.11 displays various divergences between the S&P500 Large Cap Index and both the S&P Bullish Percent Index and the MACD. This is a good example of using oscillators based on price and market breadth as a means to mitigate the adverse effects of multicollinearity.

Geometrically Based Oscillator Pattern Analysis

Buy and sell signals may be derived from applying *geometrically* based overlay indicators to window oscillators. Overlays that are usually employed include:

- Trendlines
- Channels

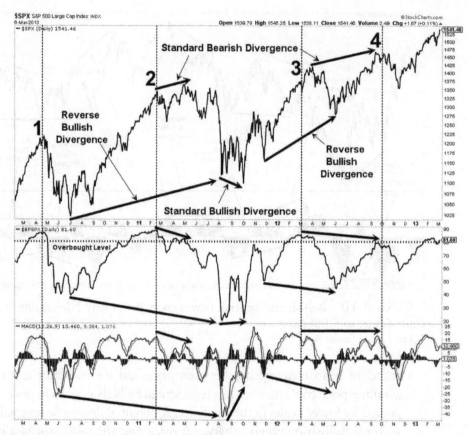

FIGURE 8.11 Price-Oscillator Divergences on the Daily Chart of the S&P500 Large Cap Index.
Courtesy of Stockcharts.com

- Chart Patterns
- Apex Reactions

Signals are indicated as follows:

- Oscillator breaching a geometrically based overlay to the *upside* is a buy (bullish) signal
- Oscillator testing a geometrically based overlay from below is a sell (bearish) signal
- Oscillator breaching a geometrically based overlay to the *downside* is a sell (bearish) signal
- Oscillator testing a geometrically based overlay from above is a buy (bullish) signal

See Figure 8.12. We see the geometrical overlays, on the momentum oscillator (MOM), generating buy and sell signals upon violation of trendlines and chart patterns on the 30-min chart of the Nikkei 225. We also see a projected channel bottom buy signal.

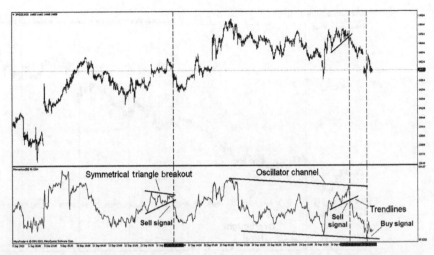

FIGURE 8.12 Oscillator Chart Pattern-Based Buy and Sell Signals on the 30-Min Chart of Nikkei 225.
Source: MetaTrader 4

Numerically Based Oscillator Pattern Analysis

Just as for geometrically based overlays, buy and sell signals may also be derived from applying *numerically* based overlay indicators to window oscillators. Overlays that are usually employed include:

- Bollinger Bands
- Moving Averages
- Moving Average Bands
- Fibonacci Levels
- Linear Regression Bands

Signals are indicated as follows:

- Oscillator breaching a numerically based overlay to the *upside* is a buy (bullish) signal
- Oscillator testing a numerically based overlay from below is a sell (bearish) signal
- Oscillator breaching a numerically based overlay to the *downside* is a sell (bearish) signal
- Oscillator testing a numerically based overlay from above is a buy (bullish) signal

See Figure 8.13. We observe that the RSI is finding support at the lower Bollinger band. Prices also bottomed every time the RSI found support at the lower band. Notice that the actual oversold was a fair distance below the Bollinger band oversold levels. This method effectively catches bottoms in a rapidly rising market, without requiring the RSI to decline all the way down to test the 30 percent oversold line.

249

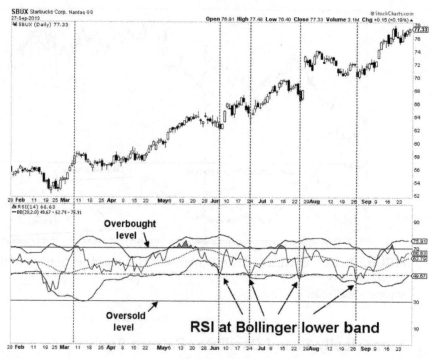

FIGURE 8.13   Oscillator Chart Pattern-Based Buy and Sell Signals on the Daily Chart of Starbucks Corp.
Courtesy of Stockcharts.com

Horizontally Based Oscillator Pattern Analysis

Buy and sell signals may also be derived from applying *horizontally* based overlay indicators to window oscillators. Hence, practitioners look for prior support and resistance in the oscillators for potential bullish and bearish indications. Signals are indicated as follows:

- Oscillator breaching a resistance level is a buy (bullish) signal
- Oscillator displaying resistance at a prior oscillator resistance level is a sell (bearish) signal
- Oscillator breaching a support level is a sell (bearish) signal
- Oscillator displaying support at a prior oscillator support level is a buy (bullish) signal

See Figure 8.14.

Oscillator-on-Oscillator Analysis

Buy and sell signals may also be derived from the interaction between window-based oscillators. We have already seen an example of indicator-on-oscillator analysis in Figure 8.13 where the RSI reacted at the upper and lower Bollinger bands. Similarly, oscillator-on-oscillator analysis may also render useful information.

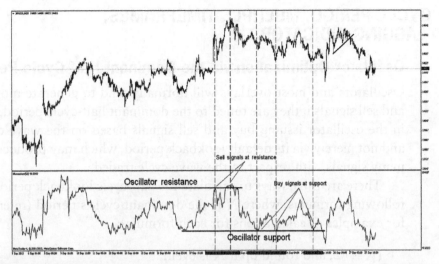

FIGURE 8.14 Oscillator Support- and Resistance-Based Buy and Sell Signals on the 30-Min Chart of Nikkei 225.
Source: MetaTrader 4

One such example is the Stochastic RSI, where the stochastic of RSI values are calculated and plotted as a window oscillator. Practitioners look for potential bullish and bearish indications via any of the previous seven approaches to analyzing an oscillator. In Figure 8.15, notice that the stochastic RSI pinpoints potential buying dips (indicated at the dotted time lines) in an uptrend on the daily chart of Apple Inc.

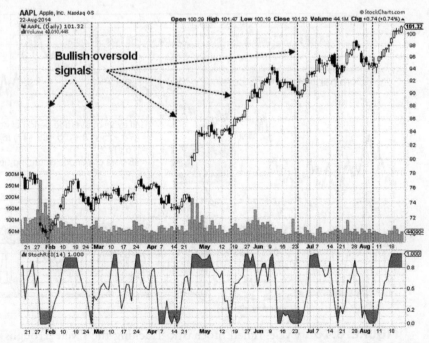

FIGURE 8.15 Oscillator-on-Oscillator Analysis on the Daily Chart of Apple Inc.
Courtesy of Stockcharts.com

8.3 CYCLE PERIOD, MULTIPLE TIMEFRAMES, AND LAGGING INDICATORS

Oscillator Optimization via the Dominant Half-Cycle Period

Oscillators and most overlays will normally tend to generate more effective buy and sell signals if they are tuned to the dominant half-cycle period. This will result in the oscillator issuing buy and sell signals based on the wave cycle of interest and not merely via its default lookback period, which may produce too few or too many signals with respect to the wave cycle traded.

There are three ways to calculate the half-cycle lookback period via any of the following formulas, where N is the dominant cycle's period (refer to Chapter 12 for examples of calculations for each formula):

- $(N+1)/2$, and round up if N is even;
- $(N/2) + 1$, and round down if N is odd; and
- $(2N+3)/4$, round to closest integer.

For example, assume that we are interested in using the stochastic to generate buy and sell signals. From Figure 8.16 we observe that the average dominant cycle period on the daily GBPUSD chart, from 2005 to 2007, was on average, 75 days (where a new cycle trough was formed at the same wave degree). The half cycle would then be, using the second formula above, $(75/2) + 1 = 38.5$ days. We round this down since N is odd (75), making the half cycle 38 days. We therefore tune our stochastic's lookback period to 38 periods. We see that it tracked and fore-casted the cycle troughs perfectly, including troughs during the period *after* the sample period was taken (out of sample data). Note that the standard 14-period

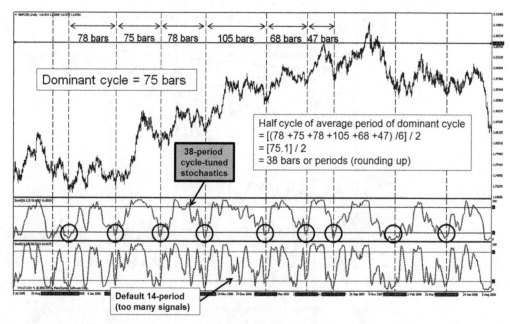

FIGURE 8.16 Cycle-Tuned Stochastic Tracking the Cycle Troughs Effectively on the Daily GBPUSD Chart.
Source: MetaTrader 4

default setting generated too many oversold signals as compared to the cycle-tuned oscillator.

Oscillator Analysis on Multiple Timeframes (MTF)

Oscillators and overlays of various timeframes may be plotted on the same chart for more effective comparison of oscillator action and its relationship to price action. Assume that we intend to set up a chart to display the 5-minute, 15-minute, and 1-hour RSI. We use a 5-minute interval chart as our basic chart. We first need to find the *multiplying factor* (MF) in order to calculate the lookback periods of the higher timeframe RSIs.

- MF (for a 15 mins interval chart) = 15 min/5 min = 3
- MF (for a 60 mins interval chart) = 60 min/5 min = 12

So, our 15-min RSI is obtained by multiplying the RSI standard default lookback period by 3, giving 14 × 3 = 42 periods. Therefore, a 42-period RSI on a 5-min chart will represent a 15-min RSI. Similarly, an hourly RSI is displayed on a 5-min chart if we increase its lookback period to 14 × 12 = 168 periods. For oscillators like the MACD, we need to increase all the variables via the MF. We use the same method to plot multiple timeframe moving averages and other overlays on charts. For example, to display an *hourly* 20-period moving average on a 5-min chart, we need to plot a 20 × 12 = 240 period moving average. This would represent a 20-period moving average as seen on the hourly chart. It should be noted that there will be very small discrepancies between an actual 20-period moving average on an hourly chart and a 240-period moving average on a 5-min chart, although they both essentially track the same average.

Lagging Indicators

Oscillators, being derived mainly from price, are usually lagging price action. But this does not mean that leading indications are not possible. Divergence is one form of oscillator analysis that is regarded as a leading indicator. Another example of leading indicators is the early reversals that tend to occur in momentum oscillators, normally reversing or slowing down before price. Horizontally and geometrically based overlays are also forms of leading indicators. Not all numerically based overlays are leading indicators. For example, Fibonacci projection, extension, expansion, and retracement are forms of leading indicators, but moving averages are not.

8.4 INPUT DATA

We may also create new oscillators from other oscillators. For example, if we replace price by RSI values for each period, we will create what is referred to as a StochRSI window oscillator. Let C be the current closing price, L_n be the lowest price of the last n periods, and H_n be the highest price of the last n periods. The raw %K is given by:

$$\%K = (C - L_n)/(H_n - L_n)$$

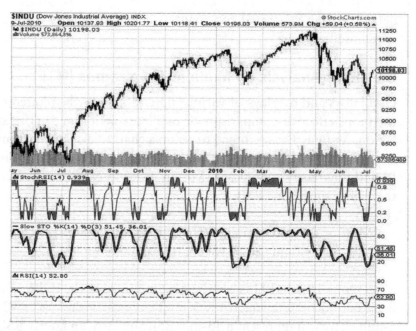

FIGURE 8.17 Creating the StochRSI from Normalizing the RSI.
Courtesy of Stockcharts.com

Replacing C with current RSI value RSI_C, L_n with the lowest RSI value of last n periods RSI_{Ln}, and H_n with the highest RSI value of last n periods RSI_{Hn}, we get:

$$Stoch\,RSI = moving\,average\,of\,(RSI_C - RSI_{Ln})/(RSI_{Hn} - RSI_{Ln})$$

The StochRSI is a bounded oscillator, due to the nature of the normalizing equation above. See Figure 8.17. It shows the stochastic, StochRSI, and RSI window oscillators, in descending order on the charts. The defaulted lookback period for the StochRSI is 14 bars. Notice that the StochRSI provides faster and more responsive signal action as compared to the original RSI.

Data Drop-Off Effect

The *drop-off effect* is fairly obvious when an oscillator or overlay drops off an old data point and substitutes it for a new one, preserving the length of the lookback period. Let us use a simple moving average to illustrate the effect. Assume that we create a seven-period simple moving average of the following prices:

$7, $4, $3, $3, $2, $4, $5

The average would be $28/7 = $4. Assume that we now move on to the next data point, dropping the last price of $7 and adding a new data point at $4:

$4, $3, $3, $2, $4, $5, $4

The new average will now be $3.57. The percentage change is ($4 – $3.75)/$4 × 100% = 10.75%. If we now replace the original last price of $7 with $9, the new percentage change will be [($30/7) − $3.57]/($30/7) × 100% = 16.72%. This illustrates that when dropping off large values and replacing them with smaller values, the average will account for this change by making sudden up and down moves, causing the moving average values to be more erratic. To reduce the impact of the drop-off effect, we could:

- Select longer lookback periods
- Use more front-weighted moving average based oscillators (e.g., exponential or linear weighting)

8.5 TREND TRADING USING OSCILLATORS

We may use oscillators to time continuations and breakouts in the direction of the existing trend. It is always best to trade in the direction of the larger existing trend. To do this effectively using oscillators, we look for the following signals to join and trade in the direction of the larger existing or predominant trend:

- In an existing uptrend, a buy signal is represented as:
  - Oscillator crossing above the equilibrium line
  - Oscillator crossing above its signal line
  - Oscillator is at oversold or rising back above oversold levels
  - Oscillator displaying bullish standard or reverse divergence with price
  - Oscillator violating a chart pattern or trendline to the upside
- In an existing downtrend, a sell signal is represented as:
  - Oscillator crossing below the equilibrium line
  - Oscillator crossing below its signal line
  - Oscillator is at overbought or declining back below overbought levels
  - Oscillator displaying bearish standard or reverse divergence with price
  - Oscillator violating a chart pattern or trendline to the downside

8.6 WINDOW OSCILLATORS

We shall now turn our attention to a few popular indicators, such as MOM, ROC, MACD, Stochastics, and so on. These oscillators are referred to as momentum oscillators since they track the underlying acceleration and deceleration of price action. Momentum tends to weaken and strengthen before price. It is this quality that makes such oscillators effective in forecasting potential trend changes.

Unfortunately, momentum oscillators are not very useful during a strong and prolonged up- or downtrend, as they tend to remain at overbought and oversold for long periods. During such periods, it would be better to use price overlay indicators such as support and resistance, trendlines, moving averages, channels, envelopes, and volatility bands to signal any potential trend change. The use of a trend change indicator such as the average directional index (ADX) may also prove useful in gauging the beginning and end of a trend.

Finally, it is always best to fully master the use and interpretation of one oscillator well instead of using multiple oscillators and not being entirely familiar with any of them. Each oscillator has its individual characteristics and it takes time to familiarize oneself with them. Nevertheless, the trader should understand that oscillators only generate trade signals, not trade triggers.

ROC (Tracking Momentum via the Ratio Method)

The rate of change oscillator (ROC) tracks the percent or ratio change in price over N periods. Note that some practitioners also use a smoothed version of the ROC for better visualization of price behavior, especially if there is significant volatility. Although the ROC usually uses closing prices, some practitioners also use typical price, midprice, and weighted close prices. The general ROC formula is:

$$ROC = (\text{Latest Price} - \text{Price } N \text{ periods back}) / \text{Price } N \text{ periods back}$$

If we multiply the ROC value above by 100 percent, we get the percentage representation of ratio change. As such, a $10 change from $1 and $90 will be displayed differently, for example:

$$(\$11 - \$1) / \$1 \times 100\% = 1000\%$$

$$(\$110 - \$100) / \$100 \times 100\% = 10\%$$

A $10 rise over 10 periods starting from $1 has a larger ROC value when compared to a $10 rise over 10 periods starting from $90. As such, assuming that prices rise $10 per every 10 periods, we would see the ROC flatten out as prices rise. This may induce the practitioner to believe that the uptrend is starting to weaken. When prices are flat or beginning to flat line, the ROC will decline to zero. For the ROC to remain flat, price needs to be rising at a steady rate. If ROC is rising, this indicates that price is accelerating, with respect to prices N periods ago.

As per any oscillator, the ROC may be analyzed for buy (bullish) and sell (bearish) signals using any of the eight forms of oscillator analysis described in a previous section. See Figure 8.18. We see the ROC remaining flat during a constant rate of ascent in price, as expected. We also see the ROC declining as prices start to range. Note that the zero line crossovers indicate buy and sell signals and the historically overbought levels, at Points 1 to 3, forecast tops and bottoms accurately on the daily chart of Goldman Sachs Group Inc. Notice how the ROC momentum oscillator *reverses before price* at Points 1 to 3. This is the most important and useful characteristic of momentum oscillators.

MOM (Tracking Momentum via the Difference Method)

Momentum can also be tracked using the *difference* method. Instead of calculating the ratio as in an ROC oscillator, the MOM tracks the price difference over the last N periods. Although the MOM usually uses closing prices, some practitioners also use typical price, midprice, and weighted close prices. The general MOM formula is:

$$MOM = \text{Latest Price} - \text{Price } N \text{ periods back}$$

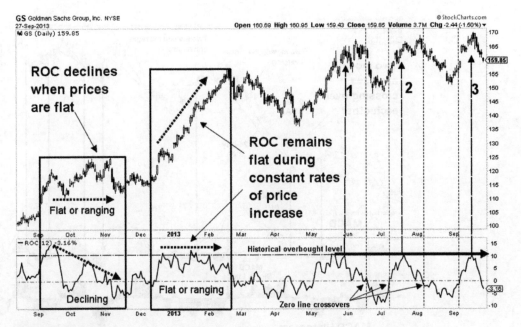

FIGURE 8.18 ROC Action of the Daily Chart of Goldman Sachs Group Inc.
Courtesy of Stockcharts.com

The MOM oscillator does not exhibit the non-linearity experienced by ROC oscillators. When prices are flat or beginning to flat line, the MOM will decline to zero. For the MOM to remain flat, price needs to be rising at a steady rate. If MOM is rising, this indicates that price is accelerating, with respect to prices N periods ago.

The MOM may be analyzed for buy (bullish) and sell (bearish) signals using any of the eight forms of oscillator analysis described in a previous section. In most ways, it is identical to ROC action.

MACD and MACD Histogram

Created by Gerald Appel, the MACD stands for moving average convergence divergence. The MACD is created by *detrending two moving averages* with each other and plotting the difference as a window oscillator. Detrending removes the trend component, leaving only the difference in values. In the case of the MACD, detrending is simply the subtraction of the values of the 26-period exponential moving average from the 12-period exponential moving average.

$$MACD == 12\text{-period EMA} - 26\text{-period EMA}$$

In Figure 8.16, we notice that every time the 12-day EMA tests or crosses the 26-day EMA, the MACD line tests the zero level (refer to the solid vertical arrows). This is because the difference between the two EMAs is zero. Whenever the two EMAs start to diverge, the MACD starts to move away from the zero line, and when they converge the MACD moves toward its zero level. If the 12-period EMA crosses above the 26-period EMA, the MACD rises above the zero level, and whenever the

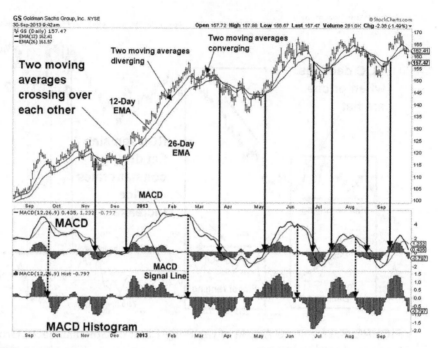

FIGURE 8.19   MACD Action of the Daily Chart of Goldman Sachs Group Inc.
Courtesy of Stockcharts.com

12-period EMA crosses below the 26-period EMA, the MACD falls below the zero level.

The MACD histogram is a double detrended oscillator. It is the difference between the MACD and its nine-period signal line. Again, as we can see from Figure 8.19, every time the MACD tests or crosses over its signal line, the histogram moves to its zero level (shown by dotted vertical arrows). The histogram tends to react faster than the MACD by reversing before it. *Detrending removes the lag from oscillators* and as such, double detrending creates an even more responsive oscillator.

The MACD and its histogram may be analyzed for buy (bullish) and sell (bearish) signals using any of the eight forms of oscillator analysis described in a previous section.

In Figure 8.20 we see historically overbought levels in the MACD signaling potential tops in the hourly USDJPY.

Average True Range (ATR)

Created by Welles Wilder, the average true range tracks the volatility associated with price activity. It does this by tracking the true range of each bar over a specified number of periods and finding the average of that value. True range is defined as the largest of the three following price ranges:

- The range of the current bar
- The difference between the previous close and the current high
- The difference between the previous close and the current low

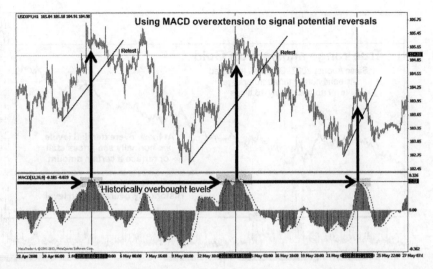

FIGURE 8.20 MACD Overbought Levels Signaling Potential Tops on the 4-Hour Chart of USDJPY.
Source: MetaTrader 4

ATR is a simple moving average of true range. It is used as a means of sizing a stoploss. Stopsizes are usually some multiple of ATR.

The ATR has the following characteristics:

- An increase in price volatility increases the value of the ATR
- Falling ATR values in an uptrend is a bearish indication
- Rising ATR values in an uptrend is a bullish indication
- Falling ATR values in an downtrend is a bullish indication
- Rising ATR values in an downtrend is a bearish indication
- High or extreme values of ATR usually accompany price peaks and troughs in the market

Figure 8.21 displays true range action on the daily chart of Gold. The lookback period is set to one period, indicating that we are observing true range rather than the average true range. We see true range signaling a correction in Gold every time it surpasses the historically overextended level.

The Stochastic Oscillator

Created by George Lane, the bounded stochastic oscillator tracks the relative position of the current price or latest close as a percentage of the price range over a specified number of periods, measured from the lowest low of the range. It is called the raw %K. See Figure 8.22. We see that the closing price is 83.3 percent of the range over a lookback period of one bar. The raw %K is usually defaulted to a lookback period of 14 bars. A 14-day lookback period was originally used to track the monthly commodity *half cycle*.

Let C be the closing price, L_n be the lowest low of the last n periods, and H_n be the highest high of the last n periods. There are two representations of the

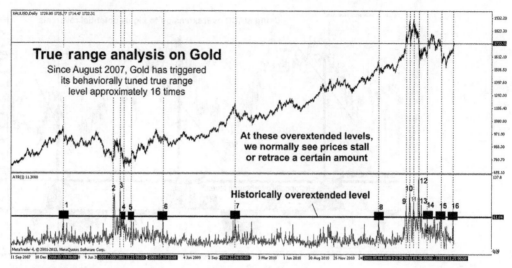

FIGURE 8.21 True Range Action of the Daily Chart of Gold.
Source: MetaTrader 4

stochastic oscillator, the fast and the slow. In each representation, there are two lines, one called the %K and its corresponding signal line called the %D. In the fast version of the stochastics we have the fast or raw %K and fast %D. The fast stochastic is calculated as follows:

$$\text{Fast or Raw }\%K = (C - L_n)/(H_n - L_n) \times 100\%$$

$$\text{Fast }\%D = 3\text{-period simple moving average of Raw }\%K$$

In the slow version of the stochastics we have the slow %K and slow %D. The slow stochastic is calculated as follows:

$$\text{Slow }\%K = 3\text{-period simple moving average of Raw }\%K$$

$$\text{Slow }\%D = 3\text{-period simple moving average of Slow }\%K$$

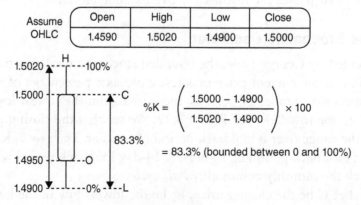

FIGURE 8.22 Percentage of Price Range.

The default lookback period for the fast or raw %K is 14 periods. If we smooth the %K by creating a simple 3-period moving average of it, we call this the fast %D. If we further create a 3-period simple moving average of fast %D, we get the slow %D.

In short, the fast %D line is a smoothed version of the raw %K line and the slow %D line is a *double smoothed* version of the raw %K line. The %D line is used to determine overbought and oversold levels, 50 percent level crossovers, divergence, and signal line crossovers. When using the raw %K, the fast %D represents its signal line, and when using the slow %K line, the slow %D becomes its signal line. As far as signal line crossovers are concerned:

- Whenever the fast %K line crosses above the fast %D signal line, it represents a buy (bullish) signal.
- Whenever the fast %K crosses below the slow %D (signal line), it represents a sell (bearish) signal.
- Whenever the slow %K crosses above the slow %D (signal line), it represents a buy (bullish) signal.
- Whenever the slow %K crosses below the slow %D (signal line), it represents a sell (bearish) signal.

The stochastic oscillator may be analyzed for buy (bullish) and sell (bearish) signals using any of the eight forms of oscillator analysis described in a previous section. Overbought and oversold levels are defaulted at 80 percent and 20 percent, respectively.

Figure 8.23 shows a cycle-tuned stochastic tracking the tops and bottoms in Silver with uncanny accuracy. Note that the *historical* overbought and oversold values were used instead of the standard 20 and 80 percent overextension levels. It is done via visual inspections and it is usually a better reflection of the behavior of market participants. We may say that when using historically

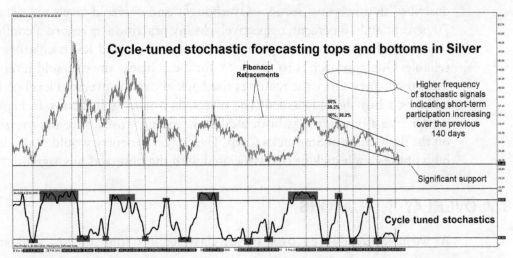

FIGURE 8.23 Cycle-Tuned Stochastic Tracking Tops and Bottoms Effectively on the Daily Silver Chart.
Source: MetaTrader 4

extreme levels that the stochastics overextension levels are *behaviorally tuned*. A higher frequency of alternation between overbought and oversold signals is also an indication of potentially greater short term participation in the markets. Note that Silver reversed at the Fibonacci retracement levels while the oscillator was at overbought.

It should be noted that the %K formula represent a normalizing process. It is in fact identical to the RSI normalizing process. To normalize data means to bind it with a range of values, with an upper and lower limit. One disadvantage of normalization in the stochastic oscillator is that it tends produce erratic swings between the overbought and oversold levels especially when the price range associated with the %K lookback period is very narrow.

Relative Strength Index (RSI)

Created by Welles Wilder, the RSI tracks the stock's underlying strength in terms of its average gain and loss of over the last n periods. Let the average gains over the last n periods be G and the average loss over the last n periods be L. Relative strength, RS, is defined as RS = $|G/L|$.

$$RSI = 100 - [100/(1 + G/L)]$$

$$\text{Re-arranging, we get, } RSI = 100 \times (G/(G + L))$$

This is similar to the stochastic normalization process where the maximum value in the numerator will always be equal to or less than the value in the denominator. Welles Wilder used a 14-period lookback and smoothed the RSI data using the Wilder's averaging, which is a form of exponential moving average. The RSI is less volatile than the stochastic action and may be a good replacement for the stochastic in volatile markets. The RSI oscillator may be analyzed for buy (bullish) and sell (bearish) signals using any of the eight forms of oscillator analysis described in a previous section. Overbought and oversold levels are defaulted at 70 percent and 30 percent, respectively. Many practitioners regard a confluence of buy and sell signals occurring on both the stochastic and RSI oscillators as more reliable. One approach is to first look for a dip below the oversold level on both these oscillators. Once the readings rise back above the oversold level on both oscillators, a buy signal is issued. The reverse is true for sell signals. In Figure 8.24, we observe a buy signal as both oscillator readings rose above the oversold level on the daily chart of Starbucks Corp. The trigger for entry would normally be the high of the candlestick or bar associated with the observed buy signal.

8.7 OVERLAY INDICATORS

As we have already seen, overlays are classified into four categories, namely:

- Numerically based overlays
- Geometrically based overlays

FIGURE 8.24 Buy Signal and Trigger on the Daily Chart of Goldman Sachs Group Inc.
Courtesy of Stockcharts.com

- Horizontally based overlays
- Algorithmically based overlays

Price interacts with these overlays, finding support and resistance. The best forms of support and resistance are resistive and supportive clusters or confluences. A concentration of bullish and bearish indicators within a narrow price range will normally result in a strong price barrier.

We have covered most of these overlays in other sections of this handbook, so we will not repeat them here. We shall instead now turn our attention to Floor Trader's Pivot Points.

What Are Floor Trader's Pivot Points?

The Floor Trader's Pivot Points is a trend-following and volatility indicator. It is a numerically based overlay. Depending on the range of the previous day, it will project various levels of resistance (R1, R2, R3, etc.) and support (S1, S2, S3, etc.) for the next day. It also projects a pivot point level, PP, around which the day's action unfolds.

To construct these pivot points, first find the previous day's typical price. This represents the next day's pivot level, PP. To construct the first pivot support level, we project the difference between the previous day's high and PP downward from the PP price. Similarly to construct the first pivot resistance level, we project the

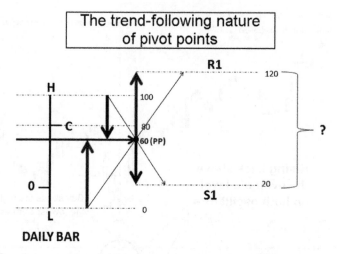

FIGURE 8.25 Constructing the First Pivot Resistance and Support Level.

difference between the previous day's low and PP upward from the PP price. See Figure 8.25. We can clearly see why it is called the *pivot* point. It is around this PP that the previous day's volatility is incorporated into the next day's projections. If the previous day was volatile, it would tend to create a larger range. This will affect the next day's projection levels. Note that if the previous day's close was above its midprice, the new projected levels would all be raised the next day. Hence, it is essentially a trend-following overlay indicator

To construct the second pivot support level, we subtract the previous day's range from the PP, and to construct the second pivot resistance level we add the previous day's range to the PP. See Figure 8.26. We see that by adding yesterday's range, we are incorporating yesterday's volatility into the current day's projections. Hence, it is essentially an indicator of potential future volatility.

To construct the third pivot support level, we subtract the previous day's range from the first support level, and to construct the third pivot resistance level we

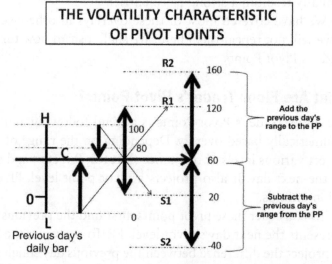

FIGURE 8.26 Constructing the Second Pivot Resistance and Support Levels.

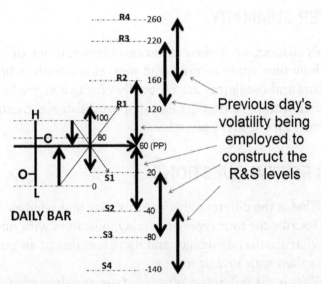

FIGURE 8.27 Constructing the Third and Fourth Pivot Resistance and Support Levels.

add the previous day's range to the first resistance level. And in similar fashion, the fourth support level is constructed by subtracting the previous day's range from the second support level, and to construct the fourth resistance level we add the previous day's range to the second resistance level. See Figure 8.27.

A popular way to gauge the day's action is to identify if price has opened below or above the PP. If it has opened below the PP, the current day's prices are expected to drift lower, and if it has opened above the PP, the current day's prices are expected to drift higher.

The violation of the second support or resistance levels indicate a strong downtrend or uptrend is in effect, while the third resistance and support levels represent extreme overbought and oversold levels, respectively. If the day is quiet and non-eventful, prices should stay within the first pivot support and resistance levels. See Figure 8.28 for price interacting with these pivot point levels. Besides using pivot point levels for initiating entries, many practitioners use the levels as a basis of exiting a position.

FIGURE 8.28 Price Reacting to Pivot Points on the Daily Chart of Goldman Sachs Group Inc.
Courtesy of Stockcharts.com

265

8.8 CHAPTER SUMMARY

In this chapter, we looked at various classifications of indicators and oscillators and how they apply to price and market action. It is important to note that indicators and oscillators are especially effective in predicting reversals when they coincide with price barriers like support/resistance, trend lines, channel boundaries, and Floor Trader's pivot levels.

CHAPTER 8 REVIEW QUESTIONS

1. What is the difference between overlay and window oscillators?
2. Describe the four types of overlay indicators with one example of each type.
3. What are the advantages and disadvantages of an unbounded oscillator?
4. Explain scale invariance.
5. What is the difference between static and dynamic overlay indicators?
6. What are the eight ways to analyze an oscillator?
7. Explain how to set up the hourly and 4-hour MACD on a 15-min chart.
8. What are the differences between the ROC and MOM momentum oscillators?

REFERENCES

Archelis, Steven B. 2001. *Technical Analysis from A to Z*. New York: McGraw-Hill.

Colby, Robert W. 2003. *The Encyclopedia of Technical Market Indicators*. New York: McGraw-Hill.

CHAPTER 9

Divergence Analysis

LEARNING OBJECTIVES

Upon completing this chapter, you should be able to:

- Understand the narrow and the broader meanings and interpretation of divergence and convergence
- Employ the concept of confirmation to categorize divergence
- Differentiate between standard, reverse, bullish, and bearish divergence
- Recognize and forecast divergent signal alternation between standard and reverse divergence
- Distinguish between George Lane's Setups and contemporary reverse divergence
- Appreciate the directional implications of divergence in terms of wave degrees, cycles, and trend referencing
- Apply divergence analysis to the market via an integrated approach

---

Divergence, when used in conjunction with other indicators, offers one of the most effective ways of forecasting potential reversals and continuations in price and market action. It may be derived from a variety of sources and technical data. Divergence can also be found on all wave degrees and timeframes. It is particularly useful when identified between non-correlated data series. One of the earliest and possibly the most significant application of divergence can be found in development of Dow Theory, where divergence between the Dow Industrials and Transportation Averages is commonly regarded as an important barometer of potential future market action. We will also attempt to bring some definitional clarity and coherence to terms such as standard and reverse divergence, direction, confirmation, continuation, and reversals with respect to divergence analysis.

9.1 DEFINITION OF DIVERGENCE

Generally speaking, *divergence* occurs when two data or time series exhibit motion in *opposing* directions. But as will be shown shortly, this is *not* always the case.

9.1.1 Main and Supporting Data Series

When trying to determine if divergence exists, we compare the *main* data series to its *supporting* data series. The main data series may have one or more supporting data series. In technical analysis, the main data series is usually *price* itself while the supporting data series comprises various *oscillators* and *indicators*.

Nevertheless, both the main and supporting data series may be comprised of any of the following, and are by no means limited to the following list:

- Price
- Oscillators
- Overlay indicators
- Volume
- Open interest
- Market breadth indicators
- Sentiment indicators
- Relative strength chart

In order to accurately and sensibly define divergence and convergence, we must first clarify what is meant by *opposing* directions.

9.1.2 Defining Direction in Divergence Analysis

Motion can only take place in three possible directions, namely *up, down,* or *sideways.* Some practitioners contend that sideways motion does not constitute a true trend. Nevertheless, for the purpose of defining divergence, this contention does not invalidate or detract from the analysis.

> **NOTE**
>
> Moving in opposing directions is defined as one data series moving in *two out of three possible directions* while the other data series is moving in the *remaining direction.*

This gives rise to *six* possible combinations for moving in opposing directions:

1. One data series is up while the other is sideways
2. One data series is up while the other is down
3. One data series is sideways while the other is up
4. One data series is sideways while the other is down

5. One data series is down while the other is up
6. One data series is down while the other is sideways

The following *three* combinations are regarded as moving in the *same general direction*:

1. Both data series are moving up
2. Both data series are moving sideways
3. Both data series are moving down

9.1.3 Determining Direction in Divergence Analysis

When trying to ascertain whether a data series is moving up or down, we examine the:

- *Sequence of peaks and troughs* (or swing highs and swing lows, respectively) to identify the direction of the data series over a specified number of cycles or oscillations
- *Slope (or angle) between two data points* to identify the direction of the data series over a specified range or duration of data (especially in the absence of visible peaks and troughs)

It must be noted that in order to determine direction by comparing peaks and troughs, the formation of the subsequent peak or trough must first be firmly established. A peak or trough is usually defined and established via the application of some kind of filter. As seen in an earlier chapter, the establishment of peaks or troughs is strictly based on price filtering. *Time-based filters are not applicable, as a certain amount of price excursion is required to establish a new peak or trough.* It is interesting to note that some practitioners also resort to using regression lines in order to establish the direction of the data series, in the hope of achieving greater consistency when analyzing divergence. But it will be shown that such an approach will only lend itself to standard and not reverse divergence analysis.

Before proceeding any further, it should be stressed that establishing direction in divergence analysis differs slightly from that of conventional trend analysis, having basically four ways to establish direction. Generally speaking, the determination of direction depends exclusively on the definition being employed; for example, an uptrend may be defined as a series of higher peaks and troughs, while a downtrend may be depicted as successively lower peaks and troughs. Notice that both *peaks and troughs* must be moving in the same direction in order to be deemed a trend. However, in divergence analysis, as will be described shortly, it suffices that the direction of the current larger trend may also be determined solely by comparing adjacent *peaks or troughs*. Note that this unique definition of direction is only applied when attempting to determine the direction of the current larger trend across a *single oscillation* at the lower wave degree and is never used to determine the direction of the prior or subsequent larger trend, both of which are defined via the conventional approach to trend analysis. Therefore directional discrepancy between the data series at the current larger trend may be based on a very specific definition, as opposed to the conventional definition of trend analysis.

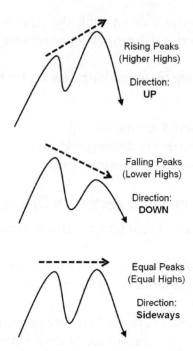

FIGURE 9.1 Defining Direction Using Adjacent Peaks (Highs).

An example may help illustrate this point. See Figure 9.1. In the process of trying to gauge direction using adjacent peak to peak analysis, we need to determine if the *subsequent peak* is higher, lower, or flat with respect to the previous peak.

Similarly, when comparing adjacent troughs to establish direction, we must determine if the *subsequent trough* is higher, lower, or flat with respect to the previous trough, as depicted in Figure 9.2.

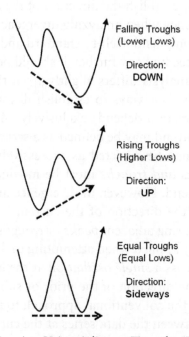

FIGURE 9.2 Defining Direction Using Adjacent Troughs (Lows).

This unique approach for determining direction is only employed at the point of non-confirmation and nowhere else. This definition of trend or direction may also seem somewhat lacking or unusual when compared to the usual strict requirement for both higher peaks and troughs in an uptrend and similarly for both lower peaks and troughs in a downtrend. One way to resolve this disparity is to imagine a trendline connecting the adjacent peaks or troughs. Once we do this, we realize that we are in fact defining trend in the same way that a trendline does, by employing just two points.

It would therefore be particularly useful at this point to subclassify direction or trend analysis in the following manner, as it relates specifically to divergence analysis:

- *Multiple Peak and Trough Analysis* is used to define and analyze uptrends and downtrends across *multiple* peaks and troughs, where an uptrend may be defined as successively higher peaks and troughs and a downtrend as successively lower peaks and troughs. In divergence analysis, this conventional approach to analyzing trends may be used to establish the direction of the prior, current, and subsequent larger trend.
- *Slope Analysis* is used to define and analyze uptrends and downtrends (a) when peaks and troughs are not clearly visible or accessible, and (b) when multiple peaks and troughs are visible but are observed as a slope at a higher wave degree. In divergence analysis, slope analysis may be used to establish the direction of the prior, current, and subsequent larger trend. When slope analysis is used, only standard divergence analysis applies. Reverse divergence is excluded from the analysis and is not accounted for, as its use would lead to definitional ambiguity. Slope analysis is also applied to trendlines or regression lines.
- *Adjacent Peak to Peak Analysis* is used to define direction between two *adjacent* peaks, representative of the market rising and falling across a single cycle on the lower wave degree. In divergence analysis, it may be used to establish the direction of the current larger trend. This kind of analysis should not be employed to determine the direction of general trends, which includes the prior and subsequent larger trends (unless reducible to two peaks at a higher wave degree).
- *Adjacent Trough to Trough Analysis* is used to define direction between two *adjacent* troughs, representative of the market rising and falling across a single cycle at the lower wave degree. In divergence analysis, it may be used to establish the direction of the current larger trend, but it should not be employed to determine the direction of general trends, which includes the prior and subsequent larger trends (unless reducible to two troughs at a higher wave degree).

It is imperative to be aware that, when comparing adjacent peaks between two data series, there are nine possible combinations that encompass motion in all possible directions of the current larger trend, six for moving in opposing directions, and three for moving in the same general direction. The total number of combinations expands to 18 when we also start to compare successive troughs in order

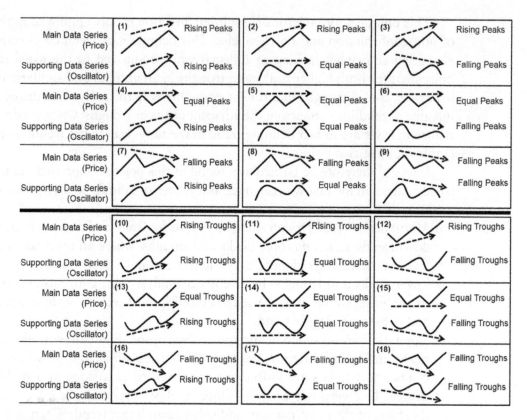

FIGURE 9.3 Defining Direction of the Current Larger Trend.

to determine direction of the current larger trend. See Figure 9.3. Boxes (1) to (9) are based on adjacent peak to peak analysis and boxes (10) to (18) are based on adjacent trough to trough analysis. Boxes (1), (5), (9), (10), (14), and (18) depict both data series moving in the same direction, lacking directional properties called *divergence* and *convergence*.

As mentioned earlier, when peaks and troughs are not available or visually accessible to determine direction, we simply refer to the angle or slope between two data points. In such cases, the existing 12 combinations that depict motion in opposing directions between the two data series collapse back to six. But in order to identify which of the six combinations indicate bullishness or bearishness in the main data series, we first need to understand the concept of divergence.

9.2 GENERAL CONCEPT OF DIVERGENCE

The term *divergence* is a constant cause of confusion in technical analysis, especially to the uninitiated. This is further exacerbated when practitioners occasionally employ the term *convergence* to imply divergence and vice versa. We shall now attempt to resolve these inconsistencies in the usage of the terms divergence and convergence by first introducing another important concept in technical analysis called *confirmation*.

9.2.1 Concept of Confirmation in Divergence Analysis

The terms *confirmation*, *non-confirmation*, and *price confirmation* are used in very specific ways when dealing with divergence:

- *Confirmation* and *Non-Confirmation* are used to describe whether the main and its supporting data series are in directional agreement with each other or otherwise, respectively.
- *Price confirmation* (applicable and relevant only to the main data series) relates to some qualifying action in price that subsequently establishes or confirms the validity of an initial bullish or bearish divergent setup, by way of penetration of some price barrier.

> **NOTE**
>
> Confirmation exists when the main and supporting data series are *in agreement* with each other *at the same wave degree.*

Being in agreement:

- Means that the successive peaks and troughs in the supporting data series are moving in the same general direction with the peaks and troughs in the main data series at the same wave degree
- Implies a continuation of the current larger trend (i.e., current trend at the next higher wave degree to the oscillations that formed the peaks and troughs).

Agreement may also be represented by the slopes of the data series pointing in the same general direction, that is, either up or down, especially when peak and trough analysis is not available or possible. The oscillators and indicators in the supporting data series indicate the potential for further price extension or momentum in the direction of the current larger trend or direction of motion. See Figure 9.4 for confirmation via adjacent peak to peak and trough to trough analysis.

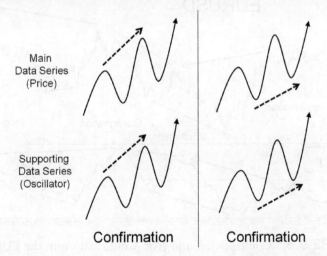

FIGURE 9.4 Confirmation via Adjacent Peak to Peak (Left) and Trough to Trough (Right) Analysis Indicating Agreement between Price and Oscillator.

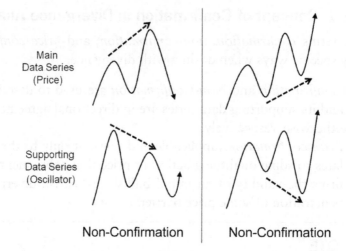

FIGURE 9.5 Non-Confirmation via Adjacent Peak to Peak (Left) and Trough to Trough (Right) Analysis Indicating Disagreement between Price and Oscillator.

Non-confirmation occurs when the main and supporting data series are *in disagreement* with each other. This means that the peaks and troughs in the supporting data series are not moving in the same general direction with the peaks and troughs in the main data series, implying a potential reversal or weakening of the current larger trend. The oscillators indicate a possible decrease in price momentum. Non-confirmation is considered potentially more reliable if it is supported or corroborated by at least three weakly or non-correlated supporting data series. See Figure 9.5 for non-confirmation via single peak to peak and trough to trough analysis.

Figure 9.6 is a chart of the EURUSD foreign exchange pair. We see confirmation and non-confirmation at various points on the chart, from both adjacent peak to peak as well as trough to trough analysis.

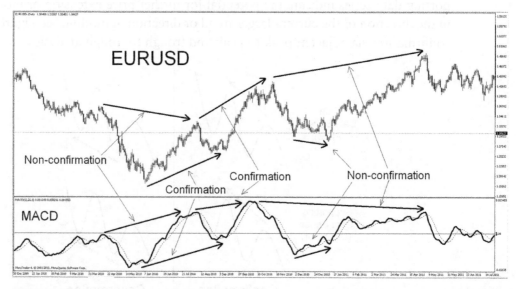

FIGURE 9.6 Confirmation and Non-Confirmation in the EURUSD via Adjacent Peak to Peak and Trough to Trough Analysis.
Source: MetaTrader 4

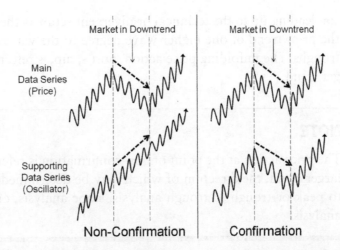

FIGURE 9.7 Non-Confirmation and Confirmation via Conventional Trend or Multiple Peak and Trough Analysis Indicating Disagreement and Agreement between Price and Oscillator.

Confirmation and non-confirmation may also be depicted as agreement and disagreement between general trends in the data series, that is, across *multiple* peaks and troughs, which represent conventional trend analysis. See Figure 9.7 for confirmation and non-confirmation, based on multiple peak and trough analysis. (Non-confirmation here may also be referred to as slope divergence, since the slopes of the two data trends are in opposition with each other.)

Figure 9.8 illustrates confirmation and non-confirmation using slope analysis, since the peaks and troughs are not clearly visible on the chart. Slopes pointing in the same general direction indicate confirmation.

9.2.2 Trend Referencing in Divergence Analysis: The Prior, Current, and Subsequent Trends

Non-confirmation may potentially result in either a continuation or reversal in price, depending on the type of divergence involved. It is useful to refer to price

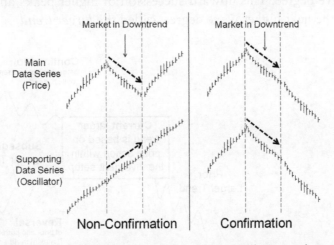

FIGURE 9.8 Non-Confirmation and Confirmation via Slope Analysis Indicating Disagreement and Agreement between Price and Oscillator.

275

action leading up to the technical or divergent setup as the *prior larger trend*, that is, the prior trend of one higher wave degree to the waves that formed the peaks or troughs. The unfolding price action, post setup, is referred to as the *subsequent* larger trend.

> **NOTE**
>
> The price action at the point of non-confirmation is referred to as the current larger trend, the direction of which may be determined using adjacent peak to peak or trough to trough analysis, slope analysis, or conventional trend analysis.

The current larger trend may either be a continuation or reversal of the prior trend. Similarly, the subsequent larger trend may be a continuation or reversal of the current or prior larger trend. See Figure 9.9.

We refer to the prior and subsequent trend of progressively higher or lower peaks and troughs as the larger trend, or trend at the next higher wave degree. The establishment of divergence is normally based on the sequence of peaks and troughs at one higher wave degree than the oscillations that created it at the point of non-confirmation. Hence, when comparing the peaks and troughs between the main and supporting data series, both divergence and convergence must be observed at the appropriate or *corresponding* wave degree in order to remain analytically consistent. The term *corresponding* refers to price action at the same wave degree. *It is impossible to determine and interpret confirmation and non-confirmation correctly without the ability to recognize and distinguish between wave degrees.*

9.2.3 Wave Degrees in Divergence Analysis

In Figure 9.10, we see price moving up and down, that is, oscillating at a lower wave degree. This upward succession of higher peaks and troughs forms a trend at the next higher wave degree, called the *larger trend*.

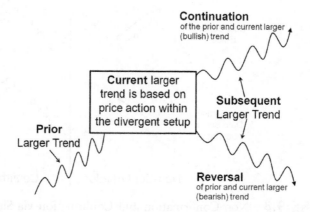

FIGURE 9.9 Trend Referencing Pre and Post Technical Setup/Signal.

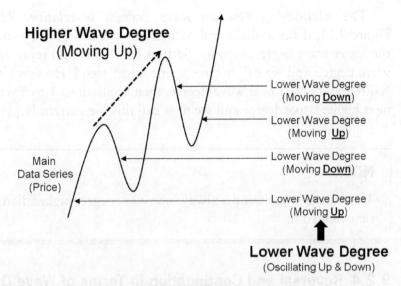

FIGURE 9.10 Cycles at a Lower Wave Degree Forming a Larger Trend.

Figure 9.11 illustrates wave cycles or oscillations at three different wave degrees. We observe price rising simultaneously on all three wave degrees, namely at the:

1. Lower wave degree between points P and Q, R and S, and so on
2. Next or first higher wave degree between I and II, III and IV, V and VI, and so on
3. Second higher wave degree between 1 and 2

It is obvious that peaks II and IV are formed from the oscillatory action at the lower wave degree between points G and Y, indicating a rise at a higher wave degree. As we shall see later, it is important to identify the wave degree that we are trying to establish as confirmation or non-confirmation, in order to tell whether the subsequent price action is a continuation or reversal of a trend at the first or second higher wave degree.

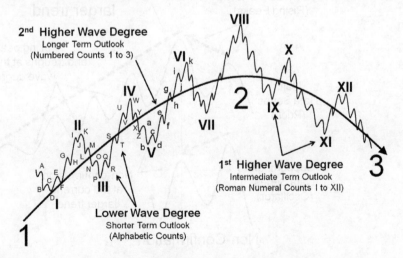

FIGURE 9.11 Trends at Various Wave Degrees.

The relationship between wave degrees is *relative*. Referring again to Figure 9.11, if the alphabetical oscillations (A, B, C, . . . , a, b, c, etc.) represent the lower wave degree, then oscillations I to XII would represent the next higher wave degree and we call it the current larger trend. However, if oscillations I to XII represent the lower wave degree, then oscillations 1 to 3 would represent the next higher wave degree and we now call this the current larger trend.

> **NOTE**
>
> The current larger trend is always one wave degree higher than the oscillations that created it.

9.2.4 Reversal and Continuation in Terms of Wave Degrees

Before we delve further into the topic of divergence per se, let us first refer to a couple of examples to better understand the meaning of *reversal* and *continuation* with respect to wave degrees in a trend. This is a critical step in understanding how standard and reverse divergence is subsequently defined. In Figure 9.12, we see higher peaks in price accompanied by lower peaks in the supporting data series giving rise to non-confirmation based on adjacent peak to peak analysis. Price subsequently makes successive lower peaks and troughs. We say that there is a reversal of the current larger trend, or trend at the next higher wave degree. As will be explained later, standard divergence indicates a potential reversal in the current larger trend. The case for reverse divergence is a little more complicated.

Referring to Figure 9.13, we observe an upside reversal of the current larger trend, with higher peaks and troughs in the EURUSD.

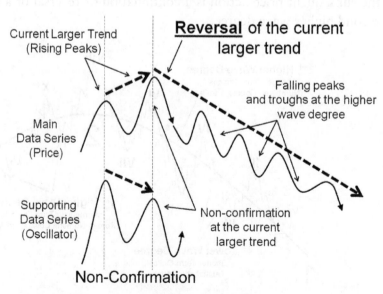

FIGURE 9.12 Reversal of the Current Larger Trend.

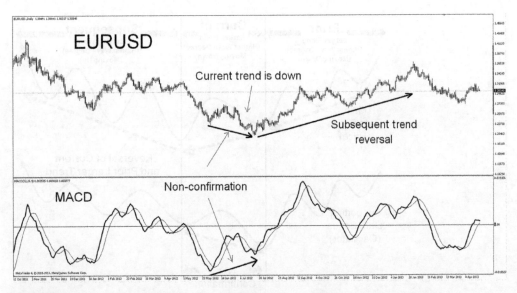

FIGURE 9.13 Subsequent Reversal of the Current Larger Trend (EURUSD).
Source: MetaTrader 4

In Figure 9.14, lower peaks in price are accompanied by higher peaks in the supporting data series giving rise to non-confirmation at the current larger trend based on adjacent trough to trough analysis. Price continues to make successive lower peaks and troughs. We say that there is a continuation of the current larger trend. As will be explained later, reverse divergence implies a potential continuation in price, which we now understand to mean a continuation at the next higher wave degree, or of the current larger trend.

We shall now observe the progression of the three main trends around a divergent setup. In Figure 9.15, the prior larger downtrend was followed by non-confirmation. Using adjacent trough to trough analysis, we see the current larger trend depicting a falling market, which subsequently reversed to the upside. Hence the subsequent larger trend is a reversal of both the current and prior larger trends.

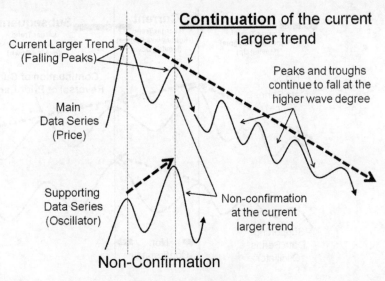

FIGURE 9.14 Continuation of the Current Larger Trend.

279

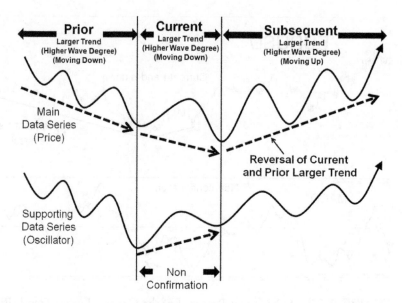

FIGURE 9.15 Reversals Based on Adjacent Trough to Trough Analysis.

It should be noted that the directions of the prior and subsequent larger trends are wholly determined using conventional peak and trough analysis (and in the absence of visible peaks and troughs, slope analysis is applied). In Figure 9.16, the subsequent larger trend represents a continuation of the current larger trend and a reversal of the prior larger trend.

9.2.5 Continuation and Reversal Indications Independent of Price Direction

As we have already seen, confirmation and non-confirmation depend on whether there is any directional agreement between the data series or otherwise, where confirmation suggests a potential continuation of the current larger trend.

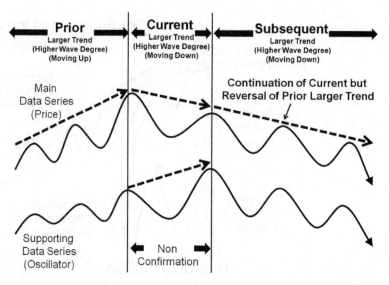

FIGURE 9.16 Reversals and Continuation Based on Adjacent Peak to Peak Analysis.

However, it must be noted that some indicators and oscillators in the supporting data series may indicate potential continuation and reversal irrespective of the direction of price. They also do not require disagreement with price for non-confirmation or agreement for confirmation. Some examples of these oscillators and indicators include volume bar action, moving average of volume, open interest, and average true range, where rising peaks and troughs (and slopes) indicate confirmation, whereas falling peaks and troughs (and slopes) indicate non-confirmation, regardless of the direction of price in the main data series. Only the direction of the supporting data series is relevant and it is the only determining factor of the potential strength or weakness underlying the trend. But to determine bullishness or bearishness, the direction of price is still required.

9.2.6 Narrow Interpretation of Divergence and Convergence

Whenever the corresponding peaks or troughs between the main and supporting data series are moving toward each other, we say that the two data series are *converging* on each other. Notice that during convergence, the main and supporting data series are moving in opposite directions, as defined in section 9.1.3, and hence there is non-confirmation. The illustrations in boxes (4), (7), (8), (13), (16), and (17) in Figure 9.3 display convergence.

Alternatively, whenever the corresponding peaks or troughs between the main and supporting data series are moving away from each other, we say that the two data series are *diverging* from each other. Referring to Figure 9.3, illustrations in boxes (2), (3), (6), (11), (12), and (15) display divergence. Notice that during divergence, as in convergence, the main and supporting data series are moving in opposing directions indicating non-confirmation. Therefore we say that both convergence and divergence exhibit *directional discrepancy*.

Convergence and divergence have bullish and bearish indications. Convergence of corresponding peaks or troughs between the data series is normally considered bullish, whereas its divergence is regarded as bearish. This is mainly attributed to the fact that the direction of the oscillators in the supporting data series is usually regarded as a prognostication of future price action. Consequently, rising peaks or troughs in the supporting data series are an indication of potential strength, and further upside in price is expected *regardless* of whether there is non-confirmation or otherwise. Similarly, falling peaks or troughs in the supporting data series are an indication of potential weakness, and further downside in price is therefore expected.

One question arises, however, when referring to scenarios depicted in boxes (5) and (14) in Figure 9.3, where no successively higher or lower peaks and troughs are observed, essentially depicting price traversing sideways. Since divergence or convergence is nonexistent in both scenarios, does that imply confirmation? As discussed earlier, confirmation must also indicate a potential for further price extension or momentum in the direction of the current larger trend. We observe no divergent or convergent behavior associated with the scenarios

281

depicted in boxes (5) and (14), and the oscillators in the supporting data series do not appear to indicate any further price extension or momentum in the direction of the current larger trend. Hence, the term confirmation is *undefined* in sideways formations and is best reserved for situations where a clear and obvious trend is in effect.

9.2.7 Broad Interpretation of Divergence

It is customary to use the term divergence in a broader sense to describe *any* disagreement or non-confirmation between the main and supporting data series. Herein lies the confusion.

NOTE

Under the broad interpretation, any and all non-confirmation is regarded as divergent and this therefore also includes any data series that are convergent on each other. As such, divergence is a consequence of both the main and supporting data series moving toward or away from each other.

Under this wider definition, all combinations depicted in Figure 9.3 are now categorized as divergent, with the exception of six combinations: four of which have no disagreement, namely (1), (9), (10), and (18), and the remaining two being undefined, that is, (5) and (14).

9.2.8 Convergence and Divergence under the Broad Interpretation of Divergence

As will be shown later, a convergence of troughs and a divergence of peaks would, under this broader interpretation, be referred to as standard bullish and standard bearish divergence, respectively. The situation is a little more complicated for reverse divergence, depending on whether the reverse divergence is predicated on George Lane's bull and bear setups, or on the newer school of thought where reverse divergences are expected to represent a pure continuation of the current larger trend. Nevertheless, regardless of whichever it is based on, reverse divergence will, in the initial stage, still represent a continuation of the current larger trend under both approaches. With this in mind, a convergence of peaks and a divergence of troughs would, under this broader interpretation, be referred to as reverse bearish and reverse bullish divergence, respectively.

9.2.9 Directionally and Non-Directionally Aligned Slope Divergence and Convergence

Divergence and convergence may also be categorized according to how much the two data series are directionally aligned with each other at the current larger trend. See Figures 9.17, 9.18, and 9.19.

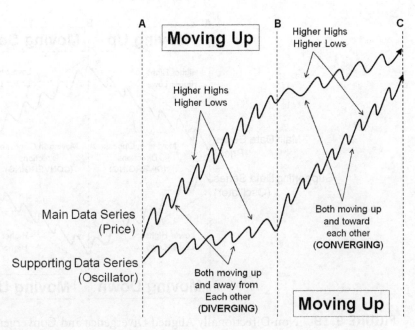

FIGURE 9.17 Directionally Aligned Slope Divergence and Convergence.

In Figure 9.17, we see that between time lines A and B, the slopes of the current larger trends of the main and supporting data series are moving away or diverging from each other. Subsequently, between time lines B and C, we see that the slopes of the current larger trends of the two data series are now moving toward or converging on each other.

In Figure 9.18, we also see divergent and convergent action both occurring in the same general direction, but this time to the downside. In both cases, there is no

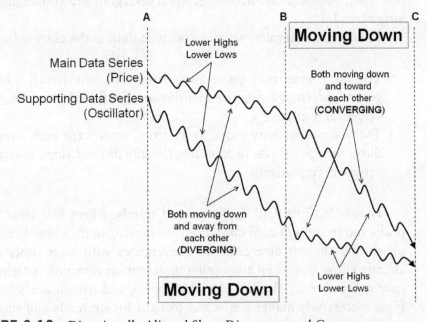

FIGURE 9.18 Directionally Aligned Slope Divergence and Convergence.

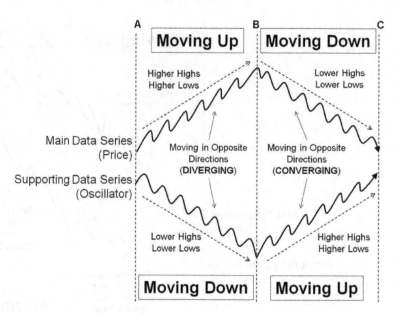

FIGURE 9.19 Non-Directionally Aligned Divergence and Convergence.

significant directional discrepancy, as the slopes of all data series are moving in the *same general direction*, namely either up or down, when diverging and converging at the current larger trend. They do not exhibit motion in opposing directions, based on the definition of direction given in Section 9.1.2.

In Figure 9.19, we observe the slopes of two data series diverging from each other between time lines A and B, and subsequently converging on each other between B and C. This time, however, significant directional discrepancy exists as the slopes of both data series are now moving in opposing directions, with one rising and the other declining, when diverging and converging at the current larger trend.

From these examples, we may conclude that, at the current larger trend:

- Two data series may move away from, or toward each other, in the *same general direction* giving rise to *directionally aligned* slope divergence and convergence, respectively.
- Two data series may move away from, or toward each other, in *opposing* directions giving rise to *non-directionally aligned* slope divergence and convergence, respectively.

Figures 9.17 to 9.19 depict general trends, where it is clear that successive peaks and troughs *in each data series* are moving in the same direction, regardless of whether there is divergence or convergence with some other data series. We already know that when attempting to determine direction for general trends, we may use conventional trend or multiple peak and trough analysis, that is, identifying successively higher peaks and troughs for uptrends and successively lower peaks and troughs for downtrends.

> **NOTE**
>
> The use of peak to peak or trough to trough analysis to determine divergence is only applicable if we are looking for non-confirmation between two *adjacent* peaks or troughs at the current larger trend. Consequently, if we are looking for divergence across *multiple* peaks and troughs, we must use conventional trend or slope analysis instead.

This has significant implications in the determination of bullishness or bearishness in divergence analysis, as we shall see in the following section.

9.2.10 Slope Analysis and Slope Divergence

Once it is determined that adjacent peak to peak or trough to trough analysis is not applicable, the practitioner may then resort to conventional trend analysis. When applying slope analysis, any disagreement between the slope in price and its supporting data series shall be referred to as *slope divergence*. The term slope divergence has also been employed by William Blau (in his book *Momentum, Direction and Divergence*) to refer to divergence between a moving average and an oscillator. Though Blau uses the term in a more specific and proprietary fashion, we will use it to refer to any divergence, under the broad interpretation, that is identified by comparing slopes between data series that are formed by either:

- Multiple peaks and troughs trending in opposing directions (Figure 9.7)
- Price excursions devoid of any visible peaks and troughs (Figure 9.8)

We see that there is an overlap between slope analysis and conventional trend analysis when multiple peaks and troughs are observed, but slope analysis distinguishes itself from conventional when slopes are formed in the absence of peaks and troughs.

Assuming that the oscillator or indicator in the supporting data series represents momentum, this would directly imply that a rising oscillator is potentially bullish for price and a declining oscillator is conversely bearish. Alternatively, under the narrow interpretation, this means that convergence between price and the oscillator always implies potential price bullishness whereas divergence always implies potential price bearishness. We can therefore also refer to these, under the broad interpretation, as *bullish or bearish slope divergence*. As seen in Section 9.1.3, there are only six combinations of divergence under the broad interpretation, and three more indicating non-divergence. As will be discussed later, this interpretation of slope divergence aligns perfectly with that of standard divergence analysis. Therefore, when encountering slope divergence, we can interpret it in the same manner as that of standard divergence in order to determine the bullish and bearish bias of any setup. Hence, bullish slope divergence may be regarded as standard bullish divergence and bearish slope divergence as standard bearish divergence.

In most situations, peaks and troughs are clearly visible on the charts, making the identification of bullish or bearish divergence a fairly simple task. However, there may be occasions when the peaks and troughs are not obvious on a chart, especially when the path of the data series approximates a straight line. This is a common occurrence when viewing data on higher timeframes, which tends to filter out the lower wave cycles, or when data trends strongly with little or no retracement during the trend. Also, divergence between the data series at a lower wave degree *does not* necessarily indicate divergence at a higher wave degree, though it may signal a potential directional change.

> **NOTE**
>
> When peak and trough analysis is not available or possible, we treat and interpret the directional discrepancy as *standard* divergence, where diverging data series is bearish and converging data series is bullish for the main data series.

This means that we must exclude reverse divergence setups when applying slope analysis. Reverse divergence analysis in the absence of visible peaks and troughs would introduce *interpretational ambiguity*. Referring to Figure 9.20, we observe trends with no visually apparent peak and trough oscillations. As a result, standard divergence analysis is applied, giving us only two possible outcomes, namely either standard bearish or standard bullish divergence.

Figure 9.21 shows *the six possible combinations for standard divergence in the absence of peaks and troughs*. They are identical to those found in Figure 9.3 in boxes (2), (3), (6), (13), (16), and (17) as well as boxes in Figure 9.28 that coincide with standard divergence based on adjacent peak to peak and trough to trough analysis.

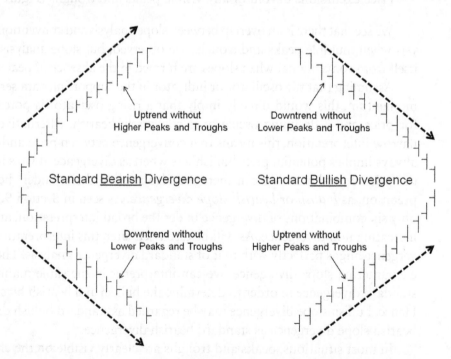

FIGURE 9.20 Slope Divergence as Standard Divergence in Trends without Peak and Trough Oscillations.

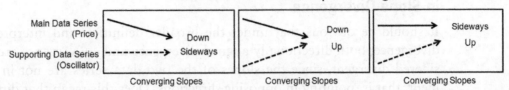

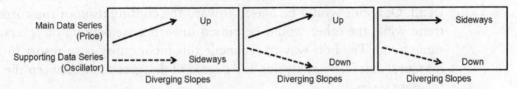

FIGURE 9.21　Standard Slope Divergence in the Absence of Peaks and Troughs.

In Figure 9.22, we observe peak and trough oscillations at a lower wave degree giving rise to a trend at a higher wave degree, that is, the current larger trend. If the current larger trend itself does not also oscillate, then it will not be possible to employ peak and trough analysis to the next larger trend in order to determine its direction. Furthermore, performing peak and trough analysis on the lower wave degree oscillations will not accurately describe the action of the next larger trend. Therefore slope analysis is employed to determine the direction of the next larger trend.

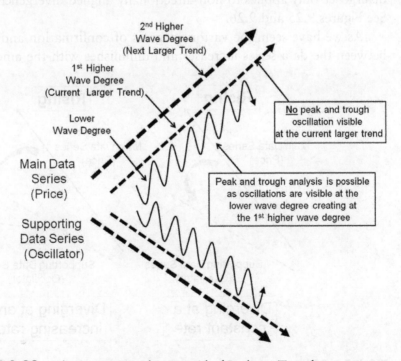

FIGURE 9.22　The Larger Trend Is Devoid of Peaks or Troughs.

9.2.11 Degree of Confirmation and Non-Confirmation in Slope Divergence

It should be obvious that under the broader definition and interpretation of divergence, both directionally aligned divergence and convergence are not considered divergent, since the slopes of the two data series are not in disagreement, that is, pointing in opposing directions. Does this mean that directionally aligned divergences and convergences represent confirmation? It would be fairly reasonable to assume that divergent and convergent behaviors have different implications and that they both cannot imply a continuation of the current larger trend. Only one would be biased toward the continuation of the current larger trend while the other would be biased toward a weakening or reversal of that same trend. The best way to reconcile this incongruity is to resort to a relative measure, that is, by analyzing the *degree* of disagreement between the slopes of the data series.

In Figure 9.23, we see the slopes of two data series trending to the upside. Although the slopes of both data series are generally moving upward and not in opposing directions, they are nonetheless not rising at similar or identical rates. Each data series is rising at a different rate, evinced by the *angle of ascent*. As long as the supporting data series is rising at a lower rate than the main data series in an uptrend, or falling at a higher rate than the main data series in a downtrend, we have directionally aligned slope divergence. See Figure 9.24.

As price rises, once the slope of the supporting data series falls to the horizontal and below, we have non-directionally aligned divergence. Similarly in a downtrend, once the slope of the supporting data series rises to the horizontal and above, we have non-directionally aligned convergence. The broad definition of divergence only applies to non-directionally aligned divergence and convergence. See Figures 9.25 and 9.26.

As we have seen, the various degrees of confirmation and non-confirmation between the data series increases and diminishes with the amount of agreement

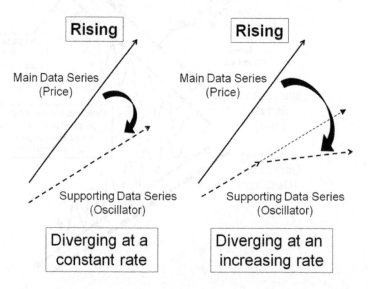

FIGURE 9.23 Varying Degrees of Directionally Aligned Slope Divergence in an Uptrend.

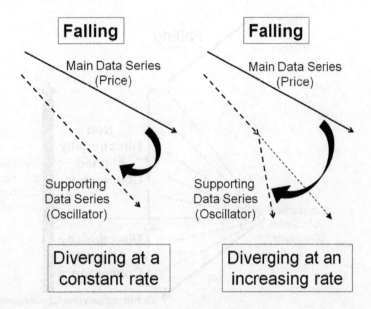

FIGURE 9.24 Varying Degrees of Directionally Aligned Slope Divergence in a Downtrend.

between the data series. When dealing with non-directionally aligned divergence, non-confirmation is represented by significantly clear and obvious disagreement. But with directionally aligned divergence, as seen in Figure 9.25, non-confirmation is technically absent as rising peaks and troughs in price are matched with rising peaks and troughs in the supporting data series, and similarly for declining peaks and troughs in a downtrend. The only distinguishing factor is the *strength* or *degree of agreement* present. A strong positive correlation between the slopes of the two data series implies a greater *degree of confirmation*.

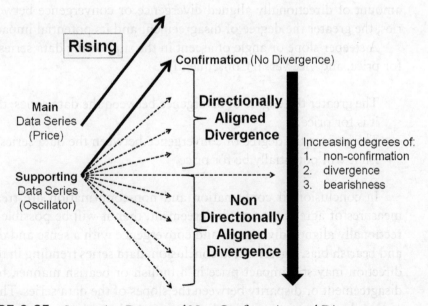

FIGURE 9.25 Increasing Degrees of Non-Confirmation and Divergence.

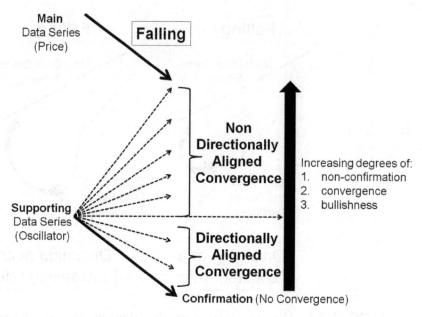

FIGURE 9.26 Increasing Degrees of Non-Confirmation and Convergence.

NOTE

In non-directionally aligned divergence, disagreement is either present or not, whereas in directionally aligned divergence, disagreement and consequently non-confirmation is measured by degrees.

The degree of non-confirmation may therefore be represented by the amount of divergence or convergence present between the data series. The larger the amount of directionally aligned divergence or convergence between the data series, the greater the degree of disagreement and its potential impact on price.

A steeper slope or angle of ascent in the supporting data series is more bullish for price, and vice versa. Consequently:

- The greater the degree of divergence between the data series, the more bearish it is for price.
- The greater the degree of convergence between the data series, the more bullish it will potentially be for price.

In conclusion, if confirmation and non-confirmation are treated as relative measures of agreement and disagreement, then it will be possible to attribute directionally aligned divergence and convergence with a sense and degree of bullish and bearish bias. Therefore, in conclusion, data series trending in the same general direction may still impact price in a bullish or bearish manner, by the degree of disagreement or disparity between the slopes of the data series. The data series do not need to move in opposite directions in order to impact price.

9.3 STANDARD AND REVERSE DIVERGENCE

With greater clarity on reversals, continuations, and the various approaches to defining trend and direction, we are now ready to deal with the topic of standard and reverse divergence.

Standard divergence is also referred to as *classic, common, regular,* or *reversal* divergence, whereas reverse divergence is popularly referred to as *hidden, inverted, trend,* or *continuation* divergence. George Lane used reverse divergence as part of his Bull and Bear setups. Unfortunately, there is still a fair amount of definitional confusion in technical analysis, especially when dealing with reverse divergence, as there seems to be two distinct schools of thought on the matter. It is important to remember that standard and reverse divergence are regarded as *non-directionally aligned divergence* and are interpreted under the broader definition. Standard and reverse divergence refer specifically to non-confirmation in the current larger trend.

When determining the nature and type of the divergence involved, we must account for the:

- *Wave degree* at which the divergence is being observed or identified
- *Approach* used when applying reverse divergence
- *Type of analysis* used to determine divergence (i.e., slope, adjacent peak/trough, or conventional peak and trough trend analysis)

In general terms, standard divergence occurs when:

- Only price, and not the supporting data series, is making equal or higher peaks (based on adjacent peak to peak analysis).
- Only price, and not the supporting data series, is making equal or lower troughs (based on adjacent trough to trough analysis).
- There is a non-directionally aligned discrepancy between the slopes in price and the supporting data series.

More specifically, standard divergence consists of any of the following 12 setups:

1. Price is making higher peaks while the oscillator is making lower peaks
2. Price is making higher peaks while the oscillator is making equal peaks
3. Price is making equal peaks while the oscillator is making lower peaks
4. Price is making lower troughs while the oscillator is making higher troughs
5. Price is making lower troughs while the oscillator is making equal troughs
6. Price is making equal troughs while the oscillator is making higher troughs
7. Price slope is rising while the oscillator slope is flat
8. Price slope is rising while the oscillator slope is falling
9. Price slope is flat while the oscillator slope is falling
10. Price slope is flat while the oscillator slope is rising
11. Price slope is falling while the oscillator slope is flat
12. Price slope is falling while the oscillator slope is rising

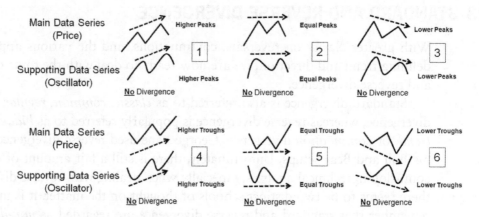

FIGURE 9.27 Non-Divergence at the Current Larger Trend Using Adjacent Peak to Peak and Trough to Trough Analysis.

In general terms, basic reverse divergence occurs when:

- Only price, and not the supporting data series, is making equal or lower peaks (based on adjacent peak to peak analysis)
- Only price, and not the supporting data series, is making equal or higher troughs (based on adjacent trough to trough analysis).

More specifically, basic reverse divergence consists of any of the following *six* setups:

1. The oscillator is making lower troughs while price is making higher troughs
2. The oscillator is making lower troughs while price is making equal troughs
3. The oscillator is making equal troughs while price is making higher troughs
4. The oscillator is making higher peaks while price is making lower peaks
5. The oscillator is making higher peaks while price is making equal peaks
6. The oscillator is making equal peaks while price is making lower peaks

Remember that slope and reverse divergence are mutually exclusive and that slope divergence is treated and interpreted in a similar manner to standard divergence. There are six out of 18 possible combinations where successive peaks and troughs between the two data series are pointing in the same direction, indicating non-divergence in the current larger trend. See Figure 9.27.

The remaining 12 consist of six combinations each, for standard and reverse divergence, where the successive peaks and troughs between the two data series are pointing in different directions, as illustrated in Figures 9.28 and 9.29, respectively.

9.3.1 Bullish and Bearish Divergence

Before delving any further, let us first turn our attention to the directional implications of divergence. Divergence may be categorized as either bullish or bearish, sometimes also referred to as *positive* or *negative*, respectively.

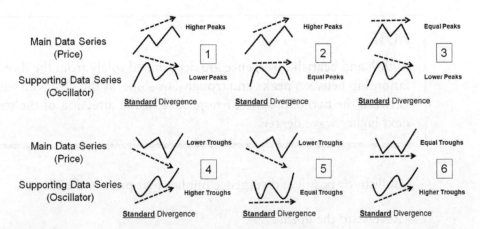

FIGURE 9.28 Representations of Standard Divergence at the Current Larger Trend Using Adjacent Peak to Peak and Trough to Trough Analysis.

It is imperative to realize that *price is expected to subsequently follow through in the direction of the supporting data series* at the next higher wave degree when applying standard divergence analysis. Therefore, if the supporting data series is moving to the upside, price is also expected to eventually move to the upside, and we say that we have *bullish divergence*. Conversely, if the supporting data series is moving to the downside, price is expected to eventually move to the downside, and we say that we have *bearish divergence*. It is assumed that the supporting data series is reflecting the underlying strength (with increasing momentum) or weakness (with diminishing momentum) in price. Regardless of its current direction, price is expected to eventually converge on the supporting data series. (This is the reason why some practitioners also call this bullish convergence, adding to the confusion. What these practitioners are actually doing is applying the narrow definition of divergence. Under the narrow definition, bullish non-confirmation is referred to as bullish convergence. Additionally, bearish non-confirmation is referred to as bearish convergence under reverse divergence analysis.)

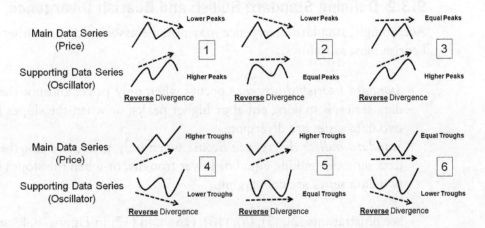

FIGURE 9.29 Representations of Reverse Divergence at the Current Larger Trend Using Adjacent Peak to Peak and Trough to Trough Analysis.

> **NOTE**
>
> Bullish and bearish divergence are determined solely from the directional relationship between peaks and troughs, or slope, at the observed wave degree between the two data series, *irrespective* of the direction of the trend at the next higher wave degree.

Bullish (or positive) divergence implies that price will either:

- Reverse to the *upside*
- Continue rising to the *upside*

Bearish (or negative) divergence implies that price will either:

- Reverse to the *downside*
- Continue declining to the *downside*

With respect to reverse divergence, price is expected to continue in the direction of its current larger trend, moving in the opposite direction to that of the supporting data series. Unfortunately, there are two approaches in reverse divergence with contrary outcomes. In either case, if the supporting data series is moving to the upside, price is expected to move to the downside, and we say that we have reverse bearish divergence. Conversely, if the supporting data series is moving to the downside, price is expected to move to the upside, and we say that we have reverse bullish divergence.

It is customary in technical analysis to assume that the supporting data series is reflecting the underlying strength or weakness in price. Regardless of its current direction, price is expected to eventually converge on the supporting data series in George Lane's Bull and Bear setups.

9.3.2 Defining Standard Bullish and Bearish Divergence

Accordingly, standard divergence may now be associated with either a bullish or bearish bias, as follows:

- *Standard bearish divergence* occurs when only price, and not the supporting data series, is making equal or higher peaks, or when the slopes between the two data series are diverging.
- *Standard bullish divergence* occurs when only price, and not the supporting data series, is making equal or lower troughs, or when the slopes between the two data series are converging.

See illustrations (2), (3), (6), (13), (16), and (17) in Figures 9.43 and 9.44.

Standard bearish divergence indicates a potential *reversal to the downside* of the current larger trend as observed at the point of non-confirmation, seen in

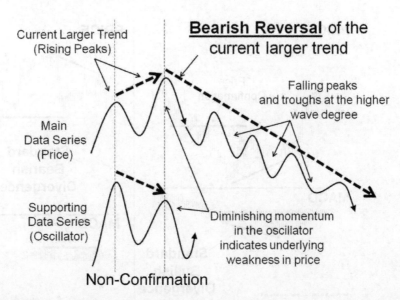

FIGURE 9.30 Standard Bearish Divergence via Adjacent Peak to Peak Analysis.

Figure 9.30. Falling peaks in the supporting data series indicate diminishing momentum, which is potentially bearish for price. Figure 9.31 illustrates standard bullish divergence where a potential *reversal to the upside* current larger trend as observed at the point of non-confirmation. Rising troughs in the supporting data series indicate strengthening momentum, which is bullish for price. Price is expected to reverse and subsequently move *in the direction of the supporting data series* in both standard bullish and bearish divergences.

Examples given in Figures 9.30 and 9.31 expand on illustration (3) in Figure 9.43, and illustration (16) in Figure 9.44, respectively.

Figure 9.32 is a chart of price and its moving average convergence divergence (MACD) indicator displaying standard bullish and bearish divergence. Also

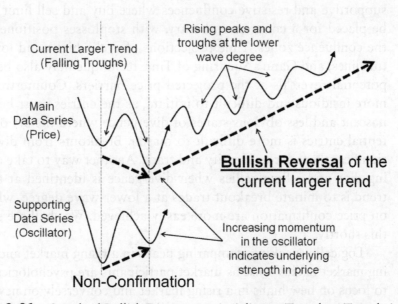

FIGURE 9.31 Standard Bullish Divergence via Adjacent Trough to Trough Analysis.

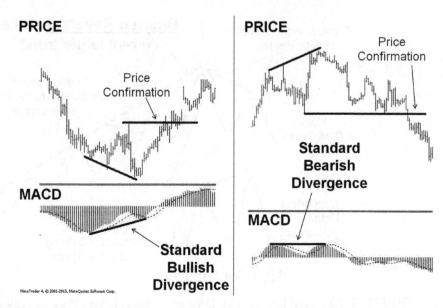

FIGURE 9.32 Standard Bullish and Bearish Divergence.
Source: MetaTrader 4

included are the *price confirmation* levels where the breakout of a prior support or resistance level confirms bullish or bearish divergence setup and provides a price trigger for participatory action.

Though divergent setups are normally traded at the breakout of some price barrier, more experienced traders sometimes also employ standard divergence to help them initiate countertrend entries like *buying on the dips* or *selling into the rallies*. The use of various price barriers and indicator overlays, which include previous supports and resistances, trendlines, price channels, popular moving averages, and various volatility bands, may be used to help identify potential supportive and resistive confluences where buy and sell limit entry orders may be placed for a countertrend entry, with stoplosses positioned slightly beyond the confluence zones. Time projections of cyclic highs and lows, apex reaction timelines, and Gann's Squaring of Time technique may also be used to pinpoint potential reversals at the projected price barriers. Countertrend trades are far more insidious and difficult to initiate, as the entries must be made during the nascent and less obvious stages of divergence where the art of anticipating potential entries is more difficult to master. Breakouts from divergent setups are significantly easier to identify and trade. Another way to take advantage of buying dips and selling rallies when divergence is identified at the current larger trend is to initiate breakout trades at a lower wave degree, where entries based on price confirmation are more easily achieved. We shall see some examples of this shortly.

Logically speaking, comparing peaks in a rising market and troughs in a falling market makes sense as market participants are psychologically more inclined to focus on new highs in a rising market and conversely on new lows in a falling market in order to make important trading and investment decisions, and it is for this reason that it is referred to as standard divergence. However, reverse divergence involves comparing peaks in a falling market and troughs in a rising market and may be somewhat counterintuitive.

9.3.3 Defining Reverse Bullish and Bearish Divergence

The case for reverse divergence is not as straightforward, as there are two distinct approaches, one predicated on George Lane's Bull and Bear setups and a more contemporary approach that anticipates a contrary outcome. Reverse divergence normally suggests a potential *continuation* of the current trend at one higher wave degree, simply referred to as the current larger trend. In George Lane's Bull and Bear setups, this continuation is expected to be short lived as price is expected to resume its original trend at the second higher wave degree. Traders frequently employ reverse divergence to help identify tradable breakouts, as well as tops or bottoms if employing Bull or Bear setups. The main difference between the two approaches is fairly easy to identify and may well serve as a guide when in doubt:

1. The first approach requires a *continuation* of the current larger trend, with traders looking for an upside or downside breakout in price. For the sake of clarity and convenience, we shall refer to divergences associated with this contemporary approach simply as *Reverse Bullish* or *Reverse Bearish Divergence*. Price moves in opposition to the direction indicated by the supporting data series at the point of non-confirmation in the current larger trend.

2. The second approach also requires a similar initial *continuation* of the current larger trend, but this is expected to be eventually followed by a *reversal*, with traders usually looking to enter the market at tops or bottoms formed by this reversal. We shall henceforth use the same terms that George Lane originally attributed to this type of divergence, namely as *Bull* and *Bear Setups*. Price eventually follows in the direction indicated by the supporting data series at the point of non-confirmation.

It is important to bear in mind that, when analyzing the market via slope divergence, neither approach to reverse divergence applies anymore, and the setup is interpreted using standard divergence. In short, reverse divergence only exists when adjacent peak to peak or trough to trough analysis is used. Therefore, there are no chart examples of reverse divergence based on conventional trend or slope analysis.

Reverse divergence, in terms of bullish or bearish bias, may be reclassified into four distinct categories, to accommodate both approaches, as follows:

1. *Bull Setups* occur when only price, and not the supporting data series, is making equal or lower peaks. Price is expected to initially reverse, making lower peaks and troughs until a bottom is formed, followed by a subsequent reversal to the upside, making higher peaks and troughs, representing an uptrend at the next higher wave degree. The rationale behind the bearishness is as

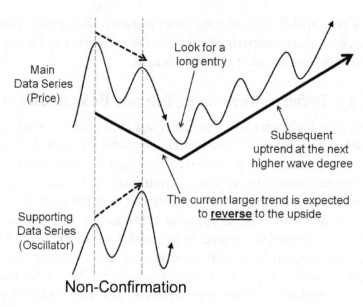

FIGURE 9.33 Reverse Divergence Seen in the Early Stages of a Bull Setup.

follows: rising peaks in the supporting data series indicate increasing momentum, which reflects underlying strength in price, and therefore are potentially bullish for price. See Figure 9.33. The divergent setup itself includes both the non-confirmation as well as the anticipated long entry signal.

Figure 9.34 shows a bull setup between points A and B on FXI (iShares FTSE China 25 Index Fund, NYSE). We see price continuing its downtrend, as expected after a reverse divergent setup. A reversal is anticipated in a bull setup and channel projection analysis identified a potential bottom in the index

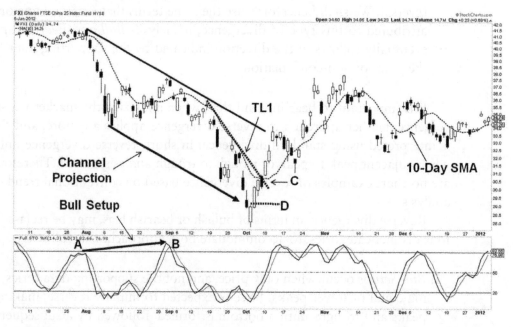

FIGURE 9.34 A Bull Setup on FXI.
Courtesy of Stockcharts.com

fund. Price confirmation of the setup is seen at point C, where price violates a couple of price barriers in the form of a downtrend line TL1 and 10-day simple moving average. The trader looks to initiate a long position at the break of either price barrier, as the current larger trend is expected to reverse to the upside. We also see the stochastics in an overbought position prior to price confirmation, which is bullish for the fund. A more aggressive entry would be one where a trader initiates a long position at the break of the high—at point D—of the lowest bullish candlestick, in proximity to the area where channel projection anticipates a bottom. The initial stoplosses are positioned just below the low of the lowest candlestick, for all entries.

With respect to wave degrees, it should be noted that if the prior larger trend was originally to the upside, then this bull setup is expected to eventually resume the original prior larger trend. In Figure 9.35, we see the current larger trend reverse twice in a bull setup at points 1 and 2 after penetrating the lower trough and higher peak respectively, establishing a continuation of not only the prior larger trend, but also of the trend that is one wave degree higher than the subsequent larger trend, referred to in Figure 9.35 as the second higher wave degree.

2. *Reverse Bearish Divergence* also occurs when only price, and not the supporting data series, is making equal or lower peaks. But in this case, price is expected to *continue to make lower peaks and troughs*, establishing the subsequent downtrend at the next higher wave degree. The underlying rationale for bearishness is as follows: although rising peaks in the supporting data series indicate increasing momentum, price still fails to rise above its previous peak, which is potentially bearish for price. (Any astute reader will immediately realize that this will lead to definitional inconsistencies when the same rationale is applied to standard divergence. This apparent contradiction will be dealt with shortly.) This type of divergence may also be likened to a failed Bull Setup, although trying to determine how much of a downside price excursion is required in order to invalidate the setup is subjective at best. Price moves

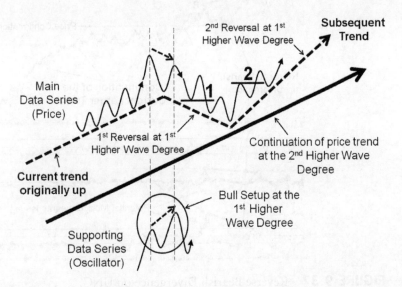

FIGURE 9.35 Bull Setup as Continuation at the Second Higher Wave Degree.

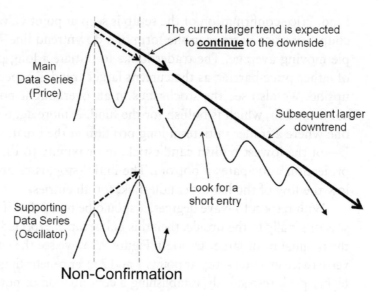

FIGURE 9.36 Reverse Bearish Divergence.

in opposition to the direction indicated by the supporting data series at non-confirmation. See Figure 9.36.

In Figure 9.37, we identify a reverse bearish divergent setup between points A and B on UNG (United States Natural Gas Fund, NYSE). The current larger trend is expected to continue to the downside, in an already declining market. The setup is confirmed once price penetrates the prior support at point 1. Traders will normally initiate short positions around the breakout with stoplosses located just above the highest point at B, trailing price all the way down until the stop is taken out. Shorts may also be entered at the retest of the prior support, now turned resistance. In this example, we see three

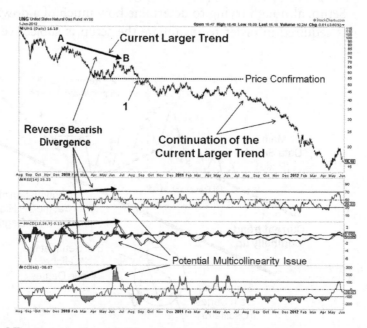

FIGURE 9.37 Reverse Bearish Divergence on UNG.
Courtesy of Stockcharts.com

fairly correlated oscillators, that is, the relative strength index (RSI), MACD, and commodity channel index (CCI) accompanying price, rendering the apparent agreement between them somewhat less credible, with the potential of misleading the trader or analyst into a false sense of confidence. Since all are constructed around price, these oscillators tend to give similar signals much of the time. We say that the oscillators are collinear. It is best to choose oscillators and indicators that provide a greater degree of independent signaling.

If a longer-term trend was originally to the downside prior to the divergence setup, then this bearish setup is expected to lead to the resumption of that original prior larger trend, recognized also as a continuation at the second higher wave degree. In Figure 9.38, we see the price continuation violating point 1, which confirms the subsequent larger downtrend, and in the process establishing a downside continuation of a trend at the second higher wave degree, that is, one wave degree higher than the subsequent larger trend.

3. *Bear Setups* occurs when only price, and not the supporting data series, is making equal or higher troughs. Price is expected to initially continue to make higher troughs and peaks until a top is formed, thereafter reversing to resume the subsequent downtrend at the next higher wave degree. The rationale behind the bearishness is as follows: falling troughs in the supporting data series indicate diminishing momentum, which reflects underlying weakness in price, and therefore is potentially bearish for price. Price eventually follows through in the direction indicated by the supporting data series at non-confirmation after a short upside continuation of the current larger trend. See Figure 9.39.

In Figure 9.40, we see a bear setup between points A and B on IYT (iShares DJ Transportation Average Index Fund, NYSE). Using channel projection techniques based on trendline TL1, we identify a potential top in the market, after which price confirmation of the bear setup in the form of either the violation of the uptrend line TL2 at point F or 20-day exponential moving average

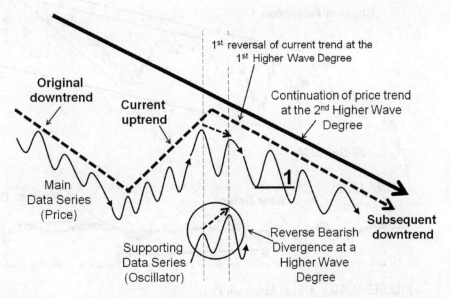

FIGURE 9.38 Reverse Bearish Divergence as Continuation at Second Higher Wave Degree.

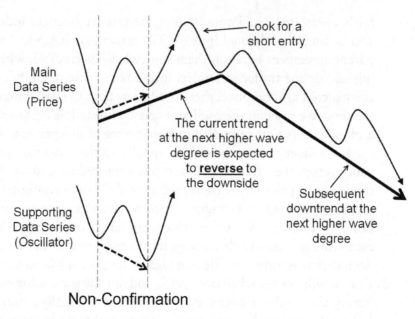

FIGURE 9.39 Reverse Divergence Seen in the Early Stages of a Bear Setup.

at point E is anticipated. Traders would normally initiate a short position at either point E or point F, with all stops positioned just above the highest high of the formation preceding the breakouts. We also see standard bearish divergence on the MACD and its histogram between points C and D, which is bearish for the fund. Once price retests TL1 after the breakout, many traders would have already executed either a full exit or partial scale out of short positions, with most protective stoplosses rolled down in a defensive move to lock in earlier profits.

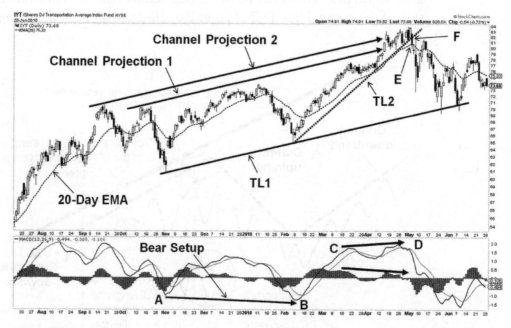

FIGURE 9.40 A Bear Setup on IYT.
Courtesy of Stockcharts.com

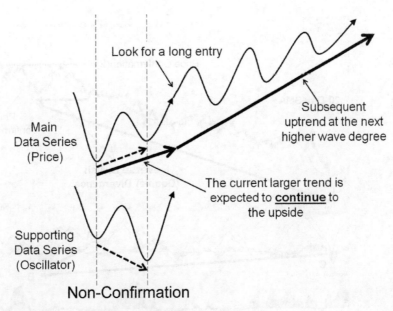

FIGURE 9.41 Reverse Bullish Divergence.

4. *Reverse Bullish Divergence* also occurs when only price, and not the supporting data series, is making equal or higher troughs. But in this case, price is expected to continue to make higher peaks and troughs, establishing the subsequent uptrend at the next higher wave degree. This type of divergence may also be likened to a failed Bear Setup. The underlying rationale for bullishness is as follows: although falling troughs in the supporting data series indicate diminishing momentum, price still fails to penetrate below its previous trough, which is potentially bullish for price. As in all reverse divergences, price moves in opposition to the direction indicated by the supporting data series at non-confirmation. See Figure 9.41.

In Figure 9.42, we observe that there is a reverse bullish divergent setup between points A and B, as well as on a higher wave degree between points B and C. This double divergence on Pfizer Inc. is regarded as more bullish than if it is accompanied by simple divergence. We see agreement between the MACD and Chaikin Money Flow (CMF) oscillators. This is a much better combination of oscillators than that observed in Figure 9.37, as the degree of collinearity between the MACD and CMF is significantly less. This is largely because the CMF oscillator takes into account volume information, and not just that of price alone. The current larger trend is expected to continue to the upside, with further price excursion being potentially precipitated by a penetration of either the prior resistance or 20-day simple moving average, indicated by price confirmation points 1 and 2, respectively. Traders will normally attempt to trade the breakout around the prior resistance and moving average. Further bullish signals prior to breakout include the CMF turning positive and the MACD signaling a bullish crossover with its signal line.

This dual interpretation of reverse divergence is summarized in illustrations (4), (7), (8), (11), (12), and (15), in Figures 9.43 and 9.44.

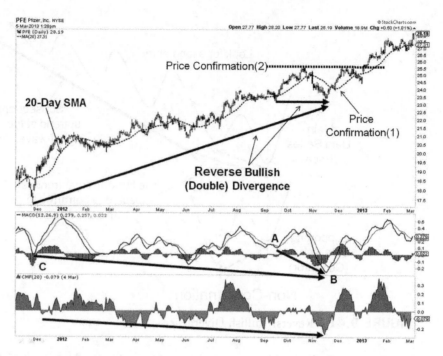

FIGURE 9.42 Reverse Bullish (Double) Divergence on Pfizer Inc., NYSE.
Courtesy of Stockcharts.com

Figures 9.45 to 9.47 are chart examples of various standard and reverse divergences in action.

In Figure 9.46, a series of consistent cyclic lows is identified on 3M stock. Standard bullish divergence can be found between points 1 and 2, while standard bearish divergence can be found between points 5 and 4 as well as between

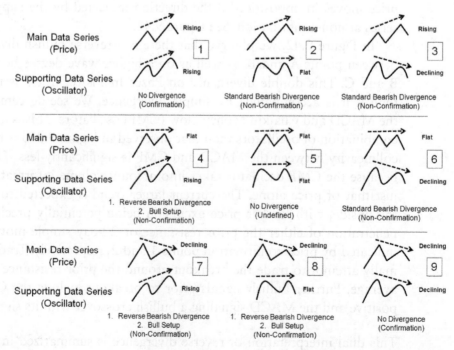

FIGURE 9.43 Bullish and Bearish (Standard and Reverse) Divergence—Part 1.

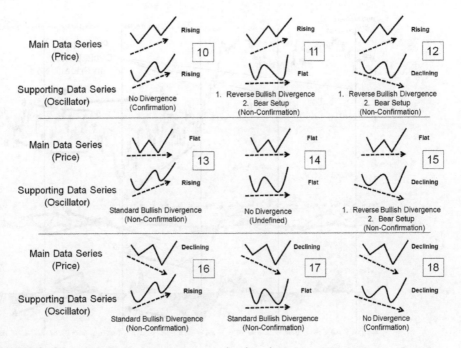

FIGURE 9.44 Bullish and Bearish (Standard and Reverse) Divergence—Part 2.

points 4 and 6. Reverse bearish divergence is seen between points 3 and 4, while reverse bullish divergence is seen between points 7 and 8 as well as between points 8 and 9. A few instances of agreement between the oscillators can be observed between points 1 and 2 as well as between points 7 and 8. The double divergence arising from the alignment of the MACD and CMF oscillators between points 1 and 2 gave rise to a significant pullback in price from around

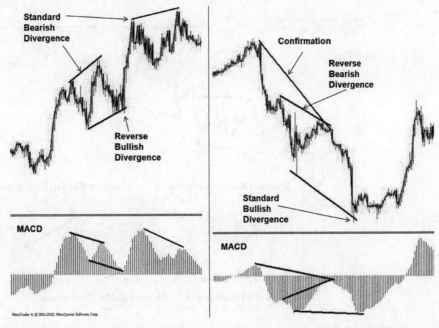

FIGURE 9.45 The Four Standard and Reverse Divergences in Action.
Source: MetaTrader 4

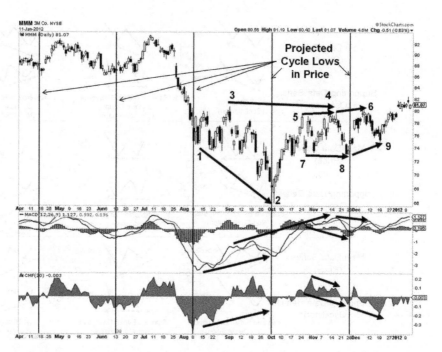

FIGURE 9.46 Combining Standard and Reverse Divergences with Cycle Projections.
Courtesy of Stockcharts.com

$66, which incidentally also coincided with the projected cyclic low near point 2. Integrating time and price projections is normally assumed to yield a more reliable analysis.

In Figure 9.47, we see alternating standard and reverse divergent signals between the Dow Jones Industrial and Transportation Averages.

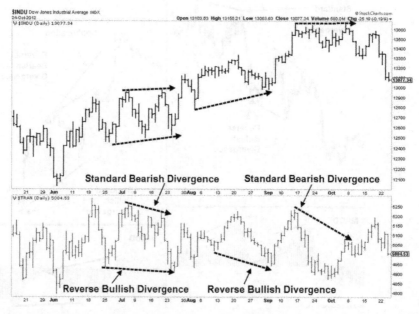

FIGURE 9.47 Divergences between the Dow Jones Industrial and Dow Jones Transportation Averages.
Courtesy of Stockcharts.com

9.3.4 The Divergence Master Heuristic

We can summarize the expected or potential follow-through action in the main data series as follows:

- If successive adjacent *peaks* in both the main and supporting data series are pointing in different directions, we expect price in the main data series to be bearish and subsequently fall in price, and
- If successive adjacent *troughs* in both the main and supporting data series are pointing in different directions, we expect price in the main data series to be bullish and subsequently rise in price.

This simple but powerful rule of thumb makes isolating and identifying bullish and bearish divergences an almost effortless task. This heuristic is applicable to both standard divergence and the contemporary approach to reverse divergence analysis. However, keep in mind that this heuristic only applies to the initial stage of a Bull and Bear Setup where a short-term continuation of the current larger trend is also expected before an eventual reversal.

9.3.5 Standard and Reverse Divergence as Continuation and Reversal at Higher Wave Degrees

Continuation and reversal may exist at a certain wave degree but not at another. As we have already seen, a reversal at one wave degree may represent continuation at a higher wave degree, which in turn could easily represent a reversal at an even higher wave degree. This leads us logically to the relationship between divergent setups and various wave degrees. In the following illustrations, we shall observe standard divergence leading to a reversal of the prior larger trend, while reverse divergence is being followed by a continuation of the prior larger trend. See Figures 9.48 to 9.51.

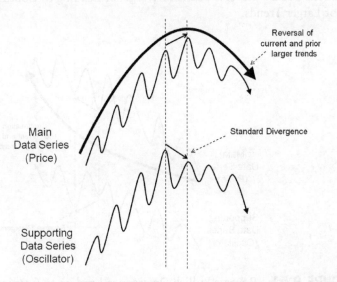

FIGURE 9.48 Standard Bearish Divergence Leading to Reversal of the Current and Prior Larger Trends.

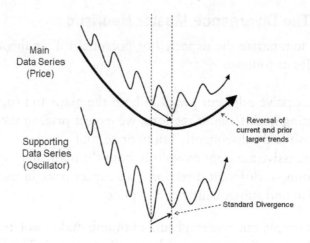

FIGURE 9.49 Standard Bullish Divergence Leading to Reversal of the Current and Prior Larger Trends.

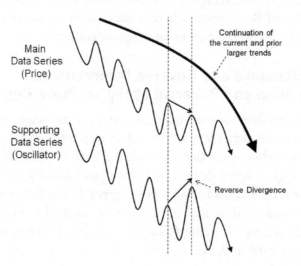

FIGURE 9.50 Reverse Bearish Divergence Leading to Continuation of the Current and Prior Larger Trends.

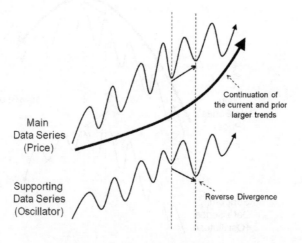

FIGURE 9.51 Reverse Bullish Divergence Leading to Continuation of the Current and Prior Larger Trends.

In Figures 9.52 to 9.55, we now instead observe standard divergence leading to a continuation of the current prior trend, whereas reverse divergence is being followed by a reversal of the prior larger trend. Therefore, we must be extremely careful when employing terms like continuation and reversal in divergence analysis without first specifying which wave degree or trend is being observed.

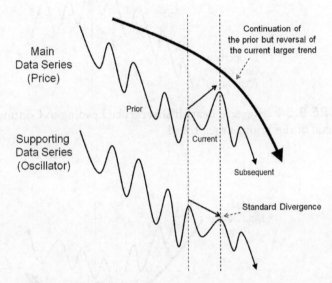

FIGURE 9.52 Standard Bearish Divergence Leading to Reversal of the Current and Continuation of the Prior Larger Trend.

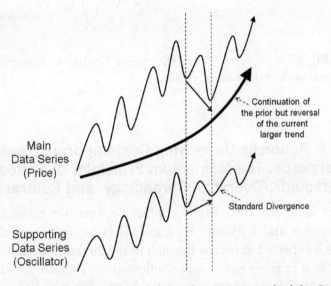

FIGURE 9.53 Standard Bullish Divergence Leading to Reversal of the Current and Continuation of the Prior Larger Trend.

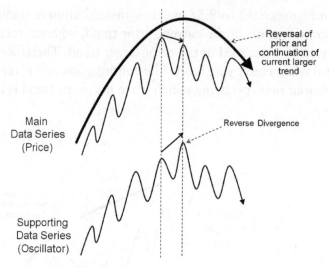

FIGURE 9.54 Reverse Bearish Divergence Leading to Continuation of the Current and Reversal of the Prior Larger Trend.

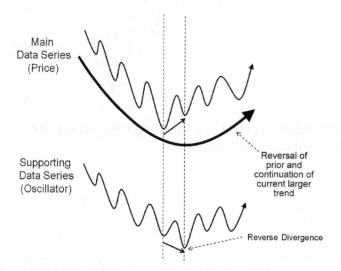

FIGURE 9.55 Reverse Bullish Divergence Leading to Continuation of the Current and Reversal of the Prior Larger Trend.

9.3.6 Rationale Underlying Contemporary Reverse Divergence: The Momentum Principle, Over-Reaction, Overbought/Oversold, Chronology, and Contrarianism

There is no real definitional conflict between the rationale underlying standard divergence and Bull/Bear Setups. This is because in both types of divergences, price is expected to follow through in the direction of the supporting data series as indicated at the point of non-confirmation. Therefore, with Bull and Bear setups, any continuation of the current larger trend is regarded as merely temporary and may be understood to represent some short-lived *expression of over-reaction* in the markets which would eventually precipitate a reversal. This makes sense since the supporting data series is regarded as representative of the potential underlying momentum in price. We may refer to this as the *momentum principle*. However, this is not the case with the contemporary approach to reverse divergence, where price is expected to move in the opposite direction to the supporting data series, that is, against the natural flow of the underlying momentum.

So far, we have managed to reconcile standard divergence with the Bull and Bear setups by combining the momentum principle and short-term over-reaction in the markets. Unfortunately, if reverse divergence is explained using the momentum principle, we very rapidly run into difficulty. Numerous attempts have been made to reconcile and make some sense of reverse divergence, with the most popular introducing a *chronological element* in order to obviate definitional inconsistencies. Unfortunately, it does very little to explain *why* divergence should be read one way for standard and another for reverse divergence. Briefly, the chronological approach states that standard divergence should be viewed *prospectively* whereas reverse divergence is best viewed *retrospectively*. In simple terms, it means that standard divergence is regarded as forward looking and predictive, whereas reverse divergence is but a record of what has transpired.

We shall now examine the definitional inconsistencies that arise when using the chronological approach to explain standard divergence. Let us first apply the chronological approach to reverse divergence, where it seems to explain why continuation of the current larger trend occurs:

- In reverse bullish divergence, troughs continue to rise in the main data series, showing strength *in spite of* falling troughs in the supporting data series that should indicate some underlying weakness in the main data series. This is therefore *bullish* for price and the current larger trend is expected to continue to rise.
- In reverse bearish divergence, peaks continue to fall in the main data series, showing weakness *in spite of* rising peaks in the supporting data series that should indicate some underlying strength in the main data series. This is therefore *bearish* for price and the current larger trend is expected to continue to decline.

Before applying the chronological approach to explain standard divergence, let us first apply the momentum principle to standard divergence:

- In standard bullish divergence, falling troughs in the main data series show weakness, *whereas* rising troughs in the supporting data series indicate the possibility of some underlying strength or gain in momentum in the main data series. This is potentially *bullish* for price and the current larger trend is expected to subsequently reverse to the upside.
- In standard bearish divergence, rising peaks in the main data series show strength, *whereas* falling peaks in the supporting data series indicate the possibility of some underlying weakness or loss in momentum in the main data series. This is potentially *bearish* and the current larger trend is expected to subsequently reverse to the downside.

As we already know, the momentum principle lends itself naturally to standard divergence, as does the chronological approach to reverse divergence. Now if we apply the chronological approach to standard divergence, we run into the following inconsistencies:

1. In standard bullish divergence, troughs continue to fall in the main data series, showing weakness *in spite of* rising troughs in the supporting data series that should indicate some underlying strength in the main data series. This is therefore *bearish* for price and the current larger trend is expected to continue to decline.
2. In standard bearish divergence, peaks continue to rise in the main data series, showing strength *in spite of* falling peaks in the supporting data series that should indicate some underlying weakness in the main data series. This is therefore *bullish* for price and the current larger trend is expected to continue to rise.

As we can clearly observe above, explanation (1) is wholly inconsistent and contradicts what is expected of standard bullish divergence, and explanation (2) is similarly inconsistent and contradicts what is expected of standard bearish divergence. Therefore, if we accept the chronological explanation for standard divergence, this will introduce serious ambiguity as it yields a diametrically opposed forecast to that indicated when applying the momentum principle.

Another approach we can adopt in order to explain reverse divergence would be to assume that it is representative of some form of *contrarian behavior*. This implies that market participants are willing to take a trade contrary to the evidence available with the belief that following the herd is ultimately unprofitable. But this line of reasoning also eventually leads to some inconsistency, especially if applied to standard divergence. In fact, such a contrarian would go long when encountering standard bearish divergence and short on standard bullish divergences. In effect, the conclusions reached using a contrarian approach are similar to those of the chronological approach, whereby traders long standard bearish divergences and short standard bullish divergences. For all practical purposes, the chronological and contrarian approaches are functionally identical.

A better explanation may be had by considering *overbought* and *oversold* levels. Some practitioners refer to overbought and oversold levels in the supporting data series as an explanation for subsequent price moves during reverse divergence. For example, it is argued that in the case of bearish reverse divergence prices are expected to continue to fall as the indicator is already at or approaching overbought levels. Similarly, with bullish reverse divergence, prices are expected to continue to rise as the indicator is already at or approaching oversold levels. *This is by far the most logical and reasonable explanation for the continuation of price in reverse divergent scenarios.*

The distinction between a setup being one of reverse divergence or a Bull and Bear setup is also of great concern since both types of divergences start out as a continuation of the current larger trend. How does one distinguish between the two setups? At which point does a reversal of the continuation represent part of a Bull/Bear setup and how can we distinguish this reversal from the one that would inevitably occur in a reverse divergent setup? In other words, at which point does a Bull or Bear setup actually fail? Though it may be somewhat difficult to resolve this conceptually, on the practical side, the trader could easily employ a bidirectional approach such as initiating a straddle breakout around the price level where a reversal is expected in a Bull/Bear setup. Should the reversal entry fail, the trader would subsequently re-enter in the opposite direction, expecting further continuation. Of course, the only downside in any bidirectional entry mechanism is the unfavorable buildup of oscillational losses across the straddle.

So in summary, the overbought/oversold rationale is probably the best explanation for price continuation during reverse divergence. The momentum principle only works to explain standard divergence, but cannot account in any way whatsoever for reverse divergence, while the chronological and contrarian approache works well to explain reverse divergence. This unfortunately begs the question of why we should not apply the chronological or contrarian approach to standard divergence as well. Maybe the real answer lies in the level of popularity of certain approaches. Applications of technical analysis evolve over time and if there is sufficient interest in a particular approach or technique, it may ignite a self-fulfilling prophecy whereby traders and investors start to trade in accordance with the new interpretation, influencing market and price action. Furthermore, for every interpretation, there will exist an equal and opposite proposition. Therefore, only through continuous market observation and constant forward testing will it be possible to determine the most reliable approach in the market.

9.3.7 Double Divergence

Divergence can be simple, double, or even complex. There are numerous representations of double divergence. Generally speaking, double divergence is considered stronger evidence for a potential reversal or continuance of the current trend. Let us now examine a few different representations of double divergence. What follows are four basic classifications of double divergence and these are by no means exhaustive.

9.3.7.1 Contiguous Peak to Peak and Trough to Trough Divergence This type of double divergence is characterized by having two contiguous or successive divergent setups that are of the same type. Some practitioners refer to three or more such successive divergent setups as *multiple* divergence. See Figure 9.56.

9.3.7.2 Inter Peak or Trough Double Divergence This type of double divergence is characterized by having one divergent setup contained within a larger divergent setup where both divergences are of the same kind, which therefore reinforces its bullish or bearish signal. This type of double divergence is not commonly found in the markets. Figures 9.57 to 9.60 illustrate the four double divergence setups. In all the following illustrations, point C is the focal or pivot point of both the smaller and larger divergent setups. Figures 9.59 and 9.60 may also refer to Bear and Bull setups, respectively.

9.3.7.3 Inter Wave Cycle/Degree Divergence This type of double divergence is characterized by having one of two divergent setups formed at a higher wave

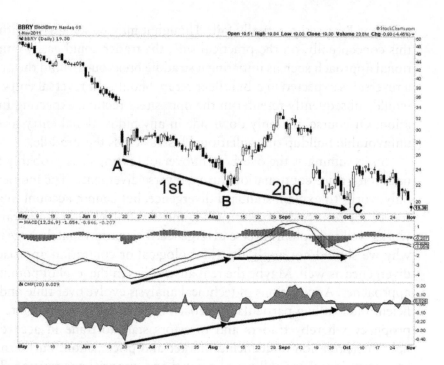

FIGURE 9.56 Standard Bullish Double Divergence on BlackBerry.
Courtesy of Stockcharts.com

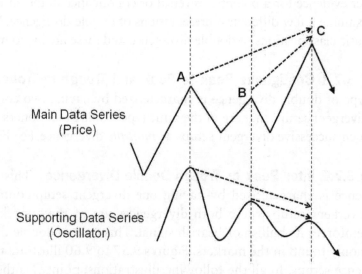

FIGURE 9.57 Standard Bearish Double Divergence (Inter Peak).

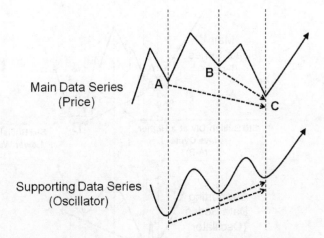

FIGURE 9.58 Standard Bullish Double Divergence (Inter Trough).

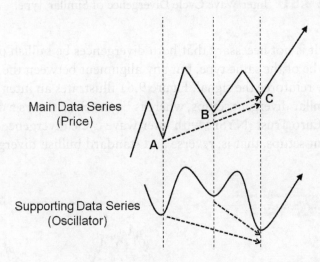

FIGURE 9.59 Reverse Bullish Double Divergence (Inter Trough).

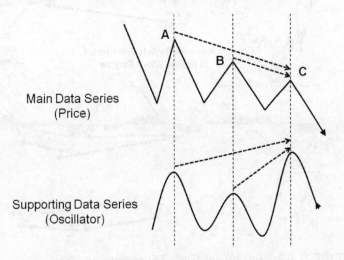

FIGURE 9.60 Reverse Bearish Double Divergence (Inter Peak).

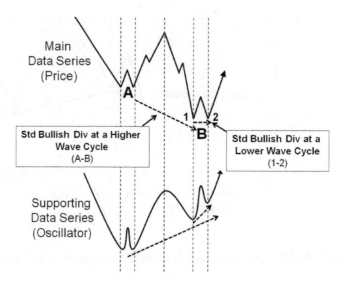

FIGURE 9.61 Inter Wave Cycle Divergence of Similar Type.

degree. It is not necessary that both divergences be bullish or bearish, nor do they need to be of the same type, but any alignment between the two setups would potentially reinforce the signal. Figure 9.61 illustrates an inter wave cycle divergence with similar divergent setups, whereas Figure 9.62 shows a chart of FXE Currency Shares Euro Trust (NYSE) with inter wave cycle divergence comprising dissimilar divergent setups, that is, reverse and standard bullish divergence.

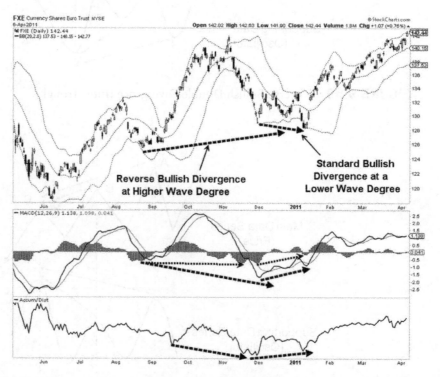

FIGURE 9.62 Inter Wave Cycle Divergence on FXE.
Courtesy of Stockcharts.com

9.3.7.4 Inter Oscillator Double Divergence Besides the MACD divergence seen in Figure 9.62, we also observe its histogram displaying similar divergences, which in itself is another form of double divergence. Many practitioners look for this combination of double MACD divergence for a potentially more reliable signal.

9.3.8 Multiple Divergence

Any chart comprising two or more divergent setups is normally referred to as a multiple divergent setup. Multiple divergence is also sometimes loosely referred to as complex divergence, but this may not always be appropriate. Having numerous overlapping or alternating divergent setups may indeed be seen as complex, however, complex divergences, in their simplest forms, may be represented by a simple divergence between two oscillators in the supporting data series that are at different phases to each other.

9.3.9 Complex Divergence

Complex divergence may be represented by any of the following:

- Triple or multiple divergences
- Phase-based divergences between oscillators
- Extensive overlapping or alternating divergent setups

We shall see numerous examples of these complex divergences throughout the rest of this chapter and handbook.

9.3.10 Detrending and Double Detrending: Inter Moving Average Divergence

Detrending allows the trader and analyst to isolate and quantify the difference between two data series by removing the trend component from the data. The most well known example of detrending is the MACD, which is constructed by detrending two exponential moving averages (EMA) of 12 and 26 periods. The MACD therefore isolates the spread or difference in price at every point along the two moving averages. Whenever the two moving averages converge on each other, the value of the MACD declines, approaching a minimum value of zero at the point where the two moving averages meet. Conversely, any divergence between the two moving averages increases its value, positively for upside divergences and negatively for downside divergences between the two moving averages. The greater the divergence between the moving averages, the farther away the MACD will move from its central or zero equilibrium value. Divergence between the two moving averages represents confirmation of the upside or downside trend and therefore implies a continuation, whereas convergence suggests a weakening of the current trend and therefore implies a reversal.

> **NOTE**
>
> The convergence of two moving averages indicates a slowing of the trend whereas divergence indicates a strengthening of the trend.

As the MACD rises and falls, peaks and troughs will form, allowing for further divergence analysis between the MACD and price itself.

Detrending can also take place between the MACD and its own signal line, thus creating the MACD histogram. The histogram therefore represents a quantitative measure of the *amount or degree of divergence* between the MACD and its own signal line. Since the MACD itself is a product of detrending two moving averages, it follows that the histogram represents a double detrended oscillator. Finally, one advantageous property of detrending is that it removes or reduces lag, or latency, in the original oscillator, and as a result, the detrended oscillator responds more rapidly to price fluctuations. Double detrending creates an even more responsive oscillator. This is particularly useful when attempting to analyze divergences at the lower wave degrees.

In Figure 9.63, we see the MACD indicator quantifying the difference in value between the 12- and 26-day EMAs. For example, at point X, the difference in value between the two moving averages is found to be 20¢. Upon tracing a vertical line between those two points on the moving averages, we see that it intersects the MACD at the expected value of 20¢, indicating that the MACD is indeed representative of the amount of convergence and divergence between the two moving averages and not merely a qualitative tool. Notice that the trend component associated with the moving averages is absent from the MACD. In the same manner, the histogram quantifies the difference between the MACD and its own signal line. In general, we observe that:

- Every time the MACD moves away from the zero or equilibrium level, we see a trend in effect
- Every time the two moving averages diverge, a strong trend is present, and when they converge, we notice a slowing of the trend

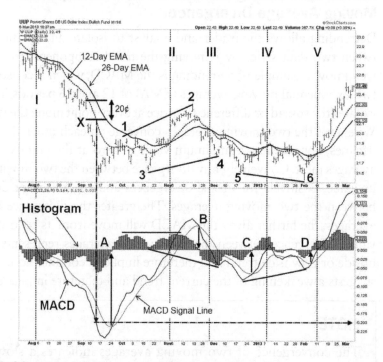

FIGURE 9.63 Creating Divergence from Detrending.
Courtesy of Stockcharts.com

- Every time the two moving averages meet, the MACD has a value of zero, that is, it will be at the zero level (see vertical lines I to V)
- Every time the MACD and its signal line meet, the histogram has a value of zero (see sample points A to D)
- The histogram reacts faster than the MACD, identifying divergences at a lower wave degree (see standard bearish divergence between points 1 and 2, and standard bullish divergence between points 3 and 4)
- There is a standard bullish double divergence between points 5 and 6, where both the MACD and its histogram display rising troughs
- There is also double divergence at points 5 and 6, resulting from two overlapping standard divergent setups, one occurring between point 5 and 6 with another from the lowest point in the MACD to point 6

9.3.11 Divergence as Leading Indicator

Divergence provides one of the best early warnings of an impending trend change or reversal. It transforms a lagging indicator into a leading indicator. Although that may be the case, it is nevertheless prudent to only act when there is price confirmation, which provides a price-based trigger for entry, as well as evidence to support a bullish or bearish forecast. As with any technical tool, divergence should be used in conjunction with other technical indicators. The objective is to locate a higher probability entry around supportive and resistive confluences. Figure 9.64 shows how divergence is used in conjunction with other indicators to locate potential reversals in Gold (XAUUSD).

The windows at the bottom of the chart show the accumulation/distribution line, along with a cycle-tuned stochastic oscillator. The overbought and oversold levels in the stochastic are indicated on the chart as OB and OS, respectively. Time lines 1 to 8 mark the points in the gold market when the overbought level was tested. Point A, which represents resistance, is the first actionable point

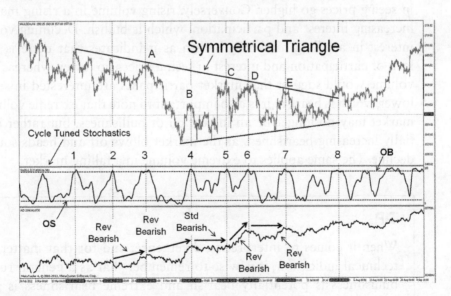

FIGURE 9.64 Divergence as a Leading Indicator.
Source: MetaTrader 4

where a trader could initiate a short position as price validates the downtrend line at its third point of contact. At this point, we see the stochastics at overbought at time line 3, which is bearish for Gold. We also observe reverse bearish divergence between the peaks located at time lines 2 and 3, indicating a potential downside continuation of the current larger trend. In similar fashion, we see standard and reverse bearish divergence acting as a leading indicator between points B and E, with the downtrend line providing resistance between C and E. The stochastics are also all at overbought at these points. This combination of divergence with other non-correlated oscillators and overlay indicators together create high probability entry points for traders interested in establishing short positions in Gold.

9.3.12 Volume Bar Action, Open Interest, and ATR Divergence

The rules for interpreting divergence are markedly different when it comes to volume bar action, open interest, and average true range (ATR). We cannot employ terms like standard or reverse divergence. We are only able to describe a setup as either bullish or bearish and divergent or confirmatory.

The rules of interpretation are as follows:

- Rising prices with declining volume bar action represent *bearish divergence*
- Rising prices with rising volume bar action represent *bullish confirmation*
- Declining prices with rising volume bar action represent *bearish confirmation*
- Declining prices with declining volume bar action represent *bullish divergence*

Note that the rules above also apply to the moving average of volume and to open interest and the ATR. Declining volume or open interest in a rising market is bearish as it indicates that there is an increasing lack of participation and interest in seeing prices go higher. Conversely, rising volume in a rising market indicates increasing interest and participation, which is bullish. Declining volume or open interest in a falling market is bullish as it indicates that there is an increasing lack of participation and interest in seeing prices go lower, whereas an increasing volume would suggest that market participants are interested in seeing price go lower, which is bearish. It is also important to note that extreme volume in a rising market may no longer be an indication of bullishness, but rather one of potentially increasing bearishness as the market blows off and heads south in a rapid decline. The same applies to extreme volume in a falling market.

TIP

When it comes to interpreting divergence, and for that matter any other technical indication, it is wise to remember that as a general rule extreme bullishness is potentially bearish and extreme bearishness is potentially bullish.

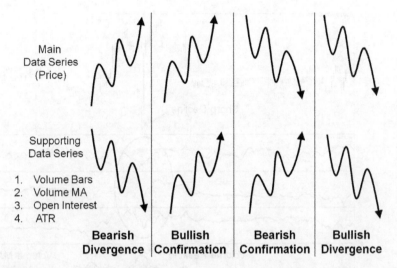

FIGURE 9.65 Volume Bars, Open Interest, and ATR Divergence.

Figure 9.106 is a good example of this general rule in action. We observe a significant blow off in Silver during the 2011 rapid run up in price. The top in Silver was accompanied by extreme volume and declining open interest, which we see, in retrospect, as representing a potentially bearish setup.

Finally, as far as open interest is concerned, a declining open interest in a rising market indicates diminishing volatility, which may adversely impact the persistence of the current trend and is therefore deemed bearish. Similarly, a declining ATR in a falling market also indicates diminishing volatility and by the same argument is deemed bullish.

From Figure 9.65, it is clear that these indicators will signal divergence and confirmation *irrespective* of the direction of price. A decline in these indicators always signals divergence, whereas a rise signals confirmation. However, in order to determine if the divergence and confirmation are bullish or bearish, we need to ascertain the current direction of price.

It is important to distinguish volume bar divergence with that of other volume indicators and oscillators. Volume indicators like OBV, Chaikin Money Flow, Percentage Volume Oscillator, Accumulation Distribution Line (ADL), and Money Flow Index (MFI) are all interpreted using conventional standard and reverse divergence analysis, and are never interpreted in the same manner as volume bar, open interest, and ATR divergence.

NOTE

The rules for interpreting volume bar divergence are completely different from those for volume oscillator divergence.

The disparity between volume bar divergence and other volume oscillator divergences is obvious, especially during a pronounced selling climax. As volume surges during a decline, reflected by rising volume bars, volume oscillators tend to decline instead. This is because volume oscillators are constructed to take into account price

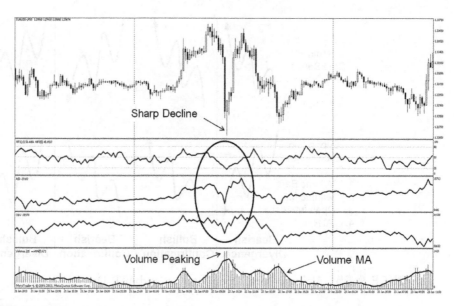

FIGURE 9.66 Volume Bar Divergence during a Sharp Decline.
Source: MetaTrader 4

action, where volume is subtracted during falling prices. This disparity only affects selling climaxes and not blow offs. In Figure 9.66, we observe that during a sharp decline in the EURUSD, the volume bars peaked, whereas all three volume oscillators—that is, the MFI, ADL, and the OBV—spiked downward. Notice also that the moving average of volume is also interpreted using the same rules as for volume bar action.

In Figure 9.67, we see volume bar divergence indicating a bearish confirmation, which is reinforced by the ADL signaling a reverse bearish divergence in the EURUSD.

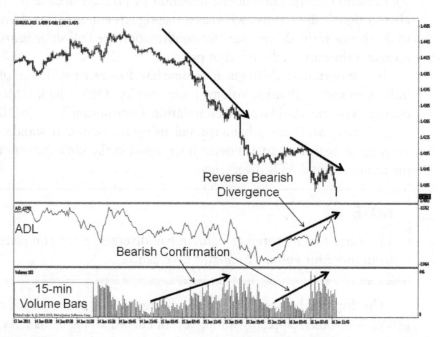

FIGURE 9.67 Volume Bar and Volume Oscillator Divergence.
Source: MetaTrader 4

9.4 PRICE CONFIRMATION IN DIVERGENCE ANALYSIS

Confirmation and non-confirmation represents the *potential* for price to either reverse or continue at the current larger trend. In other words, it is merely *evidence* that the market is either inherently weak or strong. We still require some form of qualifying action in the main data series in order to prove or *confirm* that the divergent setup in the main data series is actually reversing or continuing with its current larger trend as a result of that divergence.

This proof is referred to as *price confirmation* and is normally based on the penetration of some significant price barrier in the main data series. Price confirmation is never sought in the supporting data series. Divergence should only be confirmed by some form of qualifying price action and not on any indicator or oscillator action. Once price has violated a significant price barrier in the main data series, we say that there is *price confirmation* of the divergence setup. If price does not prove itself by unfolding in the expected manner with respect to its larger current trend, we say that the divergence setup is still *unconfirmed by price*.

> **TIP**
>
> Divergence must only be confirmed by price alone, via the penetration of some significant price barrier.

Price confirmation in the main data series is best determined by penetration or violation of any *significantly clear and obvious price barriers,* which include:

- Support or resistance levels
- Indicator overlay barriers
- Psychological levels (e.g., double- and triple-zero-digit prices)

Some popular examples of indicator overlay barriers include trendlines, moving averages, chart patterns, floor trader's pivot points, Ichimoku clouds, fixed percentage envelopes, volatility bands, Fibonacci based ratio levels, and Gann levels. Conventionally, support and resistance, trendlines, and moving averages are still the preferred price barriers for price confirmation.

> **NOTE**
>
> A divergent setup is seen as a bullish or bearish signal, while price confirmation is regarded as a *trigger* for participatory action.

The exact point of entry when initiating a long or short position based on the level of price confirmation depends on the entry filter employed, which may include any of the following:

- Price-based filtering
- Time-based filtering

- Algorithmic-based filtering
- Exogenous event-based filtering

To further increase the potential strength and reliability of the qualifying action, price confirmation is potentially most reliable when:

- Accompanied by at least three *weakly* or *non-correlated* oscillators or indicators
- All three non-correlated oscillators and indicators indicate divergence and are *in agreement* with each other
- All three non-correlated oscillators and indicators also indicate non-conflicting *double* or *multiple* divergences
- The *expected time of breakout* for price confirmation occurs in proximity to projected cycle lows for upside breakouts and cycle highs for downside breakouts.

If the three supporting data series are in some way correlated, there is a possibility that the corresponding oscillators and indicators may provide similar or identical bullish and bearish signals. We say that the oscillators and indicators are *multicollinear*. See Figure 9.37. This misleads the analyst or practitioner into believing that the apparent agreement between the oscillators and indicators are in some way strong and reliable signals.

In order to reduce the effects of multicollinearity within the supporting data series, it is best to avoid introducing supporting data series that are based on the same *technical data*, which can be categorized into various *fields*, some of which include:

- Price
- Volume
- Open interest
- Market breadth
- Sentiment

This requires that if one of the supporting data series is a momentum indicator, then the other supporting data series should be an indicator or oscillator derived from some other technical data field like volume, open interest, market breadth, sentiment, and so on. This will greatly mitigate the undesirable effects of multicollinearity between the various indicators and oscillators that make up the supporting data series, providing for potentially more independent and reliable signals. Time-based projections derived from standard cycle analysis, Fibonacci time zones, Gann's squaring of time, or triangle apex reaction analysis may also be advantageous in pinpointing the time of breakout. See Figures 9.68 to 9.83 for some idealized examples of price confirmation using moving averages, trendlines, support and resistance, chart patterns, and confluence-based breakouts on the all four types of divergences. (Price confirmation for Bull and Bear setups is not specifically depicted in the following examples, but they only require an extra step, with price confirming the breakout from the expected reversal after the initial continuation of the current larger trend.)

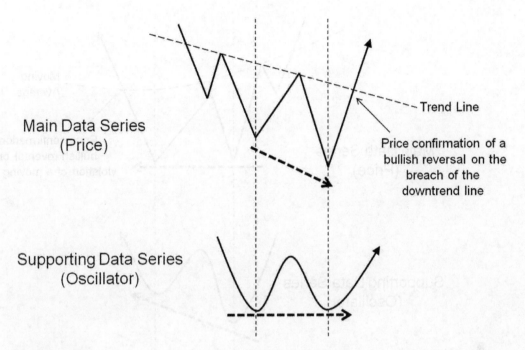

Main Data Series
(Price)

Trend Line

Price confirmation of a
bullish reversal on the
breach of the
downtrend line

Supporting Data Series
(Oscillator)

FIGURE 9.68 Price Confirmation of Standard Bullish Divergence via a Trendline Breakout.

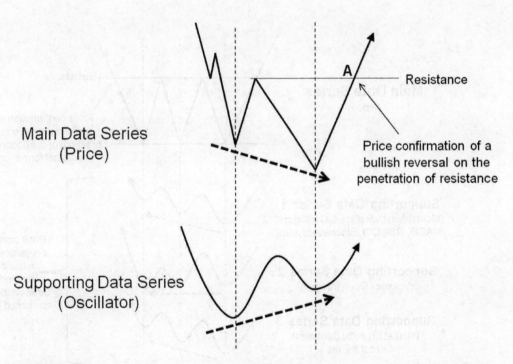

Main Data Series
(Price)

A

Resistance

Price confirmation of a
bullish reversal on the
penetration of resistance

Supporting Data Series
(Oscillator)

FIGURE 9.69 Price Confirmation of Standard Bullish Divergence via a Resistance Breakout.

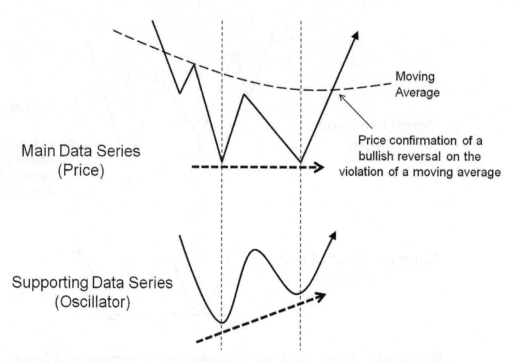

FIGURE 9.70 Price Confirmation of Standard Bullish Divergence via a Moving Average Breakout.

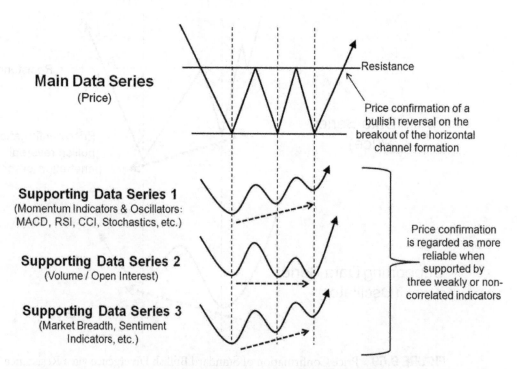

FIGURE 9.71 Price Confirmation of Standard Bullish Divergence via a Channel Breakout with Three Non-Correlated Indicators.

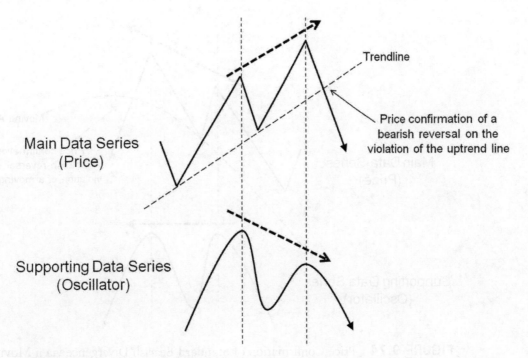

FIGURE 9.72 Price Confirmation of Standard Bearish Divergence via a Trendline Breakout.

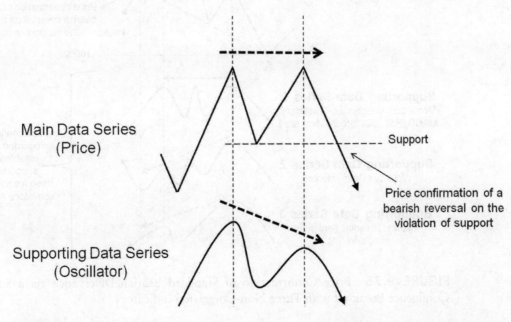

FIGURE 9.73 Price Confirmation of Standard Bearish Divergence via a Support Breakout.

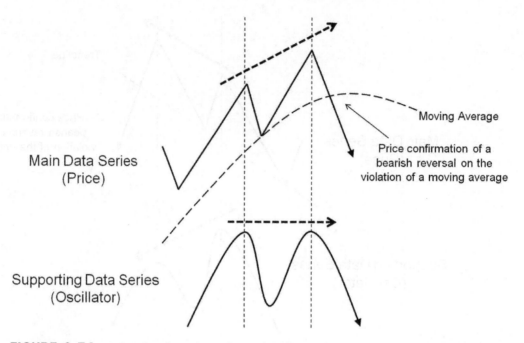

FIGURE 9.74 Price Confirmation of Standard Bearish Divergence via a Moving Average Breakout.

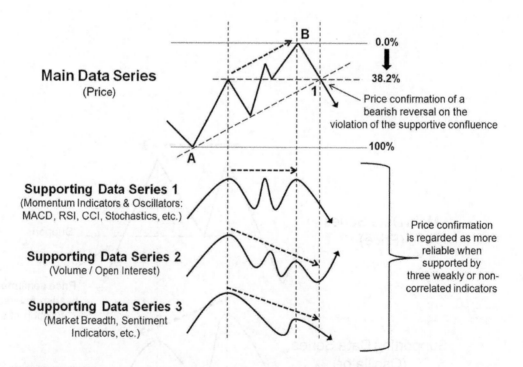

FIGURE 9.75 Price Confirmation of Standard Bearish Divergence via a Supportive Confluence Breakout with Three Non-Correlated Indicators.

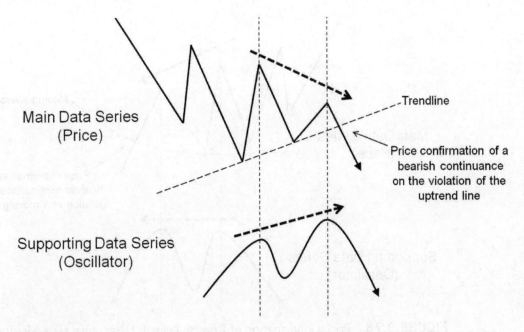

FIGURE 9.76 Price Confirmation of Reverse Bearish Divergence via a Trendline Breakout.

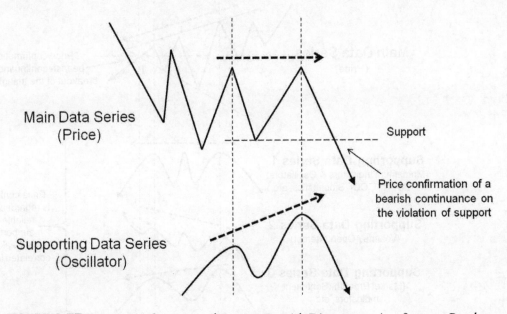

FIGURE 9.77 Price Confirmation of Reverse Bearish Divergence via a Support Breakout.

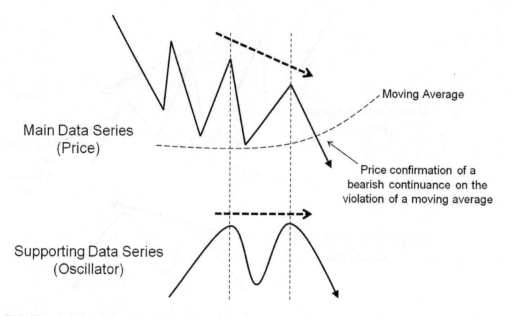

Main Data Series
(Price)

Moving Average

Price confirmation of a
bearish continuance on the
violation of a moving average

Supporting Data Series
(Oscillator)

FIGURE 9.78 Price Confirmation of Reverse Bearish Divergence via a Moving Average Breakout.

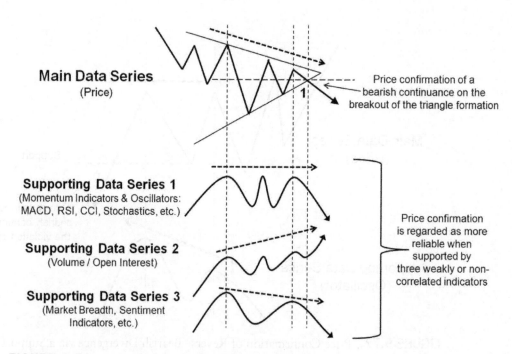

Main Data Series
(Price)

Price confirmation of a
bearish continuance on the
breakout of the triangle formation

Supporting Data Series 1
(Momentum Indicators & Oscillators:
MACD, RSI, CCI, Stochastics, etc.)

Supporting Data Series 2
(Volume / Open Interest)

Price confirmation
is regarded as more
reliable when
supported by
three weakly or non-
correlated indicators

Supporting Data Series 3
(Market Breadth, Sentiment
Indicators, etc.)

FIGURE 9.79 Price Confirmation of Reverse Bearish Divergence via a Triangle Formation Breakout with Three Non-Correlated Indicators.

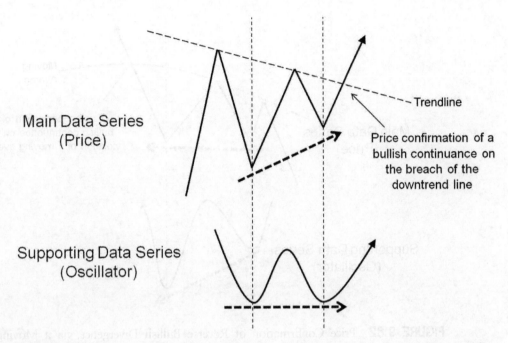

FIGURE 9.80   Price Confirmation of Reverse Bullish Divergence via a Trendline Breakout.

Figures 9.81 to 9.86 show three different price continuations applied on the same bar chart. This illustrates the point that the ensuing of price barrier formation is essentially continuous; it is therefore useful to use a significantly clear out-of-area price barrier for a more reliable entry or forecast.

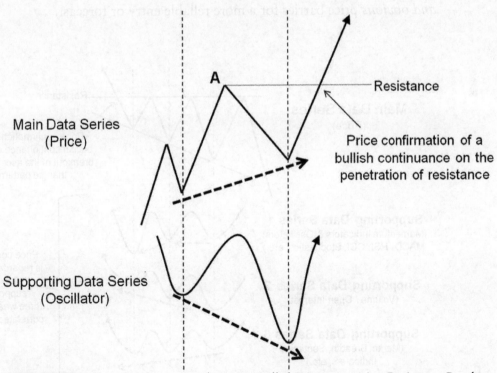

FIGURE 9.81   Price Confirmation of Reverse Bullish Divergence via a Resistance Breakout.

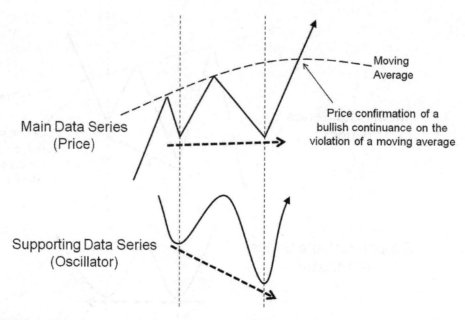

FIGURE 9.82 Price Confirmation of Reverse Bullish Divergence via a Moving Average Breakout.

Figures 9.84 to 9.86 show three different price confirmations applied on the same bar chart. This illustrates the point that the choice of price barrier for confirmation is essentially *arbitrary*. It is therefore best to choose a *significantly clear and obvious* price barrier for a more reliable entry or forecast.

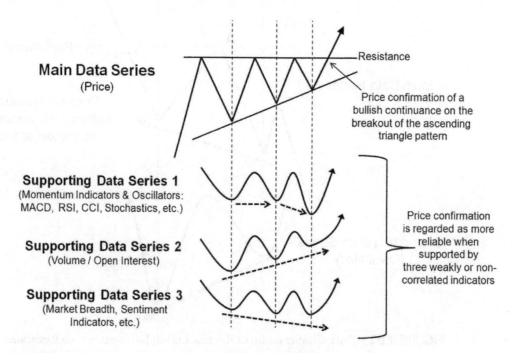

FIGURE 9.83 Price Confirmation of Reverse Bullish (Double) Divergence via a Triangle Formation Breakout with Three Non-Correlated Indicators.

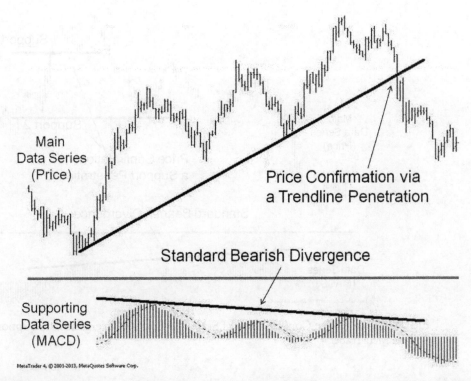

FIGURE 9.84 Price Confirmation of Standard Bearish Divergence via a Trendline Breakout.
Source: MetaTrader 4

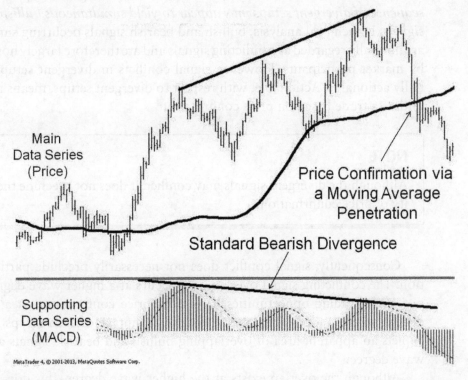

FIGURE 9.85 Price Confirmation of Standard Bearish Divergence via a Moving Average Breakout.
Source: MetaTrader 4

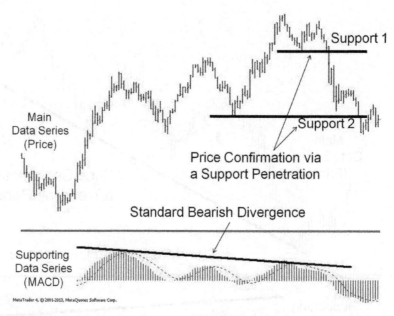

FIGURE 9.86 Price Confirmation of Standard Bearish Divergence via Support Breakouts. Source: MetaTrader 4

9.4.1 Price Confirmation in Contiguous Divergent Setups and Follow-Through

Sometimes, price oscillates continuously between divergent setups. *A continuous sequence of divergent setups may appear to yield simultaneous bullish and bearish signals.* In technical analysis, bullish and bearish signals occurring simultaneously are normally regarded as conflicting signals and are therefore largely non-actionable by market participants. However, signal conflicts in divergent setups are potentially actionable. Actionable, with respect to divergent setups, means the ability to initiate a trade based on price confirmation.

> **NOTE**
>
> Although the divergent signals may conflict, it does not preclude the possibility of price confirmation.

Consequently, signal conflict does not necessarily preclude participatory action. The conflicting signal overlap only occurs at a higher wave degree and does not affect trading opportunities if we seek price confirmation at a lower wave degree, where traders can potentially take advantage of such setups. Figure 9.87 depicts an apparent area of overlapping bullish and bearish signals at the higher wave degree.

Although the overlap exists at the higher wave degree, this does not prevent it from being a tradable setup. Once a divergent setup has been identified at the higher wave degree, the trader may initiate a trade once price has confirmed the

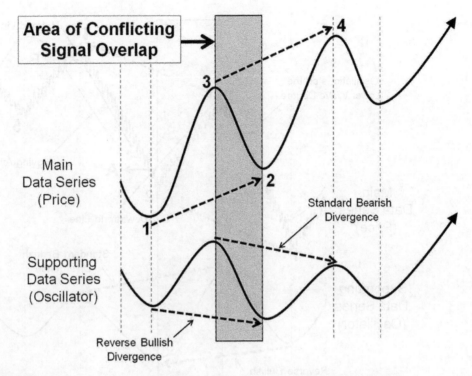

FIGURE 9.87 Conflicting Signal Overlap in Opposing Divergent Setups.

setup at a lower wave degree. The penetration of a higher peak or lower trough may be used as a price barrier for price confirmation. Alternatively, a moving average may also be employed to catch the reversal at the lower wave degree. Figure 9.88 shows price motion at a higher wave degree originating from oscillations at a lower wave degree. We see the same area of conflicting signals as in Figure 9.87. After establishing reverse bullish divergence at the higher wave degree, the trader may initiate a long entry at point A upon the breach of the first, second, or even third higher peak at the lower wave degree, depending on the parameters of the entry filter employed. Alternatively, an upside violation of a downtrend line or moving average based on the lower wave degree may also be used as an entry trigger. Similarly, a trader may use the breach of a lower trough to initiate short entry at point B after establishing standard bearish divergence at a higher wave degree, with the downside violation of the uptrend line or moving average based on the lower wave degree as alternate entry triggers.

As long as price confirmation is not wholly dependent on resistance or support levels based on the *prior peak or trough* at the higher wave degree, then signal conflicts will, in most cases, not adversely impact participatory action. For example, in Figure 9.89, a reverse bullish divergent signal overlaps a reverse bearish divergent signal. We observe that the reverse bullish divergent setup failed to gain confirmation at the prior resistance level based on the peak at point 3. The reverse bearish divergent setup also failed to gain confirmation at the prior support level based on the trough at point 2. Therefore, seeking price confirmation at the next lower wave degree is preferable in most cases.

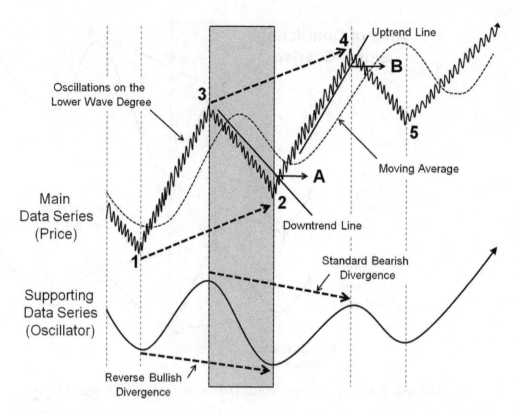

FIGURE 9.88 Trading the Conflicting Signal Overlap at a Lower Wave Degree.

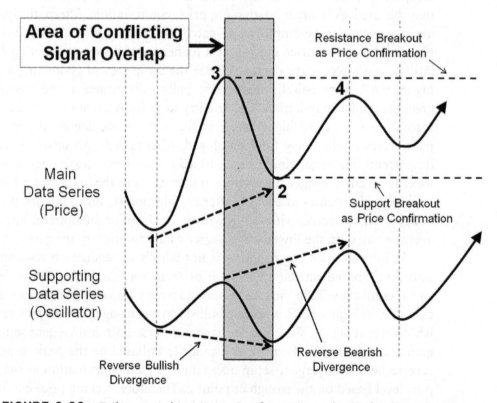

FIGURE 9.89 Failure to Achieve Price Confirmation at the Higher Wave Degree.

But there are situations where price confirmation at the higher wave degree is necessary, especially when it relates to forecasting the direction of the subsequent larger trend where we require the violation of a higher peak or lower trough in order to determine whether it is up trending or down trending.

Finally, once prices reverse and the divergent setup achieves price confirmation, we say that there is *follow-through* of the setup. It should be obvious by now that for any setup, follow-through is easier to achieve at the next lower wave degree. Therefore, in spite of overlapping areas of conflicting signals at the higher wave degree, it does not affect participatory action at the lower wave degree as there is a high level of follow-through from one setup to another.

9.5 SIGNAL ALTERNATION BETWEEN STANDARD AND REVERSE DIVERGENCE

As briefly discussed in the previous section, there may be situations where standard and reverse divergence formations may overlap and even alternate in succession, resulting in what initially appears to be contradictory signals. We shall examine 20 general scenarios where the data series trend, range, expand, and contract with respect to each other. There are only six idealized scenarios exhibiting signal alternation. We shall assume for convenience that all data series action unfolds contiguously in a consistent manner and displays no irregular action.

9.5.1 Heuristic for Determining if Signal Alternation Is Present

We can formulate a general rule of thumb for deciding if signal alternation exists between the main and supporting data series.

Signal alternation exists if the all three conditions below are satisfied:

1. *Peaks* between the two data series are trending in *different* directions
2. *Troughs* between the two data series are trending in *different* directions
3. *Peaks and troughs* within each data series are trending in the *same* direction

In the following six illustrations, we find that signal alternation only occurs when both the main and supporting data are trending in *opposite* directions (i.e., non-directionally aligned divergence). Figures 9.90 and 9.91 show two out of the six idealized scenarios where there is signal alternation.

9.5.2 Heuristic for Determining No Signal Alternation

Signal alternation between standard and reverse divergence does not occur when:

■ Both the main and supporting data series are trending in the *same* direction
■ Both the main and supporting data series are exhibiting *contrasting* sideways formations (i.e., one data series expanding while the other is contracting)

337

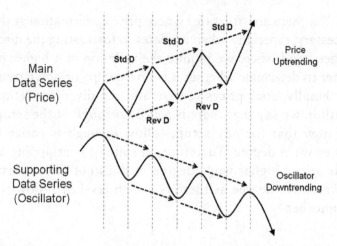

FIGURE 9.90 Signal Alternation in Opposing (Divergent) Data Trends.

- Both the main and supporting data series are exhibiting *similar* sideways formations (i.e., both data series expanding or contracting together)
- One data series is expanding or contracting while the other is flat or trending

Figures 9.92 and 9.93 show two out of the 14 idealized scenarios where there is no signal alternation.

9.6 MORE EXAMPLES OF DIVERGENCE

In the following sections, we shall examine some real world charts with various types of divergences in action.

9.6.1 Examples of Price to Price Divergence

In this section we shall look at divergence between stocks, funds, futures contracts, and various indices in lieu of oscillators and indicators.

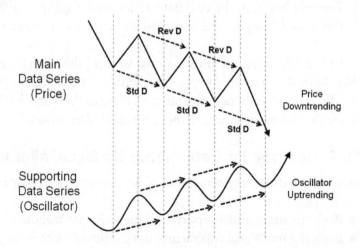

FIGURE 9.91 Signal Alternation in Opposing (Convergent) Data Trends.

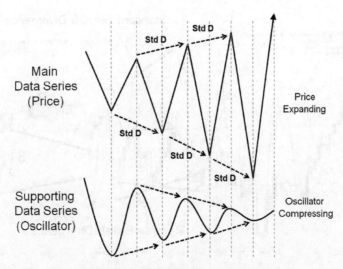

FIGURE 9.92   No Signal Alternation between Expanding and Contracting Formations.

9.6.1.1 Examples of Inter Market Divergence

The main challenge when attempting to identify divergence between stocks, commodities, and various indices is to determine which instrument would best represent the main data series. It behooves the analyst to refer to the momentum principle, described in section 9.3.6, as a guide to determining the most appropriate choice for the main data series. The momentum principle states that the main data series is expected to follow through in the direction of the supporting data series, as far as standard divergence is concerned. Therefore, based on a similar rationale, the task is to identify the stock, commodity, or index that leads the one under observation. In short, the leading instrument will represent the supporting data series, and the instrument or market under observation in the main data series is expected to follow through in the direction of the leading market or instrument. As for the application of reverse divergence analysis, we shall resort to either the contrarian or chronological approach and expect a continuation in price in main data series.

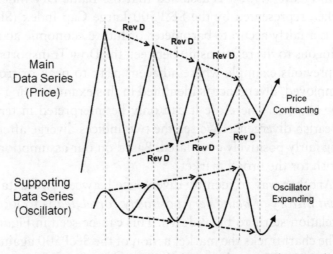

FIGURE 9.93   No Signal Alternation between Contracting and Expanding Formations.

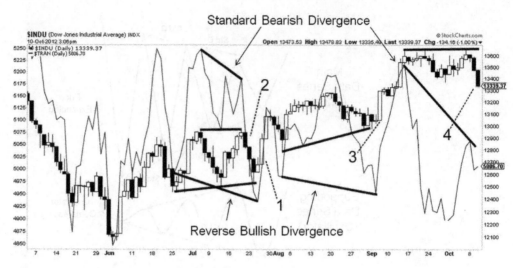

FIGURE 9.94 Intermarket Divergences.
Courtesy of Stockcharts.com

Figure 9.94 shows the various divergences that exist between the Dow Jones Industrial Average and the Dow Jones Transportation Average over a period of five months. The Transportation is represented by the line chart. Assuming that the Dow Jones Transportation Average represents the supporting data series, we expect the Industrials to follow through in the direction indicated by the Transports for standard divergence and in the opposite direction to the Transports in reverse divergence. We see that the Industrials do in fact react to the Transports in the manner expected fairly consistently, as evinced by the price excursion at points 1 to 4. For example, we see the Industrials declining at point 2 after a standard bearish divergent setup and subsequently rising, as expected, at point 1 after a reverse bullish divergent setup. The Industrials rise again in similar consistent fashion at point 3 after a second reverse bullish divergent setup and decline, as expected, at point 4 after another standard bearish divergent setup. This is all predicated on the assumption that the Transports lead the Industrials.

In Figure 9.95, it is assumed that the Baltic Dry Index will lead the broader market, represented by the S&P500 Large Cap Index (SPX). The Baltic Dry Index is a fairly accurate barometer of future economic activity, which in a way is analogous to the relationship between the Dow Transports and Industrials. Unlike the previous example where adjacent peak to peak or trough to trough analysis is employed, divergence is identified in this example using conventional trend and slope analysis. Therefore it can only be interpreted in terms of standard bullish or bearish divergence. We see the two indices diverge after a prolonged period of being fairly positively correlated. Based on our assumption, this setup is therefore bearish for the broad market.

Another way to identify divergence between two data series that have a *consistent history of being very positively correlated* is to look for periods when the correlation starts to breakdown. This can be seen in Figure 9.96 at points A and B. The chart tracks the market action of the S&P500 against an inverted Volatility Index (VIX). This is done to help better visualize the relationship between the two

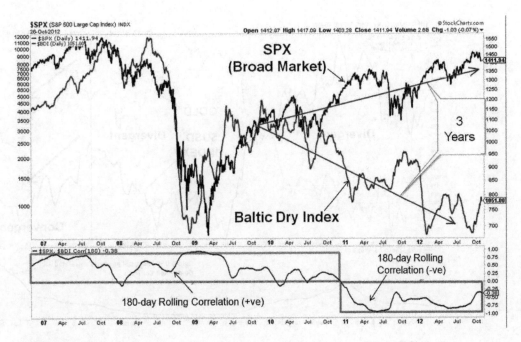

FIGURE 9.95 Intermarket Divergence.
Courtesy of Stockcharts.com

indices. We can see a significantly strong and consistent correlation between the two data series. But at points A and B, we observe larger than average divergences in correlation between the two indices.

Figure 9.97 brings up a very important point. When two markets are normally positively correlated, we look at divergence as a deviation from the norm. However when markets are normally negatively correlated, we instead look at

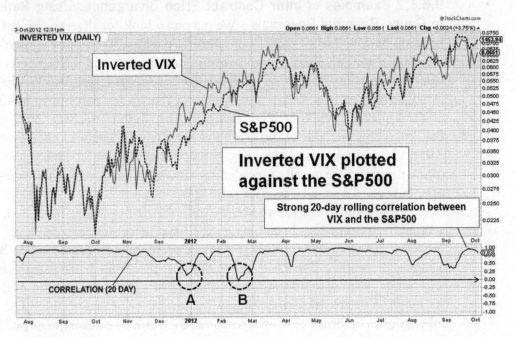

FIGURE 9.96 Intermarket Correlation and Divergence.
Courtesy of Stockcharts.com

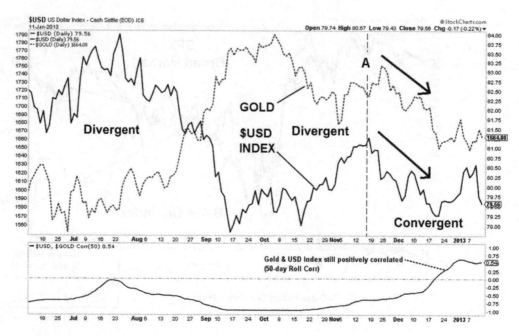

FIGURE 9.97 Naturally Divergent Markets.
Courtesy of Stockcharts.com

convergence as a deviation from the norm. Many markets have a natural inverse relationship with other markets. In such cases, divergence is actually represented by the two markets converging on each other, albeit only briefly. In Figure 9.97, the convergence begins around time line A.

9.6.1.2 Examples of Inter Contract Price Divergence: Using Ratio Spikes to Gauge Potential Reversals
We may also look for divergences between the prices in back and front months of a futures contract. We simply construct a ratio or relative strength chart of two contract months and add a fixed percentage envelope or volatility band to it. In Figure 9.98, we see reversals in Silver being accurately forecasted, at points 1 to 9, whenever the 20-day percentage band violated at the 5 percent breakout level, based on the March and May 2012 contracts. Breakouts to either side of the band give equally valid signals and provide a fairly easy and consistent way of gauging potential reversals in Silver. Larger violations of the threshold are usually preceded by more significant selling climaxes or blow offs, as evinced by the large price ratio spike at point 7.

In Figure 9.99, reversals in Brent Crude Oil are accurately predicted, at points 1 to 13, every time the thresholds on the fixed percentage envelope are tested or breached. Threshold A represents a lower percentage threshold while B is set at a higher percentage. The ratio spikes that test threshold B are usually associated with larger reversals in Brent Crude Oil. The threshold percentage levels may be set either via back testing or simply by careful visual inspection. The first significant reversal drove oil down to about $107.40. The subsequent pullback was accurately identified at point 1 where the ratio spike tested the lower percentage threshold. The pullback was followed by an extended run up in oil prices.

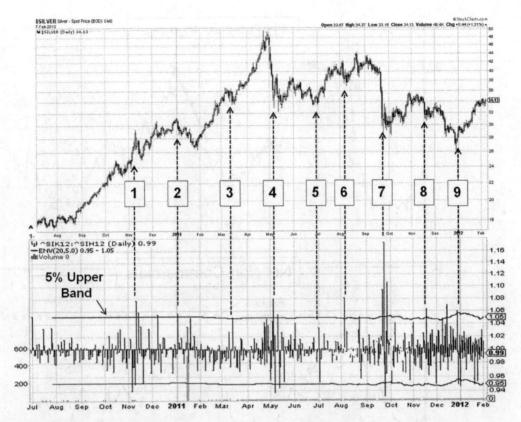

FIGURE 9.98   Forecasting Reversals in Silver via Inter Contract Divergence.
Courtesy of Stockcharts.com

9.6.1.3 Examples of Price to Net Commercial (COT Report) Divergence

Though a reading of the entire COT report is necessary for a proper analysis, we shall only focus on the historical open interest relationship between the USD Index Futures and the net non-commercials for the purpose of this brief analysis. In Figure 9.100, we observe that the net non-commercial activity exhibited

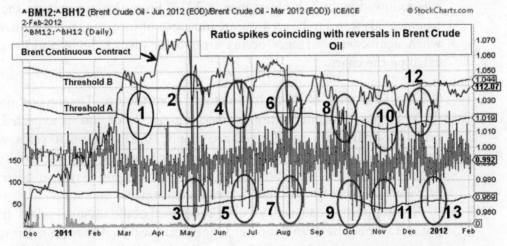

FIGURE 9.99   Forecasting Reversals in Brent Crude Oil via Inter Contract Divergence.
Courtesy of Stockcharts.com

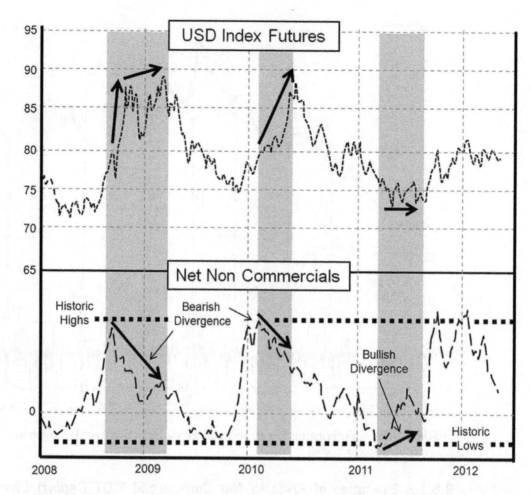

FIGURE 9.100 Forecasting Reversals via USD Index Futures to Net Non-Commercials Divergence.

significant bearish divergence around 2008 to 2009 and again in 2010. This was followed by bullish divergence in 2011. From this perspective, the net non-commercials seems to be an accurate indicator of future market action, especially when significant divergence occurs around the historic highs and lows, as indicated on the chart.

9.6.1.4 Examples of Price to Seasonal Divergence Divergence may also be derived from non-confirmation between current price and its expected seasonal price. Seasonal prices may be averaged over 5, 10, 20, or even 30 years, with some providers excluding outlier events in order to give a more representative price that is free from various distortions. The mode of averaging may also differ between providers, ranging from simple to weighted averages.

The supporting data series will be comprised of the seasonal prices. It is best to use at least one short- and another longer-term seasonal chart in order to identify any discrepancies or change in market behavior. All divergences should only entail participatory action once there is clear and significant price confirmation.

9.7.1.5 Examples of Relative Performance Divergence   This is another type of divergence that is based on the percentage performance of two data series over the same period of observation. It is a *relative* measure because:

- The performances are measured as a ratio or percentage rather than as a spread based on absolute price or index point differences
- The most recent percentage performance depends on the initial point of reference or comparison over a specified period (i.e., the performance at each point is compared to the price or index level at the start of the observed period and is measured as a percentage of this initial price or index level)

In Figure 9.101, the Housing Index is making lower peaks in terms of percentage performance while the SPY ETF is making higher peaks, where the period of comparison extends from June 1, 2010, to March 13, 2013. In this example, the Housing Index is assuming the role of supporting data series and is therefore indicating future bearishness in the broad market, represented in this example by the SPY ETF. In a sense, performance charts are useful in that they normalize performance by comparing percentages instead of absolute values, making comparison across various markets and instruments more accessible and meaningful. (To compare the relative percentage or ratio performance of two data series as a function of price *at each point* rather than with the initial price of the observed period, we resort to the use of relative or comparative strength charts.)

FIGURE 9.101   Relative Bearish Divergence between the Housing Index (PHLX) and the SPY ETF.
Courtesy of Stockcharts.com

9.6.2 Examples of Price to Overlay Indicator Divergence

In this section, we shall examine divergence between price and various overlay indicators.

9.6.2.1 Examples of Price to Moving Average Divergence

The amount of divergence between price and its own moving average plays a key role in the forecasting of potential reversal and continuations in the market. To determine the amount of divergence present, we detrend price with its moving average in the same way that the MACD is created, which is by detrending two moving averages. In Figure 9.102, a price oscillator was used to isolate and quantify the amount of divergence between price and its moving average. (The MACD was used in the example below with a period setting of 1 for price and 100 for the exponential moving average that we would like to observe.) One advantage of using a price oscillator is that it identifies the potential overbought and oversold levels in the stock, as indicated from 1 to 5. Notice that the projected overbought and oversold levels coincide with bottoms and tops in the stock.

9.6.3 Examples of Overlay to Overlay Indicator Divergence

In this section, we shall examine divergences between three popular overlay indicators, namely moving averages, Bollinger Bands, and regression lines.

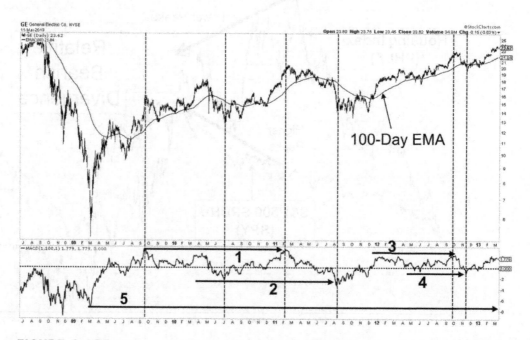

FIGURE 9.102 Forecasting Reversals in GE via Overbought and Oversold Levels in the Price Oscillator.
Courtesy of Stockcharts.com

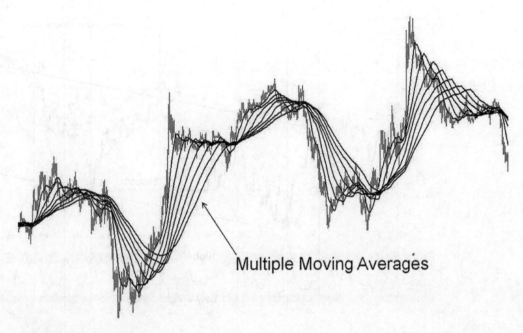

Multiple Moving Averages

FIGURE 9.103 Forecasting Consolidations and Trends via Multiple Moving Average Divergence and Convergence.

9.6.3.1 Examples of Inter Moving Average Divergence

The most popular indicator that is founded on inter moving average divergence is the MACD. As mentioned in an earlier section, we may use the divergence created between the peaks and troughs in the MACD and price itself to forecast reversals and continuations in the market.

We could also study the divergent behavior of various popular moving averages to better understand the nature and character of the market under observation. In Figure 9.103, we see multiple moving averages in action. Diverging averages indicate continuation while converging averages indicate a slowing of the trend and potential reversal. This diverging and converging behavior within the group of moving averages is of immense interest to the practitioner as it provides a means of forecasting potential consolidations and breakouts, by observing the average rate at which the group of averages contracts and expands.

9.6.3.2 Examples of Bollinger Bandwidth Divergence

We shall use the broad definition of divergence when referring to Bollinger Bandwidth divergence. Slope analysis is used when analyzing bandwidth divergence, and therefore this excludes reverse divergence from the analysis. The fluctuations in the bandwidth reflect the degree of divergence between the upper and lower bands. Under the narrow definition of divergence, these fluctuations represent the diverging and converging action between the bands. It is important to understand that we cannot use terms like standard, bullish, or bearish with bandwidth divergence. This is because the bandwidth

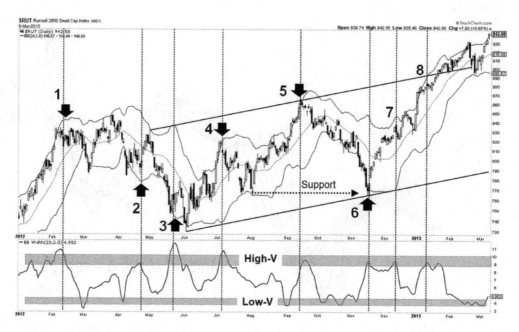

FIGURE 9.104 Forecasting Reversals in the Russell 2000 Small Cap Index with Bollinger Bandwidth Divergence.
Courtesy of Stockcharts.com

divergence provides no directional information with respect to future price action, hence it is not possible to determine if a divergent setup is bullish or bearish. Bandwidth divergence tracks the volatility in the market, and therefore converging bands represent periods of lower volatility while diverging bands represent periods of greater volatility. Bandwidth divergence is particularly useful in predicting:

- Potential breakout moves in the market especially after an extended period of low volatility (trades based on taking advantage of these low volatility breakouts are popularly referred to as *squeeze* plays)
- Reversals at historical overbought bandwidth levels

In Figure 9.104, the reversal in the Russell 2000 Small Cap Index, indicated at points 1 to 6, coincides fairly consistently with the test of the historical overbought or extreme level on the Bollinger bandwidth indicator. The upper extreme level represents periods of high volatility whereas the lower extreme reflects periods of low volatility. Point 6 may be of particular interest to traders as it represents a *supportive confluence* comprising a projected channel bottom and a prior support level, accompanied by a Bollinger bandwidth divergence peak. Hence, point 6 represents a high probability entry. As far as trading at points 7 and 8 is concerned, as with any divergent setup, there must be some form of price confirmation to trigger an entry. Assuming that we use the 20-day moving average (which happens to represent the central value of the Bollinger Band) as the barrier required for price confirmation, no trade would have been initiated at points 7 or 8 as there was no decisive closing penetration of the moving average at either points.

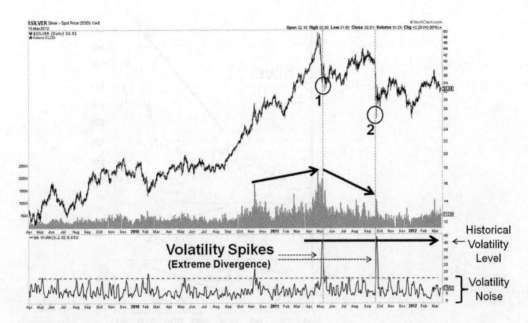

FIGURE 9.105 Forecasting Reversals in Silver with Bollinger Bandwidth Divergence. Courtesy of Stockcharts.com

Figure 9.105 is yet another example of using extreme Bollinger bandwidth divergence to forecast potential reversals in price. The Bollinger bandwidth is set to a lower lookback value of five days in order to increase its responsiveness to rapid price excursions and market shocks. We see two selling climaxes occurring at points 1 and 2, both of which were accompanied by large volatility spikes in the Bollinger bandwidth. This first spike demarcates the historical volatility level which will later serve as a threshold for potential future reversals. We see this volatility threshold being subsequently violated, with Silver forming a new bottom at point 2. The peaks of the volatility spikes lie well above its noise floor, indicating that the two bottoms are high sigma events. The noise floor is also fairly well contained, fluctuating within a 15 percent band.

9.6.3.3 Examples of Inter Regression Line Divergence

Some practitioners also employ the use of a regression line to determine the direction of a particular trend of interest. When using regression lines, slope analysis is employed, with all non-confirmation being either standard bullish or bearish divergence. As a result, reverse divergence is excluded from the analysis when employing regression lines to determine direction.

9.6.4 Examples of Price to Volume and Open Interest Divergence

In Figure 9.106, we see significant long-term bearish divergence in Silver between price and open interest, between time lines A and B. The volume action displays bullish confirmation and eventually peaks at point 1. As pointed out in section 9.4.14, any extremely bullish formation is potentially bearish, and vice versa. We

FIGURE 9.106 Price to Volume and Open Interest Divergence in Silver.

also see medium-term bearish divergence indicated between point 2 and time line B. Rising volume accompanied by declining open interest is indicative of a rally fueled by *short covering*. Though not displayed on the chart, it may be interesting to be aware of the fact that the Market Vane sentiment readings for Silver were at extreme overbought levels prior to Silver peaking in 2011. Sentiment indicators are most reliable at market extremes and should therefore be incorporated into any analysis of divergence at historic or significant price levels. Finally, market participants should only initiate short positions or exit previously profitable long positions upon price confirmation.

9.6.5 Examples of Oscillator to Oscillator Divergence

Divergence between two different oscillators is referred to as *inter-oscillator* divergence, whereas that between two identical oscillators is called *intra-oscillator* divergence. The two basic measures of divergence between oscillators are that of direction and phase. Divergence stemming from directional discrepancies is most commonly employed. It is harder to locate phase discrepancies between oscillators that usually peak and trough in lockstep with each other. That is the reason why when a phase discrepancy arises, it is regarded as a strong indication of a potential reversal.

9.7.5.1 Example of Inter-Oscillator Divergence (Directional Discrepancy)—Using OBV-ADL Indicator Pair Divergence to Gauge Market Regime Change One particularly useful technique for forecasting market behavior or regime change is via the combined use of the OBV and ADL. Whenever there is non-confirmation between the OBV and ADL, price action will fairly frequently be volatile and erratic. However, when there is confirmation between these two

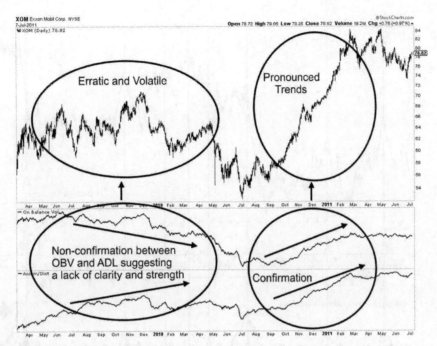

FIGURE 9.107 Forecasting Regime Changes in Exxon Mobile Corp via OBV-ADL Divergence.
Courtesy of Stockcharts.com

indicators, price action will usually be less volatile with more pronounced trends. This ability to gauge market behavior will be of great benefit to directional traders who want to avoid choppy action and only participate when the market is more predisposed to trending action. See Figure 9.107.

9.6.5.2 Examples of Inter-Oscillator Divergence: Phase Discrepancy

Phase differences are easily identified by locating peaks or troughs in the oscillators that are not in sync or aligned with each other. Though phase difference is ideally associated with sinusoidal action and is therefore perfectly identifiable and quantifiable, this is unfortunately not the case in semi-random markets where wave cycles are at best transient and seldom symmetrical. Before looking at our next example, let us first define phase divergence.

When examining phase divergence, the following guidelines apply:

1. When peaks are asynchronous, it is regarded as potentially *bearish for price*
2. When troughs are asynchronous, it is regarded as potentially *bullish for price*
3. When peaks are asynchronous, no oscillator peak should lag the peak in price
4. When troughs are asynchronous, no oscillator trough should lag the trough in price

Figure 9.108 displays a chart of the continuous contract in wheat, with two oscillators—the 60-day rolling CCI and the MACD—as the supporting data series. We notice that for the most part peaking in the CCI and MACD is fairly synchronous. But at time line A we see the CCI peaking before MACD and price.

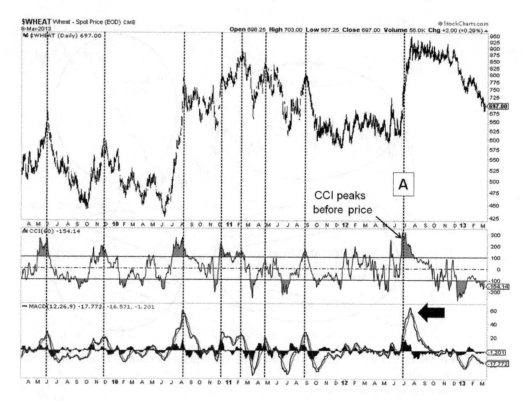

FIGURE 9.108 Forecasting Reversals in Wheat via Phase Divergence.
Courtesy of Stockcharts.com

Such phase divergences are regarded as stronger bearish signals. Guideline (3) above has not been breached.

9.6.5.3 Examples of Intra-Oscillator Divergence: Directional and Phase Divergence

Just as for inter-oscillator divergence, we also look for both directional and phase discrepancies in intra-oscillator divergence. Although the oscillators are identical, the lookback period will be different. A longer lookback period will generate slower oscillations at a higher wave degree while a shorter setting will generate more rapid oscillations at a lower wave degree. Since the two oscillators are of identical construction, the faster oscillations at the lower wave degree represent, in a sense, the harmonics of the larger oscillations at the higher wave degree. This is analogous to a guitar string being plucked, where the largest wave produces the lowest note with the smaller waves producing the harmonics and higher overtones. Figure 9.109 is a chart of spot GBPUSD displaying intra-oscillator divergence between a 100-day and 10-day price oscillator. Figure 9.110 shows phase divergence at time lines 3 and 6. The two oscillators are synchronous at all the other time lines indicated.

9.6.6 Example of Price to Market Breadth Divergence

We may also employ divergence between price and market breadth indicators to forecast potential reversals. In Figure 9.111, the two indicators plotted are the

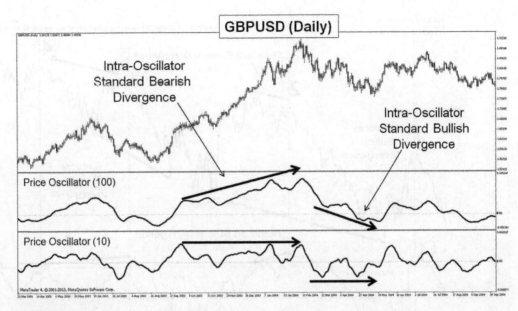

FIGURE 9.109 Forecasting Reversals in GBPUSD via Intra-Oscillator (Directional) Divergence.
Source: MetaTrader 4

S&P500 Bullish Percent Index and the MACD. We observe that every time the Bullish Percent Index tests its overbought level, as seen at time lines 1 to 4, the market eventually reverses. We see two non-correlated indicators providing almost identical signals. We also see that the market reacts in a consistent manner to the bullish and bearish divergences by following through with either an upside or downside move initiated at or soon after price confirmation.

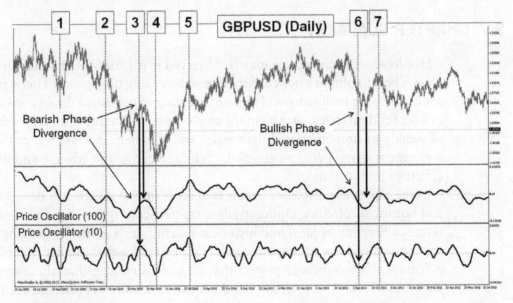

FIGURE 9.110 Forecasting Reversals in GBPUSD via Intra-Oscillator (Phase) Divergence.
Source: MetaTrader 4

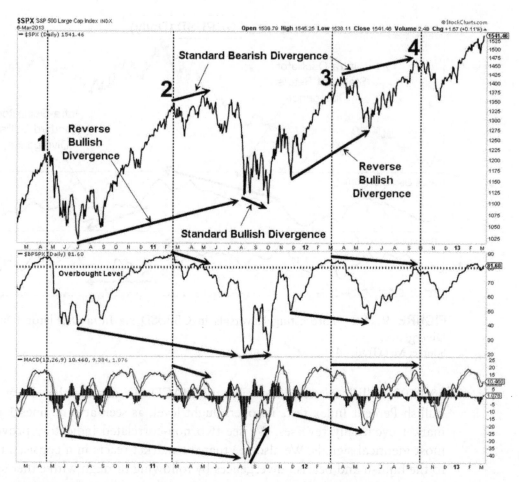

FIGURE 9.111 Forecasting Reversals in the S&P500 via Market Breadth Divergence.
Courtesy of Stockcharts.com

9.7 CHAPTER SUMMARY

As we have seen, divergence may be observed in a variety of technical setups. It is always best to obtain price confirmation when using divergence. This is because in some cases, the indicators will remain in a state of *persistent divergence* with price or another data series, such as in the case of serial or multiple divergences. The use of weakly or non-correlated data series will also help increase the probability of a divergent signal being more reliable, circumventing the adverse and misleading effects of multicollinearity.

One aspect not discussed in this chapter is that of divergence between implied and historical volatility. Option traders are particularly interested in observing divergence between implied and historical volatility as a guide for gauging the most appropriate options strategy to employ. When the level of implied volatility is significantly overbought with respect to itself and also higher than the corresponding historical volatility, a reversion to the mean is usually expected in the form of a potential volatility crush.

Finally, practitioners interested in using divergence as a tool for price projections may also want to refer to Constance Brown's book *Technical Analysis for the Trading Professional,* where she employs the spread or differential between various inflection points as a basis for price projections.

CHAPTER 9 REVIEW QUESTIONS

1. Describe the main challenges in the application of divergence analysis.
2. Explain how the adverse effects of multicollinearity could be avoided or reduced.
3. Describe George Lane's Bull and Bear setups and discuss the challenges in identifying such setups.
4. Give examples where volume divergence may be ineffective.
5. Describe the relationship between divergence and price momentum.
6. Describe an ideal divergence setup and its underlying weaknesses.
7. What are the methods for identifying divergence?
8. Explain how you would trade a divergent setup.

REFERENCES

Blau, William. 1995. *Momentum, Direction and Divergence.* New York: John Wiley & Sons.

Brown, Constance M. 1999. *Technical Analysis for the Trading Professional.* New York: McGraw-Hill.

LeBeau, Charles, and David W. Lucas. 1992. *Technical Traders Guide to Computer Analysis of the Futures Market.* Homewood, IL: Business One Irwin.

Pring, Martin J. 2002. *Technical Analysis Explained: The successful Investor's Guide to Spotting Investment Trends and Turning Points.* 4th ed. New York: McGraw-Hill.

Fibonacci Number and Ratio Analysis

The application of Fibonacci numbers and ratios in technical analysis is pervasive. It is probably one of the most popular and widely used overlay indicators in technical analysis. In this chapter, we shall study the application of Fibonacci numbers and ratios to the financial markets and how we can use them to identify potential key reversal and breakout levels.

10.1 THE FIBONACCI NUMBER SERIES

Leonardo Fibonacci, in his historic 1202 book entitled *Liber Abaci* (Book of the Abacus), introduced to Western civilization a special sequence of numbers known as the *Fibonacci series*. Before learning how Fibonacci numbers and ratios are used in the financial markets to forecast potential support and resistance levels, let us first turn our attention to the source and derivation of these interesting numbers and ratios.

10.1.1 The Fibonacci Series

A simple mathematical expression that describes a Fibonacci series is given as follows:

$$F_{n+1} = F_n + F_{n-1}$$

where F_n represents the current number, F_{n-1} the previous number, and F_{n+1} the next number in the Fibonacci series. Alternatively, due to the iterative nature of the mathematical expression, it may also be expressed as:

$$F_n = F_{n-1} + F_{n-2}$$

where F_{n-1} and F_{n-2} represent the immediately previous two numbers of the sequence.

Regardless of the way it is mathematically expressed, every number in the Fibonacci sequence is the sum of its last two previous whole numbers.

Therefore, starting with $F_{n-1} = 0$ as the previous number and $F_n = 1$ as the current number in the series, we obtain F_{n+1}, the next number in the Fibonacci series, by repeating or iterating the process for each new F_n:

0, 1, 1, 2, 3, 5, 8, 13, 21, 34, 55, 89, 144, 233, 377, . . .

where we see that: 1+0 = 1, 1+1 = 2, 2+1 = 3, 3+2 = 5, 5+3 = 8, and so on, ad infinitum.

10.1.2 The French Connection: The Lucas Series

A variant of this iterative series may be constructed by changing the initial two numbers of the series, that is, by starting with $F_{n-1} = 2$ and $F_n = 1$ instead of $F_{n-1} = 0$ and $F_{n-1} = 1$. This new series is popularly referred to as the *Lucas Series*, after Edouard Lucas, a French mathematician. Similarly, by iteration via the Fibonacci sequence, we obtain:

2, 1, 3, 4, 7, 11, 18, 29, 47, 76, 123, 199, 322, . . .

where we see that: 2+1 = 3, 3+1 = 4, 4+3 = 7, 7+4 =11, 11+7 = 18, and so on, ad infinitum.

Letting L_n be the current number in a Lucas series, the relationship between the Lucas and Fibonacci number series is given by the mathematical relationship:

$$L_n = F_n + 2F_{n-1}$$

Let us examine this formulaic relationship a little more closely. As we have seen, the tenth Fibonacci number in the sequence given above is 34. Hence, via this mathematical expression, the corresponding tenth Lucas number should be $L_{10} = F_{10} + 2F_9 = 34 + 2(21) = 34 + 42 = 76$, which turns out to be the expected answer.

As we shall see later, Fibonacci (as well as Lucas) number counts are extremely popular technical tools commonly used to forecast potential top and bottom reversals in the markets, especially when they are used in conjunction with other overlay indicators such as Bollinger Bands, Japanese Candlesticks, Ichimoku Clouds, conventional trendlines, and price channels. To further help increase the probability of identifying these potential reversals, traders and analysts often also seek supporting evidence of overbought and oversold conditions in conventional window oscillators such as Stochastics, commodity channel index (CCI), moving average convergence-divergence (MACD), rate of change (ROC), and the relative strength index (RSI) during such reversals.

10.1.3 Philosophical Significance of the Fibonacci Iterative Series

We can clearly see that the next number in the Fibonacci series, F_{n+1} (i.e., new information), is the direct result of F_n (i.e., current information) interacting with F_{n-1} (past information).

$$F_{n+1} = F_n + F_{n-1}$$
$$(\text{Future}) = (\text{Present}) + (\text{Past})$$

In a sense, this mathematical expression uncannily reflects the commonly accepted philosophical premise that eventuality and causation are the direct result of current action based on past conditions or experience. This approach seems to fits very well with the study of technical analysis, as analysts and traders rely wholly on past and current information in order to determine and predict future market action.

10.2 FIBONACCI RATIOS

One unique and rather mysterious feature of the Fibonacci series is that of the ratio of the current Fibonacci number to its immediate previous number, that is, the ratio (F_{n+1}/F_n) or (F_n/F_{n-1}). This ratio approaches 1.618 (to three decimal places) as we progress further out along the series of Fibonacci numbers. In fact, as it turns out, it really does not matter which two numbers were initially chosen to start the sequence. As we progress further along the sequence, it will always approach 1.618! In similar fashion, the Lucas numbers also approach this ratio of 1.618 in the limit. This unique ratio is referred to as the Golden Ratio, or Phi (Φ). This ratio is also sometimes referred to as the Divine Proportion. Please refer to Figure 10.1.

As can be seen from Figure 10.1, both the Fibonacci and Lucas series approach the ratio of 1.618 as we progress further out along the sequence, that is, dividing any Fibonacci number by the number that immediately precedes it. In fact this ratio oscillates slightly as it asymptotically approaches 1.618, akin to the mechanical *dampening action* as seen in vibrating springs. See Figures 10.2 and 10.3.

As an exercise, try selecting *any two random numbers* and generate a Fibonacci sequence. You will inevitably discover that the ratio of any number to its immediate previous number will always start to approach 1.618 as you progress further along that particular sequence.

N	Fibonacci Sequence	Fibonacci Ratio	Lucas Sequence	Lucas Sequence Ratio
1	0	N/A	2	N/A
2	1	N/A	1	0.5000000
3	1	1.0000000	3	3.0000000
4	2	2.0000000	4	1.3333333
5	3	1.5000000	7	1.7500000
6	5	1.6666667	11	1.5714286
7	8	1.6000000	18	1.6363636
8	13	1.6250000	29	1.6111111
9	21	1.6153846	47	1.6206897
10	34	1.6190476	76	1.6170213
11	55	1.6176471	123	1.6184211
12	89	1.6181818	199	1.6178862
13	144	1.6179775	322	1.6180905
14	233	1.6180556	521	1.6180124
15	377	1.6180258	843	1.6180422
16	610	1.6180371	1364	1.6180308
17	987	1.6180328	2207	1.6180352
18	1597	1.6180344	3571	1.6180335
19	2584	1.6180338	5778	1.6180342
20	4181	1.6180341	9349	1.6180339
21	6765	1.6180340	15127	1.6180340
22	10946	1.6180340	24476	1.6180340
23	17711	1.6180340	39603	1.6180340
24	28657	1.6180340	64079	1.6180340
25	46368	1.6180340	103682	1.6180340

FIGURE 10.1 The Fibonacci and Lucas Sequences with Their Corresponding Ratios (F_n/F_{n-1}).

10.2.1 Geometrical Significance of the Fibonacci Ratio

In addition to the unique mathematical property of asymptotically approaching the ratio of 1.618 in the limit, the Golden Ratio also has special geometrical significance. Refer to Figure 10.4 below.

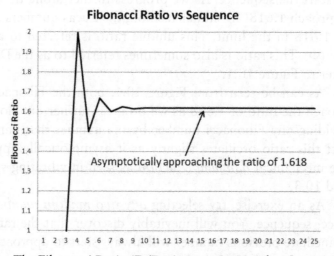

FIGURE 10.2 The Fibonacci Ratio (F_n/F_{n-1}) versus Its Number Sequence.

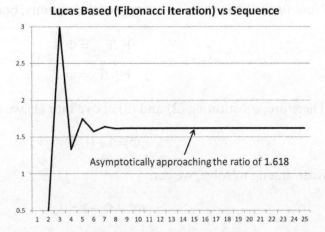

FIGURE 10.3 The Lucas-Based Fibonacci Ratio (F_n/F_{n-1}) versus the Lucas Number Sequence.

As it turns out, there is only one ratio that satisfies the following condition where the ratios of the lengths are:

$$BC/AB = AC/BC$$

That unique ratio is 1.618 (to three decimal places), which is also referred to as the *Golden Section*. This mysterious property has inspired mankind since its discovery, and as a consequence, many monuments and works of art have incorporated various aspects of the Golden Section within their construction. This ratio is also purportedly found in nature as an underlying fabric of creation.

10.2.2 The Simple Mathematical Derivation of Phi (Φ)

We can easily derive the value of Φ mathematically by extrapolating the ratio in the limit of two adjacent numbers in a Fibonacci series. Here is one of the many mathematical methods that may be employed to derive this ratio.

As seen earlier, a Fibonacci sequence may be defined as:

$$F_{n+1} = F_n + F_{n-1}$$

Let us now divide across by F_n, giving us:

$$(F_{n+1}/F_n) = (F_n/F_n) + (F_{n-1}/F_n)$$
$$(F_{n+1}/F_n) = 1 + (F_{n-1}/F_n)$$

(1)

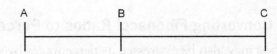

FIGURE 10.4 The Golden Ratio (or Section).

361

Now, *in the limit*, that is, as n approaches infinity, both:

$$F_n / F_{n-1} = \Phi \qquad (2)$$

$$F_{n+1} / F_n = \Phi \qquad (3)$$

Therefore, substituting (2) and (3) above into (1) we get:

$$\Phi = 1 + (1/\Phi)$$

Rearranging to solve, we get:

$$\Phi^2 - \Phi - 1 = 0$$

With the roots of the equation being:

$$\Phi = (1 \pm \sqrt{5})/2$$

Selecting the positive value, this will give us the value of $\Phi = 1.618033$ (to six decimal places).

10.2.3 Other Φ-Related Ratios Based on the Fibonacci Iterative Series

We already know that $\Phi = 1.618$ (to three decimal places). Here are some other important ratios related to Φ:

- $(1/\Phi) = 0.382$
- $\Phi \times \Phi = 2.618$
- $(2/\Phi) - 1 = 0.236$
- $\sqrt{(1/\Phi)} = 0.786$
- $\sqrt{\Phi} = 1.272$

The items in this list of Φ-related ratios are regarded as significant ratios in technical analysis and are used widely by technical traders and analysts. Please note that higher-order magnitudes of 1.618 are also employed in technical analysis, especially when calculating Fibonacci projection levels, for example, 1.618, 2.618, 3.618, and 4.618. It is customary for charting packages and platforms to also include the ratio 0.5, 1.0, 2.0, 3.0, and 4.0 within Fibonacci retracements, extensions, expansions, and projections. Some analysts contend that these ratios are not true Fibonacci ratios while others argue that 0.5 is a legitimate Fibonacci-related ratio since we can always derive 0.5 by dividing 1 by 2, which are both numbers from the Fibonacci series. By extension, multiples of 0.5 give rise to the ratios 1.0, 2.0, 3.0, and 4.0, respectively.

10.2.4 Converting Fibonacci Ratios to Percentages

These ratios may also be expressed as percentages by simply multiplying the ratio by 100. For example, the Fibonacci ratio 0.618 may be expressed as (0.618×100)

percent = 61.8 percent. Ratios and percentages may be used interchangeably to designate various Fibonacci levels.

10.3 FIBONACCI RETRACEMENTS, EXTENSIONS, PROJECTIONS, AND EXPANSIONS

Fibonacci numbers and ratios are employed as a means of determining potential support and resistance levels during:

- Price retracements
- Price extensions
- Price projections
- Price expansions

Fibonacci numbers and ratios are also employed to *time* potential reversals in the market, that is, as projections in time, as we shall see in subsequent sections.

Before proceeding, it would be best to clarify, in a general way, the terms retracement, extension, projection, and expansion.

10.3.1 Price Retracements

A retracement is a price decline or correction from a significant peak, or a rally from a significant trough. The amount of retracement is usually measured as a percentage of the *observed price range*, measured from the peak to a previous significant trough, or from a trough up to a previous significant peak. In short, we have downside as well as upside retracements. See Figure 10.5.

Figure 10.6 is an idealized example of an upside Fibonacci retracement. It is essentially just the inverse of a downside Fibonacci retracement.

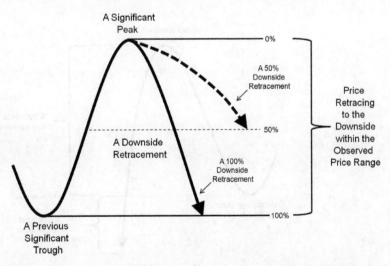

FIGURE 10.5 Downside Retracement within an Observed Price Range.

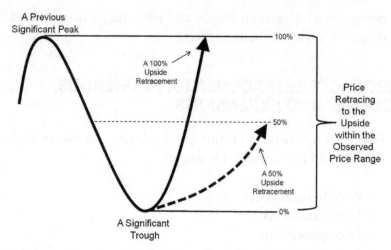

FIGURE 10.6 Upside Retracement within an Observed Price Range.

10.3.2 Price Extensions

A downside extension is any downside retracement that is *greater* than 100 percent, that is, the downside retracement extends below the previous significant trough, that is, beyond the observed price range. In similar fashion, an upside extension is any upside retracement than is greater than 100 percent, that is, the upside retracement extends above the previous significant peak that is beyond the observed price range. See Figures 10.7 and 10.8.

10.3.3 Price Expansions

Generally speaking, an *expansion* is simply an extension above or below an observed price range. It is a special form of an extension. *It is the orientation of the significant peaks and troughs that distinguishes between an expansion and an extension.*

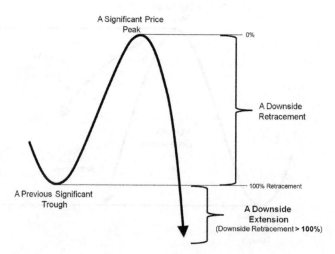

FIGURE 10.7 Downside Extension beyond a Price Range.

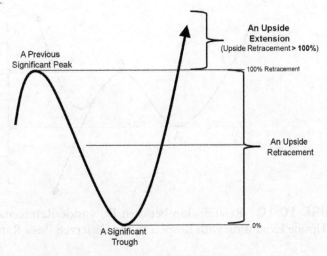

FIGURE 10.8 Upside Extension beyond a Price Range.

As we have seen in the previous section, an upside extension is defined as a percentage extension of the observed price range above its previous significant peak, and is never measured below its previous significant trough. Similarly, a downside extension is defined as a percentage extension of the observed price range below its previous significant trough, and is never measured above its previous significant peak.

But in expansions, the extensions are measured in the *opposite* direction. In the case of an upside expansion, price exceeds the observed price range where the significant trough occurs *prior* to the significant peak. For downside expansions, price extends below the observed price range where the significant peak occurs *prior* to the significant trough. See Figures 10.9 and 10.10.

From a certain perspective, an upside price expansion may also be regarded, for all practical purposes, as an *inverted or failed downside extension*. It starts off as a downside extension, with future price action expected to retrace below

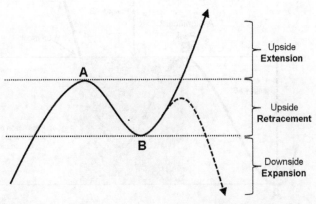

FIGURE 10.9 Relationship between Upside Retracement, Upside Extensions, and Downside Expansion with Respect to the Observed Price Range.

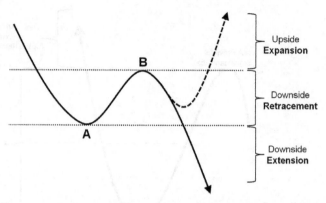

FIGURE 10.10 Relationship between Downside Retracement, Downside Extensions, and Upside Expansion with Respect to the Observed Price Range.

the previous significant trough. Price subsequently penetrates the previous peak instead. The technical trader and analyst would now be interested in identifying potential resistances with respect to the upside Fibonacci expansion levels based on the observed price range. Note that the ensuing price action within the observed price range, for the purposes of expansions and extensions, is irrelevant. Only the height of the observed price range is taken into account when calculating extensions and expansions. Please refer to Figures 10.11 and 10.12 for illustrations of upside and downside expansions, respectively.

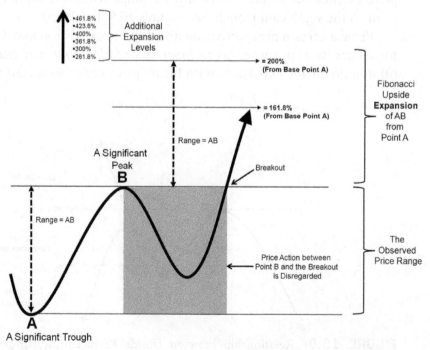

FIGURE 10.11 Upside Expansion beyond an Observed Price Range.

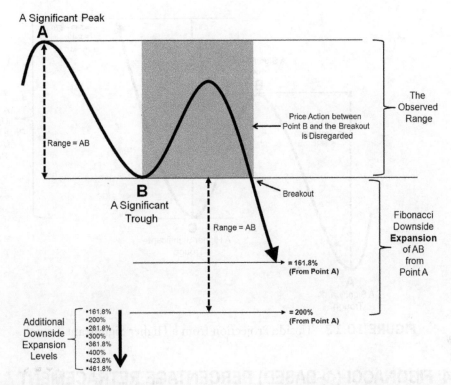

FIGURE 10.12 Downside Expansion beyond an Observed Price Range.

The reader should note that there is some confusion in the industry and literature with regard to the use of the terms extension, expansion, and projection. On some charting platforms, projections are referred to as expansions. Some authors also use extension to mean expansion. Nevertheless, as long as the user is clear as to the objective of the observation, there should not be any confusion.

10.3.4 Price Projections (also referred to as ABC Projections)

An upside price projection is a projection of an observed price range from a higher significant trough. A 100 percent price projection is simply a one to one (1:1) projection of the observed price range from some new higher significant trough. Similarly, a 200 percent price projection is a two to one (2:1) projection of the observed price range from some new higher significant trough. Fibonacci upside price projections use the Φ-related percentages for forecasting potential resistances in an uptrend. Similarly, Fibonacci downside price projections use the Φ-related percentages for forecasting potential support in a downtrend. It is interesting to note that upside price projections essentially transform into upside price extensions should the price level at point C coincide with the previous significant trough, that is, point A. Similarly, downside price projections essentially transform into downside price extensions should the price level at point C coincide with the previous significant peak, that is, point A. See Figures 10.13 and 10.14.

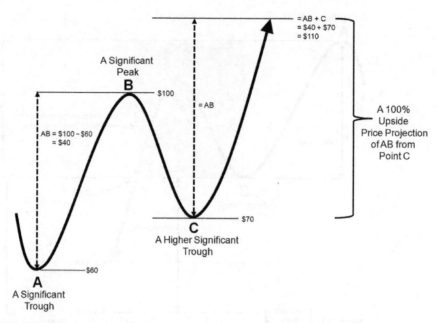

FIGURE 10.13   Upside Projection from a Higher Significant Trough.

10.4 FIBONACCI (Φ-BASED) PERCENTAGE RETRACEMENT LEVELS WITHIN AN OBSERVED PRICE RANGE

Once a significant peak A and trough B are identified in price, the observed price range between A and B may be divided into various percentage or ratio intervals as a way of measuring the amount of price retracement from the peak A. There are various ways to divide any price range in percentage or ratio terms. We could,

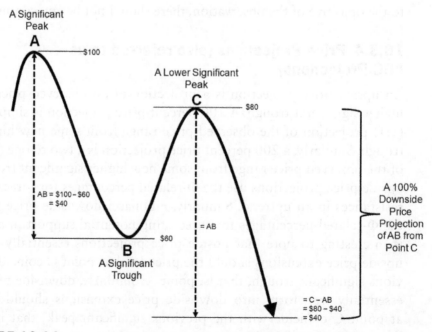

FIGURE 10.14   Downside Projection from a Lower Significant Peak.

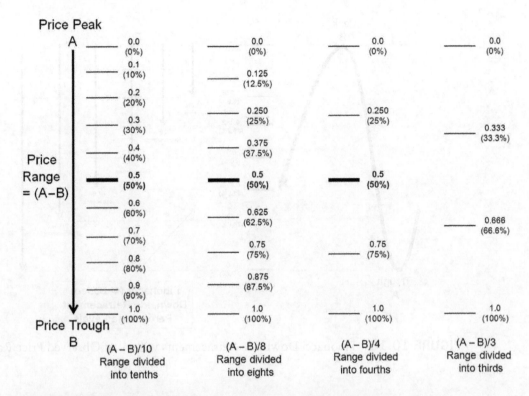

FIGURE 10.15 Percentage Downside Retracements within a Price Range.

for example, divide the price range AB into 10 equal intervals, with each interval occupying 10 percent of the price range. We could also divide the price range into any other number of *psychologically significant* intervals, like thirds, fourths, or eighths, as a way of measuring the amount of downside or upside retracement from its peak or trough and to *forecast potential support or resistance levels within an observed price range*. The greater the psychological attraction of a certain retracement percentage level, *the greater the probability that traders would react at that level*, helping to create potential support in downside retracements and potential resistance in upside retracements. The stronger the perception that a certain retracement percentage level is significant, the greater will be the potential for a stronger reaction at that level, resulting in more reliable support and resistance. Having a cluster or concentration of Fibonacci retracement levels around a price level increases the potential of creating a stronger reaction or barrier to price around that price level. These clusters or concentrations are referred to as Fibonacci *confluences*. We shall learn more about supportive and resistive confluences in a subsequent section. See Figure 10.15.

As observed in Figure 10.15, we could use any psychologically significant percentage retracement construct to mark the amount of price decline from peak A. Notice that the 50 percent retracement level runs through three of the retracement setups in Figure 10.15. This is the reason why the 50 percent retracement level is of great psychological significance and importance, as it is a common factor in three of the most widely used percentage retracement constructs in technical analysis. Both Gann and Dow recognized the significance of the 50 percent retracement level in the financial markets.

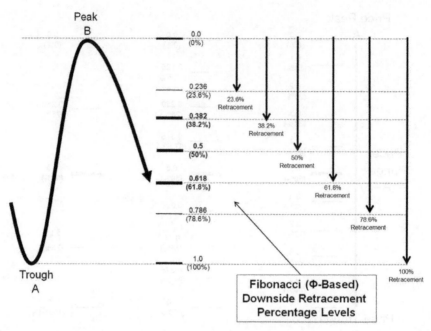

FIGURE 10.16 Fibonacci Downside Retracements within an Observed Price Range.

10.4.1 Fibonacci Φ-Based Ratio Intervals

Dividing the price range into equally sized intervals or equally spaced levels is not the only way to forecast potential support in a price decline. Dividing the observed price range according to Fibonacci (Φ-based) ratios or percentages is an extremely effective way of *forecasting potential support in downside retracements and resistance in upside retracements.*

Popular Fibonacci percentage retracements include:

- 23.6 percent
- 38.2 percent
- 61.8 percent
- 78.6 percent

It is customary for charting packages to also include the 50 percent retracement.

Fibonacci retracement percentages of 38.2 percent, 50 percent, and 61.8 percent are considered to be the most important. In Figure 10.16, we observe price retracing and finding support at the 61.8 percent Fibonacci retracement level.

Figure 10.17 shows price retracing to the upside and finding resistance at around the 38.2 percent Fibonacci retracement level.

Figure 10.18 is a chart of the daily EURUSD showing Fibonacci downside retracement support at points 2, 3, and 4. Point 1 shows price finding resistance at the 23.6 percent level. The retracement levels are only applicable after point B.

Figures 10.19 to 10.22 are examples of Fibonacci upside retracements in action on the foreign exchange cash markets.

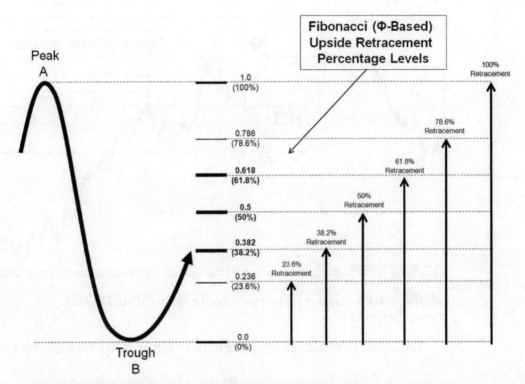

FIGURE 10.17 Fibonacci Upside Retracements within an Observed Price Range.

10.4.2 Calculating Potential Resistance via Fibonacci Upside Retracement Levels

Assume that the significant peak and trough of an observed retracement range are point A and point B, respectively. Assume that the peak at point A is at the price level of $78 and that the trough at point B is at $48. Refer to Figure 10.17 as a visualization guide.

FIGURE 10.18 Downside Retracement on the Daily EURUSD Chart.
Source: MetaTrader 4.

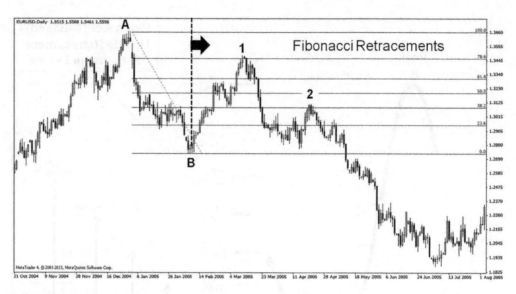

FIGURE 10.19 Upside Retracement on the Daily EURUSD Chart.
Source: MetaTrader 4

The formula for calculating upside retracement levels within a given price range is:

$$Trough + (Price\ Range \cdot Retracement\ Ratio)$$

In our example, the observed the price range AB is:

$$Price\ Range = Peak - Trough$$
$$= A - B$$
$$= \$78 - \$48$$
$$= \ \$30$$

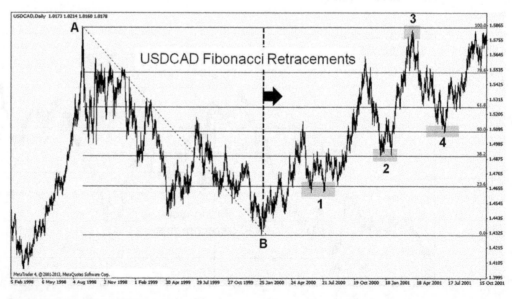

FIGURE 10.20 Upside Retracement on the Daily USDCAD Chart.
Source: MetaTrader 4

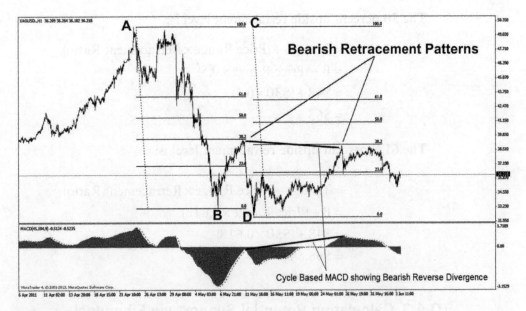

FIGURE 10.21 Upside Retracement on the Daily XAUUSD Chart.
Source: MetaTrader 4

(Note: We always subtract the trough from the peak, regardless of whether it is for a downside or upside retracement calculation, as the price range must always be a positive value.)

The 23.6 percent upside retracement level is:

$$= \text{Trough} + (\text{Price Range} \times \text{Retracement Ratio})$$
$$= B + (\text{Price Range} \times 0.236)$$
$$= \$48 + (\$30 \times 0.236)$$
$$= \$55.08$$

FIGURE 10.22 Upside Retracement on the Daily MMM Chart.
Courtesy of Stockcharts.com

The 50 percent upside retracement level is:

$$= \text{Trough} + (\text{Price Range} \times \text{Retracement Ratio})$$
$$= B + (\text{Price Range} \times 0.5)$$
$$= \$48 + (\$30 \times 0.5)$$
$$= \$63$$

The 61.8 percent upside retracement level is:

$$= \text{Trough} + (\text{Price Range} \times \text{Retracement Ratio})$$
$$= B + (\text{Price Range} \times 0.618)$$
$$= \$48 + (\$30 \times 0.618)$$
$$= \$66.54$$

10.4.3 Calculating Potential Support via Fibonacci Downside Retracement Levels

Assume that the significant trough and peak of an observed retracement range are point A and point B, respectively. Assume that the trough at point A is at the price level of $59 and that the peak at point B is at $99. Refer to Figure 10.16 as a visualization guide.

The formula for calculating downside retracement levels within a given price range is:

$$\text{Peak} - (\text{Price Range} \times \text{Retracement Ratio})$$

In our example, the observed the price range AB is:

$$\text{Price Range} = \text{Peak} - \text{Trough}$$
$$= B - A$$
$$= \$99 - \$59$$
$$= \$40$$

(Note: We always subtract the trough from the peak, regardless of whether it is for a downside or upside retracement calculation, as the price range must always be a positive value.)

The 23.6 percent downside retracement level is:

$$= \text{Peak} - (\text{Price Range} \times \text{Retracement Ratio})$$
$$= B - (\text{Price Range} \times 0.236)$$
$$= \$99 - (\$40 \times 0.236)$$
$$= \$89.56$$

The 50 percent downside retracement level is:

$$= \text{Peak} - (\text{Price Range} \times \text{Retracement Ratio})$$
$$= B - (\text{Price Range} \times 0.5)$$
$$= \$99 - (\$40 \times 0.5)$$
$$= \$79$$

The 61.8 percent downside retracement level is:

$$= \text{Peak} - (\text{Price Range} \times \text{Retracement Ratio})$$
$$= B - (\text{Price Range} \times 0.618)$$
$$= \$99 - (\$40 \times 0.618)$$
$$= \$74.28$$

10.5 FIBONACCI (Φ-BASED) PERCENTAGE EXTENSION LEVELS BEYOND AN OBSERVED PRICE RANGE

As previously mentioned, Fibonacci extensions are retracements that correct more than 100 percent.

Popular Fibonacci price percentage extension levels include:

- 127.2 percent
- 161.8 percent
- 261.8 percent
- 361.8 percent
- 423.6 percent
- 461.8 percent

It is customary to also include multiples of the 100 percent retracement, namely:

- 200 percent
- 300 percent
- 400 percent

Traders and analysts look for potential support at these significant Fibonacci downside extension levels, and potential resistance at significant Fibonacci upside extension levels. See Figures 10.23 and 10.24.

Figures 10.25 and 10.26 are examples of downside and upside extensions, respectively.

In Figure 10.26 we observe that the 161.8 percent extension level of the range AB coincides with a channel top and an overbought signal on the stochastics. This resistive confluence of indicators potentially increases the probability that price reacts or reverses at the forecasted Fibonacci expansion level.

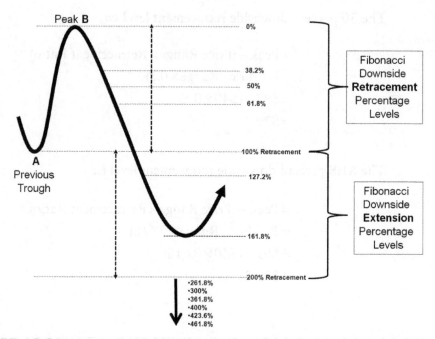

FIGURE 10.23 Fibonacci Downside Extension Support Levels below a Previous Significant Trough.

10.5.1 Calculating Potential Resistance via Fibonacci Upside Extension Levels

When calculating Fibonacci upside extension levels, we usually select the trough as the base for the extension. It is highly unconventional to use the peak as a base for extension, in spite of giving the correct price levels for the upside extension. For example, an upside extension percentage of 127.2 percent would be expressed

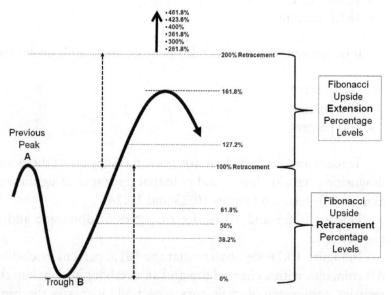

FIGURE 10.24 Fibonacci Upside Extension Resistance Levels above a Previous Significant Peak.

FIGURE 10.25 Downside Extension on the Daily EURUSD.
Source: MetaTrader 4

as 27.2 percent if we selected the peak, instead of the trough, as the base for the extension of the observed price range. We shall therefore, by convention, use the trough as the base for calculating all upside extensions and the peak as a base for calculating all downside extension levels.

Assume that the significant peak and trough of an observed retracement range are point A and point B, respectively. Assume that the peak at point A is at the price level of $115 and that the trough at point B is at $85. Refer to Figure 10.24 as a visualization guide.

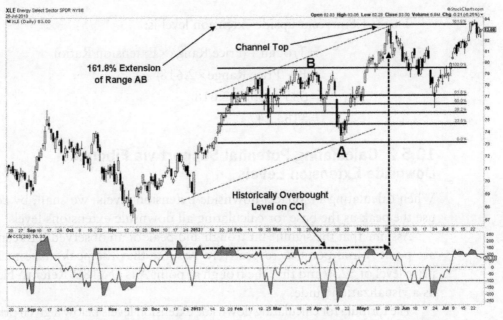

FIGURE 10.26 Upside Extension on the Daily EURUSD.
Courtesy of Stockcharts.com

The formula for calculating upside extension levels above a given price range is:

$$\textbf{Trough} + (\textbf{Price Range} \times \textbf{Extension Ratio})$$

In our example, the observed the price range AB is:

$$
\begin{aligned}
\text{Price Range} &= \text{Peak} - \text{Trough} \\
&= A - B \\
&= \$115 - \$85 \\
&= \$30
\end{aligned}
$$

(Note: We always subtract the trough from the peak, regardless of whether it is for a downside or upside extension calculation, as the price range must always be a positive value.)

The 127.2 percent upside extension level is:

$$
\begin{aligned}
&= \text{Trough} + (\text{Price Range} \times \text{Extension Ratio}) \\
&= B + (\text{Price Range} \times 1.272) \\
&= \$85 + (\$30 \times 1.272) \\
&= \$123.16
\end{aligned}
$$

The 161.8 percent upside extension level is:

$$
\begin{aligned}
&= \text{Trough} + (\text{Price Range} \times \text{Extension Ratio}) \\
&= B + (\text{Price Range} \times 1.618) \\
&= \$85 + (\$30 \times 1.618) \\
&= \$133.54
\end{aligned}
$$

The 261.8 percent upside extension level is:

$$
\begin{aligned}
&= \text{Trough} + (\text{Price Range} \times \text{Extension Ratio}) \\
&= B + (\text{Price Range} \times 2.618) \\
&= \$85 + (\$30 \times 2.618) \\
&= \$163.54
\end{aligned}
$$

10.5.2 Calculating Potential Support via Fibonacci Downside Extension Levels

When calculating Fibonacci downside extension levels, we shall, by convention, use the peak as the base for calculating all downside extensions levels.

Assume that the significant trough and peak of an observed retracement range are point A and point B, respectively. Assume that the peak at point B is at the price level of $236 and that the trough at point A is at $186. Refer to Figure 10.23 as a visualization guide.

The formula for calculating downside extension levels below a given price range is:

$$\textbf{Peak} - (\textbf{Price Range} \times \textbf{Extension Ratio})$$

In our example, the observed the price range AB is:

$$\text{Price Range} = \text{Peak} - \text{Trough}$$
$$= B - A$$
$$= \$236 - \$186$$
$$= \$50$$

(Note: We always subtract the trough from the peak, regardless of whether it is for a downside or upside extension calculation, as the price range must always be a positive value.)

The 127.2 percent downside extension level is:

$$= \text{Peak} - (\text{Price Range} \times \text{Extension Ratio})$$
$$= B - (\text{Price Range} \times 1.272)$$
$$= \$236 - (\$50 \times 1.272)$$
$$= \$172.4$$

The 161.8 percent downside extension level is:

$$= \text{Peak} - (\text{Price Range} \times \text{Extension Ratio})$$
$$= B - (\text{Price Range} \times 1.618)$$
$$= \$236 - (\$50 \times 1.618)$$
$$= \$155.1$$

The 261.8 percent downside extension level is:

$$= \text{Peak} - (\text{Price Range} \times \text{Extension Ratio})$$
$$= B - (\text{Price Range} \times 2.618)$$
$$= \$236 - (\$50 \times 2.618)$$
$$= \$105.1$$

10.6 FIBONACCI (Φ-BASED) PERCENTAGE EXPANSION LEVELS BEYOND AN OBSERVED PRICE RANGE

Fibonacci expansions are also employed to forecast potential support and resistance. Popular Fibonacci price percentage expansions levels include:

- 127.2 percent
- 161.8 percent
- 261.8 percent
- 361.8 percent
- 423.6 percent
- 461.8 percent

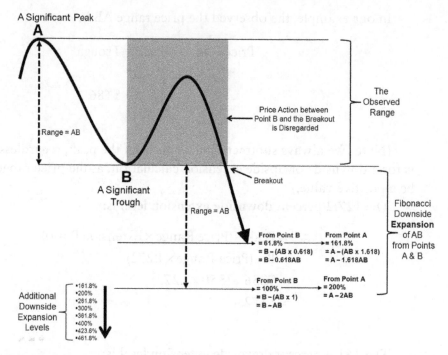

FIGURE 10.27 Fibonacci Downside Expansion Levels below the Observed Price Range.

It is customary to also include multiples of the 100 percent retracement, namely:

- 200 percent
- 300 percent
- 400 percent

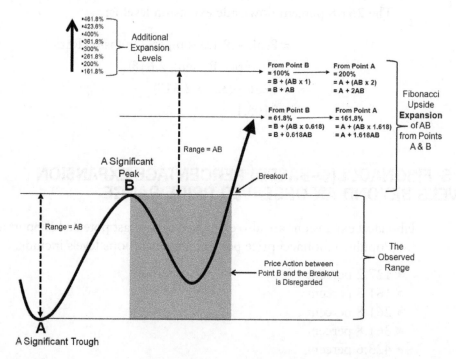

FIGURE 10.28 Fibonacci Upside Expansion Levels above the Observed Price Range.

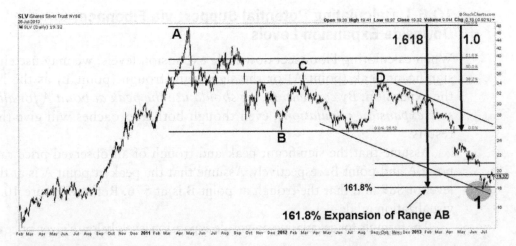

FIGURE 10.29 Fibonacci Downside Expansion on SLV (iShares Silver Trust NYSE).
Courtesy of Stockcharts.com

These percentage expansion levels are similar to the conventional or popular extension percentage levels. See Figures 10.27 and 10.28.

Figures 10.29 and 10.30 are examples of downside and upside expansions, respectively. In Figure 10.29, we see price reacting at the 161.8 percent expansion level of the range AB, at point 1. This is further supported by a channel bottom, increasing the potential for a reaction or pullback. In Figure 10.30, we also observe a resistive confluence at point 1, comprised of a 150 percent expansion level, a trendline test, and an overbought signal on the stochastics. Price subsequently retraces from the resistance zone.

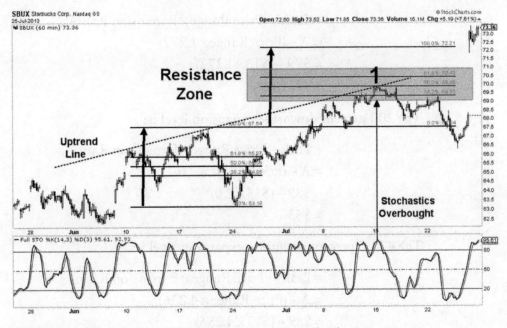

FIGURE 10.30 Fibonacci Upside Expansion on Starbucks Corp.
Courtesy of Stockcharts.com

10.6.1 Calculating Potential Support via Fibonacci Downside Expansion Levels

When calculating Fibonacci downside expansion levels, we may use either the significant peak (point A) or the significant trough (point B) as the base for the expansion. *By convention, we should use the peak at point A for all downside expansion calculations*, even though both approaches will give the same results.

Assume that the significant peak and trough of an observed price range are point A and point B, respectively. Assume that the peak at point A is at the price level of $89 and that the trough at point B is at $76. Refer to Figure 10.27 as a visualization guide.

The formula for calculating downside expansion levels below a given price range is:

$$\text{Peak} - (\text{Price Range} \times \text{Expansion Ratio})$$

In our example, the observed the price range AB is:

$$\begin{aligned}
\text{Price Range} &= \text{Peak} - \text{Trough} \\
&= A - B \\
&= \$89 - \$76 \\
&= \$13
\end{aligned}$$

(Note: We always subtract the trough from the peak, regardless of whether it is for a downside or upside expansion calculation, as the price range must always be a positive value.)

The 127.2 percent downside expansion level is:

$$\begin{aligned}
&= \text{Peak} - (\text{Price Range} \times \text{Expansion Ratio}) \\
&= A - (\text{Price Range} \times 1.272) \\
&= \$89 - (\$13 \times 1.272) \\
&= \$72.46
\end{aligned}$$

The 200 percent downside expansion level is:

$$\begin{aligned}
&= \text{Peak} - (\text{Price Range} \times \text{Expansion Ratio}) \\
&= A - (\text{Price Range} \times 2.0) \\
&= \$89 - (\$13 \times 2.0) \\
&= \$63
\end{aligned}$$

The 423.6 percent downside expansion level is:

$$\begin{aligned}
&= \text{Peak} - (\text{Price Range} \times \text{Expansion Ratio}) \\
&= A - (\text{Price Range} \times 4.236) \\
&= \$89 - (\$13 \times 4.236) \\
&= \$33.93
\end{aligned}$$

10.6.2 Calculating Potential Resistance via Fibonacci Upside Expansion Levels

When calculating Fibonacci upside expansion levels, we may use either the significant peak (point B) or the significant trough (point A) as the base for the expansion. By convention, we should use the trough at point A for all upside expansion calculations, even though both approaches will give the same results.

Assume that the significant trough and peak of an observed price range are point A and point B, respectively. Assume that the trough at point A is at the price level of $50 and that the peak at point B is at $110. Refer to Figure 10.28 as a visualization guide.

The formula for calculating downside expansion levels below a given price range is:

$$\text{Trough} + (\text{Price Range} \times \text{Expansion Ratio})$$

In our example, the observed the price range AB is:

$$\text{Price Range} = \text{Peak} - \text{Trough}$$
$$= B - A$$
$$= \$110 - \$50$$
$$= \$60$$

(Note: We always subtract the trough from the peak, regardless of whether it is for a downside or upside expansion calculation, as the price range must always be a positive value.)

The **127.2 percent upside expansion level** is:

$$= \text{Trough} + (\text{Price Range} \times \text{Expansion Ratio})$$
$$= A + (\text{Price Range} \times 1.272)$$
$$= \$50 + (\$60 \times 1.272)$$
$$= \$126.32$$

The **300 percent upside expansion level** is:

$$= \text{Peak} + (\text{Price Range} \times \text{Expansion Ratio})$$
$$= A + (\text{Price Range} \times 3.0)$$
$$= \$50 + (\$60 \times 3.0)$$
$$= \$230$$

The **423.6 percent upside expansion level** is:

$$= \text{Peak} + (\text{Price Range} \times \text{Expansion Ratio})$$
$$= A + (\text{Price Range} \times 4.236)$$
$$= \$50 + (\$60 \times 4.236)$$
$$= \$304.16$$

10.7 FIBONACCI (Φ-BASED) PERCENTAGE PROJECTION LEVELS FROM A SIGNIFICANT PEAK OR TROUGH

Fibonacci projections are especially useful for forecasting potential support and resistance when price is making *new* highs or lows, where no historical or prior support or resistance levels are available for reference. The Fibonacci trader or analyst attempts to find potential support and resistance levels beyond the original retracement range. Fibonacci projections are most reliable when they are part of a tight supportive or resistive confluence.

Besides using Fibonacci projections, potential support and resistance levels may also be determined, especially when price is making new highs or lows, via any of the following technical tools:

- Floor Trader's Pivot Point Analysis
- Channel Projections—Internal and External
- Trendline and Channel Analysis
- Gann Price Projections
- Psychological Numbers

Potential Fibonacci resistance levels may be forecasted by projecting various Fibonacci ratios of a certain *significant price range*, from a higher significant trough. Assuming that the distance between the trough at point A and the peak at point B is AB, we may choose any Fibonacci percentage with which to project AB from a higher significant trough (point C).

The main Fibonacci percentages associated with projections are:

- 61.8 percent
- 161.8 percent
- 261.8 percent
- 361.8 percent
- 423.6 percent
- 461.8 percent

By convention, the following percentages are also used along with Fibonacci projections:

- 100 percent
- 200 percent
- 300 percent
- 400 percent

Please refer to Figure 10.31.

Similarly, for downside projections, we may choose any Fibonacci percentage with which to project AB from a lower significant peak at point C, with the objective of locating potential support levels in the market. Refer to Figure 10.32.

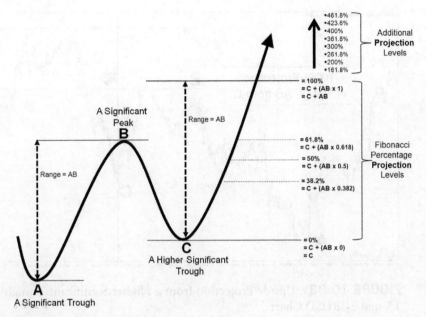

FIGURE 10.31 Fibonacci Upside Projection Resistance Levels from a Higher Significant Trough.

Figure 10.33 is an example of an upside projection on the 15-min EURUSD chart. The area of application lies after point C.

10.7.1 Calculating Potential Resistance via Fibonacci Upside Projection Levels

When calculating Fibonacci upside projection levels, we use the higher significant trough at point C as the base for the projection.

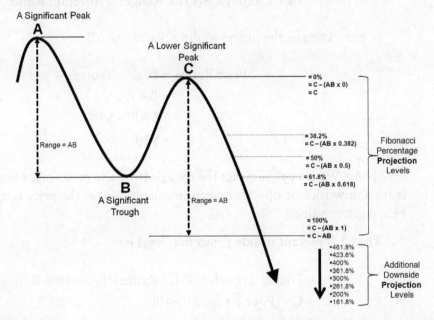

FIGURE 10.32 Fibonacci Downside Projection Support Levels from a Lower Significant Peak.

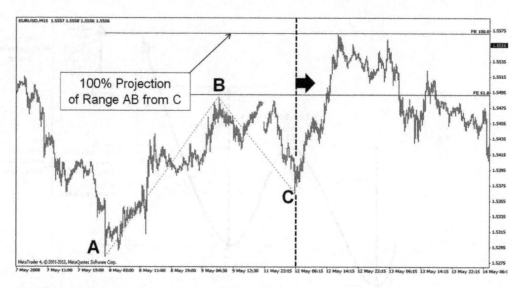

FIGURE 10.33 Upside Projection from a Higher Significant Trough at Point C on the 15-min EURUSD Chart.
Source: MetaTrader 4

Assume that the significant trough and peak of an observed price range are point A and point B, respectively. Assume that the peak at point B is at the price level of $100, the trough at point A is at $70, and the higher significant trough at point C is at $85. Refer to Figure 10.31 as a visualization guide.

The formula for calculating upside projection levels above a given price range is:

Higher Trough + (Price Range × Projection Ratio)

In our example, the observed the price range AB is:

$$
\begin{aligned}
\text{Price Range} &= \text{Peak} - \text{Trough} \\
&= B - A \\
&= \$100 - \$70 \\
&= \$30
\end{aligned}
$$

(Note: We always subtract the trough from the peak, regardless of whether it is for a downside or upside projection calculation, as the price range must always be a positive value.)

The 61.8 percent upside projection level is:

$$
\begin{aligned}
&= \text{Higher Trough} + (\text{Price Range} \times \text{Projection Ratio}) \\
&= C + (\text{Price Range} \times 0.618) \\
&= \$85 + (\$30 \times 0.618) \\
&= \$103.54
\end{aligned}
$$

The 100 percent upside projection level is:

$$= \text{Higher Trough} + (\text{Price Range} \times \text{Projection Ratio})$$
$$= C + (\text{Price Range} \times 1.0)$$
$$= \$85 + (\$30 \times 1.0)$$
$$= \$115$$

The 461.8 percent upside projection level is:

$$= \text{Higher Trough} + (\text{Price Range} \times \text{Projection Ratio})$$
$$= C + (\text{Price Range} \times 4.618)$$
$$= \$85 + (\$30 \times 4.618)$$
$$= \$223.54$$

10.7.2 Calculating Potential Support via Fibonacci Downside Projection Levels

When calculating Fibonacci downside projection levels, we use the lower significant peak at point C as the base for the projection.

Assume that the significant peak and trough of an observed price range are point A and point B, respectively. Assume that the peak at point A is at the price level of $200, the trough at point B is at $150, and the lower significant peak at point C is at $180. Refer to Figure 10.31 as a visualization guide.

The formula for calculating downside projection levels above a given price range is:

$$\text{Lower Peak} - (\text{Price Range} \times \text{Projection Ratio})$$

In our example, the observed the price range AB is:

$$\text{Price Range} = \text{Peak} - \text{Trough}$$
$$= A - B$$
$$= \$200 - \$150$$
$$= \$50$$

(Note: We always subtract the trough from the peak, regardless of whether it is for a downside or upside projection calculation, as the price range must always be a positive value.)

The 61.8 percent downside projection level is:

$$= \text{Lower Peak} - (\text{Price Range} \times \text{Projection Ratio})$$
$$= C - (\text{Price Range} \times 0.618)$$
$$= \$180 - (\$50 \times 0.618)$$
$$= \$149.10$$

The 100 percent downside projection level is:

$$= \text{Lower Peak} - (\text{Price Range} \times \text{Projection Ratio})$$
$$= C - (\text{Price Range} \times 1.0)$$
$$= \$180 - (\$50 \times 1.0)$$
$$= \$130$$

The 461.8 percent downside projection level is

$$= \text{Lower Peak} - (\text{Price Range} \times \text{Projection Ratio})$$
$$= C - (\text{Price Range} \times 4.618)$$
$$= \$180 - (\$50 \times 4.618)$$
$$= -\$50.90$$

In the last example, we find that a 461.8 percent downside projection of the observed price range from point C gives a negative price value of $50.90. This is why analysts must be prudent when attempting to forecast potential support in the market using projection, expansion, and extension techniques. The real market is subject to numerous constraints and the analyst must be cognizant of the limitations and boundaries of his or her technical tools and forecasts. Making highly unrealistic forecasts that are disconnected from actual market conditions may cause irreparable damage to one's standing and reputation as a professional technical analyst! An analyst should endeavor to see the broader picture and always strive to make forecasts and recommendations within the context of the market.

10.8 WHY SHOULD FIBONACCI RATIOS OR NUMBERS WORK AT ALL?

Indeed, why should any indicator or technical tool work for that matter? Man has always been enthralled with the geometric and mathematical properties of the Fibonacci sequence and its Φ ratio. There are literally hundreds of books and literary works on the subject. The Fibonacci sequence and Divine Ratio are purported to be the underlying matrix governing the very physiology, biology, geometry, mathematics, and physics of nature and the universe.

The fact that we may never be able to conclusively prove that such a mathematical relationship or matrix underlies all of creation, or at the very least the financial markets, does not necessarily render the application of Fibonacci ratios and numbers or indeed any indicator to the markets any less effective. This is because the markets are essentially behaviorally driven. The main reason for any technical indicator being effective or at least statistically reliable lies more with the psychology of the market participants than with the actual mathematical properties or construction of an indicator. If a sufficient number of traders react to the signals from a particular indicator or oscillator, it is highly probable that the market will be influenced by the concerted action of traders all risking capital on those signals.

Price action therefore, for the most part, is a consequence of expectation. Hence, it is not so much about whether an indicator actually works, but rather it is more about the expectation that the market participants have about an indicator that really matters. Traders and analysts observe price reacting very frequently with uncanny accuracy at various significant Fibonacci levels every day in the markets. Fibonacci levels may or may not have any real significance with respect to the underlying structure of the markets, but if there are enough market participants willing to risk capital based on a popular indicator reading, this will impact the performance of that indicator. As more traders rely and act on the signals from a certain indicator, the greater will be the potential for a larger reaction in price when those signals appear. This in turn will attract even more traders. This positive feedback cycle is an example and natural consequence of the *self-fulfilling prophecy* in action. And as with any positive feedback loop, it is essentially an unstable system, especially when there is an increasing number of traders who start to take preemptive action in the markets, eroding the reliability of the signals. This may help explain why indicators slip in and out of popularity, and on a larger scale, why markets rise and fall.

In short, *price action is essentially behaviorally driven, mainly by expectation and investor bias.* Future price action is the result of market participants acting on what they believe to be a true reflection of what is and may be transpiring in the markets. It is their collective perception that matters, be it accurate or misguided.

10.9 GEOMETRICALLY VERSUS NUMERICALLY BASED FIBONACCI OPERATIONS

We must be circumspect when applying Fibonacci ratios to charts. Basically, there are two ways to apply Fibonacci operations like retracements, extensions, expansions, and projections.

10.9.1 The Numerically Based Approach to Fibonacci Operations

The first is to assign a numerical value, that is, *price*, to various peaks and troughs used to perform these Fibonacci operations. Hence, the observed range that will be employed to calculate these Fibonacci operations is just the *difference in price* between, for example, a significant peak at point A and a significant trough at point B, that is, (A − B). As we have seen earlier, the observed price range (A − B) form the basis for all Fibonacci operations, be it to pinpoint retracement, extension, expansion, or projection price targets.

If we perform Fibonacci operations by calculating the levels using assigned numerical values, then it makes no difference whether ratio (logarithmic) or linear (arithmetic) scaling is used on the chart. There will be no discrepancy in the calculated or projected Fibonacci-based price targets. Compare the three retracement levels in Figure 10.34 to those in Figure 10.35. They give the same price levels for the retracement percentages within the observed price range.

In Figure 10.34, we see that the Fibonacci retracement price levels represent the 38.2 percent, 50.0 percent, and 61.8 percent values as calculated from the peak, within

FIGURE 10.34 Numerically and Geometrically Based Retracements on an Arithmetically Scaled Chart.
Courtesy of Stockcharts.com

the observed price range. Besides having each percentage retracement level assigned numerical values, the retracement levels are also geometrically consistent with respect to the *physical* distances measured on the chart, that is, the actual physical distance from the peak to the numerical value associated with the 38.2 percent level actually measures 38.2 percent of the entire physical range on the chart, as measured from the peak. In short, the numerical and geometrical determinations of the price associated with the 38.2 percent retracement level are consistent with each other.

If we now apply ratio or logarithmic scaling to the same stock chart, we see that the numerical values associated with the same three retracement levels are identical to those on the linear or arithmetically scaled charts. This is because the calculations use the same data points. See Figure 10.35.

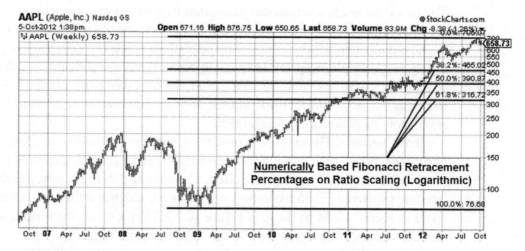

FIGURE 10.35 Numerically Based Retracements on a Logarithmically Scaled Chart.
Courtesy of Stockcharts.com

FIGURE 10.36 Geometrically Based Retracements on a Logarithmically Scaled Chart. Courtesy of Stockcharts.com

10.9.2 The Geometrically Based Approach to Fibonacci Operations

We now see what happens when we use a geometrically based approach on a logarithmically scaled chart. Refer to Figure 10.36. Notice that the three geometrically derived retracement levels are now associated with different values. The previous 38.2 percent retracement level price of $465 is now $295. The other two retracement percentages of 50 percent and 61.8 percent also display a change from $390 to $234 and $316 to $190, respectively. Due to the compression effects at higher prices inherent on logarithmically scaled charts, the percentage retracement values will tend to decline to lower values when measured geometrically.

We also see in Figure 10.36 that geometrical symmetry is not preserved on logarithmic charts. For example, we expect to find the physical distance from the 50 percent level to either the 38.2 percent or 61.8 percent to be of equal distances. But we observe that this is not the case. We find that, in our chart, there is a price difference of $61 between the 38.2 percent and 50 percent retracement levels, whereas the price difference between the 50 percent and the 61.8 percent levels is only $44. This does not occur on arithmetically scaled charts, as numerical and geometrical symmetry are preserved.

Therefore in summary, when employing arithmetically scaled charts, retracement levels may be determined by using either the numerical or geometrical approach. There will be no price discrepancy in the values of the respective retracement levels and geometric symmetry will be preserved. Conversely, when employing geometrically scaled charts, retracement levels should only be determined via the numerical approach. This will ensure that the retracement values are consistent with those on arithmetically scaled charts.

Note that since geometrical symmetry is not preserved on logarithmically scaled charts, the use of proportional dividers (a popular Fibonacci percentage measuring tool) will yield inconsistent results. Proportional dividers should therefore only be used on arithmetically scaled charts.

10.10 THE FIBONACCI TRADER'S TECHNICAL TOOLBOX

Fibonacci ratio and number counts have been applied in a myriad of ways in the financial markets. We shall cover some of the more important approaches in this chapter. Here is a list of some of the more popular Fibonacci applications:

- Fibonacci retracements
- Fibonacci extensions
- Fibonacci expansions
- Fibonacci projections
- Fibonacci fan lines
- Fibonacci channels
- Fibonacci spirals
- Fibonacci ellipses
- Fibonacci arcs
- Fibonacci circles
- Fibonacci-based moving averages
- Fibonacci time ratio projections
- Fibonacci number counts
- Fibonacci wave counts
- Fibonacci time zone projections

From the list above, we have categorized the various applications into their respective price and time elements. See Figure 10.37.

Fibonacci retracements, extensions, expansions, and projections are static or horizontal overlay indicators. A horizontal overlay indicator has no time element associated with it. Conventional support and resistance are also horizontal overlay

PRICE	PRICE & TIME	TIME
Retracements	Fan Lines	Number Counts
Extensions	Channels	Wave Counts
Expansions	Spirals	Time Ratio Projections
Projections	Ellipses	Time Zone Projections
	Arcs	
	Circles	
	Moving Averages	

FIGURE 10.37 Fibonacci Tools Categorized According to Price and Time Elements.

indicators. As a result, the prices associated with such indicators do not vary over time. This makes it easy for traders to place entry orders at these static price levels, long before prices actually test these levels, allowing the placement of buy and sell limit entry orders in the market. Horizontal overlay indicators yield identical values regardless of whether logarithmic or arithmetic scaling is employed, as long as the values of the Fibonacci levels are numerically determined. If the geometric approach is adopted, then only arithmetically scaled charts should be used, as geometrical symmetry is not preserved on logarithmically scaled charts. Finally, horizontal overlay indicators are not affected by data adjustments, dropouts, or errors resulting from the removal or addition of non-trading days like holidays and weekends from the charts.

Fan line, channel, spiral, ellipse, arc, circle, and Fibonacci-based moving average forecasts are dynamic and have both price and time elements associated with them. This means that the price forecasts vary over time. Some non-Fibonacci dynamic overlay indicators include conventional trendlines, rising or falling channels, Andrew's pitchforks, and regression lines. Unlike horizontal overlay indicators, dynamic overlay indicators have an angular component to them, that is, they tend to move diagonally or at an incline. Consequently, dynamic overlay indicators like Fibonacci channels, fan lines, arcs, and spirals yield different results depending on whether logarithmic or arithmetic scaling is employed. Other dynamic overlay indicators like Fibonacci-based moving averages are unaffected by the type of scaling employed as they are *strictly* numerically determined and possess no geometrical element. Refer to Figures 10.38 and 10.39. Notice that price tests and breaches the first declining fan line when employing arithmetic scaling but clearly remains above the fan line on the logarithmically scaled chart. This discrepancy is more pronounced on longer-term charts. We must also be aware of the fact that dynamic overlay indicators are affected by data adjustments on the charts due to non-trading days. The removal and addition of non-trading days from a chart affects the angle of trendlines and may cause inconsistent readings as the chart contracts and expands over the same period of observation.

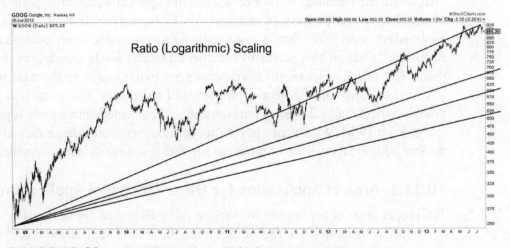

FIGURE 10.38 Logarithmically Scaled Fibonacci Fan Lines.

FIGURE 10.39 Arithmetically Scaled Fibonacci Fan Lines.

Finally, Fibonacci number counts, wave counts, time zone, and time ratio projections are purely time-based indicators with no element of price associated with them. That is why these time-based indicators cannot predict whether a reversal will result in a top or bottom formation. These indicators can only indicate when a reversal is likely to occur. Time-based indicators are completely unaffected by the type of chart scaling used, as scaling only affects the price axis. Unfortunately, these indicators are greatly affected by data adjustments on the charts for non-trading days, much more so than dynamic overlay indicators, as time-based indicators reside *strictly* in the time domain and are therefore more susceptible to changes along the time axis.

10.11 AREA OF APPLICATION

It is very important to know where and when Fibonacci levels are applicable. Generally speaking, all levels of retracement, extension, expansion, and projection are valid levels of observation once they are *beyond the last data point used to perform the Fibonacci operation*. For example, in Figure 10.40, the area of application, that is, the area where the Fibonacci retracement levels are applicable, lies after point B, the top of the observed retracement price range, AB. Fibonacci retracement levels cannot be analyzed retrospectively, that is, prior to their creation, which only occurred at point B. Any price action that seems to react to Fibonacci levels *retrospectively*, that is, points 1, 2, and 3, which on the chart occur prior to the area of application, may actually serve to corroborate potential supports and resistances. This actually occurred at point X, where the 38.2 percent retracement level coincided with a prior support level (point 3) on IWM. What seems in retrospect to be mere coincidence may in fact help provide additional evidence of potential support in a downside retracement.

10.11.1 Area of Application for Other Fibonacci Applications

The proper areas of application for various other Fibonacci applications is illustrated in the following figures. For each application, the area of application is to the right of the vertical dashed line, as indicated by the arrow. See Figures 10.41 to 10.44.

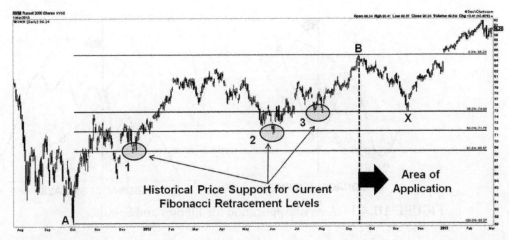

FIGURE 10.40 Historical Price Support for Retracement Levels within the Area of Application.
Courtesy of Stockcharts.com

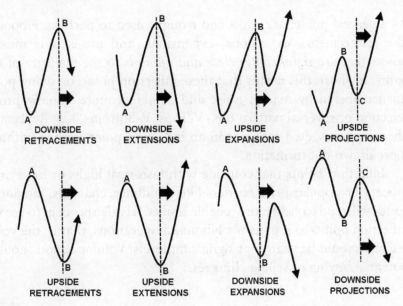

FIGURE 10.41 Area of Application for Retracements, Extensions, Expansions, and Projections.

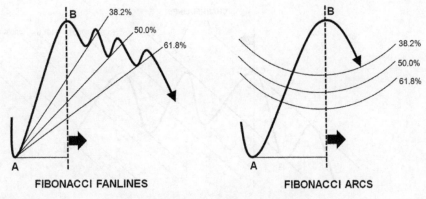

FIGURE 10.42 Area of Application for Fanlines and Arcs.

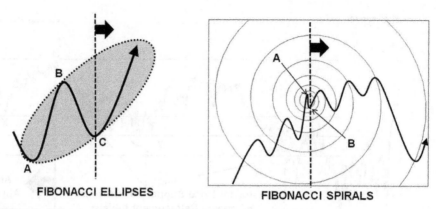

FIGURE 10.43 Area of Application for Ellipses and Spirals.

10.12 SELECTING EFFECTIVE INFLECTION POINTS FOR FIBONACCI OPERATIONS

As a general guideline, peaks and troughs used to perform Fibonacci operations like retracements, extensions, expansions, and projections must be inflection points that are *significantly clear and obvious* to the majority of market participants. In short, this means that these inflection point, or swing points, should be unencumbered by market noise and exhibit a more visually pronounced price rejection or reversal pattern (i.e., V-Tops, V-Bottoms, Key Reversal and Pin Bars, Shooting Stars, etc.) rather than an inflection point formed within a longer and more drawn out formation.

Inflection points that coincide with historical highs or lows or any other significant or popular price barriers like trendlines, channels, moving averages, and bands will tend to yield more reliable results. It is also prudent to use volume-filtered inflection points as a basis for Fibonacci operations, that is, the volume and open interest should be near or at significant levels. Volume action should also indicate potential buying or selling climaxes.

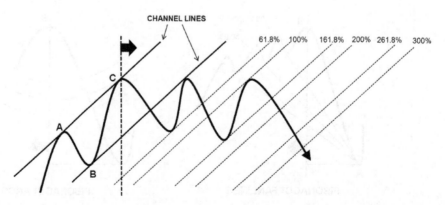

FIGURE 10.44 Area of Application for Fibonacci Channel Projections.

10.13 FIBONACCI, DOW, GANN, AND FLOOR TRADER'S PIVOT POINT LEVELS

Of all the possible percentage retracement levels, the 38.2 percent, 50 percent, and 61.8 percent levels are the most significant and widely employed. From the table in Figure 10.45, we can clearly see why this is the case.

From the table, it is obvious that the 50 percent retracement level is found in most of the popular retracement approaches. Both Gann and Dow considered the 33.3 percent (one-third), 50 percent, and 66.6 percent (two-thirds) retracements as very significant levels during market reversals, especially when trying to determine if a reversal is merely a secondary reaction or a full-blown change in the primary trend.

The Floor Trader's Pivot Point levels also contribute to the upper and lower 5 percent retracement bands. A pivot point is defined as the *typical price* based on yesterday's high (H), low (L), and closing prices (C):

$$\text{Typical price} = (H + L + C)/3 = \text{Pivot Point}$$

Let us now assume two special cases. The first is when the daily close is at the high of the day. Let us also *normalize* yesterday's range to a maximum of 100 units where the maximum high is 100 and low is 0, for the sake of clarity. Therefore, with reference to Figure 10.46, the Pivot Point level for the following day will be:

$$\text{Pivot Point Level} = (100 + 0 + 100)/3 = 66.6$$

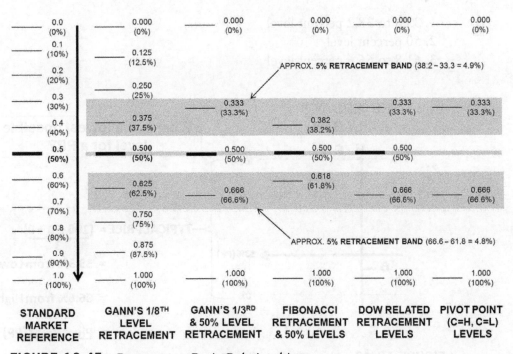

FIGURE 10.45 Retracement Ratio Relationships.

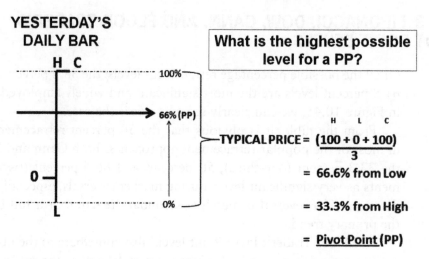

FIGURE 10.46 Floor Trader's Pivot Point 33.3 Percent Level.

The second case is when the daily close is at the low of the day. Refer to Figure 10.47:

$$\text{Pivot Point Level} = (100 + 0 + 0)/3 = 33.3$$

In short, if yesterday's close was at the high, the first support level today will be at $100 - 66.6 = 33.3$, that is, 33.3 percent below yesterday's high. On the other hand, if yesterday's close was at the low, this would mean that the next lower support level would be at $100 - 33.3 = 66.6$, that is, 66.6 percent below yesterday's high.

Looking at the table in Figure 10.45, we immediately perceive that there are three main clusters of retracement ratios, appearing around the:

1. 33.3 to 38.2 percent level
2. 50 percent level
3. 61.8 to 66.6 percent level

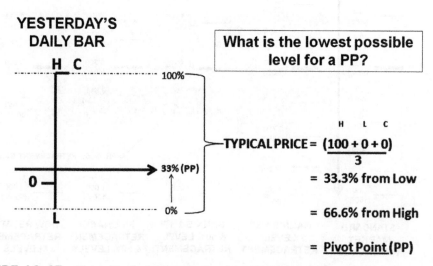

FIGURE 10.47 Floor Trader's Pivot Point 66.6 Percent Level.

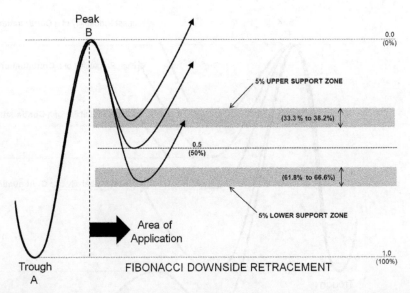

FIGURE 10.48 Upper and Lower 5 Percent Support Zones in a Downside Fibonacci Retracement.

The first and third clusters listed above occupy approximately 5 percent of the retracement range and represent a band or confluence of either supportive or resistive levels, depending on whether price is above or below these bands. Therefore when trading the markets, it is prudent to bear in mind that there is a strong possibility of price experiencing support anywhere within the upper or lower 5 percent support zones in a downside retracement, as depicted in Figure 10.48. Figure 10.49 illustrates the position for upside retracements.

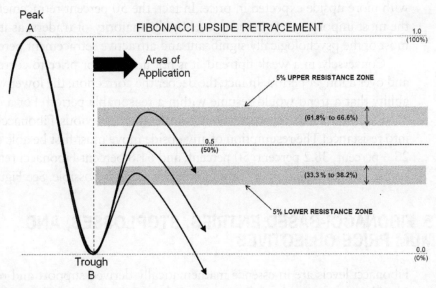

FIGURE 10.49 Upper and Lower 5 Percent Resistance Zones in an Upside Fibonacci Retracement.

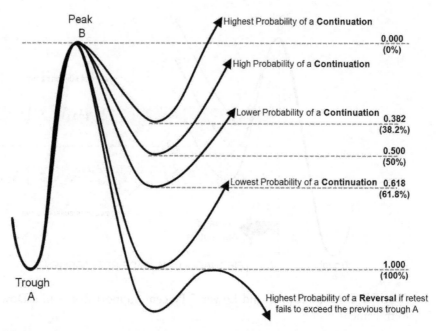

FIGURE 10.50 Probability of Continuation in a Retracement.

10.14 PROBABILITY OF CONTINUATION AND REVERSAL IN FIBONACCI RETRACEMENTS AND EXTENSIONS

The amount of retracement is considered to be an indication of the probability of price continuation. For example, in a very strong uptrend, price is not expected to correct more than 38.2 percent of the price range, otherwise it would be an indication that the uptrend may not be as inherently bullish as originally envisaged. Any correction should be followed a quick and sharp pullback resulting in the resumption of the predominant trend. A 50 percent correction is still considered a bullish indication, with more upside expected in price. In fact, the 50 percent retracement is considered the most important retracement level by the majority of traders, as it coincides with most of the psychologically significant and attractive retracement percentage levels.

Conversely, in a weak uptrend, it is not unusual for price to correct more deeply and over a longer period. In fact, the deeper the correction, the lower will be the probability that a trend would resume within a reasonable period. For a downside Fibonacci retracement, deep corrections transform all previous Fibonacci support levels into resistance! The resumption of any upside move must first be able to penetrate the 23.6 percent, 38.2 percent, 50 percent, and 61.8 percent Fibonacci retracement levels before any continuation of the predominant trend is possible. See Figure 10.50.

10.15 FIBONACCI-BASED ENTRIES, STOPLOSSES, AND MINIMUM PRICE OBJECTIVES

Fibonacci levels are in essence mathematically derived support and resistance levels. Just like conventional support and resistance, Fibonacci levels are static and are not time dependant, that is, they do not vary with time, as they are horizontally orientated.

Diagonal-type indicators like trendlines are dynamic, that is, they have a time element in determination of the current price. Moving averages are also dynamic in nature as the current moving average price is a function of time. That is why is it very difficult to forecast the exact price at which a trendline or moving average violation will occur. The steeper the trendline or angle of ascent of a moving average, the more difficult it is to predict the price at which a breach would occur, as small price movements could result in a very wide range of possible prices at which a breach could occur.

As support and resistance, the price at which a Fibonacci level would be breached is known long in advance. This makes it very convenient for the placement of stoplosses and profit targets. Fibonacci levels are traded in exactly the same way as conventional support and resistance levels. Traders may use a Fibonacci level as an:

- Entry
- Stoploss
- Profit target

10.15.1 Fibonacci Level as a Profit Target, Entry, and Stoploss Level

Once a trade is initiated for whatever reason, a Fibonacci level may be used as a profit target, exiting positions in full or partially. As prices approach Fibonacci retracement, extension, expansion, or projection levels, traders may want to start tightening their stops in anticipation of a correction or some larger reversal. In Figure 10.51, an entry is initiated at the break of the uptrend line in Gold on the four-hour chart. A Fibonacci price projection is made based on the range BC, projected downward from point E. We see price testing the 161.8 percent projection level at point D and rapidly pulling back to higher prices. A trader would be wise to exit or at least roll down the stops on a short position as price

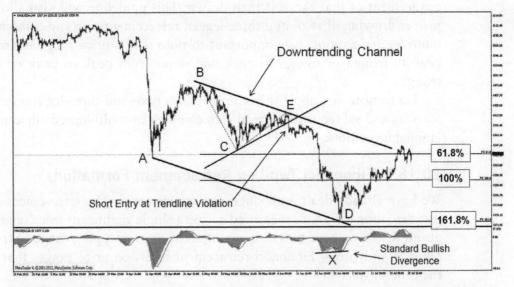

FIGURE 10.51 Fibonacci Level as a Profit Target, Entry, and Stoploss Level in Gold.
Source: MetaTrader 4

approaches point D. Standard bullish divergence on the MACD (as seen at point X) coupled with the fact that point D is also finding support at a channel line points to a potentially bullish scenario. At point D, the trader may exit all or some positions in profit and subsequently reverse into a long position with an initial stop positioned just below the 161.8 percent Fibonacci projection level. Therefore we see the 161.8 percent Fibonacci projection level being used in the first instance as a profit target, and subsequently as a point of entry for the ensuing long position, with a stop placed below it. Again, finding a confluence of bullish indications at point D strengthens the case for a more reliable price reversal forecast.

10.16 FIBONACCI TWO- AND THREE-LEG RETRACEMENTS

When applying Fibonacci retracements to adjacent or overlapping ranges we must be careful to only draw Fibonacci levels for the most significant retracement ranges. We shall employ a general rule for determining which ranges are the most significant with the area of observations.

10.16.1 General Rule for Drawing Fibonacci Retracements in Adjacent or Overlapping Ranges

As a general rule, if any preceding range engulfs *all* subsequent ranges within the area of observation, the Fibonacci retracement of that preceding range is drawn. The term *engulf* means that the range under consideration contains the highest peak and lowest trough when compared to all subsequent ranges, while *area of observation* extends from the beginning of the leftmost range up to the current price. The practitioner should start from the leftmost range within an area of observation and work through every range toward the right by checking if that range engulfs all subsequent ranges that occur after it. If it does, the Fibonacci retracement of that range is then drawn. This guideline will also allow for the proper drawing of two- and three-legged retracements, or any combinations of multi-leg formations. It is important to note that a price range is drawn from peak to trough or trough to peak and never from peak to peak or trough to trough.

Let us now first apply this simple rule to two- and three-leg retracement formations and subsequently extend it to complex or multi-legged adjacent or overlapping formations.

10.16.2 Fibonacci Two-Leg Retracement Formations

We have already dealt with single-leg retracements. The retracement levels are just the Fibonacci ratios measured across a single significant price range. In situations where we have two or more adjacent or overlapping ranges, care must be taken to only draw Fibonacci retracement levels on price ranges that abide by the general rule.

Figure 10.52 illustrates the various possible two-range formations that a practitioner may encounter in the markets.

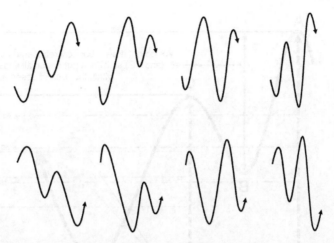

FIGURE 10.52   Various Adjacent and Overlapping Two-Range Formations.

In Figure 10.53, we see these adjacent and overlapping two-range formations on the VIX daily chart.

Figure 10.54 illustrates a typical two-leg retracement range. The area of observation spans from point A to the current price. Applying the general rule for drawing retracements, we start from the leftmost range AB, which fails to fulfill the general rule of engulfing all subsequent ranges within the area of observation. The next range under consideration would be that of BC, which also fails to fulfill the general rule. Hence, no Fibonacci retracements are drawn for these last two ranges. Conversely, the range CD satisfies the general rule of engulfing all subsequent ranges, *as long as price remains within the range CD.* Similarly, the range AD also satisfies the general rule of engulfing all subsequent ranges, as long as price remains within the range AD. Therefore, Fibonacci retracements are only drawn for ranges AD and CD, after which the practitioner may begin looking for significant Fibonacci clusters within the two-leg formation.

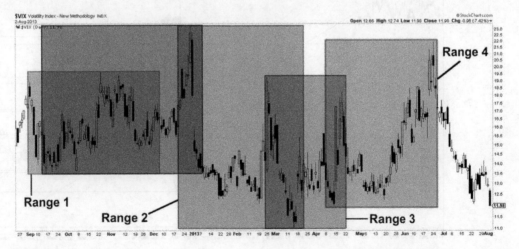

FIGURE 10.53   Various Adjacent and Overlapping Two-Range Formations on the Daily VIX (Volatility Index) Chart.
Courtesy of Stockcharts.com

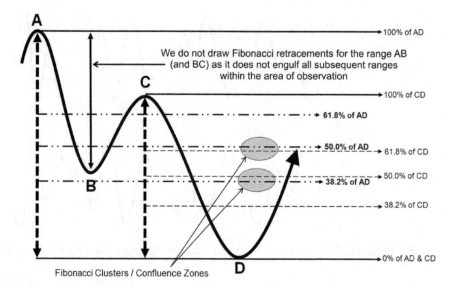

FIGURE 10.54 Fibonacci Retracement Clusters across the Combined Price Range AD and CD.

Figure 10.55 clearly depicts two-leg Fibonacci clusters on the daily USDCAD chart, with retracement measured across from ranges AB and CB.

10.16.3 Invalidating the Fibonacci Retracement Levels

It must be pointed out that should price subsequently extend beyond the *largest retracement range*, all Fibonacci retracement levels within the area of observation will be invalidated. New retracement levels need to be recalculated once a larger

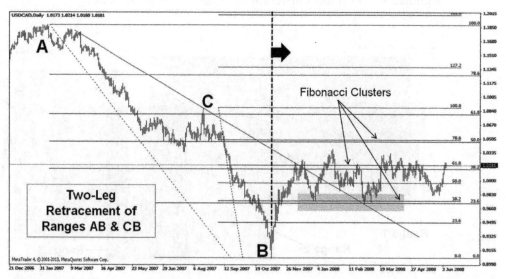

FIGURE 10.55 Fibonacci Retracement Clusters across the Combined Price Range AB and CB on the Daily USDCAD Chart.
Source: MetaTrader 4

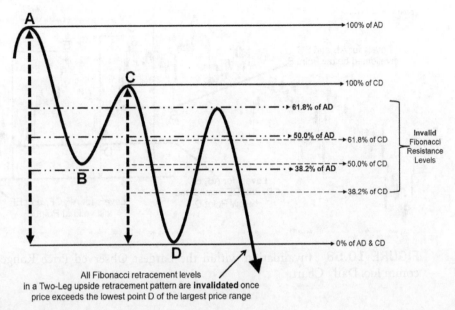

FIGURE 10.56 Fibonacci Retracements Invalidated once the Largest Retracement Range Is Exceeded.

retracement range is identified, which cannot occur until a new higher peak or lower trough is formed. In Figure 10.56, the largest range AD is exceeded, thereby invalidating all previously drawn Fibonacci retracement levels.

Note that invalidation also applies to price ranges *within* the largest range. Exceeding the largest range within the area of observation will be invalidated at all Fibonacci retracement levels within it, but exceeding smaller ranges within it will only invalidate the retracement levels of those smaller ranges that have been exceeded.

Figure 10.57 depicts several examples of invalidation within two-range formations. Once price violates a prior peak or trough, the Fibonacci levels associated with that preceding range are invalidated. The dotted lines in Figure 10.57 represent the *threshold of invalidation*.

Refer to Figure 10.58. Let us assume that we are interested in searching for potentially significant Fibonacci clusters between point A and point F, that is, the

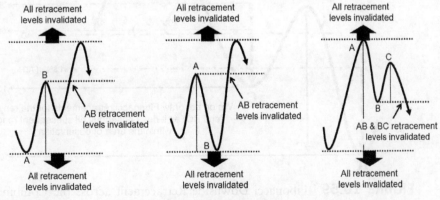

FIGURE 10.57 Invalidation within Two-Range Formations.

405

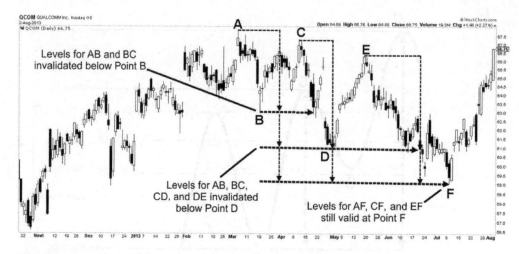

FIGURE 10.58 Invalidation within the Largest Observed Price Range on the Qualcomm Inc. Daily Chart.

area of observation. Therefore, AF represents the largest range. We observe the Fibonacci retracement levels for various ranges within the largest range, AF, being invalidated as price violates each threshold. Only Fibonacci retracement levels for ranges AF, CF, and EF are valid.

Figure 10.59 shows a two-leg downside retracement range. The area of observation spans from point A to the current price. Applying the general rule, Fibonacci retracements are only drawn for ranges AD and CD, after which the practitioner may begin looking for significant Fibonacci supportive clusters within the two-leg formation.

As before, should price subsequently exceed the largest price range AD, all Fibonacci retracement levels within that range are invalidated. Retracement levels

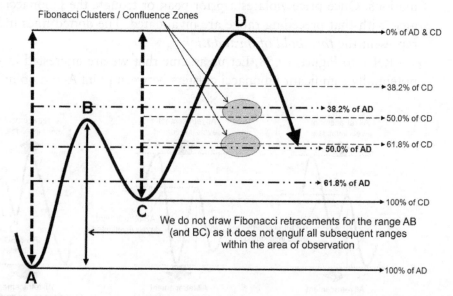

FIGURE 10.59 Fibonacci Downside Retracement across the Combined Price Range AD and CD.

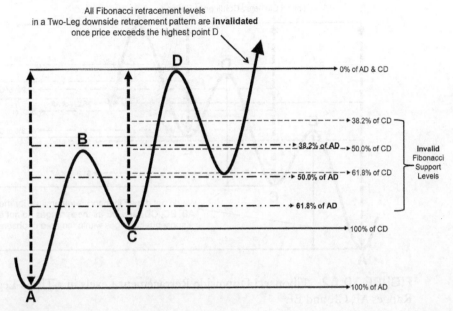

FIGURE 10.60 Fibonacci Downside Retracement Levels Invalidated Once the Retracement Reference Point Is Exceeded.

need to be recalculated at a new larger retracement range, which cannot occur until a new higher peak has formed after the upside breakout. See Figure 10.60.

10.16.4 Fibonacci Three-Leg Retracement Formations

Fibonacci three-leg retracements are calculated and plotted via the same general rule. After locating the area of observation, that is, the largest observed price range, calculate the retracement levels for all other ranges that satisfy the general rule. Refer to Figures 10.61 and 10.62.

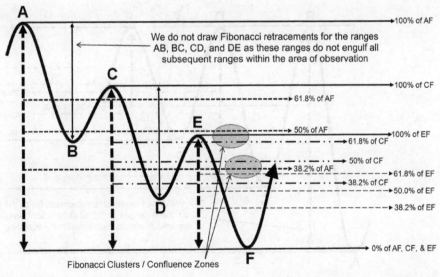

FIGURE 10.61 Fibonacci Upside Retracement Levels in a Three-Leg Formation for Ranges AF, CF, and EF.

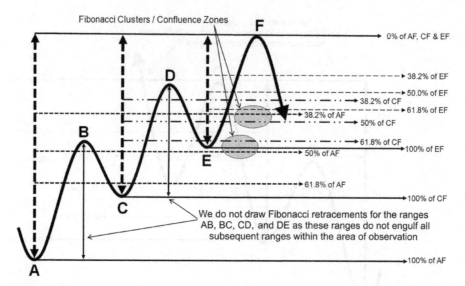

FIGURE 10.62 Fibonacci Downside Retracement Levels in a Three-Leg Formation for Ranges AF, CF, and EF.

A special case of a Fibonacci three-leg retracement formation is that of the ascending triangle pattern where the general rule is satisfied by all three price ranges within the area of observation. See Figure 10.63.

10.16.5 Fibonacci Complex Multi-Leg Retracement Formations

Even within complex multi-leg formations, we should still abide by the general rule for calculating and plotting adjacent and overlapping retracement levels. In

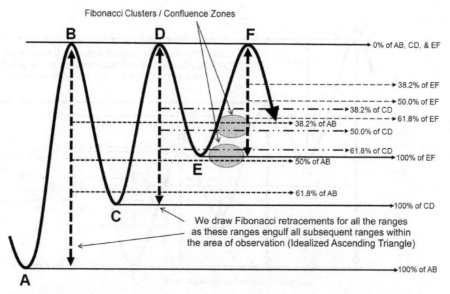

FIGURE 10.63 Fibonacci Downside Retracement Levels in an Idealized Ascending Triangle Formation for Ranges AF, CF, and EF.

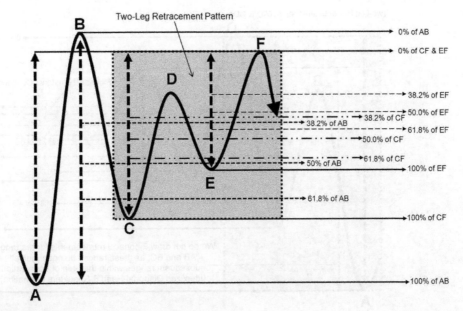

FIGURE 10.64 Fibonacci Downside Retracement Levels in a Complex Formation for Ranges AB, CF, and EF.

Figure 10.64, we see a situation where the first peak B exceeds peak F, a two-leg formation spanning from point C to point F. This makes AB the largest range. In this instance, we calculated the retracement levels for AB, CF, and EF, as these ranges satisfy the general rule. However, we do not calculate the retracement levels for BC, CD, and DE. Note that if point B were below point F, then we would not consider its Fibonacci retracement levels.

Refer to Figure 10.65. The largest range is AD. Our area of observation spans from point A to the current price. Applying the general rule to the complex formation, the leftmost range AB does not engulf all subsequent ranges, and hence the Fibonacci retracements for that range are not drawn. The next range, BC, also does not engulf all subsequent ranges, and hence the Fibonacci retracements for that range are also not drawn. The following range AD does engulf all subsequent ranges, and hence the Fibonacci retracements for range AD are drawn. The range CD also engulfs all subsequent ranges, and therefore the Fibonacci retracements for CD are drawn. In similar fashion, the Fibonacci retracements for DE and EF are drawn. In short, Fibonacci retracement levels are only drawn for ranges CD, DE, EF, and AD, as they all satisfy the general rule. The practitioner may now begin the task of identifying any significant Fibonacci clusters and any other overlay indicator–based supportive and resistive confluences. (Retracement levels for DE are not displayed for the sake of visual clarity.)

10.17 FIBONACCI FAN LINES

Fibonacci fan lines track the amount and degree of reversal in price. Fan lines are in essence merely trendlines and are therefore to be treated as barriers to price, representing either support or resistance. They are traded in the same manner

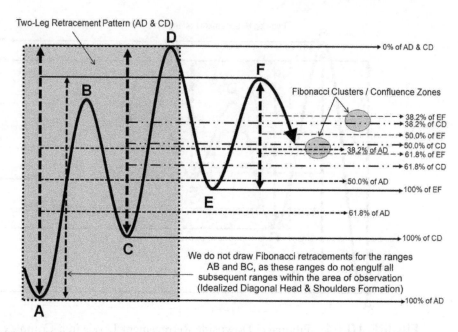

FIGURE 10.65 Fibonacci Downside Retracement Levels in a Complex Formation for Ranges AD, CD, DE, and EF.

as any trendline. One important characteristic of Fibonacci fan lines is that they are comprised of three trendlines, all plotted in accordance with the three main Fibonacci retracement ratios—38.2 percent, 50.0 percent, and 61.8 percent. Fan lines may be rising or declining. Rising fan lines are sometimes referred to as *accelerating* fan lines and declining fan lines as *decelerating* fan lines. Rising fan lines initially represent areas of resistance, turning into support once breached. In similar fashion, declining fan lines initially represent areas of support, turning into resistance once breached. Violation of the third fan line is normally considered strong evidence of potential continuation of a reversal.

To construct Fibonacci declining fan lines, refer to Figure 10.66. We first need to identify a significant peak and trough from which to plot the fan lines. Draw a vertical line from the peak to the price level at point A, the base. Calculate the three retracement-ratio values for the range AB, and then mark off the points of intersection between the vertical measuring line and the three retracement levels (points 1, 2, and 3). Plot three trendlines connecting the base to each intersect point. The same procedure applies for rising fan lines.

We see price finding support at the first and third fan lines. We also observe price finding resistance at the second fan line at point X.

In Figure 10.67, our base point is at point A. The vertical measuring line extends down from point C (not shown). We observe that price finds support at the first declining fan line at point D, which lies around a previous support level. We also see unusually large volume at point D, well above its 20-day moving average. Price subsequently reverses rapidly to the upside after testing the first fan line. It is important that all fan line tests are supported by a confluence of bullish or bearish indications. In this example, the prior support and surging volume added to the bullishness of the fan line test. Note that the area of application is after point

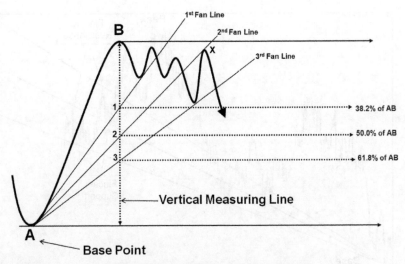

FIGURE 10.66 Constructing Declining Fibonacci Fan Lines.

C and all earlier tests of the fan lines are irrelevant and may well be regarded as coincidental.

In Figure 10.68, we see price finding support and resistance at the declining fan lines numerous times on the daily Natural Gas chart.

10.17.1 Invalidating Fibonacci Fan Lines

There are two scenarios where fan lines should be redrawn. The first scenario whereby declining fan lines should be redrawn occurs when price exceeds the peak from which they were plotted. Similarly, rising fan lines should be redrawn when price exceeds the trough from which they were plotted. Referring to Figure 10.67

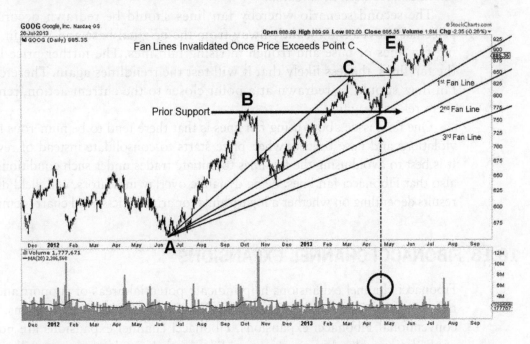

FIGURE 10.67 Declining Fibonacci Fan Lines on Google Inc.
Courtesy of Stockcharts.com

FIGURE 10.68 Price Finding Support and Resistance on Declining Fibonacci Fan Lines in Natural Gas.
Source: MetaTrader 4

again, declining Fibonacci fan lines plotted from the base A to point C are valid as long as price remains below point C. Therefore the fan line test at point D was valid. Since price has now exceeded point C, any new areas of potential support provided by declining fan lines must be determined by redrawing the fan lines from the base A to point E instead. We cannot therefore continue to use fan lines plotted from base A to point C for any future forecasts of potential support. The fan lines have been invalidated.

The second scenario whereby fan lines should be redrawn occurs when price has moved significantly away from the original base and peak in declining fan lines or base and trough in rising fan lines. The farther price is from the fan lines, the less likely that it will test the trendlines again. Therefore, the fan lines should be redrawn at a point closer to the current action, rendering them relevant again.

One final issue about using fan lines is that there tend to be numerous fan line violations and false triggers when price starts to consolidate instead of reversing. It is best to avoid using the fan lines to initiate trades under such conditions. Note also that Fibonacci fan lines, being dynamic overlay indicators, will yield different results depending on whether a logarithmic- or arithmetic-scaled chart is employed.

10.18 FIBONACCI CHANNEL EXPANSIONS

Fibonacci channel expansions help indicate potential areas of support and resistance in price. The width of the channel is the basis for the expansions. Unlike conventional Fibonacci expansions, Fibonacci channel expansions are normally applied *diagonally*. As a consequence, Fibonacci channel expansions will yield different results depending on the type of scaling used on the charts.

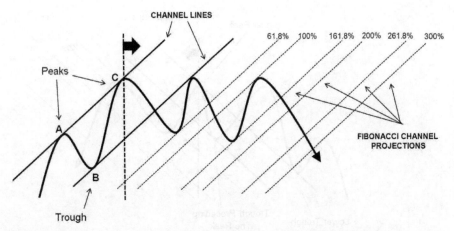

FIGURE 10.69 Conventional Fibonacci Downside Channel Expansions.

Fibonacci downside channel expansions may be formed in a number of ways. The conventional approach of constructing the main channel is by connecting the peaks and projecting a channel line from a lower trough. See Figure 10.69.

An alternative approach of constructing the main channel is to connect the troughs and projecting a channel line from a higher peak. See Figure 10.70.

A less conventional way of constructing Fibonacci downside channel expansion is by connecting a lower trough with a higher peak, and projecting the channel line from a trough preceding that higher peak, as illustrated in Figure 10.71.

In Figure 10.72, we see Fibonacci channel expansions on the daily Gold chart, based on the width of the original channel, as indicated. The chart also displays two standard Fibonacci downside projections, projecting the range AB downward from point C. Price is seen testing the 61.8 percent, 100 percent, 161.8 percent, 300 percent, and 361.8 percent Fibonacci channel lines very decisively. The various Fibonacci downside projection levels also provided added bullishness at the 100 percent and 361.8 percent channel line expansions.

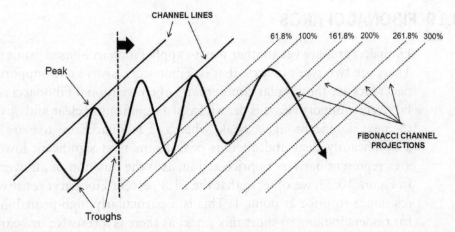

FIGURE 10.70 Conventional Fibonacci Downside Channel Expansions.

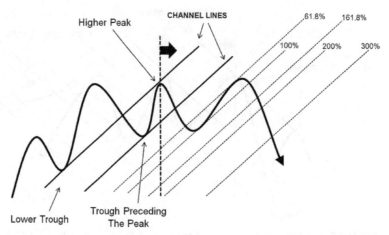

FIGURE 10.71 Less Conventional Fibonacci Downside Channel Expansions.

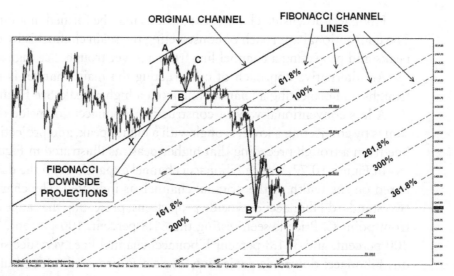

FIGURE 10.72 Fibonacci Downside Channel Expansion Lines on the Gold Daily Chart.
Source: MetaTrader 4

10.19 FIBONACCI ARCS

Fibonacci arcs are yet another way to apply Fibonacci-based ratios to price action. There are two types of arcs, that is, Fibonacci resistive and supportive arcs. Fibonacci arcs are the circular counterparts of conventional Fibonacci retracements. A Fibonacci supportive arc is drawn from a significantly clear and obvious trough to the next significant higher peak, whereas a Fibonacci resistive arc is drawn from a significantly clear and obvious peak to the next significant lower trough. The arcs represent barriers to price action, as is the function of all overlay indicators. In Figure 10.73, we observe that the 61.8 percent Fibonacci resistive arc provided resistance to price at point 1. This is a particularly high-probability entry point for traders looking to short this stock, as there is a resistive or bearish confluence comprised of a prior resistance level and an upper regression channel line. The

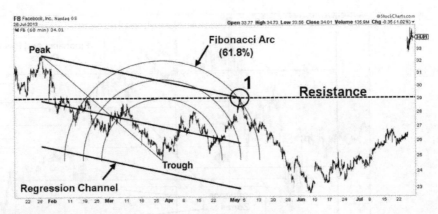

FIGURE 10.73 Fibonacci Resistive Arcs on Facebook Inc.
Courtesy of Stockcharts.com

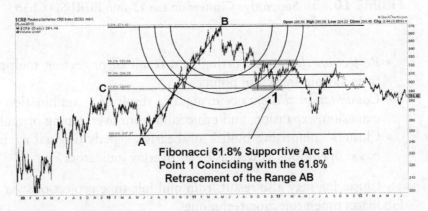

FIGURE 10.74 Fibonacci Resistive Arcs on the CRN Index.
Courtesy of Stockcharts.com

area of application is after the trough indicated on the chart. Note that Fibonacci arcs, being a dynamic overlay indicator, will yield different results depending on whether a logarithmically or arithmetically scaled chart is employed.

Figure 10.74 is an example of a supportive confluence comprised of Fibonacci arcs, retracements, and a prior support level (price at point C).

10.20 SUPPORTIVE AND RESISTIVE FIBONACCI CLUSTERS

Whenever two or more Fibonacci levels are concentrated around a certain price level, we say that there is a cluster or confluence of Fibonacci levels. These Fibonacci clusters may be either supportive or resistive, depending on whether price is above or below the cluster. If price is above it, we say that we have a *supportive confluence* or cluster of Fibonacci levels. Conversely, when price is below it, we say that we have a *resistive confluence* or cluster. This is because confluences or clusters represent barriers to price action.

There are various Fibonacci operations that may result in clustering.

- *Retracement clusters* occurring as a result of retracing overlapping price ranges
- *Extension clusters* occurring as a result of extending multiple ranges
- *Expansion clusters* occurring as a result of expanding multiple price ranges

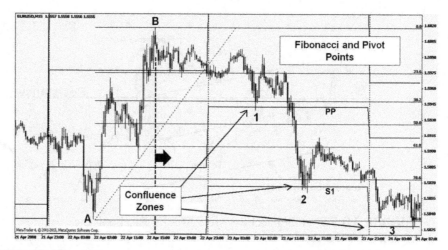

FIGURE 10.75 Supportive Clusters on the 15-min EURUSD Chart.
Source: MetaTrader 4

- *Projection clusters* occurring as a result of projecting multiple price ranges from various inflection points
- *Combination clusters* occurring as a result of a combination of retracement, extension, expansion, and projection from overlapping or multiple ranges
- Clusters comprising bullish or bearish signals originating from Fibonacci-based operations as well as other overlay indicators

Clustering may also result from multiple time projections via any of the four Fibonacci time-projection techniques.

Figure 10.75 displays supportive clusters at levels 1, 2, and 3 comprised of both Fibonacci retracement levels (measured across the range AB) and Floor Trader's Pivot levels (at PP, S1, and S2).

Figure 10.76 displays a resistive cluster at the 50 percent Fibonacci retracement level across the range AB, on the cash-settled U.S. dollar index. The resistive cluster or confluence is comprised of an upper Bollinger band, a 50 percent Fibonacci

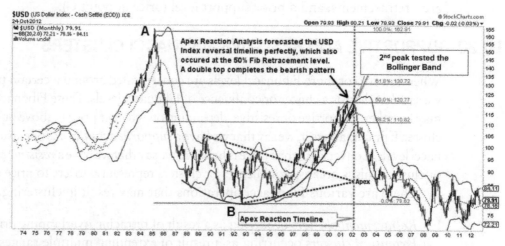

FIGURE 10.76 A Resistive Confluence on the Cash-Settled U.S. Dollar Index.
Courtesy of Stockcharts.com

retracement level, and an apex reaction time line projection. We subsequently see a rapid downside price excursion after reacting at the resistive confluence.

10.21 POTENTIAL BARRIERS IN FIBONACCI PROJECTIONS

When projecting an observed price range, there exists a Fibonacci cluster relationship between the Fibonacci *expansion* of the range and the Fibonacci *projection* levels, measured from each of the 38.2 percent, 50 percent, and 61.8 percent retracement levels of the range. Referring to Figure 10.77, we see that the upside projection for the range AB from the 38.2 percent retracement level yielded the greatest amount of resistive clustering above the range, whereas projecting the range from the 50 percent retracement level yielded the least resistive clustering above the range. This may be yet another reason why the 50 percent retracement was considered the most important and significant retracement percentage by both Gann and Dow. No trader and analyst would ever discount the 50 percent retracement potential even in today's algorithmically driven markets.

10.22 FIBONACCI TIME AND RATIO PROJECTION ANALYSIS ON ELLIOTT WAVES

Elliott waves are best described via various Fibonacci operations on its unique 5up-3down fractal wave structure. Before analyzing the potential price targets that can be ascertained by applying Fibonacci operations to impulsive and corrective waves, we must first understand the ratio relationship between two Fibonacci ratios.

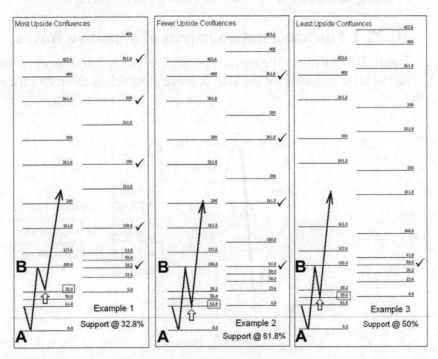

FIGURE 10.77 A Resistive Clustering Based on Expansion and Projections from the 38.2 Percent, 50 Percent, and 61.8 Percent Retracement Levels.

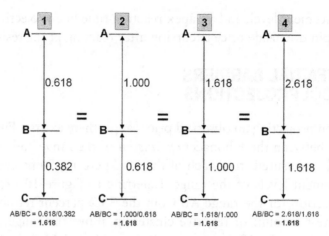

FIGURE 10.78   Ratio Invariant/Equivalent Relationships.

Figure 10.78 shows four examples of the *ratio of two Fibonacci ratios*. We observe that all four ratio relationships give 1.618. Therefore, the size or magnitude of a wave may be expressed as a ratio of another wave in more than one way. In each of the four cases, the size of wave AB is 1.618 times larger than that of wave BC. We may refer to this as either ratio equivalence or invariance. Consequently, it would be best to set the reference wave, that is, the wave that we are comparing other waves to, to a base reference ratio of 1.000. This would make the task of comparing the relative size of various waves to each other much more comprehensible. Therefore, for the sake of clarity, we shall set the reference wave to a base ratio of 1.000. Let us now turn our attention to the probable ratio relationships between various waves within the Elliott wave structure.

10.22.1 Fibonacci Ratio Analysis of Impulsive Waves

Figure 10.79 depicts the various possible Fibonacci upside *expansion* ratios for a top in wave 3, based on the size of wave 1, which is the reference wave.

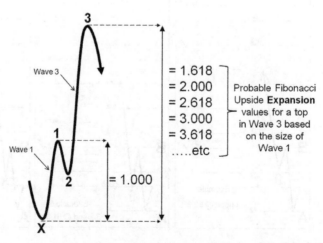

FIGURE 10.79   Probable Ratio Expansion Values of Wave 1 for a Top in Wave 3.

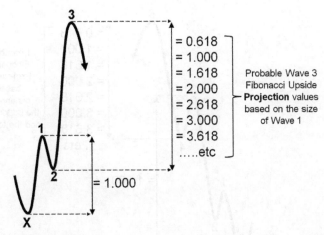

FIGURE 10.80   Probable Ratio Projection Values of Wave 1 for a Top in Wave 3.

Figure 10.80 depicts the various possible Fibonacci upside *projection* ratios for a top in wave 3, based on size of wave 1.

Figure 10.81 depicts the various possible Fibonacci upside *expansion* ratios for a top in wave 5, based on the distance measured from the bottom of wave 1 to the top of wave 3.

Figure 10.82 depicts the various possible Fibonacci upside *projection* ratios for a top in wave 5, based on the distance measured from the bottom of wave 1 to the top of wave 3.

Figure 10.83 depicts the various possible Fibonacci upside *expansion* ratios for a top in wave 5, based on the distance measured from the bottom of wave 1 to the bottom of wave 4.

Figure 10.84 depicts the various possible Fibonacci upside *projection* ratios for a top in wave 5, based on the size of wave 3.

Figure 10.85 depicts the various possible Fibonacci wave size ratios allowable for a wave 3 according to the rules of Elliott wave construction.

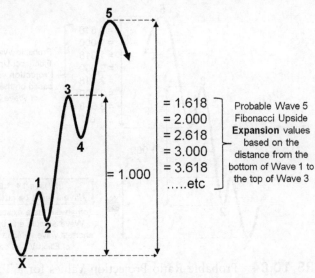

FIGURE 10.81   Probable Ratio Expansion Values for a Top in Wave 5.

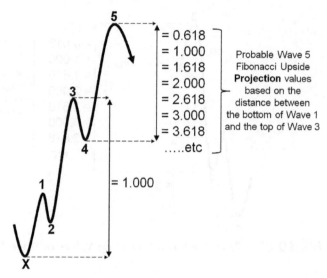

FIGURE 10.82 Probable Ratio Projection Values for a Top in Wave 5.

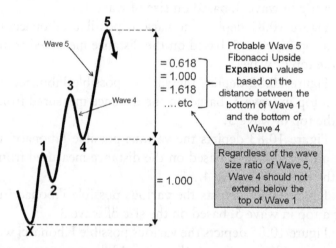

FIGURE 10.83 Probable Ratio Expansion Values for a Top in Wave 5.

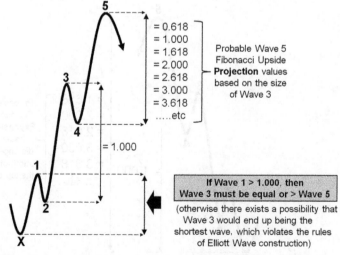

FIGURE 10.84 Probable Ratio Projection Values for a Top in Wave 5, Based on the Size of Wave 3.

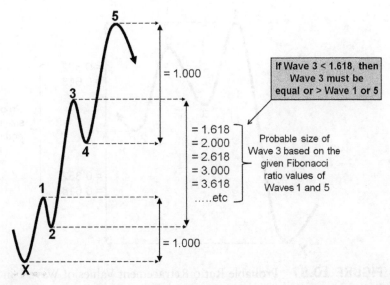

FIGURE 10.85 Allowable Wave Size Ratios for Wave 3 under the Rules of Elliott Wave Construction.

10.22.2 Fibonacci Ratio Analysis of Corrective Waves

Figure 10.86 depicts the various possible Fibonacci downside *retracement* ratios for a bottom in wave 2, based on the observed price range of wave 1.

Figure 10.87 depicts the same probable retracement ratios for a bottom in wave 2, as seen in Figure 10.86, but displayed in a *ratio equivalent* format. It is essentially identical to the ratio relationships shown in the previous diagram.

Figure 10.88 depicts the various possible Fibonacci downside *retracement* ratios for a bottom in wave 4, based on the entire observed price range as measured from the bottom of wave 1 to the top of wave 3.

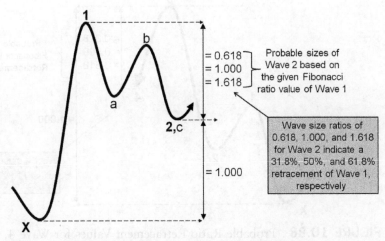

FIGURE 10.86 Probable Ratio Retracement Values of Wave 1 for a Bottom in Wave 2.

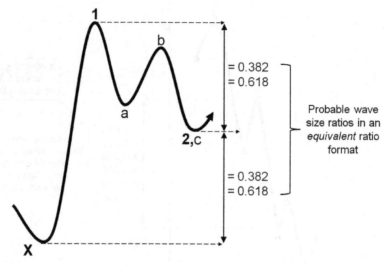

FIGURE 10.87 Probable Ratio Retracement Values of Wave 1 in an Equivalent Ratio Format.

10.22.3 Fibonacci Ratio Analysis of Corrective Waves in a Triangle Pattern

Waves that make up a triangle pattern also tend to exhibit ratio relationships with each other. Figure 10.89 depicts a series of converging waves within a symmetrical triangle pattern. It is not uncommon for subsequent alternate waves to be a factor of 0.618 shorter than the preceding wave. Refer to Figure 10.89 for an idealized version of this contraction ratio relationship.

In Figure 10.90, we observe this wave contraction on the EURUSD weekly chart, between December 2000 and September 2001. It is interesting to note that the ratio of wave heights AB to CD is approximately 1.608, which is about 1.1 percent off the idealized contraction ratio of 1.618.

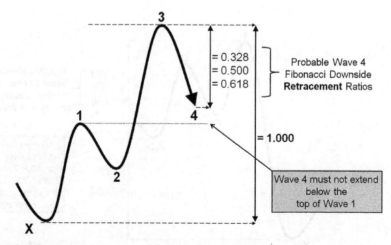

FIGURE 10.88 Probable Ratio Retracement Values for Wave 4, Based on the Size of the Entire Price Range.

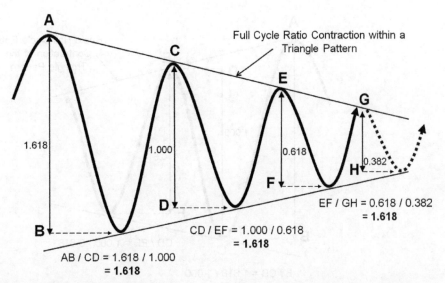

FIGURE 10.89 Possible Ratio Contraction Values for Waves within a Triangle Pattern.

Less common is a rapid *half-cycle* ratio contraction within the triangle pattern. In Figure 10.91, we observe that the wave contracts every half cycle instead. This type of price behavior normally suggests that a potential short-term breakout may be imminent.

10.22.4 Fibonacci Time Projection Analysis of Elliott Waves

We may employ Fibonacci-based time projection techniques to forecast potential tops and bottoms in the market. To forecast at which point in time a potential reversal could occur, we may use:

- Fibonacci number counts
- Fibonacci-based wave counts

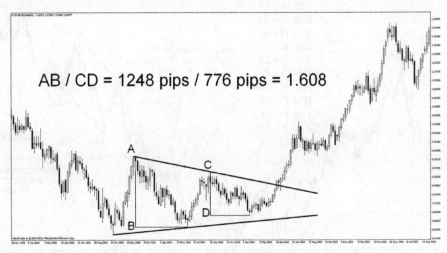

FIGURE 10.90 Fibonacci Ratio Contraction within a Triangle Pattern on the Weekly EURUSD Chart.
Source: MetaTrader 4

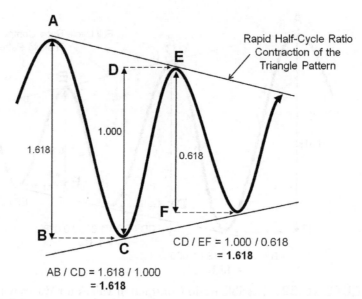

FIGURE 10.91 Rapid Half-Cycle Ratio Contraction within a Triangle Pattern.

- Fibonacci time ratio projections
- Fibonacci time zone projections

10.22.5 Fibonacci Number Counts

Figure 10.92 shows a simple Fibonacci number count for predicting potential reversals in price. It may be used on any timeframe. Start the Fibonacci number count from a significant peak or trough. The count increases as each subsequent bar or candlestick is formed. Potential reversals are then expected whenever the count approaches the next Fibonacci number in the sequence. It works best in

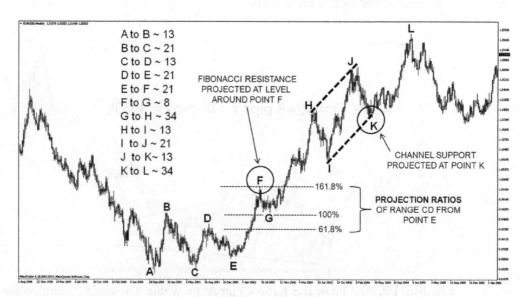

FIGURE 10.92 Fibonacci Number Counts on the Weekly EURUSD Chart.
Source: MetaTrader 4

conjunction with other indicators, and especially so when a resistive or supportive confluence is present at one of the Fibonacci numbered peaks or troughs.

We observe that, though only approximate (that is, give and take a few candlesticks at each peak and trough), the Fibonacci number count works fairly well in forecasting potential reversals on the EURUSD weekly chart from point A all the way up to point L. For example, the number of bars or candlesticks from trough A to peak B is approximately 13, and from peak B to trough C approximately 21. Fibonacci number counts may be made from:

- Peak to Peak
- Trough to Trough
- Peak to Trough
- Trough to Peak

In our example, we measured the number of bars or candlesticks from peak to trough and trough to peak repeatedly from point A to point L. The trick to using the Fibonacci number counts effectively is to locate other nearby potential resistance or support levels as price approaches the next Fibonacci number count. It is extremely rare that the reversal will always occur on the exact Fibonacci count itself, but more likely slightly before or after an expected peak or trough. Fibonacci number counts are best used as signals, requiring price confirmation before an entry or exit is initiated. The Fibonacci count at point F coincided with a 161.8 percent Fibonacci projection level of the price range CD, measured from point E. This tends to make the signal somewhat more reliable and provides an extra reason why price could reverse within the vicinity of the approaching Fibonacci count. Notice also that price is retesting a previous peak formed at point B as it consolidates around point G. Point G is also located just north of a 100 percent Fibonacci projection level. Again, this adds to the reliability of any Fibonacci count found around the vicinity of point G. Finally, we observe that the Fibonacci count around point K occurs at a channel support, giving the Fibonacci count a little more credibility.

10.22.6 Fibonacci-Based Wave Counts

Fibonacci counts may also be in the form of *wave counts*, instead of just counting the number of bars or candlesticks. Wave counts are in essence an extension of number counts. This is easy to understand when we realize that a sequence of bars on a chart in fact represents a wave in motion. Assigning Fibonacci counts to waves provides the technical analyst with yet another means of forecasting price action. Hence it is not surprising that Fibonacci wave counts naturally became an integral and significant part of Elliott Wave Theory. Figure 10.93 illustrates how Fibonacci-based wave counts are incorporated into Elliott waves. As we can see, at the highest level, that is, the highest wave cycle, the full market cycle is complete after a two-wave move, comprised of one impulsive wave up followed by a corrective wave down. The highest wave cycle is itself composed of smaller waves, that is, subwaves, being that of a five-wave up followed by a three-wave down. In this case, the full market cycle is complete after eight subwaves on the lower

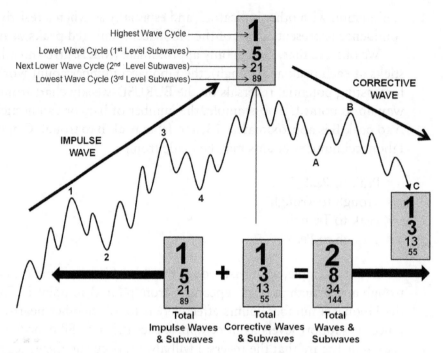

FIGURE 10.93 Elliott Wave/Fibonacci Wave Counts.

wave cycle. In fact, every wave cycle or wave degree may be broken down into yet smaller wave cycles or subwaves. We call this phenomenon *wave fractalization*. As we repeat this process, we find that the Elliott wave counts always add up to a Fibonacci number. This unique underlying structure provides yet another way for understanding and forecasting the behavior of the markets.

10.22.7 Fibonacci-Based Time Ratio Projections

Fibonacci time ratio projections may also be employed to forecast when a reversal may take place. Such projections are frequently performed on Elliott waves in conjunction with conventional Fibonacci ratio analysis to arrive at a price-time forecast for the next reversal.

When performing Fibonacci time ratio projections, we first measure the duration of our reference wave, and set it to a base ratio of 1.000. We subsequently calculate various Fibonacci-based projection ratios to predict potential turning points in the market. As always, it is best if these time ratio projections are in the proximity of other supportive or resistive confluences, with corresponding overbought or oversold indications in the oscillators. It is usually best that no technical tool or indicator be used in isolation. A confluence or cluster of technical indications around a particular price and time will generally lead to more reliable forecasts. Fibonacci time ratio projections may be made from:

- Peak to Peak
- Trough to Trough
- Peak to Trough
- Trough to Peak

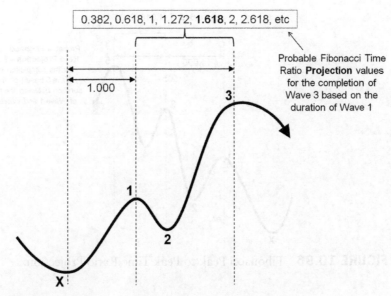

FIGURE 10.94 Fibonacci Trough to Peak Time Ratio Projection.

Figure 10.94 illustrates the probable time ratio relationships for the completion of wave 3 based on the duration of wave 1.

Figure 10.95 illustrates the probable time ratio relationships for the completion of wave 4 based on the duration between the bottoms of wave 1 and wave 2.

Figure 10.96 illustrates the probable time ratio relationships for the completion of wave 5 based on the duration between the tops of wave 1 and wave 3.

Figure 10.97 is a chart of the daily EURUSD illustrating various time ratio relationships. We observe that the ratio of the duration of BD to BG is 2, while

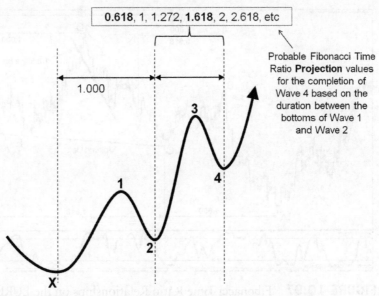

FIGURE 10.95 Fibonacci Trough to Trough Time Ratio Projection.

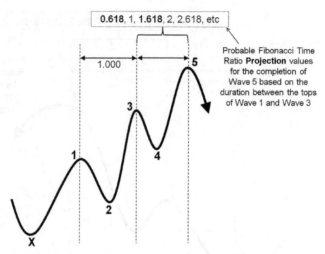

FIGURE 10.96   Fibonacci Peak to Peak Time Ratio Projection.

the ratio of the duration of BX to BD is 0.618. The ratio of the duration of BD to DG is a one to one correspondence. Point D occurs at a ratio of 1.618 of BX (i.e., 1/0.618 = 1.618). The possibility of a bearish reversal at point D is further supported by a test of the upper Bollinger band, which represents potential resistance, as well as an overbought indication on the *cycle-tuned* stochastic oscillator. The trader now awaits price confirmation before initiating a trade, which may be in the form of a simple trendline violation, as indicated on the chart. This is a good example of looking for a trade setup based on a confluence or concentration of bearish indications, and not merely relying on a single time ratio projection.

Point F is another example of only acting on a time ratio projection in the vicinity of other bullish indications. We observe that point F is 1.618 of the duration

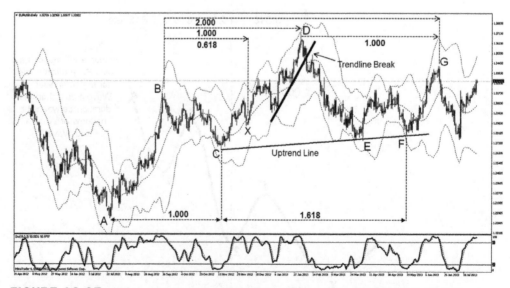

FIGURE 10.97   Fibonacci Time Ratio Relationships on the EURUSD Daily Chart.
Source: MetaTrader 4

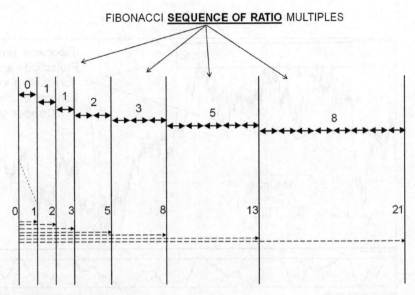

FIGURE 10.98   Fibonacci Time Zone Projections.

between points A and C, as projected from point C. The possibility of a bullish reversal at point F is further supported by a test of the lower Bollinger band, which represents potential support. This bullish indication is also corroborated by an oversold indication on the cycle-tuned stochastic oscillator. The presence of an uptrend line further increases the expectation of a bullish reversal around point F. The trader may now initiate a long entry at the test of the uptrend line or wait for confirmation of an upside move in price before pulling the trigger. Once again, we see the time ratio projection of a potential reversal being supported by a confluence of bullish indications.

10.22.8 Fibonacci Time Zone Projections

Fibonacci time zone projection is yet another way to forecast potential tops and bottoms in price. Fibonacci time zone projection is rather unique in that it is a combination of Fibonacci number counts and ratio projection. In essence, it represents the *counting of ratio multiples*, based on the Fibonacci number series. See Figure 10.98.

When applying Fibonacci time zone projections, we may set the initial zone by measuring from significant peaks and troughs, or inflection points, to be more general. The initial zone, upon which all subsequent time zone ratio multiples will be based, may be set from:

- Peak to Peak
- Trough to Trough
- Peak to Trough
- Trough to Peak

In Figure 10.99, we see Fibonacci time zone projections accurately forecasting tops and bottoms on the hourly Copper chart. The initial zone was set up using

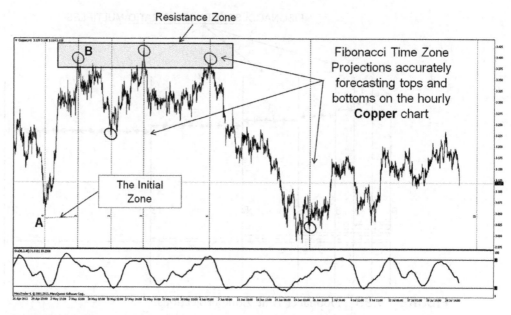

FIGURE 10.99 Fibonacci Time Zone Projections on the Hourly Copper Chart.
Source: MetaTrader 4

a significant trough at point A and the next significant peak at point B. The duration between A and B is then expanded in multiples, according to the Fibonacci sequence, 0, 1, 1, 2, 3, 5 , 8, 13, 21, 34, 55, and so on. The various tops and bottoms fell precisely on the projected time lines. This of course will not always be the case when performing time zone projections. Most of the time the projected time line for an expected reversal fails to fall on the exact peak or trough. Nevertheless, these projections are still useful especially if they are accompanied by other bullish or bearish indications. We see the projected tops in Copper testing a strong resistance zone, which suggest further bearishness. The overbought signals on the cycle-tuned stochastic oscillator coincide with the projected tops within the resistance zone. The first tradable point will be point C, since the area of application lies beyond point B.

One interesting point about Fibonacci time zone projections is that the counts can have a harmonically related Fibonacci sequence. For example, the Fibonacci sequence 0, 1, 1, 2, 3, 5, 8, 13, 21, 34, and so on may be rewritten as 0, 2, 2, 4, 6, 10, 16, 26, 42, 68, and so on. The ratio of any number in the new harmonically related series to its preceding number will still yield 1.618 in the limit. Therefore, when performing Fibonacci time zone projections, we may in fact expand the ratios according to the new series but at half of the original bar interval. For example, instead of using the original sequence on an hourly chart, we could use the new harmonically related sequence on a 30-minute chart. The time line projections will match up precisely with those projected on the hourly charts.

Fibonacci time zone projections, number counts, and time ratio projections only forecast potential reversals in price. Unlike conventional cycle analysis, these time-based projection techniques do not furnish any information as to whether the reversal will be that of a top or bottom.

430

10.23 CHAPTER SUMMARY

As we have seen, Fibonacci ratio price projections, retracements, extensions, and expansions form an important part of any practitioner's technical toolbox. We see the power of applying Fibonacci ratios to the charts especially when we combine price and time based Fibonacci ratio projections. Such confluences provide a more effective means of gauging potential price reactions and reversals in the markets.

CHAPTER 10 REVIEW QUESTIONS

1. Explain how you could potentially increase the reliability of Fibonacci forecast levels.
2. Describe the various probable Fibonacci ratio projection and expansion relationships for determining the top of wave 5 in an Elliott wave pattern.
3. What is Constance Brown's view on applying Fibonacci operations?
4. Explain how you would test the reliability of a forecasted Fibonacci level.
5. Explain how chart scaling affects Fibonacci applications.
6. In which markets, or under what scenarios, would Fibonacci forecasts be more reliable?
7. Describe how you would use oscillators to confirm Fibonacci level forecasts.
8. How would you apply Fibonacci analysis to price gaps?

REFERENCES

Boroden, Carolyn. 2008. *Fibonacci Trading.* New York: McGraw-Hill.

Brown, Constance. 1999. *Technical Analysis for the Trading Professional.* New York: McGraw-Hill.

Frost, A. J., and Robert R. Prechter. 1999. *Elliott Wave Principle.* New York: John Wiley & Sons.

Maclean, George. 2005. *Fibonacci and Gann Applications in Financial Markets.* Hoboken, NJ: Wiley Trading Series.

CHAPTER
11

Moving Averages

LEARNING OBJECTIVES

After studying this chapter, you should be able to:

- Understand the importance of moving averages as a technical tool for forecasting price reversal as well as determining the strength and direction of a trend
- Apply the concepts of moving averages to the real markets
- Identify and differentiate between detrending and smoothing
- Differentiate between reliable and unreliable entries based on moving averages
- Identify early signs of a market top or bottom using moving averages
- Understand how to calculate EMA, SMA, WMA, and VWAP

A moving average is an incredibly versatile technical tool. It can help to determine the general direction and strength of an existing trend, potential levels of support and resistance, and points of entry and exit and can be used as the central value for envelopes and bands, which are used to pinpoint levels of overextension in the market. In this chapter, we shall cover the main components of moving averages, their various forms of construction, and applications in the markets.

11.1 SEVEN MAIN COMPONENTS OF MOVING AVERAGES

Moving averages have a multitude of applications, some of which are:

- As a price filter, allowing for better clarity with regard to price activity
- In oscillator form for identifying potential levels of overselling and overbuying
- As a price barrier, providing support and resistance to price
- As a central value for envelopes and bands
- To indicate the strength and direction of a trend
- As a trigger for initiating entries and exits
- As a signal of potential bullishness and bearishness in the market

The reliability of a moving average as support and resistance depends on:

- The moving average's angle of ascent and descent
- The number of times it has been tested
- The accuracy and quality of the price test
- The amount of volatility in the market

Moving averages indicate potential bullishness and bearishness in the following ways:

- A rising moving average is an indication of potential bullishness.
- A declining moving average is an indication of potential bearishness.
- A shorter-term moving average crossing above a longer-term moving average is an indication of potential bullishness.
- A shorter-term moving average crossing below a longer-term moving average is an indication of potential bearishness.
- A shorter-term moving average rebounding off a longer-term moving average to the upside is an indication of potential bullishness.
- A shorter-term moving average rebounding off a longer-term moving average to the downside is an indication of potential bearishness.

Moving averages are not affected by the type of chart scaling used, whether it is semi-logarithmic or arithmetic. This is because moving averages are determined numerically and have no geometrical component on the charts, unlike trendlines, which are geometrically related and drawn from price inflection points on the charts. This makes trendlines and chart patterns susceptible to inconsistencies when employing different chart scaling.

We shall now study the components of moving averages and the various methods of constructing a moving average.

(1) The Data Field

Moving averages are constructed by creating a truncated or continuous *rolling average* using technical data such as:

- Price Data: Open, High, Low, and Closing Prices (OHLC)
- Volatility Data: Standard Deviation, Mean Deviation, True Range
- Transaction-Based Data: Volume, Tick Volume, Open Interest
- Market Breadth Data: Advances, Declines, Total Issues, New High, New Low, Up Volume, Down Volume, Total Volume
- Flow of Funds Data: Margin Debt, Account/Credit Balances, Cash to Asset Ratios
- Sentiment Data: Short Interest Ratio, Specialist to Public Ratio, Bullish Percent Index, Put/Call Ratio, Implied Volatilities (VIX), Bond Yields (Yield Curve), Net Commercial and Net Noncommercial Positions (COT Report)

A truncated moving average is one where data is averaged over a fixed number of data points, *dropping off* older data points with the addition of more new data, that is, a simple moving average. A continuous type moving average is one where the most recent value is the result of contributions by all data points since its inception. There is no dropping off of older data, that is, an exponential moving average.

Moving averages are also constructed by creating a rolling average of more *complex combinations* of technical data such as:

- Mid-Price: $(H + L)/2$
- Typical Price: $(H + L + C)/3$
- Weighted Close: $(H + L + 2C)/4$
- Data Differences:
  - Bar Range $(H - L)$
  - Momentum $(C_n - C_{n-1})$
  - Detrended Data (e.g., MACD) [Closing price of MA(1)—Closing price of MA(2)]
  - Net Advance Declines $(A - D)$
  - Net Advance Volume $(UV - DV)$
  - Net New Highs (New H – New L)
  - Intercontract Spread (Front Month – Back Month Price)
- Data Ratios:
  - Rate of Change, that is, Momentum $[(C_n - C_{n-1})/C_{n-1}]$
  - Advance Decline Ratio (A/D)
  - Volume Ratio (UV/DV)
  - Ratio Adjusted AD $[(A - D)/\text{Total Issues}]$
- Moving Averages: SMA, EMA, WMA, VWMA (i.e., Double and Triple Smoothing)
- Oscillator Equations: Stochastic Raw %K

(2) Longitudinal and Cross-Sectional Forms of Averaging

As seen from the lists above, a moving average may be constructed on practically any simple or complex combination of technical data. Generally, a moving average is constructed using *single-valued data*. This is referred to as the *longitudinal* form of a moving average. It tracks the current average value for each new single value added to the moving average. Most forms of moving averages are of the longitudinal type.

If we construct a moving average based double or multiple values for each period, this is referred to as the *cross-sectional* form of a moving average. For example, constructing a new moving average based on the *average value of two other moving averages* would represent a cross-sectional form of a moving average.

(3) Data Referencing

The average price over N bars is positioned on the time line in the middle of the sequence of N bars, which represents the correct position for average price within the sequence. This is referred to as a *centered* moving average. This form of moving average displays *no lag with respect to price*. As a consequence, it is a popular tool for identifying price cycles.

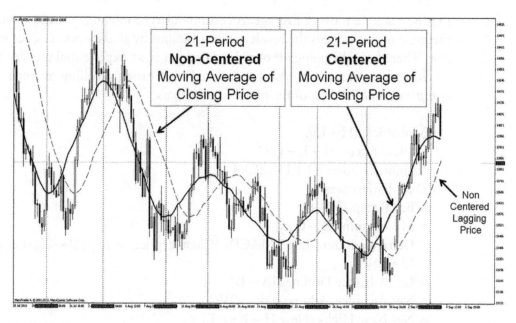

FIGURE 11.1 Centered versus Non-Centered Moving Averages on the 4-Hour Chart of the Nikkei 225.
Source: MetaTrader 4

In technical analysis, the average price is usually positioned at the last right-most bar on the chart, that is, at the current bar. This is the *non-centered* or *end-displaced* version of a moving average. It is technically incorrect to place the average price at the last bar, but in technical analysis this is done because it is being used as a barrier to price, that is, as potential levels of support and resistance, it is able to interact with price. Although there is no price lag in the centered version, the moving average does not extend to the most recent bars and therefore cannot provide a barrier to price.

It is interesting to note here that although the non-centered moving average is technically incorrect with respect to the positioning of the average price, nevertheless it tends to work well in the markets as support and resistance. This is a perfect example of the self-fulfilling prophecy at work.

In Figure 11.1, we see the 21-period centered moving average tracking price closely while the non-centered or end-displaced moving average exhibits lag with respect to price. The last few bars have been concealed for added clarity.

In Figure 11.2, we observe the same chart, but this time without concealing half of the last N bars, that is, half of the 21 bars. We see the non-centered moving average interacting with price, initially providing a sell signal and subsequently acting as resistance at the second-to-the-last bar.

Many charting platforms do not offer the centered moving average as an option when selecting the type of moving average to employ on the charts. Nevertheless, a centered moving average can easily be created by shifting the end-displaced or non-centered moving average back by half its period. The exact amount to shift back is calculated using $(N - 1) \div 2$. Hence, for our 21-period end-displaced moving average, we need to displace the moving back by $(21 - 1) \div 2 = 10$ periods. This formula works well with odd numbers. For even numbers, *round down* to the closest integer value.

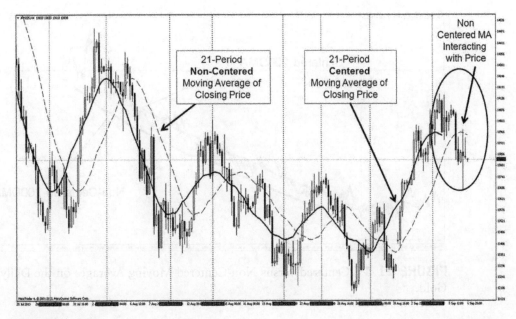

FIGURE 11.2 Centered versus Non-Centered Moving Averages on the 4-Hour Chart of the Nikkei 225.
Source: MetaTrader 4

As we will learn from cycle analysis in Chapter 20, the middle of any N-period number of bars is found using $(N + 1) \div 2$, rounding up to the closest integer if N is even. Let us now locate the middle N periods using the formula $(N + 1) \div 2$ and compare that with shifting back by half of N periods using $(N - 1) \div 2$. Figure 11.3 proves that both calculations refer to the same bar, which represents the middle of 10 periods.

Finally, centered moving averages with *very large periodicities* tend to move through the central region of price activity, representing a kind of central value

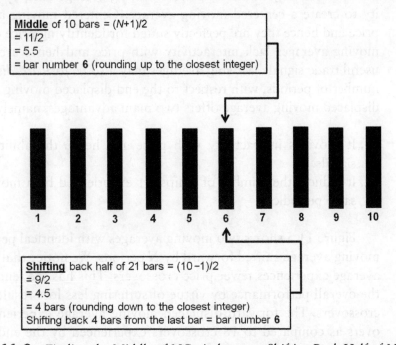

Middle of 10 bars = $(N+1)/2$
= 11/2
= 5.5
= bar number **6** (rounding up to the closest integer)

Shifting back half of 21 bars = $(10-1)/2$
= 9/2
= 4.5
= 4 bars (rounding down to the closest integer)
Shifting back 4 bars from the last bar = bar number **6**

FIGURE 11.3 Finding the Middle of N Periods versus Shifting Back Half of N Periods.

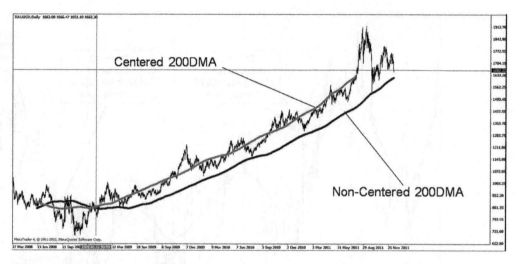

FIGURE 11.4 Centered versus Non-Centered Moving Averages on the Daily Chart of Gold.
Source: MetaTrader 4

to which prices tend to revert after a certain amount of price excursion from the line. It works well as a trend identifier in this mode, rather than tracking shorter-term cycles. Figure 11.4 shows both 200-day centered and end-displaced (non-centered) moving averages. The popular 200-day end-displaced moving average is seen providing reliable support to Gold prices.

(4) Time Adjustments/Displacements

As we have seen, we can displace a moving average back by half of its periodicity to create a centered moving average. Centered moving averages do not lag price and hence they are perfectly suited for identifying price cycles. But centered moving averages lack interactivity with price and hence are unable to provide useful trade signals. Moving averages may also be *forward displaced* by a certain number of periods, with respect to the end-displaced moving average. A forward displaced moving average offers two main advantages, namely:

1. It provides interactivity with price and hence the ability to provide trade signals.
2. It reduces the number of whipsaws experienced by a moving average of the same periodicity.

Figure 11.5 shows two moving averages with identical periodicities with one moving average shifted forward by N periods. We notice that the shifted moving average experiences fewer price crossovers. This has the tendency of improving the overall performance by virtue of suffering less loss resulting from excessive crossovers. The forward displaced moving average experiences about 6 crossovers as compared to 18 crossovers experienced by the end-displaced moving average.

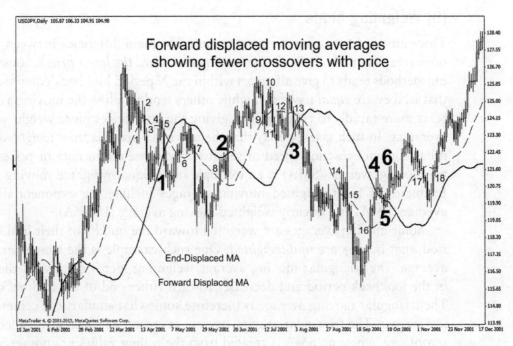

FIGURE 11.5 End-Displaced versus Forward Shifted Moving Averages on the Daily Chart of the USDJPY.
Source: MetaTrader 4

This would be more responsive than employing a longer-term trend line, which would technically also reduce the number of whipsaws. But a longer-term moving average would lag price significantly and therefore would not prove to be as profitable a strategy as compared to a shorter-term forward displaced moving average. See Figure 11.6.

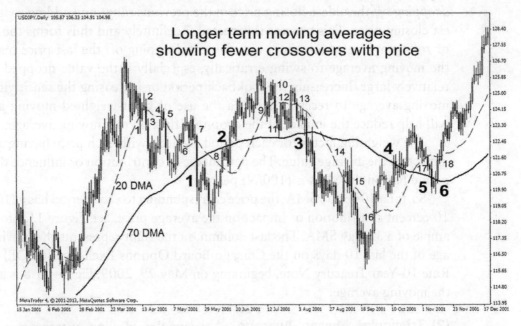

FIGURE 11.6 End-Displaced versus Longer-Term Moving Averages on the Daily Chart of the USDJPY.
Source: MetaTrader 4

(5) Weighting Mode

There are numerous ways to average data. The main difference between the various averaging methods *lies in the sensitivity toward the latest prices*. Some averaging methods tends to give all prices within the N period lookback equal weighting, that is, they are *equal weighted*, while others tend to allow the moving average to react more rapidly to recent prices, giving the later prices more weight within its averaging. In such cases, we say that the moving average is *front weighted*, that is, it has a greater reaction speed or sensitivity to more recent data or prices. A simple moving average (SMA) is an example of an equal-weighted moving average. Examples of front-weighted moving averages include the exponential moving average (EMA) and linearly weighted moving average (LWMA).

Some moving averages are weighted toward the *middle* of their lookback period, that is, they are *mid-weighted*. One such example is the triangular moving average. The triangular moving average weighting increases toward the middle of the lookback period and decreases toward either end of the lookback period. The triangular moving average is therefore somewhat similar to a centered moving average. The triangular moving average is created via a process called *double smoothing*, where an SMA is created from the rolling values of another SMA.

(1) Simple Moving Average   A simple moving average (SMA) is the most basic form of a moving average and is calculated by first dividing the sum of all prices by its number of periods. Let N equal the lookback period:

$$\text{Average over } N \text{ periods} = \sum(\text{Closing Prices over } N \text{ periods})/N$$

This average value is then rolled forward to the next most recent closing price, *dropping off* the oldest closing price in the previous range and adding to it the latest closing price. This process is repeated indefinitely and thus forms the *moving* or *rolling* average. Sometimes the effect of dropping off the last price may cause the moving average to swing erratically, especially if the value dropped off was relatively large. Increasing the lookback period or increasing the sensitivity of the moving average to recent prices via the use of front-weighted moving averages will help reduce the impact of the drop-off effect on the moving average.

The weighting factor for each period is equal, with each price having an equal impact on the average value. The percentage of contribution or influence that each period has on the SMA is (100/N) percent.

So, for a 10 period SMA, the price corresponding to each period has a (100/10) = 10 percent contribution or impact on the average price. See Figure 11.7 for an example of a 10-day SMA. The last column on the right represents the moving average of the last 10 days on the Chicago Board Options Exchange (CBOE) Interest Rate 10-Year Treasury Note, beginning on May 29, 2009. Figure 11.8 is a plot of the moving average.

(2) Triangular Moving Average   A triangular moving average is a *double smoothed moving average*. The value for each period of the first SMA is averaged a second time over the same number of periods. It is mid-weighted, as can

CBOE Interest Rate 10-Year T-Note

Start Date	Daily Closing Price	Sum Over Last 10 Periods	Average Price = Sum / 10
29-May-09	3.46		
1-Jun-09	3.71		
2-Jun-09	3.64		
3-Jun-09	3.55		
4-Jun-09	3.72		
5-Jun-09	3.86		
8-Jun-09	3.89		
9-Jun-09	3.86		
10-Jun-09	3.94		
11-Jun-09	3.86	37.49	**3.749**
12-Jun-09	3.79	37.82	**3.782**
15-Jun-09	3.71	37.82	**3.782**
16-Jun-09	3.67	37.85	**3.785**
17-Jun-09	3.65	37.95	**3.795**
18-Jun-09	3.83	38.06	**3.806**
19-Jun-09	3.79	37.99	**3.799**
22-Jun-09	3.69	37.79	**3.779**
23-Jun-09	3.64	37.57	**3.757**
24-Jun-09	3.68	37.31	**3.731**

FIGURE 11.7 Calculations for a 10-Day Simple Moving Average of the CBOE Interest Rate 10-Year Treasury Note.
Data: Yahoo Finance

be mathematically proven using basic algebra. Assume that the moving averages have a lookback period of four bars and that closing prices are used.

First find the four-period SMA:

$$\text{Average Price for Day 1} = (C_4 + C_3 + C_2 + C_1)/4$$

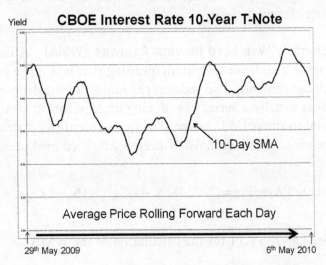

FIGURE 11.8 A 10-Day Simple Moving Average of the CBOE Interest Rate 10-Year Treasury Note.
Data: Yahoo Finance

Average of the next four bars, dropping off the last closing price C_1 gives

$$\text{Average Price for Day } 2 = (C_5 + C_4 + C_3 + C_2)/4$$

And similarly for the next two days:

$$\text{Average Price for Day } 3 = (C_6 + C_5 + C_4 + C_3)/4$$

$$\text{Average Price for Day } 4 = (C_7 + C_6 + C_5 + C_4)/4$$

We now find the average of the averages for the first four days (Double Smoothing):

$$= [(C_4 + C_3 + C_2 + C_1) + (C_5 + C_4 + C_3 + C_2) + (C_6 + C_5 + C_4 + C_3)$$
$$+ (C_7 + C_6 + C_5 + C_4)]/16$$
$$= [C_7 + 2C_6 + 3C_5 + 4C_4 + 3C_3 + 2C_2 + C_1]/16$$

Hence, we observe that the weighting for a triangular average is greater in the middle of the period (i.e., 1–2–3–4–3–2–1). In order to construct a triangular moving average, we need to first determine the period to be used.

Let us assume that we have identified a 19-period dominant cycle in the market and we want to track it using a triangular moving average. We first find the half-period value, which is given by $(N + 1)/2$ and rounding up if N is even. This gives us $(19 + 1)/2 = 10$ periods. We shall now calculate the SMA of both averages using this period. Hence, we use a 10-period triangular moving average to track a 19-period cycle in the market. See Figure 11.9 for an example of the calculation for a 10-day triangular moving average. The last column on the right represents the *moving average of the last 10 average prices* on the CBOE Interest Rate 10-Year Treasury Note, beginning on May 29, 2009. Figure 11.10 is a plot of the moving average.

(3) Linearly Weighted Moving Average (WMA) A linearly weighted moving average is also front weighted, meaning that it is more sensitive to recent prices, which conveniently also reduces the impact of the drop-off effect. The weighting factor is usually a series of reducing multiplication factors, the length of which is equal to the period chosen. The more recent the prices or data, the larger will be the weighting factor. An N-period weighted average is calculated as follows:

$$\text{Weighted Average} = [NC_N + (N - 1)C_{N-1} + (N - 2)C_{N-2} + \cdots + (1)C_1]/[N(N + 1)/2]$$

See Figure 11.11 for the calculation of the WMA.

(4) Exponential Moving Average (EMA) An exponential moving average (EMA) is a front-weighted moving average. It is very sensitive to recent prices, and

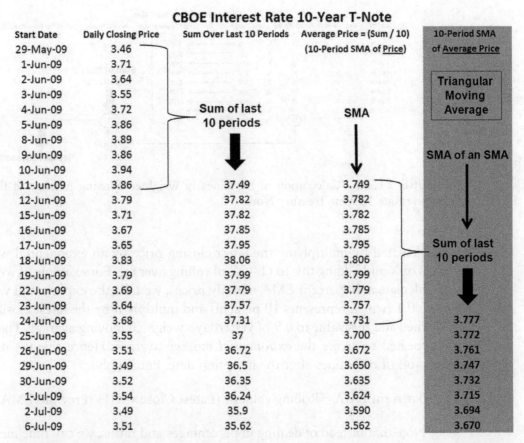

FIGURE 11.9 Calculations for a Triangular Moving Average (Double Smoothing) of the CBOE Interest Rate 10-Year Treasury Note.
Data: Yahoo Finance

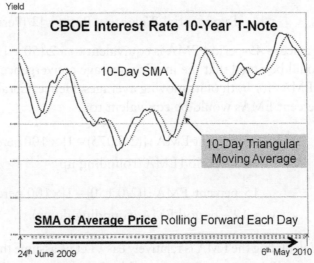

FIGURE 11.10 A Triangular Moving Average of the CBOE Interest Rate 10-Year Treasury Note.
Data: Yahoo Finance

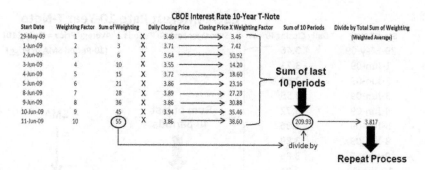

FIGURE 11.11 Calculation of the Linearly Weighted Moving Average of the CBOE Interest Rate 10-Year Treasury Note.

is calculated by multiplying the latest closing price by an exponential weighting ratio of X and adding this to $(1 - X)$ of rolling average. For example, if we wanted to calculate a 10 percent EMA of daily prices, we take the exponential weighting ratio 0.1 (which represents 10 percent) and multiply it by the latest closing price. We then add this value to 0.9 of yesterday's weighted moving average. The process is repeated to create the *exponential moving average*. Hence there is no actual drop-off of old values after the inception date. Put simply:

$$10 \text{ percent EMA} = \text{Rolling value of (Latest Close} \times 0.1) + (\text{Previous EMA} \times 0.9)$$

Note that instead of dealing in percentages and ratios, we can redefine them in terms of time periods, via the following formula:

$$\text{Periods} = [(2/\text{Exponential Weighting Ratio}) - 1]$$

Hence, a 25-period EMA is equivalent to a $(2/0.25)-1 = 8-1 = 7$ period EMA. Rearranging the equation we get:

$$\text{Exponential Weighting Ratio} = [2/(\text{Periods} + 1)]$$

Hence, a 49-period EMA is equivalent to a $2/(50 + 1) = 0.04 \sim 4$ percent EMA. It should be noted that the moving average convergence-divergence (MACD) also uses EMAs for both of its moving averages. Hence, Gerald Appel's 7.5 percent and 15 percent EMAs would be equivalent to:

$$7.5 \text{ percent EMA} : [(2/0.075) - 1] \times 100 \text{ percent} = 25.66$$
$$= 26 - \text{period EMA (rounding up)}$$

$$15 \text{ percent EMA} : [(2/0.150) - 1] \times 100 \text{ percent} = 12.33$$
$$= 12 - \text{period EMA (rounding down)}$$

Calculating the EMA is relatively easy. Let us assume that we use yesterday's EMA value of $30 as our starting value. (Most platforms use yesterday's SMA of the same lookback period as the starting point since no EMA is available.) The closing price today is $28, and the closing prices for the next two days are $26 and $24, respectively.

FIGURE 11.12 Comparing EMA and SMA Sensitivities on a Daily Chart of iShares Barclays 20+ Year Treasury Bond Fund.
Courtesy of Stockcharts.com

Let us now calculate a nine-day EMA. The first thing we need to do is determine the exponential ratio for a nine-period EMA, which is just $[2/(9 + 1)] = 0.1$ (i.e., a 10 percent EMA). Hence, the EMA for the next three days is calculated as follows:

$$\text{EMA (Day 1)} = (\text{Latest Close} \times 0.1) + (\text{Previous EMA} \times (1 - 0.1))$$
$$= (\$28 \times 0.1) + (\$30 \times 0.9) = \$29.80$$

$$\text{EMA (Day2)} = (\text{New Close} \times 0.1) + (\text{Previous EMA} \times (1 - 0.1))$$
$$= (\$26 \times 0.1) + (\$29.80 \times 0.9) = \$29.42$$

$$\text{EMA (Day 3)} = (\text{New Close} \times 0.1) + (\text{Previous EMA} \times (1 - 0.1))$$
$$= (\$24 \times 0.1) + (\$29.42 \times 0.9) = \$28.87$$

Figure 11.12 compares the sensitivities of a 40-Day EMA to that of the 40-Day SMA on a daily Chart of iShares Barclays 20+ Year Treasury Bond Fund. We observe that the EMA reacts more rapidly to price changes than the SMA, with respect to the same periodicity.

(5) Volume-Weighted Moving Average (VWMA)

A volume-weighted moving average is weighted according to the volume that accompanies the *typical price* for each period. The greater the volume at a particular price, the more the value of the moving average will be biased toward that price. Typically, tick volume is used. In our example, we shall use the period's volume instead. It is calculated by first multiplying each period's typical price by its volume and then adding it all up. This total is then divided by the total volume to get the volume-weighted average price (VWAP). See Figure 11.13. Notice that higher volume at $5 drove the volume-weighted average price up to $3.42, from the average price of $3.00.

The percentage contribution or influence that most recent price has on the moving average is ($400/$4800) × 100 percent = 8.33 percent. This is much

TYPICAL PRICE	DAY'S VOLUME	PRICE X VOLUME	CUMULATIVE VOLUME	TOTAL PRICE X VOLUME	VWAP
$1.00	200	200	200	200	**$1.00**
$4.00	200	800	400	1000	**$2.50**
$5.00	500	2500	900	3500	**$3.88**
$3.00	300	900	1200	4400	**$3.66**
$2.00	200	400	1400	4800	**$3.42**

VWAP = $4800 / Total Volume
= $4800 / 1400
= **$3.42**

Average Price = $15 / Total Periods
= $1500 / 5
= **$3.00**

FIGURE 11.13 Calculating the VWAP.

TYPICAL PRICE	DAY'S VOLUME	PRICE X VOLUME	CUMULATIVE VOLUME	TOTAL PRICE X VOLUME	VWAP
$1.00	100	100	100	100	**$1.00**
$4.00	100	400	200	500	**$2.50**
$5.00	100	500	300	1000	**$3.33**
$3.00	100	300	400	1300	**$3.25**
$2.00	100	200	500	1500	**$3.00**

VWAP = $1500 / Total Volume
= $1500 / 500
= **$3.00**

Average Price = $15 / Total Periods
= $1500 / 5
= **$3.00**

FIGURE 11.14 Calculating the Equivolume VWAP.

lower than for a five-period simple moving average, which is (100 percent /5) = 20 percent. The price that influences the moving average the most is $5, since it has the greatest volume, as it has a percentage contribution of (2500/4800) × 100 percent = 52 percent to the most recent value of the volume-weighted moving average.

Figure 11.14 shows what happens when volumes for each period are all equal. *It basically reverts back to a simple moving average of price.* This is important, as it makes the use of VWAP on constant volume charts pointless. A simple moving average of price would achieve the same result.

See Figure 11.15 for a comparison of VWAP with a standard SMA of the same periodicity.

Figure 11.16 shows VWAP acting as support and resistance. Prices below VWAP are considered bearish, whereas prices above VWAP are considered bullish.

(6) Wilder's Averaging Method   Welles Wilder introduced a form of averaging that he uses with his indicators in his book *New Concepts in Technical Trading*

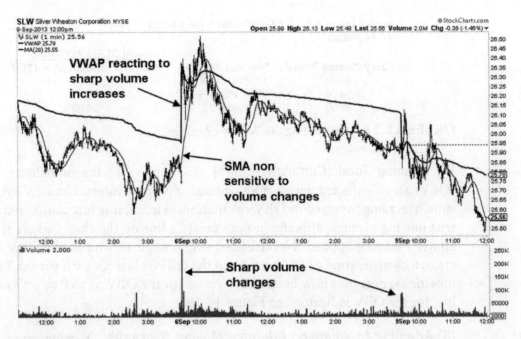

FIGURE 11.15 Comparing EMA and SMA Sensitivities on a 1-Min Chart of Silver Wheaton Corporation.
Courtesy of Stockcharts.com

Systems. Assume that the previous 14-day Wilder moving average value was $6.20. Multiply this by 13 and add the most recent closing price. Divide the total by the number of periods, which in this case is 14. Use this result as the next day's moving average value. The sequence of values represents the Wilder's moving average. See Figure 11.17.

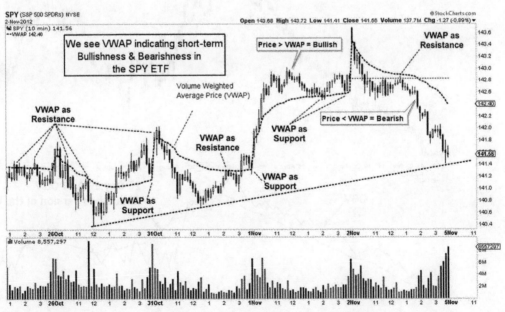

FIGURE 11.16 VWAP Action on a 10-Min Chart of SPY ETF.
Courtesy of Stockcharts.com

Assume previous day's 14-day Wilder's MA = $6.20
N = 14 periods

Daily Closing Prices	Previous MA × 13	WILDER'S AVERAGE Close+(Previous MA × 13)/N
$5.00	$6.20 x13=$80.60	$6.11
$4.00	$6.11 x13=$79.43	$5.95
$8.00	$5.95 x13=$77.35	$6.09

FIGURE 11.17 Calculating the Wilder's Average.

(7) Running Total (Cumulative Line) Indicators like the on-balance volume (OBV) are constructed with a running total of all past values. Unlike VWAP, there is no averaging involved in OBV calculations. Hence, it is not considered to be a true moving average, although it does create a line on the charts where technical analysis may be applied. Nevertheless, a smoothed version of the OBV may be created by generating an SMA based on the OBV values for each period. This new moving average may now be used as a proxy for the OBV, as well as act as a signal line for the OBV indicator. See Figure 11.18.

(8) Adapting to Volatility: Adaptive Moving Averages Moving averages may also be adjusted for volatility. There are many forms of volatility-weighted moving averages, sometimes referred to as *adaptive* moving averages. They are constructed in such a way that *as volatility increases the sensitivity of the moving averages decreases*, thereby distancing the moving averages from price. This is important so as to reduce the probability of being whipsawed by price in an erratic market.

FIGURE 11.18 VWAP Action on a Daily Chart of Utilities Select Sector SPDR. Courtesy of Stockcharts.com

This also helps protect the traders using stoploss orders from premature exits. As the volatility subsides, the sensitivity of the adaptive moving average starts to increase, drawing it closer to price action. The exponential weighting ratio, or alpha (α), is usually modified to account for volatility in price, unlike the exponential weighting ratio found in standard EMAs, which are fixed and nonadaptable. Popular adaptive moving averages include:

- Kaufman Adaptive Moving Average (KAMA)
- MESA Adaptive Moving Average (MAMA)
- Variable Index Dynamic Average (VIDYA)
- Following Adaptive Moving Average (FAMA)
- Fractal Adaptive Moving Average (FRAMA)

(6) Degree of Smoothing

Prices are usually single, double, or triple smoothed. A single SMA is a simple smoothing of the original data or prices. Sometimes, practitioners will smooth the data a second time, that is, double smooth, to either:

- Further reduce the volatility
- Create a second moving average to be used as a crossover signal for the single smoothed moving average (e.g., the stochastic oscillator's slow %D is a double smoothed SMA of the slow %K, which is itself a single smooth MA)

See Figure 11.19 for an example of double smoothing in the Slow Stochastics. The Slow %K, which is itself a seven-period moving average of Raw %K, is smoothed via a three-period SMA. If both are plotted, the three-period SMA, that is, the Slow %D, acts as a signal line, indicating potential buy and sell signals every time it crosses above and below the Slow %K, respectively. The five-period SMA of relative strength index (RSI) also provides a means of using crossovers as an indication of potential bullishness or bearishness in the market.

There are a couple of ways to smooth data or prices in lieu of double or triple smoothing, some of which are:

- Using a moving average with a longer lookback period
- Using a less-sensitive moving average, that is, an equal-weighted moving average like the SMA instead of a front-weighted moving average like the EMA or WMA

Finally, unlike for triangular moving averages, the creation of a double smooth moving average does not require the half period value to be employed. Simply calculate a new SMA of the rolling values of the first SMA.

(7) Data Periodicity

The easiest parameter to adjust on a moving average is its periodicity, that is, its lookback period. The longer the lookback period, the less sensitive the moving

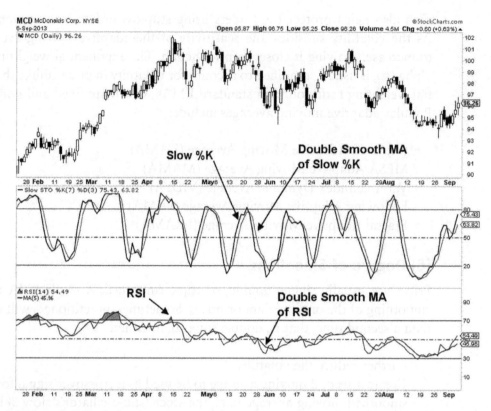

FIGURE 11.19 Double Smoothing on the Slow Stochastic Oscillator on a Daily Chart of McDonalds Corp.
Courtesy of Stockcharts.com

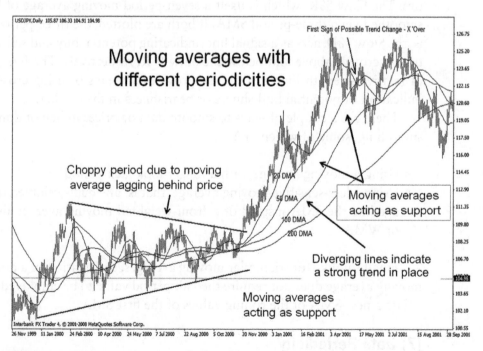

FIGURE 11.20 Moving Averages with Different Periodicities on the Daily Chart of USDJPY.
Source: MetaTrader 4

average will be to price action. In Figure 11.20, we see moving averages with different periodicities reacting at different rates to rising prices.

The most appropriate lookback period for a moving average depends on the objective at hand. Simple moving averages with *popular periodicities* tend to perform better as support and resistance, some of which include:

- 20 period
- 50 period
- 100 period
- 200 period

Some practitioners also use *Fibonacci-based periodicities* on moving averages, some of which are:

- 5 period
- 8 period
- 13 period
- 21 period
- 34 period
- 55 period
- 89 period
- 144 period

Other approaches include tuning it to the quarter, half, or full period of the dominant cycle in the market or tuning it via visual inspection. Some practitioners also perform back testing to determine the most profitable lookback period for a certain moving average, over a specified period of observation. Sometimes practitioners do not require moving averages to act as a barrier to price, but rather as a *timing indicator*, relying on the crossover of two moving averages to signal a buy or sell, or simply to signal potential bullishness or bearishness. In such cases, the periodicities are chosen to according to the frequency of signals and triggers required for a particular methodology.

11.2 NINE MAIN APPLICATIONS OF MOVING AVERAGES

(1) As a Price Cycle Filter

Moving averages are usually used to *smooth* data so that the trend component is isolated and emphasized. This is particularly useful during erratic or chaotic price activity where the trend determination is difficult. It therefore acts as a low-pass filter of market noise, filtering out all higher-frequency price cycles. The shorter the periodicity of a cycle, the higher will be its cycle frequency. As such, moving averages are therefore sometimes used as a proxy for price action in situations where the general direction of the trend is of greater importance than the actual price reactions or price rejection levels. See Figure 11.21 for an example of the 200-day moving average filtering out all the smaller price oscillations and fluctuations to indicate the *general direction of the longer-term trend*.

FIGURE 11.21 200-Day Moving Average Acting as a Filter on the Daily Chart of Dell Inc.
Courtesy of Stockcharts.com

(2) Detrended to Be an Oscillator

We may also subtract the rolling values of one moving average from another, rendering the difference between the two averages. Since the resulting data *represents only the difference in values* for each period over the lookback period, all trend information is lost. Hence, the term *detrended*. Figure 11.22 shows two EMAs, specifically, the 12-day and 26-day EMAs, converging with and diverging from each other as price rises and declines. The two EMAs are detrended against one another and the resulting difference is displayed in the form of an oscillator in the window below. This is in fact the MACD indicator. During a strong uptrend or downtrend, the 12- and 26-day EMAs *diverge*, causing the MACD to rise or fall, respectively.

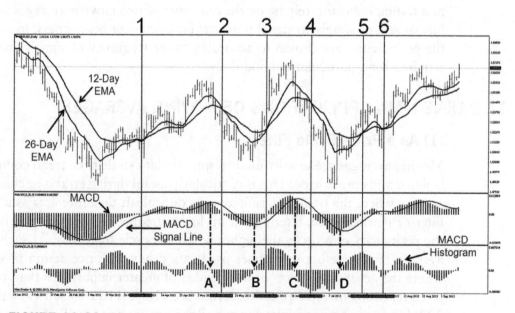

FIGURE 11.22 Detrending Moving Averages on the Daily Chart of GBPUSD.
Source: MetaTrader 4

This rising and falling creates peaks and troughs in the MACD, and allows the trader or analyst to look for standard or reverse divergences between the peaks and troughs in price and MACD. The stronger the trend, the greater will be the divergence between the two EMAs. As the uptrend or downtrend slows down, the two EMAs begin to converge, indicating weakness in the uptrend or downtrend. This is why the MACD is called the *Moving Average Convergence-Divergence* indicator. The difference between the EMAs is zero when they meet, which causes the MACD to revert back to its zero or equilibrium level. We see this clearly at time lines 1 to 6. A smoothed version of the MACD represents its signal line.

Many practitioners prefer to use the MACD-signal line crossover as buy and sell signals instead of the zero- or equilibrium-level crossovers. This is because the MACD-signal line crossover provides earlier buy and sell signals. Whichever the case may be, *price confirmation* is always required, by way of a price penetration of some barrier overlay like trendlines, moving averages, support and resistance, and so on. For more on the MACD, please refer to Gerald Appel's book *Technical Analysis: Power Tools for Active Traders.*

Notice the double detrending in Figure 11.22. If we detrend the MACD against its own signal line and plot the differences, we get the MACD Histogram. This oscillator tends to signal price reversal much more rapidly than the MACD, since double detrending reduces the lag components between price and the oscillators. As per the two EMAs, whenever the MACD and its signal line meet, the histogram will be at its zero or equilibrium level, as seen at points A to D.

Figure 11.23 displays the result of detrending a 26-day EMA with price itself. Such an indicator is called a *price oscillator*, which is essentially identical to the MACD, except for the periods used. This is very useful as it isolates the historically overbought and oversold levels in the market with respect to the behavior of price to the 26-period EMA. In the Figure 11.23 below, we observe price making tops

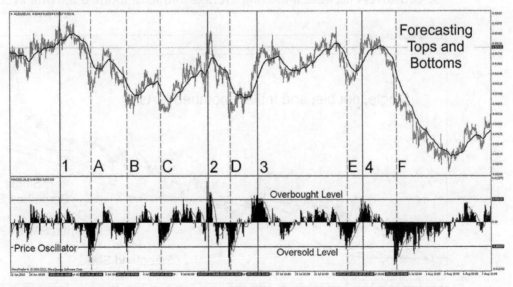

FIGURE 11.23 Detrending Price with a Moving Average on the Hourly Chart of AUDUSD.
Source: MetaTrader 4

453

every time the price oscillator tests or exceeds the upper overbought threshold level, as seen at time lines 1 to 4, and making bottoms every time the price oscillator tests or falls below the lower oversold threshold level, as seen at time lines A to F.

Therefore, detrending moving averages afford practitioners a means to do further analysis by looking for divergences between detrended oscillators and price. Also, various technical studies can be applied to the oscillators themselves with the objective of identifying potential tops and bottoms in the market as well as assessing the strength or weakness of trending action.

(3) Smoothing Price Action

Double and triple smoothing helps reduce the unwanted information like noise and short-term price cycles. Double smoothing is normally found in oscillators in the form of a signal line. The two most popular double-smoothed signal lines are the stochastic Slow %D and the MACD nine-period signal line. Double smoothing is simply creating a new moving average based on the data from another moving average. Triple smoothing is creating a new moving average from data based on a double smoothed moving average. Figure 11.24 depicts a single SMA that has been double and triple smoothed. They are all placed on the same chart. *Notice that unlike double and triple detrending, which tends to remove lag between the oscillator and price, double and triple smoothing increases the price lag.*

(4) As a Price Trigger or Signal

Moving averages may be set up to provide signals and triggers. Moving averages provide buy and sell signals in three main ways, namely as:

1. Crossovers between price and a moving average
2. Crossovers between two or more moving averages
3. Crossovers between a moving average and its smoothed moving average

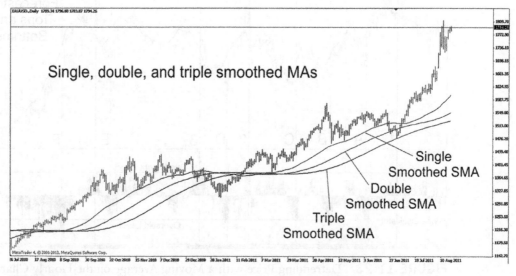

FIGURE 11.24   Smoothing Action on the Daily Chart of Gold.
Source: MetaTrader 4

FIGURE 11.25 Golden and Death Crosses on the Daily Chart of Apple Inc.
Courtesy of Stockcharts.com

The crossover of price and a moving average is by far the most important of the three forms listed above. It is the only one that represents *price confirmation* of a breakout or trend change and as such represents a trade trigger. The remaining two forms are merely signals that add to the evidence that the market is bullish or bearish.

Nevertheless, it may sometimes be better to employ a double moving average crossover in lieu of price crossing over its moving average as a trade trigger. This is because a double moving average crossover is less susceptible to whipsaws. A triple moving average crossover may also be employed as a trigger where trades are scaled in, as each faster moving average crosses above or below a slower moving average.

Two of the most popular indications of potential trend change via the use of crossovers are the Golden Cross and the Death Cross. Conventionally, a golden cross occurs when a shorter-term moving average (50 day SMA) crosses over a longer-term moving average (200 day SMA). It is seen as a bullish sign. See Figure 11.25 for double moving average crossover signals based on the 100- and 200-day SMAs.

A death cross occurs when a shorter-term moving average crosses below a longer-term moving average. It is seen as a bearish sign. Conventionally, it is based on a 50-day SMA crossing below the 200-day SMA. See Figure 11.26.

Another popular form of crossover that generates buy and sell signals is the *Open-Close Moving Average Crossover*. Two SMAs (or EMAs) are created, with one SMA based on opening price and the other on closing price. Whenever the SMA of close prices crosses above the SMA of opening prices, a buy signal is issued. Conversely, whenever the SMA of close prices crosses below the SMA of opening prices, a sell signal is issued. See Figure 11.27. We see this crossover as a fairly effective indicator of price change.

In Figure 11.28, we observe the triple moving average crossovers diverging whenever there is a strong trend present and with crisscrosses, or whipping each other, when the markets are ranging.

Trading with moving averages is fairly easy if there is a strong trend in effect. Buying as price crosses above the moving average and selling as price crosses

455

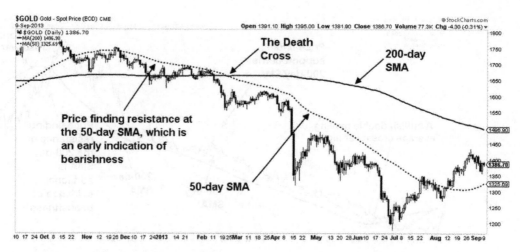

FIGURE 11.26 Death Cross on the Daily of Gold.
Courtesy of Stockcharts.com

below it is simple enough, as long as a suitable price filter is employed. As we learned in Chapter 5, filters may be:

- Price based
- Time based
- Event based
- Pattern based

Weaker trends tend to generate more false buy and sell signals. One way to reduce the incidence of whipsaws and false breakouts is to *trade the support and*

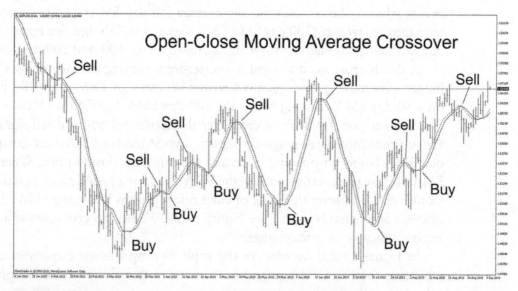

FIGURE 11.27 Open-Close Moving Average Crossover Signaling Entries on the Daily of GBPUSD.
Source: MetaTrader 4

456

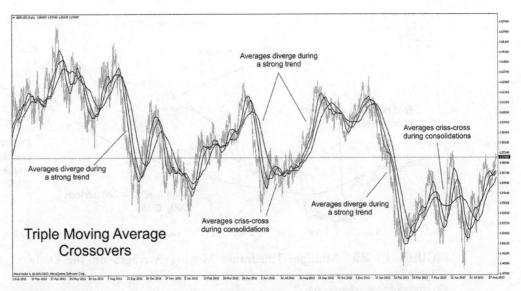

FIGURE 11.28 Triple Moving Average Crossover on the Daily of GBPUSD.
Source: MetaTrader 4

resistance levels around the moving average instead, similar to taking a double top or bottom breakout when a bullish or bearish trendline is violated in point and figure charting.

(5) As Central Value for Envelopes and Bands

Moving averages also act as central values for envelopes and bands, which attempt to *contain* price action (volatility) within a well-defined region. This is useful in gauging the relative levels of overextension or overreaction in the markets. The market is overbought if prices test or exceed the upper band and is oversold if prices test or fall below the lower band.

(6) As Trend Identifier

One effective way of determining the general strength of a trend is to see if all the moving averages are pointing in the same direction. As long as the short-, medium-, and longer-term moving averages are all pointing in the direction of the existing trend, the trader may continue to initiate entries in the direction of the trend. *Once the shorter-term moving averages start to turn or cross over a longer-term moving average, the trader should start to take defensive measures.*

It is sometimes convenient and advantageous to observe the short-, medium-, and longer-term moving averages on the same chart. Setting up a chart to display multiple timeframe moving averages is fairly straightforward. Let us use a 5-min chart to illustrate the technique. To display the one-hour moving average on a 5-min chart, simply divide the duration of moving average

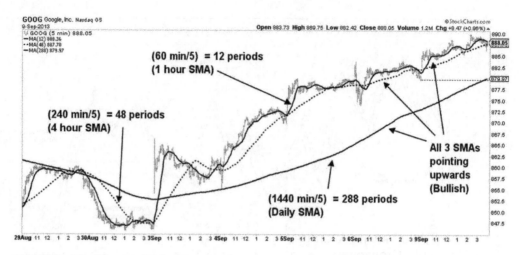

FIGURE 11.29 Multiple Timeframe Moving Averages on the Daily of Chart of Goggle Inc.
Courtesy of Stockcharts.com

you require by five. Therefore, a one-hour SMA must be set to (60mins/5) = 12 periods. A four-hour moving average must be set to (60mins × 4)/5 = 48 periods. Finally, a daily moving average must be set to (1440 mins/5) = 288 periods. See Figure 11.29 for the graphical representation of these three moving averages on a 5-min chart.

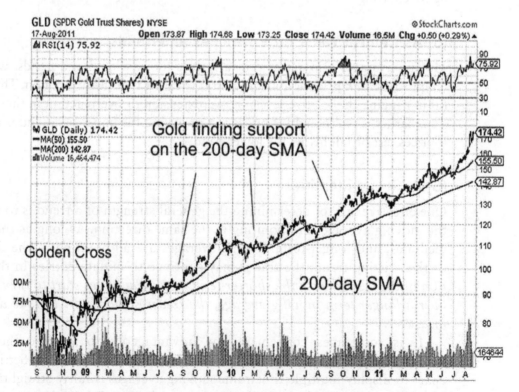

FIGURE 11.30 Finding Support on the Daily Chart of Gold.
Courtesy of Stockcharts.com

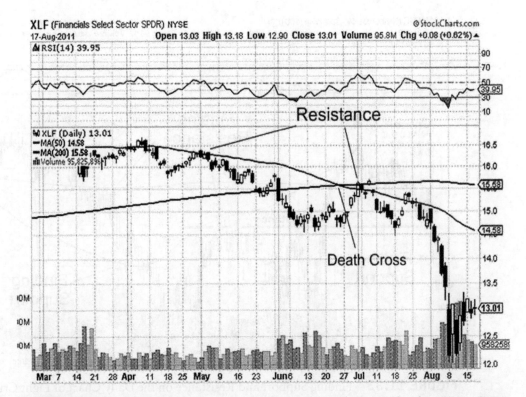

FIGURE 11.31 Finding Resistance on the Daily Chart of Financials select Sector SPDR.
Courtesy of Stockcharts.com

FIGURE 11.32 Finding Support on the Daily Chart of Apple Inc.
Courtesy of Stockcharts.com

459

FIGURE 11.33 Finding Support and Resistance on the Daily Chart of Light Crude Oil. Courtesy of Stockcharts.com

(7) As a Price Barrier

The most popular use of moving averages is to employ them as levels of potential support and resistance. As such, they may be used to also provide levels for initiating long and short trades. See Figures 11.30 and 11.31.

Figure 11.32 illustrates the ideal scenario where a moving average support is also part of a prior support level in price, which occurred around October 2011. This is an example of a bullish confluence.

Figure 11.33 illustrates another ideal scenario where a moving average resistance is also part of a prior resistance level in price, which occurred around September 2011. This is an example of a bearish confluence.

Figure 11.34 shows price finding resistance at both the 50- and 200-day SMA on the daily chart of Amazon.com Inc.

Figure 11.35 illustrates a series of bullish confluences from November 2012 onward. We find prior support levels around the levels that price test the 100-day uptrending SMA. The uptrend line also helps to create a stronger bullish confluence, giving the trader more confidence in the reliability of the SMA as a barrier to price action.

It should be noted that moving averages may also find support and resistance at other moving averages as well, where a rebound to the upside is regarded as bullish and a rebound to the downside as bearish. This is often seen occurring in oscillators, too. One typical example is that of the stochastic oscillator, where we sometimes observe the slow %K finding support or resistance at %D. See Figure 11.36.

FIGURE 11.34 Finding Resistances on the Daily Chart of Amazon.com Inc.
Courtesy of Stockcharts.com

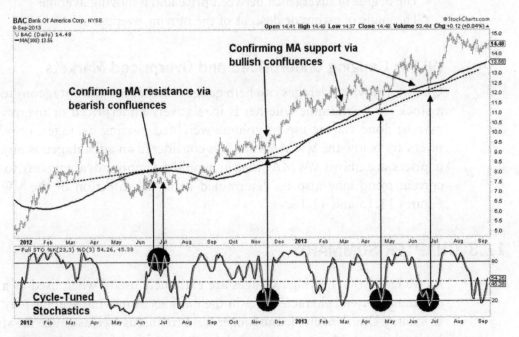

FIGURE 11.35 Finding Supportive and Resistive Confluences on the Daily Chart of
Bank of America Corp.
Courtesy of Stockcharts.com

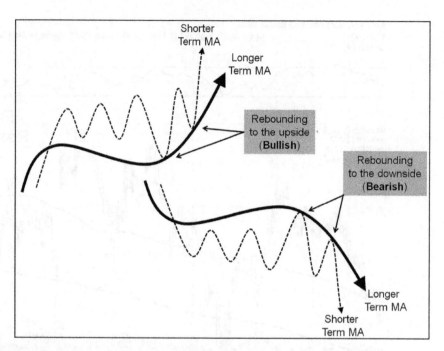

FIGURE 11.36 Moving Averages Rebounding Off Other Moving Averages.

(8) For Gauging the Strength of Trend

The strength of a trend may be gauged from:

- The degree of divergence between moving averages
- The degree of divergence between price and a moving average
- The angle of ascent or descent of the moving average

(9) For Gauging Underpriced and Overpriced Markets

One way moving averages can help gauge whether it is advantageous to buy into a stock is to determine whether is it relatively underpriced or overpriced. This may be done via the use of volume-weighted moving averages, or VWMA. If prices are below the VWMA, then it is considered an advantageous buy, whereas if prices are above VWMA, then it would be more advantageous to sell. The current trend may also be determined from the direction of the VWMA. See Figures 11.15 and 11.16.

11.3 CHAPTER SUMMARY

As we have seen, moving averages are extremely useful when used as a filter for determining trend characteristics in the markets. A moving average may be tuned to identify short, medium, and longer-term trends, as well as gauge the strength of any such trend. Moving averages also form the basis for creating price envelopes and bands. Many practitioners employ moving averages as a means of signaling entries into the market.

CHAPTER 11 REVIEW QUESTIONS

1. What are the basic functions of a moving average?
2. What is the difference between truncated and continuous-type moving averages?
3. Describe the number of ways to increase the sensitivity of moving averages.
4. How is an EMA different from an SMA?
5. How would you gauge the strength of a trend using moving averages?
6. How would you gauge the relative levels of overextension in the market using moving averages?
7. List as many ways as you can where a moving average can generate buy and sell signals.
8. Explain the difference between detrending and smoothing.

REFERENCES

Appel, Gerald. 2005. *Technical Analysis: Power Tools for Active Traders*. Upper Saddle River, NJ: Financial Times Prentice Hall.

Murphy, John. 1999. *Technical Analysis of the Financial Markets*. New York: New York Institute of Finance (NYIF).

Pring, Martin J. 002. *Technical Analysis Explained: The Successful Investor's Guide to Spotting Investment Trends and Turning Points*. 4th ed. New York: McGraw-Hill.

Wilder, J. Welles, Jr. 978. *New Concepts in Technical Trading Systems*. McLeansville, NC: Trends Research.

CHAPTER
12

Envelopes and Methods of Price Containment

LEARNING OBJECTIVES

After studying this chapter, you should be able to:

- Understand the importance of price containment as a technical tool for forecasting price reversal as well as continuation
- Apply the concepts of price containment to various stocks and markets
- Identify and differentiate between the different forms of price containment and understand their individual strengths and weaknesses
- Identify any bearish or bullish confluence that will add to the weight of the evidence about potential future price behavior
- Understand how to tune envelopes and bands to important dominant cycles

The art and science of price containment is primarily about the identification of significant price reaction levels. It helps to identify levels of potential price reversals and continuations and may be applied to practically any market. In this chapter, we shall be discussing the five basic forms of price containment and see them in action in various stocks and markets.

12.1 CONTAINING PRICE ACTION AND VOLATILITY ABOUT A CENTRAL VALUE

An envelope is an overlay indicator that comprises an upper and lower band. It is used primarily as a means of containing price action. The main areas of focus when dealing with bands include the:

- *Reaction* of price at the central value and bands
- *Direction* of the central value bands

465

- Amount of *divergence* between the bands
- *Distance* of price from the bands
- *Bandwidth* as a function of price and volatility

We shall now focus on the function and construction of various bands and envelopes.

Function of an Envelope or Band

Envelopes or bands have six main functions, namely:

1. As a means of gauging the average volatility of price action
2. As an indicator of overbought and oversold conditions
3. As a means of identifying potential levels of support and resistance
4. As a price trigger for initiating entries or exits
5. As a means of trend identification
6. As a way to trade moving averages without excessive whipsawing during consolidations

The direction of the central value and bands indicates the general direction of the trend since it contains the trend within it most of the time. The majority of the central values are in fact moving averages, which are smoothed versions of any existing trend. See Figure 12.1 bands and central value indicating trends in the S&P GSCI Energy Index.

The upper band, lower band, and the central value all represent barriers to price action. As barriers to price, the bands provide support and resistance. But here is the important difference between bands and other barriers of price action. For example, it should be noted that in a downtrend, the lower band tends to be more reliable as support than as resistance while in an uptrend, the upper band

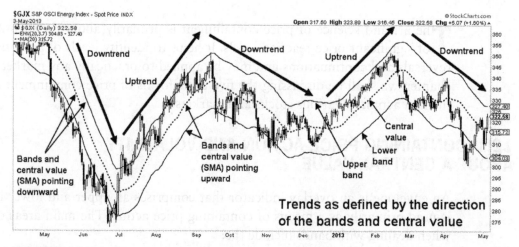

FIGURE 12.1 Bands and Central Value Indicating Trend Action on the S&P GSCI Energy Index.
Courtesy of Stockcharts.com

tends to be more reliable as resistance than as support. This is because prices tend re-enter the bands. The bands are not merely barriers to price but they also represent levels of price being overbought and oversold and as such, *prices are expected to eventually revert back to the central value.* See Figure 12.2.

Bullish and Bearish Sentiment

It is generally considered bullish if:

- The bands are pointing in an upwardly direction
- Prices are above the bands

It is generally considered bearish if:

- The bands are pointing in an downwardly direction
- Prices are below the bands

Price below the central value is a bearish indication, but price below the lower band is considered much more bearish. Similarly, price above the central value is a bullish indication, but price above the upper band is considered much more bullish.

Gauging Volatility

Volatility in price is usually indicated in the following ways:

- The bandwidth *expanding* for both bands that are based on a fixed percentage of their central value and on those that are based on average true range (ATR)
- The bands *diverging* for envelopes that are based on measures of standard deviation, such as Bollinger Bands
- Price *exceeding* the bands
- Price *whipsawing* across both the upper and lower bands

FIGURE 12.2 Bands as Reliable and Unreliable Support and Resistance on the Daily Chart of Amazon.com Inc.
Courtesy of Stockcharts.com

467

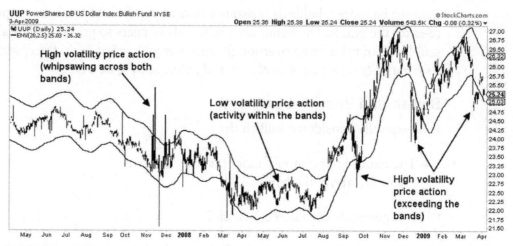

FIGURE 12.3 Volatility on the Daily Chart of PowerShares DB U.S. Dollar Index Bullish Fund.
Courtesy of Stockcharts.com

See Figure 12.3.

Central Value

An envelope comprises an upper and lower band, which may or may not be based on some central value. Popular envelopes or bands that are based on some form of central value are:

- Bollinger Bands: Simple moving average (SMA) of closing prices
- Fixed Percentage Bands: Any form of moving average
- Fixed Value Bands: Any form of moving average
- Keltner Bands: 10-period SMA of *typical price,* that is (H +L+C)/3; some modern variations include the use of a 20-day period or even an exponential moving average (EMA) as its central value
- STARC Bands: 6-period SMA of closing prices
- ATR Bands: Any form of moving average

Popular bands that are not based on some form of central value are:

- Price Channels and Donchian Channels
- Darvas Boxes

Some examples of central value are:

- Moving Average of Closing Prices
- Moving Average of Mid Prices
- Moving Average of Typical Prices
- Moving Average of Weighted Close Prices
- Regression Line

The type of moving averages that are used to calculate central values include:

- Simple Averaging
- Exponential Averaging
- Linear Weighted Averaging
- Wilder's Averaging

Band Construction

The construction of the bands may be based on any of the following measures:

- Volatility
- Percentage
- Fixed Value

Bands may also be categorized as either:

- Price dynamic
- Price static

A price-dynamic band is one where the values of the bands change with price. A price-static band is one where the values of the bands do not change with price until the bands are invalidated by a penetration, such as the upper and lower bands of horizontal channels and Darvas boxes. Price-static bands are usually also referred to as channels rather than as envelopes. See Figure 12.4.

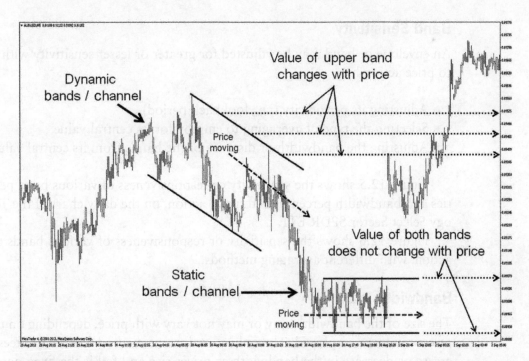

FIGURE 12.4 Price-Dynamic and Price-Static Bands/Channels on the 5-Min Chart of AUDUSD.
Source: MetaTrader 4

469

Bandwidth

The bandwidth, that is, the distance between the upper and lower bands, may be based on any of the following:

- Central value ± percentage of the central value
- Central value ± fixed dollar or point value
- Central value ± multiples of standard deviation based on the central value
- Central value ± multiples of ATR based on the central value

Here are some popular examples of bands constructed based on measures of volatility and percentage:

- Bollinger Bands: 20-period SMA of closing prices ± 2 standard deviations of the 20-period SMA
- Fixed Percentage Bands: Any moving average ± a fixed percentage of the current moving average value
- Fixed Value Bands: Any moving average ± a fixed dollar or point value of the current moving average value
- Keltner Bands: 10-period SMA of *typical price* (H+L+C)/3 ± 10-period SMA of ATR; some modern variations include the use of a 20-day SMA or even an exponential moving average (EMA) as its central value
- STARC Bands: 6-period SMA of closing prices ± multiples of a 15-period ATR; multiples are normally two or three times the 15-period ATR
- ATR Bands: Any moving average ± multiples ATRs of its central value

Band Sensitivity

An envelope or band may be adjusted for greater or lesser sensitivity with respect to price action by:

- Adjusting its periodicity (i.e., lookback period)
- Selecting the type of averaging to employ for its central value
- Adjusting the bandwidth or distance of the bands from its central value

Figure 12.5 shows the sensitivity or responsiveness of various band periodicities and bandwidth percentages to price action, on the daily chart of the Technology Select Sector SPDR ETF.

Figure 12.6 shows the sensitivity or responsiveness of various bands to price action, with different averaging methods.

Bandwidth Bias

The size of the bandwidth may or may not vary with price, depending on the type of containment employed. The only containment method that guarantees an increase or decrease in the bandwidth as prices rise and fall is the fixed percentage band. There is a bias toward larger bandwidths at higher prices because the bandwidths are based on a percentage of the central value that is greater at higher

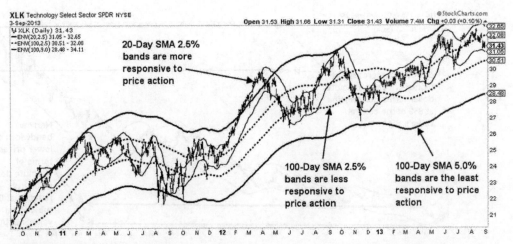

FIGURE 12.5 Various Degrees of Band Responsiveness on the Daily Chart of the Technology Select Sector SPDR ETF.
Courtesy of Stockcharts.com

prices. Other price-containment methods like Keltner and STARC bands may also see some bandwidth increase at higher prices but that is attributed to the larger ATR *values associated with the central value* that tend to accompany higher prices. As we will see in a subsequent section, the visual anomaly associated with the fixed percentage bands may be normalized by simply employing a logarithmically scaled chart. See Figure 12.7.

Trading with the Band: Entries, Exits, and Stoplosses

There are two basic approaches with respect to trading the bands, namely the:

1. Breakout Entry
2. Reversal Entry

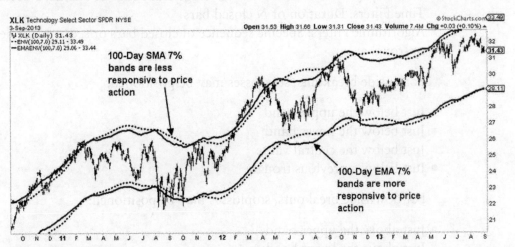

FIGURE 12.6 Band Responsiveness with Respect to Averaging Method (EMA vs SMA) on the Daily Chart of the Technology Select Sector SPDR ETF.
Courtesy of Stockcharts.com

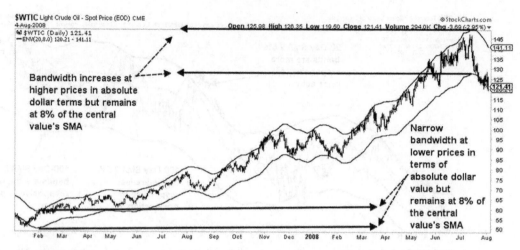

FIGURE 12.7 Bandwidth Bias on the Daily Continuous Chart of Light Crude Oil.
Courtesy of Stockcharts.com

With the breakout entry approach, the trader normally initiates an entry once price breaches either the upper band, lower band, or central value with a *closing violation*, that is, price closes outside the bands or beyond the central value. For breakout entries, the bands should be adjusted for a greater sensitivity so they will be more conducive for breakouts. A balance must be struck between trying to generate more breakouts with a more sensitive setting and avoiding being whipsawed with a wave of false breakouts.

The trader's exact point of entry will depend on the type of price filter employed, which may be any of the following (see Chapter 5 for more on price filtering):

- Event-Based Measure: Closing price or barrier retest after the breakout
- Absolute Measure: Fixed price excursion
- Relative Measure: Percentage of breakout price
- Volatility Measure: Multiples of average true range or standard deviation
- Time Filters: Duration of *N* closed bars
- Algorithmic Filters: Specific sequence of closed bars or sequence of new peaks or troughs

For upside breakouts, stoplosses may be positioned:

- Just below the upper band
- Just below the lower band
- Just below the central value
- Just below a previous trough

For downside breakouts, stoplosses may be positioned:

- Just above the upper band
- Just above the lower band
- Just above the central value
- Just below a previous peak

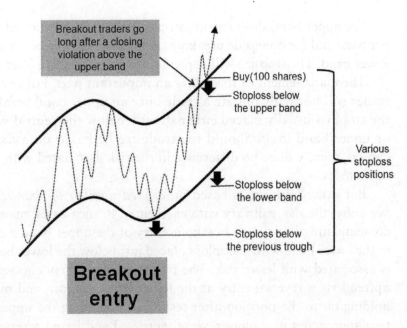

FIGURE 12.8 Buy and Sell Triggers on the Weekly Chart of the Russell 2000 Growth iShares.

See Figure 12.8 for buy and sell triggers as well as possible stoploss levels using the standard breakout approach.

See Figure 12.9 for buy and sell triggers as well as possible stoploss levels on the weekly chart of the Russell 2000 Growth iShares.

The reversal entry approach requires the trader to initiate a long entry once price tests the lower band and a short entry if the upper band is tested. *With reversal entries, no price filter is required.* The trader may initiate an entry at the exact level where price tests the upper or lower bands. But if the trader chooses to seek price confirmation for a reversal entry instead, then the application of a price filter is required in order to determine the point of entry *after* testing the bands.

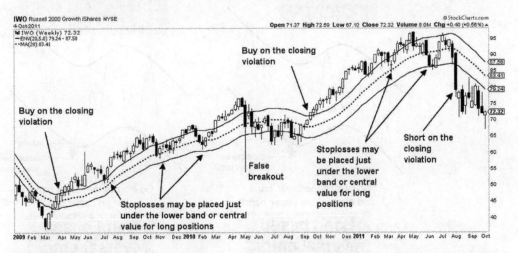

FIGURE 12.9 Buy and Sell Triggers on the Weekly Chart of the Russell 2000 Growth iShares.
Courtesy of Stockcharts.com

For upper band short entries, stoplosses may be positioned just above the upper band and for downside breakouts, stoplosses may be positioned just below the lower band. The stopsize will depend on the type of price filter used.

The management of risk plays an important part. For example, a breakout trader will normally initiate a trade once an upper band breakout occurs, with the stoploss usually placed either slightly below the central value, lower band, or upper band itself. Should the tradesize be based on a fixed percentage of capital, there will be no difference in the risk associated with any of the breakout entries.

But if the tradesize is based on *a fixed number of shares, lots, or contracts per entry*, the risk will vary with each entry. In such cases, many traders who are contemplating initiating a breakout entry of the upper band may instead go long at the lower band with a stoploss placed just below the lower band instead, which is associated with lesser risk. The trader therefore may choose to go long in an uptrend via a reversal entry at the lower band support, and may also decide on holding on to the position after testing or breaching the upper band. There are two approaches in trading reversal entries. Band based reversal traders go long at the lower band and short at the upper band, regardless of the market trend. Trend based reversal traders only go long at the lower band in an uptrend and short at the upper band in a downtrend. It should be noted that reversal entries buy and sell at more advantageous prices when compared to breakout entries. See Figure 12.10

Finally, positioning stoplosses just beyond the bands for breakouts and reversal entries will work fairly well with most bands except Bollinger Bands. This is because Bollinger Bands *diverge* during high periods of volatility. This makes it difficult to position the stoplosses effectively. One solution is to use the central value, which is a simple moving average, for stop placement.

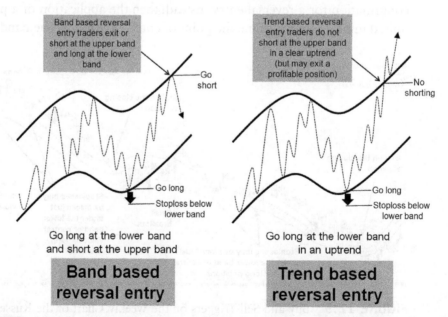

FIGURE 12.10 Difference between Band Based Reversal Entry and Trend Based Reversal Entry.

12.2 ADJUSTING BANDS FOR EFFECTIVE PRICE CONTAINMENT

There are basically two main approaches for adjusting the bands to effectively contain price action, namely:

1. By visual inspection
2. By tuning to a dominant cycle

Tuning by Visual Inspection

Tuning or adjusting an envelope or band to effectively contain price by visual inspection is by far the more reliable approach. This is because the bands are adjusted with respect to actual price action over a certain period of observation. Tuning by visual inspection *automatically accounts for any dominant cycles* that may be present over the period of observation. It also accounts for the average market noise that accompanies all cyclic activity in the market. Tuning the bands visually involves adjusting the periodicity and sensitivity of the bands until *most of the price action is contained within the bands* over the period of observation. It should be noted that the periodicity and sensitivity may need to be re-optimized after some time due to regime changes in the market.

Tuning via Half- and Quarter-Cycle Periodicities

Many practitioners also adjust bands with respect to some dominant cycle over the period of observation. This is usually done by first isolating the periodicity of a dominant cycle. The band's lookback period is then set to its half cycle. The quarter cycles are also employed, as we shall see shortly.

Calculating the Half-Cycle Period   For example, let us assume that you have isolated a dominant cycle and found that the *average* distance between cycle troughs is 40 bars, or periods. Let N be the average cycle period. In this case, $N = 40$. There are three ways to calculate the half-cycle lookback period via any of the following formulas:

- $(N+1)/2$ and round up if N is even
- $(N/2)+1$ and round down if N is odd
- $(2N+3)/4$ round to closest integer

The last formula is advantageous from the perspective that you need not remember whether you are required to round up or down. Instead, you simply round to the *closest integer*. The formula is derived by finding the average of the first two formulas and will always yield a result that ends with either a 0.25 or 0.75, making it easy to round to the closest integer:

$$((N+1)/2 + (N/2) + 1))/2 = (N + 2 + N + 1)/4 = \underline{(2N+3)/4}$$

475

For Even Dominant-Cycle Periods   Since $N = 40$ (even number of periods), each formula will yield the following half-cycle lookback period:

First Formula: $(N+1)/2$

$$(N+1)/2 = (40+1)/2 = 20.5$$

Rounding up as N is even = $\underline{21\ periods}$

Second Formula: $(N/2)+1$

$$(N/2)+1 = (40/2)+1 = \underline{21\ periods}$$

No rounding down required as N is not odd.

Third Formula: $(2N+3)/4$

$$(2N+3)/4 = ((2\times40)+3)/4 = 83/4 = 20.75\ periods$$

Rounding to the *closest* integer = $\underline{21\ periods}$

For Odd Dominant-Cycle Periods   Let us now assume that the dominant cycle period is an odd number of periods, that is, $N = 47$. Each formula will now yield the following half cycle lookback period:

First Formula: $(N+1)/2$

$$(N+1)/2 = (47+1)/2 = \underline{24\ periods}$$

No rounding up required as N is not even.

Second Formula: $(N/2)+1$

$$(N/2)+1 = (47/2)+1 = 24.5\ periods$$

Rounding down as N is odd = $\underline{24\ periods}$

Third Formula: $(2N+3)/4$

$$(2N+3)/4 = ((2\times47)+3)/4 = 97/4 = 24.25\ periods$$

Rounding to the *closest* integer = $\underline{24\ periods}$

Figure 12.11 is an example of tuning the fixed percentage bands to a dominant cycle on the four-hour chart of GBPUSD. The trough-to-trough cycle period was 133 bars. Using the third formula would also yield $((2\times133)+3)/4 = 67.25$. Rounding to the closest integer would give us 67 periods or bars. We therefore set the band periodicity to 67 bars. The band's percentage of central value was derived via visual inspection.

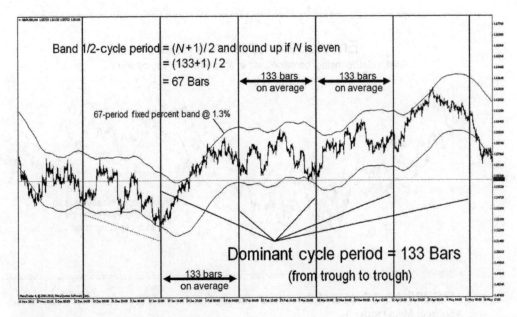

FIGURE 12.11 Tuning the Fixed Percentage Bands to the Dominant Half-Cycle Period on the 4-Hour Chart of GBPUSD.
Source: MetaTrader 4

Calculating the Quarter-Cycle Period   To find the quarter-cycle period for an average dominant cycle of N periods, we use $(N+1)/4$ and round to the closest integer, or round up to the next integer if the value falls on a 0.50 decimal or higher. We shall be focusing on the application of quarter-cycle lookback periods in a later section.

12.3 METHODS OF PRICE CONTAINMENT

There are basically five approaches to contain price. Let us now focus on each price containment indicator's character and behavior.

Fixed Value Bands

Fixed value bands comprise any moving average with upper and lower bands that are at *equal dollar or point value distance from the central moving average*. They are not as popular as the fixed percentage bands for two reasons:

1. Fixed value bands cannot adapt to market volatility and as such will give many false buy and sell signals during periods of increased volatility.
2. They cannot adapt to the larger ATR values at higher prices and will require frequent re-optimization to account for the wider bars.

Relative Value Bands

Fixed percentage moving average bands are the popular form of price containment. Market participants use them to indicate trend, potential support, and resistance and as a trigger for initiating buy and sell positions. Entries may be executed via any of the three approaches, that is, via breakouts, reversal entries, or reversal

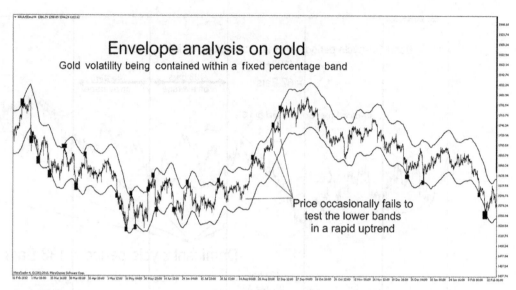

FIGURE 12.12 Fixed Percentage Bands Containing Price Volatility in Gold.
Source: MetaTrader 4

entry breakouts. In Figure 12.12, we observe Gold prices being very effectively contained by the visually tuned fixed percentage bands over a period of one year from February 2012 to February 2013. Notice that in very quickly rising markets, price sometimes fails to test the lower bands during dips in the uptrend.

As mentioned in an earlier section, the bandwidth of fixed percentage bands maintains a fixed percentage value of its SMA. Therefore on a linear or arithmetically scaled chart, the bandwidth will be seen to increase in size as prices rise. One way to resolve this is to employ logarithmically scaled charting where an equal distance on the charts corresponds to equal percentage increments. Since fixed percentage bands are also of a fixed percentage nature, the bandwidth will remain unchanged at all prices. Figure 12.13 compares Google's fixed percentage bands on both logarithmically and arithmetically scaled charts.

Volatility Bands

There are three popular of volatility band overlay indicators:

1. Bollinger Bands
2. Keltner Bands
3. Stoller Average Range Channels (STARC Bands)

Bollinger Bands are by far one of the most widely used price containment indicators. It is a simple moving average with an upper and lower band. Each band is exactly two standard deviations away from its simple moving average. A closing violation above or below either band represents an entry signal. The bands represent levels of *relative overextension* in price. Hence price may be overbought at low or high prices. Price occasionally *tags* or walks the bands

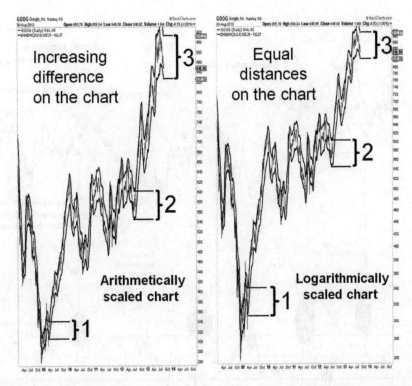

FIGURE 12.13 Comparing Fixed Percentage Bands via Different Chart Scaling on the Daily Chart of Goggle Inc.
Courtesy of Stockcharts.com

during a strong price excursion. Rapid price moves will cause the bands to diverge and a period of low volatility will cause it to *squeeze*, that is, the upper and lower bands converge. The squeeze is normally a precursor to a strong price move. Many traders will wait for a squeeze before trying to catch the subsequent move.

Though a close beyond the bands is a breakout trigger, many traders employ either the standard reversal entry or the reversal entry breakout approach with regard to trading the bands.

One interesting pattern is the double top with only the second peak located within the Bollinger Bands. This pattern is considered bearish and traders should seek price confirmation before participating, should a downside move subsequently unfold. (Similar confirmation is advised for a double bottom pattern with only the second trough located within the Bollinger Bands—a bullish formation.)

Associated with the Bollinger overlays are two oscillators that help chartists gauge potential reversals and continuations in price while using the bands. The first oscillator is the *Bollinger bandwidth,* which simply tracks the percentage difference between the lower and upper bands. When the Bollinger bandwidth indicator declines and remains at lower readings, it is a warning of a potential volatility breakout. It helps to identify the squeeze formation.

The second is the *Percent B* indicator that tracks the position of price relative to the bands. A reading of one corresponds to price being at the upper band, while a reading of zero corresponds to price being at the lower band. The readings will

479

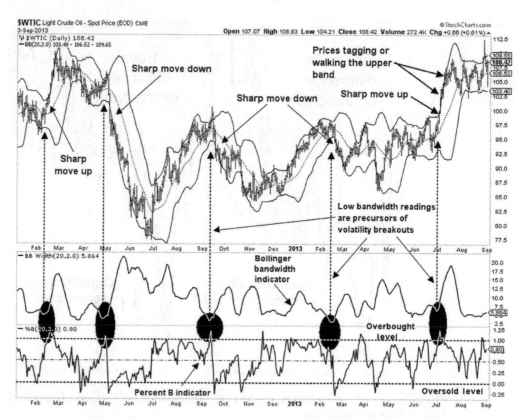

FIGURE 12.14 Bollinger Bands Working in Conjunction with the Bollinger Oscillator Pinpointing Potential Moves on the Daily Chart of Light Crude Oil.
Courtesy of Stockcharts.com

exceed one if price is above the upper band and will be below zero if price is below the lower band. High readings indicate overbought conditions while low readings indicate oversold conditions. Figure 12.14 show the Bollinger band and its two indicators working together to pinpoint potential moves in the market.

Although the Bollinger band may be employed to initiate breakout entries, Figure 12.15 shows Bollinger bands working effectively in pinpointing sell and buy reversal entries on the Silver 30-min chart.

Note that to reduce false or ineffective entry signals while trying to trade with a larger trend, a trader should use the reversal entry breakout technique for Bollinger band entries. Many of the failed buy signals found on the chart in Figure 12.15 would have been successfully avoided or filtered out had the reversal entry breakout technique been employed.

Many traders also set up *multiple* Bollinger bands. There are numerous approaches when employing multiple bands. A popular approach employed by volatility traders using a Bollinger *double-band* setup has an inner one-standard deviation (one-SD) upper and lower band flanked by both two-standard deviation (two-SD) and three-standard deviation (three-SD) upper and lower bands.

Bollinger Band Setup 1 Once price closes above the SMA, enter long at the upper one-SD band with a profit target at the two-SD upper band. The stoploss is placed

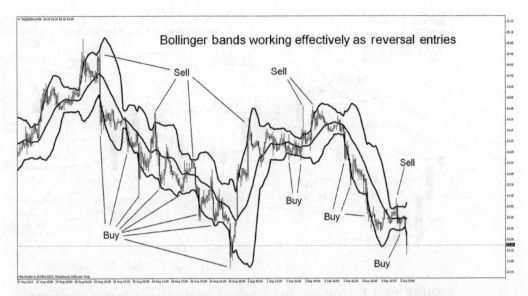

FIGURE 12.15 Reversal Entries on Bollinger Bands Working Effectively in Pinpointing Potential Reversals on the 30-Min Chart of Silver.
Source: MetaTrader 4

just under the SMA. Conversely, if price closes below the SMA, enter short at the lower one-SD band with a profit target at the two-SD lower band. To improve the effectiveness of this approach, look for any trendline, chart pattern, or overlay break-outs that coincide with the Bollinger one-SD entry, with oversold conditions for an upside breakout and overbought conditions for a downside breakout on the momentum oscillators. See Figure 12.16.

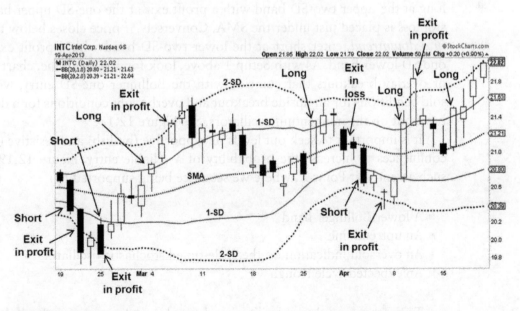

FIGURE 12.16 Bollinger Bands Setup 1 on the Daily Chart of Intel Corp.
Courtesy of Stockcharts.com

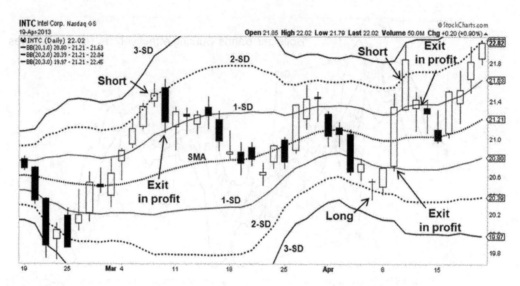

FIGURE 12.17 Bollinger Bands Setup 2 on the Daily Chart of Intel Corp.
Courtesy of Stockcharts.com

Bollinger Band Setup 2 Enter short at the upper two-SD band with a profit target at the one-SD upper band. The stoploss is placed just above the three-SD upper band. Conversely, enter long at the upper two-SD band with a profit target at the one-SD upper band. The stoploss is placed just below the three-SD lower band. For more reliable entries, look for a resistive confluence around the upper two-SD band when shorting and a supportive confluence around the lower two-SD band when going long. See Figure 12.17.

Bollinger Band Setup 3 Once price closes above the SMA *in an uptrend*, enter long at the upper two-SD band with a profit exit at the one-SD upper band. The stoploss is placed just under the SMA. Conversely, if price closes below the SMA *in a downtrend*, enter short at the lower two-SD band with a profit exit at the one-SD lower band. As with Setup 1 above, look for any trendline, chart pattern, or overlay breakouts that coincide with the Bollinger one-SD entry, with oversold conditions for an upside breakout and overbought conditions for a downside breakout on the momentum oscillators. See Figure 12.18.

It is important to seek out levels of supportive (bullish) and resistive (bearish) confluences to increase the probability of a reliable entry. Figure 12.19 depicts such an entry at Point X, where we see price being supported by:

- A lower Bollinger band
- An uptrend line
- An oversold indication on the cycle-tuned stochastic oscillator
- An expected cycle trough

Two other popular volatility band overlay indicators are the Keltner and STARC bands. The Keltner band comprises a 10-period SMA of *typical price*

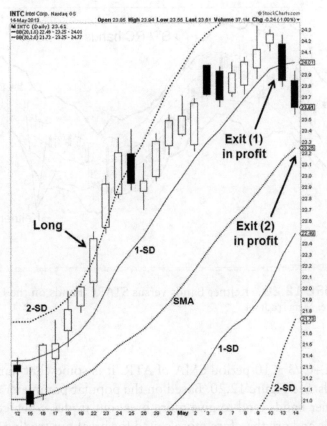

FIGURE 12.18 Bollinger Bands Setup 3 on the Daily Chart of Intel Corp.
Courtesy of Stockcharts.com

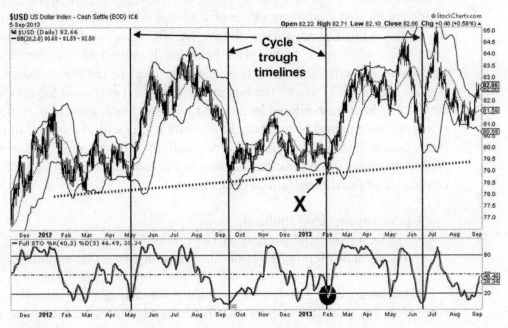

FIGURE 12.19 Supportive (Bullish) Confluence at the Lower Bollinger Band on the Daily Chart of U.S. Dollar Index.
Courtesy of Stockcharts.com

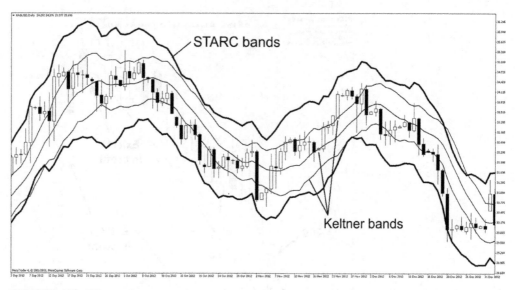

FIGURE 12.20 Keltner Bands versus STARC Bands on the Daily Chart of Silver.
Source: MetaTrader 4

(H+L+C)/3 ± 10-period SMA of ATR. It is somewhat narrower than the STARC bands. See Figure 12.20. Based on the popular parameter settings, we see that the Keltner bands tend to give more breakout trades when compared to the STARC bands and are therefore more suited for breakout trading. It should be noted that many practitioners also use a 10- or 20-period exponential moving average instead of the 10-period SMA of typical price.

Starc Bands comprise a six-day SMA of typical price, that is, (H+L+C)/3. The bands are located at some multiple of a 15-day ATR, usually two or three times the 15-day ATR. The advantage of using STARC bands is that its parameters are not usually adjusted to fit the price behavior. It is used as it is and that makes this a very objective indicator. It is normally used to initiate standard reversal entries. Figure 12.21 shows the buy and sell reversal entries in Silver. We initiate entries that have been filtered by a cycle-tuned stochastic oscillator. Hence we sell if it is within a period of overbought and buy if it is within a period of oversold. Nevertheless, it should be noted that no oscillator works perfectly all of the time. Notice that Point X on the chart represents a potentially strong buy level due to a confluence of *bullish* indications comprising:

- A prior support level (bullish)
- A STARC lower band support barrier (bullish)
- Oversold indication on the cycle-tuned stochastic oscillator (bullish)

Linear regression bands also contain price action. The central value is a regression line flanked by upper and lower bands that are exactly one (or two) standard deviations away from the regression line. Again, if the bands are not too steep, it may lend itself to breakout trades. But if it is very steep, reversal entries only should be taken. Note that linear regression bands only contain

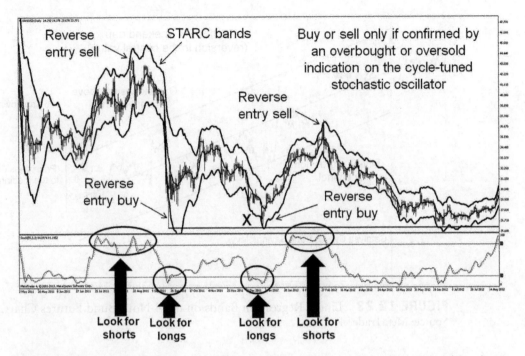

FIGURE 12.21 STARC Bands Working in Conjunction with the Cycle-Tuned Stochastic Oscillator in Pinpointing Potential Tops and Bottoms on the Daily Chart of Silver. Source: MetaTrader 4

current price action. *It cannot be projected into the future for potential barrier levels.* See Figure 12.22.

Figures 12.23 show price reverting back to its central value, that is, the regression line, during a gap down in the exchange rates on the 30-min chart of EURUSD. As with any price-containment band, price is expected to revert to its mean or central value.

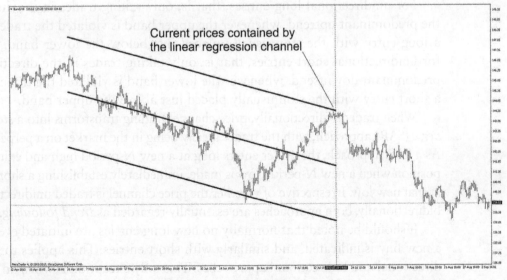

FIGURE 12.22 Linear Regression Bands on the 4-Hour Bund Futures Chart.
Source: MetaTrader 4

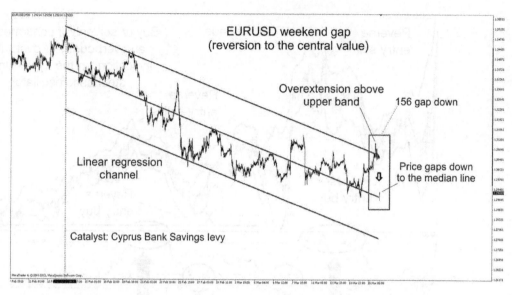

FIGURE 12.23 Linear Regression Bands on the 4-Hour Bund Futures Chart.
Source: MetaTrader 4

Algorithmic-Based Bands

Price channels comprise upper and lower bands that signal *new breakout trades*. The upper band represents the highest high of the last N periods and similarly, the lower band represents the lowest low of the last N periods. The price channel may be employed either:

1. Unidirectionally
2. Bidirectionally (Stop and Reverse, SAR)

For unidirectional long entries, that is, only taking trades in the direction of the predominant uptrend, whenever the upper band is violated the trader initiates a long entry with the stop usually placed just below the lower band. Similarly, for unidirectional short entries, that is, only taking trades in the direction of the predominant downtrend, whenever the lower band is violated the trader initiates a short entry with the stop usually placed just above the upper band.

When traded bidirectionally, price channel trading transforms into a *stop and reverse* (SAR) approach, with the trader ideally being in the market on a perpetual basis. As a SAR approach, the trader enters long at a new N-period high and exits the long position when a new N-period low is made, immediately establishing a short position at that new low. Irrespective of whether the price channel is traded unidirectionally or bidirectionally, both approaches are essentially regarded as *trend following*.

It should be noted that normally no new long entries are initiated even though a new buy is indicated, and similarly with short entries. This applies to both unidirectional and bidirectional approaches. This only exception is when an entry has been rendered riskless by rolling the initial stoploss into a protective position. This way, the overall percentage risk never exceeds the maximum risk allowable. To maximize longer-term profitability, all risk-free positions should be allowed to run over longer periods in the market, scaling out some profit along the way.

As far as channel periodicities are concerned, the most popular lookback period for a price channel is probably 20 periods. This may be attributed to Richard Donchian's four-week price channel, which equated to a 20-day trading period. Even the famous Turtle traders used a form of price channeling with incredible success in the markets. Richard Donchian used a 20-day lookback period for the price channel because he was trying to track a four-week commodity cycle in the market. See Figure 12.24 for an example of a typical bidirectional price channel signaling long and short re-entries.

One serious disadvantage of using price channels is that it does not take into account any significantly clear and obvious support or resistance that may be in proximity with a new channel entry. We clearly see this occurring at Point 4 where a *long entry was initiated just below a clear and obvious resistance level* created near the middle of May 2013. This weakness may potentially lead to many premature entries.

Being *trend following* by construction, price channels tend to work better in stronger trends. They perform very poorly in consolidations. In fact, unless the trend is *strong enough*, price channels tend to perform relatively poorly. The chart in Figure 12.24 shows a series of bidirectional trades. The short entry at Point 1 was exited at Point 2 for a loss. A new long was established at Point 2, which was exited at Point 3 for a small gain. A new short established at Point 3 experienced another loss when it was exited at Point 4. Needless to say, the new long position initiated at Point 4 was exited with a loss at Point 5. In such a situation, it is obvious that a 20-period lookback is inappropriate across the period of observation in Google.

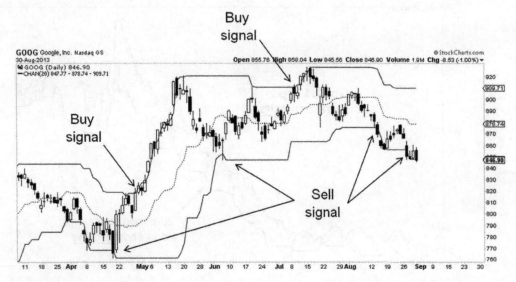

FIGURE 12.24 20-Day Bidirectional (SAR) Price Channel Signaling Long and Short Re-Entries on the Daily Chart of Google Inc.
Courtesy of Stockcharts.com

487

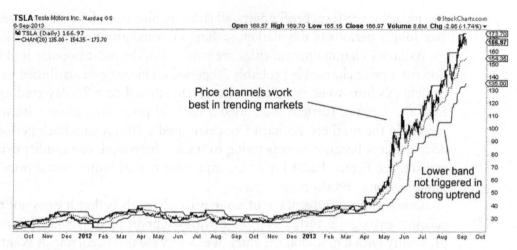

FIGURE 12.25 Price Channels Working Effectively in Strong Trends as Seen on the Daily Chart of Tesla Motors Inc.
Courtesy of Stockcharts.com

Fortunately, the situation improves once a strong trend is present. Figure 12.25 depicts a buy signal in Tesla Motors in November 2012. There was no subsequent sell indication even through September 2013. A trader would have gotten in at around $40 and could ride the trend all the way up to $166.97 without any exit signals being issued.

Some traders opt to exit with a more responsive lower band, that is, with a shorter lookback period or via a different technical exit. Here are a few popular exit mechanisms typically applied to price channels:

■ For long entries, exit with a more responsive lower band, with periods ranging from 2 to 10 periods, depending on the degree of responsiveness required (see Figure 12.26).

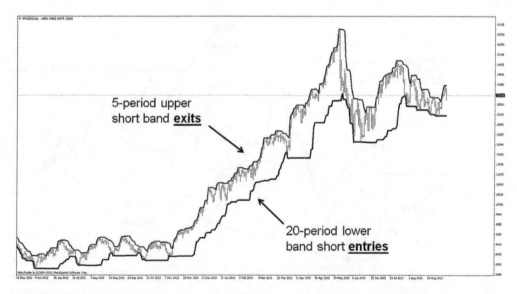

FIGURE 12.26 A Price Channel with Relatively Faster Long Exits on the Daily Nikkei 225 Chart.
Source: MetaTrader 4

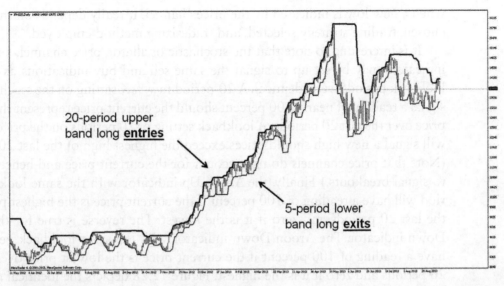

FIGURE 12.27 A Price Channel with Relatively Faster Short Exits on the Daily Nikkei 225 Chart.
Source: MetaTrader 4

- For long entries, exit after price breaches the significant low of the last 2 or 3 bars.
- For short entries, exit with a more responsive upper band, with periods ranging from 2 to 10 periods, depending on the degree of responsiveness required (see Figure 12.27).
- For short entries, exit after price breaches the significant high of the last 2 or 3 bars.
- Execute a chandelier exit.
- Use an appropriate moving average exit.

Bollinger bands are able to adapt to volatility based on the activity of their central value. Fixed-percentage bands are able to account for larger fluctuations at higher prices based on the price of their central value. Most bands except price channels and Darvas boxes are able to account for, or adjust to, price activity. Unfortunately, price channels can only adjust to volatility by continuously changing the lookback period. There is no central value that the bands may use as a means of determining price activity. So it is up to the user to determine the appropriate lookback period for a particular period in the market.

The best way to set the lookback period for a price channel is to first determine the periodicity of a dominant cycle in the market. Once the periodicity of a dominant cycle is known, the trader may set the price channel to the quarter-, half-, or full-cycle period lookback. The quarter cycle provides for a faster turnover in profit but it is potentially more susceptible to market noise and false breakouts, being closer to price action.

It must be noted that with price channels, traders do not buy at support and sell at resistance. The upper and lower bands of the price channel do not represent support and resistance, but rather new highs and new lows based on a selected lookback period. Nevertheless, some traders have reported that a reverse strategy may be more profitable, that is, by selling when a new high is indicated and buying when a new low is indicated by the price channel. It really depends on the market chosen, trading strategy selected, and tradesizing method employed.

It is interesting to note that the stochastic oscillator, price channel, and Aroon indicators may be set up to signal the same sell and buy indications as if all the lookback periods were identical. A 20-period raw %K setting on the stochastic will signal a reading of nearly 100 percent should the current price represent the highest price over the last 20 periods. A lookback setting of 20 periods on the price channel will signal a new high should prices exceed the highest high of the last 20 periods. (Note that price channels do not account for the current price and hence are able to signal breakouts.) Finally, the Aroon Up indicator with the same lookback period will have a reading of 100 percent if the current price is the highest price over the last 20 periods and zero if it is the lowest. The reverse is true for the Aroon Down indicator. The Aroon Down indicator with the same lookback period will have a reading of 100 percent if the current price is the lowest price over the last 20 periods and zero if it is the highest. Figure 12.28 depicts the identical matching buy signals from all three indicators. This combination of indicators and oscillators represents the highest level of multicollinearity. As such, *confirmation of the new price channel breakouts via the Aroon Up and Stochastics Oscillator are therefore redundant or superfluous as all three indicators are mathematically constructed to give virtually identical signals over the same lookback period.*

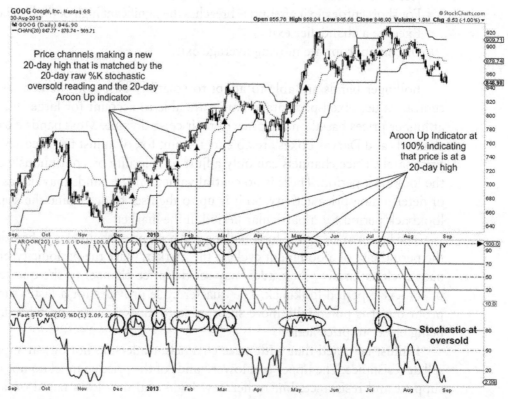

FIGURE 12.28 Multicollinearity on the Daily Chart of Google Inc.
Courtesy of Stockcharts.com

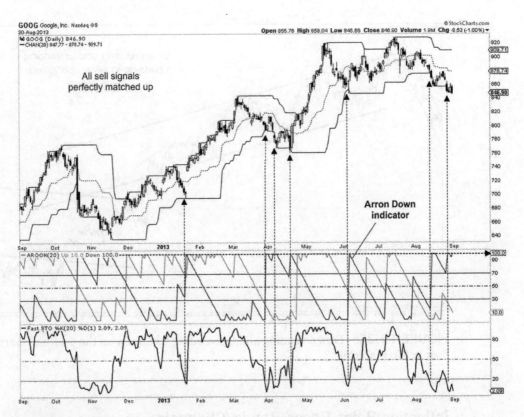

FIGURE 12.29 More Multicollinearity on the Daily Chart of Google Inc.
Courtesy of Stockcharts.com

Figure 12.29 depicts the same multicollinearity for downside breakout signals on the price channel.

The next example depicts a standard 20-period breakout channel in action. It should be noted that channels work best in stronger trends. In Figure 12.30, we see a channel experiencing losses in ranging action and profiting during trends.

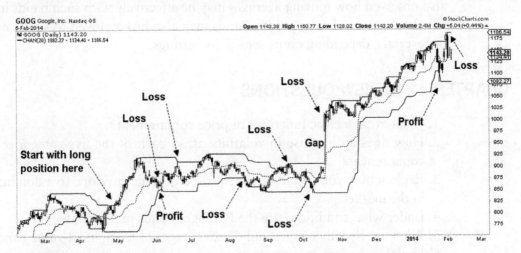

FIGURE 12.30 20-Period Channel Action on the Daily Chart of Google Inc.
Courtesy of Stockcharts.com

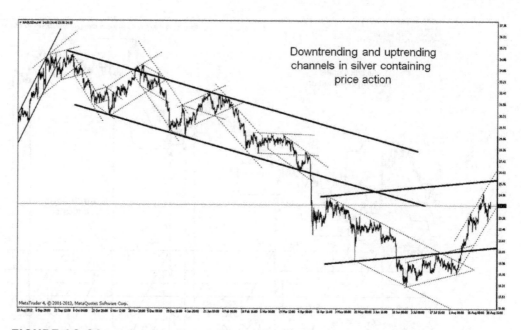

FIGURE 12.31 Downtrending and Uptrending Channels on the 4-Hour Chart of Silver. Source: MetaTrader 4

Inflection Point–Based Bands/Channels

Finally, price may also be contained via the classical uptrending, downtrending, and horizontal channels. It is important to choose significant inflection points for drawing the channel lines. See Chapter 13 for more details on channel formations. See Figure 12.31.

12.4 CHAPTER SUMMARY

We have seen how price is effectively contained within various bands. We have also observed how moving averages may be effectively with such bands in providing clear entry and exits points. Bands may also be employed to signal breakouts or reversals, depending on its sensitivity settings.

CHAPTER 12 REVIEW QUESTIONS

1. What are the basic functions of price containment?
2. How does an increase in volatility affect each of the five categories of price containment?
3. Explain how you would tune a fixed-percentage envelope to a dominant cycle in the market.
4. Under what conditions are the Bollinger bands more reliable?
5. What are the advantages and disadvantages of using fixed-value bands?
6. Explain why it is unnecessary to confirm buy and sell signals with a stochastic or Aroon oscillator that is of the same periodicity as a price channel.

7. How is Andrew's pitchfork different from other price-containment indicators?
8. What are the effects of employing logarithmic and arithmetic scaled charts with fixed-percentage envelopes?

REFERENCES

Bollinger, John. 2001. *Bollinger on Bollinger Bands*. New York: McGraw-Hill.

Kirkpatrick, Charles, and Julie Dahlquist. 2007. *Technical Analysis: The Complete Resource for Financial Market Technicians*. Upper Saddle River, NJ: Pearson Education.

Murphy, John. 1999. *Technical Analysis of the Financial Markets*. New York: New York Institute of Finance (NYIF).

Pring, Martin J. 2002. *Technical Analysis Explained: The Successful Investor's Guide to Spotting Investment Trends and Turning Points*. 4th ed. New York: McGraw-Hill.

Chart Pattern Analysis

LEARNING OBJECTIVES

After studying this chapter, you should be able to:

- Understand how to identify important chart patterns and how to use them to forecast potential reversals and continuations in the market
- Describe the five modes of chart pattern completion including the various price filters that are appropriate for each type of pattern completion
- Calculate the minimum price objectives for various chart patterns
- Distinguish between passive and aggressive trading approaches with respect to chart patterns

Chart pattern analysis is probably one of the most popular forms of technical analysis. Chart patterns help to identify market tops and bottoms as well as trend continuations. Chart patterns also indicate the minimum price movement expected once the pattern is completed. In this chapter, we shall cover various reversal and continuation chart patterns and their characteristics, guidelines for pattern completion, minimum price objectives, and various trading approaches with respect to chart patterns.

13.1 ELEMENTS OF CHART PATTERN ANALYSIS

In this chapter we will be studying various chart pattern constructs, including the:

- Preconditions required for an effective and reliable chart pattern reversal or continuation
- Minimum measuring objectives (price target projections)
- Characteristics of reversal and continuation patterns
- Expected volume action for a reliable chart pattern reversal or continuation

The Real Building Blocks of Chart Patterns: The Underlying Behavioral Component

Chart patterns are a consequence of human behavior. They are a direct result of knowledge-based bias at work in the markets. Market participants tend to place buy orders above a price barrier and sell orders below it. This learned behavior is therefore responsible for making a barrier resistant to price. When price approaches any overlay barrier such as a trendline, channel, percentage band, Ichimoku overlay, or moving average, it will initially encounter orders that inhibit further price movement incident upon it. This causes a reaction in the form of pullback from the barrier. These reactions explain why chart patterns exist. Price tends to rebound off price barriers and in the process forms trendlines, triangles, channels, wedges, pennants, and flags. For a more detailed discussion on the trade and behavioral mechanisms underlying these reactions, refer to Chapter 25.

Two Conditions for Determining Reversal or Continuation of Chart Patterns

In order to determine whether a chart pattern is a reversal or continuation pattern, two pieces of information are required, namely:

- The intrinsic sentiment associated with the pattern
- The direction of the existing trend (trend sentiment)

A bullish chart pattern in an uptrend and a bearish chart pattern in a downtrend are regarded as continuation patterns. A bearish chart pattern in an uptrend and a bullish chart pattern in a downtrend are regarded as reversal patterns. Trend sentiment is bullish for uptrends and bearish for downtrends. Therefore, we may also state that:

- When the intrinsic and trend sentiments agree (that is, both bullish or bearish), the chart pattern is regarded as a continuation pattern.
- When the intrinsic and trend sentiments disagrees, the chart pattern is regarded as a reversal pattern.

The following can be said about intrinsically neutral chart patterns like the symmetrical triangle and horizontal channel:

- They are generally considered to be reversal patterns if they occur in proximity to previous market tops or bottoms (being neutral in sentiment, they tend to adopt external or extrinsic sentiment, which in this case is bearish at previous market tops and bullish at previous market bottoms).
- They are generally considered to be reversal patterns if they occur in proximity to a projected cycle extreme.
- They are generally considered continuation patterns if they occur near the midpoint of a price cycle.

The following chart patterns are regarded as *intrinsically bullish* patterns irrespective of their locations on the chart:

- Inverted head and shoulders patterns
- Falling wedges
- Ascending triangles
- Bullish flags and pennants
- Double/triple/multiple Bottoms

The following chart patterns are regarded as *intrinsically bearish* patterns irrespective of their locations on the chart:

- Standard head and shoulders patterns
- Rising wedges
- Descending triangles
- Bearish flags and pennants
- Double/triple/multiple Tops

The following chart patterns are regarded as *bearish reversal* chart patterns:

- Broadening formations in uptrends
- Standard head and shoulders in uptrends
- Island formations in uptrends
- Rounding tops in uptrends
- Diamond formations in uptrends
- Rising wedges in uptrends
- Double/triple/multiple tops
- Descending triangles in uptrends
- V tops

The following chart patterns are regarded as *bullish reversal* chart patterns:

- Broadening formations in downtrends
- Inverted head and shoulders in downtrends
- Island formations in downtrends
- Cup and handles in downtrends
- Rounding bottoms in downtrends
- Diamond formations in downtrends
- Falling wedges in downtrends
- Double/triple/multiple bottoms
- Ascending triangles in downtrends
- V bottoms

The following chart patterns, although regarded as *intrinsically neutral*, are nevertheless regarded as reversal chart patterns:

- Diamond formations
- Expanding (broadening) formations

The following chart patterns are regarded as *continuation* chart patterns:

- Bullish pennants and flags in uptrends
- Bearish pennants and flags in downtrends
- Symmetrical triangles in uptrends and downtrends
- Horizontal channels in uptrends and downtrends
- Ascending triangles in uptrends
- Descending triangles in downtrends
- Inverted head and shoulders in uptrends
- Standard head and shoulders in downtrends
- Falling wedges in uptrends
- Rising wedges in downtrends

Consolidation and Non-Consolidation Patterns

Most chart patterns are regarded as *consolidation* patterns. This is because for a chart pattern to form, price has to decelerate and remain within some confined region of price. A few exceptions are V-tops and V-bottoms. These V-patterns are not usually regarded as consolidation patterns as they do not decelerate and then range within a certain region of price. On the contrary, *they reverse very abruptly and begin to trend strongly in the opposite direction.* Refer to Figure 13.1 for a summary of chart pattern classifications.

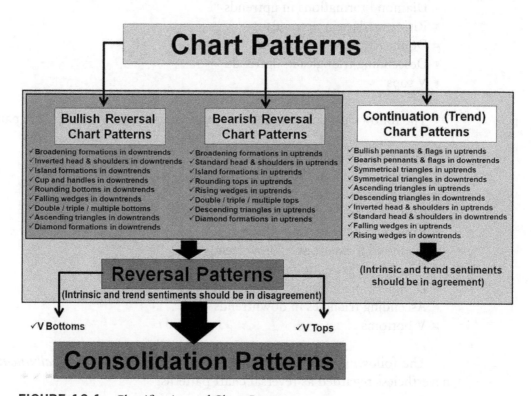

FIGURE 13.1 Classifications of Chart Patterns.

13.2 PRECONDITIONS FOR RELIABLE CHART PATTERN REVERSALS

Sixteen Main Preconditions for a Reliable Reversal

For a reliable reversal, a significantly clear and obvious trend has to be in effect. *The more extended and pronounced a trend, the more likely will be a potential reversal.* A reversal (or continuation) move is also regarded as more reliable if it is accompanied by decreasing volume. A bearish chart formation in proximity to any downside violation of significant trendlines or price barriers is also regarded as more reliable. The reverse applies for bullish chart patterns.

It should also be noted that bullish reversal formations tend to last longer than bearish reversal formations, especially in the equity markets. This is because much more capital and unrealized profit are at risk at market tops as compared to market bottoms where prices are low and the corresponding capital at risk is less significant. This discrepancy is less obvious in the commodity markets where traders and investors trade and invest on very low margins.

Besides studying the individual price behavior associated with each chart pattern, the practitioner should also be aware of the 16 basic price and volume preconditions that are indicative of a potential reversal, namely:

1. Decrease in price cycle amplitude during a trend
2. Decrease in price cycle period during a trend
3. Change in bar retracement symmetry during a trend
4. Decrease in average bar range during a trend
5. Lack of quality of price persistence (price becoming more volatile) during a trend
6. Decrease in average bar stochastic ratio during a trend
7. Decrease in average candlestick real body to range ratio during a trend
8. Changes in angular symmetry and momentum
9. Proximity to a price barrier
10. Reduction in frequency and decrease in depth of trend-based oscillations
11. Relative size of chart pattern and its duration
12. Appearance of a third (exhaustion) gap prior to the formation of a chart pattern
13. Completion of the average range for the period under observation
14. Overextended price action with respect to a price barrier
15. Price accompanied by extremely high or low volume
16. Divergence between price and volume and oscillators

If a chart pattern is preceded by any of these 16 preconditions, a potential reversal is more likely to occur. These 16 preconditions are discussed in more detail in Chapter 5.

The Minimum Measuring Objective: The One-to-One Price-Target Projection Level

Most charts patterns have a minimum price objective or target associated with them, with the exception of V tops and bottoms. The minimum price objective of most chart patterns is usually a *one-to-one projection (1:1) of the height of the pattern from the breakout point.* This also corresponds to the reward-risk ratio setup for a trade based on a chart pattern. The one-to-one, two-to-one, and three-to-one projections are popular profit-taking levels and the practitioner should treat these levels as potential reversal levels. These hidden profit-taking levels also represent barriers to price action of which most novice traders are totally unaware when trading chart patterns. In some chart formations like the flag and pennant, the height of the *pole* is used for the determination of minimum price objectives or targets.

Pattern Completion

Chart patterns are usually considered complete or confirmed when one of the following five scenarios occurs:

1. Price breaches a level associated with a significant inflection point with respect to the chart pattern.
2. Price breaches a trendline associated with the chart pattern.
3. A minimum number of significant price inflection points are formed.
4. A price gap is formed.
5. The formation is visually discernible.

For example, chart patterns that require a breach of a price level associated with a significant inflection point in order to be considered as complete or confirmed include:

- Double tops and bottoms: The breach of a price level associated with a significant price inflection point between the two peaks in a double top or two troughs in a double bottom completes the pattern. See Figures 13.14 and 13.15.
- Triple and multiple tops and bottoms: The breach of significant price inflection points between triple and multiple peaks in a topping formation or triple and multiple troughs in a bottoming formation completes the pattern. See Figure 13.19.
- Rounding tops and bottoms: A breach of the previous significant peak in a rounding bottom formation or breach of the previous significant trough in a rounding top formation completes the pattern.

Chart patterns that require a breach of a trendline in order to be considered complete or confirmed include standard and inverted head and shoulders patterns. A breach of the head and shoulders neckline completes the pattern. See Figures 13.4 and 13.5.

Chart patterns that require a minimum number of significant price inflection points to be formed in order to be considered complete or confirmed include any chart pattern that is formed by two (or four) trendlines, such as:

- Expanding (broadening) and contracting triangles which include ascending, descending, and symmetrical triangles
- Rising, falling, and horizontal channels
- Wedges
- Pennants

- Flags
- Diamond formations, which require the formation of four trendlines

Once the two (or four) trendlines encapsulating any of these patterns are formed, the pattern is complete and no breakout is required.

Chart formations that are considered complete or confirmed once gaps are formed are the top and bottom island formations. A top island formation requires a gap up followed by a gap down in price for completion. In similar fashion, a bottom island formation requires a gap down followed by a gap up in price for completion.

Finally, chart patterns that are considered complete or confirmed once they are obvious or visually discernible include V tops and V bottoms. These patterns cannot be confirmed until they become obvious, that is, they can only be clearly identified in hindsight.

Price Filters Associated with Chart Pattern Completion

For a valid pattern completion or confirmation via the penetration of trendlines or price levels associated with significant inflection points, a close beyond the trendline or price level is usually employed. For intraday or intra-period penetrations, a price filter based on one of the following may be employed to determine pattern completion:

- A minimum percentage of price move
- A minimum fixed dollar, pip, or point move
- A minimum move based on some multiple of standard deviation or average true range (ATR)

For pattern completion or confirmation via the formation of two or more trendlines, trendlines should be drawn based on *significantly clear and obvious* peaks for downtrending lines and troughs for uptrending lines. A pattern is said to be tentative until it is confirmed.

Chart Pattern Failure

In order for a chart pattern to fail, it must be first completed or confirmed. Technically, a pattern does not exist until it is confirmed. *A completed chart pattern is said to have failed if price moves in a direction opposite to the expected follow-through action.* For example, a head and shoulders formation cannot fail unless it is first completed via a valid neckline violation. Once a valid violation has occurred, price is expected to move in the direction of the neckline breakout. If it does not, the pattern is said to have failed.

The main problem with determining whether failure has occurred is a question of degree. An example will help clarify this issue. Traders A and B selected one percent and three percent breakout filters, respectively. Assume that price extended beyond the neckline by two percent and immediately reversed in the opposite direction, extending beyond the right shoulder. Has the chart pattern failed? It would be classified as a failure as far as Trader A is concerned since according to Trader A's filter setting, the chart pattern was completed but failed to follow through in the direction of the breakout. As far as Trader B is concerned, no failure has yet occurred as the pattern is not yet confirmed or completed, since there is still no valid breakout. For Trader B, the pattern only failed to complete.

But one could also argue that there is no real failure as far as Trader A's scenario is concerned since price did move an extra one percent beyond the one percent filter in the direction of the breakout. The question will now be the amount of price excursion required after a valid breakout in order for a pattern to avoid failure. *Many practitioners solve this problem by requiring that a completed pattern achieves its minimum one-to-one projected price objective or target in order to avoid any future possibility of pattern failure.*

Chart Patterns and Scaling

The type of chart scaling employed will affect the analysis of chart patterns. This is because chart patterns are geometrically based. As such, the construction and subsequent angle of trendlines will vary when being expanded at the lower price levels and compressed at higher price levels on the logarithmically scaled charts. There will be a discrepancy in the chart pattern breakout levels between arithmetically and logarithmically scaled charts.

13.3 POPULAR CHART PATTERNS

V Tops and V Bottoms

A V top is a formation that makes a very clear and distinctive top in the market, which is usually accompanied by a large spike in volume, popularly referred to as a blow off. Similarly, a V bottom is a formation that makes a very clear and distinctive bottom in the market, which is usually accompanied by a selling climax. The uptrends and downtrends associated with V tops and V bottoms are characterized by very little trend oscillation and may even trace out a parabolic path in some cases. The formation is usually not visually discernible until most of the subsequent retracement is done. There is no clear way to determine pattern completion in V tops and V bottoms. There is also no minimum price objective associated with this pattern. The best way to catch a V top or bottom is to employ a simple trendline violation. See Figure 13.2.

V tops and V bottoms may peak and trough respectively at:

- Historical support and resistance levels
- The test of some significant trendline
- Significant Floor Trader's Pivot Point levels
- Significant Fibonacci levels
- Important psychological prices ending with double and triple zeros
- Significant resistive and supportive confluences

Volume testing its historical highs is probably the clearest indication of a potential V top or V bottom forming in the market. In Figure 13.3, we observe the USDCAD forming a V bottom on the four-hour chart.

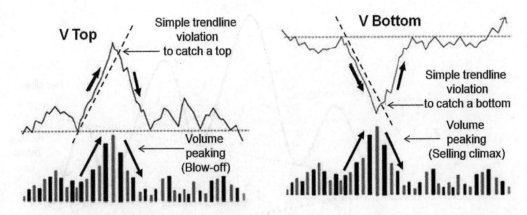

FIGURE 13.2   V-Top and V-Bottom Formations.

Head and Shoulders Top Formation

A simple *head and shoulders top* formation is characterized by a peak representing the left shoulder, followed by a higher peak which is referred to as the head of the formation. A lower peak representing the right shoulder is found on the right-hand side of the head. The head should be the highest peak in the formation. The *neckline* is a trendline that connects the troughs that lie on either side of the head. Necklines may be horizontal or inclined. *A complex head and shoulders formation consists of multiple left and right shoulders.* Volume should ideally be greatest at the left shoulder and gradually diminish at each subsequent peak as the formation develops. Volume should start to increase as price breaks out from the neckline, but should decline on the retest of it. In an inverted head and shoulders formation (also referred to as a head and shoulders bottom), the head is the lowest trough within the formation, but the volume action remains similar to that of a

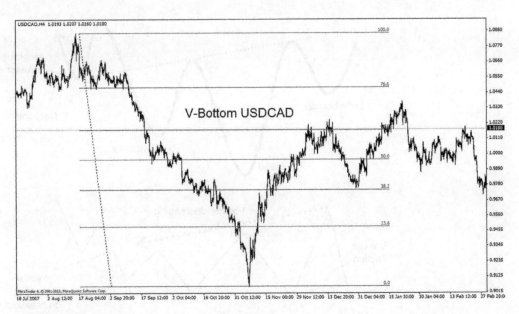

FIGURE 13.3   V-Top and V-Bottom Formations.
Source: MetaTrader 4

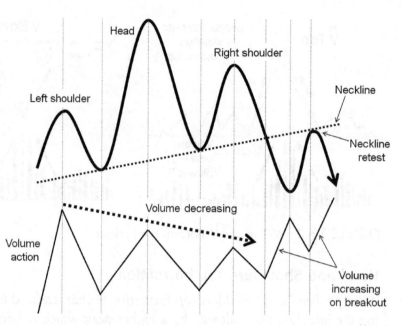

FIGURE 13.4   A Head and Shoulders Top Formation.

head and shoulders top formation. The inverted head and shoulders formation is completed with a valid upside breakout of the neckline. See Figures 13.4 and 13.5.

The pattern is completed once there is a valid penetration of the neckline. Until a valid penetration has occurred, the formation is regarded as merely tentative. In order for the pattern to avoid failure, the minimum one-to-one price objective or target should be met before price reverses back up above the neckline or any peak within the formation.

It should be noted that a valid penetration of the neckline is required in order to distinguish it from triangle formations, which do not require a breakout for

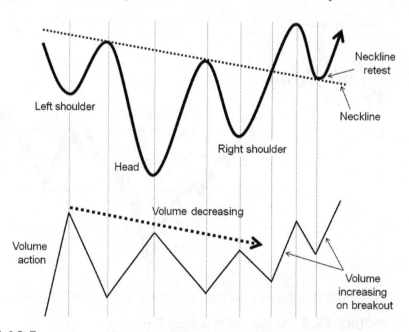

FIGURE 13.5   An Inverted Head and Shoulders Formation.

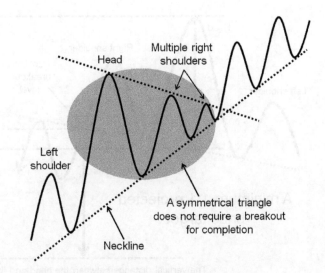

FIGURE 13.6　An Inverted Head and Shoulders Formation.

pattern completion. In Figure 13.6, we see a completed symmetrical triangle formation, but the head and shoulders formation is still merely tentative.

A head and shoulders top formation is regarded as a continuation pattern in a downtrend and a reversal formation in an uptrend. In similar fashion, an inverted head and shoulders formation is regarded as a continuation pattern in an uptrend and a reversal formation in a downtrend. See Figure 13.7.

The minimum one-to-one price objective or target for a head and shoulders top formation is simply the vertical distance between the head and the neckline projected downward from the neckline breakout level. For an inverted head and shoulders formation, the vertical distance is projected upward from the neckline breakout level. *Once the minimum projected target is met, a formation will have avoided any further possibility of failure.* See Figure 13.8.

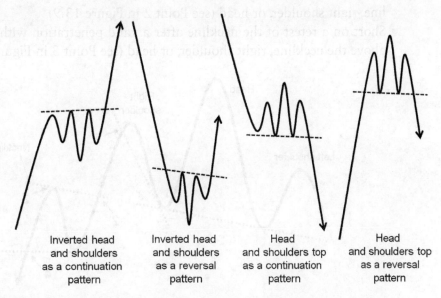

FIGURE 13.7　Continuation and Reversal Head and Shoulders Formation.

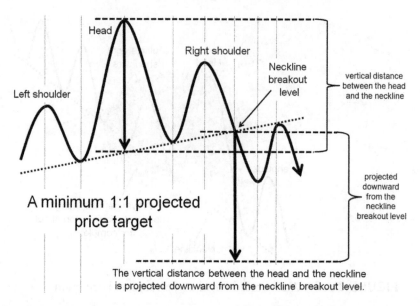

FIGURE 13.8 The Minimum One-to-One Projected Price Target.

A trader may initiate an entry in a head and shoulders top formation in any of the following ways (the reverse applies for inverted head and shoulders formations):

- Short at a break of the right shoulder's uptrend line with a stop placed above the right shoulder or head (see Point 1 in Figure 13.9)
- Short at the peak of the right shoulder with a stop placed above the right shoulder or head, especially when there is a significant resistive confluence comprising of significant Fibonacci retracement levels, Floor Trader's Pivot Point levels, and psychologically important price levels associated with double and triple zeros
- Short at the right shoulder when it is testing the left shoulder's resistance level, with a stop placed above the resistance level or head
- Short on a valid penetration of the neckline with a stop placed above the neckline, right shoulder, or head (see Point 2 in Figure 13.9)
- Short on a retest of the neckline after a valid penetration with a stop placed above the neckline, right shoulder, or head (see Point 3 in Figure 13.9)

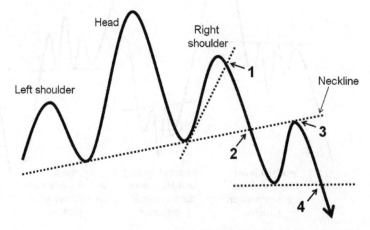

FIGURE 13.9 The Minimum One-to-One Projected Price Target.

■ Short on the penetration of the price associated with the trough created by the retest action, with a stop placed above the trough, neckline, right shoulder, or head (see Point 4 in Figure 13.9)

Advantages of entering at the right shoulder of a head and shoulders top formation:

■ If the head and shoulders top formation completes, traders will already be in profit at the moment the neckline was validly breached, which will help minimize the risk of having the stoploss taken out.
■ Shorting at the top of the right shoulder helps to reduce the effects of whipsaws at the neckline break.
■ There is no danger of a neckline retest endangering profits.

Disadvantages of entering at the right shoulder of a head and shoulders top formation:

■ It might not be a head and shoulders top formation after all, and price rallies to form a double top instead, in the process taking out the stoploss.
■ There is insufficient clarity and the formation may turn out to be a symmetrical or ascending triangle, which suggests a continuation of the existing trend instead.
■ A head and shoulders top formation could well turn out to be a consolidation pattern and remain in a range.

In Figure 13.10, we observe an inverted head and shoulders formation meeting its minimum one-to-one price objective on the 5-min chart of the EURUSD.

FIGURE 13.10   The Minimum One-to-One Projected Price Target for an Inverted Head and Shoulders Formation on the 5-Min Chart of EURUSD.
Source: MetaTrader 4

FIGURE 13.11 The Minimum One-to-One Projected Price Target for a Head and Shoulder Top Formation on the 15-Min Chart of EURUSD.
Source: MetaTrader 4

In Figure 13.11, we observe a head and shoulders top formation meeting its minimum one-to-one price objective on the 15-min chart of the EURUSD.

In Figure 13.12, we observe an inverted head and shoulders top formation meeting its minimum one-to-one price objective on the 30-min chart of the EURUSD. Notice that there is a smaller head and shoulders formation nested within a larger head and shoulders formation. Although not shown on the chart,

FIGURE 13.12 The Minimum One-to-One Projected Price Target for an Inverted Head and Shoulders Formation on the 30-Min Chart of EURUSD.
Source: MetaTrader 4

FIGURE 13.13 The Minimum One-to-One Projected Price Target for an Inverted Head and Shoulders Formation on the 30-Min Chart of the U.S. Oil Fund.
Courtesy of Stockcharts.com

the minimum one-to-one price objective of the smaller inverted head and shoulders formation coincides with the neckline of the larger formation. This is an example of a complex head and shoulders formation, that is, a formation with multiple shoulders.

In Figure 13.13, we observe an inverted head and shoulders top formation meeting its minimum one-to-one price objective on the daily chart of the U.S. Oil Fund. We also see a rising channel meeting its minimum one-to-one downside price objective. Bearish divergence with respect to the MACD is additional evidence for a more reliable rising channel downside breakout.

Double Tops and Bottoms

A double top formation is simply a retest of a prior resistance level and a double bottom is a retest of a prior support level. A double top is a bearish reversal formation, whereas a double bottom is a bullish reversal formation. A double top formation is completed once the lowest trough between the two peaks in a double top formation is violated. In similar fashion, a double bottom formation is completed once the highest peak between the two troughs in a double bottom formation is violated. *This price level associated with the completion of a double top and bottom formation is referred to as the validation level.* The formation is considered tentative until it is completed via a valid penetration of the validation level. Volume should be lighter on both the second peak in a double top formation and second trough in a double bottom formation. Volume should ideally begin to increase on breakout. The minimum one-to-one measuring objective for a double top formation is simply the downside projection measured from the validation level of

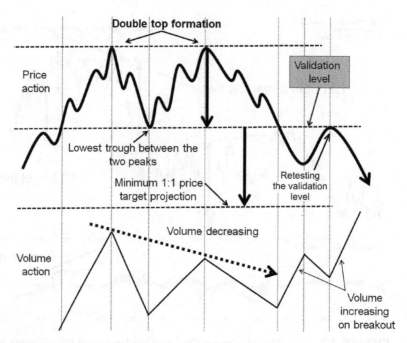

FIGURE 13.14 An Ideal Double Top Formation.

vertical distance between the resistance level in a double top formation and its validation level. Similarly, the minimum one-to-one measuring objective for a double bottom formation is simply the upside projection measured from the validation level of vertical distance between the support level in a double bottom formation and its validation level. Once this minimum price objective is met, the formation would have obviated any possibility of a failure. See Figures 13.14 and 13.15.

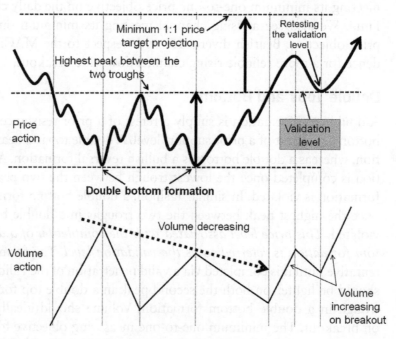

FIGURE 13.15 An Ideal Double Bottom Formation.

Short entries may be initiated in a double top formation at (the reverse applies for double bottom formations):

- The second peak with a stoploss positioned just above it
- The breakout of the validation level with a stoploss positioned just above it or the second peak
- The retest of the validation level after a valid breakout with a stoploss positioned just above it or the second peak
- The breakout of the new support level created during a retest of the validation level with a stoploss positioned just above the support level, the validation level, or the second peak

In Figure 13.16, we observe the completion of a double top and bottom formation on the four-hour chart of EURUSD.

In Figure 13.17, we observe the various double top and bottom formations with their corresponding follow-through reversal action.

In Figure 13.18, we observe various double top and bottom formations on the daily chart of Delcath Systems Inc. Notice a one-to-one horizontal channel price target coinciding with a double top three-to-one downside target projection.

Triple Tops/Bottoms

A triple top formation is simply a double retest of a prior resistance level and a triple bottom is a double retest of a prior support level. A triple top is a bearish reversal formation, whereas a triple bottom is a bullish reversal formation. A

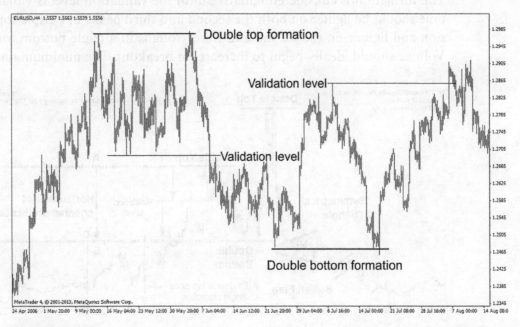

FIGURE 13.16 A Completed Double Top and Bottom Formation on the 4-Hour Chart of EURUSD.
Source: MetaTrader 4

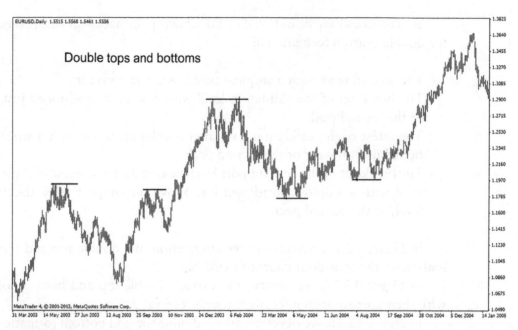

FIGURE 13.17 Various Double Top and Bottom Formations on the Daily Chart of EURUSD.
Source: MetaTrader 4

triple top formation is completed once the lowest trough between the first and last peak in a triple top formation is violated. In similar fashion, a triple bottom formation is completed once the highest peak between the first and last trough in a triple bottom formation is violated. The price level associated the completion of a triple top and bottom formation is referred to as the validation level. The formation is considered tentative until the validation level is violated. Volume should be lighter on both the second and third peaks in a triple top formation and lighter on the second and third troughs in a triple bottom formation. Volume should ideally begin to increase on breakout. The minimum one-to-one

FIGURE 13.18 A Minimum One-to-One Downside Projected Price Target for a Double Top and a Horizontal Channel Formation on the Daily Chart of Delcath Systems Inc.
Courtesy of Stockcharts.com

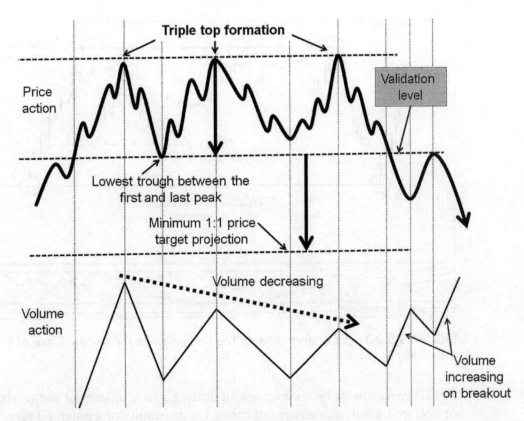

FIGURE 13.19 An Ideal Triple Top Formation.

measuring objective for a triple top formation is simply the downside projection measured from the validation level of vertical distance between the resistance level in a triple top formation and its validation level. Similarly, the minimum one-to-one measuring objective for a triple bottom formation is simply the upside projection measured from the validation level of vertical distance between the support level in a triple bottom formation and its validation level. Once this minimum price objective is met, the formation would have obviated any possibility of a failure. See Figure 13.19 for an illustration of an idealized triple top formation.

In Figure 13.20, we observe a completed triple top formation on the 15-min chart of EURUSD. Notice that it has not met the minimum one-to-one price objective and is therefore susceptible to pattern failure if price reverses back above the resistance level formed by the three peaks.

Island Tops and Bottoms

Island tops and bottoms are reversal formations. Island top formations are preceded by an upside gap and subsequently followed by a downside gap, completing the formation. Island bottom formations are preceded by an upside gap and completed by a subsequent downside gap. Volume could well be very heavy around the peak in an island top formation or trough in an island bottom formation, indicating a buying and selling climax, respectively. Conversely, volume could also

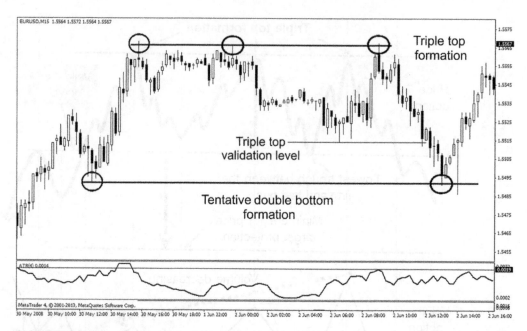

FIGURE 13.20 A Completed Triple Top Formation on the 15-Min Chart of EURUSD.
Source: MetaTrader 4

be extremely low or below average, indicating a lack of interest in the island top or bottom formation, thereby indicating the possibility of a potential reversal. See Figures 13.21 and 13.22. Island reversal formations tend to be more reliable if the island tops or bottoms develop in a price range where:

- There are prior resistance or support levels or
- There are other resistive confluences in an island top formation or supportive confluences in an island bottom formation comprising Fibonacci or Gann levels, Floor Traders Pivot Point levels, psychologically important price levels,

FIGURE 13.21 An Island Top Formation within a Larger Descending Triangle Formation on the Daily Chart of PowerShares DB U.S. Dollar Bullish Fund.
Courtesy of Stockcharts.com

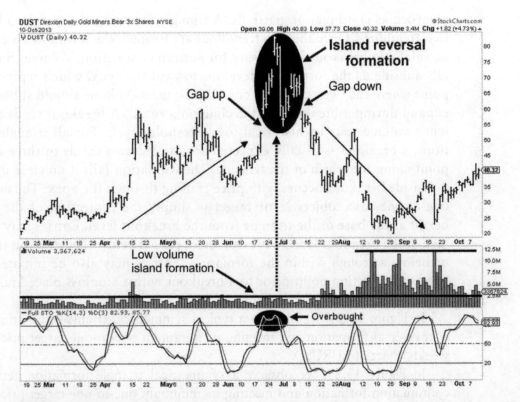

FIGURE 13.22 An Island Top Formation on the Daily Chart of Direxion Daily Gold Miners Bear 3X Shares.
Courtesy of Stockcharts.com

and any other price overlays such as trendlines, channels, moving averages, Ichimoku clouds, and so on.

Notice that in Figure 13.21, the island top forms at the previous resistance level, making it potentially more reliable as a reversal pattern.

In Figure 13.22, we observe a completed island top formation occurring on low volume during an overbought condition on the daily stochastics oscillator.

Symmetrical, Ascending, and Descending Triangles

There are basically four types of triangle formations:

1. Ascending (characterized by converging trendlines)
2. Descending (characterized by converging trendlines)
3. Expanding (characterized by diverging trendlines)
4. Symmetrical (characterized by converging trendlines)

Symmetrical triangles are neutral formations. They are characterized by successively lower peaks and higher troughs. There are generally regarded as reversal formations if they are located at cycle extremes or at previous significant resistance or support levels. At or near cycle midpoints, they are regarded as continuation patterns. A triangle formation is contained between two trendlines. Once the two trendlines are formed, the formation is complete or valid. No breakout is necessary for pattern completion. Volume should ideally subside as the formation develops toward the apex, which represents the point where the two trendlines converge or meet. Volume should subsequently expand during a breakout and decline on a retest. A breakout tends to occur when volume tests its historical low threshold levels. For all triangle formations, a breakout is usually expected around the two-thirds to three-quarters point along the width of the triangle. The formation fails if no clear upside or downside breakout occurs with price trading through the apex. The minimum one-to-one price objective or target is simply the projection of the vertical height at the base of the triangle from the breakout level. Entries may be initiated at the breakout level, with stoplosses placed below the breakout trendline or below a trough within the formation. Entries may also be initiated at the opposite inflection point prior to a breakout with a stoploss placed just below the opposite trendline. See Figure 13.23.

In Figure 13.24, we observe a typical symmetrical triangle formation acting as a reversal formation and meeting its minimum one-to-one target price on the weekly chart of EURUSD.

In Figure 13.25, we observe a symmetrical triangle formation acting as a continuation formation and meeting its minimum one-to-one target price on the 15-min chart of EURUSD.

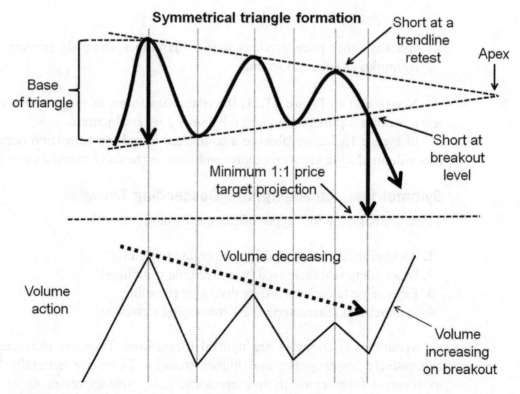

FIGURE 13.23 An Idealized Symmetrical Triangle Formation.

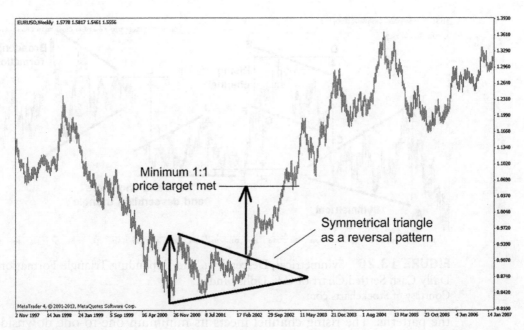

FIGURE 13.24 A Symmetrical Triangle as a Reversal Formation on the Weekly Chart of EURUSD.
Source: MetaTrader 4

In Figure 13.26, we observe a symmetrical formation acting as a continuation formation and meeting its minimum one-to-one target price on the 15-min chart of EURUSD. The height of the base of the triangle, AB, is projected from the breakout level at Point C, which is met exactly at the market top indicated at the price level DE. CD is the projection of AB from Point C. We also see other chart patterns meeting their minimum one-to-one price targets based on the height of

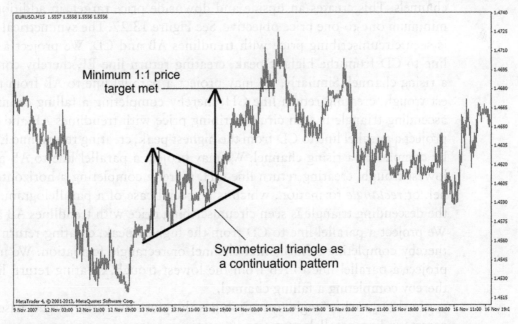

FIGURE 13.25 A Symmetrical Triangle Formation as a Continuation Formation on the 15-Min Chart of EURUSD.
Source: MetaTrader 4

FIGURE 13.26 Symmetrical, Descending, and Expanding Triangle Formations on the Daily Cash Settled Chart of U.S. Dollar Index.
Courtesy of Stockcharts.com

the patterns. The rising channel meets its minimum one-to-one downside target price at the projection of the height of the channel, EF, from the breakout point. GH is the projection of EF from Point G. We also see a failed descending triangle meeting its minimum one-to-one upside price target based on the projection of the height of the base, IJ, from the breakout point. KL is the projection of IJ from Point K.

It should be noted that since two trendlines circumscribe price within a triangle formation, a parallel line may also be drawn based on each trendline. In short, two *parallelograms* can be created for any single triangle formation; in other words, a single triangle formation produces two corresponding price channels. This creates an upside and downside price target, in addition to the minimum one-to-one price objective. See Figure 13.27. The symmetrical triangle is seen circumscribing price with trendlines AB and CD. We project a parallel line to CD from the highest peak, creating return line EF, thereby completing a rising channel. Similarly, we may project a parallel line to AB from the lowest trough, creating return line GH, thereby completing a falling channel. The ascending triangle is seen circumscribing price with trendlines AB and CD. We project a parallel line to CD from the highest peak, creating return line EF, thereby completing a rising channel. We may project a parallel line to AB from the lowest trough, creating return line GH, thereby completing a horizontal channel, or *rectangle* formation, which is a special case of a parallelogram. Finally, the descending triangle is seen circumscribing price with trendlines AB and CD. We project a parallel line to CD from the highest peak, creating return line EF, thereby completing a horizontal channel or rectangle formation. We may also project a parallel line to AB from the lowest trough, creating return line GH, thereby completing a falling channel.

In short, each triangle formation has therefore two price targets based on its corresponding parallelograms and a minimum one-to-one price target based on the projection of the vertical height of the base from the triangle breakout level.

518

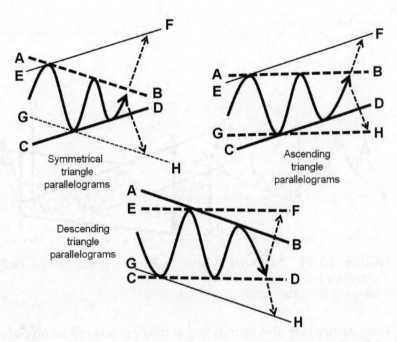

FIGURE 13.27 Symmetrical, Descending, and Ascending Triangle Parallelograms.

In Figure 13.28, we observe a symmetrical triangle circumscribing price between trendlines FG and EI, meeting its minimum one-to-one price objective with the projection of its base EF from the breakout level at G. GH is the projection of the base EF from the breakout level G. A parallel line to EI is projected from Point X, creating a return line XK, thereby completing its corresponding rising channel. The minimum one-to-one price target of this rising channel is simply the height of the channel IJ, which is projected as KL, from the rising channel breakout level at Point K. Hence we have three price targets associated with the symmetrical triangle, namely the return line XK and the minimum one-to-one price target level at Points H and L.

Ascending triangles are bullish formations. They are characterized by successively higher troughs with equal or matching peaks. There are regarded as continuation formations in an uptrend and reversal formations in a downtrend. Once the two trendlines are formed, the formation is complete or valid. No breakout is necessary for pattern completion. Volume should ideally subside as the formation develops toward the triangle apex. Volume should subsequently expand during a breakout and decline on a retest. A breakout tends to occur when volume tests its historical low threshold levels. A breakout is usually expected around the two-thirds to three-quarters point along the width of the triangle. The formation fails if no clear upside breakout occurs, with price trading through the apex or breaking out toward the downside. The minimum one-to-one price objective is simply the projection of the vertical height at the base of the triangle from the upside breakout level. Further price objectives are derived from its two parallelogram-based price targets. Long entries may be initiated at the breakout level with stoplosses placed below the resistance or below a trough within the formation.

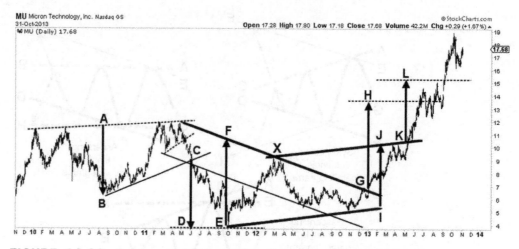

FIGURE 13.28 Symmetrical Triangle Parallelograms on the Daily Chart of Micron Technology Inc.
Courtesy of Stockcharts.com

Long entries may also be initiated at the opposite inflection point prior to a breakout with a stoploss placed just below the opposite trendline. *It should be noted that if the breakout occurs to the downside, the minimum one-to-one projected target price may also be used to determine the minimum price excursion for the failed formation.* The associated parallelogram-based targets may also be used in such cases. See Figure 13.29.

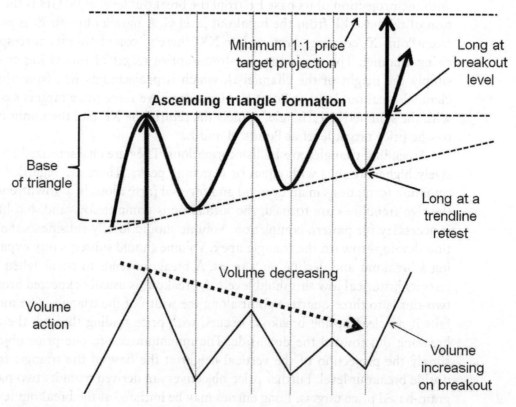

FIGURE 13.29 An Idealized Ascending Triangle Formation.

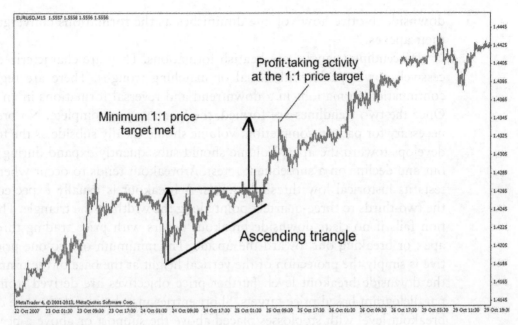

FIGURE 13.30 An Ascending Triangle Formation as a Continuation Formation on the 15-Min Chart of EURUSD.
Source: MetaTrader 4

In Figure 13.30, we see an ascending triangle meeting its minimum one-to-one price objective. Notice how price retraces at this one-to-one profit-taking level.

In Figure 13.31, we see various ascending triangles meeting their minimum one-to-one price targets. The ascending triangle formed between July and August is the only one that did not fail, that is, it did not break out to the

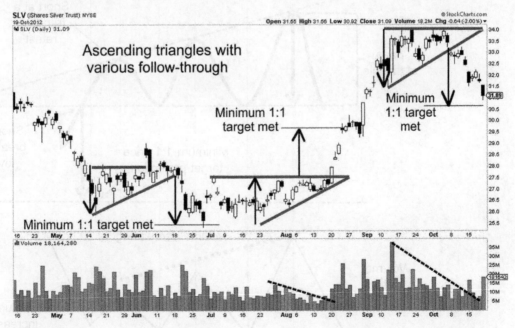

FIGURE 13.31 Ascending Triangles as Reversal Formations on the Daily Chart of Micron Technology Inc.
Courtesy of Stockcharts.com

downside. Notice how volume diminishes as the formations converge toward their apexes.

Descending triangles are bearish formations. They are characterized by successively lower peaks with equal or matching troughs. There are regarded as continuation formations in a downtrend and reversal formations in an uptrend. Once the two trendlines are formed, the formation is complete. No breakout is necessary for pattern completion. Volume should ideally subside as the formation develops toward the apex. Volume should subsequently expand during a breakout and decline on a subsequent retest. A breakout tends to occur when volume tests its historical low threshold levels. A breakout is usually expected around the two-thirds to three-quarters point along the width of the triangle. The formation fails if no clear downside breakout occurs with price trading through the apex or breaking out toward the upside. The minimum one-to-one price objective is simply the projection of the vertical height at the base of the triangle from the downside breakout level. Further price objectives are derived from its two parallelogram-based price targets. Short entries may be initiated at the downside breakout level with stoplosses placed above the support or above a peak within the formation. Short entries may also be initiated at the opposite inflection point prior to a breakout, with a stoploss placed just above the opposite trendline. It should be noted that if the breakout occurs to the upside, the minimum one-to-one price projected target may also be used to determine the minimum price excursion for the failed formation. The associated parallelogram-based targets may also be used. See Figure 13.32.

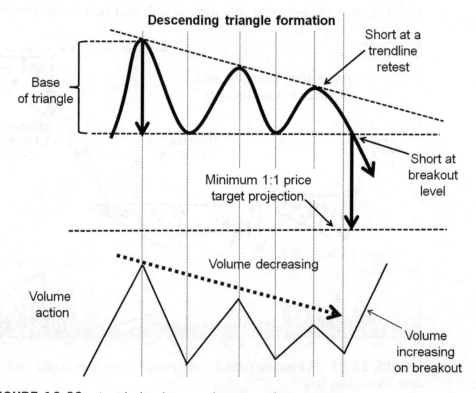

FIGURE 13.32 An Idealized Descending Triangle Formation.

FIGURE 13.33 Ascending Triangles as Reversal Formations on the Daily Chart of S&P 500 Large Cap Index.
Courtesy of Stockcharts.com

In Figure 13.33, we see various descending triangles forming around Black Monday in October 1987. Notice the bearish descending triangle formation just prior to the market collapse. It met its target before opening lower in the next trading session.

Broadening Formations

Broadening formations are also referred to as expanding triangles or megaphonic patterns and are characterized by successively higher peaks and lower troughs. Broadening formations are regarded as reversal formations. At market tops they represent bearish reversal formations and at market bottoms they are regarded as bullish reversal formations. *The broadening formation is usually a precursor of increasing volatility in the markets*. Stoplosses are normally taken out when attempting to trade support or resistance levels during a price expansion. The pattern is complete once the two diverging trendlines are established. No breakout is required for pattern completion. There is no clear minimum target projection associated with this formation. Entries may be initiated at the retest of either trendline, with stoplosses placed slightly beyond it. Notice the increase in volatility after a broadening formation is formed in Figures 13.34 and 13.35.

Bullish and Bearish Flags

Bull and bear flag formations represent short-term trend interruptions and as such are regarded as continuation formations. The flag forms as a parallelogram and it slopes slightly against the direction of the existing trend. In uptrends it slopes downward and in downtrends it slopes upward. The flag parallelogram is preceded by a pole that represents a short and rapid thrust in price, and is ideally accompanied by heavy volume. The volume should gradually subside as the flag parallelogram unfolds and increase on

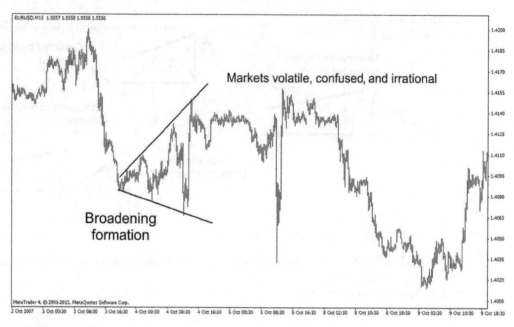

FIGURE 13.34 A Broadening Formation as a Precursor of Increasing Volatility on the 15-Min Chart of EURUSD.
Source: MetaTrader 4

breakout. Once volume tests its historical lows, a potential breakout from the parallelogram may be imminent. The formation is complete once the parallelogram is formed and no breakout is required for pattern completion. The minimum upside and downside price targets are simply one-to-one price projections based on the height of the pole, measured from the parallelogram breakout level. *It should be noted that minimum one-to-one price tar-*

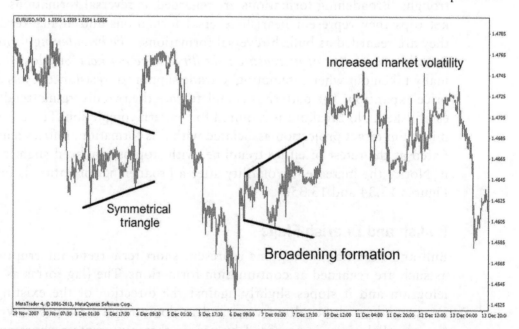

FIGURE 13.35 A Broadening Formation as a Precursor of Increasing Volatility on the 30-Min Chart of EURUSD.
Source: MetaTrader 4

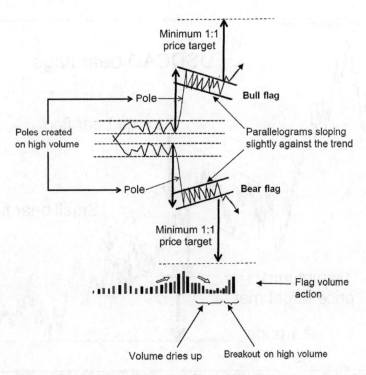

FIGURE 13.36 Idealized Bull and Bear Flag Formations.

gets may also be obtained based on the parallelogram itself. A two-to-one parallelogram-based price projection coinciding with a one-to-one pole-based price projection tends to result in the creation of a potentially strong price barrier. Entries may be initiated at the breakout of the parallelograms. See Figure 13.36.

In Figure 13.37, we see two bear flags meeting their minimum one-to-one price objective. In addition we notice that price also reacted at the two-to-one downside price projection based on the larger bear flag.

In Figure 13.38, we observe a bull flag meeting its minimum one-to-one price objective based on the height of the entire formation from the parallelogram upside breakout level. We also notice the two-to-one price target based on the height of the parallelogram being met at nearly the same price level on the 15-min chart of the EURUSD.

Bullish and Bearish Pennants

Bullish and bearish pennant formations also represent short-term trend interruptions and as such are regarded as continuation formations. The pennant typically forms as a small symmetrical triangle. The pennant is preceded by a pole which represents a short and rapid thrust in price, and is ideally accompanied by heavy volume. The volume should gradually subside as the pennant develops and increase on breakout. Once volume tests its historical lows, a potential breakout from the parallelogram may be imminent. The formation is complete once the symmetrical triangle is formed and no breakout is required for pattern completion. The minimum upside and downside price targets are simply

FIGURE 13.37 Bear Flag Formations on the Daily Chart of USDCAD.
Source: MetaTrader 4

FIGURE 13.38 A Bull Flag Formation on the 15-Min Chart of EURUSD.
Source: MetaTrader 4

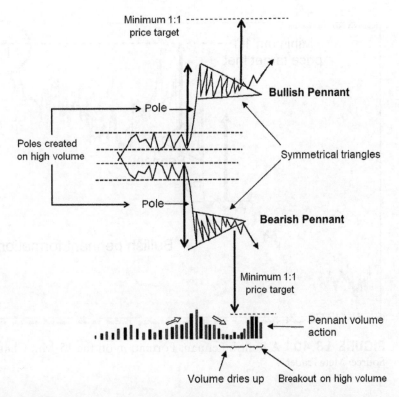

FIGURE 13.39 An Idealized Bullish and Bearish Pennant Formation.

one-to-one price projections based on the height of the pole, measured from the symmetrical triangle breakout level. It should be noted that minimum one-to-one price targets may also be obtained based on the symmetrical triangle itself. A two-to-one triangle-based price projection coinciding with a one-to-one pole-based price projection tends to result in the creation of a potentially strong price barrier. Entries may be initiated at the breakout of the small symmetrical triangles. See Figure 13.39.

In Figure 13.40, we see a pennant formation meeting its minimum one-to-one price target based on the height of the pole, measured from the breakout level, on the 15-min chart of the EURUSD. Notice how price retraces once the target is met. Again this can be attributed to profit taking at the anticipated price target level.

Rising and Falling Wedges

Wedges are price formations that slant either upward or downward. The main difference between wedges and triangles is that the two trendlines that circumscribe price within a wedge formation point in the same direction. A rising wedge is intrinsically bearish and a falling wedge is intrinsically bullish. Therefore, a rising wedge is regarded as a reversal formation in an uptrend and a continuation in a downtrend. In similar fashion, a falling wedge is regarded as a reversal formation in a downtrend and a continuation in an uptrend. The formation is complete once the two converging trendlines are established. No breakout is required for pattern completion. The volume should gradually subside as the wedge formation develops and increase on breakout. Once volume

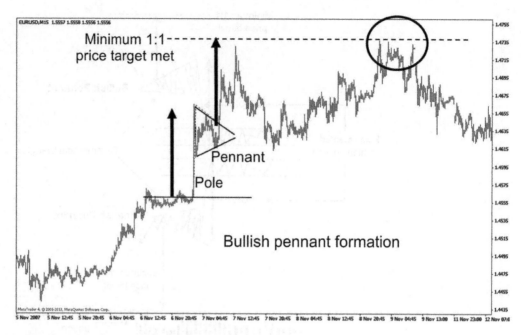

FIGURE 13.40 A Bullish Pennant Formation on the 15-Min Chart of EURUSD.
Source: MetaTrader 4

tests its historical lows, a potential breakout from the wedge formation may be imminent. The minimum upside and downside price targets are simply one-to-one price projections based on the greatest height within the wedge formation, measured from the breakout. Entries may be initiated at the breakout of the wedge formations. See Figures 13.41.

In Figures 13.42 and 13.43 we see rising wedge formations meeting their minimum one-to-one price targets. Notice how price retraces at these price target levels, indicative of profit taking. Figure 13.43 also depicts various other chart pattern formations meeting their minimum price targets.

Rounding Tops and Bottoms

Rounding tops are regarded as bearish reversal formations and rounding bottoms as bullish reversal formations. Volume should gradually subside toward the middle of the formation and should ideally start to increase thereafter, in anticipation of a breakout. This formation tends to develop over longer periods as compared to other chart patterns. *The determination of the exact point of completion is not always clear and obvious with rounding formations.* Many practitioners use a significantly clear and obvious inflection point at the inception of the formation as a guide to pattern completion. Once price retests the previous significantly clear and obvious peak in a rounding bottom formation, the pattern is complete. Similarly, once price retests the previous significantly clear and obvious trough in a rounding top formation, the pattern is complete. The minimum upside and downside price targets are simply one-to-one price projections based on the greatest height within the rounding formation, measured from the breakout of the previous significant peaks or troughs. See Figures 13.44.

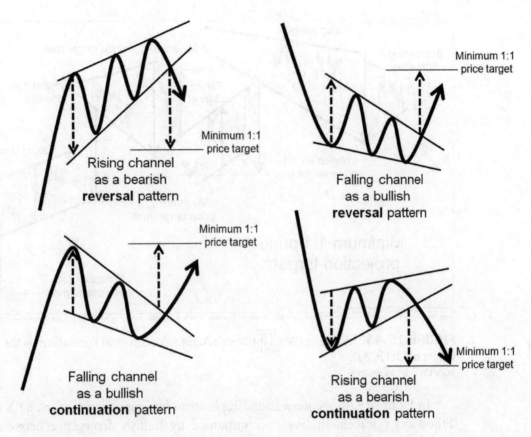

FIGURE 13.41 Rising and Falling Wedges as Reversal and Continuation Formations.

FIGURE 13.42 A Rising (Bearish) Wedge Formation Acting as a Reversal Formation on the 14-Hour Chart of EURUSD.
Source: MetaTrader 4

FIGURE 13.43 A Rising (Bearish) Wedge Acting as a Reversal Formation on the 4-Hour Chart of USDCAD.
Source: MetaTrader 4

In Figure 13.45 we see a rounding bottom finding support at the 61.8 percent Fibonacci retracement level, accompanied by bullish divergence between price and the MACD oscillator.

In Figure 13.46 we see a rounding top forming in the vicinity of a head and shoulders minimum one-to-one price target. This rounding top formation has no clear prior trough that may be used as a breakout level.

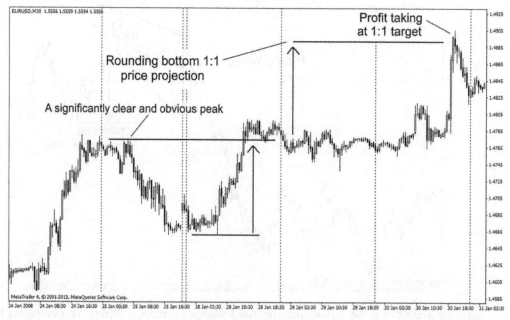

FIGURE 13.44 A Rounding Bottom Formation on the 30-Min Chart of EURUSD.
Source: MetaTrader 4

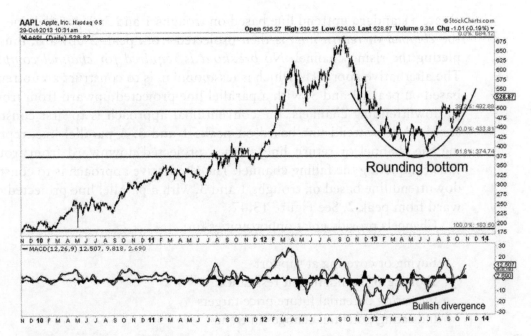

FIGURE 13.45 A Rounding Bottom Formation on the Daily Chart of Apple Inc.
Courtesy of Stockcharts.com

Horizontal, Rising, and Falling Channels

Channels are characterized by price being contained between two parallel lines, which may be flat, rising, or declining. It takes three inflection points to construct a channel. There are two basic ways of constructing a channel. In a rising channel, the conventional approach to constructing a channel is to first

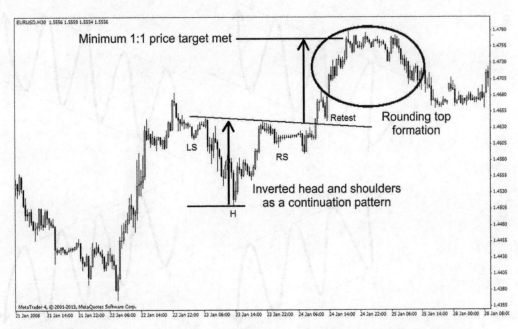

FIGURE 13.46 A Rounding Top Formation on the 30-Min Chart of EURUSD.
Source: MetaTrader 4

531

create a standard uptrend line based on troughs 1 and 3. A parallel line, called the *channel* or *return line*, is then projected from peak 2 upward, thus completing the rising channel. *No breakout is required for channel completion.* The alternative approach, which is less popular, is to construct an uptrend line based on peaks 1 and 3, with a parallel line projected upward from trough 2. In downtrending channels, the conventional approach is to first construct a standard downtrend line based on peaks 1 and 3. A parallel line, representing the channel or return line, is then projected downward from trough 2, thus completing the falling channel. The alternative approach is to construct a downtrend line based on troughs 1 and 3, with a parallel line projected downward from peak·2. See Figure 13.47.

Channels provide great opportunities for:

- Buying or covering at support
- Shorting or liquidating at resistance
- Indicating potential future price targets
- Indicating potential changes in trend

It should be noted that the *first tradable point* will be Point 4 in all cases, either by buying at Point 4 in a rising channel or selling at Point 4 in a falling channel with a stoploss placed just beyond the up- or downtrend lines, respectively. Should price violate the channel at Point 4, a breakout trade is initiated. It is important to also note that it is safer to establish:

- A short position in a downside breakout of a rising channel
- A long position in an upside breakout of a falling channel

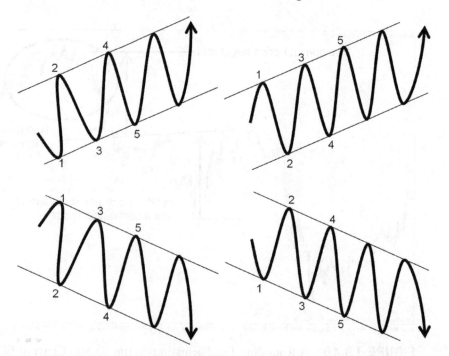

FIGURE 13.47 Constructing Channels.

- A long position at the standard uptrend line of support rather than at the return line in a rising channel
- A short position at the standard downtrend line of resistance rather than at the return line in a falling channel

Channels are also particularly useful in helping define an Elliott wave. *It is much easier to visualize an Elliott wave when it can be circumscribed by a channel.* It is also not unusual to find bearish chart patterns within a falling channel and bullish chart patterns with a rising channel. In Figure 13.55, we observe two bearish head and shoulders formations within a falling channel followed by a bullish broadening formation that led to an upside reversal, penetrating the downtrend line.

The minimum price excursion associated with channels will be the one-to-one price objective or target based in the height of the channel, projected from the breakout level, irrespective of where the breakout occurs.

Volume should gradually subside as the channel develops and increase on breakout. The longer it takes for a channel to unfold, the stronger and more persistent will be its subsequent breakout. Horizontal channels are useful because they provide numerous opportunities for buying low and selling high, as long as price remains within the channel. This is popularly referred to as *range trading*. It should be noted that once price fails to retest either the resistance or support within a horizontal channel, it should be taken as an indication of a potential breakout, in the direction opposite to the failed retest. See Figure 13.48.

In Figure 13.49, we see a rising channel meeting its minimum one-to-one price objective. Notice the profit-taking activity at that level, causing price to retrace. We notice that price fails to test the channel support just prior to breaking to the upside. This failure to retest tends to be an early indication of a bullish upside breakout. Similarly, the failure to retest a resistance level tends to be an early indication of a bearish downside breakout.

In Figure 13.50, we see a rising channel meeting its minimum downside one-to-one price target, on the four-hour chart of EURUSD. As before, we tend to see price reversing at the minimum target level.

In Figure 13.51, an uptrend line was drawn based on Points C and D, and a return line projected from Point A. Notice how price reacted to the return line

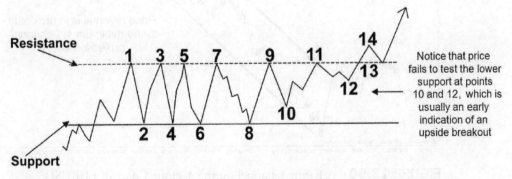

FIGURE 13.48   A Horizontal Channel Providing Range Trading Opportunities.

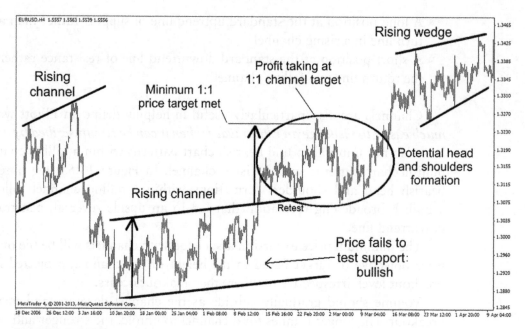

FIGURE 13.49 A Rising Channel on the 4-Hour Chart of EURUSD.
Source: MetaTrader 4

at Point B, with a sharp retracement. Another uptrend line was drawn based on Points D and F, and a return line projected from Point B. Again, notice how price reacted to the return line BE at Point B.

In Figure 13.52, price reacted at a rising channel's return line at Point X, which coincided with a 161.8 percent Fibonacci projection level. Notice that the cycle-tuned stochastic is also at overbought. These three conditions tend to produce a more reliable bearish reaction at Point X.

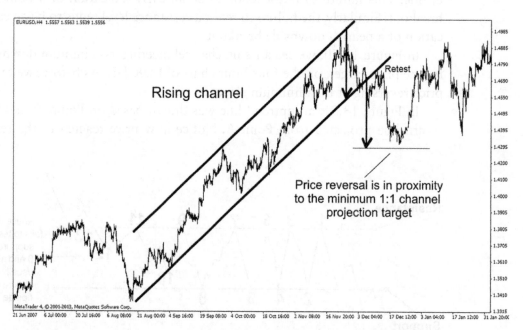

FIGURE 13.50 A Rising Channel on the 4-Hour Chart of EURUSD.
Source: MetaTrader 4

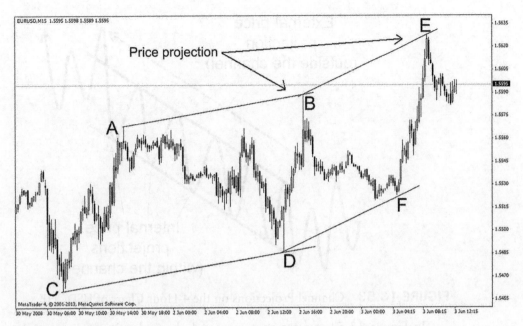

FIGURE 13.51 Channel Projections on the 15-Min Chart of EURUSD.
Source: MetaTrader 4

Channel projections may be determined internally and externally. Internal price projections occur within the original channel, whereas external projections occur outside the original channel, with the creation of a new larger channel parallel to the original channel with the return line projected from a higher peak that is located further back in time in a rising channel and from a lower trough that is located further back in time in a falling channel. Figure 13.53 depicts an external price projection in a rising channel.

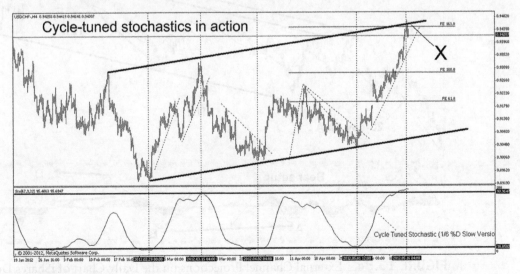

FIGURE 13.52 Channel Projections on the 4-Hour Chart of USDCHF.
Source: MetaTrader 4

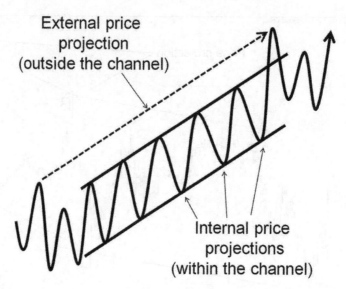

FIGURE 13.53 Channel Projections on the 4-Hour Chart of USDCHF.

In Figure 13.54, we see that a second channel price target may be obtained externally with respect to the first channel, by constructing a new parallel line to TL1 and projecting it from a higher peak located further back in time, which accurately identified a top at Point F on the daily chart of iShares Dow Jones Transportation Average Index.

In Figure 13.55, we observe numerous bearish chart formations within a falling channel, followed by a bullish broadening or megaphonic formation. Notice how the cycle troughs recur at consistent intervals. We also see a diamond formation starting to break out to the downside to the left-hand side on the chart.

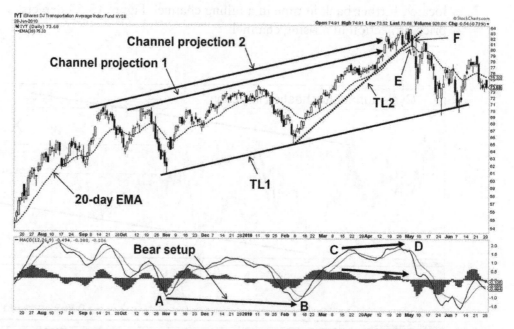

FIGURE 13.54 External Channel Projections on the Daily Chart of iShares Dow Jones Transportation Average Index Fund.
Courtesy of Stockcharts.com

536

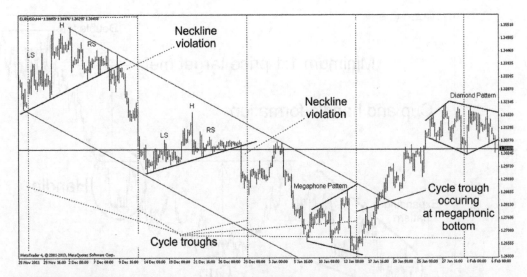

FIGURE 13.55 Downtrending Channel Action on the 4-Hour Chart of EURUSD.
Source: MetaTrader 4

In Figure 13.56, we see a horizontal channel (or rectangle formation) meeting its minimum one-to-one price target. Notice how price retraces after the target is met.

Cup and Handle Pattern

A cup and handle formation is simply a rounding bottom with a handle. Cup and handle formations are regarded as bullish reversal formations. Volume should gradually subside toward the middle of the formation and should ideally start to increase thereafter, in anticipation of a breakout. This formation tends to develop

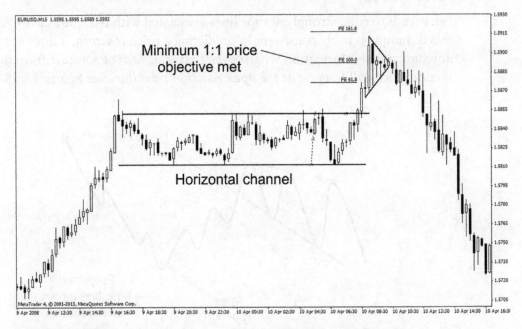

FIGURE 13.56 Channel Action on the 15-Min Chart of EURUSD.
Source: MetaTrader 4

FIGURE 13.57 Cup and Handle Formation on the 4-Hour Chart of EURUSD.
Source: MetaTrader 4

over longer periods as compared to other chart patterns. The minimum upside price target is simply a one-to-one price projection based on the greatest height within the cup and handle formation, measured from the breakout at the handle. See Figure 13.57.

Using Apex Reaction Analysis to Forecast Potential Price Activity

Price tends to react strongly at time lines associated with triangle apexes. Although this technique is fairly consistent in predicting a price reaction, it does not provide any directional information whatsoever, that is, *it cannot forecast from which direction price will traverse at the apex reaction time line*. See Figure 13.58.

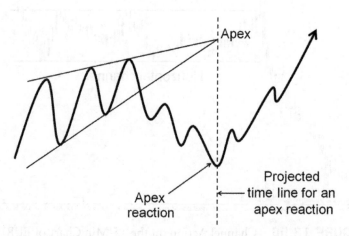

FIGURE 13.58 Projected Time line for an Apex Reaction.

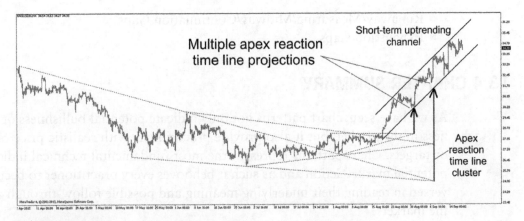

FIGURE 13.59 Apex Reactions on the 4-Hour Chart of Silver.
Source: MetaTrader 4

In Figure 13.59, we observe Silver reacting at the apex time lines. Notice a time line cluster occurring at the second apex reaction time line.

In Figure 13.60, we observe the U.S. Dollar index reversing at the apex reaction time line, which coincided with a test of the Bollinger upper band and 50 percent Fibonacci retracement level. This resistive confluence tends to create a strong barrier to price.

Price Gaps

Price gaps are also a critical part of chart pattern analysis as they usually represent potential support and resistance zones for future price tests. Please refer to Chapters 4 and 5 for more on price gaps. Here is a list of commonly found price gaps in the market:

- Common Gaps
- Breakaway Gaps

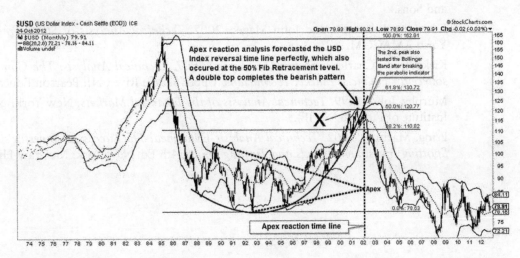

FIGURE 13.60 External Channel Projections on the Daily Chart of Cash Settled U.S. Dollar Index.
Courtesy of Stockcharts.com

- Runaway/Measuring/Midway/Continuation Gaps
- Exhaustion Gaps

13.4 CHAPTER SUMMARY

As we have seen, chart patterns not only indicate potential bullishness or bearishness in the market, but it also provide practitioners with realistic price objectives or targets. Chart patterns represent the most fundamental technical indicators of potential market action and as such it behooves every practitioner to become well versed in reading their underlying meaning and possible follow-through action in the markets.

CHAPTER 13 REVIEW QUESTIONS

1. Explain the behavioral basis for the existence of chart patterns.
2. How do we determine if a chart pattern is a reversal or continuation pattern?
3. List as many chart patterns that are intrinsically bullish as you can.
4. When does a chart pattern fail?
5. What is the difference between a rising wedge with a very shallow angle of ascent and an ascending triangle?
6. Describe the measuring objectives for a bullish flag.
7. List the preconditions for a more reliable chart pattern reversal.
8. Describe the five ways to determine chart pattern completion and list the chart patterns that are associated with each of those ways.

REFERENCES

Bulkowski, Thomas N. 2005. *Encyclopedia of Chart Patterns*. Hoboken, NJ: John Wiley and Sons.

Edwards, Robert D., and John Magee. 2007. *Technical Analysis of Stock Trends*. New York: AMACOM.

Kirkpatrick, Charles, and Julie Dahlquist. 2007. *Technical Analysis: The Complete Resource for Financial Market Technicians*. Upper Saddle River, NJ: Pearson Education.

Murphy, John. 1999. *Technical Analysis of the Financial Markets*. New York: New York Institute of Finance (NYIF).

Pring, Martin J. 2002. *Technical Analysis Explained: The Successful Investor's Guide to Spotting Investment Trends and Turning Points*. 4th Ed. New York: McGraw-Hill.

CHAPTER 14

Japanese Candlestick Analysis

Just as with bar charts, Japanese Candlestick charting represents the study of pure price action. It takes into account the price range, relative positions of its open, high, low, and close (OHLC) prices, the location of the price activity, and trend characteristics in order to effectively forecast potential breakouts and reversals in the market. In this chapter, we shall be covering various Japanese candlestick formations, their classifications, price action behavior, and their integration with other technical tools.

14.1 ELEMENTS OF CANDLESTICK ANALYSIS

Construction and Classification of Japanese Candlesticks Formations

Japanese candlesticks are constructed using OHLC data. They are identical to standard price bars except for the boxing up of the price range between the opening and closing prices. See Figure 14.1. We refer to the boxed up area as the real body. Unlike standard price bars, the existence of real bodies provides for better

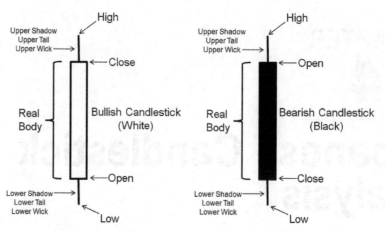

FIGURE 14.1 The Construction of Japanese Candlesticks.

visualization of price action on the charts, especially from a distance. Real bodies may be black or white, filled or hollow. The price ranges beyond the open and close prices are referred to as upper and lower tails, wicks, or shadows.

The Composite Candlestick

As with standard price bars, we can also create higher time-period or larger-interval candlesticks by combining the OHLC data from numerous lower time-period or smaller-interval candlestick action. See Figure 14.2.

There is a simple procedure for creating larger-interval candlesticks from a number of smaller- or shorter-interval candlesticks:

1. Use the opening price (O) of the first smaller-interval candlestick as the opening of the larger-interval composite candlestick.
2. Use the closing price (C) of the last smaller-interval candlestick as the closing price of the larger-interval composite candlestick.

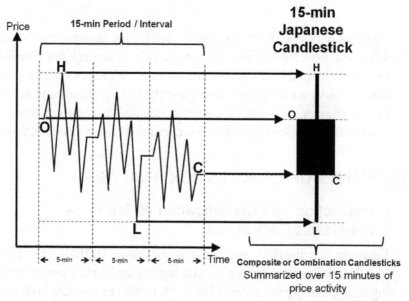

FIGURE 14.2 The Construction of Higher Time-Period Japanese Candlesticks.

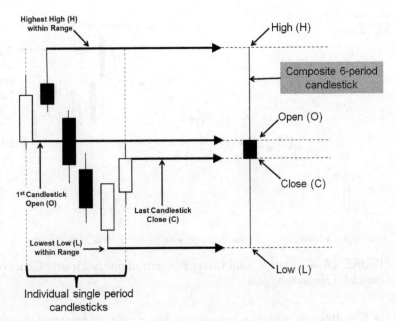

FIGURE 14.3 Creating Larger-Interval (Higher Time-Period) Japanese Candlesticks.

3. Use the highest-high (H) and lowest-low (L) price within the range of the smaller-interval candlesticks as the highest and lowest price of the larger-interval composite candlestick.

See Figure 14.3.

Multi-Timeframe Based Candlestick Confirmation

We may also look for additional evidence of bullishness and bearishness by accessing higher time-period candlesticks. There is a higher probability of a potential reversal occurring if the higher timeframe candlestick is in agreement with the bullish or bearish sentiment indicated on the lower timeframe candlestick formation. It is a form of multi-timeframe corroboration of candlestick sentiment. For example, Figure 14.4 shows a dark cloud cover formation on the hourly chart of Icahn Enterprises occurring on February 15, 2013. The probability of this bearish formation following through with the expected downside move increases if there is higher timeframe formation that supports this bearish sentiment. This is because larger or higher timeframe formations have greater influence on price action.

In Figure 14.5, we observe a similar daily dark cloud cover formation on February 15, providing additional bearish evidence for a probable downside move on the hourly chart.

Strengths and Weaknesses of Japanese Candlestick Charting

The strengths of candlestick charting include the following:

■ It allows for clearer visualization of price action.
■ Candlestick patterns are extremely popular and are heavily traded by market participants, thus making them more reliable via the effect of the self-fulfilling prophecy.

FIGURE 14.4 Dark Cloud Cover Formation on the Hourly Chart of Icahn Enterprises.
Courtesy of Stockcharts.com

- Candlestick patterns are easy to learn and understand.
- Candlestick patterns provide clear and objective entry and exit price levels.
- Candlestick charting may be combined with other technical studies for more effective forecasting of potential reversals and breakouts in the market.
- Candlestick charting is a form of constant-time charting and as such allows for the accurate plotting of trendlines, channels, and chart patterns (since the time axis is scaled in a linear fashion).

The weaknesses of candlestick charting include the following:

- Higher timeframe candlesticks do not provide information regarding the lower timeframe price activity which may be relevant for effective forecasting of more reliable breakouts on the higher timeframe candlesticks.
- It is impossible to tell whether the high or low was created first.

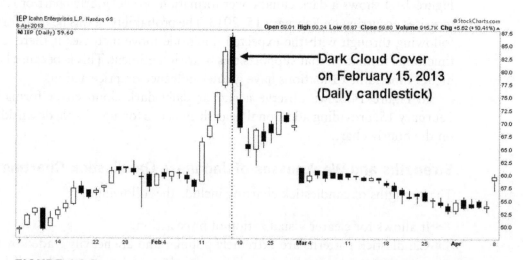

FIGURE 14.5 Dark Cloud Cover Formation on the Daily Chart of Icahn Enterprises.
Courtesy of Stockcharts.com

- There are hundreds of Japanese candlestick patterns making learning a challenge.
- The majority of Japanese candlestick patterns are reversal patterns and as such require the trader to establish a position against the direction of the existing trend.

Single, Double, Triple, and Multiple Candlestick Formations

Japanese candlestick patterns consist of single, double, triple, and multiple candlestick formations. Price confirmation is usually based on the price level of a preceding candlestick, rather than on the latest or current candlestick OHLC price.

Some Single Japanese candlestick patterns include:

- Hammer
- Inverted Hammer
- Hanging Man
- Spinning Top
- Shooting Star
- Marubozu

Some Double Japanese candlestick patterns include:

- Bullish and Bearish Harami
- Bullish and Bearish Harami Crosses
- Bullish and Bearish Engulfing Patterns
- *One White Soldier
- *One Black Crow
- Doji Stars
- Dark Cloud Cover
- Piercing Line
- Separating Line
- Kicking Line
- Meeting Line
- On-Neck and In-Neck Patterns
- Tweezers Tops and Bottoms

*There are many labels for the One White Soldier and One Black Crow. The labels used here were created by Gregory Morris, in his book *Candlestick Charting Explained*. Thomas Bulkowski uses the labels "Below the Stomach" and "Above the Stomach" in his book *Encyclopedia of Candlestick Charts*.

Some Triple Japanese candlestick patterns include:

- Three Black Crows
- Identical Three Crows
- Three White Soldiers
- Abandoned Baby
- Evening and Morning Stars

- Doji Stars
- Stick Sandwich
- Upside and Downside Tasuki Gaps
- Deliberation
- Advance Block
- Triple Star Patterns
- Two Crows

Multiple Japanese candlestick patterns include:

- Concealing Baby Swallow
- Ladder Top and Bottom
- Three Line Engulfing
- Triple Gap Up and Triple Gap Down
- Bullish and Bearish Breakaways

Reversal and Continuation Candlestick Patterns

Candlestick patterns may also be categorized as either reversal or continuation. Some reversal Japanese candlestick patterns include:

- Hammer
- Hanging Man
- Shooting Star
- Piercing Line
- Dark Cloud Cover
- Bullish and Bearish Harami
- Bullish and Bearish Harami Crosses
- Bullish and Bearish Engulfing Patterns
- Abandoned Baby
- Evening and Morning Stars
- Concealing Baby Swallow
- Ladder Top and Bottom
- Three Line Engulfing
- Triple Gap Up and Triple Gap Down
- Triple Star Patterns
- Three Black Crows
- Three White Soldiers
- Bullish and Bearish Breakaways

Some continuation Japanese candlestick patterns include:

- On-Neck and In-Neck Patterns
- Separating Lines
- Falling Three and Rising Three Method
- Upside and Downside Tasuki Gaps
- Thrusting Lines
- Mat Hold Pattern

Candlestick to Bar Chart Correspondence It should be noted that there is a fair amount of correspondence between bar chart patterns and candlestick patterns. But in some cases they do differ. For example, all outside days are essentially equivalent to candlestick engulfing patterns, but not all inside days are equivalent to Harami patterns. This is because there is no requirement that the first bar of an inside day pattern be less than one-quarter to one-third of the range of the second bar. In Harami patterns, the second small real-bodied candlestick must be at most one-quarter to one-third of the range of the first candlestick.

Price Action Guide for Analyzing Candlestick Action

Before we delve into the analysis of individual Japanese candlestick patterns and their underlying psychology, we need to first understand the behavioral characteristics of price and candlestick action from a broader perspective.

Here are some elements that influence pure price action and candlestick behavior:

1. Sentiment Bias Most individual candlesticks and candlestick patterns have *intrinsic sentiment bias*. Intrinsic sentiment bias is a condition or state of having an inherent bullish or bearish bias or sentiment, *with all other external or extrinsic factors excluded*. Many individual candlesticks and candlestick patterns are, in and of themselves, bullish or bearish. As a general rule, individual candlesticks or candlestick patterns that have no intrinsic sentiment bias, that is, they are neither bearish nor bullish, will fully adopt any sentiment derived from external factors such as location, overextension, relative proportionality, trend interruptions, including prior activity.

Nevertheless, the intrinsic sentiment is often overwhelmed by extrinsic sentiment, causing the formation's sentiment to be influenced by the extrinsic factors. This means that a bullish candlestick or formation may be regarded as less or more bullish and a bearish formation as less bearish or more bearish, depending on external factors such as location, overextension, relative proportionality, and prior activity. Extrinsic or external factors do not alter the intrinsic sentiment, but rather the *degree* of bullishness and bearishness inherent within the formation. *This means that not all similar candlestick formations will be equally bullish or bearish.*

An example will help crystallize this concept of sentiment adoption. Refer to Figure 14.6. The *rising three method* is a bullish pattern, that is, it is intrinsically bullish. It is obvious that the pattern is more bullish at the start of the uptrend where the bullish candlesticks have a much larger range. As the trend proceeds upward, the bullish candlesticks start to shrink in height, that is, their ranges start to decrease gradually as the prices rise. The bullish candlesticks associated with the last rising three pattern have by far the smallest candlestick ranges, which in itself is already an indication of decreasing bullishness. Although the last rising three pattern is still inherently bullish, the external sentiment is turning potentially bearish. We notice that not only are the candlestick ranges decreasing, but the entire trend is being constricted to move in a narrow and converging manner, forming what is referred to as a rising wedge, which is bearish. This potentially bearish scenario is further corroborated by bearish volume and absolute true range (ATR) divergence. Prices at the last rising three formation are also testing a prior resistance level in the market. Hence, it is easy to see why traders would be less

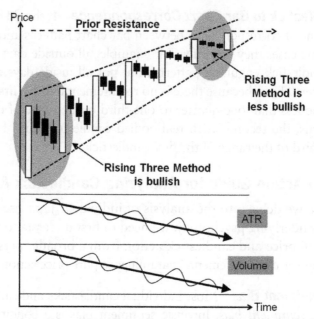

FIGURE 14.6 Intrinsic Sentiment Diminished by Extrinsic Factors.

confident in participating in the last rising three pattern breakout, even though it is essentially still a bullish pattern. It is now regarded as *less bullish*.

In our example above, the bullish candlestick formation was affected by external factors such as:

Location: The last rising three formation was located near prior resistance. This contributed to the reduction in the degree of bullishness.

Overextension: The combination of being in a state of divergence and being in proximity with a significant prior resistance level puts prices in an overbought state, which is potentially bearish.

Relative Proportionality: The gradual decrease in candlestick ranges relative to the preceding candlestick ranges is an indication of diminishing bullishness within the uptrend. This can clearly be seen from the falling ATR values.

Prior Activity: The last rising three formations were preceded by a weakening and tapering trend. Prices are not rising as fast and are in fact gradually slowing down.

Hence we see that external sentiment influences the degree of intrinsic bullishness and bearishness. Figure 14.7 shows the converse of the price action seen in the previous example. In this example, the external or extrinsic factors actually *augment the degree of bullishness* that is intrinsic in the rising three pattern. We say that the intrinsic and extrinsic sentiment is *in agreement*.

Hence, in short:

- If intrinsic and extrinsic sentiment bias are in agreement, the degree of bullishness or bearishness associated with the candlestick or pattern is *augmented*.
- If intrinsic and extrinsic sentiment bias are not in agreement, the degree of bullishness or bearishness associated with the candlestick or pattern is *diminished*.

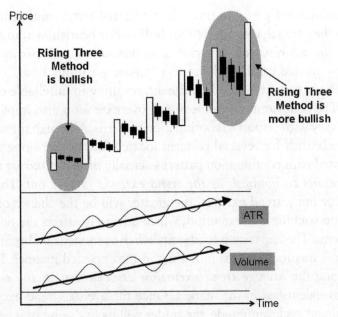

FIGURE 14.7 Intrinsic Sentiment Augmented by Extrinsic Factors.

2. Trend Sentiment If the candlestick or candlestick formation has intrinsic sentiment, then it logically follows that:

- If it is in agreement with the existing or predominant trend sentiment, it will generally be regarded as a *continuation* pattern.
- If it is not in agreement with the existing or predominant trend sentiment, it will generally be regarded as a *reversal* pattern.

Trend sentiment augments the reversal and continuation expectations associated with the candlesticks and candlestick patterns. *Trend sentiment represents the sentiment or expectation associated with a reversal or continuation pattern occurring within the context of a trend.* The further a reversal pattern occurs along in a trend, the greater the trend sentiment or expectation that it will potentially reverse. This is because trend sentiment is affected by the behavioral phenomenon of overextension in the markets. The more prolonged the trend, the greater the chance it will be overextended or approaching overextension and hence the greater will be the level of trend sentiment or expectation associated with it. Trend sentiment may be bullish, bearish, or neutral. With overextension, a bullish trend sentiment begins to become potentially more bearish, whereas a bearish trend sentiment begins to become potentially more bullish.

As a general guideline, the greater the trend sentiment, the stronger will be the potential reversal. This is why shooting stars, hammers, engulfing formations, dark cloud cover, and piercing lines represent stronger reversal patterns when located further along in the trend. Harami formations represent reversal patterns if there is sufficient bearish trend sentiment. Harami formations located within tight or narrow consolidations have very little associated trend sentiment and will not normally be regarded as reversal patterns. In fact, all candlesticks and candlestick patterns (including rising and falling windows, which represent common gaps within a consolidation) possess very little associated trend sentiment and this is the reason why they are regarded as neither bullish nor bearish, within the consolidation. *They also do not represent reversal or continuation patterns within the consolidation.* Many novice candlestick traders initiate positions based on candlestick patterns that have very little trend sentiment, resulting in unreliable entries.

The behavioral phenomenon of overextension also implies that trend sentiment will vary with respect to continuation patterns. Although the trend sentiment becomes more bearish for reversal patterns located further out along the trend, sentiment associated with continuation patterns actually *increases during the early part of a trend and starts to diminish as the trend extends further out.* This is again because the further out a trend extends, the greater will be the chance of it being overextended or approaching overextension, which adversely affects the reliability of continuation patterns. The real trick is to identify *when* overextension begins to erode the reliability of continuation patterns unfolding in the expected manner. This can be achieved by gauging the *average trend excursion associated with the amplitudes of dominant cycles* indentified in the market. Once the average trend excursion is found for the dominant cycle amplitude, the trader will have a sense of when contextual sentiment will start to wane, rendering the candlestick continuation pattern less reliable.

3. Size As a general rule, the larger the size of a candlestick or pattern, the more influence it will have on market action. A large candlestick like a Marubozu tends to have greater impact on price action as compared to a smaller candlestick. Large bullish candlesticks or patterns are more bullish than smaller ones and in similar fashion, large bearish candlesticks or patterns are more bearish than smaller ones. Larger formations tend to have greater impact and will *dominate the sentiment* of more diminutive formations. Figure 14.8 depicts a Marubozu in action.

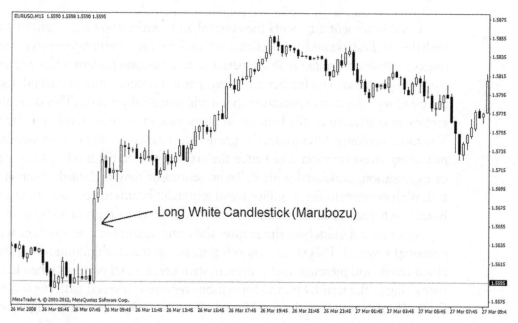

FIGURE 14.8 A Large Candlestick Impacting Subsequent the Market Action on the 15-min EURUSD Chart.
Source: MetaTrader 4

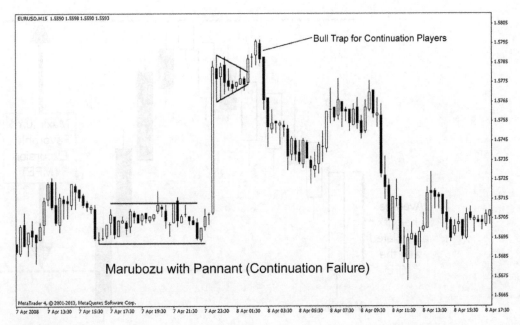

FIGURE 14.9 Marubozu Continuation Failure on the 15-min EURUSD Chart.
Source: MetaTrader 4

Unfortunately, a very large bar or candlestick does not always have the expected follow-through action, that is, long white Marubozus are not always bullish and long black Marubozus are not always bearish. See Figure 14.9.

One reason may be because the Marubozu candlestick is already *relatively overextended* with respect to other candlesticks and with other similar Marubozus of the same time period. One way to filter out overextended Marubozus is to do a backtest to gauge the *average height of a Marubozu* associated with the average maximum favorable excursion of all preceding Marubozus. Maximum favorable excursion, in this case, would simply be the maximum amount of price excursion beyond the high or low of a candlestick before price reverses back below or above the candlestick, depending whether it is a bullish or bearish Marubozu. Such data would give the trader a good idea of how overextended a Marubozu really is with respect to historical action. If a Marubozu extends beyond this average height, the trader should avoid initiating an entry. See Figure 14.10.

4. Color The color of the real body of a candlestick decreases in importance as the:

- Range of the candlestick decreases (Range = |H–L|)
- Range of the real body decreases (Real Body Range = |O–C|)

This is because smaller-sized candlesticks have a lesser impact on subsequent price action. This is why the color of the real bodies associated with spinning tops and bottoms, shooting stars, hammers, inverted hammers, and hangman patterns are of little significance.

But there are always a few exceptions to the rule! Harami and Tweezers Tops and Bottoms are some examples where the color of the larger candlesticks is

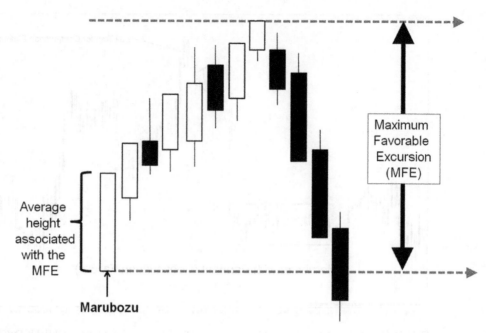

FIGURE 14.10 Example of Maximum Favorable Excursion.

irrelevant. A bullish or bearish Harami formation is also affected by contextual sentiment, augmenting or diminishing the reversal expectation of the pattern itself. Within the context of a trend, a Harami formation is regarded as more bearish if it is located further up along an uptrend and more bullish if it is located further down along a downtrend. The color of both the first large candlestick's real body and the second smaller-bodied candlestick is of lesser importance and may be black or white. This means that the first large candlestick of a Harami formation may well be bullish or bearish. See Figure 14.11.

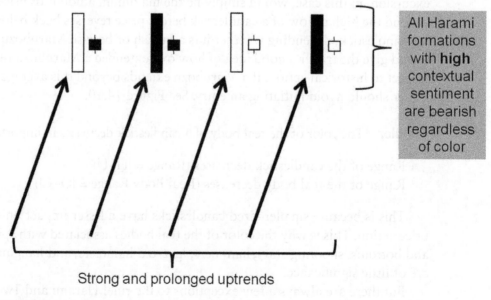

FIGURE 14.11 Color Independence in Harami Patterns.

Although the color of the first candlestick in a Harami formation is of lesser importance, it is not completely insignificant as we will see in a subsequent section on internal proportions.

5. Location   The location of the candlestick pattern is also critical to the success of its application. The best location to employ candlestick analysis will be at a price barrier. In short:

- Bearish reversal candlestick patterns work best *at or near* resistance.
- Bullish reversal candlestick patterns work best *at or near* support.
- Bearish continuation candlestick patterns work best *after* a top reversal.
- Bullish continuation candlestick patterns work best *after* a bottom reversal.

Candlestick patterns do not work well within tight or narrow price consolidations. For example, a Doji works well interrupting trends, but it is of little use within a narrow consolidation.

6. Trend Interruptions   Trend interruptions are always regarded as a sign of potential trend change. Some examples of candlestick patterns that represent trend interruptions include:

- The appearance of a Doji or small real-bodied candlestick
- The appearance of candlestick patterns that include a small real-bodied candlestick or Doji within its price range (not applicable to most candlestick patterns)
- The appearance of a large candlestick reversal formation

It is for this reason that the Harami's color is irrelevant. The inclusion of a Doji or small real-bodied candlestick within a pattern renders it a reversal pattern, which may be augmented or diminished by contextual sentiment.

7. Preceding Activity   Preceding price activity influences the extrinsic and contextual sentiment of subsequent candlestick patterns. Some examples of preceding activity that *diminishes* the bullishness and bearishness of candlestick patterns include:

- The slowing down of a trend (trend-rate deceasing)
- ATR values decreasing as the trend proceeds (meaning that the candlestick ranges are decreasing; smaller ranges indicate less bullish and bearish candlesticks)
- Prices are converging, tapering, or narrowing (e.g., rising and falling wedges).
- Rising candlesticks have successively lower closes.

8. Relative Proportions   The relative size of preceding candlesticks to that of later ones will affect the extrinsic and contextual sentiment of subsequent candlestick patterns. As already mentioned under preceding activity, a gradual reduction in the average candlestick range indicates:

- Increasing bearishness in an uptrend
- Increasing bullishness in a downtrend

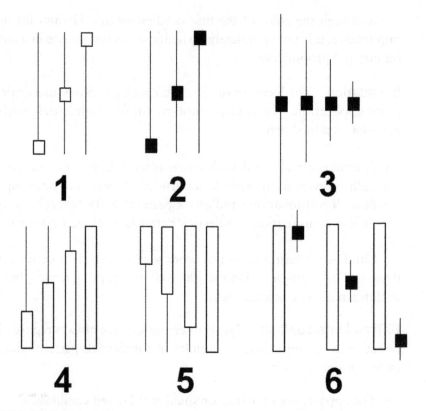

FIGURE 14.12 Internal Proportions.

9. Internal Proportions
Relative Position of Real Body and to Real Body Range to Candlestick Range
The position of the opening and closing price with respect to the high and low prices also plays a part in determining the sentiment, that is, the bullishness or bearishness of the candlestick pattern. Figure 14.12 displays a few examples of this interplay.

For example, Example 6 depicts a Harami pattern. By itself, without reference to the existing trend, it is impossible to determine if it is a bearish or bullish reversal pattern. Some practitioners would say that it should represent a bearish reversal pattern, but upon deeper reflection, it can also be fit well into a bullish reversal pattern. But what is the sentiment if we ignore location, preceding activity, and all other exogenous factors? In such cases, the only information or variable would be the position of the small real-bodied candlestick, or spinning top. Hence, in Example 6, the first Harami would be the most bullish of the three since the spinning top is situated at the top of the first candlestick range. Using the same logic, Example 2 would be bullish from the start, but the first candlestick would represent the least bullish of the three. In Example 4, the first candlestick on the left is the least bullish. With respect to Examples 1 and 2, there should be no difference between them in terms of sentiment. But with all things being equal, Example 2 would be fractionally more bearish than the patterns in Example 1. Finally, in Example 3, which candlestick would offer the most interruption to a trend? This would not be as straightforward or easy to answer. What we can say is that the first spinning top displays more market confusion as compared to the last spinning top with the smallest range. Hence the internal proportions of a candlestick or candlestick pattern play a role on determining the overall message of the markets.

14.2 POPULAR CANDLESTICK PATTERNS AND THEIR PSYCHOLOGY

Before we study individual candlestick patterns, we first need to turn our attention to the guidelines for:

1. Preferred Pre-Entry Conditions
   a) Quality of Trend: All bullish and bearish reversal candlestick formations require an uptrend to be in place. Bullish and bearish reversal candlestick formations occurring within narrow price consolidations are ignored. A parabolic uptrend on low volume would be ideal conditions for a bearish reversal candlestick formation, while a parabolic downtrend on low volume would be ideal conditions for a bullish reversal candlestick formation.
   b) Proximity to Price Barriers: Bullish and bearish reversal candlestick formations are more reliable if located near strong price barriers. It is preferred that bearish reversal candlestick formations be found near strong resistances and bullish reversal candlestick formations be found near strong support levels or zones. Barriers represent indicator overlays, such as:
   - Standard support and resistance levels
   - Fibonacci and Gann levels
   - Trendlines
   - Channels
   - Chart pattern boundaries
   - Moving averages
   - Envelopes and bands
   - Ichimoku clouds
   - Floor Trader's Pivot Point levels
   c) Divergent Pre-Conditions: It is preferred if bearish reversal candlestick formations are in a state of bearish divergence with their oscillators and indicators, while bullish reversal candlestick formations are in a state of bullish divergence with their oscillators and indicators. It is also best if both bullish and bearish reversal candlestick formations are also divergent with respect to volume and open interest.
   d) Overextended Conditions: It is also preferred if both bullish and bearish reversal candlestick formations are in a state of overextension, that is, in a state of overbought and oversold with respect to their oscillators and indicators.

2. Guidelines for Potential Trigger Levels and Stoplosses

Trading candlestick formations involves four important pieces of information:

1. The trigger level
2. The stoploss level
3. The OHLC prices of the preceding candlestick
4. Price confirmation via the closing price

Below are some general guidelines for determining the most appropriate trigger level based on variations in height of the preceding and reversal candlestick. These levels do not refer to any specific pattern or formation, but are intended to provide a logical basis for the decision-making process. It is sometimes necessary to select alternate trigger levels due to variations within the pattern that render the original or standard entry inappropriate. Here are some general guidelines for single candlestick trigger levels.

For most double and triple candlestick patterns, the trigger or entry level will usually be based on the *first candlestick of the formation*. For single candlestick reversals, the trigger or entry level will be based on the *preceding candlestick*. Here are the various trigger level options:

- Either midway or at the low of the first or preceding candlestick in a bearish reversal
- Either midway or at the high of the first or preceding candlestick in a bullish reversal
- At the low of the reversal candlestick itself in a bearish reversal
- At the high of the reversal candlestick itself in a bullish reversal
- At the lowest low of the entire formation in a bearish reversal
- At the highest high of the entire formation in a bullish reversal

An entry is usually only initiated once price closes beyond the trigger level. This is referred to as *price confirmation*. The candlestick that penetrates the trigger level may or may not belong to the reversal or continuation pattern.

Figures 14.13 and 14.14 show the four possible reversal scenarios for initiating a sell position. In scenarios 1 and 2, should the preceding candlestick be of relatively average size, the sell trigger may be either at the midpoint or low of the preceding candlestick. Should the preceding candlestick be relatively long or overextended, as depicted in scenario 3, the sell trigger should ideally be at the low of the last candlestick. This helps the Japanese candlestick trader to avoid getting in at a less advantageous price. Scenario 4 depicts the sell trigger at the low of a group of relatively short candlesticks, which is preceded by a long candlestick.

For highly complex patterns, or situations where the exact entry level is visually indistinct or not obvious to the trader, the trigger level may be based on significant inflection points in proximity to the complex pattern. This is rarely used in Japanese candlestick, but nevertheless provides an alternative for challenging entries. See Figure 14.15.

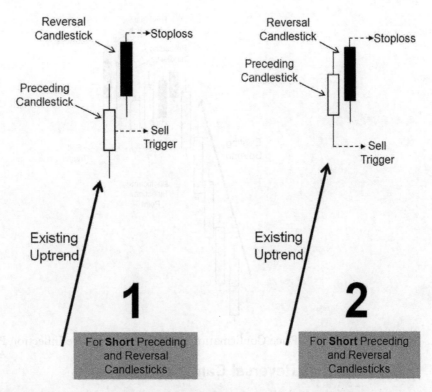

FIGURE 14.13 Price Confirmation for Short Preceding Candlesticks.

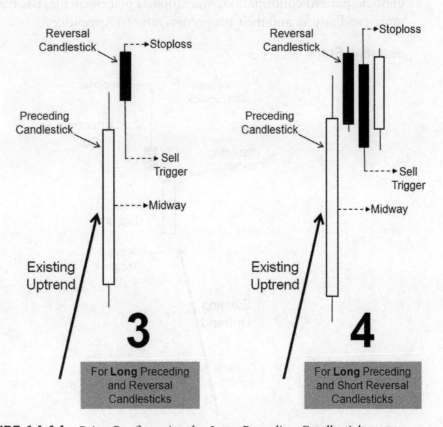

FIGURE 14.14 Price Confirmation for Long Preceding Candlesticks.

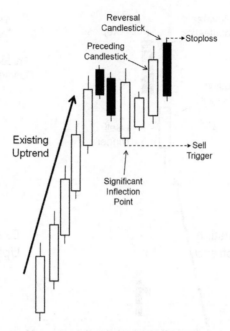

FIGURE 14.15   Price Confirmation via a Significant Price Inflection Point.

Some Bearish Reversal Candlestick Patterns

In this section we shall examine a few popular bearish reversal candlestick patterns. We shall be looking at their construction, potential trigger levels, penetration candlestick, pattern confirmation, and stoploss placements levels. For a summary of more candlesticks and their properties, refer to Appendix A.

Shooting Stars

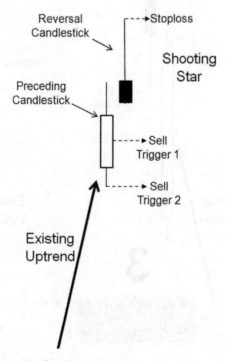

FIGURE 14.16   A Shooting Star Formation.

Desciption:

- The shooting star is a single candlestick reversal pattern. See Figure 14.16.
- It has a small real body that should be no larger than one-quarter to one-third of the entire candlestick range.
- Longer upper shadows indicate greater bearishness.
- It is best found in a protracted uptrend that is beginning to display weakness.
- The color of the real body is insignificant.
- There should not be any lower shadow, though a very short one is acceptable.
- Its corresponding bullish version is the inverted hammer.

Psychology:

- The shooting star depicts buyers struggling to drive prices higher but they are finally overwhelmed by the sellers, who drive prices back down near the low of the candlestick. The bears are potentially in control.

Trigger, Stoploss, and Confirmation:

- If the preceding candlestick is of average height, the trigger would be midway of the preceding candlestick (this is the standard shooting star entry).
- If the preceding candlestick low is close to midway, the trigger would be the low of the preceding candlestick.
- To confirm the reversal, price needs to close below the trigger level.
- The stoploss is placed at the high of the reversal candlestick.
- A buystop entry order may be placed at the high of the reversal candlestick only if there is evidence that the trend is still in effect.

See Figure 14.17. We observe an upper shadow of a shooting star extending beyond the upper channel line on the hourly EURUSD chart. This extension above the channel line represents a state of exhaustion that saw prices decline rapidly.

FIGURE 14.17 An Overextended Shooting Star on the Hourly EURUSD Chart.
Source: MetaTrader 4

Dark Cloud Cover

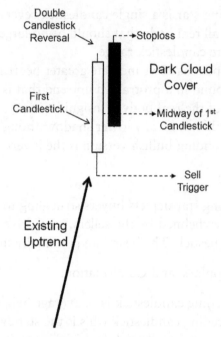

FIGURE 14.18 A Dark Cloud Cover Formation.

Description:

- The dark cloud cover is a double candlestick reversal pattern. See Figure 14.18.
- The second bearish candlestick gaps up above the high of the first candlestick and subsequently reverses back down to at least midway or more of the first candlestick.
- A longer second bearish candlestick is indicative of greater bearishness.
- It is best found in a protracted uptrend that is beginning to display weakness.
- Its corresponding bullish version is the piercing line.

Psychology:

- The dark cloud cover depicts buyers driving prices higher aggressively. Prices eventually gap up, indicating that the buyers may have the upper hand. The sellers subsequently resume control and drive prices back down to below the midpoint of the first candlestick. This essentially puts the bears in control.

Trigger, Stoploss, and Confirmation:

- The trigger is at the low of the first candlestick.
- To confirm the reversal, price needs to close below the trigger level.
- The stoploss is placed at the high of the second candlestick.
- A buystop entry order may be placed at the high of the second candlestick only if there is evidence that the trend is still in effect.

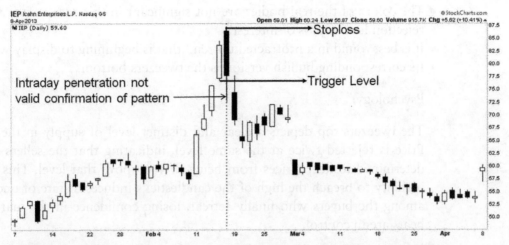

FIGURE 14.19 Dark Could Cover on the Daily Chart of Icahn Enterprises.
Source: MetaTrader 4

See Figure 14.19. The intraday penetration of the trigger level is not considered a valid confirmation of the reversal pattern.

Tweezers Top

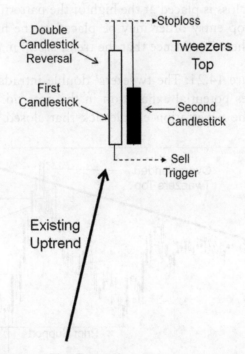

FIGURE 14.20 A Tweezers Top Formation.

Description:

- The tweezers top is a double candlestick reversal pattern. See Figure 14.20.
- Both candlesticks share the same high (it is this double test of the same high that is the most important characteristic of this pattern).
- Longer upper shadows or real bodies are indicative of greater bearishness.

- The colors of the real bodies are not significant in this case as it is the price rejection level that is of interest.
- It is best found in a protracted uptrend that is beginning to display weakness.
- Its corresponding bullish version is the tweezers bottom.

Psychology:

- The tweezers top depicts a clear and distinct level of supply in the market. Price is rejected twice at the same level, indicating that the sellers are very determined to keep prices from being driven above that level. This obvious inability to breach the high of the candlesticks induces a state of uncertainty among the buyers who finally retreat, losing confidence in the market. The bears are in control.

Trigger, Stoploss, and Confirmation:

- The trigger is at the low of the pattern.
- To confirm the reversal, price needs to close below the trigger level.
- If both candlesticks share the same low, then refer to the midway or low of the candlestick that precedes the double candlestick pattern as a possible level for a trigger.
- The stoploss is placed at the high of the pattern.
- A buystop entry order may be placed at the high of the second candlestick only if there is evidence that the trend is still in effect.

See Figure 14.21. The tweezers' double intraday penetration of the uptrend line indicates potential exhaustion in the uptrend. The pattern was finally confirmed by the penetration candlestick that closed below the trigger level. Price

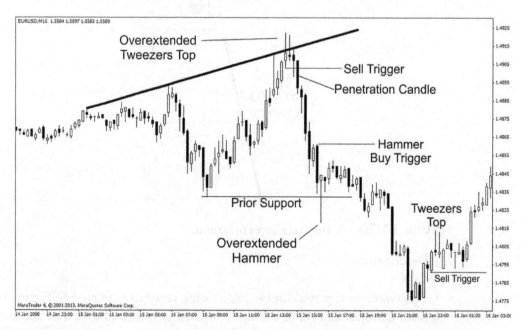

FIGURE 14.21 An Overextended Tweezers Top on the 15-min Chart of EURUSD.
Source: MetaTrader 4

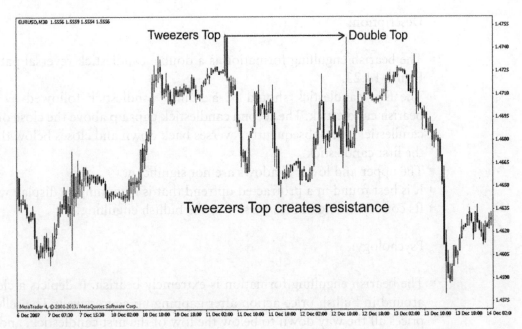

FIGURE 14.22 Tweezers and Double Top on the 30-Min Chart of EURUSD.
Source: MetaTrader 4

subsequently declined rapidly. Notice too, at the bottom right-hand side of the chart that another tweezers top pattern was formed, but it is not located at the end of an uptrend, and hence unreliable. It was not confirmed by price. The over-extended hammer was also not confirmed by price, but would have if the trigger was set to the midpoint of the preceding candlestick.

Figure 14.22 shows a tweezers top being subsequently retested, creating a double top in the process.

Bearish Engulfing

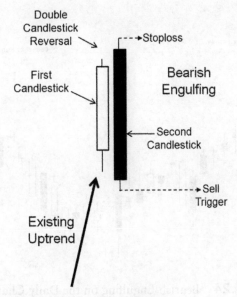

FIGURE 14.23 A Bearish Engulfing Formation.

Description:

- The bearish engulfing formation is a double candlestick reversal pattern. See Figure 14.23.
- The first candlestick should be a bullish candlestick followed by a larger bearish candlestick. The second candlestick gaps up above the close of the first candlestick and subsequently reverses back down and closes below the low of the first candlestick.
- The upper and lower shadows are not significant.
- It is best found in a protracted uptrend that is beginning to display weakness.
- Its corresponding bullish version is the bullish engulfing.

Psychology:

- The bearish engulfing formation is extremely bearish. It depicts a clear turn-around in bullish price action after gapping up aggressively. The sellers drive prices all the way down to below the low of the first candlestick, and make it very clear that the bears are now in control.

Trigger, Stoploss, and Confirmation:

- The trigger is at the low of the second candlestick.
- To confirm the reversal, price needs to close below the trigger level.
- The stoploss is placed at the high of the second candlestick or pattern.
- A buystop entry order may be placed at the high of the second candlestick only if there is evidence that the trend is still in effect.

See Figure 14.24.

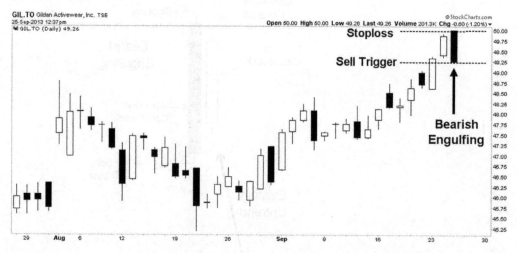

FIGURE 14.24 Bearish Engulfing on the Daily Chart of Gildan Activewear Inc.
Courtesy of Stockcharts.com

Evening Star

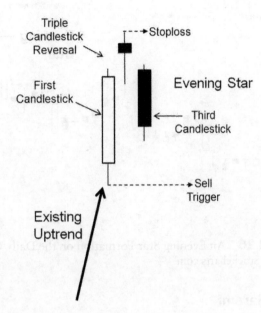

FIGURE 14.25   An Evening Star Formation.

Description:

- The evening star formation is a triple candlestick reversal pattern. See Figure 14.25.
- The first candlestick should be a strong bullish candlestick followed by a small-bodied candlestick like a spinning top gapping up above the first candlestick. The third candlestick gaps down below the second candlestick and is bearish.
- The upper and lower shadows are not significant.
- It is best found in a protracted uptrend that is beginning to display weakness.
- Its corresponding bullish version is the morning star formation.

Psychology:

- The evening star formation begins as a bullish candlestick where buyers aggressively drive the price up. The price gaps up but halts, indicating that the sellers are now putting a cap on prices. The buyers begin to lose confidence and start to retreat. The sellers subsequently drive prices down, showing that the bears are now in control.

Trigger, Stoploss, and Confirmation:

- The trigger is at the low of the first candlestick.
- To confirm the reversal, price needs to close below the trigger level.
- The stoploss is placed at the high of the second candlestick or pattern.
- A buystop entry order may be placed at the high of the second candlestick only if there is evidence that the trend is still in effect.

See Figure 14.26.

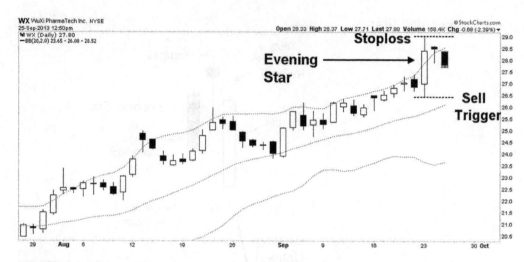

FIGURE 14.26   An Evening Star Formation on the Daily Chart of WuXi Pharma Tech Inc. Courtesy of Stockcharts.com

Bearish Harami

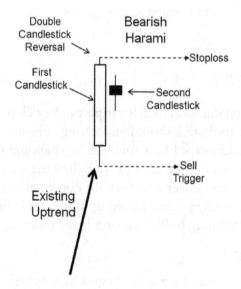

FIGURE 14.27   A Bearish Harami Formation.

Description:

- The bearish Harami formation is a double candlestick reversal pattern. See Figure 14.27.
- The first candlestick may be either a strong bullish or bearish candlestick followed by a small-bodied candlestick like a spinning top gapping into the range

FIGURE 14.28   Bearish Harami on the Daily Chart of Illinois Toll Works Inc.
Courtesy of Stockcharts.com

of the first candlestick. The second small-bodied candlestick can be of any color as well.

- The upper and lower shadows are not significant.
- It is best found in a protracted uptrend that is beginning to display weakness.
- Its corresponding bullish version is the bullish Harami formation.

Psychology:

- The bearish Harami formation begins as either a bullish or bearish candlestick. The price suddenly gaps into the range of the first candlestick and halts, indicating that the sellers are now at play in the existing uptrend. Eventually the sellers take over by driving price down below the low of the first candlestick, showing that the bears are now in control.

Trigger, Stoploss, and Confirmation:

- The trigger is at the low of the first candlestick.
- To confirm the reversal, price needs to close below this trigger level.
- The stoploss is placed at the high of the first candlestick or pattern.
- A buystop entry order may be placed at the high of the candlestick pattern only if there is evidence that the uptrend is still in effect.

See Figure 14.28.

Three Black Crows

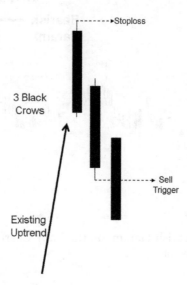

FIGURE 14.29 A Three Black Crow Formation.

Description:

- The three black crows formation is a triple candlestick reversal pattern. See Figure 14.29.
- All three candlesticks are bearish and their real bodies should overlap (otherwise it would be called three identical crows). The three real bodies should close with successively lower lows.
- The upper and lower shadows are not significant.
- The color of the three candlesticks is highly significant.
- It is best found in a protracted uptrend that is beginning to display weakness.
- Its corresponding bullish version is the three white soldiers formation.

Psychology:

- The three black crows formation is found at the top of a bullish trend where the buyers were initially in control. Then the sellers begin to drive the prices down with the appearance of the first strong bearish candle. The buyers try to resume control, evidenced by the upside opening gap in the second candlestick. But the sellers drive prices down further. The process is repeated one last time before the buyers retreat, relinquishing whatever control they had left in the market. The bears are now in control.

Trigger, Stoploss, and Confirmation:

- The trigger is at the low of the second bearish candlestick.
- To confirm the reversal, the third candlestick needs to close below this trigger level.
- The stoploss is placed at the high of the first bearish candlestick or pattern.
- A buystop entry order may be placed at the high of the candlestick pattern only if there is evidence that the trend is still in effect.

Some Bullish Reversal Candlestick Patterns

In this section we shall examine a few popular bullish reversal candlestick patterns. We shall be looking at their construction, potential trigger levels, penetration candlestick, pattern confirmation, and stoploss placements levels. For a summary of more candlesticks and their properties, refer to Appendix A.

Bullish Harami

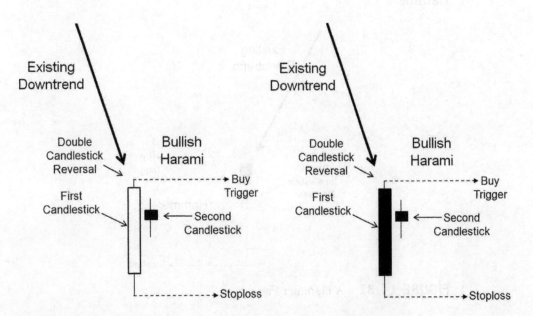

FIGURE 14.30 Color Independence of Bullish Harami Formations.

Description:

- The bullish Harami formation is a double candlestick reversal pattern. See Figure 14.30.
- The first candlestick may be either a strong bullish or bearish candlestick, followed by a small-bodied candlestick like a spinning top gapping into the range of the first candlestick. The second small-bodied candlestick can be of any color as well.
- The upper and lower shadows are not significant.
- It is best found in a protracted downtrend that is beginning to display weakness.
- Its corresponding bearish version is the bearish Harami formation.

Psychology:

- The bullish Harami formation begins as either a bullish or bearish candlestick. The price suddenly gaps into the range of the first candlestick and halts, indicating that the buyers are now at play in the existing downtrend. Eventually the buyers take over by driving price up above the high of the first candlestick, showing that the bulls are now in control.

Trigger, Stoploss, and Confirmation:

- The trigger is at the high of the first candlestick.
- To confirm the reversal, price needs to close above this trigger level.
- The stoploss is placed at the low of the first candlestick or pattern.
- A sellstop entry order may be placed at the low of the candlestick pattern only if there is evidence that the downtrend is still in effect.

Hammer

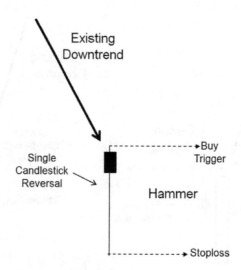

FIGURE 14.31   A Hammer Pattern.

Description:

- The Hammer is a single candlestick pattern. See Figure 14.31.
- The Hammer is a small-bodied candlestick with a long lower shadow. The real body should not be larger than 1/4th to 1/3rd of the range of the Hammer formation.
- The lower shadow should be long and extended compared to the real body.
- It is best found in a protracted downtrend that is beginning to display weakness.
- Its corresponding bearish version is the shooting star formation.

Psychology:

- Initially, the sellers or bears attempt to drive price lower in Hammer formation. The buyers finally drive prices up aggressively, above the midpoint of the candlestick, showing that the bulls are now in control.

Trigger, Stoploss, and Confirmation:

- The trigger is at the high of the Hammer itself.
- To confirm the reversal, price needs to close above the trigger level.
- The stoploss is placed at the low of the first candlestick or pattern.

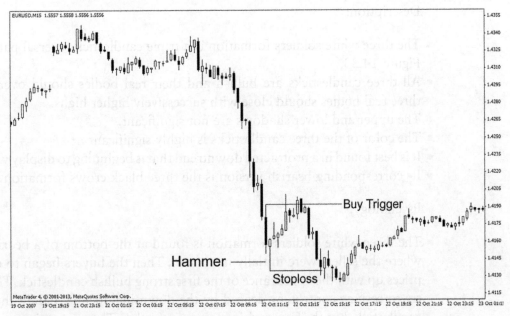

FIGURE 14.32 A Failed Hammer Pattern on the 15-Min Chart of EURUSD.
Source: MetaTrader 4

■ A sellstop entry order may be placed at the low of the candlestick only if there is evidence that the downtrend is still in effect.

See Figure 14.32. This is an example of a Hammer that was confirmed using the high of the preceding candlestick. It was eventually confirmed but prices subsequently reversed and the stoploss was taken out for a loss.

Three White Soldiers

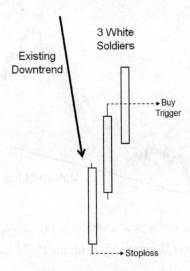

FIGURE 14.33 A Three White Soldiers Formation.

Description:

- The three white soldiers formation is a triple candlestick reversal pattern. See Figure 14.33.
- All three candlesticks are bullish and their real bodies should overlap. The three real bodies should close with successively higher highs.
- The upper and lower shadows are not significant.
- The color of the three candlesticks is highly significant.
- It is best found in a protracted downtrend that is beginning to display weakness.
- Its corresponding bearish version is the three black crows formation.

Psychology:

- The three white soldiers formation is found at the bottom of a bearish trend where the sellers were initially in control. Then the buyers began to drive the prices up with the appearance of the first strong bullish candlestick. The sellers try to resume control, evidenced by the downside opening gap in the second candlestick. But the buyers drive prices up further. The process is repeated one last time before the sellers retreat by relinquishing whatever control they had left in the market. The bulls are now in control.

Trigger, Stoploss, and Confirmation:

- The trigger is at the high of the second bullish candlestick.
- To confirm the reversal, the third candlestick needs to close above this trigger level.
- The stoploss is placed at the low of the first bullish candlestick or pattern.
- A sellstop entry order may be placed at the low of the candlestick pattern only if there is evidence that the downtrend is still in effect.

See Figure 14.34. The three white soldiers rebounded on the uptrend line and lower Bollinger Band.

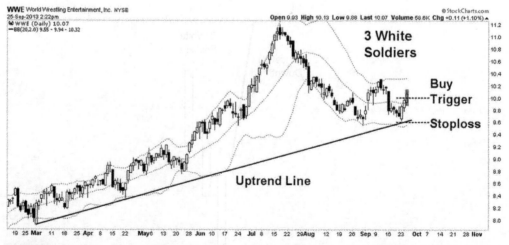

FIGURE 14.34 Three White Soldiers on the Daily Chart of World Wrestling Entertainment Inc.

Courtesy of Stockcharts.com

Bullish Engulfing

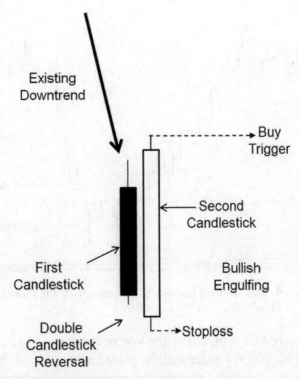

FIGURE 14.35 A Bullish Engulfing Formation.

Description:

- The bullish engulfing formation is a double candlestick reversal pattern. See Figure 14.35.
- The first candlestick should be a bearish candlestick followed by a larger bullish candlestick. The second candlestick gaps down below the close of the first candlestick and subsequently reverses back up and closes above the high of the first candlestick.
- The upper and lower shadows are not significant.
- It is best found in a protracted downtrend that is beginning to display weakness.
- Its corresponding bearish version is the bearish engulfing.

Psychology:

- The bullish engulfing formation is extremely bullish. It depicts a clear turnaround in bearish price action after gapping down aggressively. The buyers drive prices all the way up to above the high of the first candlestick, making it very clear who is in control.

Trigger, Stoploss, and Confirmation:

- The trigger is at the high of the second candlestick.
- To confirm the reversal, price needs to close above this trigger level.

FIGURE 14.36 Bullish Engulfing Formation on the Hourly Chart of EURUSD.
Source: MetaTrader 4

- The stoploss is placed at the low of the second candlestick or pattern.
- A sellstop entry order may be placed at the low of the second candlestick only if there is evidence that the downtrend is still in effect.

See Figure 14.36.

Piercing Line

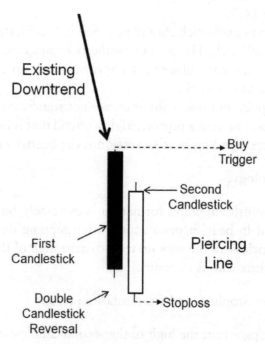

FIGURE 14.37 A Piercing Line Pattern.

Description:

- The piercing line is a double candlestick reversal pattern. See Figure 14.37.
- The second bullish candlestick gaps down below the low of the first bearish candlestick and subsequently reverses back up to at least the midpoint or more of the first candlestick.
- A longer second bullish candlestick is indicative of greater bullishness.
- It is best found in a protracted downtrend that is beginning to display weakness.
- Its corresponding bearish version is the dark cloud cover.

Psychology:

- The piercing line depicts sellers driving prices lower aggressively. Prices eventually gap down, indicating that the seller may have the upper hand. The buyers subsequently resume control and drive prices back up to above the midpoint of the first candlestick. This essentially puts the bulls back in control.

Trigger, Stoploss, and Confirmation:

- The trigger is at the high of the first candlestick.
- To confirm the reversal, price needs to close above this trigger level.
- The stoploss is placed at the low of the second candlestick.
- A sellstop entry order may be placed at the low of the second candlestick only if there is evidence that the downtrend is still in effect.

Some Candlestick Continuation Patterns

In this section we shall examine a couple of popular continuation candlestick patterns. We will be looking at their construction, potential trigger levels, penetration candlestick, pattern confirmation, and stoploss placement levels. For a summary of more candlesticks and their properties, refer to Appendix A.

Rising Three Method

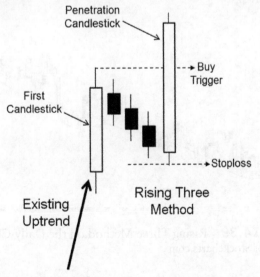

FIGURE 14.38 A Rising Three Method Continuation Formation.

Description:

- The rising three method is a multiple candlestick continuation pattern. See Figure 14.38.
- The second bullish candlestick gaps down below the low of the first bearish candlestick and subsequently reverses back up to at least midway or more of the first candlestick.
- The longer the first and last candlesticks, the more bullish will be the formation.
- It is best found in an uptrend that is beginning to display strength.

Psychology:

- The rising three method depicts bulls driving prices higher aggressively. Price subsequently declines as the bears try to take control. The buyers eventually resume control and drive prices back up to above the high of the first candlestick. This clearly puts the bulls back in control.

Trigger, Stoploss, and Confirmation:

- The trigger is at the high of the first candlestick.
- To confirm the continuation, price needs to close above this trigger level.
- The stoploss is placed at the low of the formation or last penetration candlestick.

See Figure 14.39.

FIGURE 14.39 Rising Three Method on the Daily Chart of SunOpta Inc.
Courtesy of Stockcharts.com

Upside Tasuki Gap

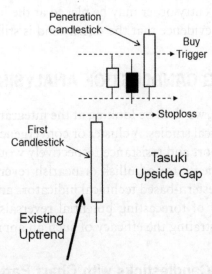

FIGURE 14.40   A Tasuki Upside Gap Formation.

Description:

- The upside Tasuki gap is a multiple candlestick continuation pattern. See Figure 14.40.
- The first candlestick should be a strong bullish candlestick. A second small real-bodied candlestick gaps up and opens above the first candlestick. This is followed by a third small real-bodied bearish candlestick opening within the second candlestick and closing below the second candlestick, but above the first candlestick.
- The upper and lower shadows are not significant.
- It is best found in an uptrend that is beginning to display strength.
- Its corresponding bearish version is the downside Tasuki gap.

Psychology:

- The upside Tasuki gap is a bullish formation. The buyers, who are in control, drive prices up in an existing uptrend, with a long white candlestick appearing. Buyers drive prices up aggressively as evidenced by a second small real-bodied candlestick gapping above the first candlestick. The sellers try to take control, but are unable to drive prices down to the top of the first candlestick. The buyers finally resume control by driving prices above the highest high of the two small real-bodied candlestick formations. The bulls are now in control.

Trigger, Stoploss, and Confirmation:

- The trigger is at the high of the second candlestick.
- To confirm the reversal, price needs to close above this trigger level.

- The stoploss is placed at the low of the second candlestick or pattern.
- A sellstop entry order may be placed at the low of the second candlestick only if there is evidence that the downtrend is still in effect.

14.3 INTEGRATING CANDLESTICK ANALYSIS

In this section, we shall be looking at the integration of Japanese candlesticks with various technical studies. A cluster or convergence of bullish or bearish indications found at support and resistance respectively would be ideal and would add to the weight of evidence for a bullish or bearish reversal. Combining Japanese candlesticks with Western-based technical indicators and oscillators is an extremely very powerful way of forecasting potential reversals in the market. Below are some examples illustrating the efficacy of such an approach.

Integrating Candlesticks with Chart Patterns

In Figure 14.41 we see candlesticks reacting at various chart pattern boundaries. Points X and Y represent potentially good entries. Notice also how the Hammer at Point Y tests the intersecting trendlines, while the small real body remains within the Bollinger Bands. Notice also the Marubozu candlestick driven by excessive volume.

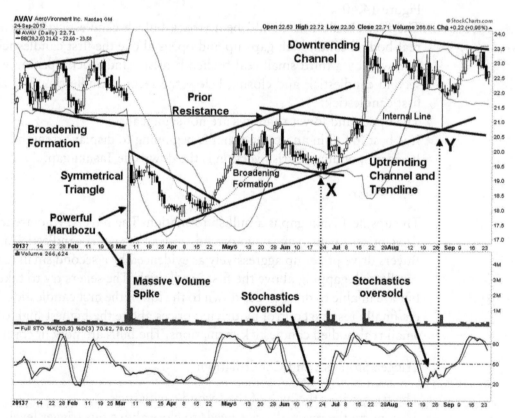

FIGURE 14.41 Integrating Candlesticks with Chart Patterns on the Daily Chart of AeroVironment Inc.
Courtesy of Stockcharts.com

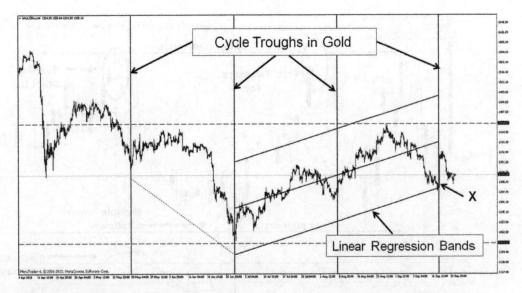

FIGURE 14.42 Identifying the Dominant Cycle on the 4-Hour Chart of Gold.
Source: MetaTrader 4

Integrating Candlesticks with Cycle Analysis

In Figure 14.42 we observe consistent cycle troughs on the daily chart in Gold. The last cycle trough rebounded strongly off a linear regression lower band.

Refer to Figure 14.43 for a close up on the Marubozu reaction of the linear regression lower band at Point X on the 4-hour charts. Again, a convergence of bullish indications will normally result in more reliable forecasting of potential reaction levels in the market. This dominant cycle in Gold represents significant information of its future behavior.

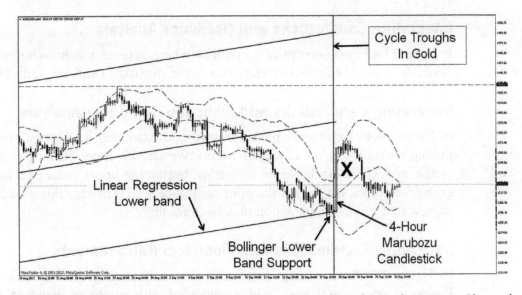

FIGURE 14.43 Integrating Cycle Troughs with Candlesticks on the 4-Hour Chart of Gold.
Source: MetaTrader 4

579

FIGURE 14.44 Integrating Candlesticks with Support and Resistance on the Weekly Chart of GLD SPDR Gold Trust Shares.
Courtesy of Stockcharts.com

Integrating Candlesticks with Support and Resistance

Some of the most reliable signals in technical analysis are based on the interaction of candlesticks at support and resistance. In Figure 14.44 we observe the GLD SPDR Gold Trust Shares reacting at support and resistance on the weekly chart, via bearish and bullish reversal candlesticks. We also notice that the stochastics are confirming the reactions at the support and resistant levels.

Integrating Candlesticks with Oscillator Analysis

In Figure 14.45 we observe price in a position where there are numerous bullish indications like channel bottoms, overextension on the stochastic oscillator, and a Hammer.

Integrating Candlesticks with Ichimoku Kinko Hyu Analysis

In Figure 14.46 we observe price penetrating the cloud at its thinnest point after finding resistance at the cloud, or Kumo. We see the upper shadow of the first candle in a Three Black Crows formation testing the upper band of a linear regression channel, which is at the prior resistance level. The very thin clouds ahead suggest that more bearish action may be unfolding.

Integrating Candlesticks with Fibonacci Retracements

In Figure 14.47 we observe a piercing line rebounding off the 38.2 percent Fibonacci retracement level, which coincided with the lower band of a linear regression channel. The Fibonacci retracement level also occurs around the prior support zone.

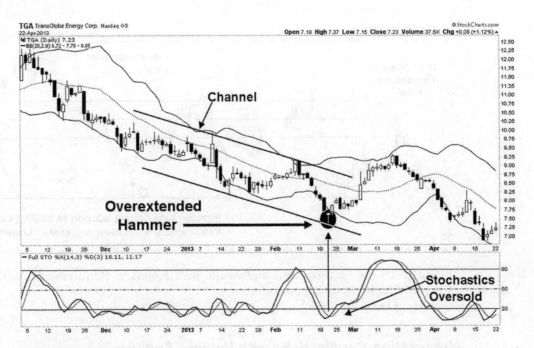

FIGURE 14.45 Integrating Candlesticks with Oscillator Analysis on the Daily Chart of TransGlobe Energy Corp.
Courtesy of Stockcharts.com

In Figure 14.45 we observe two candlesticks (denoted by overlapping red circle) on very high volume. The volume has eased recently and the momentum oscillator is simply the two-sigma or standard deviation upper Band, available via the application of a bollinger band on volume. There is also an oversold condition associated with the May breakout.

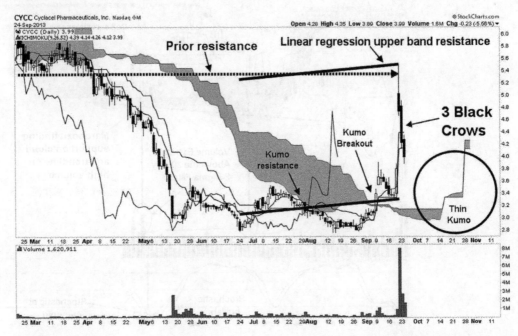

FIGURE 14.46 Integrating Candlesticks with Ichimoku Analysis on the Daily Chart of Cyclacel Pharmaceuticals Inc.
Courtesy of Stockcharts.com

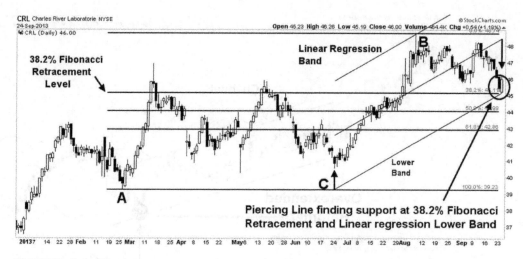

FIGURE 14.47 Integrating Candlesticks with Fibonacci Retracements on the Daily Chart of Charles River Laboratorie.
Courtesy of Stockcharts.com

Integrating Candlesticks with Volume Analysis

In Figure 14.48 we observe two Marubozus rebounding off the Ichimoku cloud on very high volume. The volume filter used to identify significant volume action is simply the two-sigma filter standard deviation upper band, available via the application of a Bollinger Band on volume. There is also an oversold indication associated with the Marubozu rebound.

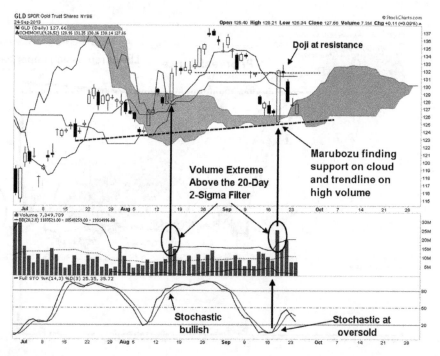

FIGURE 14.48 Integrating Candlesticks with Volume Analysis on the Daily Chart of GLD SPDR Gold Trust Shares.
Courtesy of Stockcharts.com

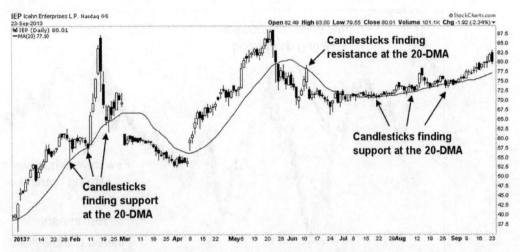

FIGURE 14.49 Integrating Candlesticks with Moving Averages on the Daily Chart of Icahn Enterprises.
Courtesy of Stockcharts.com

Integrating Candlesticks with Moving Averages

In Figure 14.49 we observe candlesticks reacting at the 20-day moving average of Icahn Enterprises.

We have seen how combining Japanese candlesticks helps to provide more effective and accurate forecasts of potential tops and bottoms in the market, including potential breakouts and continuations.

14.4 FILTERED CANDLESTICKS

Heikin Ashi Candlesticks

Heikin Ashi candlesticks are a form of *filtered* candlesticks. Each OHLC price is determined from a combination the current OHLC data and the previous period's OHLC data. When observed on the chart, it assumes a smoother appearance. Rising and declining Heikin Ashi candlesticks have different colors, making trend identification very easy. One popular way of using Heikin Ashi candlesticks is to observe the tops of falling candlesticks and bottoms of rising candlesticks. When there is a strong trend present:

- Rising Heikin Ashi candlesticks exhibit little or no lower shadows. The appearance of lower shadows is an indication of a potential trend slowdown or reversal.
- Declining Heikin Ashi candlesticks exhibit little or no upper shadows. The appearance of upper shadows is an indication of a potential trend slowdown or reversal.

See Figure 14.50.

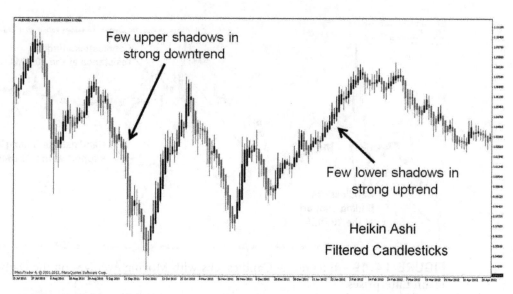

FIGURE 14.50   Heikin Ashi Candlesticks on the Daily AUDUSD Chart.
Source: MetaTrader 4

14.5 TRADING WITH CANDLESTICKS

Trading Candlestick Reversals Reliably: Trading Cyclic-Barrier Confluences

It is best to combine both price and time elements when trading the markets. It would be ideal if the dominant cycle could first be identified. This will allow the trader to gauge the best moment of entry at the most overbought and oversold conditions. Trading breakouts would also be more effective if the trader knew the phase of the dominant cycle.

Having knowledge of the market cycle activity will also help the trader fine-tune entries. For example, the period between 8 a.m. GMT to 5 p.m. GMT represents the *impulsive* period. This is when most action takes place in the markets, leading to more trend activity where breakout trading is more reliable, as opposed to the *inertial* period where prices tend to range and consolidate. See Figure 14.51.

Figure 14.52 shows potential reversal times across the trading day. Although this is an idealized indication of potential reversals, it is based on the cycles of trading activity in the market.

Price-Error Analysis

Consider a perfectly strong uptrend. The trend is strong and very symmetrical. It does not vary and price action is very regular in time and price range. See Figure 14.53.

By shifting the time line, we can manipulate the type of candle/bar to represent any formation. If we quantized price from between the Ys, that is, Y1 to Y2, Y2 to Y3, and so on, we get a series of rising shooting stars. This may fool the novice trader into believing that the uptrend was weak or flawed in some manner. See Figure 14.54.

If we quantized price from between the Xs, that is, X1 to X2, X2 to X3, and so on, we get a series of rising Hangmans. See Figure 14.55.

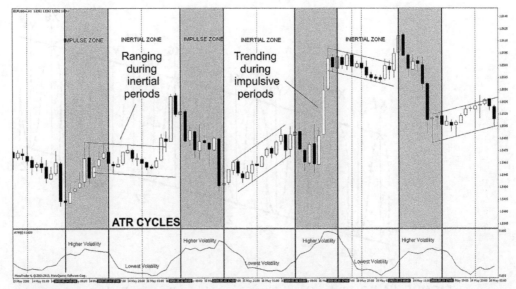

FIGURE 14.51 Integrating Candlesticks with Chart Patterns on the Hourly Chart of EURUSD.
Source: MetaTrader 4

If we quantized price from between the Zs, that is, Z1 to Z2, Z2 to Z3, and so on, we get a series of rising Dojis or a Spinning Top. See Figure 14.56.

Therefore we see that selecting the *right chart timeframe* is critical to having the most representative price displayed. To ensure that most traders and analysts observe the same candlestick representation on the charts, only use the hourly timeframe and any timeframe below it such as the 1-min, 2-min, 5-min, 15-min, and so on. *The problem starts when we employ charts above the one-hour timeframe,* as charting and trading platform providers may be based in a different time zone. A two-hour candlestick that begins at noon and another at 1 p.m. will look very

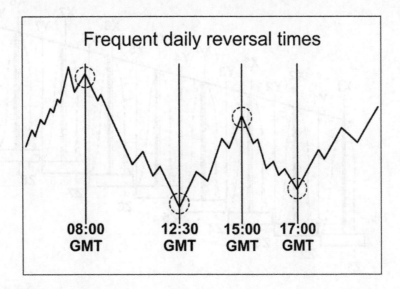

FIGURE 14.52 Potential Daily Reversal Times.

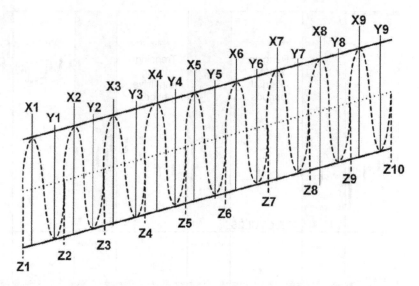

FIGURE 14.53 Price Oscillating Upward in a Regular Fashion.

different. It gets worse for the four-hour candlestick, as there will be four different versions of candlestick action. Therefore the best solution is to use a provider that offers chart action based on the trading activity of the most liquid market, that being the London/European period. As such, charts using timeframes above the one hour should preferably be based on GMT time. This will align traders with the strongest and most reliable price reactions based on technical analysis of charts synched to the most active markets in the world. Knowledge of the Asian, European, and U.S. trading sessions, including the four-hour U.S.-European trading session overlap, is critical for shorter-term trading.

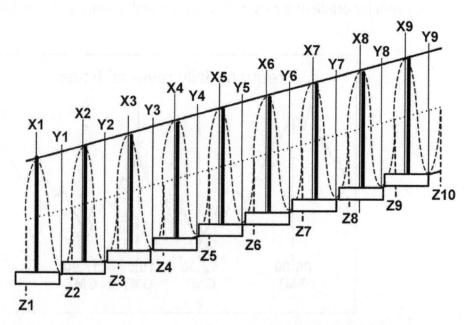

FIGURE 14.54 Regular Upside Oscillations Portrayed as Shooting Stars.

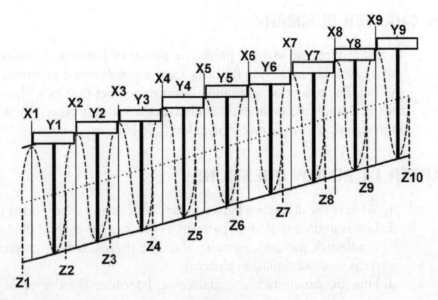

FIGURE 14.55 Regular Upside Oscillations Portrayed as Hangman Candlesticks.

FOREX Candlesticks

Foreign Exchange (FOREX) candlestick action differs slightly from candlestick action based on equity action. Due to the high level of liquidity, price gapping is minimal, except over the weekends. As such, candlestick patterns that require gaps as part of their formation will take on a different look in the FOREX market. Some patterns that are affected by this include the evening and morning stars, kicking, in-neck and on-neck patterns, separating lines, and upside and downside Tasuki gaps.

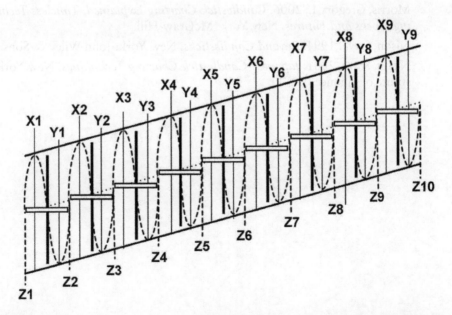

FIGURE 14.56 Regular Upside Oscillations Portrayed as a Series of Rising Dojis.

14.6 CHAPTER SUMMARY

In this chapter, we saw the predictive power of Japanese Candlestick analysis. In most cases, Japanese Candlesticks are used to forecast potential reversals in the market. The practitioner should always remember that as with any other form of technical analysis, Japanese Candlesticks work best especially when it coincides with significant or historical price levels or barriers.

CHAPTER 14 REVIEW QUESTIONS

1. What is the difference between candlesticks and other forms of charting?
2. List as many candlestick patterns as you can for each of the four categories of candlestick patterns, namely: bearish patterns, bullish patterns, reversal patterns, and continuation patterns.
3. How do candlestick size and color determine the degree of bullishness and bearishness?
4. What is the difference between intrinsic, extrinsic, trend, and contextual sentiment?
5. Explain the difference between a hammer and an inverted hammer formation.
6. How are FOREX candlesticks different?
7. What is the difference in sentiment between a Doji and a Doji with tremendous volume?
8. How can a bullish Marubozu turn bearish?

REFERENCES

Bulkowski, Thomas N. 2008. *Encyclopedia of Candlestick Charts*. Hoboken, NJ: John Wiley and Sons.

Lambert, Clive. 2011. *Candlestick Charts*. Petersfield, UK: Harriman House Ltd.

Morris, Gregory L. 2006. *Candlestick Charting Explained: Timeless Techniques for Trading Stocks and Futures*. New York: McGraw-Hill.

Nison, Steve. 1994. *Beyond Candlesticks*. New York: John Wiley & Sons.

Nison, Steve. 2001. *Japanese Candlestick Charting Techniques*. New York: New York Institute of Finance (NYIF).

CHAPTER 15

Point-and-Figure Charting

Point-and-Figure charting is essentially an exercise in reading pure price action. Volume and time are excluded and only price is observed, strictly for potential support and resistance levels. In this chapter, we will cover Point-and-Figure chart construction, minimum price projections, trade-related issues, and various Point-and-Figure forecasting techniques.

15.1 BASIC ELEMENTS OF POINT-AND-FIGURE CHARTS

As we saw in Chapter 4, there are *four* basic ways to plot price action on the charts, namely as:

1. Constant range bars
2. Constant time bars
3. Constant tick bars
4. Constant volume bars

Point-and-Figure charting is a form of *constant range* bars where each unit move in price is of a fixed or constant amount. Therefore each unit move in price is not dependent on the amount of:

- Time that has elapsed
- Volume that was traded
- Transactions that were made

As a consequence, there is no time axis on a Point-and-Figure chart. The vertical axis tracks price, while the horizontal axis tracks the progression of price once it has satisfied a certain criterion. Time therefore is implicit in the charts by virtue of its progressive motion toward the right, rather than an explicit feature on the charts. Nevertheless, Point-and-Figure practitioners may still incorporate a certain element of time into the charts by annotating the hour, day, month, or year directly on the chart. We shall see examples of such annotation in a subsequent section.

Since there is no explicit representation of time as an axis in Point-and-Figure charting, conventional volume bars are also not usually displayed on Point-and-Figure charts. As we have already seen in Chapter 6, volume may be plotted in two ways, that is, either with respect to time or with respect to price. *Volume by time* records the number of shares or contracts bought or sold over a certain interval of time and this is plotted below each price bar on the chart's time axis. It tracks volume as a function of time. Alternatively, *volume by price* records the total number of shares or contracts bought or sold at a certain price and is plotted on the price axis instead. It tracks volume as a function of price. Many Point-and-Figure practitioners opt to plot volume by price in order to track the level of market participation at each price level. Prices that are associated with large volume activity represent a potentially more effective barrier to future price action. Notice in Figure 15.1 that the S&P 500 Large Cap Index found support between 1350 and 1410 points, in the price range where large volume activity was observed.

Devoted advocates for Point-and-Figure charting argue that the omission of time and conventional volume by time is of no real consequence and that price is all that truly matters since all information is already reflected or discounted in price itself. They also contend that there is also no need to track volume since price action is in itself a consequence of volume action. They argue that if there is sufficient interest or demand, prices will rise, and vice versa. Hence, keeping track of the effect of supply and demand is all that is required and there is no need to also keep track of the cause for it.

In spite of this view, many technical analysts do still refer to conventional bar or candlestick charting for time and volume information. It is important to bear in mind that not all significant upside or downside movements in price are precipitated by strong demand or supply. *Prices may still rise on declining volume, signaling a potential reversal or deceleration in price.* Without access to volume information that directly reflects the level of demand and supply in the market, there is no way for a technical analyst to infer whether a trend is potentially weakening or strengthening.

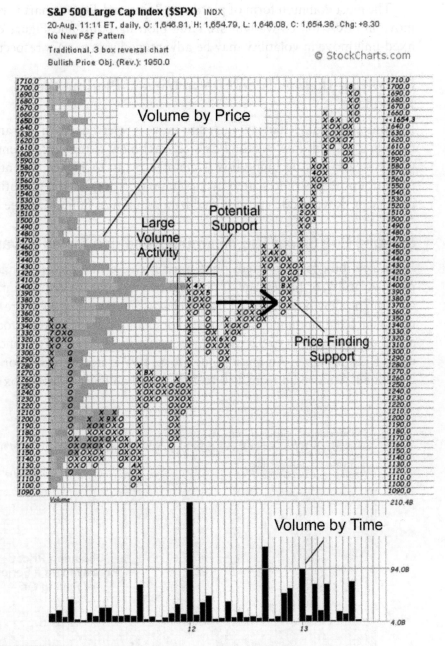

FIGURE 15.1 Representing Volume in a Point-and-Figure Chart.
Courtesy of Stockcharts.com

Measures of Unit Move

As a form of constant range bars, each unit move itself may be constant with respect to a fixed unit move in:

- Price
- Volatility (based on ATR or standard deviation)
- Percentage

The most common form of plotting a Point-and-Figure chart is via a fixed-unit move in price. But as we will see later, plotting Point-and-Figure charts using a fixed-unit move in volatility may be advantageous in certain respects.

Portraying Up Moves and Down Moves: Plotting the Xs and Os

In Point-and-Figure charting, each unit move is referred to as a *box* and the amount of each fixed-unit move is the *box size*. Each new rising box is denoted by an X, whereas each new declining box is denoted by an O. Hence, a continuous rise in price or uptrend is represented by a column of rising Xs and a continuous decline in price or downtrend is represented by a column of falling Os. See Figure 15.2.

Box and Box Sizes: The Minimum Condition for an Advance

For a new box to be plotted, price must traverse the *minimum* fixed amount in price, volatility, or percentage. If price fails to traverse the required minimum fixed amount, no new box is plotted on the charts. The box size therefore represents the minimum fixed amount per unit move. For example, if the current stock price is $10 and the box size is set to $2, then a new box may only be plotted once price moves up to $12, *or higher*. An upside move to $11.99 is not sufficient for a new box to be plotted. A move up from $10 to $13.99 only allows a single box to be plotted.

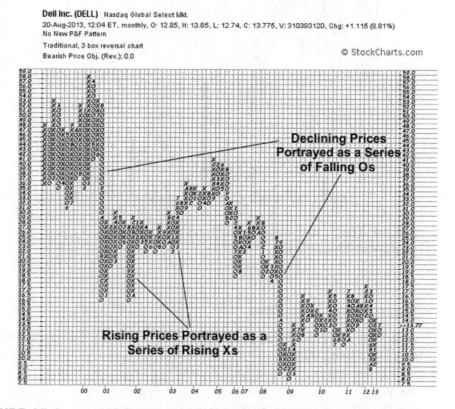

FIGURE 15.2 Rising Xs and Declining Os on a Point-and-Figure Chart.
Courtesy of Stockcharts.com

Similarly, for a box size of $2, a box is plotted for a downside unit move from $10 to $8, *or lower*. A move down from $10 to $6.01 only allows a single box to be plotted whereas a move down to $6 or $5.99 allows two boxes to be plotted.

Defining and Quantifying Continuation and Reversals

In Point-and-Figure charting, the number of boxes may be specified for a continuation or reversal move. Normally, the box size itself represents the minimum move required to create a new box *in the direction* of the current trend, whereas the reversal size represents the minimum number of boxes required to create a new box *in the opposite direction*. An X followed by another X, or an O followed by another O are both considered as continuation moves. But if an X is followed by an O or an O is followed by an X, both moves are considered to be potential conditions for a reversal. By convention, a Point-and-Figure chart is usually referred to by its reversal size rather than its continuation criterion, since its continuation criterion is usually set to one box. As such, Point-and-Figure charts are referred to as one-box, two-box, or three-box reversal charts.

We usually refer to Point-and-Figure charts in terms of their box size and reversal size, denoted as, for example, an $N \times M$ configuration, where N is the box size and M the reversal size. Therefore a 1×3 reversal chart means that a minimum unit move equivalent to one box is required for a continuation in price and three boxes for a reversal in price. Sometimes the continuation box amount is denoted as an actual unit move in price, such as $10. In such a configuration, a 1×3 chart is identical to a 10×3 chart. Some practitioners write it as a $10 \times $30 chart. In all three configurations, a $10 move is required for a new continuation box to be plotted, while a $30 move in the opposite direction is required in order for a three-box reversal to be plotted.

Let us now examine the three most widely used Point-and-Figure reversal charts.

(1) One-Box Reversal Charts   For one-box reversal charts, that is, 1×1 charts,, both the continuation and reversal sizes are one box. Let us assume that box size is $1. This means that the reverse size of one box is also $1. See Figure 15.3.

The column of 26 numbers on the far right is a chronological sequence depicting how the market moved over the entire period under observation. Initially, price rises from $20 to $25. We therefore plot six continuation boxes, in the form of rising Xs, as seen in column 1. At $25, price starts to decline. A new reversal box is not drawn until price reverses a minimum distance of one box, that is, $1. This means that once price reaches $25 – $1 = $24 or lower, a new reversal box is plotted. As prices continue to fall from $23 to $22, new continuation boxes are plotted as a column of declining Os, as seen in column 2. The reason for shifting to column 2 in order to plot the Os is simply because the space that occupies $24 in column 1 is already filled by an X. We have therefore no choice but to shift to the next column to plot the O at $24. From $22, price reverses back to $23 and a new reversal is plotted. As before, the space occupying $23 is already filled by an O in column 2. We therefore need to shift to column 3 in order to plot an X at the $23 level. Price continues up to $24 and another continuation box is plotted, and so on.

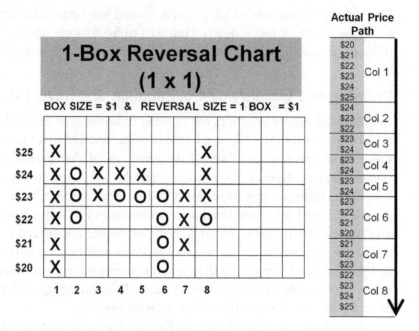

FIGURE 15.3 One-Box Reversal Chart.

We observe that for one-box reversal charts, Xs and Os may share the same column. Note that this only occurs in one-box reversal charts. For reversal two-box charts and higher, Xs and Os never share the same column and the minimum number of boxes in any column is equal to its reversal box amount.

(2) Two-Box Reversal Charts Let us now plot the same price path as found in Figure 15.3 on a two-box reversal chart in order to observe the differences. See Figure 15.4.

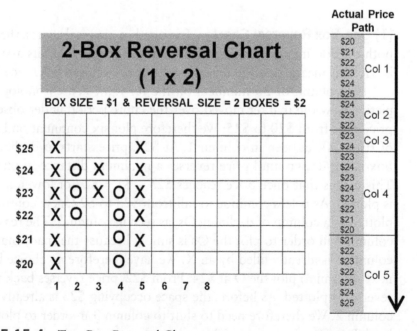

FIGURE 15.4 Two-Box Reversal Chart.

594

As before, prices rose from $20 to $25 and five new continuation boxes are plotted as a column of rising Xs. Prices subsequently fell from $25 to $24. But since this is a two-box reversal chart, no reversal box is plotted until prices fall to at least $25 – $2 = $23. Price eventually declines to $23 and two boxes are finally plotted in the next column, filling both the $24 and $23 spaces with falling Os. Price continues to fall to $22 and a new continuation box is plotted at $22 with another O, as seen in column 2. Price then reverses back to the upside and no box is plotted until prices reach $22 + $2 = $24, where two new Xs are plotted in the next column, filling in the $23 and $24 spaces, as seen in column 3. From $24, prices fell back down to $23, but this does not satisfy the two-box reversal criteria, and hence no reversal box is plotted until price reaches at least $24 – $2 = $22, upon which two falling Os would be plotted, as seen in column 4. Two new continuation boxes are plotted as prices continue to decline another $2 to $20. Finally, price reverses again to the upside, where two new reversal boxes are only plotted once price reaches $20 + $2 = $22. Prices continue to rise from $22 to $25, where three new continuation boxes are plotted as a column of rising Xs, as seen in column 5.

We therefore observe that it only took five columns to plot the same price path using a two-box chart, instead of eight columns as seen on the one-box reversal chart in Figure 15.3. We may therefore conclude that consolidations plotted on a one-box reversal chart will take up many more columns than on a two- or three-box reversal chart.

(3) Three-Box Reversal Charts We will now repeat the same procedure again by plotting the same price path as found in Figure 15.3, but this time on a three-box reversal chart. See Figure 15.5.

As before, prices rose from $20 to $25 and five new continuation boxes are plotted as a column of rising Xs. Prices subsequently fell from $25 to $24. But

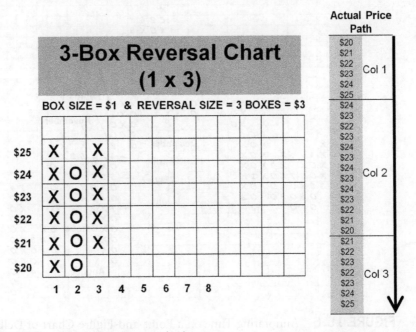

FIGURE 15.5 Three-Box Reversal Chart.

since this is a three-box reversal chart, no reversal box is plotted until prices fall to at least $25 − $3 = $22. Price eventually declines to $22 and three boxes are finally plotted in the next column, filling the $24, $23, and $22 spaces with falling Os. Price then reverses back to the upside, and no box is plotted unless prices reach $22 + $3 = $25. Prices do not reach $25 and therefore no new reversal boxes are plotted. Price finally falls to back down from $24 to $20, and two new continuation boxes are plotted at $21 and $20, as seen in column 2. Finally, price reverses again to the upside, where three new reversal boxes are plotted once price reaches $20 + $3 = $23, as seen in column 3. Prices continue to rise from $24 to $25, where two new continuation boxes are plotted as a column of rising Xs.

We now observe that it only took three columns to plot the same price path using a three-box reversal chart, instead of eight columns as seen on the one-box reversal chart, or five columns on the two-box reversal chart. Therefore the larger the reversal size, the less price action is revealed on the charts, making the charts less sensitive. Larger box sizes and reversal sizes correspond to a longer horizon outlook. It is akin to switching to a *higher timeframe* in conventional charting.

Annotating Time in Point-and-Figure Charts

We may incorporate an element of time into the charts by marking the hour, day, month, or year directly into a box. January to September months are usually denoted by the numbers 1 through 9, while October to December are denoted by the letters A to C. This is done to avoid the annotation of double digits with the boxes. Occasionally certain months may be missing due to non-activity. See Figure 15.6.

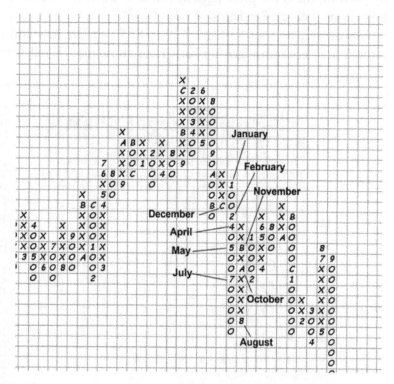

FIGURE 15.6 Annotating Time on a Point-and-Figure Chart of Dell Inc.
Courtesy of Stockcharts.com

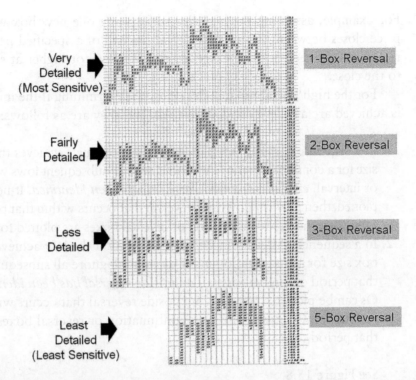

FIGURE 15.7 Comparing Reversal Sizes on a Point-and-Figure Chart of iShares Barclays 20+ Year Treasury Bond Fund.
Courtesy of Stockcharts.com

Price Sensitivity: Box Size and Reversal Box Amount

The sensitivity of a Point-and-Figure chart depends on its box size and reversal box amount. Larger box sizes require more movement in price before a box may be plotted. Increasing the box size filters out more price action, making the charts reflect only the larger movements in price. Similarly, larger reversal box amounts require more movement in price before a reversal may be plotted, in the process filtering out all extraneous market noise below the minimum reversal amount. Selecting the most appropriate box size and reversal box amount is largely dependent on market volatility and the objective of the analysis. See Figure 15.7.

We observe in the chart above that as the reversal size increases, the amount of detail in box action reduces significantly, becoming less sensitive to smaller price movements and general market noise.

Filtering Box Sizes: Closing versus High/Low Prices

The construction of a box depends on how the fixed-unit move is determined. If price is used as a measure for box size, the size of the box will then depend on whether closing prices or the period's high and low prices are used in its determination. If closing prices are used, then the box size will ignore all intervening prices, using only the final closing price to determine if prices have indeed traversed the necessary minimum amount to allow for the plotting of a new box.

For example, assuming the box size of $2, only one new box will be plotted if price closes between $12 and $13.99 at the end of a specified period or interval, regardless of whether price exceeded the $14 level or higher at some point prior to the close.

For the high/low approach, the rules for determining if the minimum box size is achieved are a little more complicated, and they are as follows:

1. In a sequence of rising Xs, plot a new X if the high achieves the minimum box size for a continuation move up and ignore all subsequent lows within that period or interval, *even if a downside reversal has been identified*. If no new Xs can be plotted, then plot any downside reversal that occurs within that period or interval. Otherwise, no new continuation or reversal boxes are plotted for that period.

2. In a sequence of declining Os, plot a new O if the low achieves the minimum box size for a continuation move down and ignore all subsequent highs within that period or interval, *even if an upside reversal has been identified*. If no new Os can be plotted, then plot any upside reversal that occurs within that period or interval. Otherwise, no new continuation or reversal boxes are plotted for that period.

See Figure 15.8.

Notice the discrepancy in the displayed price action between box sizes that employ the closing price and high/low price. We also observe some differences in the volume by price data.

Non-Accounting of Significant Price Action

It should be noted that detractors of the high/low approach argue that this method of plotting tends to misrepresent significant moves in the market. Once the high

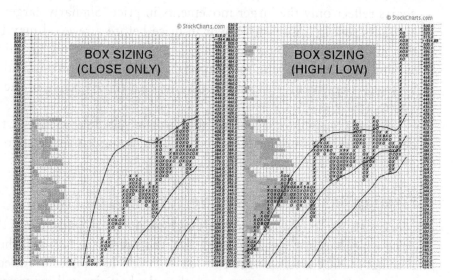

FIGURE 15.8 Comparing Closing Price versus High/Low Price on a Point-and-Figure Chart of Apple Inc.
Courtesy of Stockcharts.com

or low allows for the plotting of a new continuation box, all subsequent reversals are ignored, no matter how large the reversal may be within the period or interval. The high/low method does not account for significant reversals within the period of observation once a continuation box is plotted.

Unfortunately, the closing price approach is no better, as it only plots the number of continuation boxes that satisfy the minimum box-size requirements with respect to the final closing price, regardless of how high or low prices have moved within the period of observation. The closing price method does not account for significant continuations in price within the period of observation, especially if it closes near or just beyond the previous continuation box.

Since the plotting of new continuation or reversal boxes is totally dependent on achieving a minimum move in price, it is important to note that Point-and-Figure charts do not account for:

- Price gapping
- Periods of inactivity in the markets, which include weekends and holidays

Box Scaling

Some practitioners scale box sizes with respect to the level of price. They use smaller box sizes at lower prices and gradually increase the size of the box as prices increase. For example, they may use a box size of say $0.25 for stock prices $5 and below and $0.50 for prices between $5 and $20, and so on. The purpose for such an approach is to help visualize prices in a more balanced fashion, by expanding the box action at lower prices and compressing box action at higher prices. Employing large box sizes of say $10 would filter out virtually all price action on stocks below $10, let alone penny stocks.

Unfortunately, this approach may cause distortions when using dynamic overlay indicators such as trendlines, channels, chart patterns, and so on. Drawing trendlines based on inflection points at different box scales will result in inconsistent trendlines. It is for this reason that many Point-and-Figure practitioners have abandoned box scaling, preferring a single box size that applies across the entire range of price.

Arithmetic versus Logarithmic Scaling

Arithmetic scaling represents box action in a linear manner on a Point-and-Figure chart, whereas logarithmic or ratio scaling provides for a non-linear representation of box action. Logarithmic scaling, just like box scaling, expands price action at lower prices and compresses it at higher prices. Logarithmic scaling achieves the same objective as box scaling without the element of arbitrariness that accompanies box scaling. Box scales may be set differently from one practitioner to the next, but logarithmic scaling has only one scale, albeit non-linear. Hence it is more objective as well as consistent in its application.

Nevertheless, one must exercise caution when drawing trendlines using logarithmic charts, as uptrend lines tend to be violated much sooner and downtrend lines much later, when compared to the same trendlines drawn on arithmetic charts.

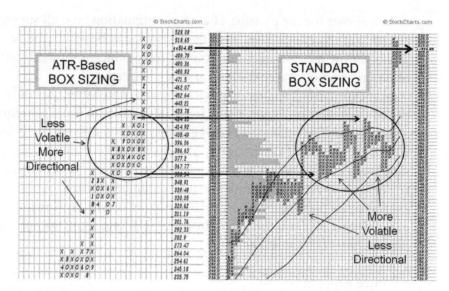

FIGURE 15.9 Comparing Fixed ATR versus Fixed Box Price on a Point-and-Figure Chart of Apple Inc.
Courtesy of Stockcharts.com

Volatility-Based Box Sizing

The box size may adopt any of the following measures:

- Fixed box *price*
- Fixed box *percentage*
- Fixed box *average true range* (ATR)

In most cases, the fixed box price is the preferred choice of measure. But as can be seen in Figure 15.9, using the volatility measure has its advantages. By selecting the box size to be one unit of volatility, we essentially filter out a significant amount of market noise, making trends more visible. We observe in Figure 15.9 that the price action is much less volatile when a volatility filter is applied.

15.2 BASIC POINT-AND-FIGURE CHART PATTERNS

We will now turn our attention to some popular Point-and-Figure chart patterns. Most patterns discussed in this section will be based on three-box reversals, unless stated otherwise. We will begin with the most fundamental of all formations, the Double Top and Bottom pattern.

Double Top and Bottom Formations

These represent the most basic bullish and bearish signals in Point-and-Figure charting. They also represent the most fundamental buy and sell *triggers*. Once price exceeds the previous X and a new X is plotted, a buy signal is issued.

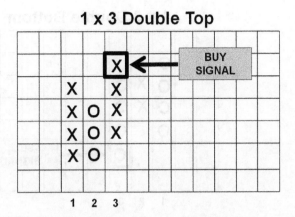

FIGURE 15.10 A Basic Three-Box Reversal Double Top Breakout.

Similarly, for double bottoms, once price breaks below the previous O and a new O is plotted, a sell signal is issued. These are essentially classified as continuation patterns. See Figure 15.10 for the basic setup.

Figure 15.11 depicts a three-box reversal double top breakout on Bank of America Corp.

Similarly, for double bottoms, once price breaks below the previous O and a new O is plotted, a sell signal is issued. See Figure 15.12.

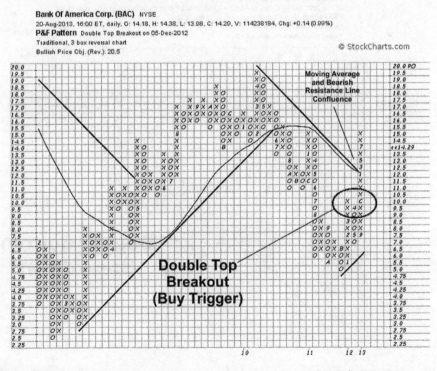

FIGURE 15.11 A Basic Three-Box Reversal Double Top Breakout on a Point-and-Figure Chart of Bank of America Corp.
Courtesy of Stockcharts.com

1 x 3 Double Bottom

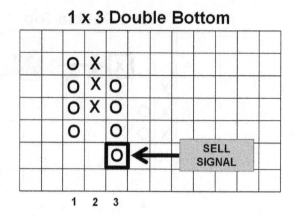

FIGURE 15.12 A Basic Three-Box Reversal Double Bottom Breakout.

Figure 15.13 depicts three-box reversal double bottom breakout in Exxon Mobil Corp.

Rising Double Tops and Declining Double Bottoms

Double top formations that are accompanied by a rising or ascending pattern of Os and Xs at the base of the formation are considered more bullish than standard double top formations. See Figure 15.14 for the basic setup.

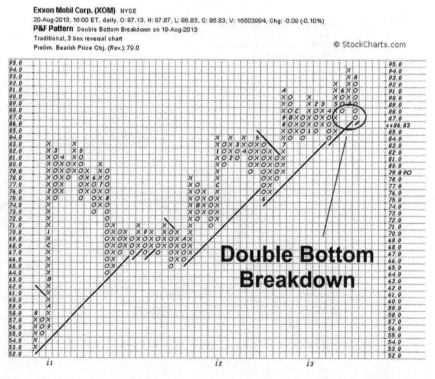

FIGURE 15.13 A Basic Three-Box Reversal Double Bottom Breakdown on a Point-and-Figure Chart of Exxon Mobil Corp.
Courtesy of Stockcharts.com

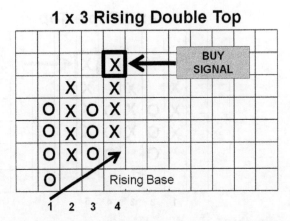

FIGURE 15.14 A Basic Three-Box Reversal Rising Double Top Breakout.

Double bottom formations that are accompanied by a declining or descending pattern of Os and Xs at the top of the formation are considered more bearish than standard double bottom formations. See Figure 15.15 for the basic setup.

Triple Tops and Bottoms

Triple tops are basically an extension of a double top formation. They represent very significant bullish signals and buy triggers. This formation takes five columns to develop. See Figure 15.16 for the basic setup.

Figure 15.17 depicts a typical triple top breakout in Chesapeake Energy Corp.

Figure 15.18 illustrates the setup for a triple bottom breakdown. They represent very significant bearish signals and sell triggers. The formation also takes five columns to develop.

Figure 15.19 depicts a typical triple bottom breakdown in Goliath Film and Media Holdings at $0.13.

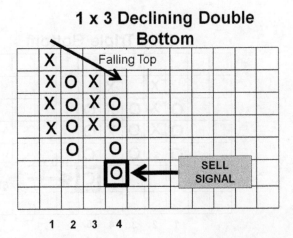

FIGURE 15.15 A Basic Three-Box Reversal Declining Double Bottom Breakdown.

1 x 3 Triple Top

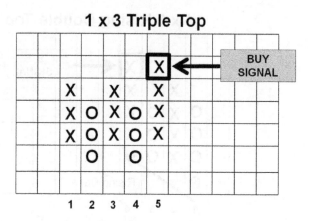

FIGURE 15.16   A Basic Three-Box Reversal Triple Top Breakout.

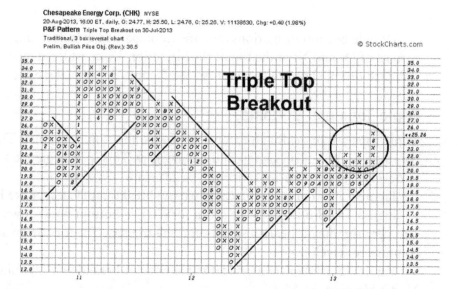

FIGURE 15.17   A Basic Three-Box Reversal Triple Top Breakout on a Point-and-Figure Chart of Chesapeake Energy Corp.
Courtesy of Stockcharts.com

1 x 3 Triple Bottom

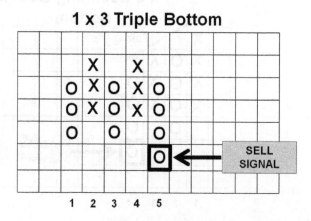

FIGURE 15.18   A Basic Three-Box Reversal Triple Bottom Breakdown.

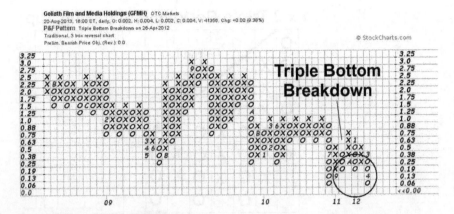

FIGURE 15.19 A Basic Three-Box Reversal Triple Bottom Breakdown on a Point-and-Figure Chart of Goliath Film and Media Holdings.
Courtesy of Stockcharts.com

Triple Tops with Rising Base and Triple Bottoms with Falling Top

Just as for rising double top formations, triple top formations that are accompanied by a rising or ascending pattern of Os and Xs at the base of the formation are considered more bullish than standard triple top formations. See Figure 15.20 for the basic setup and Figure 15.17 for an example of a triple top breakout with a rising base in Chesapeake Energy Corp.

Triple top formations that are accompanied by a falling pattern of Os and Xs at the top of the formation are considered more bearish than standard triple bottom formations. See Figure 15.21 for the basic setup.

It is important to note that, regardless of how many rising or falling columns within such formations, the actual triple top or bottom breakout itself comprises only five columns.

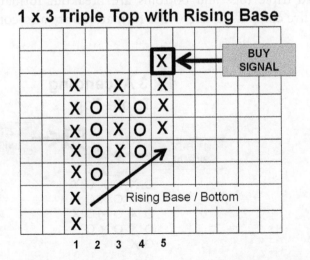

FIGURE 15.20 A Basic Three-Box Reversal Triple Top Bullish Breakout with a Rising Base.

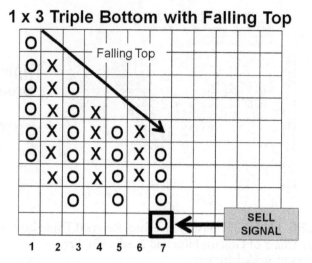

FIGURE 15.21 A Basic Three-Box Reversal Triple Bottom Bearish Breakout with a Falling Top.

Ascending and Descending Triple Tops and Bottoms

Ascending and descending triple top formations are in essence two successive double top or bottom formations. For an ascending double top formation, the first double top is breached, followed by the breach of a higher double top pattern. The reverse applies for descending triple top formations. See Figure 15.22.

Figure 15.23 depicts a typical ascending triple top in Financial Select Sector SPDR. Notice the upper Bollinger Band coinciding with the double top breakout.

Figure 15.24 is an illustration of a three-box descending triple bottom.

Spread Triple Tops and Bottoms

Spread triple tops and bottoms are breakout formations that comprise more than five columns. These wider formations are also considered to be very strong

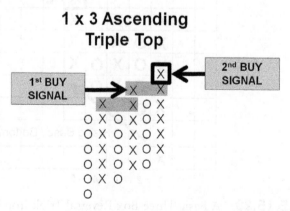

FIGURE 15.22 A Basic Three-Box Ascending Triple Top Breakout.

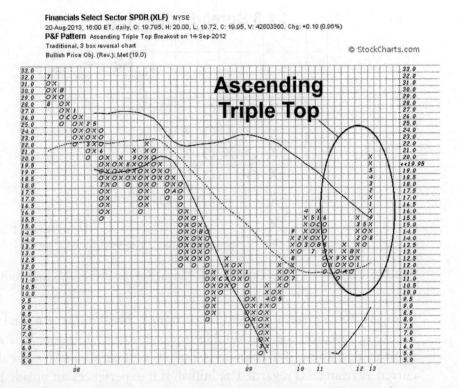

FIGURE 15.23 A Basic Three-Box Reversal Ascending Triple Top Breakout on a Point-and-Figure Chart of Financial Select Sector SPDR.
Courtesy of Stockcharts.com

bullish and bearish signals for further continuation beyond the breakout. See Figure 15.25 for an illustration of the basic setup for a spread triple top.

Figure 15.26 is an example of a spread triple top breakout in Keycorp.

See Figure 15.27 for an illustration of the basic setup for a spread triple bottom.

Figure 15.28 is an example of a spread triple bottom breakdown in Tesoro Petroleum Corp.

Bullish and Bearish Triangles

Just as in conventional bar charts, Point-and-Figure charts also contain triangular formations where boxes are converging toward an apex, not unlike symmetrical

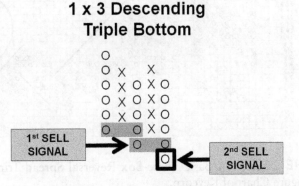

FIGURE 15.24 A Basic Three-Box Descending Triple Bottom Breakout.

607

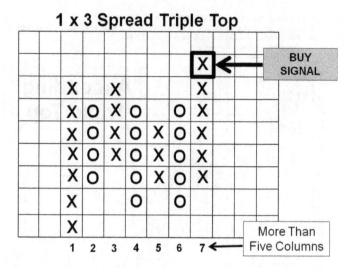

FIGURE 15.25 A Basic Three-Box Reversal Spread Triple Top Bullish Breakout.

triangles. But unlike a conventional triangle breakout, the actual buy and sell trigger is based on the first double top or bottom violation. It is normally difficult to determine if a triangle is bullish or bearish *until* a breakout has occurred. A triangle is regarded as bullish if it experiences an upside breakout and bearish if it has a downside breakout, or breakdown. Another approach is to determine if a triangle is bullish or bearish *with respect to its existing or predominant trend.* As such, all triangles would then be expected to be potentially

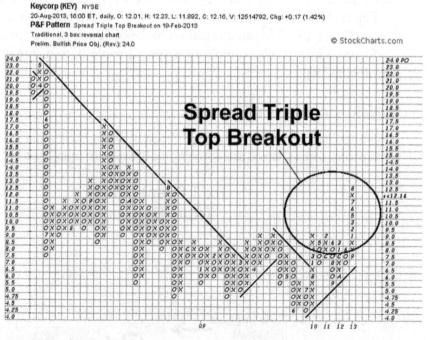

FIGURE 15.26 A Basic Three-Box Reversal Spread Triple Top Breakout on a Point-and-Figure Chart of Keycorp.
Courtesy of Stockcharts.com

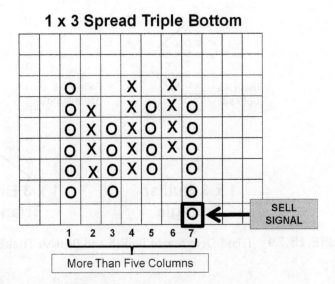

FIGURE 15.27 A Basic Three-Box Reversal Spread Triple Bottom Breakdown.

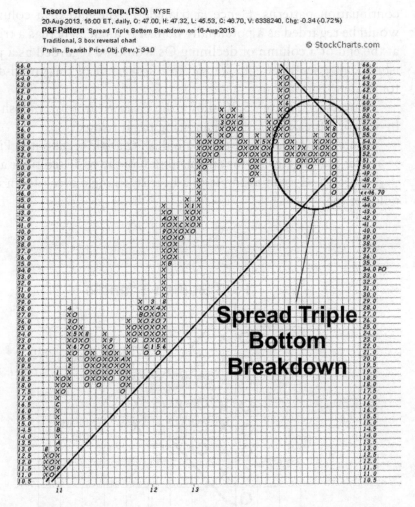

FIGURE 15.28 A Basic Three-Box Reversal Spread Triple Bottom Breakdown on a Point-and-Figure Chart of Tesoro Petroleum Corp.
Courtesy of Stockcharts.com

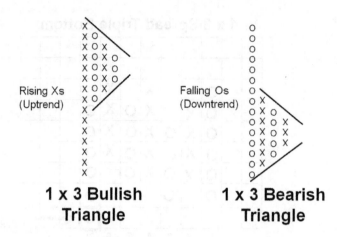

1 x 3 Bullish Triangle

1 x 3 Bearish Triangle

FIGURE 15.29 Trend-Determined Bullish and Bearish Triangle.

continuation patterns. Hence, a triangle at the end of a column of rising Xs would be regarded as a potentially bullish triangle, whereas a triangle appearing at the end of a column of declining Os would be regarded as a potentially bearish triangle. See Figure 15.29 for an illustration of this trend-driven sentiment for triangle formations.

Conversely, Figure 15.30 shows the basic setup for a bullish triangle defined by way of a breakout rather than being trend related.

Figure 15.31 is an example of a bullish triangle breakout in Pitney Bowes, Inc.

Refer to Figure 15.32 for an illustration of the basic setup for a bearish triangle.

Figure 15.33 is an example of a bearish triangle breakdown in CraiLar Technologies Inc.

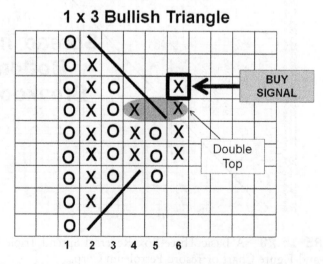

FIGURE 15.30 A Basic Three-Box Reversal Bullish Triangle by Way of Breakout.

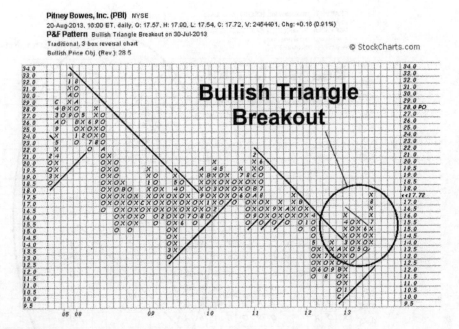

FIGURE 15.31 A Basic Three-Box Reversal Bullish Triangle Breakout on a Point-and-Figure Chart of Pitney Bowes, Inc.
Courtesy of Stockcharts.com

Bullish and Bearish Catapults

The catapult pattern is probably the most well-known complex pattern in Point-and-Figure charting. It consists of two formations, that is, a triple top or bottom and a double top or bottom. For example, a bullish catapult starts off with a breakout of a triple top, which is followed by a retreat back into the triple top formation. It then catapults beyond the original triple top breakout and forms a tentative

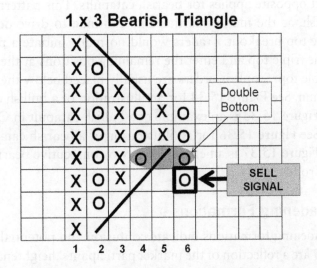

FIGURE 15.32 A Basic Three-Box Reversal Bearish Triangle by Way of Breakout.

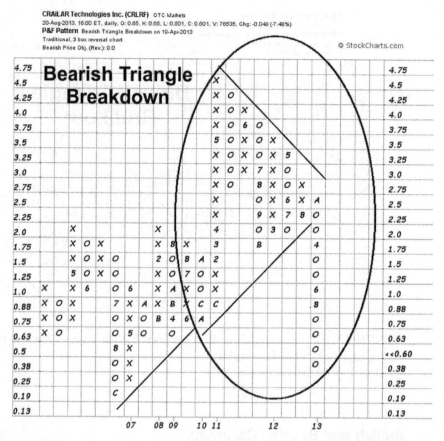

FIGURE 15.33 A Basic Three-Box Reversal Bearish Triangle Breakout on a Point-and-Figure Chart of CraiLar Technologies Inc.
Courtesy of Stockcharts.com

double top. Once the double top is breached, the catapult pattern is complete. The exact opposite applies for bearish catapults. This pattern is regarded as extremely bullish, as the market participants continue to drive demand even after a failed triple top breakout. Traders would normally initiate a partial entry at the breach of the triple top and enter the remaining positions at the breach of the subsequent double top. Stoploss orders are usually placed below the lowest X in the breakout column. See Figure 15.34 for an illustration of a bullish catapult formation.

Figure 15.35 is an example of a bullish catapult in CNO Financial Group Inc. See Figure 15.36 for an illustration of a bearish catapult formation.

Figure 15.37 is an example of two consecutive bearish catapults unfolding in Oclaro Inc.

Broadening Formations

Broadening formations indicate confusion and potential volatility in the markets. They are a reflection of the market participants' heightened emotional involvement and response in the markets. The pattern expands, making higher and lower boxes

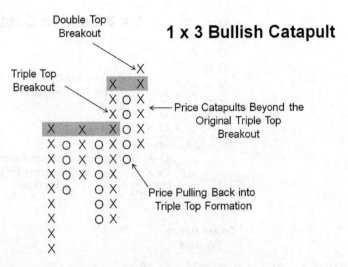

FIGURE 15.34 A Basic Three-Box Reversal Bullish Catapult.

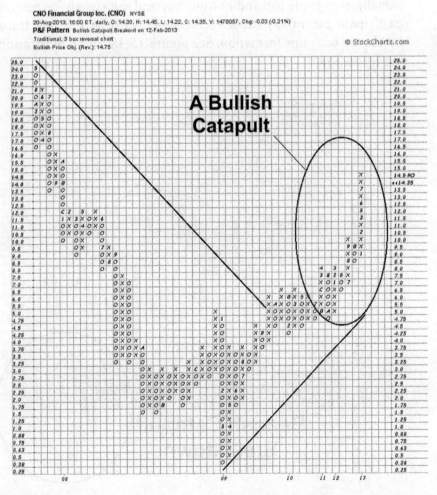

FIGURE 15.35 A Basic Three-Box Reversal Bullish Catapult on a Point-and-Figure Chart of CNO Financial Group Inc.
Courtesy of Stockcharts.com

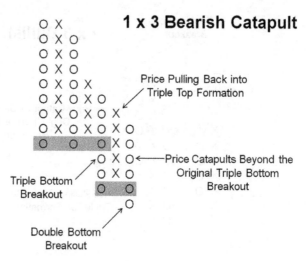

FIGURE 15.36 A Basic Three-Box Reversal Bearish Catapult.

as the formation progresses. This expansion triggers successive double and occasionally even triple top and bottom buy and sell signals, respectively. The market participant potentially experiences numerous bear and bull traps when trading breakouts with this formation. See Figure 15.38 for an illustration of a broadening formation.

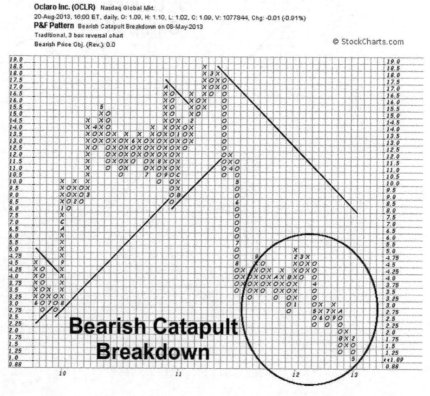

FIGURE 15.37 A Basic Three-Box Reversal Bearish Catapult on a Point-and-Figure Chart of Oclaro Inc.
Courtesy of Stockcharts.com

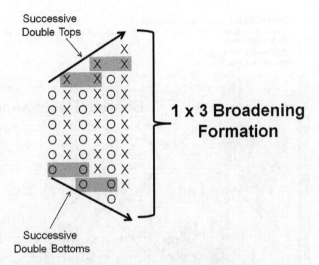

FIGURE 15.38 A Basic Three-Box Reversal Broadening Formation.

Bullish Support and Bearish Resistance Lines

Trendlines are also used in Point-and-Figure charting. The practitioner has a choice of drawing either the ±45-degree trendline or can opt to draw conventional trendlines. The 45-degree lines are somewhat unique to Point-and-Figure charts due to the square nature of the plot. Unlike conventional trendlines, only one point is required to draw a Point-and-Figure 45-degree trendline. There are four 45-degree trendlines employed in Point-and-Figure charting, namely:

1. Bullish Support Line
2. Bearish Resistance Line
3. Bullish Resistance Line
4. Bearish Support Line

The main uptrend line is the bullish support line, while the main downtrend line is the bearish resistance line. The bullish support line is drawn at a 45-degree angle upward from the space just below the lowest O of a column of Os. The bearish resistance line is drawn at a 45-degree angle downward from the space just above the highest X of a column of Xs. Uptrending channels may be created by combining the bullish support and bullish resistance lines, whereas downtrending channels may be created by combining the bearish support and bearish resistance lines. These lines are not traded as per any conventional trendline. Once a trendline is breached, the trigger for an entry must be based on a subsequent double top or bottom violation. Therefore, a trendline breach merely represents a bullish or bearish signal, and not a trigger in itself for entry. See Figure 15.39 for an illustration of these trendlines.

Reversal of Bullish and Bearish Signals

Assume that prices move to the upside, with each successive X exceeding the previous X, and with each lowest O also exceeding the previous O. This would

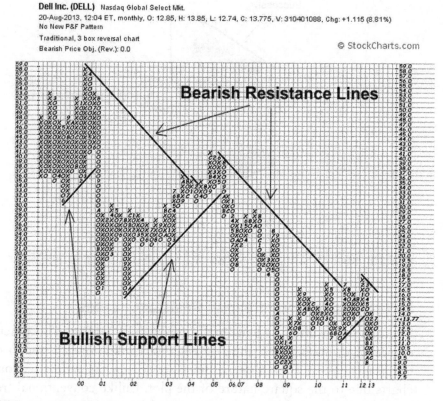

FIGURE 15.39 Trendlines on a Three-Box Reversal Point-and-Figure Chart of Dell Inc. Courtesy of Stockcharts.com

in fact represent a bullish formation. Hence, any opposing move that triggers a subsequent double bottom sell would negate all previous bullish sentiment. We say that the original bullish signal has now reversed, and the sentiment is now bearish. This formation requires that the bullish formation be at least seven to nine columns. The reverse applies for bearish signal reversed. See Figure 15.40.

Figure 15.41 depicts a bearish reversed signal on Alcatel-Lucent.

The Bullish and Bearish Fulcrum Formation

The fulcrum pattern is basically a reversal pattern in the form of a congestion or consolidation area. The use of one- or two-box reversal charts creates a more visible congestion area as opposed to congestions viewed on three-box reversal charts. As prices begin to reverse, triple and double tops begin to get violated, many times completing single or multiple catapult formations. See Figure 15.42.

High Pole/Extended Column Warning

A high pole or extended column warning is any retracement of more than 50 percent in the opposite direction of the preceding column of rising Xs. The pole should preferably be as extended as possible in price, that is, as many Xs as possible to provide more effective bearish signals. The minimum number of rising boxes should be at least three or four boxes. A 50 percent retracement from the

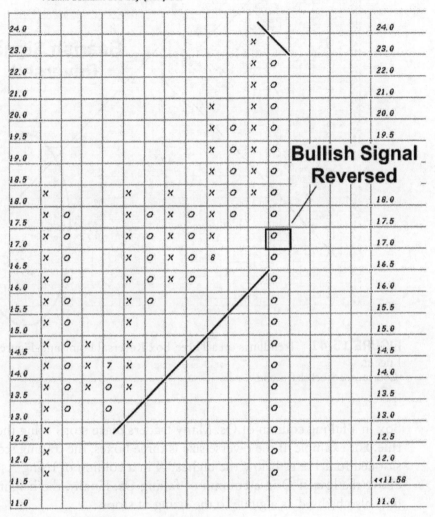

Lightinthebox Holding Co. Ltd. (LITB) NYSE
20-Aug, 16:00 ET, daily, O: 11.58, H: 12.90, L: 11.40, C: 11.58, V: 13.1M, Chg: -7.69
P&F Pattern Bullish Signal Reversed on 20-Aug-2013
Traditional, 3 box reversal chart
Prelim. Bearish Price Obj. (Rev.): 0.0

© StockCharts.com

FIGURE 15.40 Reversal of a Bullish Formation on a Three-Box Reversal Point-and-Figure Chart of Lightinthebox Holding Co Ltd.
Courtesy of Stockcharts.com

top of the column of rising Xs is an indication that there may be more supply in the market than expected. See Figure 15.43.

Placement of Stoplosses on Point-and-Figure Charts

Stoplosses are usually placed:

- Below the lowest X in the breakout column of an upside move
- Above the highest O in the breakout column of a downside move

Some traders also place trailing stops a certain number of boxes below the highest box in a rising column of Xs or a certain number of boxes above the lowest

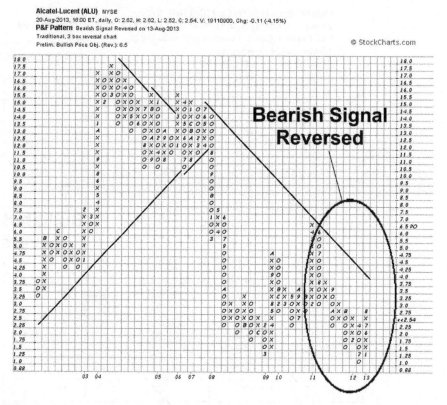

FIGURE 15.41 Trendlines on a Three-Box Reversal Point-and-Figure Chart of Alcatel-Lucent.
Courtesy of Stockcharts.com

box in a falling column of Os. Many traders place stops using the *reverse size +1* rule. For example, if the reverse size is three boxes, the trailing stop would be positioned four boxes below the highest X in a column of rising Xs and four boxes above the lowest O in a column of falling Os. Finally, the height of a formation may also be used as a guide to the sizing of stops.

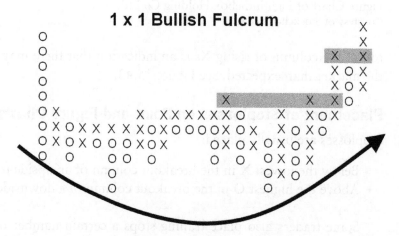

FIGURE 15.42 A Basic One-Box Reversal Fulcrum Formation.

FIGURE 15.43 High Pole Warning on a Three-Box Reversal Point-and-Figure Chart of Comcast Corp.
Courtesy of Stockcharts.com

Using Moving Averages and Bollinger Bands on Point-and-Figure Charts

Moving averages are sometimes also used on Point-and-Figure charts. The average is calculated by finding the average price of a column of boxes, that is,

$$\text{Average Price} = (\text{Highest Box Price} + \text{Lowest Box Price})/2$$

A simple moving average is then calculated based on the lookback period selected, that is, the number of lookback columns. Note that a Bollinger Band also uses the same moving average calculation for its central value. In Figure 15.44, we see the upper Bollinger band providing resistance to price while the moving average provides support.

15.3 POINT-AND-FIGURE MINIMUM PRICE OBJECTIVES

There are two approaches that the Point-and-Figure practitioner may employ to gauge the minimum potential price targets of various Point-and-Figure formations.

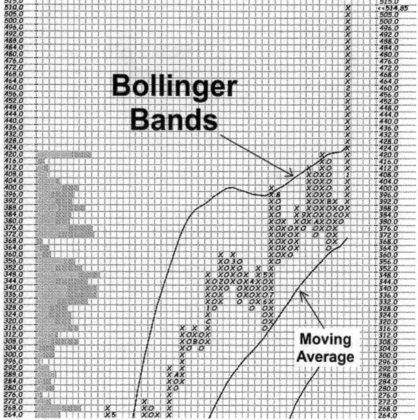

FIGURE 15.44 Bollinger Band and Its Moving Average on a Three-Box Reversal Point-and-Figure Chart of Apple Inc.
Courtesy of Stockcharts.com

The Horizontal Count

The first is called the *horizontal count,* where upside or downside minimum price targets are based on the:

- Maximum number of boxes found across a number of columns
- Average number of boxes found across a number of columns and rows within a consolidation
- Number of boxes between the initial and breakout columns
- Box size
- Reversal size

For upside horizontal counts, a practitioner usually finds the number of boxes across the widest part of the consolidation or the number of boxes between the initial and breakout columns, or finds the average number of boxes by adding up

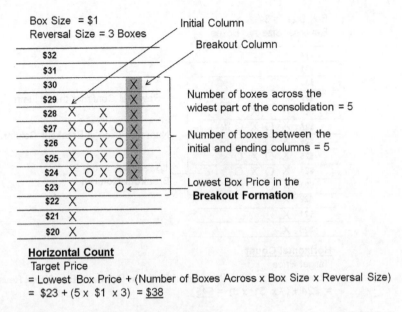

Box Size = $1
Reversal Size = 3 Boxes

Horizontal Count
Target Price
= Lowest Box Price + (Number of Boxes Across x Box Size x Reversal Size)
= $23 + (5 x $1 x 3) = $38

FIGURE 15.45 The Upside Horizontal Count.

all the rows of boxes and dividing the total by the number of rows, then multiplying the number of boxes by the box size and reversal size. This total is then added to the price of the lowest box in the formation. See Figure 15.45.

The same applies for the downside vertical count, except that we subtract the total from the highest part of the formation.

The Vertical Count

The second approach for gauging the minimum potential upside or a downside price target is called the *vertical count,* where minimum price targets are based on the:

- Number of boxes in the *breakout column*
- Average number of boxes found across a number of columns and rows within a consolidation
- Box size
- Reversal size
- Reversal to confirm breakout column
- The two-thirds reduction (for downside vertical counts)

For upside vertical counts, find the number of boxes in the breakout column after a subsequent reversal has confirmed the column action. Multiply the number of boxes in the breakout column by the box size and reversal size. Add this total to the price of the lowest box in the breakout column. See Figure 15.46.

The calculation is similar for downside vertical price projections. Multiply the number of boxes in the breakout column by the box size and reversal size after a subsequent reversal has confirmed the column action. Subtract this total from the price of the highest box in the downside breakout column. *Note that some*

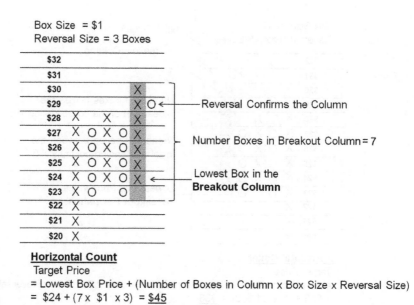

FIGURE 15.46 The Upside Vertical Count.

practitioners employ the '2/3 rule' to further reduce the amount of the projected downside to account for the upside bias in the markets. In our example, our original target of $15 thus becomes $30 − ($15 × 2/3) = $20. The practitioner has a choice as to which he or she believes is more a more appropriate downside projection approach. See Figure 15.47.

Note that we have confined our calculations for determining price objectives to arithmetically scaled Point-and-Figure charts. For calculating related price targets on logarithmically scaled chats, please refer to the Jeremy Du Plessis book *The Definitive Guide to Point and Figure*, published by Harriman House Publishing.

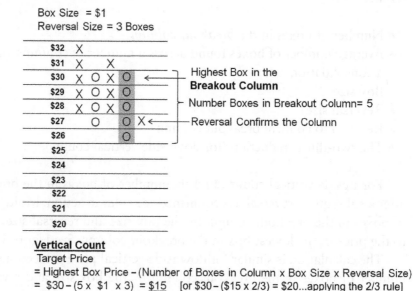

FIGURE 15.47 The Downside Vertical Count.

Fibonacci Analysis as an Alternate Means of Price Projection

Some practitioners also opt to apply Fibonacci extensions, expansions, projections, and retracements on Point-and-Figure charts. This represents an alternative way of making price projections, other than using the horizontal and vertical counts.

15.4 BULLISH PERCENT INDEX AND RELATIVE STRENGTH

The Bullish Percent Index is the ratio of all component stocks within a certain sector or index group currently on a basic Point-and-Figure buy signal (i.e., double top breakout) divided by the total number of stocks in that sector or index group. A reading of 70 is considered as overbought and 30 as oversold. It is essentially a market-breadth indicator. In Figure 15.48, we see that every time the S&P 500 Bullish Percent Index tests the historical 80 percent overbought level, the market eventually retraces, as seen at Points 1, 2, 3, and 4. There are Bullish Percent Indexes for major indexes, sectors, and industry groups.

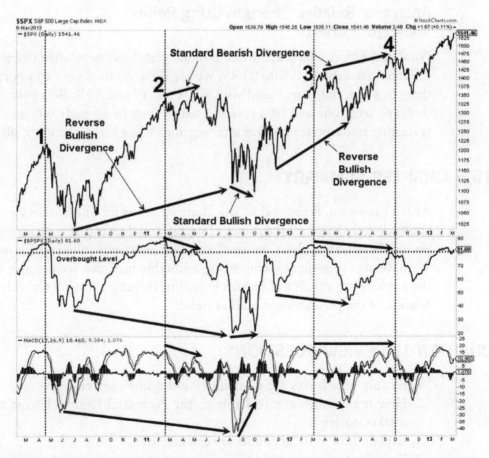

FIGURE 15.48 S&P 500 Bullish Percent Index versus the S&P 500 Large Cap Index. Courtesy of Stockcharts.com

FIGURE 15.49 S&P 500 Gold to Silver Ratio with a Long Tail Down Pattern.
Courtesy of Stockcharts.com

Analyzing Relative Strength Using Point-and-Figure Charts

Point-and-Figure charts are also a popular way to view relative strength between different markets. In Figure 15.49, we see the gold to silver ratio portrayed on a three-box reversal chart based with a box size of one ATR. We observe a long tail down pattern followed by a reversal, which may be an early indication that gold is starting to outperform silver after significantly underperforming silver.

15.5 CHAPTER SUMMARY

As we have seen, Point and Figure charting offers an alternative view of market action, largely based on the forces of supply and demand. It is, in a very real sense, pure price action analysis, as time and volume are not fully explicit in the charts. We have also seen that by employing a suitable box size, we are able to filter out the appropriate amount of market volatility, thereby allowing for a clearer identification of the predominant market trend.

CHAPTER 15 REVIEW QUESTIONS

1. Explain how boxes are plotted in Point-and-Figure charts.
2. How many ways are available to the Point-and-Figure chartist to filter out market noise?
3. Explain how vertical counts are calculated.
4. Describe how you would trade a Bullish Pattern Reversed.
5. Explain how trendlines are drawn on Point-and-Figure charts.

6. What are the disadvantages of using closing prices and high/low prices to determine box size?
7. Why is it better to use one-box reversal charts to track fulcrum formations?
8. Describe a double top pattern using three different reversal sizes.

REFERENCES

Du Plessis, Jeremy. 2005. *The Definitive Guide to Point and Figure*. Cambridge, UK: Harriman House Publishing.

Dorsey, Thomas J. 2001. *Point and Figure Charting*. Hoboken, NJ: John Wiley & Sons.

Wheelan, Alexander. 1954. *Study Helps in Point and Figure Technique*. New York: Morgan, Rogers and Roberts.

CHAPTER
16

Ichimoku Charting and Analysis

Ichimoku Kinko Hyo analysis is very rapidly gaining popularity in Western-based technical analysis. It offers traders and analysts a unique and powerful way of reading current market behavior and also acts as a leading indicator of potential future support and resistance. It is a surprisingly easy overlay indicator to use despite its complex appearance on the charts. Once mastered, it will afford practitioners a fast and straightforward way of determining market regime changes and future market reaction levels.

16.1 CONSTRUCTING THE FIVE ICHIMOKU OVERLAYS

Goichi Hosoda, also known as Ichimoku Sanjin, introduced his work based on Japanese candlestick charting in the late 1960s. It is basically a candlestick chart superimposed with five overlays comprising moving-average-type overlay indicators. Ichimoku Kinko Hyo loosely translates into *single glance balance* or *one glance equilibrium* chart. Goichi Hosoda was interested in presenting a way of encapsulating the entire current market sentiment and future outlook on a single chart.

Components of an Ichimoku Chart

An Ichimoku chart is essentially a Japanese candlestick chart superimposed with five moving-average-type overlay indicators. Ichimoku charting was originally intended to offer a longer-term outlook on the markets, and as a consequence the daily chart was the *preferred timeframe* when conducting Ichimoku chart analysis. As will be explained later, there is another reason why the daily chart was chosen with respect to the lookback periods selected for the Ichimoku overlays. Nevertheless, many modern-day practitioners also apply Ichimoku analysis to the sub-hourly and hourly timeframes. As popularity for hourly and sub-hourly applications of Ichimoku chart analysis increases, so will its reliability and potential impact on market action, all fueled by the effects of self-fulfilling prophecy.

The five overlay indicators found on the Ichimoku Japanese candlestick chart are:

1. Tenkan-sen (Conversion or Turning Line)
2. Kijun-sen (Base Line)
3. Senkou Span A (Cloud Span A or Leading Span A)
4. Senkou Span B (Cloud Span B or Leading Span B)
5. Chikou Span (Lagging Line)

The area between the Senkou Span A and Senkou Span B is known as the Ichimoku cloud, or *kumo*. The cloud is the most important element on an Ichimoku chart, and the majority of trades initiated are based on the interaction of price with the cloud. Generally speaking, all five overlays act for the most part as bullish or bearish signals, while the cloud has the added function of being the main and single most important trigger for entry to, and exit from, the markets. See Figure 16.1 for an example of a typical Ichimoku chart, that is, a standard daily Japanese candlestick chart with five overlay indicators.

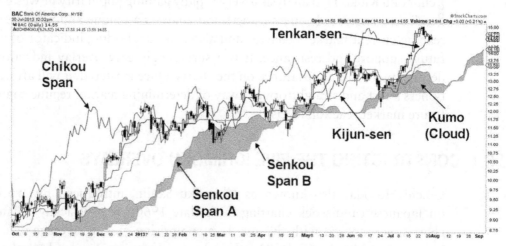

FIGURE 16.1 Ichimoku Daily Chart of Bank of America Corp.
Courtesy of Stockcharts.com

Time Displacement, Lookback Characteristics, and Price Averaging of the Ichimoku Overlay Components

Some unique properties of Ichimoku overlays include:

- Time-displacement characteristics
- Lookback characteristics
- Price-averaging approach

The Tenkan-sen is calculated by taking the rolling *mid-range* price of the last nine periods, while the Kijun-sen is calculated by taking the rolling mid-range price of the last 26 periods. Care must be taken here to distinguish between conventional average mid-price and mid-range price. Though both represent a form of *average price*, the approach to averaging is markedly different. Mid-range price is the average price between the highest peak and the lowest trough of the last N periods, while conventional average mid-price represents the average of all the mid-prices of each bar over the last N periods. In Figure 16.2, H represents the high of each bar, while L represents the low. Notice the difference between the two average price calculations.

In short, Ichimoku charts use the rolling mid-*range price* while conventional moving averages employ the *average mid-price*. Figure 16.3 highlights the visual contrast between the two types of averaging by comparing the 26-day simple moving average to the 26-day Kijun-sen. Rolling mid-range prices do not possess a smooth appearance, unlike simple moving averages. This is because the rolling average mid-range price only changes if there is a higher peak or lower trough

CALCULATING THE ICHIMOKU AVERAGE

Mid-price of each bar is averaged over last 9 bars	Mid-range price of the last 9 bars

$$\text{Average Mid-price} = \frac{(H1+L1)/2+(H2+L2)/2+\ldots+(H9+L9)/2}{9}$$

[Average Mid-price]

$$\text{Mid-range price} = \frac{(H7+L4)}{2}$$

[Mid-range Price]

FIGURE 16.2 Average Mid-Price versus Range Mid-Price.

629

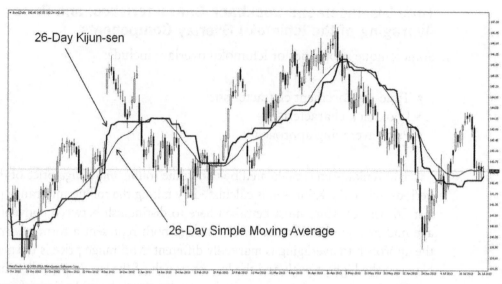

FIGURE 16.3 26-Day SMA versus Kijun-sen on the Daily Bund Chart.
Source: MetaTrader 4

over the last twenty-six periods. This characteristic is shared by the Tenkan-sen, Senkou Span B, and—to a *lesser* extent—the Senkou Span A (since Span A is a simple moving average of two rolling mid-range prices).

The Senkou Span A is calculated by taking the *average of the Tenkan-sen and Kijun-sen,* and plotting its 26 periods into the future. See Figure 16.4.

Senkou Span B is calculated by taking the *mid-range* price of the last 52 periods and plotting it 26 periods into the future. As mentioned earlier, the additional simple average smoothing action on Senkou Span A gives it a smoother appearance than that of Senkou Span B. See Figure 16.5.

Chikou Span is just the current or closing price plotted 26 periods back in time. It is in fact the equivalent of a conventional line chart that has been displaced

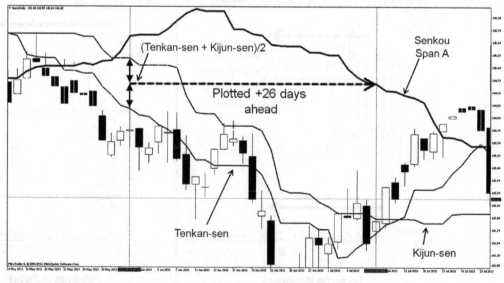

FIGURE 16.4 Senkou Span A on the Daily Bund Chart.
Source: MetaTrader 4

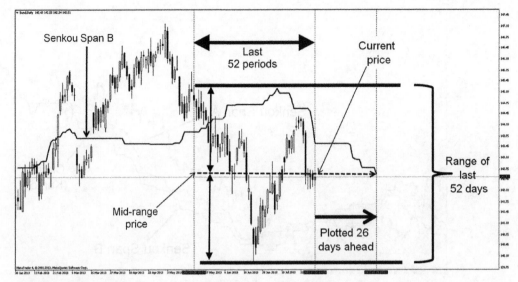

FIGURE 16.5 Senkou Span B on the Daily Bund Chart.
Source: MetaTrader 4

backward. It should be noted that it is the only Ichimoku overlay that does not use mid-range pricing. See Figure 16.6.

The Ichimoku Cloud, or Kumo, is represented by the area bounded by Senkou Span A and Span B. As the market rises and falls, Senkou Span A will flip above and below Senkou Span B. The color of the cloud is of no relevance whatsoever. Only the *thickness* and the *angle* of ascent or descent are of any importance in cloud analysis. See Figure 16.7.

Figures 16.8 and 16.9 summarize the main three characteristics of all five Ichimoku overlays.

Figure 16.10 displays a summary of all calculations required to construct each of the five Ichimoku overlays.

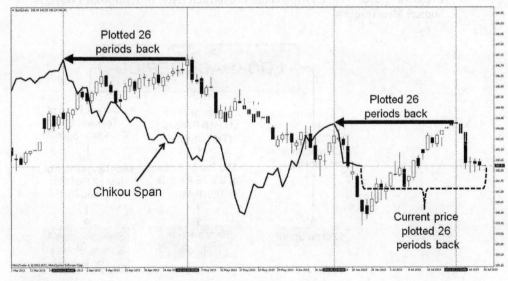

FIGURE 16.6 Chikou Span on the Daily Bund Chart.
Source: MetaTrader 4

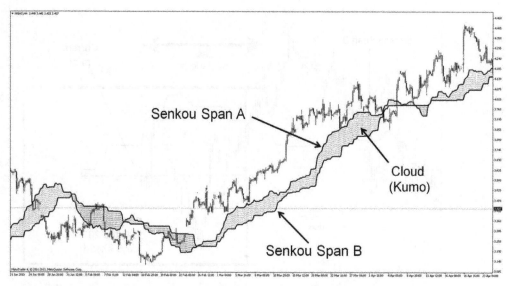

FIGURE 16.7 Cloud Action on the 4-Hour Natural Gas Chart.
Source: MetaTrader 4

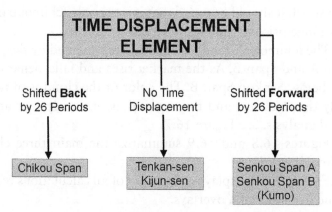

FIGURE 16.8 Time Displacement Characteristic of Ichimoku Overlays.
Source: MetaTrader 4

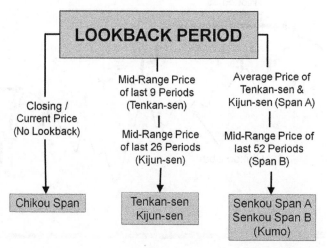

FIGURE 16.9 Lookback Period Characteristic of Ichimoku Overlays.
Source: MetaTrader 4

$$\text{Tenkan-sen} = \frac{\text{(Highest High + Lowest Low) over last 9 periods}}{2}$$

$$\text{Kijun-sen} = \frac{\text{(Highest High + Lowest Low) over last 26 periods}}{2}$$

$$\text{Span A} = \frac{\text{(Tenkan-sen + Kijun-sen)}}{2} \longrightarrow \boxed{\text{Plotted 26 days forward}}$$

$$\text{Span B} = \frac{\text{(Highest High + Lowest Low) over last 52 periods}}{2} \longrightarrow \boxed{\text{Plotted 26 days forward}}$$

$$\text{Chikou Span} = \text{Current or Closing Price} \longrightarrow \boxed{\text{Plotted 26 days back}}$$

FIGURE 16.10   Calculations for Ichimoku Overlays.

16.2 FUNCTIONAL ASPECT OF ICHIMOKU OVERLAYS

As with all technical overlays, Ichimoku overlays function as:

- Trend-identification indicators
- Barriers to price action, that is, as support and resistance (except for Chikou Span, which lags price)
- Bullish and bearish signals
- Leading indicators of future price barriers
- Trade triggers (mainly when price interacts with the cloud)

Trend-Identification Indicators

Being primarily based on moving averages, Ichimoku charts are particularly good at identifying the presence of a trend. Here are some trend-identification signals found on Ichimoku charts:

- Tenkan-sen rising above and falling below the Kijun-sen. Whenever the Tenkan-sen crosses above the Kijun-sen, it is an indication that a potential uptrend may be in effect. Conversely, whenever the Tenkan-sen crosses below the Kijun-sen, it is an indication that a potential downtrend may be in effect.
- Both Tenkan-sen and Kijun-sen rising above and falling below the cloud. Whenever the Tenkan-sen and Kijun-sen cross above the cloud, it is an indication that a potential uptrend may be in effect. Conversely, whenever the Tenkan-sen and Kijun-sen cross below the cloud, it is an indication that a potential downtrend may be in effect.
- Price rising above and falling below the Tenkan-sen, Kijun-sen, and cloud. Whenever price crosses above the Tenkan-sen, Kijun-sen, or cloud, it is an indication that a potential uptrend may be in effect. Conversely, whenever price crosses below the Tenkan-sen, Kijun-sen, or cloud, it is an indication that a potential downtrend may be in effect.

- Senkou Span A rising above and falling below Senkou Span B. Whenever the Senkou Span A crosses above the Senkou Span B, it is an indication that a potential uptrend may be in effect. Conversely, whenever the Senkou Span A crosses below the Senkou Span B, it is an indication that a potential downtrend may be in effect.
- Chikou Span rising above and falling retroactively below Tenkan-sen, Kijun-sen, price, and cloud. Whenever the Chikou Span crosses above the Tenkan-sen, Kijun-sen, price, or cloud, it is an indication that an uptrend may be in effect. Conversely, whenever the Chikou Span crosses retroactively below the Tenkan-sen, Kijun-sen, price, or cloud, it is an indication that a downtrend may be in effect.
- The angle of ascent and descent of the Tenkan-sen, Kijun-sen, cloud, and Chikou Span.

The angle of ascent and descent of the Tenkan-sen, Kijun-sen, cloud, and Chikou Span is an indication of the strength or conviction of the trend. Generally speaking, an angle of ascent of approximately 35 to 45 degrees is generally considered most favorable, as it suggests the possibility of a more steady and sustained move, with more upside expected, resulting in greater returns for market participants. Steeper angles normally suggest shorter-term action as the possibility of trend exhaustion is greater as market participants become more nervous about the rapid rise in price. In such scenarios, corrections tend to occur much more quickly and more deeply than with trends that show a more balance relationship with price and time. Finally, a shallow angle of ascent tends to suggest that a trend may be inherently weak and lack conviction, and is expected to remain as such for some time. Traders may choose to opt out of such lethargic trends and risk capital in more animated trends. See Figure 16.11.

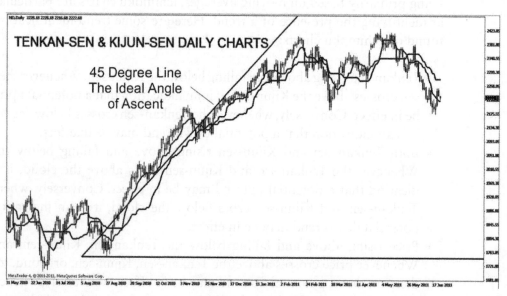

FIGURE 16.11 Tenkan-Sen and Kijun-Sen Angle of Ascent on the Daily Nasdaq Chart.
Source: MetaTrader 4

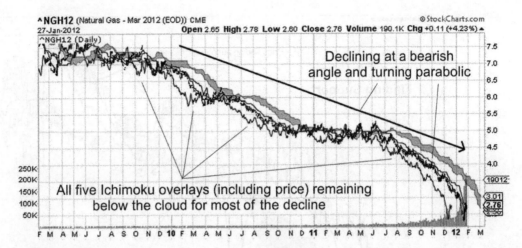

FIGURE 16.12   Downtrend Signaled on Daily Natural Gas Chart.
Courtesy of Stockcharts.com

Figure 16.12 shows Natural Gas descending at a bearish angle, with all five Ichimoku overlay indicators signaling that a strong downtrend is in effect.

Barriers to Price and Overlay Action

All technical overlay indicators represent barriers to price. The reason that they are barriers to price is simply because they represent support or resistance, and as such, market participants will normally place long orders above a support and short or sell orders below a resistance. Consequently, as price approaches support from above, it will encounter a proportionally larger degree of interest from market participants to go long and as a consequence vie for a better fill, which may cause price to initially rebound. Similarly, as price approaches resistance from below, it will encounter a proportionally larger degree of interest from market participants to go short or sell, which may cause price to initially correct. It is the actual placement of orders and competition for a more advantageous fill that causes both support and resistance to act as barriers to price action.

Price may find support or resistance at the:

- Tenkan-sen
- Kijun-sen
- Upper and lower cloud boundaries

Not only can price find support or resistance at any of the four Ichimoku moving averages, but all five Ichimoku overlays can also find support or resistance with each other. For example:

- Tanken-sen may find support or resistance at the Kijun-sen.
- Both the Tanken-sen and Kijun-sen may find support or resistance at the cloud.
- Chikou Span may find support or resistance retroactively at the cloud, price, Tenkan-sen, and Kijun-sen.

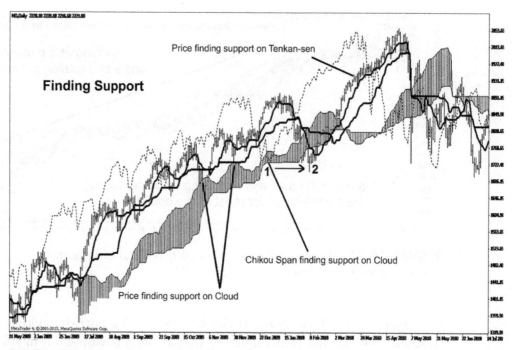

FIGURE 16.13 Finding Ichimoku Supports on the Daily Natural Gas Chart.
Source: MetaTrader 4

In Figure 16.13, it is interesting to note that the Chikou Span found support retroactively on Senkou B at Point 1, which may explain why price found support at Point 2.

In Figure 16.14, we again observe price finding support and resistance at various points on Senkou B and Senkou A.

The thickness of the Ichimoku clouds is of particular importance when referring to barriers. *The thinner the cloud, the greater will be the tendency for price to penetrate it.* In short, a thicker cloud represents a potentially stronger barrier to price and is therefore bullish if price lies above it, whereas a thinner cloud

FIGURE 16.14 Finding Ichimoku Support and Resistance on the Daily Soybean Chart.
Courtesy of Stockcharts.com

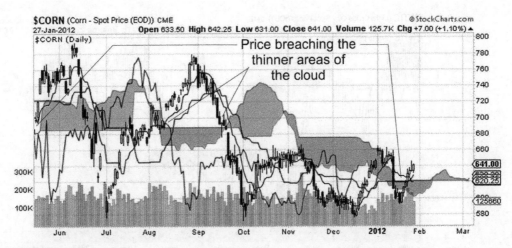

FIGURE 16.15 Price Violating the Thinner Clouds on the Daily Corn Chart.
Courtesy of Stockcharts.com

represents a potentially weaker barrier to price and is therefore relatively less bullish if price is above it. See Figure 16.15.

Figure 16.16 is another example of price having a tendency to violate the thinner areas of the cloud.

In Figure 16.17, we see Light Crude Oil finding resistance at the cloud at Points 1 and 2, and subsequently finding support at Points 3 and 4. Notice that the cloud is particularly thick at Points 1, 3, and 4, acting as a stronger barrier to price.

It is important to realize that although price can never find support or resistance at the Chikou Span, the Chikou Span itself can find support or resistance *retroactively* at the Ichimoku cloud, price, and at both the Tenkan-sen and Kijun-sen. We have already saw an example of this at Points 1 and 2 in Figure 16.13.

FIGURE 16.16 Violating the Thinner Clouds on the Daily Spot Gold Chart.
Courtesy of Stockcharts.com

FIGURE 16.17 Thick Clouds at Support and Resistance on the Daily Light Crude Oil (Spot) Chart.
Courtesy of Stockcharts.com

Combining Ichimoku and Fibonacci Retracements

Employing Fibonacci ratio analysis on the Ichimoku barrier overlays is particularly effective in identifying potential areas of support and resistance. In Figure 16.18, we observe the Chikou Span finding resistance at price. We also see a confluence of bearish signals at Point 1 where price was rejected after testing the cloud, which was incidentally at a 38.2 percent Fibonacci retracement level, measured over the observed price range AB. Subsequently, at Point 2 we see price finding support at the cloud, coinciding perfectly with the 50 percent retracement level. See Figure 16.18.

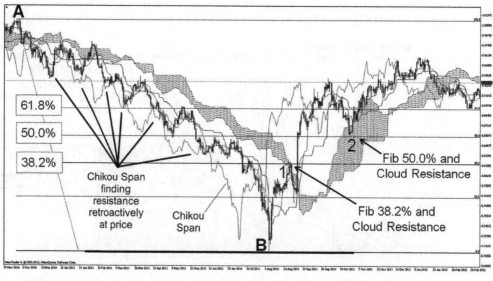

FIGURE 16.18 Fibonacci-Cloud Confluences on the Daily Natural Gas Chart.
Source: MetaTrader 4

Bullish and Bearish Ichimoku Indications

Among the five Ichimoku overlays, both the cloud and Chikou Span are considered the most important indicators of sentiment. Here are some bullish indications or signals found on Ichimoku charts.

Price is considered bullish if it is:

- above the Tenkan-sen,
- above the Kijun-sen,
- above the cloud, or
- rising at a bullish angle.

The market is also considered bullish if:

- Tenkan-sen crosses above the Kijun-sen,
- Tenkan-sen and the Kijun-sen cross above the cloud,
- Chikou Span is retroactively above price,
- Chikou Span is retroactively above the Tenkan-sen, Kijun-sen, or cloud,
- Tenkan-sen and the Kijun-sen are rising at a bullish angle,
- the cloud is rising at a bullish angle, or
- the cloud is thick when price is above it.

For bearish indications, price is considered bearish if it is:

- below the Tenkan-sen,
- below the Kijun-sen,
- below the cloud, or
- is declining at a bearish angle.

The market is also considered bearish if:

- Tenkan-sen crosses below the Kijun-sen,
- Tenkan-sen and the Kijun-sen cross below the cloud,
- Chikou Span is retroactively below price,
- Chikou Span is retroactively below the Tenkan-sen, Kijun-sen, or cloud,
- Tenkan-sen and the Kijun-sen are declining at a bearish angle,
- The cloud is declining at a bearish angle, or
- The cloud is thick when price is below it.

Only in a strong uptrend will all five Ichimoku overlays be in agreement with each other on whether the market is bullish or bearish. Most of the time, some signals will conflict with others. When that happens, the market is usually in or about to go into, ranging mode.

The Japanese candlesticks play an important role in revealing the current sentiment in the market. The candlestick formation that unfolds at support and resistance is often a significant factor in forecasting price action. The candlestick behavior within the clouds is also an important clue as to the potential direction of price breakout.

639

FIGURE 16.19 Indentifying Bullish and Bearish Signals on the Daily Dow Jones Shanghai Index.
Courtesy of Stockcharts.com

Let us now examine a couple of charts and attempt to work out their bullish and bearish indications. See Figure 16.19.

From Figure 16.19, the bearish indications are:

- The cloud is in a downtrend.
- Price is below the cloud.
- Both the Tenkan-sen and Kijun-sen are below the cloud.
- The Chikou Span is retroactively below the cloud, Tenkan-sen, and Kijun-sen, as seen at Time line 1

From Figure 16.19, the bullish indications are:

- Price is above both the Tenkan-sen and Kijun-sen.
- Tenkan-sen has crossed above the Kijun-sen.
- The cloud is relatively thin above current price, indicating potentially weaker resistance at the cloud.
- Although the overall sentiment is still bearish as price, Tenkan-sen, Kijun-sen, and Chikou Span are all below the cloud, early signs of potential bullishness are beginning to appear on the shorter-term Ichimoku moving averages.

For our next example, refer to Figure 16.20.
From Figure 16.20, the bullish indications are:

- Price is above Kijun-sen and the cloud.
- Tenkan-sen has crossed above the Kijun-sen.
- Both the Tenkan-sen and Kijun-sen are above the cloud.

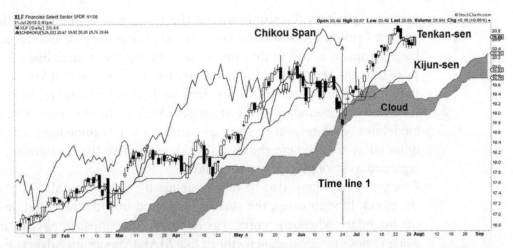

FIGURE 16.20 Indentifying Bullish and Bearish Signals on the Daily Financial Select Sector SPDR.
Courtesy of Stockcharts.com

- The Chikou Span is retroactively above the cloud, price, and both the Tenkan-sen and Kijun-sen, as seen at Time line 1.
- The cloud is ascending at a bullish angle.
- The cloud is relatively thick below current price, indicating potentially strong resistance at the cloud.

From Figure 16.20, the bearish indications are:

- Price is below Tenkan-sen.
- Price is approaching a relatively thin area of the cloud, which may potentially see price breaching any support provided by the cloud.

Ichimoku Cloud-Based Trade Triggers

Employing the use of Ichimoku overlays as a means of initiating or managing trades is gaining popularity, in addition to being a very effective method of analyzing market behavior. The overlays may be used to:

- Initiate full or partial entries or exits
- Position and size stoplosses

Initiating simple entries is predominantly executed at the cloud boundaries. Here are the various options available for initiating an entry at the cloud:

1. When price tests the upper or lower cloud boundary, the trader may initiate an entry *against* that boundary, in the form of a *reversal entry*. A reversal entry simply means to go long at support and go short at resistance, as opposed to a breakout entry, which means to go long if price breaches resistance and to go short if it breaches support. If price tests the Senkou A cloud boundary from above, the stoploss is positioned within the cloud, just below the Senkou A cloud boundary If the cloud is not too thick at the point of entry, the trader

may also position the stoplosses on the other side of the cloud, that is, below the Senkou B cloud boundary, assuming that the risk associated with the larger stopsize is still within the money management guidelines. Similarly, if price tests the Senkou B cloud boundary from below, the stoploss is positioned within the cloud, just above the Senkou B cloud boundary, or even above the Senkou A boundary if the stopsize is well within its money management guidelines. With respect to reversal entries, it is recommended that entries be initiated at areas where the cloud is thicker, where the barriers are generally regarded as strongest and most reliable

- Reversal entries may also be taken against the cloud boundaries from *within* the cloud. In such cases, the stoploss is placed outside the cloud, just beyond the boundary where the entry was initiated. The stopsize may be determined using various price-filtering methods like MAE (Maximum Adverse Excursion), volatility based stopsizing using multiples of ATR or standard deviation, fixed and variable percentage stopsizing, algorithmic or pattern based stops (e.g., Guppy's Count Back Line, 2-Bar exits, etc.), and the use of other overlay barriers like Fibonacci, Gann, or Floor Trader's Pivot point levels for a loss exit.

- Entries after a failed cloud breakout may also be initiated. The trade is initiated once price retreats back within the cloud. The actual point of entry depends on the price filtering employed. The stoploss should be placed just beyond the highest high of a failed upside breakout formation and just beyond the lowest low of a failed downside breakout formation.

- For cloud breakouts, it is best to initiate entries at areas where the cloud is relatively thin, that is where the barriers to price are generally regarded as weakest. The actual entry point depends again on the type of price filtering used, whether it is closing price, absolute dollar or point move, volatility based, percentage of price, or pattern based. The stop is usually positioned on the other side of the thin cloud.

See Figure 16.21 for a visual guide of the various ways to initiate a potential entry at the cloud boundaries.

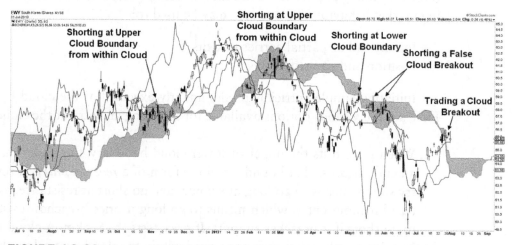

FIGURE 16.21 Indentifying Potential Trade Entries on the Daily South Korea iShares. Courtesy of Stockcharts.com

Initiating Entries via Ichimoku Moving Mid-Range Price Averages

Many traders also initiate entries when the moving averages cross over. For example, a long trade is occasionally initiated when the Tenkan-sen crosses above the Kijun-sen. But care must be taken that this trade is taken in the direction of the larger trend. It is therefore best to only initiate such an entry when there are other supportive or bullish indications, like having the cloud or other overlays rising at a bullish angle. The Chikou Span should also be retroactively above both cloud and price. Finally, the cloud itself should be favorably thick before the Ichimoku moving average crossover long trade is taken. The converse is true for initiating trades in a downtrend.

Use of Japanese Candlesticks at the Ichimoku Overlays

It is important to note that practitioners of Ichimoku charting use Japanese candlestick pattern analysis at the Ichimoku overlays as a means of defining entry and exit levels in the market. For example, the appearance of a shooting star at Senkou A resistance is a strong indication of a potential correction or reversal in price toward the lower range of the cloud. Similarly, the appearance of a bullish engulfing pattern at Senkou B support is a strong indication of a potential correction or reversal in price toward the upper range of the cloud. Japanese candlestick analysis is an integral part of Ichimoku chart analysis.

Note that many practitioners also combine Western-based oscillators as an additional means of identifying potential price reaction and reversal at the various Ichimoku overlay barriers. For a detailed analysis of Japanese candlestick patterns, please refer to Chapter 14.

16.3 ADVANTAGES AND DISADVANTAGES OF USING ICHIMOKU CHARTING

One major disadvantage of using moving averages is that they perform rather poorly during ranging action or consolidation. Since most of the Ichimoku overlays are based on some kind of moving average construction, they tend to suffer from whipsaws in ranging markets with the issuance of too many buy and sell signals. Just as with conventional moving averages, this renders Ichimoku charting highly susceptible to false signals being generated as price whipsaws around the four moving averages (with the exception of Chikou Span). Ichimoku therefore performs better during trending action. See Figure 16.22.

Such whipsaws affect the Tenkan-sen and Kijun-sen much more than the cloud. This is because the cloud is forward displaced by 26 periods, making it less sensitive and susceptible to market noise and whipsaws. This is the very same reason Joe DiNapoli and Bill Williams incorporate forward-shifted moving averages within their popular Double Repo and Alligator trade setups, respectively.

Another issue associated with using multiple moving-average-type overlay indicators in Ichimoku charting is that it increases the probability of generating conflicting signals. This usually confuses practitioners new to Ichimoku cloud analysis.

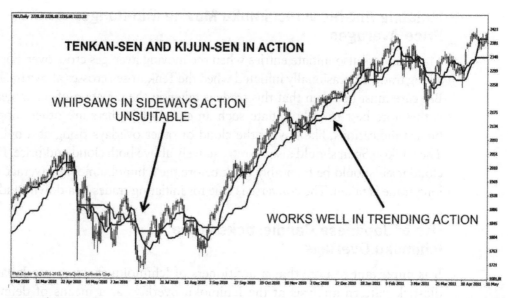

FIGURE 16.22 Whipsaw Action Across Ichimoku Moving Averages on the Natural Gas Daily Chart.
Source: MetaTrader 4

One advantage of using Ichimoku indicator overlays is that they forecast future price barriers. Practitioners are able to easily visualize potential future cloud support in an uptrend and potential future cloud resistance in a downtrend. Again, this is a consequence of using forward-displaced moving averages. It is also useful to note that Ichimoku charting is not affected by the type of scaling used on its charts. Switching from arithmetic to logarithmic scaling does not have an impact on the analysis. This is because moving averages are strictly numerically determined.

16.4 TIME AND PRICE DOMAIN CHARACTERISTICS OF ICHIMOKU OVERLAYS

The method of construction of the overlays lends itself naturally to the identification and favorable interaction of natural market-based cycle harmonics. The prevalent use of harmonically related periods like 26 and 52 (which is 2×26) is especially effective on the daily charts, as this takes full advantage of the underlying monthly or four-week cycle in the markets. Extending the lookback period to 52 days helps to seek out larger harmonically related cycles that may potentially corroborate shorter-term signals. The cloud, which is forward displaced by 26 days, is essentially projecting future support and resistance levels that are one monthly cycle ahead. Senkou Span B tracks the next larger harmonic cycle and uses this information to forecast support and resistance over a period of the next shorter-term cycle. The harmonicity appears on the charts when the chosen cycle periods actually reflect some real underlying repetitive market behavior. See Figure 16.23.

Ichimoku charting is really about the significance of the 50 percent retracement level. This is fairly obvious as three Ichimoku overlays use mid-range prices, that is, the 50 percent retracement level over three separate but harmonically related lookback periods—9, 26, and 52, where the 52-day period represents the

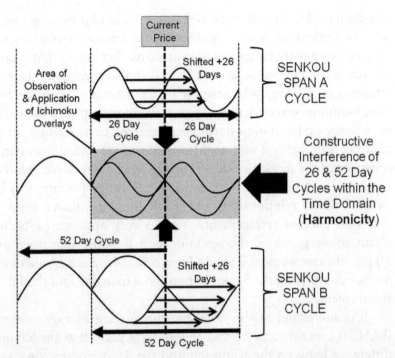

FIGURE 16.23 Harmonic Relationship between Senkou Span A and Senkou Span B within the Time Domain.

first harmonic cycle, the 26-day period the second, and the 9-day period the third harmonic cycle in the market. The mid-range prices of the Senkou Span A (which contain the two Ichimoku mid-range priced moving averages) and Senkou Span B are all forward displaced by 26 days. This shows the degree of importance that the 50 percent level has in Ichimoku cloud analysis. The 50 percent level represents the balance between the top and bottom halves of the market over harmonically related lookback periods. They are, in reality, the *lines of balance* or *equilibrium* in the markets. These lines of balance are then expected to remain relevant over the next monthly or second harmonic cycle, that is, over the next 26 days.

There is another aspect of balance within Ichimoku charting that is somewhat more subtle. It lies in the time domain. It is easy to see how a 52-period cycle is harmonically related to the 26-period cycle. They belong to a set of even harmonics, that is, periods related by a factor of 2 or ½. The 9-period cycle of the Tenkan-sen belongs to the set of odd harmonics, that is, periods related by a factor of ⅓, 3, ⅕, 5, ⅐, 7, and so on. Therefore, balance in Ichimoku *Kinko* Hyo is reflected not only in the construction and projection of the balance lines—which represents balance or equilibrium within the price domain—but is also reflected in the balance between the use of odd and even harmonic cycles in order to capture the *full expression* of the markets. Therefore, the Tenkan-sen 9-period lookback is really about tracking the odd harmonic cycle, which occurs approximately three times within a monthly cycle (3 cycles × 9 days = 27 days). We see that the 26-day lookback cycle *almost perfectly* matches up with a 27-day cycle lookback period, and may therefore be regarded, for all practical purposes, as a fairly accurate representation of a one-third odd harmonic cycle within the Ichimoku moving average setup. That is why the Tanken-sen is so unique among the Ichimoku overlays, in that it is the only moving average that attempts to capture market action that is not related to the set of even harmonic cycles. Senkou Span A is also special in this respect as it captures whatever remaining cycles result from the *interaction* or *superposition* of odd and even harmonic waves. Senkou Span A therefore captures the harmonics that reside *in between* odd and even harmonics, referred to as *partials*. In essence, Ichimoku charting is in reality a very sophisticated market cycle forecaster, capturing the full spectrum of the market's odd, even, and partial harmonic behaviors.

Because Ichimoku charts employ mid-range pricing, this implies that there exists a direct relationship between Ichimoku *balance lines* and Fibonacci or Gann 50 percent retracements. This is very apparent, especially with the frequent convergence of the Senkou Span B mid-range price and the Fibonacci 50 percent retracement level. In Figure 16.24 we see a bullish or supportive confluence comprising the Senkou Span B balance line and the Fibonacci 50 percent retracement.

It is interesting to also note that the moving average convergence-divergence (MACD) uses the same 12 and 26 lookback periods as the Ichimoku overlays. The difference between the Kijun-sen and the 26-period moving average used in the MACD is that the moving average used in the MACD is an exponential moving average of closing prices, whereas the Kijun-sen is a moving average of mid-range prices. The MACD only tracks the even harmonic cycles in the markets.

In summary, the Senkou Span B and Kijun-sen attempt to capture even harmonic cycles over both the two-month and one-month periods respectively, while the Tenkan-sen attempts to capture market action expressed in odd harmonic cycles. The Senkou Span A bridges the gap by being in the unique position of attempting to capture more complex market expression resulting from the superposition or interaction of odd and even harmonic wave action. See Figure 16.25.

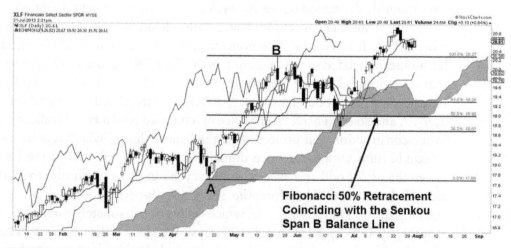

FIGURE 16.24 Senkou Span B Aligning with the Fibonacci 50 Percent Retracement Level. Courtesy of Stockcharts.com

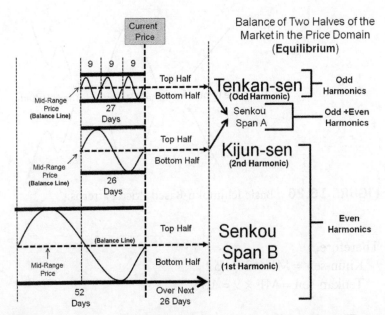

FIGURE 16.25 Projection of Mid-Range Price for the Four Ichimoku Overlays within the Price Domain.
Source: MetaTrader 4

Timeframe Implications and Setting the Ichimoku to an Underlying Cycle

The implication of all this is that the Ichimoku charting was specifically designed for use on the daily timeframe, or daily interval chart. It was constructed to exploit the natural monthly (i.e., 26-day) market cycle. *There was a reason to use the daily charts.* Applying Ichimoku charting on other timeframes where no real underlying 26-period cycle exists will generally render it less effective. The Ichimoku chart is essentially a harmonic wave analyzer, and as such either the Kijun-sen or Senkou Span A lookback periods are tuned to the main underlying cycle, allowing the Senkou Span B to analyze the next lower (even) harmonic cycle, while the Tenkan-sen analyzes the odd harmonic cycle period above that of the Senkou Span A. Therefore, in order to employ Ichimoku analysis on other market cycles, set either the Kijun-sen or Senkou Span B to the new cycle period. But the ratio of the lookback periods must be preserved.

For example, the lookback-period ratio between the Ichimoku overlays is 9 to 26 to 52. So if the new cycle period under observation is 104, we either set the Kijun-sen or Senkou Span B to this new value.

For setting it to Senkou Span B (as the first harmonic cycle), we calculate it as follows:

First, find the multiplication factor, MF.
  MF = (new cycle period/Senkou Span B)
  = 104/52
  = 2

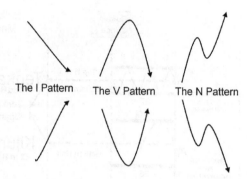

FIGURE 16.26 Basic Ichimoku-Based Price Patterns.

Therefore,

Kijun-sen = MF × 26 = 52

Tenkan-sen = MF × 9 = 18

Therefore, the new lookback periods are 18 to 52 to 104. The ratio of the lookback periods is preserved. Note that 18 to 52 to 104 can be reduced to 9 to 26 to 52 by dividing across the ratios by MF.

For setting it to Kijun-sen (as the first harmonic cycle), we calculate it as follows:

First find the multiplication factor, MF.

MF = (new cycle period/Kijun-sen)

= 104/26

= 4

Therefore,

Senkou Span B = MF × 52 = 208

Tenkan-sen = MF × 9 = 36

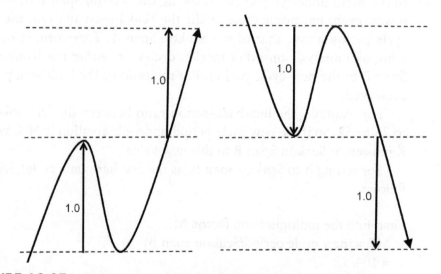

FIGURE 16.27 Ichimoku-Based Price Expansions for the V Pattern.

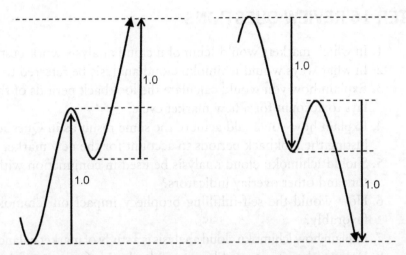

FIGURE 16.28   Ichimoku-Based Price Projections for the *N* Pattern.

The new lookback periods are now 36 to 104 to 208. Again, the ratio of the lookback periods is preserved. In this case the ratio of the lookback periods may be reduced to 9 to 26 to 52 by dividing across the ratios by MF.

Notice that to analyze and track smaller wave cycles or higher harmonics via Ichimoku charting, we set the Senkou Span B to the new underlying cycle period. For analysis of larger wave cycles or lower harmonics, we set the Kijun-sen to the new underlying cycle period instead.

16.5 BASIC ICHIMOKU PRICE-PROJECTION TECHNIQUES

Ichimoku cloud analysis also allows for the determination of minimum price objectives. This is done using price projections based on price patterns. A few basic Ichimoku-based price patterns are displayed in Figure 16.26.

Minimum price objectives are just 1-to-1 ratio expansions of the height of the pattern. For the V-pattern expansions, see Figure 16.27.

For the N-pattern expansions, see Figure 16.28.

The Ichimoku V patterns are not unlike the Western V-Top/Bottom formations. The Ichimoku *N* patterns are essentially identical to the A-B-C-D pattern, also referred to as the measured move. Similar patterns and their price expansions and projections have been dealt with in detail in Chapter 13.

16.6 CHAPTER SUMMARY

We have seen that Ichimoku charting is more than just a simple set of moving averages on a daily Japanese candlestick chart. The lookback periods of its overlays are based on the monthly cycle in the commodity markets. Each overlay tracks a specific monthly cycle harmonic, capturing the behavioral nuances of market action. It then uses this as a basis for projecting potential support and resistance levels for subsequent monthly cycles.

CHAPTER 16 REVIEW QUESTIONS

1. In which markets would Ichimoku cloud analysis work best?
2. In what ways would Ichimoku cloud analysis be referred to as subjective?
3. Explain how you would calculate the lookback periods of the Ichimoku overlays to account for a new market cycle.
4. Explain how you could achieve the same result as in Questions 3 without adjusting the lookback periods to account for the new market cycle.
5. Should Ichimoku cloud analysis be used in conjunction with Western oscillators and other overlay indicators?
6. How would the self-fulfilling prophecy impact on Ichimoku cloud analysis favorably?
7. Explain how Ichimoku cloud analysis is a study of market balance and equilibrium.
8. Describe how you would use a multiple timeframe setup based on Ichimoku cloud analysis.

REFERENCES

Elliott, Nicole. 2007. *Ichimoku Charts*. Harriman House Ltd.

Linton, David. 2010. *Cloud Charts*. Updata PLC.

Patel, Manesh. 2010. *Trading with Ichimoku Charts*. Hoboken, NJ: Wiley Trading.

CHAPTER
17

Market Profile

LEARNING OBJECTIVES

After studying this chapter, you should be able to:

- Understand how to interpret the market in terms of its balance between price and value
- Use Market Profile to define trends and consolidations
- Identify and differentiate between short- and longer-term market participant activity
- Understand the difference between responsive and initiative buying and selling in the markets
- Calculate the value area in term of Time Price Opportunities (TPOs) and volume
- Determine if there is upside buying or downside selling pressure in the markets over the short and longer term

Market Profile is essentially the charting of the balance between supply and demand, in terms of the level of agreement between price and its perceived value. It is an extremely useful way of viewing market action in terms of whether the participants believe prices are fair or unfair, disadvantageous or advantageous, with respect to their shorter- or longer-term outlook. And unlike conventional charting, trends are determined with respect to the previous day's perception of fair value. This makes Market Profile an indispensable form of analysis to the serious practitioner of technical analysis.

17.1 THE SEARCH FOR FAIR PRICE OR VALUE

The price discovery mechanism unfolds in response to the overall market participants' belief as to whether prices represent a fair reflection of value. If market participants do not perceive value around the current prices, they will react accordingly by buying or selling the market, causing markets to move or trend toward an area where they believe prices are a true reflection of value. This *agreement* between price and value is wholly dependent on the perceptions of market participants.

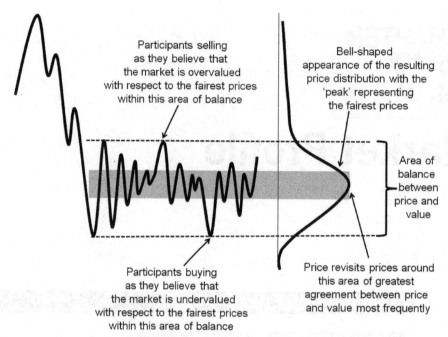

FIGURE 17.1 Area of Balance Between Price and Value.

Markets do not trend all the time. Once prices start to find agreement with value, market participants will have potentially less cause or reason to initiate any further activity until either new information enters the market or a bullish or bearish technical signal invites further participatory activity. It is during the period of balance between price and value that price starts to form a distribution as it oscillates and fluctuates around the new area of balance. This distribution of prices tends to form a bell-curve-like appearance, with the greatest agreement between price and value being found around the *fairest* price, as perceived by the majority of the market participants. Prices will rise and fall within this area of general agreement, trading back to the fairest price should prices appear unfairly high or low. See Figure 17.1.

This distribution, resulting from the behavioral responses of market participants, is not unlike those obtained from the sampling of other empirical data. For example, if we sampled the IQ of one thousand students, we would find that most of the IQs would fall around an average value, with fewer IQs lying at the upper and lower ends of the scale. We would also obtain the same bell-shaped distribution if we sampled the heights, weights, or the number coins that each student had in their pocket. If we plotted the distribution of IQs, it would look something similar to the plot seen in Figure 17.2.

Hence we see most IQ test scores gathering around a central value, normally represented by the mode, which in many cases is typically close to the average IQ value. This distribution may also be illustrated by turning it 90-degrees clockwise, as seen in Figure 17.3.

In the same manner, we may also represent price *as a function of its activity at each price level*, that is, the number of times it revisited a particular price level

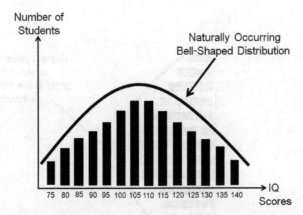

FIGURE 17.2 Frequency Distribution of IQ Test Scores Approximating a Bell-Shaped Curve.

within a specified duration. By representing price in this manner, we can easily observe its activity across various price levels, identifying the areas of balance between price and value simply by the degree and shape of the resulting distribution. See Figure 17.4. Note that the vertical axis tracks the direction of price, whereas the horizontal axis tracks the frequency of price activity at each price level. This cannot be easily observed on conventional bar or candlestick charting since they do not provide a clear graphic record of price frequency distribution.

So, how can we devise a chart that will enable us to see this distribution of price activity and hence identify areas of potential balance between price and value?

We can do this easily if we first record price activity over a specified period and subsequently collapse each separate segment of price activity into a composite profile of its price activity as time elapses. See Figure 17.5.

Referring to Figure 17.5, let us denote price movements within each half-hour period by a letter. Let us assign each successive half-hour period the letters A, B, C,

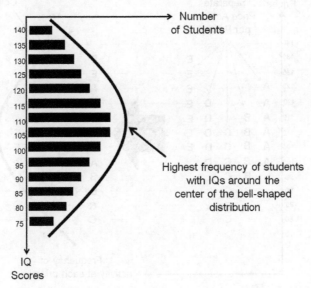

FIGURE 17.3 Frequency Distribution of IQ Test Scores Displayed Sideways.

FIGURE 17.4 Representing Price as Frequency Distribution Displayed Sideways.

D, and so on. We observe prices moving between $100 and $125 within the first half hour. In the second half hour, prices moves between $90 and $115. We continue assigning a new letter to all half-hour price movements for each successive period. In the illustration, we tracked exactly two-and-one-half hours worth of price activity, that is, A to E. We now collapse all the letters to the left-hand side, filling up all empty spaces to the left, and we end up with a bell-shaped distribution of price activity. It is now obvious that the prices with the most activity over the two-and-one-half hours are $105 and $110. This represents the prices with the greatest agreement with value. This distribution represents the *profile* of market action.

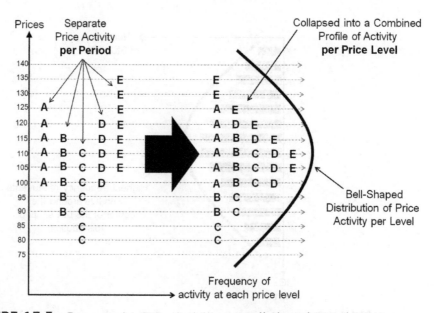

FIGURE 17.5 Representing Price Activity as a Bell-Shaped Distribution.

Note that not all distributions are perfectly distributed in the real markets. Nevertheless, prices are assumed to form a fairly symmetrical and balanced bell-shaped distribution *over time*. Therefore any skew to the lower or upper ends in the distribution is expected to gradually re-balance toward a more symmetrical profile as time passes. Prices are expected to eventually revert to the mean or average value of the distribution, which represents the fairest price.

The Value Area

This bell-shaped distribution of price activity occurs frequently and naturally in the markets as price searches for value. It is therefore not surprising and rather useful that it may be assumed to approximate a *normal* distribution, where its properties are very well known. As such, 68 percent of all activity is expected to lie within one standard deviation of the mean price of the distribution. This area of balance between price and value is called the *value area*. It represents the area where there is the greatest agreement between price and value. The further price is away from the mean, the greater the disagreement between price and value, that is, becoming more overvalued or undervalued with respect to the market. As prices continue to revert to fair price, such activity helps to balance the profile toward a more symmetrical distribution of prices. See Figure 17.6.

Calculating the Value Area via the TPO Count

In Market Profile, each half hour period is assigned or designated a letter and is called the *Time Price Opportunity* (TPO). It represents the time or period over which the market looks for an opportunity in price. The part of the distribution that lies closest to the middle of the distribution's range and contains the most letters, or TPOs, is called the *Point of Control* (POC). Should there be two equal

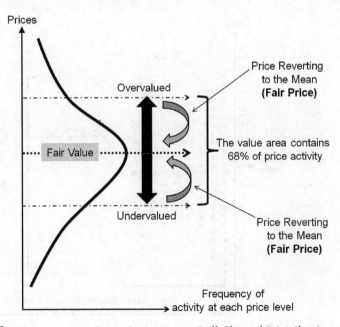

FIGURE 17.6 Representing Price Activity as a Bell-Shaped Distribution.

lines of TPOs that appear close to the middle of the distribution, the lower line of TPOs will be the POC.

To calculate the value area, we need to first locate the POC. To find the POC, find the range of the distribution and locate the middle of it. The range of a distribution is simply the difference between the highest- and lowest-priced TPOs. Finally, identify the longest line of TPOs that is closest to the middle of the range. That will represent the POC. See Figure 17.7.

In Figure 17.7, the range is $24 and the middle of the range is $84. The longest line of TPOs closest to the middle price is $84. Therefore, the POC is located at $84 and it comprises nine TPOs. Sometimes the opening price is denoted by the letter O, as seen at $88. If each period of lettering represents a half hour, the total duration of the entire distribution, assuming that M is the last price, is simply 13 × ½ hour = 6 ½ hours long (since M represents the thirteenth letter).

The value area is now calculated by:

1. Adding up all the TPOs in the distribution
2. Calculate 68 percent of the total number of TPOs
3. Compare the number of TPOs two prices above and two prices below the POC
4. Add the side with the larger amount of TPOs to the number of TPOs along the POC
5. Go two prices further on the side that was just included and add the side with the larger amount to the running total
6. Continue until 68 percent of the TPOs are accounted for within the distribution

See Figure 17.8.

Therefore, the area containing approximately 68 percent of all TPOs represents the value area. See Figure 17.9.

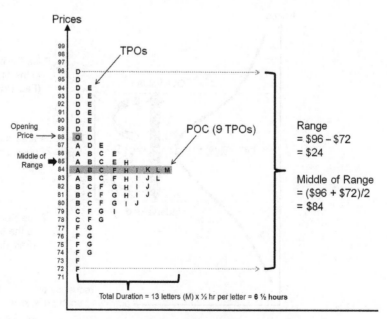

FIGURE 17.7 Finding the Point of Control (POC).

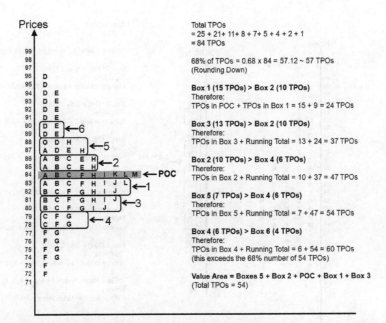

FIGURE 17.8 Finding the Value Area via the TPO Count.

Calculating the Value Area via Volume

We can also calculate the value area with respect to volume. It is calculated in a similar fashion to the TPO-based value area, with the only difference being the use of the price with highest volume instead of the POC as the central value for comparing volumes two prices above and below it. See Figure 17.10 for the calculations of volume-based value area.

Therefore, the area containing 68 percent of all volume represents the volume-based value area. See Figure 17.11.

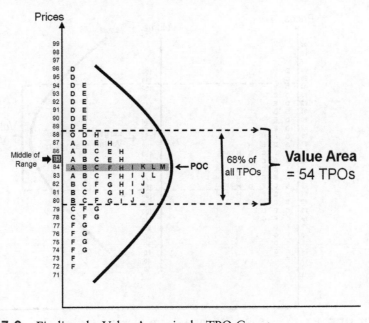

FIGURE 17.9 Finding the Value Area via the TPO Count.

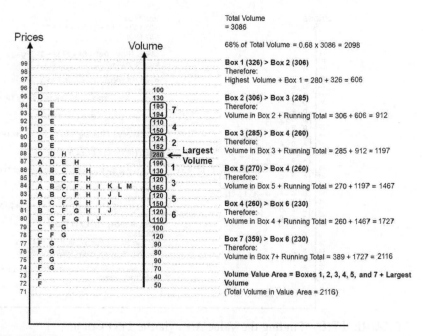

FIGURE 17.10   Finding the Volume-Based Value Area.

TPO Lettering Convention

In Market Profile, each half hour is assigned a letter ranging from capital A to X for the initial 12 hours and then followed by a to x for the remaining 12 hours, accounting for a full day's worth of trading activity. Many markets do not trade for 24 hours a day, and therefore not all of the letters are used. The practitioner may of course assign a different time period to the TPOs instead of

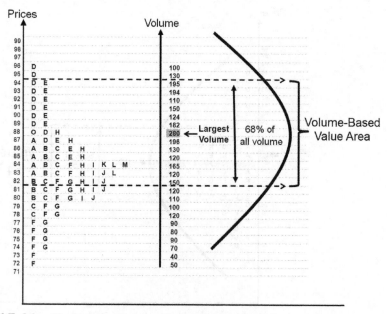

FIGURE 17.11   Finding the Volume-Based Value Area.

the conventional half-hour period in order to view the profile across a longer or shorter time horizon.

It is important to also realize that price gapping is not visually accounted for in the profile's graphic within each set of lettering. In a series of As for example, any gaps in price during that period of As is not visually displayed in the profile. But gaps in price are visually displayed if they exist between the new day's opening price and yesterday's value area, closing price, range extreme, and so on. They are not visually identifiable on an intraday basis.

Market Profile Elements

There are various chart elements that are unique to Market Profile. Refer to Figure 17.12.

In Figure 17.12, the range of TPOs indicated at 1 represents the *initial balance* of the profile's graphic. The initial balance represents the first hour of trading in the market (since it consists of letters A and B, each designated to one half-hour period). Trading within the initial balance is usually populated by the shorter-term participants, which includes the locals, day traders, and so on. Any move beyond the initial balance represents participation by the longer-term participants. *Although the shorter-term participants perceive prices as being a fair reflection of value within the initial balance*, the longer-term participants may perceive current prices as being undervalued and start driving prices higher, beyond the initial balance. Conversely, the longer-term participants may perceive current prices as being overvalued and start driving prices lower, below the initial balance. Hence all price movements or trends beyond the initial balance are generally regarded as activity by the longer-term participants who are not usually concerned whether

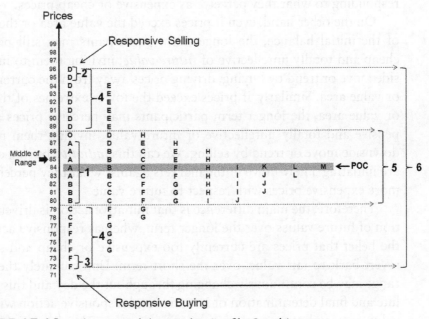

FIGURE 17.12 Elements of the Market Profile Graphic.

prices are fair or otherwise across shorter time horizons. Prices that seem expensive or unfair to the shorter-term or daily traders may in fact be regarded as cheap by the longer-term participants, if they believe that value will increase in the future. Similarly, prices that seem cheap to the shorter-term or daily traders may in fact be regarded as expensive by the longer-term participants if they believe that value will decrease in the future.

The range of TPOs indicated at 4 represents the *range extension*, that is, prices that exceed the initial balance. Range extension is regarded as evidence of activity by the longer-term participants.

The two uppermost extreme TPOs indicated at 2 represent the *single print selling tail*, whereas the lowermost TPOs indicated at 3 represent the *single print buying tail*. Tails must consist of at least two or three TPOs in order to be significant. Longer tails indicate greater conviction by the market participants. These extremes in price within the distribution range indicate very vigorous buying and selling behavior and reflect greater divergence between price and value. The range of prices indicated at 5 represents the value area based on the TPO count. Finally, the range of the distribution is indicated at 6, which is just the difference between the highest- and lowest-priced TPOs.

Market Participants of the Profile

If prices are at the upper extremes of the initial balance or value area, the daily or shorter-term participants may perceive prices as expensive, unfair, and totally unreflective of *current value*, inviting them to respond by selling, thereby returning prices to a fairer expression of value. Similarly, if prices are at the lower extremes of the initial balance or value area, the daily or shorter-term participants may perceive prices as being cheap and totally unreflective of current value, inviting them to respond by buying. We call this *responsive* buying and selling. They are responding to what they perceive as expensive or cheap prices.

On the other hand, even if prices exceed the value area or the upper extremes of the initial balance, the longer-term participants may still perceive prices as cheap and totally unreflective of *future value*, inviting them to initiate a new upside move or trend by buying, driving prices away from the current initial balance or value area. Similarly, if prices exceed the lower extremes of the initial balance or value area, the longer-term participants may perceive prices as being too expensive and totally unreflective of future value, inviting them to initiate a new downside move or trend by selling. We call this *initiative* buying and selling. They are initiating a new move in the markets against what they perceive as cheaper or more expensive prices with respect to future value.

Therefore, the main difference is that initiative action is driven by the expectation of future values over the longer term, whereas responsive action is driven by the belief that prices are currently too expensive or cheap and should return or revert back to fair value, over the short term. Unfortunately the value area and range may be continuously changing throughout the day and this makes the absolute and final determination of initiative and responsive action with respect to the value area and range extremities less consistent. The determination of initiative and responsive action with respect to the initial balance is not affected, as it does not change after the first hour, being fully defined.

Initiative and Responsive Action Based on an Objective Reference Point

Initiative or responsive action should therefore be based on a reference point that has *already been established* for a more consistent, objective, and reliable determination of:

- The market participants' buying and selling behavior
- The market's trend

The previous day's value area is the most logical choice for a fixed and absolute reference point for such a determination. Once market participants perceive a disagreement between price and value, they will respond in any of the *four* following ways:

1. Initiative Buying: Initiative buying occurs above the previous day's value area. The participants buy if they believe that prices are going higher in a rising market and that the market is currently undervalued. Initiative buying drives prices away from the previous day's value area and in the process gives rise to uptrends in the markets.

2. Responsive Buying: Responsive buying occurs below the previous day's value area. Participants buy if they believe that prices are too low or cheap and that the market is currently undervalued. Responsive buying reverts prices back toward the previous day's value area and in the process promotes balance between price and value in the markets.

3. Initiative Selling: Initiative selling occurs below the previous day's value area. Participants sell or go short if they believe that prices are going lower in a declining market and that the market is currently overvalued. Initiative selling drives prices away from the previous day's value area and in the process gives rise to downtrends in the markets.

4. Responsive Selling: Responsive selling occurs above the previous day's value area. Participants sell or go short if they believe that prices are too high or expensive and that the market is currently overvalued. Responsive selling reverts prices back toward the previous day's value area and in the process promotes balance between price and value in the markets.

Upon closer observation, one can see that both the longer-term activity of initiative buying and responsive selling occurs above the previous day's value area. Similarly, both initiative selling and responsive buying occurs below the previous day's value area. See Figures 17.13 to 17.16.

Trend followers try to decipher the actions of the *longer-term participants*, looking for signs of initiative buying or selling, which include breakouts from both the current day's initial balance and value areas, as well as from the previous day's value area and range.

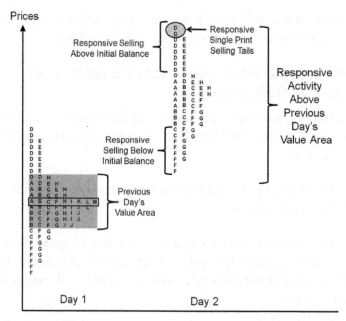

FIGURE 17.13   Responsive Activity above the Previous Day's Value Area.

Trends, Degrees of Bullishness and Bearishness, and the TPO Count

In a Market Profile, an uptrend is defined as initiative activity above the previous day's value area while a downtrend is initiative activity below the previous day's value area. The greater the distance in price from the previous day's value area, the greater will be the potential persistence and strength of the unfolding trend. See Figure 17.17.

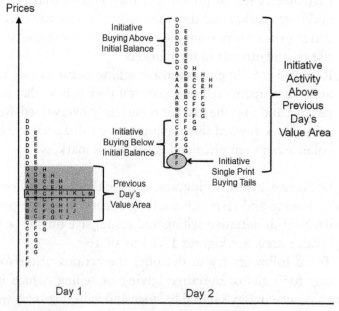

FIGURE 17.14   Initiative Activity above the Previous Day's Value Area.

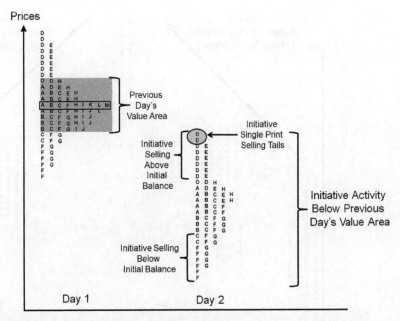

FIGURE 17.15 Initiative Activity below the Previous Day's Value Area.

Listed below are the six basic degrees of bullishness of any subsequent trend, in order of bullishness:

1. Current day's activity is within its own initial balance and above the previous day's value area (Least Bullish Scenario).
2. Current day's activity is above its own initial balance but within its value area. It is also above the previous day's value area.

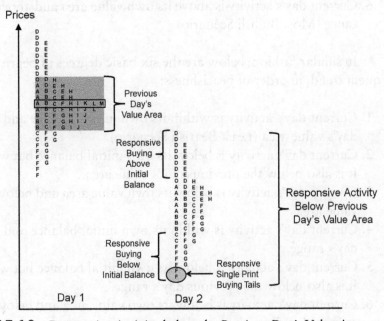

FIGURE 17.16 Responsive Activity below the Previous Day's Value Area.

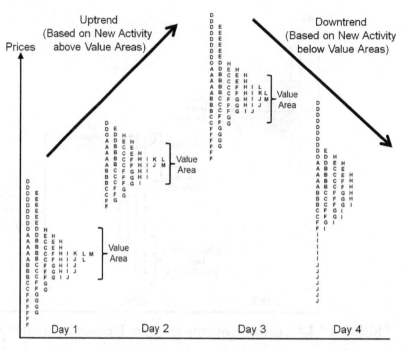

FIGURE 17.17 Profile Trend Activity Based on the Previous Day's Value Area.

3. Current day's activity is above its own value area and above the previous day's value area.

4. Current day's activity is within its own initial balance and above the previous day's range.

5. Current day's activity is above its own initial balance but within its value area. It is also above the previous day's range.

6. Current day's activity is above its own value area and above the previous day's range (Most Bullish Scenario).

In similar fashion, below are the six basic degrees of bearishness of any subsequent trend, in order of bearishness:

1. Current day's activity is within its own initial balance and below the previous day's value area (Least Bearish Scenario).

2. Current day's activity is below its own initial balance but within its value area. It is also below the previous day's value area.

3. Current day's activity is below its own value area and below the previous day's value area.

4. Current day's activity is within its own initial balance and below the previous day's range.

5. Current day's activity is below its own initial balance but within its value area. It is also below the previous day's range.

6. Current day's activity is below its own value area and below the previous day's range (Most Bearish Scenario).

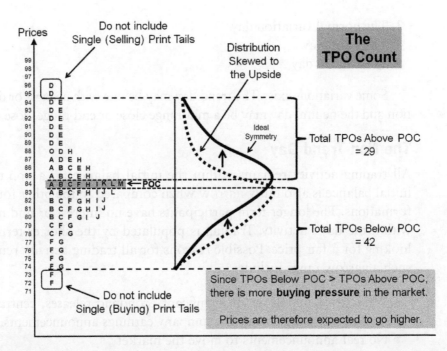

FIGURE 17.18 The TPO Count for Identifying Buying and Selling Pressure in the Market.

A novel approach to gauge the degree of buying or selling pressure in the market on any given day that is unique to Market Profile charting is the *TPO Count*. An underlying assumption in Market Profile is that the markets are expected to move toward a balance between price and value, and in the process to ideally achieve a *symmetrical distribution* of price activity around these areas of balance or value, over the longer term. Hence, any upside or downside skew within the distribution is expected to even out over time. The TPO count compares the number of TPOs above and below the POC. TPOs above the POC represent sellers or market participants with a bearish conviction while TPOs below the POC represent buyers or market participants with a bullish conviction. A larger number of TPOs above the POC suggests that there is potentially greater selling pressure in the market, and similarly, a larger number of TPOs below the POC suggests that there is potentially greater buying pressure in the market. Any imbalance of TPOs on either side of the POC skews the distribution.

To find the TPO count, count all the TPOs above and below the POC, excluding TPOs along the POC and all single tail TPOs. See Figure 17.18.

Therefore, if we identify buying pressure in an uptrend, that would indicate an added dimension of bullishness to the uptrend. Similarly, selling pressure in a downtrend would be a more bearish indication.

17.2 THE DAILY PROFILE FORMATIONS

There are five basic daily profile distributions that may unfold in the markets, namely:

1. The non-trend day
2. The normal day

3. The normal variation day
4. The trend day
5. The neutral day

Some variations exist. The trend day may be one with a single or double distribution and the neutral day may be a mid-range close or end-range close neutral days.

The Non-Trend Day

All trading activity remains within the initial balance on a non-trend day. The initial balance is also fairly narrow when compared to the other four daily profile formations. The longer-term participants have no interest or find no opportunity within the day's activity. Trading is populated by the shorter-term participants, looking for a fair price. Possible reasons for all trading activity remaining within such a narrow range include:

- Waiting for important or significant economic releases, central bank policy, interest rate announcements, company earnings announcements, and so on
- No real announcements to move the market

Trading opportunities include selling at the top and buying at the bottom of the initial balance range. See Figure 17.19.

The Normal Day

All trading activity remains mostly within the initial balance on a normal day. It differs from the non-trend day in that its initial balance is relatively wider. Note that there is some discrepancy here among various authors with respect to the violation of the initial balance on a normal day. According to Steven Hawkins, in *Steidlmayer on Markets*, the day's trading activity "produces a directionally biased range extension of about 50 percent beyond the first hour's range." Alternatively,

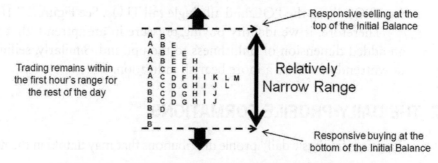

FIGURE 17.19 A Non-Trend Day.

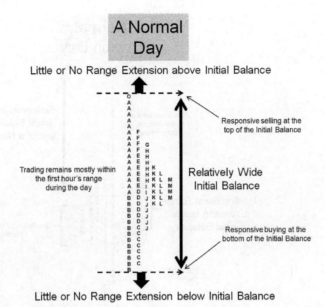

FIGURE 17.20 A Normal Day.

James Dalton, in his book *Mind over Markets*, states that the initial balance is not breached during the day's trading activity. Nevertheless, it is still best to assume, especially in today's more volatile markets, a position whereby trading activity is not generally expected to breach a relatively wider-than-normal initial balance, but if it does, it will not be a significant extension, not more than a very small percentage of the initial balance. See Figure 17.20 for a typical normal day.

The Normal Variation Day

In a normal variation day, prices breach the initial balance with a range extension that may measure up to twice the range of the initial balance. The breach is unidirectional, that is, only to one side of the initial balance. There is a stronger trend component associated with the normal variation day, though not as strong as that of a trend day. The longer-term participants drive prices beyond the initial balance once they perceive a mismatch between price and future value. The day's action may end with some responsive buying or selling by the longer-term participants, shutting off all further trend-related trading activity. Figure 17.21 illustrates an example of a normal variation day with a downside breakout of the initial range.

The Trend Day

In a trend day, prices breach the initial balance swiftly with a significant range extension created throughout the rest of the day. The initial balance experiences a breakout only to one side of the initial balance, that is, a unidirectional breakout. The initial balance is not as wide as that of the normal or normal variation day. The closing price should be at or in proximity to the upper or lower extremes of the day, depending on whether it is an uptrending or downtrending day, respectively.

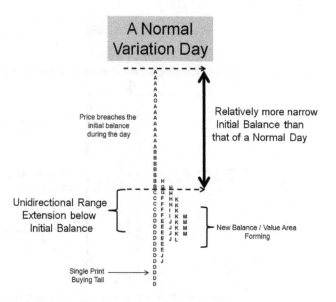

FIGURE 17.21   A Normal Variation Day.

The opening price should also be near or at the other end of the day's range. The initial balance is relatively narrow because the longer-term participants start off the day acting on a strong bullish or bearish view of the markets. Similarly, the width of the profile is also relatively narrow as compared to the normal or normal variation day, as fast-moving prices make it hard to build areas of balance at any one price during a strong trend. There is great disagreement between price and value during a trend day. Prices should finally settle around a new area of value or balance at or near the extreme end of the day's range extension. Prices should not revert back toward the initial balance if the longer-term participants have a strong directional conviction. Occasionally, prices form a double distribution, that is, two areas of value or balance between the end of the range extension and the breakout level of initial balance. Such a profile is called a *double distribution day*. Double distributions indicate that there is some uncertainty in the markets and that the trend may not be as strong as previously thought. The profile indicative of a very strong and aggressive trend would not display any clear areas of balance, and prices would extend in a pronounced series of single-print TPOs. See Figures 17.22 and 17.23.

The Neutral Day

In a neutral day, a bidirectional breach of the initial balance occurs during the day. This means that price breaches *both* the upper and lower boundaries of the initial balance. Since the initial balance is wider than that of a trend day, it indicates there is a battle between the daily short- and longer-term participants. The closing price is expected to be around the center of the distribution, that is, a *mid-range close neutral day*. If it closes near the end of either side of the range, then such a profile is expected to also exhibit a greater amount of volatility, with larger range

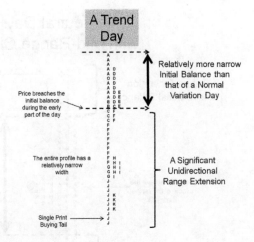

FIGURE 17.22 A Trend Day.

extensions on either side of the initial balance. Such a profile is called the *end-range close neutral day*. See Figures 17.24 and 17.25.

Profile Action Points

Traders may use the daily profile graphics as a means of determining entry and exit points. Trigger points for entries and exits include:

- The POC: Traders frequently use the previous day's POC as a support and resistance level for entry to, or exit from, the markets. The previous day's POC is traded just as any support or resistance barrier.

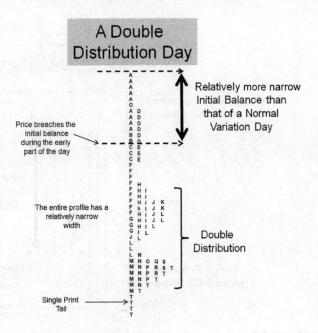

FIGURE 17.23 A Double Distribution Day.

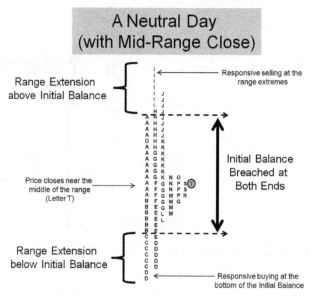

FIGURE 17.24 A Mid-Range Close Neutral Day.

- The Range Extremes: Traders also use the previous day's range extremes as support and resistance levels for entry to, or exit from, the markets.
- The Value Area: Traders may also use the previous day's value area as a zone of potential support or resistance.

The Profile's Big Picture

The tendency of price to seek balance in skewed distributions applies to longer time horizons as well. Look at the overall pattern of all daily profiles. Notice that

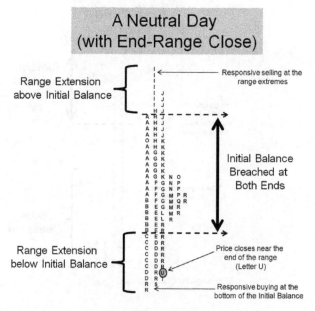

FIGURE 17.25 An End-Range Close Neutral Day.

the profiles create a larger composite profile. Locate the monthly POC of all daily TPOs. Find the monthly TPO count above and below the monthly POC. This should give the practitioner an idea of the monthly buying and selling pressure, as well as an indication of potential future price direction. A larger TPO count below the POC is bullish, and vice versa. Hence some profile traders only initiate a trade if the daily, weekly, and monthly TPO counts are all bullish or bearish. It is a form of multiple timeframe analysis of market sentiment, based on the profile graphic.

17.3 CHAPTER SUMMARY

As we have learned in this chapter, Market Profile is extremely effective in determining the behavior of market participants and on how they react to current and future value. It is predicated on the belief that price and value tend to agree over the longer term and as such trace out a predictable price path based on achieving that equilibrium. Market Profile charting is unique in that sense.

CHAPTER 17 REVIEW QUESTIONS

1. Explain how you would determine if there is more buying or selling pressure on any particular day using Market Profile charting.
2. Describe how you would calculate the value area using both the TPO and volume count methods.
3. What does the value area represent?
4. Define trend as it relates to the value area.
5. Define the potential points of entry for a trader using Market Profile as a means of trading the market.
6. What do single print buying and selling tails represent in Market Profile?
7. How would you use Market Profile to forecast potential future price direction? What is the basis for your forecast?
8. Explain how *reversion to the mean* is an underlying characteristic of Market Profile.

REFERENCES

Dalton, James F., Eric T. Jones, and Robert B. Dalton. 2013. *Mind over Markets*. Hoboken, NJ: John Wiley & Sons.

Keppler, John. 2011. *Profit with Market Profile*. Marketplace Books.

Steidlmayer, J. Peter, and Steven B. Hawkins. 2003. *Steidlmayer on Markets*. Hoboken, NJ: John Wiley & Sons.

CHAPTER
18

Basic Elliott Wave Analysis

Elliott wave analysis is widely used by institutional traders and analysts. The wave principle provides traders and analysts with a unique way of understanding market action, forecasting potential breakouts and significant reversals. This chapter covers all the basics of Elliott wave analysis with various chart examples.

18.1 ELEMENTS OF ELLIOTT WAVE ANALYSIS

Motive, Impulsive, and Corrective Waves

The reader is strongly advised to refer to the original writings of Ralph Nelson Elliott for a comprehensive and concise description of Elliott wave analysis. The references are located at the end of this chapter. Readers are advised to refer to *Elliott Wave Principle* by Frost and Prechter, which, in the author's opinion, represents the leading authority in the study and advancement of Elliott wave analysis.

The basic construct of Elliott waves consists of a 5-3 wave formation. This simply means that for every advance in price that consists of a five-wave move

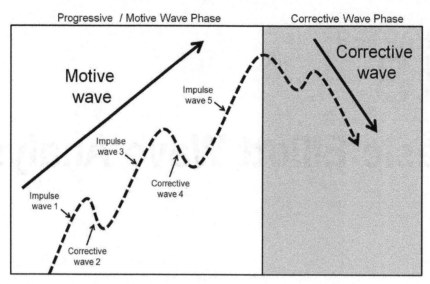

FIGURE 18.1 Motive and Corrective Waves.

up or down, which Robert Prechter refers to as a *motive wave*, there will be a reaction consisting of a three-wave move in the opposite direction, referred to as *corrective* waves. Each motive wave subdivides into three advancing waves called *impulse* waves and two corrective waves. See Figure 18.1.

It should be noted that each impulse wave also subdivides into five waves at a lower degree (labeled 1 to 5) and similarly, each corrective wave itself subdivides into three waves at a lower degree (labeled A to C), in the opposite direction to the motive wave. Waves 2 and 4 correct impulse waves 1, 3, and 5 whereas waves (A), (B), and (C) correct the motive wave itself, labeled as encircled number 1. See Figure 18.2.

In general, the distance traversed by the corrective waves should not retrace more than the distance traversed by motive or impulsive waves. This basic tendency allows for the development of trends in the market. *Motive waves are responsible*

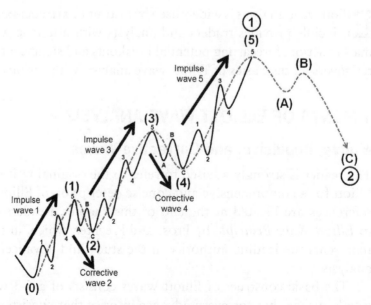

FIGURE 18.2 Impulsive and Corrective Wave Subdivisions.

for trend action, while corrective waves are responsible for retracements against a trend. It is important to note that impulsive waves are waves that move in the direction of a wave of one larger degree. This means that for a corrective wave, waves A and C are considered impulsive waves and wave B a corrective wave. This recursive subdivision represents the fractal-like nature of Elliott waves, where all wave degrees display a quality of self similarity. No matter which wave degree is observed, the wave structure will always manifest itself in the form of a 5-3 construct. Notice, in Figure 18.2, that the 5-3 wave structure in the subdivisions of waves (1) and (2) is replicated at a higher wave degree, labeled as waves encircled numbers 1 and 2.

Referring again to Figure 18.2, motive waves are *numbered* whereas corrective waves are *lettered*. Hence motive waves are numbered as (1), (2), (3), (4), and (5) with the corresponding corrective waves labeled as (A), (B), and (C). The impulse waves within the motive wave are numbered (1), (3), and (5) with its corrective waves labeled as (2) and (4). We observe that impulse waves (1), (3), and (5) subdivide into waves 1, 2, 3, 4, and 5. Corrective waves (2) and (4) subdivide into waves A, B, and C.

Each wave degree is numbered and lettered differently in order to distinguish between the various wave degrees that make up market action. Elliott listed nine important wave degrees spanning from the Grand Supercycle down to the Subminuette. See Figure 18.3 for the most widely used labeling conventions.

The time spans associated with four of the most recognizable wave degrees are as follows:

- Cycle wave degree spans from years to decades
- Primary wave degree spans from months to years
- Intermediate wave degree spans from weeks to months
- Minor wave degree spans from days to weeks

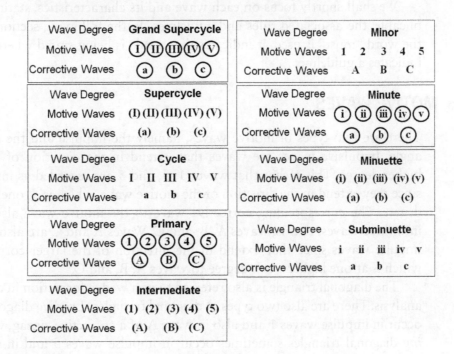

FIGURE 18.3 Labeling Conventions for Various Wave Degrees.

Referring to Figure 18.2 again, notice that the motive wave is labeled as encircled number 1, indicating a wave at the primary degree. The motive wave subdivides into three impulsive and two corrective waves, labeled as (1), (2), (3), (4), and (5), indicating a wave at the intermediate degree. Waves labeled 1 to 5 and A to C represents waves at the minor degree of trend.

Elliott waves are defined in terms of form, ratio, and time. Of the three, the preservation of the 5-3 form or pattern is of the highest importance. Fibonacci price and time ratios are considered less important than form. Although the wave structure is best described via Fibonacci ratio analysis, wave form (or structure) takes precedence.

18.2 RULES AND GUIDELINES

The identification of Elliott waves are governed by *rules* and *guidelines*. Unlike guidelines, *rules must not be breached, otherwise the wave count is invalidated*. The three main rules that govern the subwaves or waves of a lower degree with respect to a progressive or motive wave are as follows:

1. Wave 2 must not extend beyond the start of wave 1
2. Wave 3 must not be the shortest wave
3. Wave 4 must not extend into the price range of wave 1

In addition to the three main rules above, motive waves must subdivide into five waves and consequently all impulse waves must also subdivide into five waves. Although wave 5 may not extend beyond the end of wave 3 in some cases (especially when truncation is present), wave 3 must always extend beyond the end of wave 1.

We shall shortly focus on each wave and its characteristics, stating where applicable, the associated rules and guidelines. In the following sections, whenever the word "must" is used, it indicates that a rule is being stated whereas "should" indicates a guideline.

18.3 MOTIVE WAVES

There are two types of motive waves, namely the impulse and the diagonal triangle. Impulsive waves are waves that extend in the direction of a wave at a higher degree. This means that waves 1, 3, and 5 are regarded as impulse waves since they extend in the direction of the motive wave, which is at one higher wave degree. The corresponding corrective wave to the motive wave also subdivides into three waves, that is, waves A, B, and C. Waves A and C are also regarded as impulse waves since they extend in the direction of the larger corrective wave, which is at one higher wave degree to waves A, B, and C.

The diagonal triangle is also referred to as a wedge formation in chart pattern analysis. There are also two types of diagonal triangles. *Leading* diagonal triangles occur in impulse waves 1 and also in wave A of a corrective zigzag, whereas *ending* diagonal triangles sometimes occur in impulse waves 5 and in wave C of a corrective zigzag. See Figure 18.4.

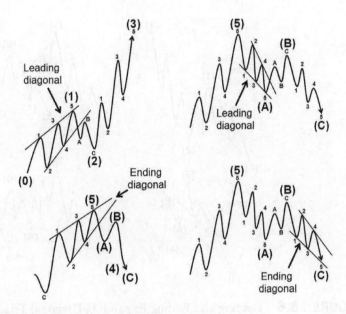

FIGURE 18.4 Leading and Ending Diagonal Triangles.

As a rule, leading and ending diagonal triangles always subdivide into five waves where leading diagonal triangles unfold in a 3-3-3-3-3 or 5-3-5-3-5 pattern and ending diagonal triangles as a 3-3-3-3-3 pattern. See Figure 18.5.

It should be noted that both leading and ending diagonal triangles may occasionally be of the expanding type, instead of the regular contracting or converging diagonal triangle. See Figure 18.6.

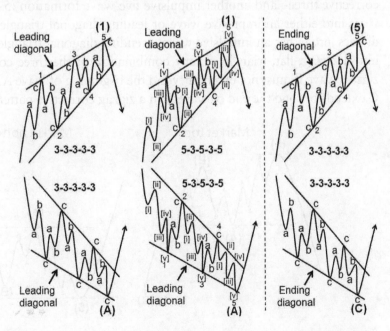

FIGURE 18.5 Subdivisions within Leading and Ending Diagonal Triangles.

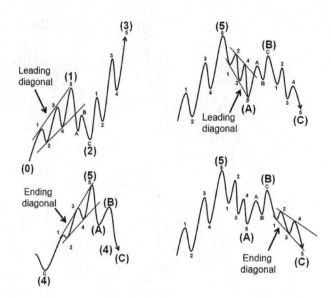

FIGURE 18.6 Leading and Ending Expanding Diagonal Triangles.

18.4 CORRECTIVE WAVES

There are four types of corrective waves, namely the:

1. Zigzag
2. Flat
3. Triangle
4. Any combination of zigzag, flat, or triangle

As a rule, a zigzag subdivides into three waves and unfolds as impulsive five-, a corrective three-, and another impulsive five-wave formation (5-3-5). Wave A subdivides into either an impulsive wave or leading diagonal triangle, while wave C subdivides into either an impulsive wave or ending diagonal triangle. Wave B subdivides into a zigzag, flat, triangle, or any combination of the three corrective waves. In a zigzag, wave B must not extend beyond the beginning of wave A. In most cases, wave C extends beyond the end of wave A in a zigzag corrective pattern. See Figure 18.7.

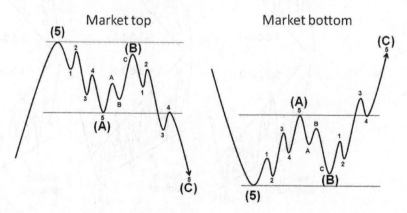

FIGURE 18.7 Zigzag Corrective Pattern.

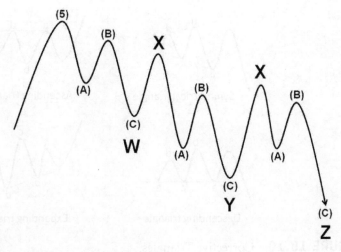

FIGURE 18.8 Double and Triple Zigzags.

Zigzags may also unfold as a double or triple pattern, called a double or triple zigzag. Double and triple zigzags are connected by an intervening wave X. Prechter included points W, Y, and Z to represent the first, second, and third completed zigzag formations. See Figure 18.8.

Flats come in three different forms, namely:

1. Regular flat
2. Expanded flat
3. Running flat

As a rule, all flats subdivide into three waves and unfold in a 3-3-5 pattern. In a flat, wave A must not be a triangle formation and wave C unfolds as either an impulsive wave or diagonal triangle. To retain its classification as a flat and to distinguish it from a zigzag pattern, wave B must retrace close or slightly beyond the start of wave A. In a regular flat, wave B retraces close to the start of wave A and wave C ends near the end of wave A. In an expanded flat, wave B retraces beyond the start of wave A and wave C extends beyond the end of wave A. Finally, in a running flat, wave B retraces slightly beyond the start of wave A and wave C fails to extend beyond the end of wave A. See Figure 18.9.

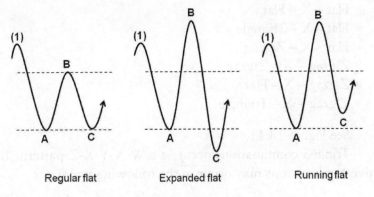

Regular flat   Expanded flat   Running flat

FIGURE 18.9 Regular, Expanded, and Running Flats.

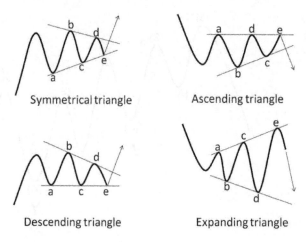

FIGURE 18.10 Corrective Triangles.

There are two types of corrective triangles, namely:

1. Contracting/converging: This includes ascending, descending, and symmetrical triangles
2. Expanding: Sometimes referred to as reverse symmetrical triangles

As a rule, all triangles must subdivide into five waves and at least four waves must unfold a zigzag-based pattern. One difference between contracting and expanding triangles is that wave C is allowed to extend beyond the start of wave B in an expanding triangle. See Figure 18.10.

Triangles never occur in impulse wave 2 unless it is part of a corrective combination. Triangles are expected to unfold in the following waves:

- Impulse wave 4
- Wave B
- Final wave in a double or triple 3 combination
- Intervening wave X

Double 3 combinations occur as a W-X-Y pattern. Double 3-based corrective combinations may occur in the following ways:

- Flat – X – Flat
- Flat – X – Triangle
- Flat – X – Zigzag
- Zigzag – X – Zigzag
- Zigzag – X – Flat
- Zigzag – X – Triangle

See Figure 18.11.

Triple 3 combinations occur as a W-X-Y-X-Z pattern. Triple 3-based corrective combinations may occur in the following ways:

- Flat – X – Flat – X – Flat

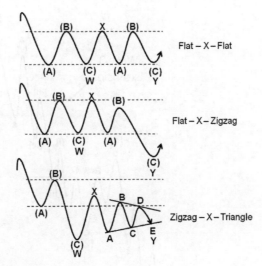

FIGURE 18.11 Double 3 Corrective Combinations.

- Flat – X – Flat –X – Zigzag
- Flat – X – Flat – X – Triangle
- Flat – X – Zigzag –X – Flat
- Flat – X – Zigzag –X – Triangle
- Flat – X – Zigzag –X – Zigzag
- Zigzag – X – Zigzag – X – Zigzag
- Zigzag – X – Zigzag – X – Flat
- Zigzag – X – Zigzag – X – Triangle
- Zigzag – X – Flat – X – Zigzag
- Zigzag – X – Flat – X – Flat
- Zigzag – X – Flat – X – Triangle

See Figure 18.12.

Note that the intervening wave X may unfold as any of the three corrective patterns. Triangles must never unfold as the first corrective pattern or occur more than once in a combination.

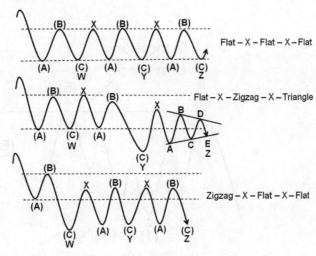

FIGURE 18.12 Triple 3 Corrective Combinations.

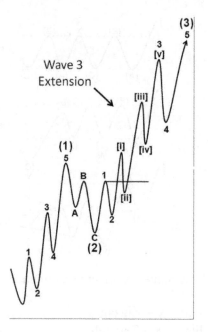

FIGURE 18.13 Triple 3 Corrective Combinations.

18.5 WAVE EXTENSIONS AND TRUNCATION

An extended wave is one where it has additional subdivisions and as a consequence will be more elongated. As a rule, wave extensions can only occur in one of three impulse waves. It occurs most frequently in wave 3 in the equity markets and in wave 5 in commodity markets. There can also be extensions of extensions within a wave. See Figure 18.13.

There are instances where wave 5 fails to extend beyond the end of wave 3. We refer to this failure as a *truncation*. Truncation can also occur within wave 5 of an ending diagonal triangle. See Figure 18.14.

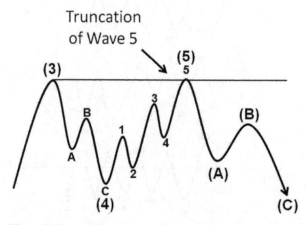

FIGURE 18.14 Wave 5 Truncation.

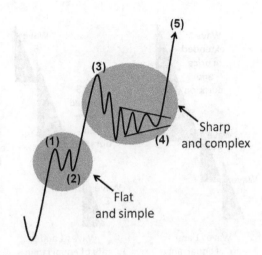

FIGURE 18.15 Alternation.

18.6 ALTERNATION

Alternation is a guideline with broad applications. It suggests that some pattern or behavior should alternate with another different pattern or behavior. Alternation expresses itself in the following ways:

- If corrective wave 2 is a simple and sharp correction, then corrective wave 4 should be a complex flat correction (and vice versa).
- Within a three-wave corrective pattern, alternation suggests that wave pattern B should be different from wave pattern A or C.
- Within a three-wave corrective pattern, alternation suggests that if wave A is simple, then wave B should be complex.

See Figure 18.15.

It should be noted that alternation also applies to the corrective sequence of a W-X-Y pattern. It is important to note that there is one exception to the general application of alternation. Alternation does not occur between waves 2 and 4 within a triangle pattern.

18.7 WAVE EQUALITY

Wave equality is a guideline that suggests that when one of the impulse waves is extended, which is usually wave 3, the remaining two impulse waves with a motive wave should be of equal length and duration. Similarly, although less common an occurrence, if wave 1 is extended, then waves 3 and 5 should be of equal length and duration. Finally, wave equality would then suggest that if waves 1 and 3 are of equal length and duration, then there is a possibility that wave 5 would be extended. This would be useful as an early warning to a commodity trader where wave 5 would often be extended in commodity markets. See Figure 18.16.

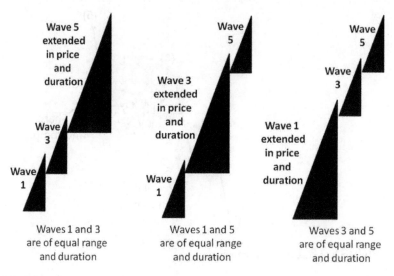

FIGURE 18.16 Wave Equality.

18.8 FIBONACCI RATIO AND NUMBER ANALYSIS OF ELLIOTT WAVES

Elliott waves are best understood in terms of Fibonacci price and time ratios and Fibonacci number sequences. For a full treatment of how Elliott waves are analyzed using Fibonacci ratios and number sequences, please refer to Chapter 10.

18.9 CHAPTER SUMMARY

As we have seen, Elliott wave analysis gives the practitioner a sense of where and how far the market may be traversing. Combining form, which is the most important characteristic of Elliott wave analysis, with Fibonacci ratio analysis provides a powerful way of forecasting potential market action. The reader is advised to read Frost and Prechter's excellent book entitled *Wave Principle: Key to Market Behavior* for a more detailed treatment of the topic.

CHAPTER 18 REVIEW QUESTIONS

1. Explain the difference between motive and corrective waves.
2. Describe the various corrective flat patterns found in Elliott waves.
3. What is alternation? Give two examples of alternation.
4. What are the rules associated with corrective triangles?
5. List the most common Fibonacci price and time ratios associated with impulse and corrective waves.
6. List all nine wave degrees and their labeling conventions from the Grand Supercycle down to the Subminuette.
7. List as many wave guidelines as you can.
8. Describe two W-X-Y corrective combinations in detail.

REFERENCES

Elliott, R. N. 2004. *R.N. Elliott's Masterworks*. Gainesville, GA: New Classics Library.

Neely, Glenn, with Eric Hall. 1990. *Mastering Elliott Wave: Presenting the Neely Method: The First Scientific, Objective Approach to Market Forecasting with Elliott Wave Theory*. Brightwaters, NY: Windsor Books.

Poser, Steven W. 2003. *Applying Elliott Wave Theory Profitably*. Hoboken, NJ: John Wiley & Sons.

Prechter, Robert R., Jr., and A. J. Frost. 2001. *Elliott Wave Principle: Key to Market Behavior* Hoboken, NJ: John Wiley & Sons.

CHAPTER 19

Basics of Gann Analysis

LEARNING OBJECTIVES

After studying this chapter, you should be able to:

- Understand the meaning of price-time balance in the markets
- Describe how one-eighth, one-third, and 50-percent retracement charts forecast potential support and resistance in the markets
- Identify and differentiate between the square of nine price and time projections
- Understand how to calculate the scale or trend rate for any commodity or market
- Construct various charts using Gann Fans and Grids using the appropriate scale or trend rate
- Set up Gann charts with various oscillators to identify overbought, oversold, and divergence with respect to price

Gann techniques for forecasting potential reaction levels in the markets have fascinated practitioners for decades, especially with his use of market geometry, symmetry, and corresponding number systems. Many of Gann's approaches are fairly esoteric, and practitioners have spent decades trying to decipher Gann's rather cryptic documentation of his techniques in his few books, personal charts, and training notes. Due to the complexity of Gann analysis, the best that can be presented here is but a brief description of some of his more popular techniques for forecasting potential areas of support and resistance, as well as potential tops and bottoms in the market, with some modern variations. We shall cover Gann angles and fans, Gann grids, Square of Nine price and time projections, as well as Gann percentage retracements.

19.1 TECHNIQUES OF W. D. GANN

William Delbert Gann believed that the markets are ruled by the interaction of price and time elements and that there should be a *balance* between them. This requirement of balance is best represented by the application of his 45 degree or

1×1 line, also referred to as the *Gann line*. Gann's preoccupation with balance between price and time led him to the study of market symmetry and cycles, with an especially strong focus on the geometrical properties of price action. He was not only intrigued by the geometry of price and time, but also by the underlying number systems that are representative of market geometry. He was fascinated by the employment of even numbers and the squares of simple number series like 2, 4, 8, 16, 32, 64, 81, 100, 121, 144 for forecasting potential turning points in the commodity markets. Gann also applied psychologically significant number ratios like halves, thirds, fourths, and eighths to both price and time. Due to the scaling of price action with respect to *specially selected units of time*, Gann kept a tremendous number of hand-drawn charts depicting various scale settings for different commodities at different price ranges. Gann was meticulous in the application of numbers, ratios, and geometry to the markets and is best known for his squaring of price and time, price-time angles, and percentage-retracement approaches to market forecasting. Some books written by W. D. Gann include:

- *Tunnel Thru the Air*
- *45 Years in Wall Street*
- *Truth of the Stock Tape*
- *The Magic Word*
- *How to Make Profits Trading in Commodities*

Cardinal, Ordinal, and Nominal Numbers

Before we begin our study of Gann's forecasting techniques, it would be best to review the definitions of a few number-related terms. A *cardinal* number describes amount or quantity, that is, the number of items or events such as 5 cars, 24 bars, 7 days, and so on. *Ordinal* numbers describe the order of things, such as first, second, third, and so on. Ordinal numbers do not represent quantity, but rather indicate rank and position, such as the fifth car, the twenty-fourth bar, the second highest marks, and so on. A *nominal* number labels something, such as phone numbers, car license plate numbers, social security numbers, and so on. Nominal numbers are not representative of quantity or rank, but are rather used for identification purposes.

Anniversaries, Seasonals, and Psychologically Significant Numbers

Due to the obvious parallel between the number of days in a year and the total number of degrees within a full circle, *Gann equated days to degrees* in his analysis. As such, 360 degrees represents one year or 360 days, 180 degrees represents one half of a year or 180 days, and 90 degrees represents a quarter of a year or 90 days. Since Gann regarded ratios such one fourth, one half, three fourths, and four fourths as numerically significant, he paid special importance to price action occurring over the 90-day, 180-day, 270-day, and yearly periods.

Gann also studied important anniversary dates of repetitive market tops and bottoms, including the seasonal behavior of price, especially for agricultural commodities. Gann placed great importance *in using only historical market peaks and troughs* in his calculations and geometrical annotations. Modern Gann practitioners tend to use significant peaks and troughs in lieu of historical peaks and troughs in the commodity markets, as much trading today is carried out on lower timeframes and over shorter time horizons. Nevertheless, firm proponents of Gann methods will insist that only historically significant prices should be employed usually based on the weekly charts.

Squaring of Price and Range and the Cycle Connection

The phrase *squaring of price* is unique to Gann analysis. It refers to the forecasting of potential peaks and troughs in the market based on a carefully selected price-time scale, or *trend rate*. Gann was seeking to graphically represent the balance between price and time on the charts and therefore had to select a chart scale where *equal units of price excursion tend to occur over equal units or intervals of time*. If drawn correctly, this would ideally represent that 45-degree or 1×1 line on the charts, an indication that price is moving at a linear rate with respect to time. If price were to move at a greater rate than time, price would be seen to rise above the 45-degree line in an uptrend, and conversely will be below the negative 45-degree line (315 degree line) in a downtrend. Therefore in order to correctly draw Gann charts, the scale or trend rate must first be determined. See Figure 19.1.

Once the scale is determined, an uptrending 45-degree line may be drawn from a significant trough and a downtrending 45-degree line may be drawn from a significant peak.

Assume that we have already determined the scale or average trend rate that best describes the balance between price and time along the 1×1 line. Gann believed that once price traces out the complete range, referred to as the *squaring of the range* that is represented by equal price excursion and equal time intervals, the trader should

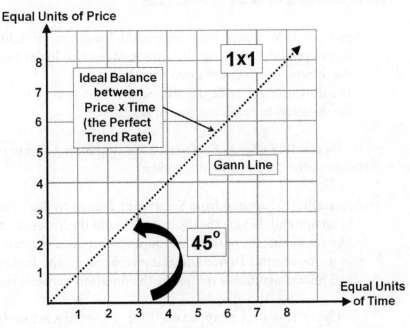

FIGURE 19.1 The 1×1 (45-Degree) Line of Balance between Price and Time.

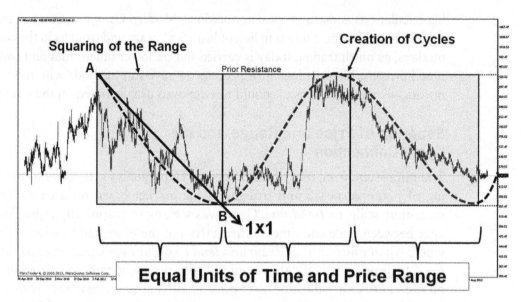

FIGURE 19.2 Squaring of the Range and the Creation of Price Cycles.

expect a top or bottom in the market. Assume that it took 40 units of time for price to traverse 40 units of price, and in the process a market top or bottom was created. A subsequent top or bottom is expected to occur after the next 40 units of time have elapsed. As long as price continues to oscillate within this range at or close to the ideal trend rate, a *price cycle* will develop. This is one reason why Gann's study of squaring the range led him to the study of price cycles. See Figure 19.2 for an actual squaring of the range on the continuous chart of wheat. We observe a price cycle developing as price oscillates within the range at the selected trend rate or scale.

There are three main approaches that modern Gann practitioners take in order to determine the scale or trend rate:

- Approach 1: Measured from Significant Trough to Trough/Peak to Peak
  - In an uptrend: Divide the distance between two lower significant troughs by the duration between the two troughs.
  - In a downtrend: Divide the distance between two higher significant peaks by the duration between the two peaks.

    Figure 19.3 depicts approach 1 for uptrending action (the reverse applies for downtrending action, not shown).

- Approach 2: Measured from Significant Trough to Peak/Peak to Trough
  - In an uptrend: Divide the distance between the lowest significant trough and highest significant peak by the duration between the two.
  - In a downtrend: Divide the distance between the highest significant peak and lowest significant trough by the duration between the two.

    Figure 19.4 depicts approach 2 for uptrending action (the reverse applies for downtrending action, not shown).

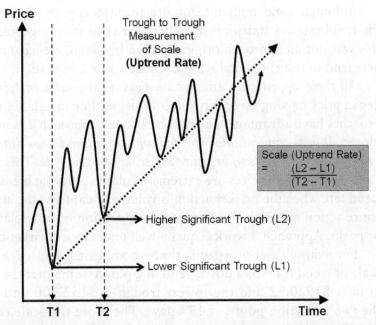

FIGURE 19.3   Finding the Scale or Trend Rate in an Uptrend via Approach 1.

- Approach 3: Regression Line Measured from Significant Trough to Peak/Peak to Trough
  - In an uptrend: Construct a regression line between the lowest significant trough and highest significant peak.
  - In a downtrend: Construct a regression line between the highest significant peak and lowest significant trough.

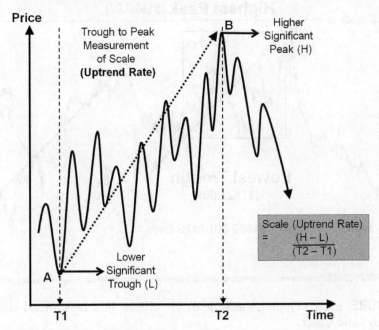

FIGURE 19.4   Finding the Scale or Trend Rate in an Uptrend via Approach 2.

Although some modern Gann practitioners employ Approach 3 to determine the trend rate via statistical means (rather than from a geometrical perspective), this was not an approach originally used by Gann. Hence, most Gann practitioners tend to resort to employing Approach 1 or 2 instead.

All three approaches attempt to measure the scale or trend rate that would depict price moving up or down the 45-degree line in balance with time. Both approaches have advantages and disadvantages. Approach 1 is most commonly employed. *It uses conventional uptrend and downtrend lines drawn from significant price inflection points to measure the scale or trend rate.* This works well in most cases, except when prices are extremely volatile. Approach 2 is more indicative of trend rate when the market action is volatile. It captures the actual rate across the entire action rather than relying on the extension of two relatively close troughs or peaks. Approach 3 works equally well under most market conditions.

For example, let us assume that we are using Approach 2 to calculate the scale or trend rate for a downtrend in Gold. Assume that the highest significant peak is \$1920.92 and the lowest trough is \$1527.00 and duration between the two inflection points is 179 days. Therefore the scale equals (\$1920.92 − \$1527.00)/179 = \$2.20 per day. The chart is now drawn so that each price unit is \$2.20 and each time interval or unit is 1 day. *When plotted, the 1×1 line is drawn at a 45-degree angle.* See Figure 19.5. We observe that Approach 2 produced a 1×1 line that proved to reflect subsequent Gold prices very closely, acting somewhat as a median line, or balance line, that is parallel to the original 1×1 line.

Note that in order to determine the scale most representative of price action, it is best to sample at least a couple or more trend rates and find the *average* trend rate. This is may be done on daily, weekly, or monthly charts.

FIGURE 19.5 Finding the Scale or Trend Rate in a Downtrend via Approach 2 on a Daily Gold Chart.
Source: MetaTrader 4

Gann's One-Eighth Retracements

Gann one-eighth retracements are constructed by dividing the range between significant historic peaks and troughs into eight equal price intervals. It is usually used to identify potential support and resistance during a retracement. Once price penetrates the highest previous peak or lowest trough in a retracement range, the entire retracement chart is redrawn as the previous levels are essentially invalidated (although these old levels may still be somewhat predictive over the near term). There is no requirement for using the scale or trend rate when drawing percentage retracement charts since retracement levels represent static overlay indicators and are not affected by the element of time, and only readings that reside on the price axis matter. It should be noted that though uncommon, some modern Gann practitioners reverse engineer the approach by identifying four initial intervals of reliable price reaction and subsequently projecting or extending the remaining four intervals in the direction of the existing trend in the hope of forecasting potential levels of support and resistance. Figure 19.6 shows the continuous chart of wheat reacting at the one-eighth retracements levels at Points 1 to 7. The range between points A and B is divided into eight equal price intervals. Point X depicts prior resistance turning into support at Points 2 and 4 at the two-eighths level, which subsequently turned into resistance at Points 5 and 6.

For all subsequent charts, the *area of application*, that is, the area where the retracement levels are valid for use, lies after the time line located at Point B. For best results, use longer-term charts such as the weekly charts and base the retracement range on a historically significant peak and trough.

Figure 19.7 depicts the Dow Jones Industrial Average reacting to various one-eighth retracements levels, as seen at Points 1 to 10, with many of the supports and resistances coinciding with oversold and overbought indications on the cycle-tuned stochastic oscillator.

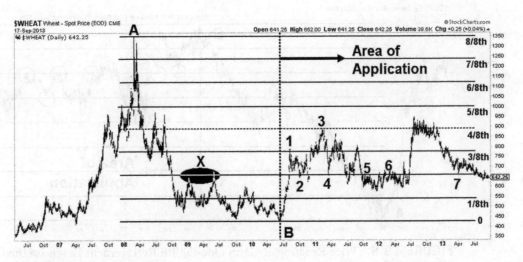

FIGURE 19.6 Filtering Price Action into Four Pieces of Information (OHLC).
Courtesy of Stockcharts.com

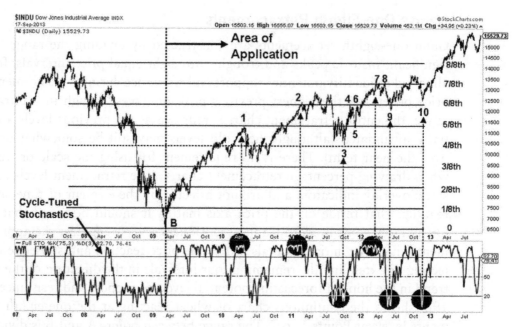

FIGURE 19.7 Price Reacting at Gann One-Eighth Retracement Levels on the Daily Chart of the Dow Jones Industrial Average.
Courtesy of Stockcharts.com

Figure 19.8 depicts copper prices reacting to various one-eighth retracement levels as seen within the circles indicated in the chart.

Gann's One-Third Retracements

In similar fashion, Gann also believed that one-third retracement levels are of significant importance. Figure 19.9 shows soybean prices reacting to the one-third and two-thirds retracement levels.

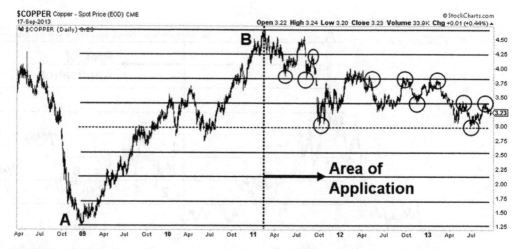

FIGURE 19.8 Price Reacting at Gann One-Eighth Retracement Levels on the Continuous Daily Chart of Copper.
Courtesy of Stockcharts.com

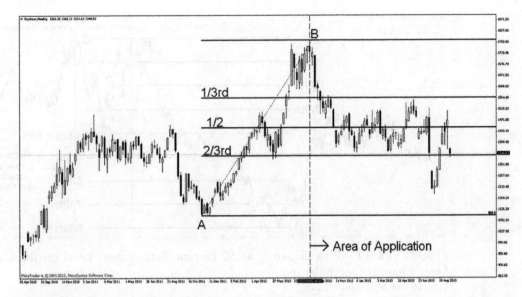

FIGURE 19.9 Price Reacting at Gann One-Third Retracement Levels on the Weekly Chart of Soybean.
Source: MetaTrader 4

Gann 50 Percent Retracement Level

Of all the retracement levels used by Gann, Gann regarded the 50 percent level as the most important retracement level. The 50 percent retracement level is psychologically significant and therefore attractive to the majority of market participants, and many investment decisions are based on the violation of this level. Figure 19.10 shows copper finding support at the 50 percent level (shown as the four-eighth level).

Figure 19.11 shows the stock price of Caterpillar Inc. finding support at the 50 percent level, as well as at various other one-eighth retracement levels as seen at Points 1 to 3. Note that the levels are not valid after the time line associated

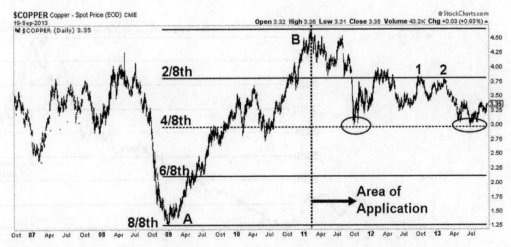

FIGURE 19.10 Price Reacting at 50 Percent Retracement Level on the Continuous Daily Chart of Copper.
Courtesy of Stockcharts.com

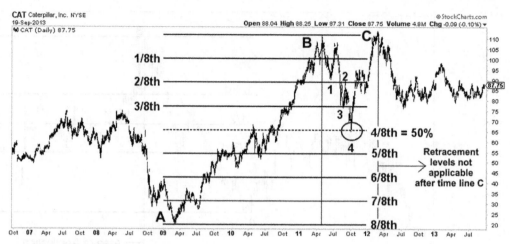

FIGURE 19.11 Price Reacting at 50 Percent Retracement Level on the Continuous Daily Chart of Caterpillar Inc.
Courtesy of Stockcharts.com

with Point C, since the price at Point C has exceeded the previous peak at Point B. The new levels have to be redrawn based on the new range, AC.

Figure 19.12 shows Apple Inc. finding support at the 50 percent level, as well as at various other one-eighth retracement levels as indicated at Points 1 and 2.

Gann Grids and the 45-Degree Line

Once the scale or trend rate has been calculated, using either Approach 1 or 2 (as described earlier), a Gann grid may be applied to the chart. Gann grids represent lines of balance between price and time since half the lines are parallel to the main 1×1 *line of balance*. The other half of the lines run perpendicular to the parallel lines of balance and represent an important barrier to price action. *The grid size is based on some ratio of the squared range*, normally full size, half, or quarter of the squared

FIGURE 19.12 Price Reacting at 50 Percent Retracement Level on the Daily Chart of Apple Inc.
Courtesy of Stockcharts.com

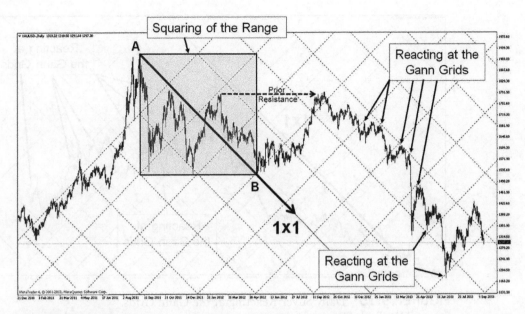

FIGURE 19.13 Gold Prices Reacting at the Gann Grids.
Source: MetaTrader 4

range. Gann only used even numbered squares on his charts. In Figure 19.13, we set the squared range to accommodate the length of four grids, measured from Point A to Point B. The grid is then expanded across the chart. The area of application is always after Point B. We observe Gold prices reacting effectively at the Gann grids at various points. The scale was calculated using Approach 2.

Figure 19.14 shows the daily wheat prices reacting at the Gann grids and cycling within the squared range. The scale was calculated using Approach 2.

In Figure 19.15, we see the daily Silver prices reacting effectively at the Gann grids. The scale was calculated using Approach 2.

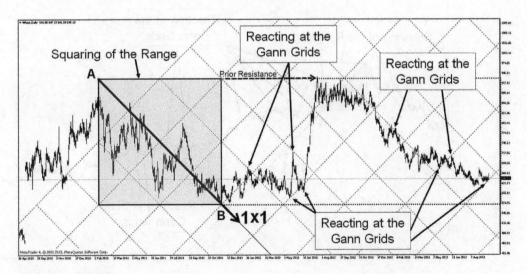

FIGURE 19.14 Daily Wheat Prices Reacting at the Gann Grids.
Source: MetaTrader 4

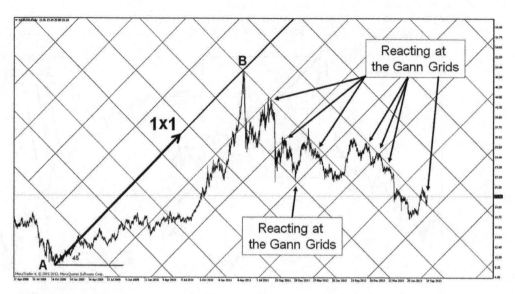

FIGURE 19.15 Daily Silver Reacting at the Gann Grids.
Source: MetaTrader 4

In Figure 19.16, we see the daily Coffee prices reacting effectively at the Gann grids. The scale was also calculated using Approach 2.

In Figure 19.17, we see the weekly Corn prices reacting effectively at the Gann grids. The scale was calculated using Approach 2.

In Figure 19.18, we see the four-hour Sugar prices reacting effectively at the Gann grids. The scale was calculated using Approach 2.

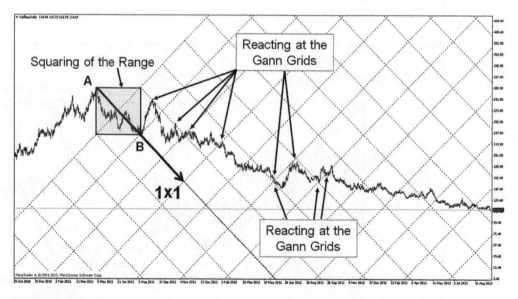

FIGURE 19.16 Daily Coffee Reacting at the Gann Grids.
Source: MetaTrader 4

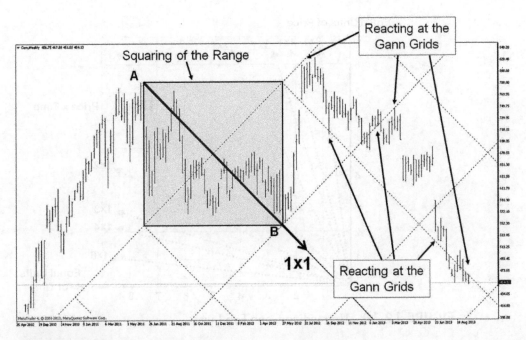

FIGURE 19.17 Weekly Corn Reacting at the Gann Grids.
Source: MetaTrader 4

Gann Fan Lines

Gann fan lines describe specific ratio relationships between price units and time units in the form of Price Units × Time Units. Gann fan lines tracks the:

- Number of price units traversed over one unit of time below the 1×1 line in a downtrend and above the 1×1 line in an uptrend

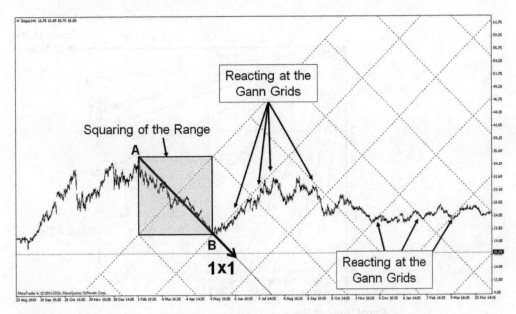

FIGURE 19.18 4-Hour Chart of Sugar Prices Reacting to the Gann Grids.
Source: MetaTrader 4

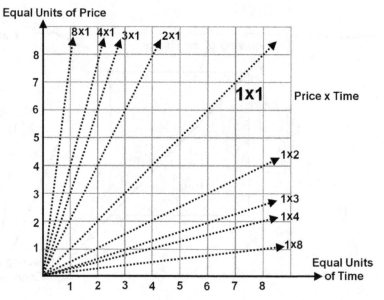

FIGURE 19.19 Uptrending Gann Fan Lines.

- Number of time units traversed over one unit of price above the 1×1 line in a downtrend and below the 1×1 line in an uptrend

See Figures 19.19 and 19.20.

Price trending upward above the 1×1 fan line is considered a strong bull trend, whereas price trending upward below the 1×1 fan line is considered a weak bull trend. Gann fan lines are treated in the same fashion as any other trendlines, that is, *as areas of support and resistance, changing roles when penetrated*. Whenever price breaches an uptrending Gann fan line to the downside, it is expected to move to the next lower

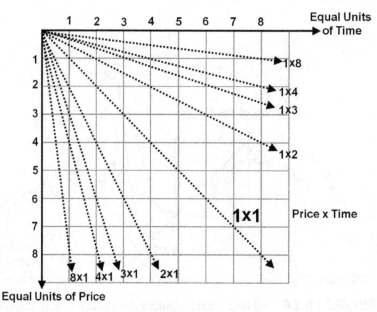

FIGURE 19.20 Downtrending Gann Fan Lines.

Gann fan line. For example, if price breaches the 3×1 fan line, price is expected to move toward the 2×1 fan line, and so on. Whenever price breaches a downtrending Gann fan line to the upside, it is expected to move to the next Gann higher fan line. For example, if price breaches the 1×4 fan line, price is expected to move toward the 1×8 fan line. This expected behavior is referred to by Gann as the *Rule of All Angles*.

Gann fan lines are drawn from historical and significant peaks and troughs. Uptrending Gann fan lines are drawn from historical or significant troughs while downtrending Gann fan lines are drawn from historical or significant peaks. Uptrending Gann fan lines are invalidated once price falls below the trough from which it was drawn and downtrending Gann fan lines are invalidated once price exceeds the peak from which it was drawn.

For a 1×1 line to be plotted, the scale or trend rate must be known in advance. Figure 19.21 shows the daily Gold prices reacting to the Gann fan lines based on trend rates calculated using Approach 2.

Figure 19.22 shows the weekly Soybean prices reacting to the Gann fan lines based on trend rates calculated using Approach 2.

Figure 19.23 shows the daily Coffee prices reacting to the Gann fan lines based on trend rates calculated using Approach 2.

Figure 19.24 shows the four-hour Sugar prices reacting to the Gann fan lines based on trend rates calculated using Approach 2.

Figure 19.25 shows the weekly Corn prices reacting to the Gann fan lines based on trend rates calculated using Approach 2. Note that the Gann fan lines were invalidated after the time line associated with Point C, since the price at Point C exceeded the previous peak A from which the original fan lines were drawn.

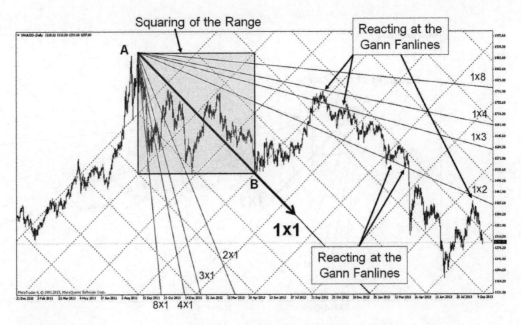

FIGURE 19.21 Prices Reacting at Downtrending Gann Fan Lines on the Daily Chart of Gold.
Source: MetaTrader 4

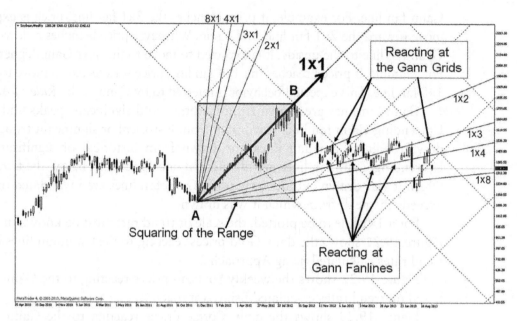

FIGURE 19.22 Prices Reacting at Uptrending Gann Fan Lines on the Weekly Chart of Soybean.
Source: MetaTrader 4

Figure 19.26 shows the weekly Corn Gann fan lines redrawn from Point C, the new peak, based on a parallel 1×1 degree line. We see the new 1×1 fan line tracking prices closely, acting somewhat like a median line, that is, a line of balance between price and time. We observe price breaking below the 1×1 fan line, indicating a strong downtrend in effect.

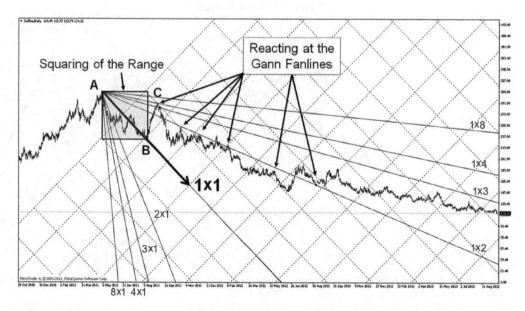

FIGURE 19.23 Prices Reacting at Uptrending Gann Fan Lines on the Daily Chart of Coffee.
Source: MetaTrader 4

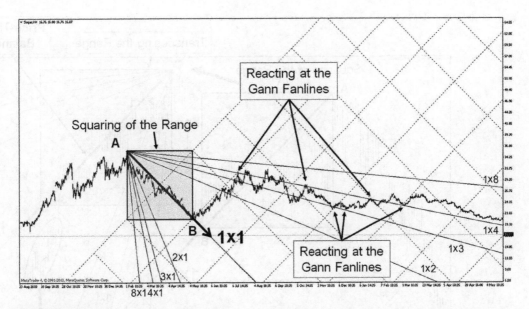

FIGURE 19.24 Prices Reacting at Downtrending Gann Fan Lines on the 4-Hour Chart of Sugar.
Source: MetaTrader 4

Gann's Square of Nine: Price Projections (Circle of Price)

Gann's Square of Nine is an extremely popular Gann technique for forecasting potential future support and resistance in the market. Once current price is identified on the Gann square, future resistances can easily be identified by locating, in a *clockwise* direction, prices that correspond to higher prices occurring at the following angles: 90, 180, 270, 360, and so on.

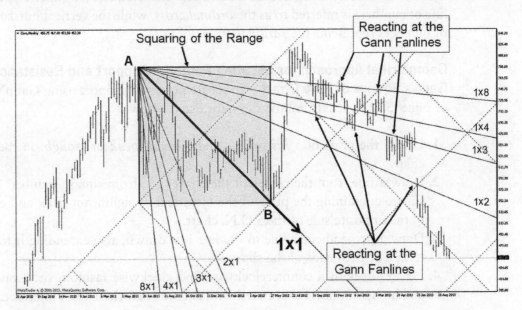

FIGURE 19.25 Prices Reacting at Downtrending Gann Fan Lines on the Weekly Chart of Corn.
Source: MetaTrader 4

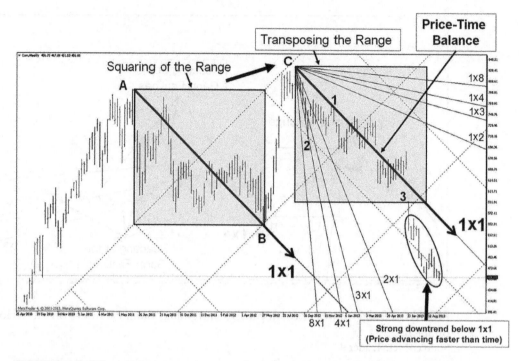

FIGURE 19.26 Transposing the Downtrending Gann Fan Lines to a New Peak on the Weekly Chart of Corn.
Source: MetaTrader 4

In a similar fashion, future support levels can easily be found by locating, in a *counterclockwise* direction, prices that correspond to lower prices occurring at the following angles: −90, −180, −270, −360, and so on.

Refer to Figure 19.27 for an illustration of the Square of Nine. The diagonal line of numbers is referred to as the *ordinal cross,* while the vertical/horizontal line of numbers represents the *cardinal cross.*

Geometrical Approach for Locating Potential Support and Resistance Using Gann's Square of Nine Chart

To locate potential support using Gann's Square of Nine (S.O.N.) chart, follow the steps listed below:

1. Locate the price of a *historical or significant peak or trough* on the S.O.N. chart.
2. Draw a line from the center of the chart (i.e., from square number 1) to the square containing the price of the historical or significant peak and extend it to the opposite side of the S.O.N. chart.
3. Draw a perpendicular line to the line just drawn, also extending it to the extremes at both ends of the chart.
4. Locate, in both a counterclockwise and clockwise fashion, successive lower and higher numbers associated with squares that these lines intersect.

These numbers represent the price levels of potential future support and resistance. For example, assume that the price of a commodity was $105 per

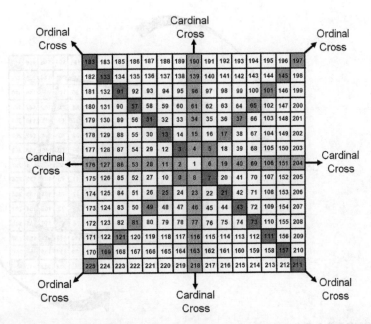

FIGURE 19.27 The Cardinal and Ordinal Crosses within the Square of Nine Chart.

kilogram of weight. After drawing a straight line through the center of the square containing the price $105, and a line perpendicular to this first line which is also drawn through the center of the square, simply count down from the price of $105, *in a counterclockwise fashion*, until the next lower price is located at the perpendicular line, which in this case, turns out to be $95, which represents the −90-degree support level from $105, in Gann's unique terminology. Continuing to count backward, the next lower support level would potentially occur at the next line at $85, which represents the −180-degree support level from $105. The next two lower supports would be $76 and $68, representing the −270- and −360-degree support levels, respectively, as measured from $105. See Figure 19.28.

To locate potential future resistance, count up from the price of $105, *in a clockwise fashion*, finding the next higher price located at the perpendicular line, which in this case, turns out to be $115, which represents the 90-degree resistance level from $105, in Gann speak. Continuing counting forward, the next higher resistance level would potentially occur at the next line at $126, which represents a 180-degree resistance level from $105. The next two higher resistances would be $138 and $150, representing the 270- and 360-degree resistance levels, respectively, as measured from $105.

Numerical Method for Locating Potential Support and Resistance Using Gann's Square of Nine Gann identified *numerical angular values* in the following manner:

- 360 degrees (full cycle) corresponds to a value of 2
- 180 degrees (one half cycle) is equivalent to a value of 1
- 90 degrees (one quarter cycle) is equivalent to a value of 0.5
- 45 degrees (one eighth cycle) is equivalent to a value of 0.25

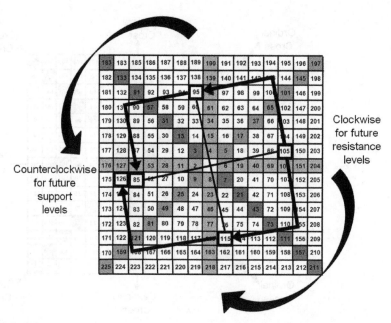

Clockwise
for future
resistance
levels

Counterclockwise
for future
support
levels

FIGURE 19.28 Locating Support and Resistance Geometrically on the Square of Nine Chart.

To locate the next Gann quarter-cycle support and resistance levels, *simply add or subtract 0.5 to the square of the commodity price and subsequently find the square root of that total* (add for resistance and subtract for support). Assume that the commodity is priced at $105 per kilogram.

Square root of $105 = 10.24$

- To find the next 90-degree resistance from $105, add 0.5 to $10.24
- $10.24 + $0.5 = $10.74
- Square this number to get $115.35
- Rounding down to the closest integer we get $115 (which matches our geometrical result obtained earlier)

Similarly, to find the 90-degree support level:

- Subtract 0.5 from $10.24 = $9.74
- Square this number to get $94.86
- Rounding up to the closest integer we get $95 (which matches our geometrical result obtained earlier)

To find the 180-, 270-, and 360-degree support levels, just repeat the procedure above replacing 0.5 with 1, 1.5, and 2, respectively, which should yield $85, $76, and $68. To find the 180-, 270-, and 360-degree resistance levels, replace 0.5 with 1, 1.5, and 2, respectively. This should yield potential resistance levels at $126, $138, and $150.

Figure 19.29 is a chart of four-hour gold prices. We observe the price range around the $1518 to $1522 support zone being forecasted *weeks before it was*

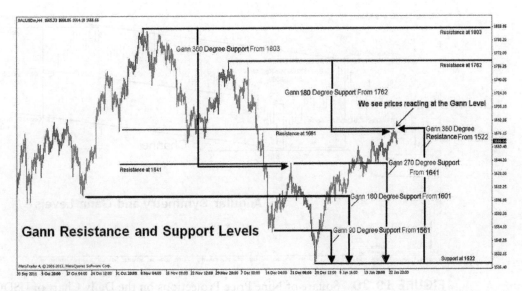

FIGURE 19.29 Square of Nine Price Projections on the 4-Hour Chart of Gold.
Source: MetaTrader 4

formed in the following S.O.N. calculations (some prices have been rounded up to the closest integer):

- 90-degree support from $1561: $[(\sqrt{1561}) - 0.5]^2 = \$1522$
- 180-degree support from $1601: $[(\sqrt{1601}) - 1.0]^2 = \$1522$
- 270-degree support from $1641: $[(\sqrt{1641}) - 1.5]^2 = \$1522$
- 540-degree support from $1762: $[(\sqrt{1762}) - 3.0]^2 = \$1519$
- 630-degree support from $1803: $[(\sqrt{1803}) - 3.5]^2 = \$1518$

This represents a *confluence or cluster of bullish indications* around the $1518 to $1522 price zone. Price subsequently found resistance at 360 degrees above $1522, at around $[(\sqrt{1522}) + 2]^2 = \$1682$.

In Figure 19.30, we observe the USDCHF finding support at 0.8558 to 0.8566, which is approximately 720 degrees (two full cyclic revolutions) below 0.9315. We also observe the USDCHF finding support at the 360- and 720-degree support levels from 0.9594, which coincided with a channel bottom. This represents a confluence of bullish indications.

In Figure 19.31, we observe the daily Gold prices finding resistance at $1431, which is very close to the 360-degree level from the prior resistance level at $1265, that is, $[(\sqrt{1265}) + 2]^2 = \$1411$. Price found resistance once more at $1586, which is very close to 360 degrees above $1431, that is, $[(\sqrt{1431}) + 2]^2 = \$1584$. Notice the MACD at historically overbought levels at Point B, coinciding closely to an expected cyclic high.

Variation on Gann's Square of Nine Technique for Price Projections

We may also position the price of a significant peak or trough at the center of the square and have it revolve outward, in the usual counterclockwise and clockwise

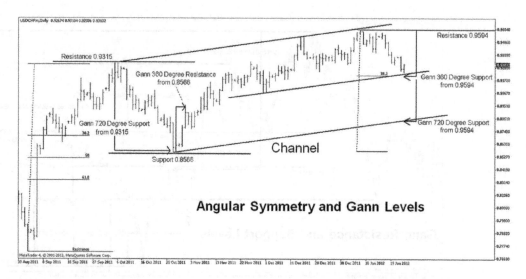

FIGURE 19.30 Square of Nine Price Projections on the Daily Chart of USDCHF.
Source: MetaTrader 4

fashion. Prices that intercept or are in proximity to the ordinal and cardinal crosses represent prices at which potential reactions or reversals may occur in the market.

For example, let us assume that we want to forecast the next important reversal in the Gold market. We position the price of gold's highest peak of $1920 at the center of the square. We now have gold prices revolve counterclockwise around the center, expanding outwards at $1 decrements per square (replacing the numbers 1, 2, 3, etc. with decreasing prices instead). We then look for prices that lie on or are in proximity to either the cardinal or ordinal crosses. These prices represent potential reaction levels or bottoms in the Gold market. Similarly, we may then repeat the process by moving clockwise, looking for potential reaction levels or tops in the Gold market.

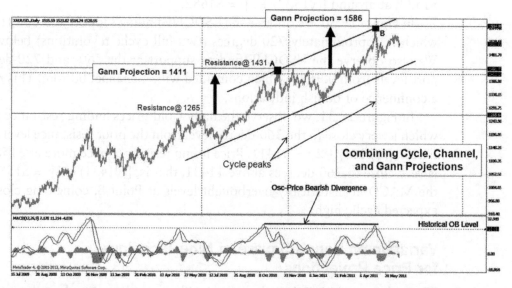

FIGURE 19.31 Square of Nine Price Projections on the Daily Chart of Gold.
Source: MetaTrader 4

We may also position the price of a significant trough at the center of the square and have it revolve outward in standard counterclockwise and clockwise fashion. As before, prices that intercept or are in proximity to the ordinal and cardinal crosses represent prices at which potential reactions or reversals may occur in the commodity market.

Gann's Square of Nine: Time Projections (Circle of Time)

We may also replace the data within a Square of Nine to forecast *when a potential top or bottom is to be expected*, instead of forecasting the potential price at which a reversal occurs in the market. We can do this by positioning the date of a significant peak or trough at the center of the square and have it revolve outward, in the usual counterclockwise fashion, in an increasing manner. Dates that intercept or are in proximity to the ordinal and cardinal crosses represent the dates at which potential reversal may occur in the market.

Squaring of the Low and High

Besides squaring the range, Gann also introduced a couple of techniques called the *Squaring of the High* and *Squaring of the Low*. These approaches attempt to forecast potential market tops and bottoms via a very simple mathematical process. Again, the practitioner should have had some experience calculating the scale or trend rate of the market under observation before embarking on a campaign of forecasting potential market tops and bottoms via the squaring of the high and low values.

We may forecast potential tops and bottoms by *squaring of the high* as follows:

- Locate a historic or significant peak in the commodity market.
- Calculate the scale or trend rate for the timeframe used.
- Divide the price at the peak by the trend rate.
- The resulting number represents the number of periods to the next potential top or bottom.

For example, we have already found the trend rate of gold to be currently around \$2.20. Therefore to square the high, we divide the peak price with the trend rate giving (\$1920.92/\$2.20) = 873 days to the next potential top or bottom in the market, as measured from the date of the formation of the peak.

Squaring the low is identical to the squaring of the high except that we replace the peak price with a historic or significant trough price to forecast potential tops and bottoms in the market.

Comparing Gann, Dow Theory, and Fibonacci Retracement Levels

There are some similarities between Gann-, Dow-, and Fibonacci-based retracement levels. There are a few Gann, Dow, and Fibonacci retracement levels that are in proximity to each other, *making these levels a significant zone for potential*

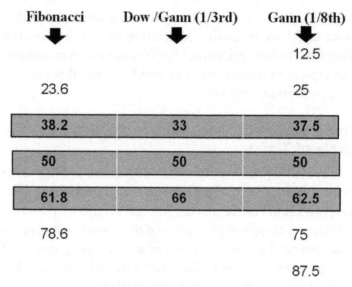

FIGURE 19.32 Closely Related Retracement Ratios.

price rejections in the markets. We see from Figure 19.32 that there are three significant barrier zones, located at or ranging from:

- 33 percent to 38.2 percent
- 50 percent
- 61.8 percent to 66 percent

The trader should therefore always be vigilant for a clustering or confluence of these different retracement levels once identified, as prices may react strongly at these barrier zones.

The Data Dropout Effect

Charting platforms may omit or include non-trading days, depending on the service provider. The addition or removal of such data from the charts will impact dynamic overlay indicators such as trendlines, channels, and chart patterns, that is, overlays that depend on the drawing of diagonal lines connecting different price inflection points. The addition, removal, or unintentional dropout of such data will affect the angle of trendlines on the charts. As such, Gann fan lines and grids would be the most affected. Conversely, such data variations will not have an impact on numerically determined forecasts such as percentage reversal levels and Square of Nine price projections.

19.4 CHAPTER SUMMARY

In this chapter, we learned about the importance of balance between price and time, which forms the basis of most of Gann's analytical approaches. The practitioner should note that there are many modern variations to Gann's original techniques. Gann's method of price forecasting works in most markets, but it appears to work especially well in the commodity markets.

CHAPTER 19 REVIEW QUESTIONS

1. Describe a few number systems that Gann used in his analysis.
2. How would you calculate the most appropriate scale or trend rate for a particular market?
3. Explain how one squares the highs and the lows.
4. What is the connection between squaring the range and price cycles?
5. Briefly describe how Gann fan lines are created.
6. What does the rule of all angles mean?
7. Describe the various retracement approaches that Gann used in his analysis of the markets.
8. Calculate, using the Square of Nine, the 90-degree support and resistance for a price peak at $310.

REFERENCES

Gann, W. D. 2008. *Tunnel Thru the Air*. The Richest Man in Babylon.

Gann, W. D. 2009 *45 Years in Wall Street*. Eastford, CT: Martino Fine Books.

Gann, W. D. 2008 *Truth of the Stock Tape*. The Richest Man in Babylon.

Gann, W. D. 2008 *The Magic Word*. New York: BN Publishing.

Gann, W. D. 2010 *How to Make Profits Trading in Commodities*. Eastford, CT: Martino Fine Books.

CHAPTER 20

Cycle Analysis

LEARNING OBJECTIVES

After studying this chapter, you should be able to:

- Understand how to identify important price cycles in the market and use them to forecast potential reversals and continuations in the market
- Describe the various cyclic principles and how they affect market action
- Calculate the correct lookback periods for centered moving averages, window oscillators, and overlay indicators
- Understand how chart patterns are formed from cyclic and trend components

Cycle analysis is an important part of technical analysis. In this chapter we will cover the most important principles of cycle analysis, including the various approaches to identifying price cycles. We will also learn how to effectively tune oscillators and overlay indicators to the most significant cycles within the period of observation.

20.1 ELEMENTS OF CYCLE ANALYSIS

Price Cycles

Price cycles are simply *oscillations* in price. They are characterized by price making peaks and troughs in a fairly regular and consistent manner. Many practitioners refer to price cycles as time cycles. This is erroneous. Time only moves forward, as required by the laws of thermodynamics. Time does not cycle or oscillate. As time progresses along its forward path, it is price that exhibits cycles. The highest part of a cycle is referred to as the peak, crest, or high, whereas the lowest part a cycle is referred to as the trough, bottom, or low. Refer to Figure 20.1.

713

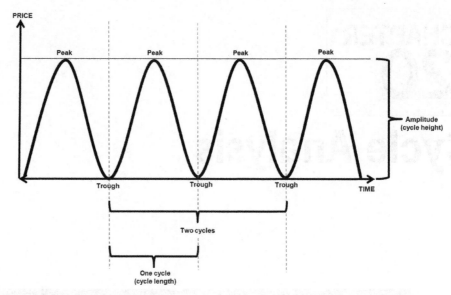

FIGURE 20.1 Cycles.

A price cycle may be defined in terms of:

- **Amplitude:** This refers to the magnitude or size of a cycle and is represented by the distance measured from peak to trough in terms of dollar, pip, or point value. The amplitude of price cycles may be classified into:
  - Up cycle amplitude
  - Down cycle amplitude

When the absolute values of the average up and down cycle amplitudes are equal, the market tends to move sideways. A larger absolute value in the average up cycle amplitude suggests that the market is bullish and rising, whereas a larger absolute value in the average down cycle amplitude suggests that the market is bearish and declining. See Figure 20.2.

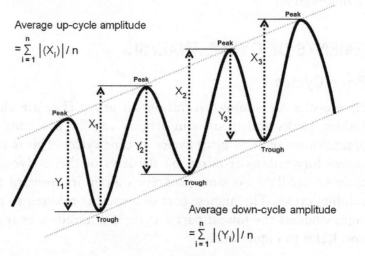

Average up-cycle amplitude

$$= \sum_{i=1}^{n} |(X_i)| / n$$

Average down-cycle amplitude

$$= \sum_{i=1}^{n} |(Y_i)| / n$$

FIGURE 20.2 Average Up and Down Cycle Amplitudes.

- Length: The cycle length is simply the time it takes to complete one cycle or oscillation. It is usually measured from *trough to trough* (although peak-to-peak measurements are sometimes used when the troughs are indistinct or visually indiscernible. Peak-to-peak measurements are less reliable and are not usually used as they are susceptible to the effects of *cycle translation*). Cycle length is normally measured by the number of periods or time intervals, which is represented by the *number of bars* it takes to complete one cycle. As such, cycle length is also referred to in terms of cycle *periodicity*.

- Phase: Cycle phase represents the point in the cycle at which price is current, and the difference between any two points is referred to as the phase difference. Phase difference is measured in time, the number of bars, or in angular form such as degrees or radians. In Figure 20.3, we observe that wave B is 180 degrees out of phase with wave A.

- Frequency: Cycle frequency represents the number of cycles completed within a similar reference time period. For example, cycle A completes one full cycle or oscillation within 20 bars. Cycle B makes two full cycles within the same 20 bars. We say that cycle B is twice the frequency of cycle A.

- Resonance: The wave amplitudes will be greatest at the point where all the peaks or troughs of the small, medium, and large wave cycles coincide. We say that the waves are in phase. This convergence of phases produces the largest amplitude, which we called resonance, usually seen during blow-offs and selling climaxes.

    Once a cycle is identified, the analyst is able forecast:

- Potential peaks and troughs in price (that is, bullish and bearish reversals)
- The price of the projected cycle peak or trough based on the average up and down cycle amplitudes

Various other technical indicators may also be made more effective by observing the locations at which they occur within a dominant cycle. A dominant cycle is the cycle that most influences price and market action within the observed time

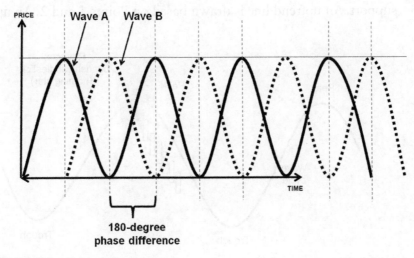

FIGURE 20.3 Phase Difference.

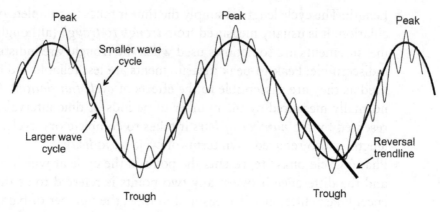

FIGURE 20.4 Reversal Trendlines.

span or horizon. Practitioners frequently tune indicator and oscillator lookback periods to one half the dominant cycle period in order to track the underlying market activity more accurately and effectively.

Price cycles may also be used to confirm trendline retests and breakouts, chart patterns, bar and candlestick patterns, and other indicator barriers. For example, in Figure 20.4, we observe a larger wave cycle making peaks and troughs. All wave cycles are comprised of smaller wave cycles, or subwaves. Assuming that the cycle length remains consistent, a trader will be able to time a trendline breakout at a projected peak or trough. We may refer to these cycle-based trendline breakouts as bullish or bearish *reversal trendlines*. Reversal trendlines associated with troughs are referred to as bullish reversal trendlines and those associated with peaks are referred to as bearish reversal trendlines.

In Figure 20.5 we observe a price cycle being used to confirm bearish and bullish candlestick patterns. A bearish pattern occurring at a projected cycle peak is more reliable than a bearish pattern occurring at a cycle midpoint or trough. Similarly, a bullish pattern occurring at a projected cycle trough is more reliable than a bullish pattern occurring at a cycle midpoint or peak.

In Figure 20.6 we observe a price cycle being used to confirm an uptrend line support. An uptrend line is drawn based on Points 1 and 2. An uptrend line retest

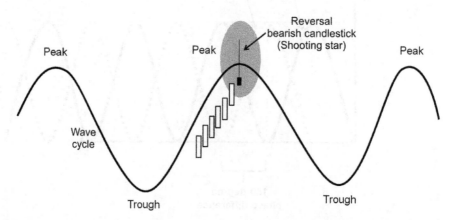

FIGURE 20.5 Bearish Patterns and Formations at Cycle Peaks.

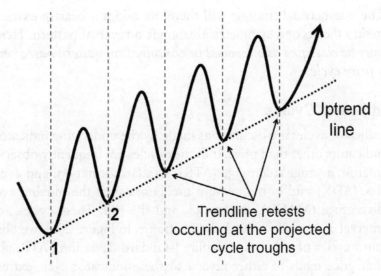

FIGURE 20.6 Bullish Trendline Retests of Support at Cycle Troughs.

of support occurring at a projected cycle trough is more reliable than an uptrend line retest of support occurring at a cycle midpoint or peak. Similarly, a downtrend line retest of resistance occurring at a projected cycle peak is more reliable than a downtrend line retest of resistance occurring at a cycle midpoint or trough.

Price cycles may also be used to confirm continuation patterns. An intrinsically bullish pattern or formation occurring *after a cycle trough* or near a cycle midpoint will potentially be more reliable as a continuation pattern. The reliability of a continuation pattern starts to diminish as it approaches the projected cycle extremes. In Figure 20.7, we observe a symmetrical triangle at two locations within a price cycle. Being an intrinsically neutral pattern, it is neither bullish nor bearish. Its sentiment is therefore wholly dependent on the contextual and extrinsic sentiment. The first symmetrical triangle is located at the midpoint of a cycle. This is bullish based on the assumption that price will continue moving toward a cycle peak. The symmetrical triangle is therefore regarded as a continuation pattern. The subsequent symmetrical triangle occurs at a cycle peak.

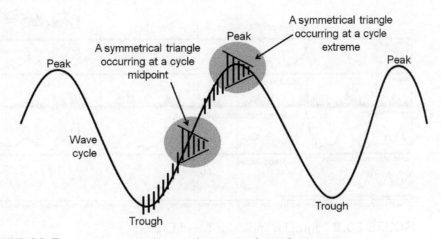

FIGURE 20.7 A Symmetrical Triangle at a Cycle Midpoint.

The symmetrical triangle will therefore adopt a bearish extrinsic sentiment. This makes the second symmetrical triangle a reversal pattern. *Hence, a chart pattern may be classified as a reversal or continuation pattern based on its location within a price cycle.*

Indicator Cycles

Indicator cycles are oscillations made by the underlying indicators that also include indicators other than price. Indicator cycles are frequently observed in volume, open interest, average true range (ATR), standard deviation, and average directional index (ADX) and in momentum oscillators such the moving average convergence-divergence (MACD), stochastics, and the RSI. These cycles are most evident on interval charts below the daily timeframe. In Figure 20.8, we observe intraday indicator cycles of volumes, volatility (standard deviation), ATR, and ADX. We notice that price tends to either reverse at these indicator cycle extremes or continue in the direction of the existing trend in a decisive manner. It seldom remains sideways. Many traders will therefore take advantage of this by placing straddles or bidirectional orders to catch price in either direction at these indicator cycle peaks.

Market Cycles

Business cycles are larger market oscillations based on the cycles in the commodity, equity, and bond markets. Cycles in these markets help determine the overall economic climate. Normally, when the markets are overheated, interest rates will rise to combat the rapidly rising cost of living. Bond prices, being directly tied to interest rates, will be the first to react by declining in a bullish environment. This represents an early indication of potential bearishness. As the bond market

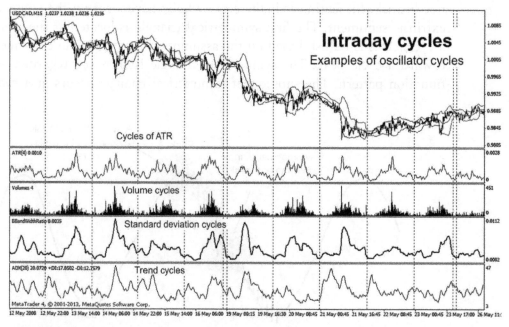

FIGURE 20.8 Intraday Indicator-Based Cycles.
Source: MetaTrader 4

declines, commodity prices will be the next to react by declining due to the higher borrowing cost caused by rising interest rates. This will affect many companies dependent on the cost of raw materials. Eventually, the equity markets will start to decline. Once inflation is under control, interest rates will begin to decline, causing bond prices to rise again. With falling interest rates, the cost of borrowing declines and commodity prices begin to rise as liquidity floods the markets. Companies begin to recover as businesses start to flourish. The equity market turns bullish again. In short, the bond market is regarded as a leading indicator of potential market tops and bottoms. The bond market turns first, followed by the commodities and finally by the equity market.

Business Cycles

Business cycles are usually tracked via oscillations in the level and growth rate of the gross domestic product (GDP), which is used as an indicator of economic health and activity. Business cycles reflect periods of expansion and contraction in the economy, depicted by economic recession, recovery, prosperity, and growth. It is usually the longer-term wave cycles that determine the primary trend in the market.

The four dominant economic cycles that are frequently referred to are the:

1. **Kondratieff Cycle:** This represents a 54-year economic cycle and it affects all markets including equities, commodities, and interest rates. It was discovered by Nikolai Kondratieff. This large economic cycle has accurately predicted market tops between the years 1810 to 1820, 1865 to 1875, 1910 to 1920, and 1970 to 1980. There have been many modern interpretations and modifications with respect to the Kondratieff theory of economic cycles since the 1920s.
2. **Juglar Cycle:** A 7- to 11-year economic cycle is also purported to exist affecting all markets and economies. This was proposed by Clement Juglar in 1860.
3. **Kitchin Cycle:** The Kitchin cycle is a four-year economic cycle that also affects all markets and economies. It is considered to be one of the most reliable prognosticators of economic health. It was discovered by Joseph Kitchin.
4. **Schumpeter Cycle:** The Schumpeter wave or cycle is an economic model that is based on the superposition of the Kondratieff, Juglar, and Kitchin cycles. It represents the sum of these three cycles. It was proposed by Joseph Alois Schumpeter. It has been found that when all three cycles within the model top or bottom are in sync with each other, the model tends to accurately predict potential economic expansions and contractions.

Seasonal Cycles

Seasonal cycles in agricultural commodities exist due to the climatic impact on crop seeding and harvesting. Seasonal cycles usually span across one year. The four-week commodity cycle is also predominant and many traders design trading systems around the four-week (or 20- to 26-day) cycle. Famous examples include the Donchian 20-day price channel, the MACD 12- and 26-day EMAs, and the Ichimoku 26- and 52-day (four- and eight-week) market overlays. When trading seasonal data, it is always wise to use the seasonals as a *signal* and *look for price confirmation in the near or front month futures contract.* The 20-period cycle is also harmonically related to 5-, 10-, and 40-period cycles. This is the effect of cycle nominality and harmonicity in the markets.

20.2 PRINCIPLES OF CYCLE ANALYSIS

Principle of Superposition (Summation)

The principle of superposition or summation suggests that the resultant wave cycle is the *sum of all short- and longer-term wave amplitudes*, comprising:

- A trend component
- An oscillatory component
- A random component

The trend component is usually driven by longer-term market participation. The oscillatory component represents the shorter-term activity driven by medium- to short-term trading activity. The random component accounts for the volatility surrounding the trend and oscillatory components.

For a more detailed account of the principles of cycle analysis, the reader is advised to read J. M. Hurst's excellent book entitled *The Magic of Stock Transaction Timing.*

The principle of summation helps explain the formation of various chart patterns such as head and shoulders, double tops and bottoms, triangles, rising and falling channels, and so on. In Figure 20.9, we see that a rising channel formation is the result of a long-term trend component being impacted by shorter-term price cycles.

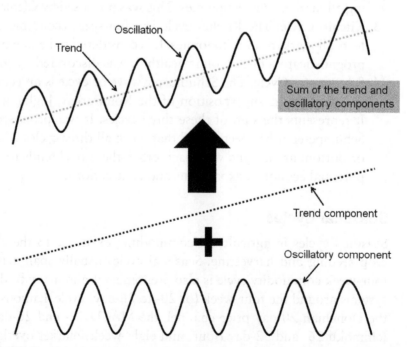

FIGURE 20.9 Principle of Summation in Action in the Creation of a Rising Channel.

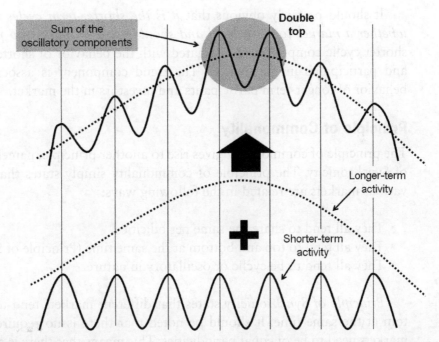

FIGURE 20.10 Principle of Summation in Action in the Creation of a Double Top Formation.

In similar fashion, a head and shoulders formation is the result of adding the amplitudes of a larger and smaller wave. See Figure 20.10.

Figure 20.11 shows a head and shoulders formation as a sum of both a longer- and shorter-term wave cycle.

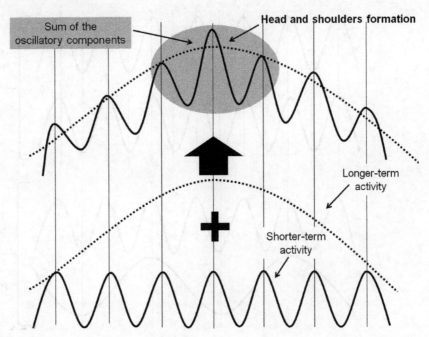

FIGURE 20.11 Principle of Summation in Action in the Creation of a Head and Shoulders Formation.

It should be fairly obvious that *it is the shorter-term cycles that determine whether a market top is a head and shoulders or a double top formation.* The shorter cyclic component is associated with the behavior of shorter-term traders and participants in the market. The trend component is associated with the behavior of longer-term participants and investors in the market.

Principle of Commonality

The principle of commonality gives rise to another principle, namely the Principle of Synchronicity. The principle of commonality simply states that cycles across various markets are related in the following ways:

- They all tend to share the same periodicities.
- They all tend to top and bottom at the same time (Principle of Synchronicity).
- They all tend to be cyclic or oscillatory in nature.

Principle of Synchronicity states that different markets tend to top and bottom at the same time. It should be noted that there is no requirement that the markets need to be of equal periodicities. This means that there is also a tendency for markets with different periodicities to top and bottom at the same time. See Figure 20.12.

This is clearly evident during periods of severe market reversal. Markets tend to move in lock step during a crisis. In Figure 20.13, we see the global markets moving in synchronicity with each other. This is a global expression of the principle of commonality in action.

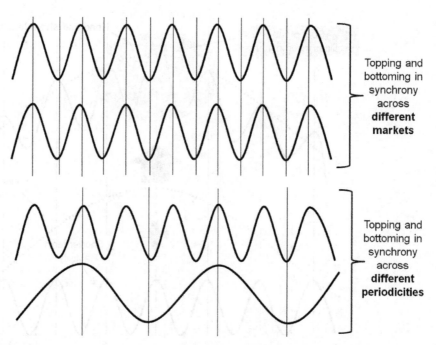

FIGURE 20.12 Principle of Synchronicity in Action across Different Markets and Periodicities.

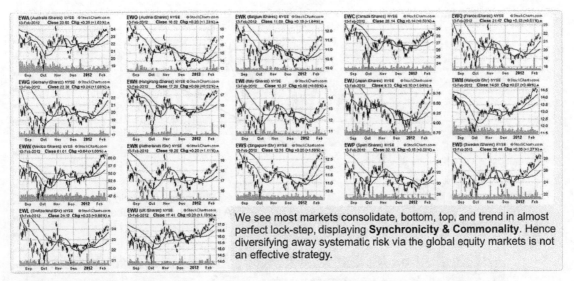

We see most markets consolidate, bottom, top, and trend in almost perfect lock-step, displaying **Synchronicity & Commonality**. Hence diversifying away systematic risk via the global equity markets is not an effective strategy.

FIGURE 20.13 Principle of Commonality (and Synchronicity) in Action Globally.
Courtesy of Stockcharts.com

Principle of Proportionality

The principle of proportionality suggests that cycles with larger amplitudes tend to have longer cycle lengths or durations. This is fairly intuitive, as larger cycles usually take longer to complete one full cycle.

Principle of Harmonicity

The principle of harmonicity suggests that cycle periodicities tend to be harmonically related, that is, cycle periodicities tend to occur in:

- Multiples of two
- Subdivisions of two (halves, 1/2) or three (thirds, 1/3)

There is usually a mathematical relationship based on the doubling, halving, tripling, or one-third subdivisions of the wave periodicities. This means that a 20-period wave is related harmonically to a 5- (1/4), 10- (1/2), 40- (×2), and 80- (×4) period wave. A 30-period wave is harmonically related to a 10- (1/3), 15- (1/2), 60- (×2), and 90- (×3) period wave. Waves with periodicities that are harmonically related by multiples or subdivisions of two tend to top and bottom together.

Principle of Variation

The principle of variation simply suggests that all cyclic principles are subject to fluctuations in the markets and as such will not always unfold as the principle suggests. In other words, the principles are merely guidelines of wave behavior tendencies. Market do not always top and bottom perfectly in sync. Cycle amplitudes are also not always preserved and will tend to change over time. One simple example of variation is a *cycle inversion*. A cycle inversion is a peak forming in

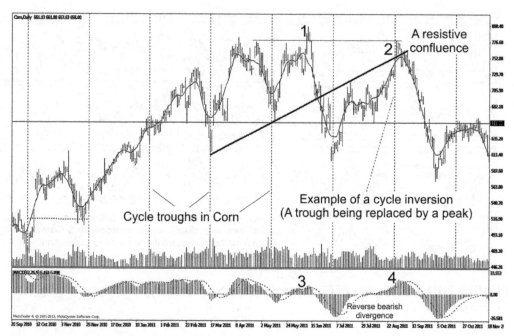

FIGURE 20.14 Cycle Inversion on the Daily Chart of Corn.
Source: MetaTrader 4

place of a trough, and vice versa. Figure 20.14 is an example of a cycle inversion where a peak forms in place of a trough. We also observe reverse bearish divergence forming between price and the MACD with a lower high between points 1 and 2 in price and a higher high between points 3 and 4 on the MACD.

Principle of Nominality

Based on the principle of commonality, markets share common harmonic elements. They are usually related in multiples of subdivisions of two and three. For example, an 18-year cycle tends to have a related 9-, 4.5-, 3-, 1.5-, and 1-year related cycles. Similarly, a 1.5-year cycle (18 month) tends to have a related 9-, 6-, 3-, 1.5-, and 0.75-month cycles. A 6-month cycle (26 weeks) tends to have a related 13-, 6.5-, and 3.25-week cycle. These cycles may be used as a starting point for the search of dominant cycles in various markets. It should be noted that these relationships are merely tendencies and will not always unfold exactly as expected.

20.3 ADDITIONAL CYCLIC CHARACTERISTICS

One interesting characteristic of cycles is that the cycle peaks tend to lean to the right of the idealized cycle-length midpoint in a rising market and this phenomenon is referred to as *right translation*. In declining markets, the peaks tend to lean to the left of the idealized cycle-length midpoint and are referred to as *left translation*. As such, right translation is bullish and left translation is bearish. See Figure 20.15.

Longer-term wave cycles tend to dominate and overwhelm the shorter-term wave cycle action. This also means that the trend of shorter-term wave cycles is determined by the trend of larger wave cycles.

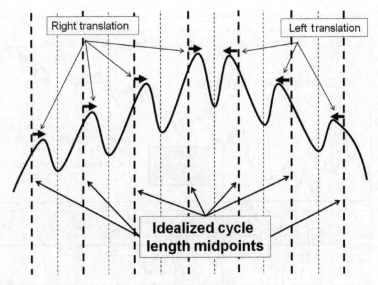

FIGURE 20.15 Right and Left Cycle Translation.

20.4 TUNING OSCILLATOR AND OVERLAY INDICATORS TO THE DOMINANT CYCLE PERIOD

For every time horizon, there exists a *dominant wave cycle* that influences most price activity. This dominant wave is usually easily identifiable as compared to other less significant cycles across the period of observation or interest. The trader should attempt to tie in the oscillator lookback periods to that of *one-half* the dominant cycle period. This will allow the trader to effectively track the most significant cyclic action within the period of observation. The main advantages of tuning window-based oscillators and price overlay indicators to one half the dominant cycle period are threefold:

- It allows the oscillator to generate only the most significant and relevant buy and sell signals.
- It allows the trader to tune price bands and envelopes to contain price effectively.
- It allows the trader to tune moving averages to track price accurately.

There are three ways to calculate the half-cycle lookback period (using any of the following formulas):

- $(N+1)/2$ and round up if N is even
- $(N/2) +1$ and round down if N is odd
- $(2N+3)/4$ round to closest integer

The last formula is advantageous from the perspective that you need not remember whether you are required to round up or down. Instead, you simply round to the *closest integer*. (Refer to Chapter 12 for more details on calculations using these formulas.)

Let us now recall how we tuned a stochastic oscillator to the dominant cycle period in Chapter 8. Refer to Figure 20.16. The average dominant cycle period on

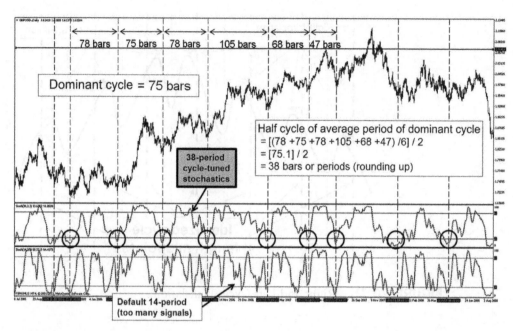

FIGURE 20.16 Tuning the Stochastic to the Dominant Cycle on the Daily Chart of GBPUSD.
Source: MetaTrader 4

the daily GBPUSD chart from 2005 to 2007 was approximately 75 days. The half cycle would then be (75/2) + 1 = 38.5 days. We round this down since N is odd (75), making the half cycle 38 days. We therefore tune our stochastic's lookback period to 38 periods. We see that it tracked and forecasted the cycle troughs perfectly, including troughs during the period *after* the sample was taken. Note that the standard 14-period default setting generated too many oversold signals as compared to the cycle-tuned oscillator. This illustrates the importance of tying the oscillators to the dominant cycle in order to generate only significant and relevant buy and sell signals.

Let us also recall how we tuned an overlay indicator to the dominant cycle period in Chapter 12. Refer to Figure 20.17. Here is an example of tuning the fixed percentage bands to a dominant cycle based on the four-hour chart of GBPUSD. The average trough-to-trough cycle period was 133 bars. Using the third formula would also yield ((2×133) + 3)/4 = 67.25. Rounding to the closest integer would give us 67 periods or bars. We therefore set the band periodicity to 67 bars. The band's percentage of central value was derived via visual inspection. Notice how the price band effectively contains price activity.

20.5 IDENTIFYING PRICE CYCLES

Trading in the direction of the trend is always recommended. Traders employ cycle analysis to provide effective entries by indicating:

- Cycle peaks in a downtrend for selling into the rallies
- Cycle troughs in an uptrend for buying the dips

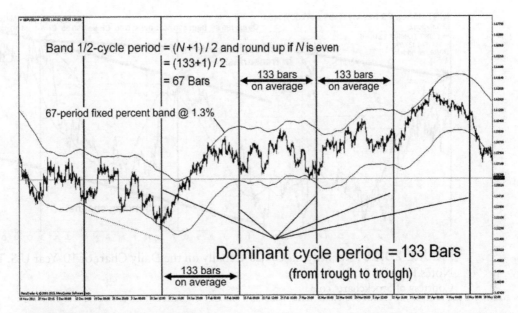

FIGURE 20.17 Tuning the Percentage Bands to the Dominant Cycle on the Daily Chart of GBPUSD.
Source: MetaTrader 4

There are five basic methods for identifying cycles in the market, namely via:

1. **Visual inspection:** The easiest way to identify price cycles is via visual inspection. Unfortunately, this requires some experience and familiarity with the markets. In Figure 20.18, we see longer- and shorter-term cycle troughs on the daily chart of 3M Co. These can be easily identified visually with some experience.

FIGURE 20.18 Identifying Cycles Visually on the Daily Chart of 3M Co.
Courtesy of Stockcharts.com

FIGURE 20.19 Identifying Cycles Visually on the Daily Chart of 10-Year U.S. Treasury Notes Price.
Courtesy of Stockcharts.com

It is important to locate some bearish formation or resistance at cycle peaks to ensure greater signal reliability. In Figure 20.19, we see a bearish convergence consisting of a channel top resistance occurring at a projected cycle peak, at Point X.

In Figure 20.20, we see a bearish convergence consisting of an uptrend line resistance occurring at a projected cycle peak, at the far right-hand side of the chart.

In Figure 20.21, we see a bearish convergence consisting of a channel resistance occurring at a projected cycle peak, at Point X on the daily chart of the AUDUSD.

2. Centered moving average: Centered moving averages are moving averages that are back shifted by one half of the cycle period. A centered moving

FIGURE 20.20 Identifying Cycles Visually on the Daily Chart of PowerShares DB U.S. Dollar Index Bullish Fund.
Courtesy of Stockcharts.com

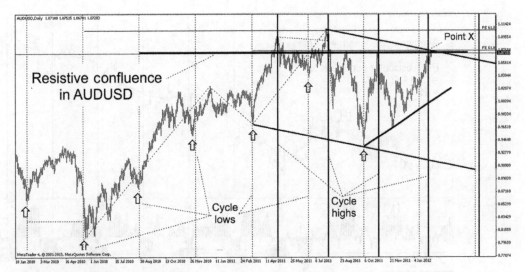

FIGURE 20.21 Identifying Cycles Visually on the Daily Chart of AUDUSD.
Source: MetaTrader 4

average can easily be created by shifting the end-displaced or non-centered moving average back by half its period. As we saw in Chapter 11, the exact amount to shift back is calculated using $(N-1)/2$. Hence, for an 11-period end-displaced moving average, we need to displace the moving average back by $(11-1)/2 = 5$ periods. This formula works well with odd numbers. For even numbers, *round down* to the closest integer value. A centered moving average tracks price cycles very closely. In Figure 20.22, we notice the centered moving average tracing out the peaks and troughs very clearly from the price action. This makes the search for potential cycles much more visually accessible. The centered moving average filters out all extraneous price activity, revealing the underlying cycles with greater clarity.

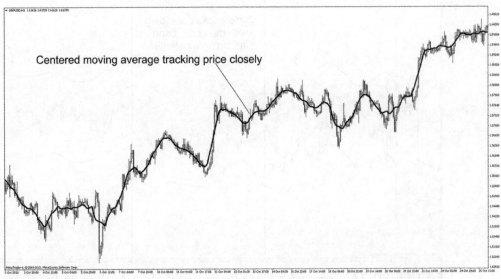

FIGURE 20.22 Centered Moving Average on the Hourly Chart of GBPUSD.
Source: MetaTrader 4

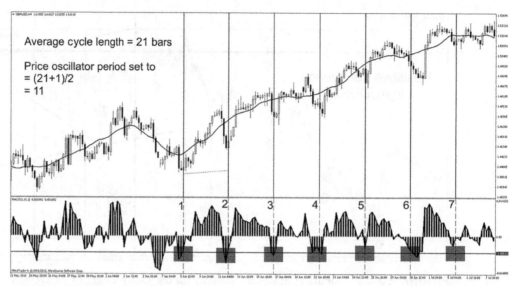

FIGURE 20.23 Identifying Cycles via a Price Oscillator on the 4-Hour Chart of GBPUSD.
Source: MetaTrader 4

3. Detrending moving averages (price oscillator, etc): We may also employ a price oscillator when trying to isolate potential cycles in the market. A price oscillator tracks the difference between price and a moving average. It helps to identify periods of overextensions that are usually related to peaks or troughs. In Figure 20.23, we tuned the price oscillator to detrend price against an 11-period moving average, which represents half the cycle period length of a cycle identified on the four-hour chart of the GBPUSD. Cycle troughs at time lines 1 and 2 were used to project the cycle lines forward in time. Notice how cycle troughs tend to occur at time lines 3 to 7 every time the oscillator tests

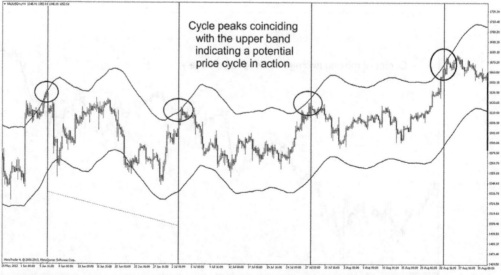

FIGURE 20.24 Identifying Cycle Peaks via Envelope Analysis on the 4-Hour Chart of GBPUSD.
Source: MetaTrader 4

the lower oversold level. We see the principle of variation in action at point 6 where the price cycle is beginning to fall out of sync with the existing cycle.

4. OBOS on popular indicators: We may also use overbought and oversold (OBOS) indications with the window oscillators to identify potential cycles in the markets. By looking for correspondence between the historical highs and lows in the oscillator and peaks and troughs in price, the chances of locating a potential cycle are greatly increased.

5. Price envelopes: Price envelopes are also extremely effective in isolating cycles in the market. As we saw in Figure 20.17, a properly tuned price band helps identify potential cycle peaks and troughs in the market. In Figure 20.24, we see peaks occurring at the upper moving average percentage band, indicative of a potential cycle in action. The upper band tests turn out to be peaks belonging to a 111-period cycle on the four-hour gold chart. It should be noted that when trying to identify cycles using price bands or envelopes, only arithmetically scaled charts should be employed. Logarithmically scaled charts will compress the bands and envelopes at higher price levels and expand them at the lower price levels, making it very hard to analyze price cycles accurately.

20.6 CHAPTER SUMMARY

As we have seen, cycle analysis studies the underlying repetitive behavior of price and market action. Although cyclic behavior is potentially predictive of market bottoms and tops, there will always be random or unexpected events or forces in the markets that may upset the periodicity and magnitude of any cycle. It is always prudent to combine cycle analysis with sentiment readings for a better forecast, especially in highly emotionally charged market environments.

CHAPTER 20 REVIEW QUESTIONS

1. Describe the different parts of a cycle.
2. Explain cycle translation.
3. What is the principle of proportionality?
4. Explain how you would calculate the half period of a given cycle.
5. What role does a centered moving average play in cycle analysis?
6. Describe the five methods for identifying a cycle in the market.
7. Explain how cycles may be used to classify reversal and continuation patterns.
8. List at least five advantages of using cycle analysis.

REFERENCES

Grafton, Christopher. 2011. *Mastering Hurst Cycle Analysis: A Modern Treatment of Hurst's Original System of Financial Market Analysis*. Hampshire, UK: Harriman House.

Hurst, J. M. 2000. *The Magic of Stock Transaction Timing*. Greenville, SC: Traders Press.

Millard, Brian J. 1999. *Channels and Cycles: A Tribute to J.M. Hurst*. Greenville, SC: Traders Press.

Schumpeter, Joseph. *Business Cycles: A Theoretical, Historical, and Statistical Analysis of the Capitalist Process*. Eastford, CT: Martino Publishing.

CHAPTER 21

Volatility Analysis

LEARNING OBJECTIVES

After studying this chapter, you should be able to:

- Understand the basic measures of central tendency, dispersion, and their associated geometrical representations
- Employ the five measure of volatility to determine market behavior
- Distinguish between trend and range volatility measures
- Identify volatility when it appears in price, oscillators, and overlay indicators
- Describe the various volatility-based indicators and how they can be used to forecast potential market tops
- Identify volatility cycles in the market
- Compare and contrast the different applications of ATR as a filter of volatility or market noise

---

The ability to gauge the degree of market volatility is crucial to any forecast or to trading decisions. Volatility impacts the degree of risk in investments, so it is an element of market behavior that should be mastered. In this chapter, we will cover the various measures for gauging volatility in the markets.

21.1 THE CONCEPT OF CHANGE AND VOLATILITY

There are many ways to measure or quantify volatility. Depending on which mode of measure is employed, different aspects of price-action volatility will be quantified. Price action may be characterized by the following five measures of volatility:

1. The change in the rate of change in price over a specified duration
2. The maximum amount of price change over equal durations
3. The number of price fluctuations over equal durations

4. The degree of interval activity over equal durations
5. The degree of relative interval activity over equal durations

Volatility in price may also be classified as:

- Directional, trend, or vectorial
- Non-directional, range, or scalar

The following are a few examples to help illustrate the various modes of volatility measure.

(1) First Measure of Volatility: Volatility as the Change in the Rate of Change in Price over a Specified Duration

The first way to quantify volatility is by the change in the rate of change in price. See Figure 21.1.

From Figure 21.1 we observe two stocks rising in price, with Stock A moving from $1 to $10 and Stock B moving from $2 to $20, over the same duration of 10 periods.

Let n represent the period. Therefore, *price change* from one period to the next is just:

$$PC_n = Price_n - Price_{n-1}$$

The rate of change (ROC) of price change is also tabulated, and is calculated (as a percentage) as:

$$ROC \text{ of } PC = (PC_n - PC_{n-1})/PC_{n-1} \times 100 \text{ percent}$$

Figure 21.2 shows the two stocks rising at different changes in price per period. Applying the first measure of volatility, which is the change in the *rate of change in price*, we find that both stocks are rising at constant rates. This means

Hypothetical Prices		Price Change		ROC in Price Change	
Stock A	Stock B	Stock A	Stock B	Stock A	Stock B
$1	$2	N/A	N/A	N/A	N/A
$2	$4	$1	$2	N/A	N/A
$3	$6	$1	$2	0%	0%
$4	$8	$1	$2	0%	0%
$5	$10	$1	$2	0%	0%
$6	$12	$1	$2	0%	0%
$7	$14	$1	$2	0%	0%
$8	$16	$1	$2	0%	0%
$9	$18	$1	$2	0%	0%
$10	$20	$1	$2	0%	0%

FIGURE 21.1 Table of Hypothetical Stock Prices and Rates of Change.

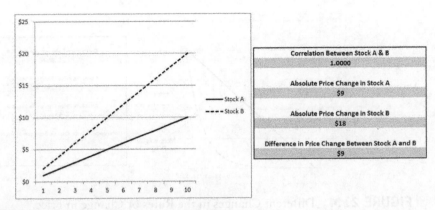

FIGURE 21.2 Constant Rates of Change in Price.

that the change in the rate of change for both stocks is zero per period. Stock B would not be regarded as more volatile, even though it is rising at a rate of $2 per period as compared to Stock A's $1 per period. It is the change in the rate of change in price from one period to the next that we are measuring, not the amount of price change per period. In short, when stocks are rising at constant amounts of price change per period, the change in the rate of change in price will be zero. Hence, it is not possible to determine which stock is more volatile via the first measure. Changes in the rate of change are characterized as *acceleration* and *deceleration* in price, unlike a constant rate of change in price.

Let us now consider a scenario of a stock rising by increasing changes in price per period. See Figure 21.3.

In this scenario, Stock B has a greater change in the rate of change in price, rising at a rate of 100 percent per period, whereas Stock A's change in the rate of change in price is 0 percent per period, that is, a constant change in price per period. Therefore, by way of the first measure of volatility, Stock B is now regarded as more volatile. Notice that Stock B is undergoing acceleration in price whereas Stock A is moving at a constant speed. See Figure 21.4.

Hypothetical Prices		Price Change		ROC in Price Change	
Stock A	Stock B	Stock A	Stock B	Stock A	Stock B
$1	$1	N/A	N/A	N/A	N/A
$171	$1	$170	$0	N/A	N/A
$341	$2	$171	$1	N/A	N/A
$512	$4	$171	$2	0%	100%
$683	$8	$171	$4	0%	100%
$853	$16	$171	$8	0%	100%
$1,024	$32	$171	$16	0%	100%
$1,195	$64	$171	$32	0%	100%
$1,365	$128	$171	$64	0%	100%
$1,536	$256	$171	$128	0%	100%
$1,707	$512	$171	$256	0%	100%
$1,877	$1024	$171	$512	0%	100%
$2,048	$2048	$171	$1,024	0%	100%

FIGURE 21.3 Different Rates of Change in Price.

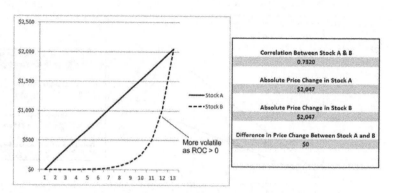

FIGURE 21.4 Different Changes in the Rates of Change in Price.

We may therefore, represent volatility in various *orders of change*, where:

- First-Order Change—Represents a simple change in price that is not considered volatile with respect to the first measure of volatility and is characterized by a constant rate of change in price
- Second-Order Change—Represents a change in the rate of change in price, which is considered to be volatile with respect to the first measure of volatility, and is characterized by acceleration or deceleration in price
- Third-Order Change—Represents "a change in the change in a rate of change in price" which is considered to be extremely volatile with respect to the first measure of volatility and is characterized by an increasing rate of acceleration or deceleration in price.

We may therefore track volatility on the charts by trying to identify change in the increasing angular increment of price, measured over equal durations. See Figure 21.5.

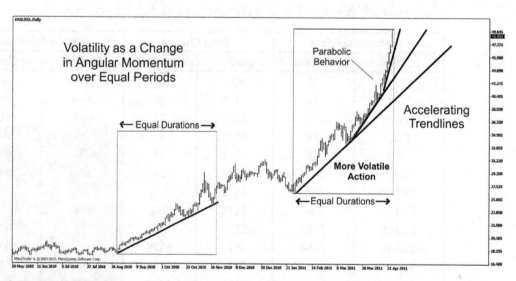

FIGURE 21.5 Increasing Angular Increment Indicating Volatility with Respect to the First Measure of Volatility on the Daily Gold Chart.
Source: MetaTrader 4

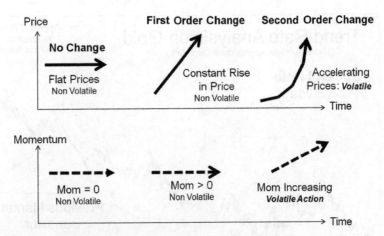

FIGURE 21.6 Relationship between Price and Momentum.

Volatility is therefore represented, with respect to the first measure of volatility, by any change above the first order. Hence price *momentum*, which represents a change in price, that is, Price$_n$ – Price$_{n-1}$, will only indicate volatility if it is either rising or falling. This only occurs at the second order of change. Flatlining momentum on the chart does not indicate the presence of volatility with respect to the first measure. See Figure 21.6.

As seen in the relationship between price and momentum in Figure 21.6, a constant change in the rate of change in price is characterized by flattened momentum action. A change in the rate of change in price is called acceleration and is depicted by a constant rate of change in momentum. An exponential or parabolic move in momentum depicts extreme volatility with respect to the first measure. See Figure 21.7. It is the same chart as in Figure 21.5, but with the 20-day momentum oscillator attached.

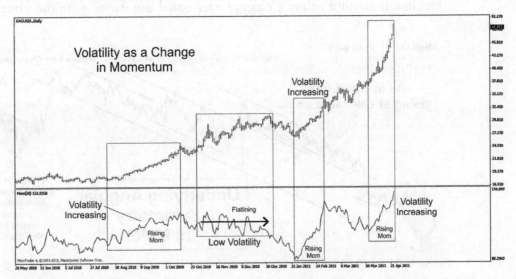

FIGURE 21.7 Angular Increment Indicating Volatility with Respect to the First Measure of Volatility on the Daily Gold Chart.
Source: MetaTrader 4

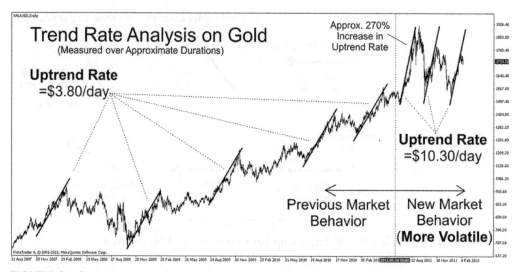

FIGURE 21.8 Trend Rate Change Indicating Potential Volatility on the Daily Gold Chart.
Source: MetaTrader 4

(2) The Second Measure of Volatility: Volatility as the Maximum Amount of Price Change over a Specified Duration

Refer to Figure 21.1 again. If we now employ the second measure of volatility, that is, the *maximum amount of price change* over equal durations, then Stock B would be considered more volatile, as the amount of price change over the 10 periods was $20 – $2 = $18, whereas the amount of price change for Stock A was only $10 – $1 = $9. (Note that all volatility measures must be made over equal durations for proper comparison.)

By applying the second measure of volatility to the example in Figure 21.3, we observe that we could not determine which stock was more volatile since the maximum amount of price change over equal durations were the same for both

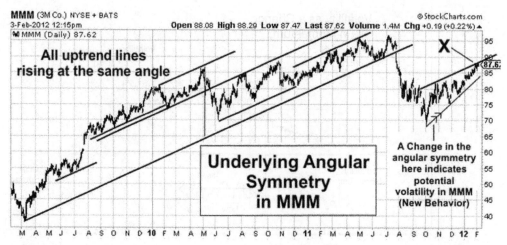

FIGURE 21.9 Trend Rate Change Indicating Potential Volatility on the Daily 3M Co. Chart.
Courtesy of Stockcharts.com

stocks, that is, $2047. Therefore, depending on the situation, different measures of volatility afford the practitioner different interpretations of price behavior.

Figure 21.8 depicts the approximate rate of change in the daily Gold prices. We notice that from June 2011, the trend rate increases from approximately $3.80 per day to $10.30 per day. This new trend rate increases the average *maximum amount of price change* over approximately similar durations, reflecting the increase in the potential underlying volatility in Gold, with respect to the second measure of volatility.

Figure 21.9 depicts the underlying angular symmetry in 3M Co., indicating a constant rate of change. We observe that from about September 2011, the trend rate increases to a new higher constant rate of change. This increases the average *maximum amount of price change* over approximately similar durations, reflecting the increase in the potential underlying volatility in 3M Co., with respect to the second measure of volatility. Notice price approaching an uptrend line at point X, where prices may experience potential resistance from an overbought angular perspective. This is further confirmed by the bearish rising wedge formation.

(3) The Third Measure of Volatility: The Number of Price Fluctuations over Equal Durations

The third measure of volatility is characterized by *the number of price fluctuations over equal durations*. In Figure 21.10, we see three trends with varying amounts of price fluctuation. The greater the fluctuations, the more volatile the trend is expected to be over the same duration. Notice that all three trends have, over the same duration:

- The same rate of change in price
- The same maximum price change

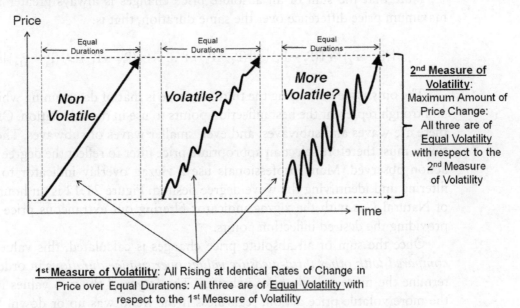

FIGURE 21.10 Increase in Price Fluctuations over Equal Durations Indicating Potential Rise in Volatility.

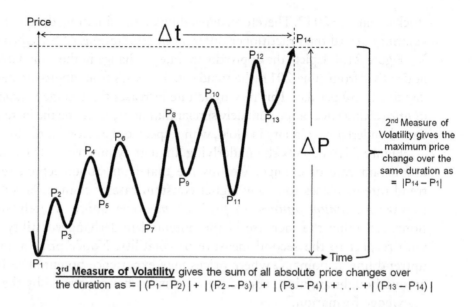

FIGURE 21.11 The Sum of All Price Changes as a Measure of Potential Volatility.

As a consequence, volatility arising from price fluctuation *cannot be properly accounted for using the first two measures of volatility*, namely, the change in the rate of change in price and maximum amount of price change over equal intervals.

As such, we have to resort to the third measure of volatility, that is, the capture of price fluctuations via the sum of all price movement over the specified duration. This is done by calculating the sum of all price changes. Note that we only take the sum of the absolute values of all price changes. See Figure 21.11.

Note that the sum of all absolute price changes is always greater than the maximum price difference over the same duration, that is:

$$|(P_1 - P_2)| + |(P_2 - P_3)| + |(P_3 - P_4)| + \ldots + |(P_{13} - P_{14})| > |(P_1 - P_{14})|$$

The only issue with using the third measure is that of determining which peak and trough represent the best inflection points to use in the calculation. Of course, there are waves and subwaves, and even smaller waves of subwaves. The practitioner must therefore select an appropriate price filter to reflect the degree of wave action observed. Many professionals use a zigzag overlay indicator to help in filtering and identifying the wave degree desired. Figure 21.12 is an hourly chart of Natural Gas with the zigzag indicator filtering out extraneous price activity, providing the desired inflection points.

Once the sum of all absolute price changes is calculated, this value is then *compared with other third-measure values over similar durations* in order to determine the more volatile price behavior. The *larger* of the two values indicates the more volatile price action, regardless if the trend was up or down. Without comparing volatility measurements over similar durations, there is no way of determining the more volatile action. It is essentially a *comparative* study.

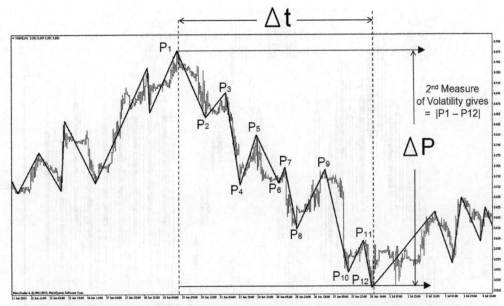

3rd Measure of Volatility gives the sum of all absolute price changes over
the duration Δt as = | (P₁ – P₂) | + | (P₂ – P₃) | + | (P₃ – P₄) | + . . . + | (P₁₁ – P₁₂) |

FIGURE 21.12 The Sum of All Price Changes as a Measure of Potential Volatility.
Source: MetaTrader 4

(4) The Fourth Measure of Volatility: The Degree of Interval Activity over Equal Durations

The fourth measure of volatility is characterized by the average *interval* activity over the duration observed. It measures that *average of all true range (ATR) action* for each interval over the duration. Therefore, when comparing two similar durations, the duration that gives the larger average true range value is considered more volatile, *with respect to the fourth measure of volatility*. See Figure 21.13.

From the idealized illustration in Figure 21.13, we observe three sets of Japanese candlestick action over the same duration, that is, 18 periods, each with a fixed candlestick range for the sake of convenience. Let us assume that the average true range, ATR, over 18 periods yields $1.50 over the first duration of candlesticks, $1.00 over the second duration, and $4.00 over the third duration. Though this is merely an illustration, notice that the fixed candlestick range for the second duration of candlesticks is $0.70, which is less than its ATR value of $1.00. This is because we assume that gapping action has contributed to the increase in the true range values of a number of candlesticks. ATR values and the fixed candlestick ranges are identical for the remaining two durations of candlestick action, as no gapping action is assumed. Notice that both the candlestick action over the first and second durations has a maximum price range of $9, whereas the third duration of candlestick action has a maximum price range of only $6. Therefore, by way of the second measure of volatility, the last duration has the lowest volatility of the three durations. Conversely, if we measure volatility via the fourth measure, that is, ATR size, the last duration of candlestick action now has the highest

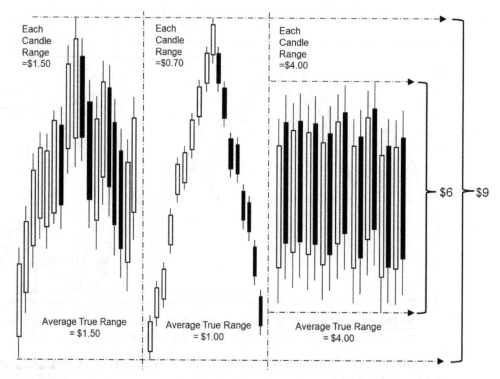

FIGURE 21.13 ATR Size: The Fourth Measure of Volatility.

volatility of the three durations. Therefore, depending on what type of volatility is being observed or analyzed, the measure of volatility may vary.

Figure 21.14 shows the ATR cycles of (fourth measure) volatility on the hourly Natural Gas chart. Notice the peaks in the ATR indicating a higher-than-normal average candlestick size over the last seven periods of lookback in the ATR oscillator. The troughs in the ATR indicate areas of smaller-than-normal average candlestick size. *It is very important to realize that high ATR readings do not necessarily correspond to trending action in price.* It merely indicates a larger average candlestick size over the selected lookback period on the ATR indicator. Points 1, 2, 3, and 4 correspond to areas of high (fourth measure) volatility *consolidations,* whereas Points X, Y, and Z correspond to areas of high (fourth measure) volatility trend action. Points A to H indicate areas of low volatility, which is usually accompanied by very little trend activity.

The bidirectional trader may also take advantage of such cyclical action by anticipating potential areas of low volatility consolidation for the placement of breakout straddles. The trader may also use the average ATR values during periods of *high volatility consolidations* as a basis for determining the most appropriate stopsize for a trend-following setup.

(5) The Fifth Measure of Volatility: The Degree of Relative Interval Activity over Equal Durations

The fifth measure of volatility identifies trend-related volatility. The first measure of volatility gauges the change in the rate of change in price as a guide to the degree of volatility in a trend. The fifth measure, on the other hand, only compares

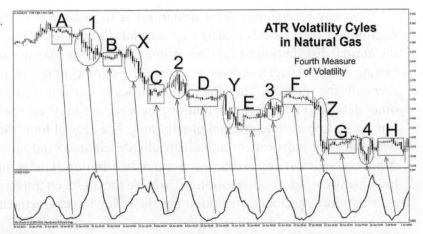

FIGURE 21.14 ATR Cycles of Volatility on the Hourly Natural Gas Chart.
Source: MetaTrader 4

the *relative average amount of price excursion* over a selected duration. The duration with the greater relative average excursion is considered the more volatile trend, again, with respect to the fifth measure of volatility.

The fifth measure of volatility is determined by dividing the larger period's ATR by the smaller period's ATR. For example, let us assume a currency trader is interested in trading the hourly EURUSD. But to gauge the potential profit, the trader would like to know the average daily excursion of the EURUSD. Assume that the hourly ATR value for the EURUSD is 20 pips and that its daily ATR is approximately 120 pips. To obtain the relative interval activity, we need to find the average *trend ratio*. Dividing the daily by the hourly ATR values gives us, in this case, an average trend ratio of 120/20 = 6.

Higher trend ratio values indicate a greater trend potential with respect to the hourly time horizon. A relative trend ratio of 10 is considered more volatile, from a trend-based perspective, than one with a value of 5.

21.2 SOME STATISTICAL MEASURES OF PRICE VOLATILITY

There are four popular statistical measures of price volatility, namely:

1. Standard Deviation (SD)
2. Mean Deviation
3. Average True Range (ATR)
4. Stock Beta

Standard deviation measures the amount of *spread* or *dispersion* from the mean or average value. If price or price returns indicate values that are close to the mean, resulting in a narrower distribution or dispersion of values, we say there is low standard deviation. This implies that there is low volatility in the price or the price-returns data. Higher standard deviation corresponds to a wider distribution of values, hence more volatility.

One way to quantify these deviations is to assume that the empirical data distribution corresponds closely to a *normal distribution*. This is very helpful as the normal distribution has various properties that one may use as a basis for forecasting potential overreactions or statistically significant prices, returns, or related events in the markets. The closer an empirically derived distribution of price or other data is to a normal distribution, the more we may use the normal distribution as a proxy for the original distribution. The central limit theorem states that with sufficient independent and identically distributed random variables, the distribution begins to approximate a normal distribution. This is important, as it allows many empirical observations to assume the useful characteristics of a normal distribution. A normal distribution has the following characteristics:

- The mean, mode, and median have the same values
- It has a symmetrical distribution
- 68.2 percent of the values lie between ± 1SD
- 95.4 percent of the values lie between ± 2SD
- 99.7 percent of the values lie between ± 3SD

The last three dispersion characteristics are by far the most useful properties of a normal distribution. Useful and effective forecasts may be made based on dispersion statistics such as these. See Figure 21.15.

The mean, mode, and median are all measures of *central tendency* where:

- The mean represents the average of all data
- The mode represents the most frequently recurring data
- The median represents the middle of all data

A very rudimentary test of how well our data approximates to a normal distribution may be determined by the amount of discrepancy between the values of the mean, mode, and median. In a normal distribution, all three measures of central tendency have the same value.

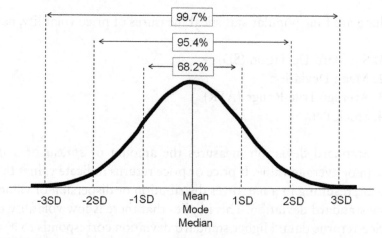

FIGURE 21.15 The Normal Distribution Dispersion Characteristics.

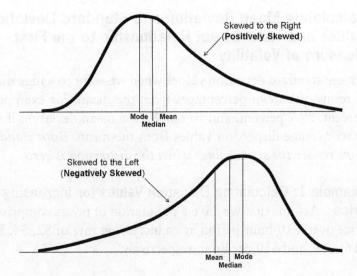

FIGURE 21.16 Left and Right Skewed Distributions.

When analyzing statistical data, we study the dispersion and geometry of the distribution. Geometry has two basic components:

1. Skewness: the bias in the data set where the tail of the distribution is pointing to either left or right side of the mean. If the tail in the data set is shifted to the left, we say that the distribution is skewed to the left, that is, negatively skewed. In such a case, the mode is usually greater than the median, which in turn is greater than the mean. If the tail in the data set is shifted to the right, we say that the distribution is skewed to the right, that is, positively skewed, where the mode is usually less than the median, which in turn is less than the mean. See Figure 21.16.

2. Kurtosis: is a measure of the distribution's peakedness. Distributions that are flatter and more spread out than the normal distributions are called platykurtic distributions, whereas distributions that are taller and more concentrated around the mean are called leptokurtic distributions. See Figures 21.16 and 21.17.

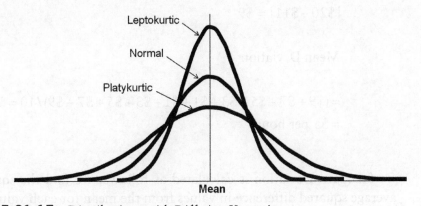

FIGURE 21.17 Distributions with Differing Kurtosis.

Calculating Mean Deviation and Standard Deviation Values and Their Direct Relationship to the First Measure of Volatility

We use standard deviation values when we want to gauge the degree of dispersion in terms of known percentages from the mean, for example, 68.2 percent, 95.4 percent, 99.7 percent, and so on. We use mean deviation if we want to know the exact average dispersion values from the mean. *Both standard and mean deviations render the same values when the dispersion is zero.*

Example 1: Calculating Deviation Values for Increasing Rates of Change in Price
Assume that we have a population of prices comprising a parabolic rise in price over a 10-hour period at an increasing rate of $2, $4, $6, $8, $10, $12, $14, $16, $18, and $20 per hour, respectively.

Mean rate of increase per hour

$$= (\$2 + \$4 + \$6 + \$8 + \$10 + \$12 + \$14 + \$16 + \$18 + \$20)/10 = \$110/10 = \$11$$

Mean Deviation is calculated as follows. We find the average of the differences in absolute values from the mean for each value:

$$|\$2 - \$11| = \$9$$
$$|\$4 - \$11| = \$7$$
$$|\$6 - \$11| = \$5$$
$$|\$8 - \$11| = \$3$$
$$|\$10 - \$11| = \$1$$
$$|\$12 - \$11| = \$1$$
$$|\$14 - \$11| = \$3$$
$$|\$16 - \$11| = \$5$$
$$|\$18 - \$11| = \$7$$
$$|\$20 - \$11| = \$9$$

Mean Deviation

$$= (\$9 + \$7 + \$5 + \$3 + \$1 + \$1 + \$3 + \$5 + \$7 + \$9)/10 = \$50/10$$
$$= \$5 \text{ per hour}$$

Standard Deviation is calculated as follows. We find the square root of the average squared difference in values from the mean for each value:

$$(\$2 - \$11)^2 = \$81$$
$$(\$4 - \$11)^2 = \$49$$
$$(\$6 - \$11)^2 = \$25$$
$$(\$8 - \$11)^2 = \$9$$
$$(\$10 - \$11)^2 = \$1$$
$$(\$12 - \$11)^2 = \$1$$
$$(\$14 - \$11)^2 = \$9$$
$$(\$16 - \$11)^2 = \$25$$
$$(\$18 - \$11)^2 = \$49$$
$$(\$20 - \$11)^2 = \$81$$

Standard Deviation

$$= \sqrt{((\$81 + \$49 + \$25 + \$9 + \$1 + \$1 + \$9 + \$25 + \$49 + 81)/10)}$$
$$= \sqrt{(\$330/10)} = \$5.74 \text{ per hour}$$

Since the standard and mean deviations are greater than zero, there is a second-order change in prices where momentum is rising. This therefore represents volatile trend action, with respect to the first measure of volatility. If the rates of change in price were constant, then the standard and mean deviations will be zero. *These are therefore useful quantitative tests for the first measure of volatility.* In this example, the actual average deviation from the mean rate of increase is $5 per hour, as indicated by the mean deviation value.

If we now assume that the rates of change in price were in fact *randomly distributed* instead of rising in a parabolic fashion, and assuming that the random distribution approximates a normal distribution, we may then use this to find the statistical properties of the given random rates of change in price. Since one standard deviation, 1SD, is $5.74, we know that 68.2 percent and 95 percent of the random rates of change in price over a 10-hour period will occur between ± 1SD and ± 2SD of the mean rate, respectively. Therefore, 68.2 percent of increases in rate of change in prices over a 10-hour period would stay within $11 ± $5.74 per hour, that is, between $5.26 and $16.74 per hour. At the 2SD level, 95.4 percent of the increases in rate of change in prices over the same number of periods would stay below an upper value of $11 + (2 × $5.74), that is, $22.48 per hour. This is especially useful information for the trader and analyst. This means that whenever the increase in the rates of change in prices falls or rises, there is a 68.2 percent chance that the rates of change in prices over a 10-hour period may potentially start to increase once they decline to a rate of $5.26 per hour, and conversely start to decline once they reach a rate of $16.74 per hour. At the 2SD level, there is a 95.4 percent chance that the rates of change in prices may potentially start to decline once they reach a rate of $22.48 per hour.

Example 2: Calculating Deviation Values for a Constant Rate of Change in Price

Assume prices are rising at a constant rate of $2 per hour over a 10-hour period. This represents a first-order change in prices—momentum is flat.

Mean rate of increase per hour

$$= (\$2 + \$2 + \$2 + \$2 + \$2 + \$2 + \$2 + \$2 + \$2 + \$2)/10 = \$20/10 = \$2$$

Mean Deviation is calculated as follows. We find the average of the difference in absolute values from the mean for each value:

$$|\$2 - \$2| = \$0$$
$$|\$2 - \$2| = \$0$$
$$|\$2 - \$2| = \$0$$
$$|\$2 - \$2| = \$0$$
$$|\$2 - \$2| = \$0$$
$$|\$2 - \$2| = \$0$$
$$|\$2 - \$2| = \$0$$
$$|\$2 - \$2| = \$0$$
$$|\$2 - \$2| = \$0$$
$$|\$2 - \$2| = \$0$$

Mean Deviation

$$= (\$0 + \$0 + \$0 + \$0 + \$0 + \$0 + \$0 + \$0 + \$0 + \$0)/10 = \$0/10$$
$$= \$0\,\text{per hour}$$

Obviously, the standard deviation value would also be zero since it uses the same difference in values between each rate of change and the mean, which are all zero in this example.

Since the standard and mean deviations are both zero, there is only a first-order change in prices, that is, a constant rate of change in prices where momentum is flattening. Therefore, there is no volatility in price as far as the first measure of volatility is concerned. Again, statistical measures of deviation are useful quantitative tests of the *first measure of volatility*.

We may also use the statistical measures of deviation to quantitatively examine if *reversals that occur at a constant rate of change in price* represent volatility with respect to the first measure. Assume that we have a market that reverses every hour and trends at a constant rate of $2 per hour. See Figure 21.18.

Does this represent volatile behavior? As we have already observed, the question as to whether a market is volatile or otherwise is a meaningless question. It is similar to asking if the trend is up or down. Without reference to the lookback duration, it is impossible to answer the question if a trend is currently up or down.

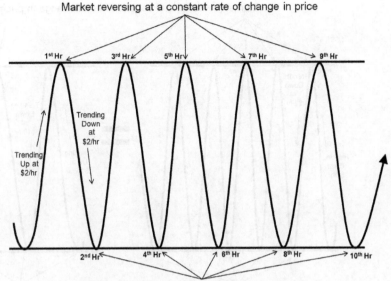

FIGURE 21.18 First Measure of Volatility in Reversing Markets at a Constant Rate of Change in Price.

A trend may be up over the last five hours but still very much down if compared to prices over the last five days. Similarly, the market may be volatile with respect to the third measure of volatility, but regarded as non-volatile if gauged by other measures of volatility. These questions need a basis of reference in order to represent meaningful queries. Getting back to Figure 21.18, let us examine if such price action is considered volatile or otherwise.

Since the mean rate of change in price is still $2 per hour, the mean and standard deviation values are zero. This is because the difference between each rate of change and the mean is zero, that is,

- For mean deviations: |$2−Mean| = |$2−$2| = $0
- For standard deviations: ($2−Mean)² = ($2−$2)² = $0

Hence, the sum of all differences for both deviations would yield zero. This means that as far as the first measure of volatility is concerned, ranging action of this sort is considered to be non-volatile. Therefore, comparing durations with ranging action that comprises constant rates of change in prices for the purposes of ascertaining the more volatile behavior is not possible via the first measure of volatility. It does not even matter if the lengths of the durations are equal or whether the rate of changing prices is occurring at the same rate. As long as the rates of change in prices are constant, there is no volatility in ranging action and it is practically indistinguishable via the first measure of volatility. See Figure 21.19.

The second measure of volatility will also be unable to distinguish between ranges of equal maximum price ranges. For consolidations of equal sizes, we need to apply either the third or fourth measures of volatility in order to find out which duration of price action is more volatile when compared to the other. For

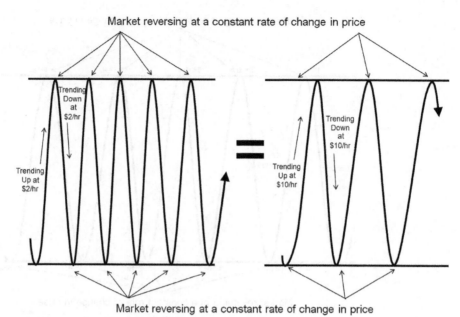

FIGURE 21.19 Non-Volatility in Ranges with Constant Rate of Change.

example, if we applied the third measure of volatility to our current example, the consolidation on the left-hand side of Figure 21.19 will be considered more volatile. The sum of all absolute price differences is greater than the consolidation on the right-hand side of the illustration.

Standard deviation is also used to measure the dispersion behavior of prices from a simple moving average of prices. In our earlier example, we used it to forecast the overreaction in trend rates, but it may also be used to examine the overreactions in price fluctuations. One such overlay indicator that does this wonderfully is the Bollinger Bands, created by John Bollinger. Bollinger bands use a 2-sigma band around a simple moving average of closing prices. (Sigma is used interchangeably with SD.) Prices testing the upper and lower band of the 2-sigma range represent, in the first instance, a strongly trending behavior. It also indicates a possibility of overreaction, with the potential for a reversal. Hence, Bollinger bands are an effective way of portraying volatility in prices. By detrending the values between the upper and lower Bollinger bands, we derive a bandwidth oscillator that clearly depicts periods of low and high volatility in price. See Figures 21.20 and 21.21.

Average True Range (ATR)

The average true range, ATR, measures the amount of interval volatility in prices. It tracks the average true range of a specified number of bars. It was introduced by Welles Wilder in his groundbreaking book, *New Concepts in Technical Trading Systems*. True range is the largest value of any of the three following possibilities:

1. Difference in price between the high and low of the current bar

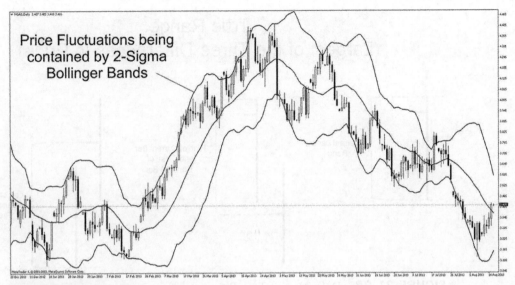

FIGURE 21.20 Volatility in Price Fluctuations Contained by Bollinger Bands on the Natural Gas Daily Chart.
Source: MetaTrader 4

2. Difference in price between the high of the current bar and the close of the previous bar

3. Difference in price between the low of the current bar and the close of the previous bar

See Figure 21.22.

A simple average of the true ranges over a specified number of bars is first calculated. The conventional or default lookback period is 14 periods. Once this

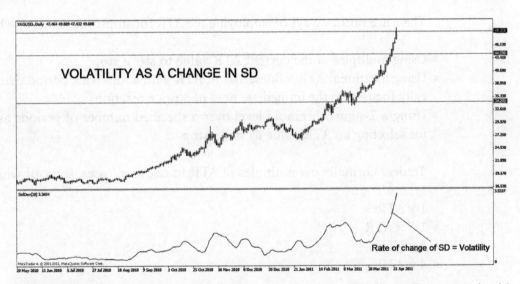

FIGURE 21.21 Volatility in Price Fluctuations Tracked by the Bollinger Bandwidth Indicator on the Natural Gas Daily Chart.
Source: MetaTrader 4

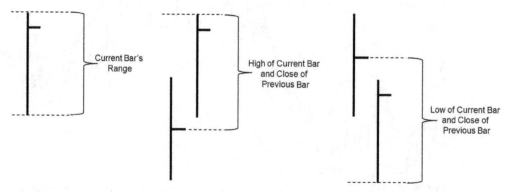

FIGURE 21.22 Definition of True Range.

is done, a rolling average based on Wilder's averaging method is calculated as follows:

$$\text{Average True Range} = ((\text{Previous ATR} \times 13) + \text{NewTR}) / 14$$

Therefore, it is obvious that the ATR reflects the degree of volatility in price fluctuations. The choice in the number of lookback periods applied is also dependent on market behavior. ATR is usually used:

- As a price filter for determining stopsize
- As a price filter for confirming a breakout

There are various ways of employing the ATR for stopsizing, some of which are:

- Using multiples of the current ATR value to size a stop
- Using locational ATR values, that is, ATR with a lookback period that specifically focuses on the immediate area of a price reaction
- Using a 2-sigma threshold level over a specified number of periods as a filter for selecting an ATR value to size a stop

Traders normally use multiples of ATR to size stoplosses, some of which are:

- $1 \times \text{ATR}$
- $1.5 \times \text{ATR}$
- $2 \times \text{ATR}$
- $4 \times \text{ATR}$

More advanced traders use some multiple of either an average or simply the highest ATR value that exceeds the 2-sigma upper Bollinger band filter level. In

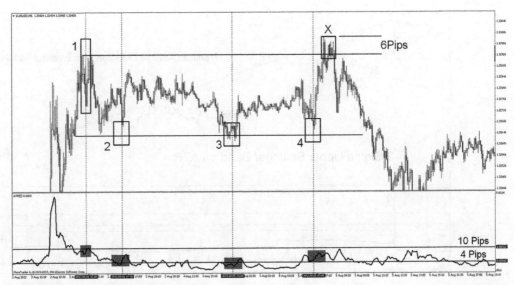

FIGURE 21.23 Using Location Centric ATR to Size a Stop on the 5-Min EURUSD Chart.
Source: MetaTrader 4

Figure 21.23, a consolidation is tested by price on numerous occasions. The trader is only interested in the volatility that surrounds the immediate area of reaction with the support and resistance levels. The trader may select a short lookback period for the ATR in order to identify the locational volatility at support and resistance. Let us assume that the trader chose a five-period lookback in this example. The trader may either look for the highest corresponding ATR value associated with Points 1 to 4, or just chose the highest ATR value if the range of ATR values is fairly close. The average ATR in this case would be approximately (10 + 5 + 4 + 5)/4 = 6 pips, and the highest would be 10 pips. The trader now must decide on what multiple of ATR to apply to the average or highest ATR value obtained from the analysis. Assuming that the trader uses 2 × ATR = 2 × 6 = 12 pips as the stopsize, this would have been an effective filter at Point X where the maximum adverse price excursion from the breakout was only 6 pips.

Figure 21.24 is an example of using a 2-sigma threshold level over a specified number of periods as a filter for selecting an ATR value to size a stop. As before, the trader may opt to size the stop using some multiple of either the average of the most significant ATR values that exceed the upper 2-sigma band or simply choose the highest value if it is not too large as compared to the rest of the ATR values. Assuming that the trader uses 2 multiples of the highest ATR value, that is, 2 × 15 pips = 30 pips, that would have acted as an effective stop for the subsequent trendline breakout, which had a maximum price excursion of approximately 25 pips.

In short, the ATR may be used as a volatility gauge of price fluctuations. Similar durations with larger ATR values are considered more volatile *with respect to the third measure of volatility.*

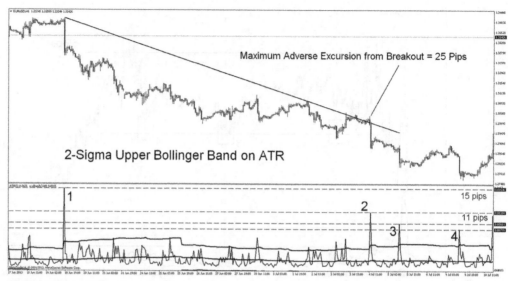

FIGURE 21.24 Using a 2-Sigma ATR Filter to Size a Stoploss on the Hourly EURUSD Chart.
Source: MetaTrader 4

Stock Beta

Stock beta is derived from the statistical regression of a particular stock's returns against the market. It describes the relationship between stock and market returns. Here are the some of the characteristics associated with beta:

- When beta = 0, the stock returns tend to be uncorrelated with market returns and the stock moves independently of the market
- When beta < 0, the stock tends to move in the opposite direction of the market
- When 1 > beta > 0, the stock returns tend to underperform the market, but the stock moves in the same direction as the market
- When beta = 1, the stock returns tend to match the market and the stock moves in the same direction as the market
- When beta > 1, the stock returns tend to outperform the market and the stock moves at a greater rate than market

Therefore, if the stock beta = 0, the stock tends to be fairly unaffected by market volatility, under conditions of normal market volatility. If the stock beta is relatively high, say at a value of about 3 to 5, the stock will experience greater volatility than the market.

21.3 OTHER MEASURES OF MARKET VOLATILITY

There are a few other measures of gauging market volatility. One popular approach is by referencing a volatility index, one of which is the VIX. The VIX is usually referred to as the *fear index*. It gauges the sentiment of the market participants and measures the amount of bullishness or bearishness in the market based on the market participants' option activity and the implied volatilities.

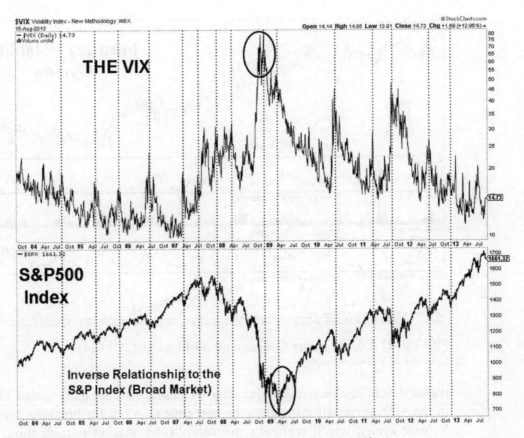

FIGURE 21.25 Volatility Cycles on the 15-Min USDCAD Chart.
Courtesy of Stockcharts.com

When the market expectation is bearish, for example, this will spark a flurry of traders and investors buying puts and selling calls. On the contrary, if the market expectation is bullish, traders and investors would instead be buying calls and selling puts. If such activity is significant, the readings in the VIX will rise. A very high VIX reading is normally seen as an early warning of a market bottom. Figure 21.25 shows the inverse relationship between the VIX and the S&P500 Index.

Another popular measure of market volatility is the Put-Call ratio, which tracks the premiums and volume of puts against calls. In a bearish market, the put-call ratio is normally much higher, as more investors and traders attempt to protect their portfolio asset values in a falling or plummeting market. At historic highs in the put-call ratio, a potential market bottom is expected.

One question that many practitioners ask is whether volatility provides any indication of future market behavior or direction.

Volatility cycles can be seen in the markets on a daily basis. Figure 21.26 below show a 15-min chart of the USDCAD currency pair. Each vertical line separates one day from the next. We clearly observe regular and fairly consistent cycles in ATR, volume, standard deviation of average price (via the Bollinger Bandwidth Indicator), and trend action (via the ADX indicator). Therefore, volatility does provide forecastable market behavior in the form of consistent cycle action. A

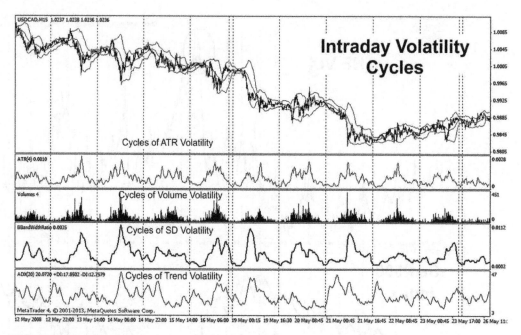

FIGURE 21.26 Volatility Cycles on the 15-Min USDCAD Chart.
Courtesy of Stockcharts.com

trader should be able to take advantage of these consistent daily cycles. The cycles in the ADX cycles afford traders the best time to get in for breakout type trades. Volume cycles, which represent the volatility in market participation, provide traders with a high probability daily reversal point in the markets, which normally occurs at the daily volume blow-off point. The ATR cycles also provide traders with a basis for determining their stop sizes, allowing for larger stops during the most volatile phase of the ATR cycle. Another instance where there may be possibility of a sudden burst of activity is when very high levels of open interest are seen in the futures market during the consolidation phase, especially if they are located near historical market highs. The tremendous volume of traders buying, selling, liquidating, and covering during such a consolidation usually precipitates strong breakout.

But does volatility indicate possible future market direction? *The answer is affirmative.* There are a few basic scenarios where this occurs:

- Price testing the upper or lower Bollinger bands has a greater tendency to reverse at the bands than elsewhere within the bands.
- Whenever a large broadening formation (which is regarded as a highly volatile chart pattern) is identified at the end of an aggressive and protracted trend, it is usually a bearish indication of a potential reversal. It is more bearish at market tops than bottoms.
- Any large and complex formation appearing and interrupting a strong trend is an indication that the market dynamics have changed and therefore may be regarded as a prognostication of a potential change in market direction.
- Historic highs in the VIX and Put-Call ratio are an early indicator of a potential market bottom.

21.4 CHAPTER SUMMARY

As we have observed, volatility may be characterized in various ways. Being able to gauge market volatility will afford the practitioner an effective means of identifying the most appropriate approach in managing positions in the market. Extreme volatility readings also indicate potential market tops and bottoms. Finally, volatility cycles also offer the practitioners a potentially consistent way of forecasting volatility in the market.

CHAPTER 21 REVIEW QUESTIONS

1. Define volatility.
2. Explain how you would measure trend-based volatility.
3. What is the difference between the first and second measures of volatility?
4. Explain how you would size a stop using ATR.
5. What is the significance of the normal distribution?
6. Describe how you would identify volatility in a consolidation.
7. Can volatility indicate the potential future direction of the markets?
8. Describe some popular market indicators of volatility.

REFERENCES

Edwards, Robert D., and John Magee. 2007. *Technical Analysis of Stock Trends*. New York: AMACOM.

Kirkpatrick, Charles, and Julie Dahlquist. 2007. *Technical Analysis: The Complete Resource For Financial Market Technicians*. Upper Saddle River, NJ: Pearson Education.

Murphy, John. 1999. *Technical Analysis of the Financial Markets*. New York: New York Institute of Finance (NYIF).

CHAPTER
22

Market Breadth

LEARNING OBJECTIVES

After studying this chapter, you should be able to:

- Understand the meaning of market breadth in terms of the broader market action
- Apply the concepts of market-breadth analysis to forecast potential tops and bottoms in the market
- Identify and differentiate between breadth data and its operations
- Calculate breadth differences, ratio, and line indicators
- Understand how to adjust an indicator to account for changing volume of issues at an exchange
- Apply technical analysis effectively to breadth-based charts

---

Market breadth is a critical form of analysis that every practitioner should be familiar with for reliable forecasting of potential market action. It is the study of the behavior of the universe of stocks that populate the markets. It concentrates on the wider market action in contrast to the narrow focus and application of technical analysis on single stocks alone. Technical analysis on single stocks without regard to the overall market action or environment is not a particularly effective approach to reliable forecasting. In this chapter, we will cover various market-breadth operators, associated indicators, and their technical interpretation.

22.1 ELEMENTS OF BROAD MARKET ACTION

Market breadth is essentially about the study of *broad market action*, as opposed to market depth, which focuses on the amount of supply and demand at various price levels of individual stocks. That is, it focuses on the components of overall market action rather than on the price action of individual stocks. For example, market breadth measures the degree of market participation by analyzing the percentage of issues rising and the amount of volume that accompanies such a rise. The prices of all individual stocks are affected by the sentiment of the broader market environment. Individual rising stocks are regarded as less bullish when viewed within the context of a bearish market environment.

Since market breadth uses data other than single stock prices, this also makes it extremely useful when attempting to ameliorate the adverse effects of multicollinearity among indicators and oscillators.

The study of market breadth, that is, broad market action, basically focuses on the:

- General behavior of the broader markets (i.e., stock index action),
- Number of issues rising and falling,
- Number of issues making new highs and lows,
- Amount of volume that accompanies upside and downside broad market action,
- Number of issues above or below psychologically significant technical filter levels (i.e., Diffusion Index),
- Number of issues on a technical buy signal (e.g., Bullish Percent Index), and
- Behavior of indexes that track the sentiment of the broader market (e.g., Volatility Indices, VIX, etc.)

Objectives of Market-Breadth Analysis

The main purpose of analyzing market breadth is to identify potential tops and bottoms in the market. This is accomplished by looking for:

- *Nonconfirmation* between market-breadth indicators and the broad market itself
- Signs of *overextension* in market behavior based on overbought and oversold indications on market-breadth indicators and oscillators

Nonconfirmation, or *divergence*, is one of the most effective methods of identifying potential tops and bottoms in the markets. It is a leading indicator, providing early warnings of potential market turns. The four types of divergence (previously covered in detail in Chapter 9) are:

- Standard Bullish Divergence
- Standard Bearish Divergence
- Reverse Bullish Divergence
- Reverse Bearish Divergence

When standard or reverse bearish divergence is spotted between market-breadth indicators and a certain index, a potential reversal in the market is expected. *The practitioner should never forget that when dealing with divergence, price confirmation is always recommended.* A bullish or bearish divergent indication in itself is insufficient evidence of a reversal. It is merely an indication of a potential reversal.

We also look for signs of overextension in market behavior based on over-bought and oversold indications in the market-breadth indicators and oscillators. As with divergence, such indications are merely signals of potential overreactions in the broad market and are not in themselves sufficient evidence of a reversal in progress. Again, price confirmation is necessary.

It should be noted that *without some form of contrary indication* like divergence and indicator overextension, market-breadth indicators may not provide much help insofar as forecasting potential market behavior is concerned. At best, the lack of contrary indications only confirms the current direction of the broad market. In short, if both market breadth and price are moving in the same direction, market breadth is confirming the market move. If they are not moving in the same direction, then market breath is seen as an early indication of potential corrections or reversals in the market.

Factors Affecting the Reliability and Consistency of Market-Breadth Analysis

There are ten main factors that have an adverse impact on the integrity of the market-breadth data and its indications, which are:

1. Changes in the number of issues at the exchange affect the calculation of many market-breadth indicators. The number of issues at most exchanges today has increased over the past few decades. This causes discrepancies between the new and older market-breadth indicator readings, disrupting the line of continuity of such readings. For example, an increase from two thousand to ten thousand issues would affect the number of net advancing issues. This will gradually introduce distortions in the indicator values. One solution is to use the *ratio-adjusted* form of the market-breadth indicator, which is simply to divide the readings by the total issues. This would essentially account for any increase or decrease in issues and help provide a more consistent indicator reading.

2. Interest rate-sensitive issues such as utility stocks, housing stocks, and various bond funds influence the broader market action. The number of interest rate–sensitive issues has risen over the years.

3. The behavior of foreign-listed stocks on the exchange like American Depository Receipts, or ADRs, may not be representative of the local market action. One solution is to use market-breadth data based on *common stocks* that represent true contributive components to the local market activity and are a truer reflection of the overall economy.

4. Nonoperating issues like various mutual funds and preferred stocks are not representative or a true reflection of the broader market action. Again, the solution is to use market-breadth data that is based on common stocks.

5. Changes in policy affecting the method and criteria for selecting stocks for inclusion on the exchange or in an index will affect the continuity of indicator readings, rendering past breadth data useless for future reference. One solution is to use the ratio-adjusted form of a market-breadth indicator that accounts for changes in the volume on the exchange.

6. The decimalization of stock prices on the NYSE in 2002 affected the number of daily unchanged issues reported. This rendered past references to breadth data unusable and incompatible.

7. A measure of downside bias is associated with various market-breadth indicator readings due to the replacement of individual stocks with poorer performing stocks that fail to satisfy the criteria for continued membership at an exchange.

8. Discrepancies in market-breadth data between various data vendors give rise to incompatible readings among charting platforms. Some data vendors provide market-breadth data based on all stocks, while others base breadth data specifically on common stocks alone.

9. Many market-breadth indicators employ a cumulative operator in their calculations, that is, current readings are added to a running total, giving rise to inconsistencies resulting from different commencement dates on which the running total is based.

10. Changes in the way market-breadth components are calculated by the exchange also affects the integrity of breadth data, as was the case in the way new highs and new lows were calculated prior to 1978 on the NYSE.

22.2 COMPONENTS OF MARKET BREADTH

We shall now turn our attention to the components that make up the majority of breadth indicators. Breadth components may be classified into three distinct groups:

1. The Breadth Data Field
2. The Breadth Operators
3. The Breadth Market Field

Breadth Data Fields

There are nine main pieces of raw breadth data consisting of:

1. Advances (A): The daily number of issues that have risen in price
2. Declines (D): The daily number of issues that have declined in price
3. Unchanged Issues (U): The daily number of issues that have not changed in price
4. Total Issues (A + D + U): The total number of tradable issues at the exchange
5. New Highs (H): Issues that have reached a new 52-week high in price
6. New Lows (L): Issues that have reached a new 52-week low in price
7. Up Volume (UV): Total daily volume of all advancing issues
8. Down Volume (DV): Total daily volume of all declining issues
9. Total Volume (T): Total daily traded volume

Note that total volume (T) is usually used as a ratio-adjustment parameter to overcome the problem of changing volume of issues at an exchange.

Breadth Operations

There are 12 main ways of manipulating the raw breadth data. The ten operations are:

1. **Subtraction:** Breadth difference is just subtracting one piece of raw breadth data from another. For example, we could find the *net advances* by subtracting the advancing issues from the declining issues, that is, (A – D). In a similar manner, *net up volume* would be (UV – DV). Some popular breadth indicators that employ breadth differences with respect to advances and declines are the Advance Decline Line, McClellan Oscillator, Haurlan Index, Plurality Index, Eakle AD Line, Fugler AD Line, and the NYSE Tick. Popular breadth indicators that employ differences in new highs and lows are New Highs-New Lows and the New High-New Low Line. Breadth indicators that employ differences in volume are the Up Volume-Down Volume Line and the McClellan Oscillator-Volume. It is important to note that the sum of the daily net advances does not add up to the weekly advances, that is, it is non-summative. The reason for not being summative over time is due to the fact that advances and declines do not take into account the *amount* of price excursion that a stock experiences. If the stock is up for the day, this is recorded as an advance of +1. If a stock closed at \$48 on Friday and had three days of advances and two days of declines, with the stock finishing at \$45 on the following Friday, the total net advance over the five days would be (3 – 2) = 1. But the net advance for the week would instead be –1, since the stock prices had in fact declined by (\$48 – \$45) = \$3 for the week.

2. **Division:** Breadth ratio is just dividing one piece of raw breadth data by another. For example, we could divide the advancing issues by the declining issues, that is, A/D, or the up volume by the down volume, that is, UV/DV. Some popular breadth indicators that use this mathematical ratio constructed on advances and declines include the Advance Decline Ratio, Breadth Thrust, and Hughes Momentum Oscillator. One breadth indicator that employs ratio calculations on volume is the New High New Low Ratio.

3. **Addition:** We could also add pieces of raw breadth data to each other, such as A + D or UV + DV. One popular breadth indicator that employs the addition operation is the Changed Volume indicator.

4. **Multiplication:** Raw breadth data pieces may also be multiplied by each other, such as A × D. One popular breadth indicator that employs multiplication is the Thrust Oscillator: $[(A \times UV) - (D \times DV)]/[(A \times UV) + (D \times DV)]$.

5. **Ratio Adjusting:** To account for changing volume of issues at an exchange, we may divide the results obtained from the other operations by the total number of issues or total volume. For example, to account for changing volume of issues, we could convert the operator results into a ratio or percentage of the total number of issues at an exchange, that is, (A – D)/(A + D + U). This would represent a ratio-adjusted form of the net advances. A ratio-adjusted form of the net up volume would simply be (UV – DV)/T. One popular breadth indicator that employs ratio adjusting is the Schultz indicator, which calculates the running total of the ratio of all advances over the total number of issues,

that is, A/(A + D + U). Another breadth indicator that uses total issues in its denominator is the High Low Logic Index, created by Norman Fosback.

6. Accumulation: Sometimes it is useful to represent raw data as a daily running total. We can do this by simply adding the daily operator results to the previous day's running total. For example, the *cumulative form* of the daily net advances would simply be: (A – D) + Previous Day's Running Total Net Advances. Popular breadth indicators that use the cumulative form include the Advance Decline Line, New High New Low Line, and the McClellan Summation Index.

7. Smoothing: The resulting values obtained by various raw data operations may frequently be too visually erratic or volatile. This erratic line may be smoothed by applying a moving average to the resulting operator values. Normally a simple moving average is sufficient to smooth the erratic operator readings, that is, ($\sum$ (A – D) over last N days)/N. It is not uncommon to employ weighted, double, or triple smoothing to the resulting operator values.

8. Crossover Triggering: In order to reduce the lag in the smoothed operator values caused by the application of single moving averages, the crossover of two moving averages is sometimes employed. This results in less erratic readings.

9. Detrending: Many breadth indicators are designed to isolate the difference between the values of two moving averages by subtracting the values of one moving average from the other, for each successive period. Such operations are termed *detrending*. One popular breadth indicator that employs the detrending of two exponential moving averages is the McClellan Oscillator. (The McClellan Oscillator is in fact mathematically identical to the MACD [moving average convergence-divergence, except for the two lookback periods and the data used.)

10. Normalization: Many oscillators are *unbounded*, that is, the indicator values have no upper or lower limit. Many of these indicators may be transformed into bounded indicators via the process of *normalizing*. Although unbounded oscillators may still indicate periods of overbought or oversold by comparing highs and lows with historically significant levels, bounded oscillators sometimes provide a simpler and more objective representation of such overextensions, where readings near or above 80 percent represent overbought conditions and those near or below 20 percent represent oversold conditions. Normalizing involves subtracting the lowest value over the last N periods from the current or closing value and dividing this by the difference between the highest and lowest values across the last N periods. (This is in fact the basic mathematical construct of George Lane's Stochastic Oscillator.) For example, we could design a normalized Advance Decline indicator such as in Figure 22.1.

$$\left\{ \frac{\text{Current (A–D)} - [\text{Lowest (A–D) over the last } N \text{ period}]}{[\text{Highest (A–D)} - \text{Lowest (A–D)}] \text{ over the last } N \text{ period}} \right\} \times 100\%$$

FIGURE 22.1 Normalizing Breadth Data.

11. Combination: Some breadth indicators are more complex in design, requiring a combination of breadth operations. For example, the Arms Index is based on a ratio of a ratio mathematical construct, that is, (A/D)/(UV/DV). The Thrust Oscillator as seen in item (4) above, is a perfect example of more complex operations.

12. Absolute Revaluation: There are some breadth indicators that require only positive values from breadth operations, also termed *absolute* values. For example, the absolute value of (10 – 20) is 10, and not –10. One popular breadth indicator that uses absolute values is the Plurality Index, which it uses the sum of the absolute differences between the advances and declines over the last 25 days, that is, $\sum |A - D|$ over the last 25 days.

Market-Breadth Fields

Market breadth data may be calculated for:

- Issues within an exchange (e.g., NYSE, NASDAQ, TSE, AMEX, CDNX, LSE, KLSE, ASE, BSE, etc.)
- Issues within an index (e.g., S&P 400, S&P 500, S&P 600, Russell 2000, etc.)
- Issues within an ETF (e.g., Select Sector SPDRs for Consumer Staples, Industrials, Financials, Energy, Materials, Utilities, etc.)

Summarizing, we may therefore briefly categorize the breadth operations and data fields as:

- Advance Decline Differences (A – D), Ratios (A/D), Cumulative, and Complex Operations
- New High New Low Differences (H – L), Ratios (H/L) and (H/(H+L)), Cumulative, and Complex Operations
- Volume Differences (UV – DV), Ratios (UV/DV), Cumulative, and Complex Operations

See Figure 22.2 for a summary of all market fields, breadth-data fields, breadth operators, and indicators.

22.3 MARKET-BREADTH INDICATORS IN ACTION

Advance Decline Indicators

It is important to note that the value of the Advance Decline Line (AD Line) indicator depends on when the calculation begins. Different start dates will result in different running totals. This does not affect the shape or direction and hence this allows the practitioner to use:

- Chart pattern analysis
- Trendlines and channels
- Divergence
- Historical extremes

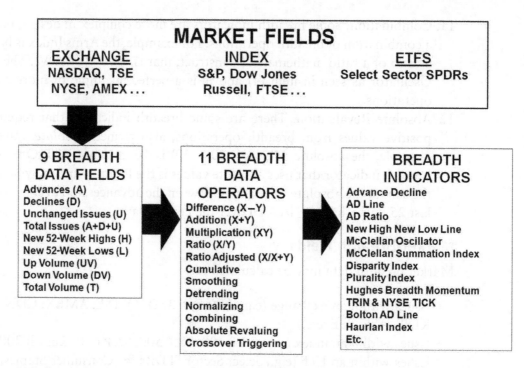

FIGURE 22.2 NYSE Summary of Market-Breadth Components.

The historical indicator extreme levels may be used although the absolute readings may differ from another Advance Decline Line indicator that started its running total from a different date. The absolute level readings of historical extremes are not important, as long as it remains consistent with respect to past action.

The basic Advance Decline (AD) indicator is just the difference between the number of daily Advances and Declines. The Advance Decline Line is a daily running total of the differences between Advances and Declines. In Figure 22.3, we observe reverse bearish divergence between time lines 1 and 2, as well as between 1 and 3, as the NYSE index makes lower highs while the NYSE AD Line makes higher highs. This is bearish for the NYSE index and we see the market fall just after time lines 2 and 3. We also observe standard bullish divergence at point X between the NYSE AD Line and the NYSE index. The NYSE index rose rapidly thereafter. The overbought levels on the NYSE Net Advances window indicator coincides fairly accurately with the market tops, as seen at time lines 1, 2, 3, and 4.

Figure 22.4 displays numerous divergences between the NYSE index and its AD Line. We see the divergences working very well in forecasting turns in the NYSE. Again, price confirmation is required whenever divergence is employed.

Figure 22.5 displays the Energy Select Sector SPDR Advance Decline Percent. This is the ratio of the AD difference over the total number of issues in the ETF, that is, $(A - D)/T$. In this example the Advance Decline Percent is smoothed by a five-day simple moving average. We observe that a test of the historically overbought level accurately coincides fairly accurately with the various smaller and larger market tops in the Energy Select Sector SPDR ETF.

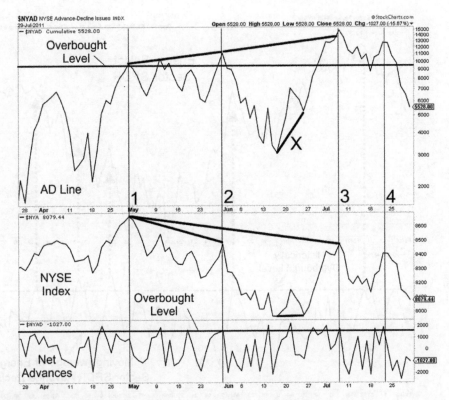

FIGURE 22.3 NYSE Net Advances and Advance Decline Line.
Courtesy of Stockcharts.com

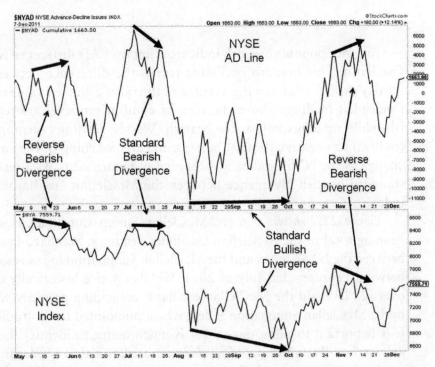

FIGURE 22.4 Divergences between the NYSE Index and Advance Decline Line.
Courtesy of Stockcharts.com

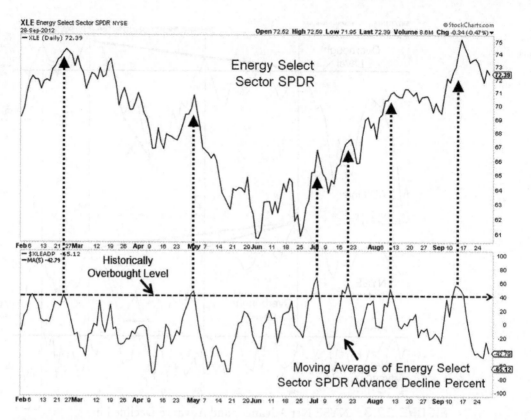

FIGURE 22.5 Divergences between the NYSE Index and the Five-Day Moving Average of the Advance Decline Percent of the Energy Select Sector SPDR.
Courtesy of Stockcharts.com

Another popular breadth indicator that uses AD difference is the McClellan Oscillator. This breadth oscillator tracks the difference between the 19- and 39-day exponential moving average of the ratio-adjusted value of net advances. Detrended readings above the zero or equilibrium level are regarded as bullish while readings below are bearish. We see readings turning from positive (bullish) to negative (bearish) giving an early warning of the subsequent trend change in the NYSE index, as observed in Figure 22.6. As a result, we also see standard bearish divergence between the McClellan Oscillator and the NYSE index.

Figure 22.7 shows that the McClellan Summation Index is simply the daily running total of the McClellan Oscillator readings. Standard bearish divergence between the NYSE index and the McClellan Summation Index is seen in the period between February and July of 2011. We also notice historically overbought and oversold levels in the McClellan oscillator coinciding perfectly with the troughs in the McClellan Summation Index, which pinpointed the bottoms in the market. It is important to point out that it is much better to identify the *actual historical overbought and oversold levels* in an oscillator that is relevant to the current market behavior instead of relying on popular preconceived levels of overbought and oversold.

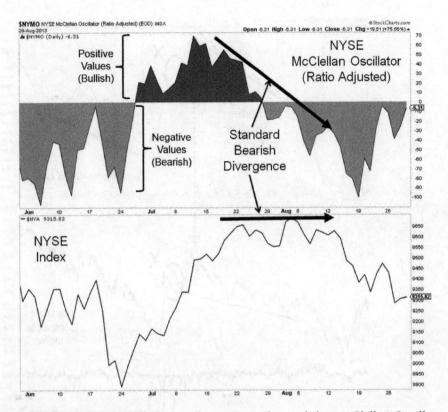

FIGURE 22.6 Divergences between the NYSE Index and the McClellan Oscillator.
Courtesy of Stockcharts.com

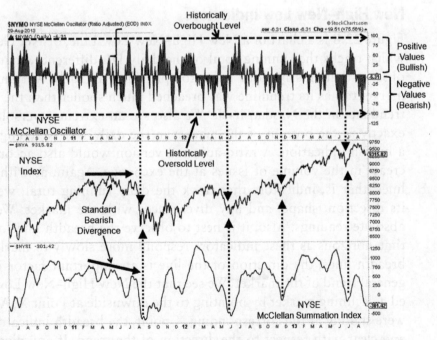

FIGURE 22.7 Divergences between the NYSE Index and the McClellan Summation Index.
Courtesy of Stockcharts.com

FIGURE 22.8 Divergences between the NYSE Index and the McClellan Summation Index.

Courtesy of Stockcharts.com

New High–New Low Indicators

Figure 22.8 is a chart of a New High–New Low Line, or Net New Highs Line, which tracks the running total of the daily HL difference, that is, (H–L). We observe that this breadth indicator provided an early warning of the 2008 market top as its trendline was breached much sooner than the corresponding trendline on the Nasdaq itself. We also see an extreme oversold level created exactly at the bottom of the market in the daily Net New Highs, which was a bullish indication. A ratio-adjusted version would also account for any increase in the volume of issues at the exchange. Again, as with most breadth lines, that is, indicators that track the daily running total, we only observe its direction, shape, and any divergences with the market. We disregard its absolute readings. Also, it is best to observe the breadth lines over the longer time horizons as these indicators respond more slowly to market action. For breadth lines, the direction of the line is an important factor in gauging the general trend of the market. We see that the New High–New Low Line indicated a declining market by pointing to the downside at Point X. Although prices were stalling at the corresponding X point, the breadth indicator was decisive and clear with respect to the direction of the trend. If any divergence should manifest on the charts between a breadth line and the market, the practitioner would be wise not to disregard it.

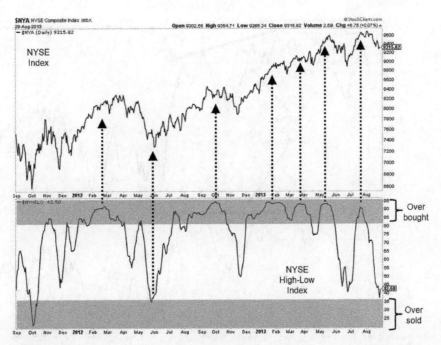

FIGURE 22.9 The High-Low Index Indicating Potential Tops and Bottoms in the NYSE Index.
Courtesy of Stockcharts.com

Figure 22.9 displays numerous overbought and oversold indications between the NYSE index and its High-Low Index. The NYSE High-Low Index is a 10-day simple moving average of the ratio of new highs over the total number of new highs and new lows. We see the overbought levels in the NYSE High-Low Index line up fairly well with both smaller market downside corrections and larger reversals. The market also tends to rebound strongly every time the NYSE High-Low Index tests the 30 to 35 percent oversold region.

Volume-Based Breadth Indicators

Figure 22.10 is a chart of a Nasdaq AD Volume Line, or Net Advancing Volume Line. The Nasdaq AD Volume Line tracks the daily running total of the net up volumes. Some practitioners also use the ratio-adjusted version. From the chart, we immediately observe a significantly clear and obvious standard bearish divergence between the Net Advancing Volume Line and the Nasdaq Composite Index, indicating a potential top in the market. Notice the market's subsequent rapid decline.

The TRIN (Arms Index) Indicator

Figure 22.11 shows a chart of the TRIN indicators. TRIN is the ratio of advances to declines over the ratio of up volume to down volume, that is, (A/D)/(UV/DV). It is a contrary indicator. Readings near or above 3.0 are bullish, while those near or below 0.5 are bearish. In the chart, we notice that every time the TRIN penetrates both the upper Bollinger band and the 2-sigma level, it coincides with a market bottom.

FIGURE 22.10 The Divergence between the Nasdaq AD Volume Index and Composite Index, Indicating a Potential Top.
Courtesy of Stockcharts.com

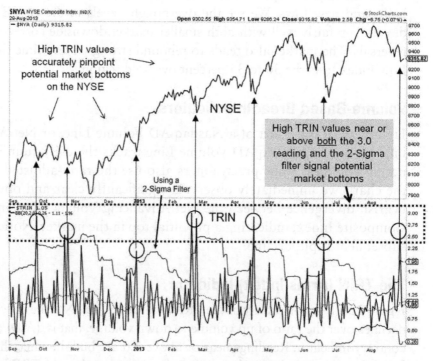

FIGURE 22.11 TRIN Indicator Signaling Potential Bottoms in the NYSE Index.
Courtesy of Stockcharts.com

Unfortunately the TRIN has some flaws. One it is that it sometimes misrepresents real demand in the markets. A high ratio of 3.0 basically means that the advances are not accompanied by a corresponding increase in net advancing volume. But this is not always true. The advance/decline ratio may be 8 and the up volume/down volume ratio may be 2.6. A ratio of 2.6 may represent an advancing volume of 2.6 million over a declining volume of 1 million shares, or it could also represent advancing volume of 26,000 over a declining volume of 10,000 shares. Hence it does not account for the numbers behind the ratios, and as such may misrepresent demand in the markets. A version called the *Modified Arms Index* was created to try to resolve this by smoothing the sum of the difference between the product of advances and the up volume less the product of declines and the down volume, over a specified number of days.

The TICK Indicator

Figure 22.12 shows a chart of the NYSE TICK indicator. The TICK tracks the difference in the number of stocks that are trading on an uptick versus those on a downtick. The TICK tracks the frequency of transaction rather than the actual volume of a transaction. It is generally regarded as a short-term indicator. From the chart, we observe that the market tends to decline on increased TICK volatility. This can easily be tracked using a 2-sigma filter, that is, the upper Bollinger band, as a filter for TICK volatility. Another way of gauging TICK volatility is to observe the width of the TICK bars. Greater widths are an indication of larger volatility, and consequently a potential for a market decline. Upper-band penetrations represent overbought conditions.

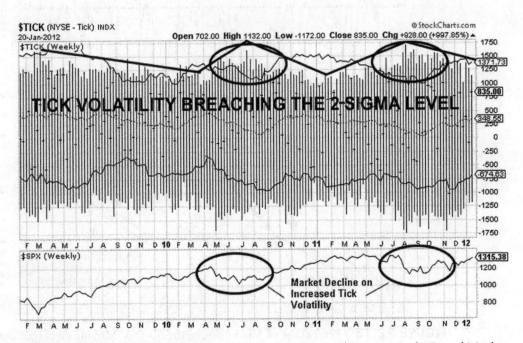

FIGURE 22.12 NYSE TICK Indicator Signaling Potential Bottoms in the Broad Market. Courtesy of Stockcharts.com

TICK–TRIN Short-Term and Longer-Term Interplay

Many traders use a combination of TICK and TRIN to time short-term entries and exits, where a rising (but not overbought) TICK and a falling (but not oversold) TRIN represents a bullish signal where the trader looks for an appropriate long entry. Conversely, a falling (but not oversold) TICK and a rising (but not overbought) TRIN represents a bearish signal where the trader looks for an appropriate short entry.

For longer-term trading, when the TICK is oversold, that is, above the 2-sigma level on a weekly chart, with the TRIN also overbought, that is, near or above the 3.0 level on the daily charts, this signals a bullish scenario and the trader looks for an appropriate long entry. Conversely, if both the TICK is overbought and the TRIN is oversold, this signals a bearish scenario and the trader looks for an appropriate short entry.

Percentage of Stocks above a Moving Average

The normal lookback periods employed to determine the percentage of stocks above a moving average are 50, 100, 150, and 200. See Figure 22.13. There is a tendency for the S&P 500 index to decline every time it tests the 80 percent overbought level. Traders still need price confirmation to ensure that there is an actual change in the trend. In this example, trendline violations are used as price confirmation.

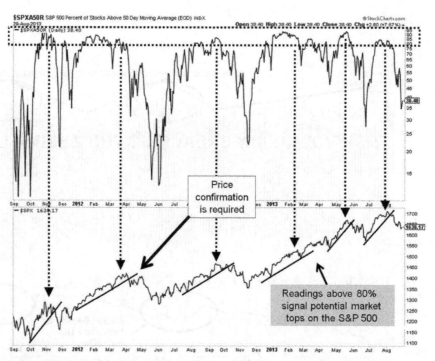

FIGURE 22.13 Percentage of Stocks above the 50-Day Moving Average Signaling Potential Tops in the S&P 500 Index.
Courtesy of Stockcharts.com

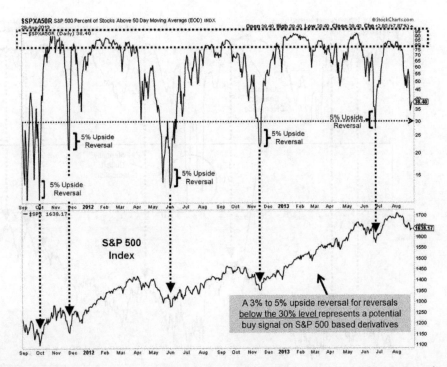

FIGURE 22.14 Percentage of Stocks above the 50-Day Moving Average Signaling Potential Buy Signals in the S&P 500 Index.
Courtesy of Stockcharts.com

One particularly effective buy signal is the 3 to 5 percent upside reversal for reversals near or below the 30 percent oversold level. See Figure 22.14. Once a buy signal is identified, look for price confirmation on the S&P 500 near month futures or SPY ETF.

Bullish Percent Index

The Bullish Percent Index tracks the number stocks in a group or index that are on Point-and-Figure buy signals, which is represented by a Point-and-Figure Double Top upside breakout. When the percentage of stocks on a buy signal is near or breaks above the 80 percent level, it is considered overbought and a potential correction or reversal in expected, which is to be confirmed by price. Figure 22.15 depicts the tendency for the market to reverse every time it tests the overbought level. Conversely, when the bullish percent index is near or below its 30 percent oversold level, as it was around the end of 2011, a trader is afforded a very advantageous long entry.

The Volatility Index

Volatility indexes are also particularly effective in gauging the general broad market sentiment. Figure 22.16 shows how the Russell 2000 Volatility Index tracks the amount of fear in declining markets. We can see that tops in the volatility indexes correspond very closely to bottoms in the markets. We may use historically extreme levels to time future market bottoms.

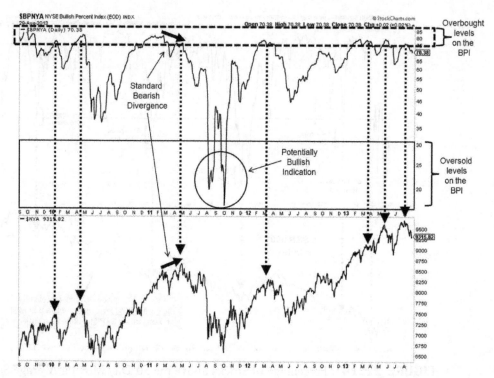

FIGURE 22.15 NYSE Bullish Percent Index Signaling Potential Tops in the NYSE Index.
Courtesy of Stockcharts.com

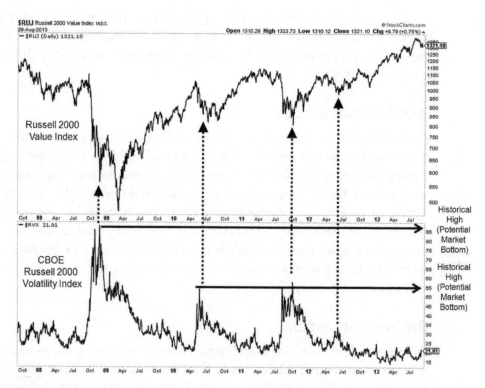

FIGURE 22.16 Russell 2000 Volatility Index Signaling Potential Bottoms in the Russell 2000 Value Index.
Courtesy of Stockcharts.com

Because some volatility indexes are now tradable, many have criticized the ever-popular VIX as being less of a true reflection of the market participants' general sentiment. The ability to impact or influence the VIX makes the index susceptible to manipulation and abuse. This distorts original function of the index, which was to track implied volatility of market participants in the broad market.

22.4 CHAPTER SUMMARY

As we have seen, it behooves the practitioner to cross-reference the behavior of individual issues with that of the broader market activity. We have also observed the effectiveness of identifying divergences and overextended levels of activity between market breadth data and price as a more reliable means of pinpointing potential tops and bottoms in the market. As such, the use of market breadth data is an indispensable tool for all serious practitioners.

CHAPTER 22 REVIEW QUESTIONS

1. Explain the term market breadth and how is it different from market depth.
2. Describe the type of market-breadth indicator that would allow you to gauge the strength of a trend.
3. List five breadth operations and their corresponding breadth indicators.
4. Name and describe eight main challenges associated with using breadth indicators.
5. Explain why you cannot add up five daily net advances to represent a week's net advance.
6. Describe how you would use the McClellan Oscillator with volume.
7. What are the weaknesses associated with the Arms Index and how would you rectify the issues?
8. What is the advantage of a ratio-adjusted breadth indicator?

REFERENCES

Arms, Richard W., Jr. 1989. *The Arms Index*. Dow Jones-Irwin.

Kirkpatrick, Charles, and Julie Dahlquist. 2007. *Technical Analysis: The Complete Resource for Financial Market Technicians*. Upper Saddle River, NJ: Pearson Education.

Morris, Greg. 2006. *The Complete Guide to Market Breadth Indicators*. New York: McGraw-Hill.

Murphy, John. 1999. *Technical Analysis of the Financial Markets*. New York: New York Institute of Finance (NYIF).

Pring, Martin J. 2002. *Technical Analysis Explained: The Successful Investor's Guide to Spotting Investment Trends and Turning Points*. 4th ed. New York: McGraw-Hill.

Sentiment Indicators and Contrary Opinion

Market sentiment offers the practitioner additional insight into the underlying factors that drive the markets. It is the study of the actions and opinions of market participants. It focuses on the behavioral dynamics that accompany the formations of market tops and bottoms. In this chapter, we will be discussing various sentiment indicators and how they provide an early indication of potential market turns.

23.1 ASSESSING THE EMOTION AND PSYCHOLOGY OF MARKET PARTICIPANTS

Market sentiment represents the overall view and emotions of all participants about the market environment, with particular regard for the degrees of pessimism and optimism displayed by its participants through their actions and opinions.

The study of its participants' emotions, beliefs, expectations, biases, and overall psychology especially during highly or overly emotional periods in the markets and their subsequent reactions help identify consistent patterns of behavioral excess. These patterns of behavioral excess are reflected in the action of the participants *by the way they risk capital in the markets* during such highly emotional periods. Polls of expert and public opinions also give insight as to the general sentiment of market participants.

Market Participants and the Mechanics of Contrary Opinion

Market participants may be broadly divided into two groups, namely the:

1. Well-informed
2. Under-informed

The well-informed are usually the insiders, specialists, and various locals operating at the exchange, while the under-informed are mostly represented by the general public or crowd. It should be noted that to be well-informed requires the participants to be contrarian in their outlook near market tops and bottoms, and to never buck a strong trend. They usually buy at or near market tops and sell at or near the market bottoms. Conversely, under-informed participants tend to be trend following instead. They tend to get into, and subsequently get out of, the markets too late, and as a consequence are usually involved in climatic buying at or near market tops and panic selling at or near market bottoms. See Figure 23.1.

Unfortunately not all insiders, specialists, locals, professional fund managers, and other industry experts are well-informed. In fact, many of them tend to underperform the market and even sustain losses due to bad or inefficient market timing. Similarly, not all members of the general public are under-informed.

It should be noted here that the term well-informed is not restricted to only being privy to some form of exclusive inside information or special pre-knowledge of an impending event. To be well-informed requires the participant to be contrarian near market tops and bottoms and to be a trend follower during a strong trend. Hence, it does not really matter, for all practical purposes, whether

FIGURE 23.1 Market Participants.

this is achieved by being privy to unique and exclusive information or by the application of some form of analysis that affords the participants such opportune market timing. For example, if the application sentiment or classical technical analysis allows a trader to consistently buy at or near market bottoms and sell at or near market tops, he or she is also said to be a well-informed market participant. In this case, the information was derived on analysis.

Crowd Irrationality at Market Extremes

It is generally accepted that the public usually overestimates the duration and extent of market uptrends while underestimating the duration and extent of market downtrends. The well-informed begin their buying campaigns by accumulating positions at cheap prices at market bottoms, usually after a large decline in prices and when the sentiment is most bearish. They are careful to accumulate in a gradual manner so as not to drive prices up too fast, allowing them to continue to accumulate as much as possible, by buying from the under-informed, at the most advantageous prices. The under-informed, at that point, are in a state of extreme panic, liquidating at whatever prices are available in order to expedite their exit from the market. They are overly pessimistic about the market. As prices start to climb, more savvy investors begin to buy into the market. It is when the uptrend becomes somewhat more obvious that the public starts to notice the rising prices. Public participation starts to increase, driving prices up substantially, which in turn attracts even more public participation, in a self-perpetuating positive feedback cycle, causing prices to spiral upward very rapidly. The under-informed public gets swept up in a wave of frenzied buying, not wanting to miss out on participating in the exceedingly bullish trend. As the ability to buy starts to wane due to the lack of access to any additional funds and having used up all available margin in brokerage accounts, prices start to decelerate.

As the market tops, the well-informed participants start distributing at highly advantageous prices, selling to the overly confident under-informed who still believe that the trend is very much intact or will shortly resume in momentous fashion. The under-informed are behaving and reacting to prices in an irrationally exuberant manner. Market sentiment is extremely bullish, with the under-informed being overly optimistic at this point. Prices start to decline after all buying has been shut off. Many of the under-informed are still holding on to their positions, believing that the decline is only a small healthy correction after an extensive run up in prices. Some even less-informed participants continue to buy into the market, hoping to get in before the market takes off again. The entire process repeats in a cycle of booms and busts.

Even Contrarians Must Follow the Herd

It should be noted that the well-informed are not contrarians all of the time. Being stubbornly contrarian during an extensive and prolonged uptrend in prices will prove exceedingly costly. *It is only at or near market tops and bottoms that a contrarian view is adopted by the well-informed participants*, with the rest of the time spent profiting by riding the trend that is being fueled and driven up or down by the larger mass of under-informed participants.

781

Gauging Market Tops and Bottoms

In order to effectively gauge market tops and bottoms and to subsequently profit from them, the well-informed should use a combination of sentiment indicators and classical technical analysis. The gauging of market tops and bottoms tends to be more effective if the sentiment data from both the flow of funds and opinion polls indicate a level of extreme bullishness or bearishness, occurring at historically or statically significant levels. The trader or analysts may then employ a range of time- and price-projection techniques to seek further evidence for a potential market reversal.

Most important, once a potential top or bottom is forecast, the trader should always seek *price confirmation of the reversal* before contemplating risking any capital in the markets. See Figure 23.2.

Reliability of Sentiment Readings

The majority of sentiment indicators are *contrary indicators*, especially if they track the trading activity or opinions of the under-informed. This is because when they are most bullish it usually signifies that everyone who wanted to buy into the market has already done so, drastically diminishing demand. Similarly, when they are most bearish, most selling would have already taken place, frequently in the form of a selling climax, and in the process drastically reducing supply. Unfortunately, the opinions polled from the supposedly well-informed have on numerous occasions proven to be more reliable as contrary indicators.

It should be noted that *sentiment indicators work best at market extremes*. Sentiment indicators do not give conclusive indications if the participants are not experiencing extreme levels of fear or exuberance and acting on those emotions. Furthermore, the most effective way to gauge if the sentiment of the under-informed

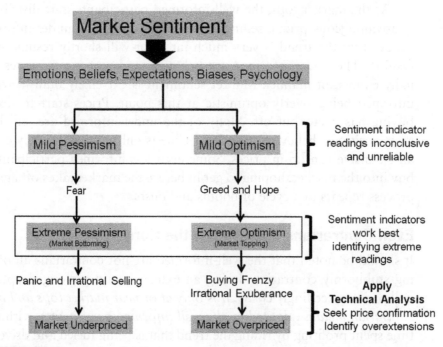

FIGURE 23.2 Market Sentiment.

participants is inordinately pessimistic or optimistic is to see if the sentiment-indicator readings are in proximity to historically extreme levels. It also behooves the practitioner to confirm extreme readings with that of other sentiment indicators.

23.2 PRICE-BASED INDICATORS VERSUS SENTIMENT INDICATORS

Very often, price-based indicators and oscillators tend to signal historically overbought and oversold conditions in sync with extreme sentiment readings. Hence, appropriately tuned oscillators based on market behavior may be used as a proxy for markets where no sentiment data is available for scrutiny. In Figure 23.3, we observe a cycle-tuned stochastic oscillator pinpointing potential bottoms in Silver, which coincides with readings at and above the historically extreme readings on the Chicago Board Options Exchange (CBOE) Options Total Put-Call Ratio sentiment indicators.

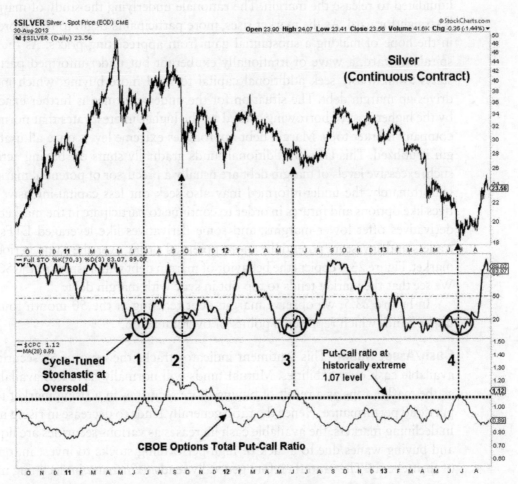

FIGURE 23.3 Convergent Signals from a Cycle-Tuned Stochastic Oscillator and the CBOE Options Total Put-Call Ratio Indicating Potential Market Bottoms.
Courtesy of Stockcharts.com

23.3 ASSESSING PARTICIPANT ACTIONS

We can gauge the sentiment of the market by the participants':

- *Participatory actions* via the analysis of the flow of funds, open interest, and trading activity
- *Expectation* via opinion polls

In this section we will be looking at some basic:

- Flow of funds data
- Open interest via the commitments of traders (COT) report
- Trading activity via the volatility based indices

(1) Flow of Funds Data

Margin Debt   Margin debt is the amount of funds borrowed from the broker in order to purchase more shares or positions. Unlike buying with cash, where shares may be held indefinitely, buying on margin incurs borrowing costs and must inevitably be liquidated to release the margin. The rationale underlying the study of margin debt is straightforward. As the market rises, more participants begin to risk more capital in the hope of making a substantial gain from appreciating prices. As the market spirals upward, a wave of irrationally exuberant but under-informed participants starts to anxiously seek additional capital to fund more buying, which inevitably drives up margin debt. The situation for the under-informed is further exacerbated by the higher cost of borrowing caused by the higher interest rates that normally accompany market tops. Margin debt approaches extreme levels once all usable margin is utilized. This lack of additional funds gradually shuts off buying activity. As such, excessive levels of margin debt are usually a precursor of potential market tops. Unfortunately, the under-informed may also seek out less capital-intensive derivatives like options and futures in order to continue to participate in the markets. These derivatives offer lower margins, and some derivatives like leveraged ETFs, afford traders and investors potentially more potential profit over the same period in the market. Figure 23.4 depicts the behavior of margin debt with respect to the S&P 500. We see that the market tends to top out in sync with margin debt.

In Figure 23.5, we observe margin debt reacting at the 50-month four-sigma upper band, which represents points of overextension.

Cash/Asset Ratio   This sentiment indicator tracks the ratio of all securities and available cash over liabilities. Mutual funds will normally have less available cash as the market tops as a result of buying more securities in a rising market to boost portfolio performance. Hence the ratio generally tends to decrease in rising markets. In declining markets, the available cash increases as various securities are liquidated and buying wanes due to a lack of high-performing stocks to invest in, on behalf of their clients. The ratio therefore generally tends to increase in declining markets.

Public Short Ratio   This sentiment indicator tracks the amount of short selling by the public over the total short sales. It is a contrary indicator, since it tracks the

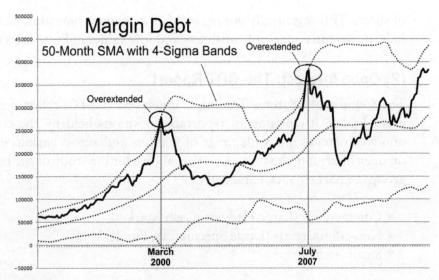

FIGURE 23.4 Margin Debt Coinciding with Market Tops. (Data: NYSE)

trading activity of the under-informed who are presumed to be largely wrong in their estimation of market tops and bottoms. High or extreme readings in this flow of funds indicator are bullish for the markets while extremely low readings are bearish.

Member Short Ratio This indicator tracks the amount of short selling by the well-informed. It is the ratio of the difference between the number of shorts sold by the members of the NYSE and the number of public shorts over the total number

FIGURE 23.5 Margin Debt Reacting at the 50-Month SMA with Four-Sigma Bands. (Data: NYSE)
Courtesy of Stockcharts.com

of shorts. *This is generally not regarded as a contrary indicator*. Hence, high values indicate potential market bearishness and low values indicate market bullishness.

(2) Open Interest: The COT Report

The Commodity Futures Trading Commission (CFTC) releases the COT report every Friday. It contains all reportable positions held by the commercials and non-commercials in a wide range of markets and across various exchanges. Data on *open interest* in the futures market allows for the study of the behavior of three groups of participants, namely the:

- Commercials (Large Hedgers, Cash Market)
- Non-commercials (Large Speculators, Funds)
- Small traders

The commercials represent large hedgers operating in the cash market, whereas the non-commercials comprise large speculators, hedge funds, and so on. The third group represents the small traders. By watching the smart money movement, traders and investors get a better idea of where the markets may be heading.

Many practitioners track and follow the non-commercials, as they are generally regarded as the better informed. Nevertheless, one may also track the movements of the hedgers, watching for an upturn or downturn in the *net commercial positions* before participating in the markets. It would be best if the upturn or downturn also occurred at previous extreme levels in the net commercial position.

In Figure 23.6, we see the net commercial positions providing simple buy and sell signals on the daily EURUSD chart. *A clear upturn in the net commercial*

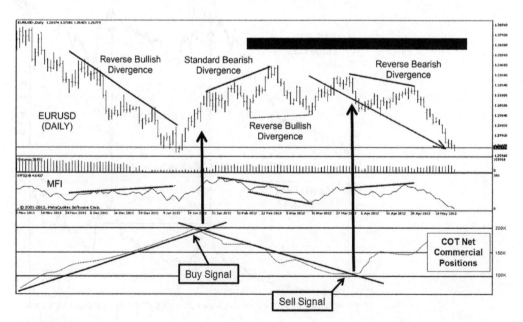

FIGURE 23.6 COT Net Commercial Positions Indicating Potential Buy and Sell Signals on the Daily EURUSD. (Data: cftc.gov)
Source: MetaTrader

positions represents a sell signal, whereas a clear downturn represents a buy signal. A simple trendline penetration is employed as a filter for directional change in the net commercial positions. We also see the Money Flow Index based on tick volume diverging from price at various points. The reverse bullish divergence coincided well with the buy signal and so did the reverse bearish divergence, with the subsequent sell signal on the net commercial positions.

(3) Trading Activity

In this section, we will observe how options may be used to define and track the behavioral characteristics of market participants. We will see how the under-informed participants behave under adverse market conditions and we can use this to track market bottoms and tops.

Put/Call Ratio: Using Option Volume and Premium This sentiment indicator tracks total put volume over the total call volume, although there are a few variations to the basic calculation that may involve the use of premium values. Put options, or puts, are bought if the participants believe that the market is going to decline, while call options, or calls, are bought if the participants believe that the market is going to rise. Hence if the ratio of puts to calls is rising, this suggests that the under-informed are bearish or lacking confidence in the market. Extremely high values indicate the potential of a market bottom being formed, while extremely low values indicate the potential of a market top being formed. It is more effective in signaling tops than bottoms.

In Figure 23.7 we see a 20-day rolling linear regression slope of the CBOE Options Total Put-Call Ratio signaling potential market bottoms whenever it tests or crosses its historically overextended level. A 20-day exponential moving average (EMA) smoothes out the CBOE Options Total Put-Call Ratio, signaling the same market bottoms as the rolling linear regression slope.

The Volatility Indices: The VIX—Using Implied Volatility The VIX has an inverse relationship with the S&P 500, as seen in Figure 23.8. This sentiment indicator of trading activity tracks the degree of *implied volatility* in the options traded on the S&P 500. It measures the fear of participants in the markets by the amount of options activity on the S&P 500. Normally, higher readings on the VIX signal the formation of potential market bottoms, while lower readings point to a more bullish scenario. In Figure 23.8, we see the large decline in the market beginning around the end of 2008, culminating in an extreme reading on the VIX, after which the market rose rapidly. We may use its previous extreme readings on the VIX as a guide to potential future bottoms.

A 20-day rolling correlation of the VIX and the S&P 500 clearly shows that, on average, the two indices are negatively correlated. See Figure 23.9.

Using Net Open Position and Pending Order Analytics Some brokerages report the total number of open positions and pending orders associated at each price level. This is valuable information. The net open position shows the level of

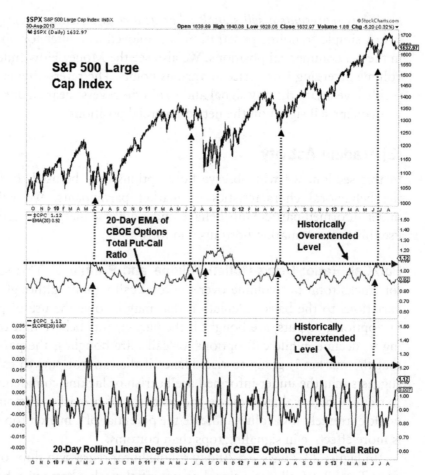

FIGURE 23.7 20-Day Rolling Linear Regression Slope of the CBOE Options Total Put-Call Ratio Signaling Potential Market Bottoms.
Courtesy of Stockcharts.com

conviction of the participants as a whole about a certain market environment. In addition, pending orders reveal potential levels of support and resistance in the market, or the depth of the market.

The downside of using such information is that pending orders may be removed with the click of a button or placed there to fool the under-informed into believing that the market has genuine supply and demand above and below its current price.

23.4 ASSESSING PARTICIPANTS' OPINIONS

Market sentiment may also be ascertained by polls, questionnaires, and interviews with both the well-informed and the under-informed. Here are but a few examples of such sentiment indicators.

Consumer Confidence Index

The Consumer Confidence Index, or CCI, is compiled from opinions based on questionnaires asked of 5,000 households inquiring about the state of the current

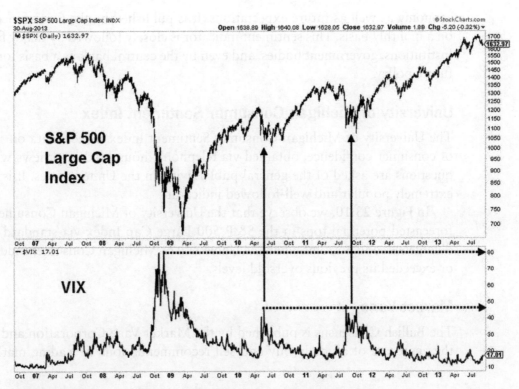

FIGURE 23.8 The VIX Signaling Potential Market Bottoms.
Courtesy of Stockcharts.com

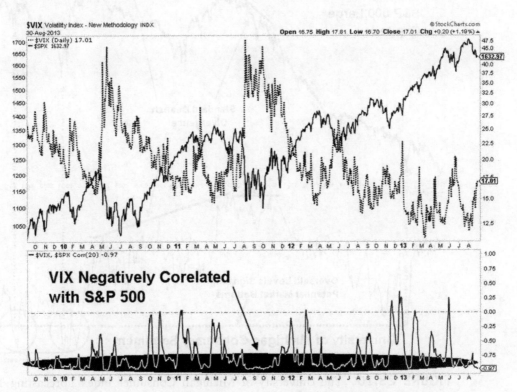

FIGURE 23.9 The VIX Is Negatively Correlated with the S&P 500 Large Cap Index.
Courtesy of Stockcharts.com

economy as well as future expectations. It is published by the Conference Board on a monthly basis. This sentiment indicator is closely followed by major financial institutions, government bodies, and even by the central bank as a basis for setting future policy.

University of Michigan Consumer Sentiment Index

The University of Michigan Consumer Sentiment Index reflects data on the level of consumer confidence, obtained via telephonic household interviews where 50 questions are asked of the general public living in the United States. It is also an extremely popular and well-followed indicator.

In Figure 23.10, we observe that the University of Michigan Consumer Index forecasted potential tops in the S&P 500 Large Cap Index via standard bearish divergences and bottoms when the University of Michigan Consumer Index tested or exceeded its previous oversold levels.

Market Vane

The Bullish Consensus is published by the Market Vane Corporation and reflects the aggregate of all daily buy and sell recommendations of leading market and

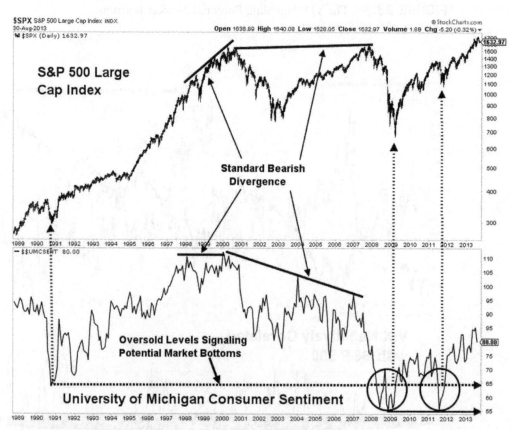

FIGURE 23.10 The University of Michigan Consumer Index Forecasting Tops and Bottoms in the S&P 500 Large Cap Index.
Courtesy of Stockcharts.com

commodity trading advisers. Generally, a rising percentage indicates a bullish market while a declining one reflects a bearish market, except at extremely high or low readings, which then turns the Bullish Consensus into a contrary indicator where extreme highs indicate the potential of a market top forming, and vice versa.

Consensus Bullish Sentiment Index

The Consensus Bullish Sentiment Index reflects the published recommendations, analysis, and advice from brokerage house analysts and independent advisory services covering 32 major markets. Just as for Market Vane's Bullish Consensus, extremely high or low readings indicate the potential of a market top or bottom forming. The Consensus Bullish Sentiment Index is also published by Barrons.

Other Indicators

There are also other measures of sentiment like cultural sentiment indicators which include corporate spending, war, rumors of war, changes of feminine fashion, and so on. This also includes media and magazine headlines. It is generally observed that media and magazine headlines are the most bullish at market tops and most bearish at market bottoms. Therefore these indications may offer further evidence of an impending market reversal. Unfortunately it is difficult to quantify such indications.

23.5 CHAPTER SUMMARY

We have seen how various sentiment indicators provide a fairly reliable indication of potential market bottoms and tops, largely via the underlying behavior of the under-informed. We must remember that these indicators are most reliable when reading are at extreme or historically significant levels. Every practitioner should therefore include sentiment indicators as an indispensable part of their technical toolkit.

CHAPTER 23 REVIEW QUESTIONS

1. Describe what is meant by the term *market sentiment*.
2. What is the difference between flow of funds and poll-based sentiment indicators?
3. Explain how you would use a flow of funds-type sentiment indicator to gauge market tops and bottoms.
4. How would you distinguish between the well-informed and the under-informed?
5. Describe the cycle of emotions and reactions for both the well-informed and under-informed at various stages of a market cycle.
6. How does the Put-Call Ratio differ from the VIX?
7. What is meant by a contrary indicator?
8. Why are price-based indicators sometimes a proxy for sentiment indicators?

REFERENCES

Briese, Stephen. 2008. *The Commitment of Traders Bible*. Hoboken, NJ: John Wiley & Sons.

Fosback, Norman. 1991. *Stock Market Logic*. New York: Dearborn Financial Publishing.

Weir, Deborah. 2006. *Timing the Market*. Hoboken, NJ: John Wiley & Sons.

Relative Strength Analysis

Relative strength charting is an extremely important technical tool for comparing the performance of one market with another. It also helps the practitioner to effectively forecast potential reversals and breakouts based on a change in percentage performance. In this chapter we will cover the construction and the application of technical analysis to relative strength charts.

24.1 MEASURING RELATIVE PERFORMANCE

There are numerous ways of studying the relationship between two or more data series, some of which include:

- Identifying the degree of correlation over a range of data points between two data series
- Identifying the spread or difference of each corresponding data point between two data series
- Identifying the ratio of each corresponding data point between two data series
- Identifying leading and lagging data series

■ Identifying divergence via peak and trough analysis
■ Comparing the percentage or ratio performance of two or more price ratio charts from a common reference point or time line

Relative strength measures the performance of one security, index, or commodity against another. There are basically two ways to create a relative strength chart, that is, either by the ratio or difference method:

■ Ratio method: *Divide* the closing or open, high, low, and close (OHLC) price of one security by another for each period and plot the ratio on a chart.
■ Difference Method: *Subtract* the closing or OHLC price of one security from another for each period and plot the difference on a chart.

Relative strength charts are usually used to compare the performance of:

■ A security against another security, index, or commodity
■ An index against another index or commodity
■ A commodity against another commodity
■ One interest rate against another interest rate

Normally, relative strength charts are employed to gauge the strength of a security within the market environment by comparing it to a broad market index. Some markets are actually based on the charting of relative strength, such as the foreign exchange (fx) markets, where the price of one currency is divided by the corresponding price of another currency for each period and the ratio is plotted as a currency pair. Many commodity traders also use relative strength charts that are based on the spread between the price of one commodity and another, usually either between different contract months or between different futures exchanges.

Applying Technical Analysis on Relative Strength Charts

We can apply technical studies on relative strength charts since they are simply derivatives of actual prices. We may employ trendlines, channels, moving averages, chart patterns, and oscillator analysis. Identifying divergence between a security and its relative strength with respect to an index or another security is a very popular way of forecasting potential reversals in the security.

Being derived from regular price charts, relative strength action shares all the same characteristics as price. Just like price action, it displays:

■ Trends
■ Reversals
■ Consolidation
■ Chart patterns
■ Gapping action
■ Volatility

Price Confirmation

When using relative strength charts to signal potential reversals or breakouts in the security, price confirmation is required. This is because any bullish or bearish indications are merely signals and are not representative of actual price movement in the main security that is being traded. Price confirmation is usually in the form of price breaching some significant price barrier, such as support or resistance, as well as some popular overlay indicators such as trendlines, channels, piece envelopes, volatility bands, chart patterns, Ichimoku clouds, Fibonacci projection levels, and so on.

Characteristics of Relative Strength Lines

The action of relative strength on the chart is referred to as a *relative strength line*, that is, RS line. The RS line is usually a form of constant-time charting where each new RS point or bar is plotted at some regular interval. But this is not always the case, as RS data may also be plotted as Point and Figure charts, which represent constant-range charting.

It should be noted that RS lines will adopt the volatility characteristics of both underlying data series, and as a consequence, RS lines tend to be much more volatile. Many practitioners therefore employ various trend identifiers to help indicate the trend of RS lines. Popular trend identifiers include:

- Trendlines
- Simple moving averages
- Double and triple moving average crossovers
- Linear regression lines

Moving averages are by far the most popular form of trend identification. Moving averages help smooth out volatile RS action, rendering the trend more obvious. The amount of smoothing may be adjusted by:

- Changing the lookback period of the moving average, where larger periodicities provide greater smoothing action
- Changing the sensitivity by selecting the most appropriate weighting factor whether it is exponential, linearly weighted, triangular, simple, and so on
- Changing the price data structure from closing, typical, or midway to weighted close prices
- Using double or triple smoothing on the original RS line

Instead of smoothing single moving averages, practitioners also use double or triple moving average crossovers to signal the start and end points of uptrends and downtrends. Practitioners tend to avoid using crossovers between a single moving average and the RS line, as volatility in the RS line would generate an inordinate number of whipsaws. Double or triple crossovers have the advantage of generating less erratic signals as compared to crossovers between the RS line and its simple moving average. Finally, many practitioners also employ crossovers between the RS line and a forward-shifted moving average as a means of generating trend signals, with the added advantage of reduced whipsaws. Unfortunately, such crossovers signals suffer relatively more lag as compared to non-displaced moving average signals.

Specific Terms for Describing Relative Strength Performance

When describing performance between two data series, whether securities, indices, interest rates, or commodities, we always use the following terms:

- Outperforming/strengthening against/stronger than
- Underperforming/weakening against/weaker than

We cannot use absolute terms like *strong* or *weak*. This is because we are only measuring the ratio or spread and *not the actual or absolute prices* of a security or index. As such:

- Underperformance does not mean that the security is necessarily falling in price, as prices could still be rising, just not as fast as the market or another security.
- Outperformance does not mean that the security is necessarily rising in price, as prices could still be falling, just not as fast as the market or another security.

Assume that we created an RS line using the ratio method, that is, by dividing Stock A's prices by Stock B's prices for each period. When the RS line is rising, we say that Stock A is outperforming Stock B. Alternatively, we could also say that Stock B is underperforming Stock A. Both expressions have the same meaning with respect to an uptrending RS line.

When the RS line is declining, we say that Stock A is underperforming Stock B. We could also say that Stock B is outperforming Stock A. Again, both expressions have the same meaning with respect to a downtrending RS line.

Assume that we created an RS line by dividing Stock A's prices with that of a broad market index (like the S&P 500, for example). Figure 24.1 illustrates how the terms outperforming and underperforming are used in such a case.

The Construction of RS Lines

In this section we are going to study the construction and behavioral characteristics of RS lines. In the following charts, the ratio method was used, dividing Stock A's closing price by Stock B's closing price to form an RS line. The RS line therefore represents a *ratio line*. It tracks the percentage moves between Stock A and Stock B, and not the absolute dollar moves.

In Figure 24.2, we observe that Stock A was flat whereas Stock B was displaying extreme volatility. Stock A remained unchanged. Upon closer examination, we see that the RS line has absorbed all of Stock B's volatility, and is now perfectly reflecting Stock B's volatility. If we took the highest RS value (2) and divide it by the lowest RS value (0.25), we see that the RS line experienced an eightfold increase between two price points. If we also took Stock B's

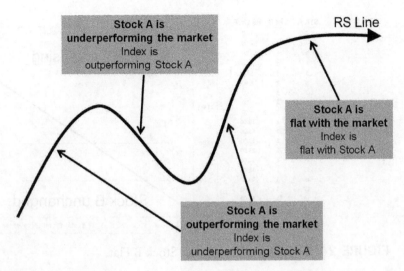

FIGURE 24.1 Outperformance and Underperformance Based on RS Line Action.

highest price ($40) and divided it by its lowest price ($5) we see that Stock B also experienced an eightfold increase between the same two price points. This clearly shows that the RS line perfectly reflects all volatility, be it from one or both of its underlying stocks.

Figure 24.3 shows Stock A outperforming Stock B. Because Stock B remained unchanged, the RS line will mimic Stock A's percentage moves perfectly.

Figure 24.4 shows both stocks rising. The RS line is rising, indicating that Stock A is rising at a faster rate than Stock B. Even though both stocks rose by the same dollar amount, that is, $20, the RS line is oblivious to absolute dollar moves. It only tracks the percentage moves.

Figure 24.5 shows both stocks rising at the same percentage rate, rendering the RS line flat. Here we see that even though both stocks rose in price, the RS line can in such situations portray non-activity. Hence practitioners must be careful when interpreting RS charts. Flat RS lines do not necessarily imply that the underlying stocks are ranging or flatlining.

Figure 24.6 shows both stocks rising. Stock A is rising at a slower rate as compared to Stock B, rendering a declining the RS line. Here we see that even though

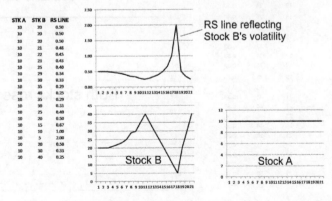

FIGURE 24.2 RS Line Absorbing and Reflecting Volatility from Underlying Stocks.

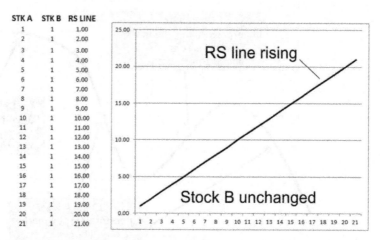

STK A	STK B	RS LINE
1	1	1.00
2	1	2.00
3	1	3.00
4	1	4.00
5	1	5.00
6	1	6.00
7	1	7.00
8	1	8.00
9	1	9.00
10	1	10.00
11	1	11.00
12	1	12.00
13	1	13.00
14	1	14.00
15	1	15.00
16	1	16.00
17	1	17.00
18	1	18.00
19	1	19.00
20	1	20.00
21	1	21.00

FIGURE 24.3 RS Line Rising with Stock B Flat.

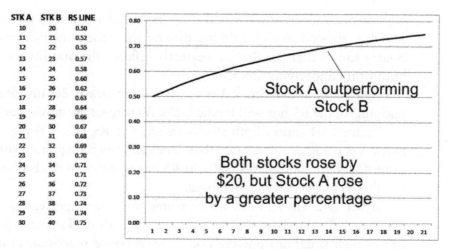

STK A	STK B	RS LINE
10	20	0.50
11	21	0.52
12	22	0.55
13	23	0.57
14	24	0.58
15	25	0.60
16	26	0.62
17	27	0.63
18	28	0.64
19	29	0.66
20	30	0.67
21	31	0.68
22	32	0.69
23	33	0.70
24	34	0.71
25	35	0.71
26	36	0.72
27	37	0.73
28	38	0.74
29	39	0.74
30	40	0.75

FIGURE 24.4 Stock A Rising at a Faster Rate than Stock B.

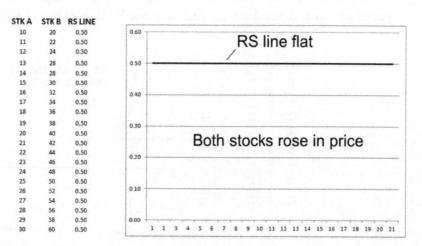

STK A	STK B	RS LINE
10	20	0.50
11	22	0.50
12	24	0.50
13	26	0.50
14	28	0.50
15	30	0.50
16	32	0.50
17	34	0.50
18	36	0.50
19	38	0.50
20	40	0.50
21	42	0.50
22	44	0.50
23	46	0.50
24	48	0.50
25	50	0.50
26	52	0.50
27	54	0.50
28	56	0.50
29	58	0.50
30	60	0.50

FIGURE 24.5 Both Stock A and Stock B Rising at the Same Rate.

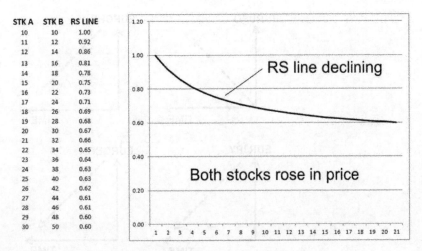

STK A	STK B	RS LINE
10	10	1.00
11	12	0.92
12	14	0.86
13	16	0.81
14	18	0.78
15	20	0.75
16	22	0.73
17	24	0.71
18	26	0.69
19	28	0.68
20	30	0.67
21	32	0.66
22	34	0.65
23	36	0.64
24	38	0.63
25	40	0.63
26	42	0.62
27	44	0.61
28	46	0.61
29	48	0.60
30	50	0.60

FIGURE 24.6   Stock A Rising at a Slower Rate than Stock B.

both stocks may be rising, the RS line can in fact trend downward. That is why we cannot refer to Stock A as weak, because it is not. Stock A had in fact risen 200 percent. But we can refer to Stock A as being *weaker* than Stock B. Stock A has underperformed Stock B. Hence, when we use the term underperformance, it is merely relative to the price movement of another stock and does not reflect the real price movement of Stock A.

Directional Implications of RS Line Action

We shall now study the directional implications of the RS line. In the following examples, we will be referring to an RS chart of Stock A prices being divided by Stock B prices. There are three scenarios that we must consider.

Scenario 1: RS line is rising
   A rising RS line can imply any of the five following possibilities:
   1. Stock A is rising and Stock B is declining.
   2. Stock A is rising and Stock B is flat.
   3. Stock A is rising at a faster rate than Stock B.
   4. Stock A is declining at a slower rate than Stock B.
   5. Stock A is flat and Stock B declining.

   In all five possibilities above, Stock A is outperforming Stock B.

Scenario 2: RS line is declining
   A declining RS line can imply any of the five following possibilities:
   1. Stock A is declining and Stock B is rising.
   2. Stock A is declining and Stock B is flat.
   3. Stock A is declining at a faster rate than Stock B.
   4. Stock A is rising at a slower rate than Stock B.
   5. Stock A is flat and Stock B rising.

   In all five possibilities above, Stock A is underperforming Stock B.

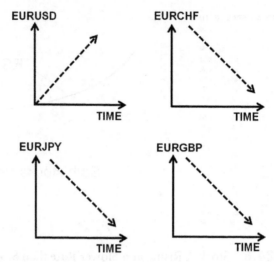

FIGURE 24.7 Which Is the Weakest Currency?

Scenario 3: RS line is flatlining

A flat RS line can imply any of the three following possibilities:

1. Stock A is flat and Stock B is flat.
2. Stock A and Stock B are both declining at equal rates.
3. Stock A and Stock B are both rising at equal rates.

In all three possibilities above, Stock A matches Stock B's performance.

Let us now look at an example from the foreign exchange (FOREX) market. Refer to Figure 24.7. Can you work out which currency is the most underperforming or weakest among the five currencies displayed?

Since the Euro is weaker than the JPY, GBP, and CHF, this makes the USD the weakest of the entire group, as the Euro is still stronger than the USD.

Bullish and Bearish Divergence

In an earlier section we observed that *outperformance and underperformance do not necessarily imply bullishness or bearishness* in the stock. There are five possibilities associated rising or falling RS lines. It is only by referencing the actual stock chart that we are able to determine whether *outperformance and underperformance imply that* a stock is bullish or bearish. It is important to note that when practitioners refer to a rising RS line as "bullish," this term is used in its *relative* sense. The actual stock may in fact be declining at a slower rate with respect to the market, but it is still "bullish" relative to market performance. It is only when the actual chart of the stock is available for comparison that a practitioner can use the terms bullish or bearish in their absolute sense. In the following illustrations, the terms bullish and bearish are used in their absolute sense since the chart of the stock is available for comparison against its RS line.

Figure 24.8 depicts bearish divergence between the RS line and price. It shows that although the stock is making higher peaks, it is underperforming the market

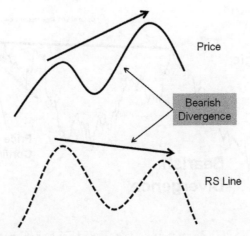

FIGURE 24.8 Standard Bearish Divergence between the RS Line and Price.

and is thus a bearish indication. There may be some underlying weakness in the stock. Again, all moves in the stock must be confirmed by price.

Figure 24.9 depicts bullish divergence between the RS line and price. It shows that although the stock is making lower troughs, it is outperforming the market and is thus a bullish indication. There may be some underlying strength in the stock. As usual, all moves in the stock must be confirmed by price.

Figure 24.10 shows Google Inc. and its RS line, with respect to the S&P500 Index (Google/S&P500). We observe bearish divergence between Google and its RS line, which indicates a potential weakening in prices since Google is seen underperforming the broad market. Price finally declined, with price breaching an uptrend line, representing price confirmation.

Divergence may also be found by comparing the percentage or ratio performance of two or more price ratio charts from a common reference point or time line. These are also popularly referred to as *performance charts*. Figure 24.11 depicts bearish divergence between Gold and the Gold Miners and Gold Bugs Index.

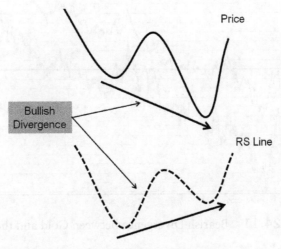

FIGURE 24.9 Standard Bullish Divergence between the RS Line and Price.

FIGURE 24.10 Bearish Divergence between the RS Line and Google Inc.
Source: StockCharts.com

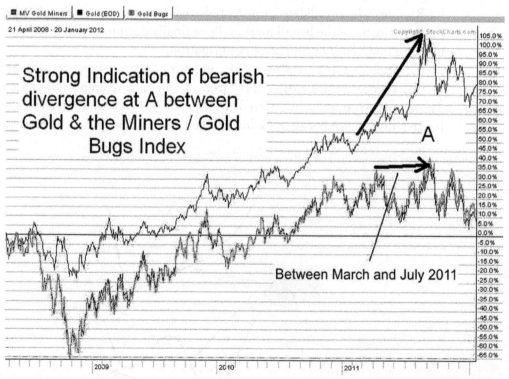

FIGURE 24.11 Bearish Divergence between Gold and the Gold Miners and Gold Bugs Index.
Source: StockCharts.com

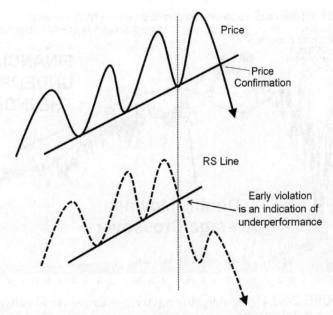

FIGURE 24.12   Bearish Divergence between Gold and the Gold Miners and Gold Bugs Index.

Examples of Applying Technical Analysis on RS Lines

Figure 24.12 illustrates an RS line breaking down prior to price confirmation. Such formations provide an early indication of potential breakouts and reversals in price.

Figure 24.13 illustrates the usefulness of a double moving average crossover of an RS line in identifying the start of the downtrend in the RS line of the CBN China 600 Index/the CRB Index ratio.

Figure 24.14 is another example of the usefulness of a double moving average crossover in identifying a downtrend in the RS line of the Financial/Industrials

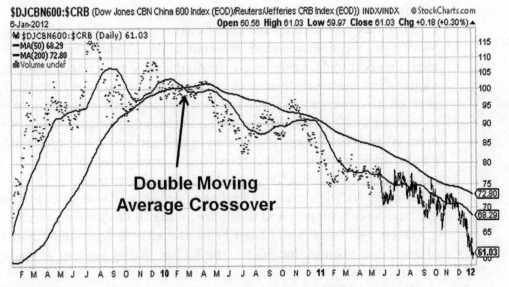

FIGURE 24.13   Double Moving Average Crossover Identifying the RS Line Trend.
Source: StockCharts.com

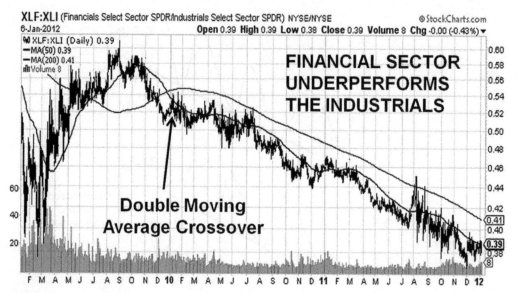

FIGURE 24.14 Double Moving Average Crossover Identifying the RS Line Trend. Source: StockCharts.com

Select Sector SPDR ratio. We see the 200-day moving average providing resistance to the RS line.

Figure 24.15 illustrates the 200-day moving average providing resistance to the RS line of the Dow Jones CBN China 600 Index/CRB Index ratio. We also see the moving average convergence-divergence (MACD) oscillator working very effectively in identifying potential reversal in the RS line, via the testing of its historical overextended upper threshold. It is important to note that we cannot refer to this overextension as an overbought level since we have no reference to the actual chart of the Jones CBN China 600 Index and hence no indication as to whether the index itself is declining or rising.

Figure 24.16 illustrates the use of chart patterns on the RS line of the Gold/Silver ratio. We observe a clear breakout to the downside from an ascending triangle that occurred slightly before the double moving average crossover, signaling a significant underperformance in gold with respect to silver. The double moving average crossover subsequently signaled a change in the direction of the RS line in October of 2011. We also see the RS line reacting twice at the 61.8 percent Fibonacci level. The RS line is also seen to be contained by an uptrending channel. Finally, apex reaction analysis forecasted a strong reversal in the RS line at the time line associated with the apex of the ascending triangle.

Figure 24.17 illustrates the RS line of Apple Inc./Dow Jones Industrials Average ratio finding support and resistance on the 50-day moving average.

Figure 24.18 shows an RS line being plotted on a Point-and-Figure ratio chart of Apple Inc. / Google Inc. Notice the RS line finding support at the bullish support trendlines.

Figure 24.19 illustrates the use of performance charts to indicate the inverse relationship between the S&P 500 and the 30-year bond price.

FIGURE 24.15 Using Oscillators with RS Charts.
Source: StockCharts.com

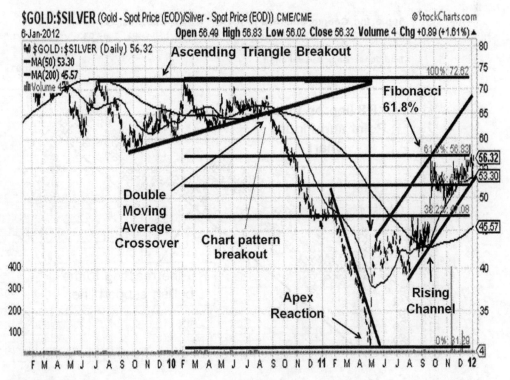

FIGURE 24.16 Application of Technical Analysis to RS Charts.
Source: StockCharts.com

FIGURE 24.17 RS Line Finding Support and Resistance on Its 50-day Moving Average.
Source: StockCharts.com

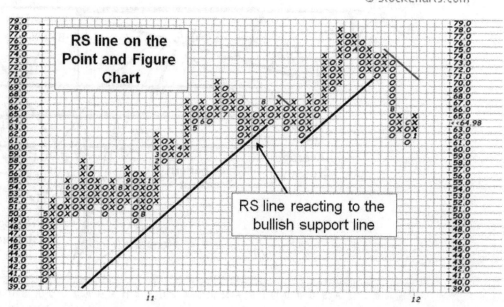

FIGURE 24.18 RS Line Plotted on a Point-and-Figure Chart.
Source: StockCharts.com

FIGURE 24.19 Performance Charts Indicating Inverse Relationships.
Source: StockCharts.com

Figure 24.20 illustrates the correlation between the RS line of the Consumer Staple SPDR/Consumer Discretionary ratio and the S&P 500 Index. We see that they are negatively correlated after 2008, once the quantitative easing commenced. Notice also that the RS line reacts to its own historical highs, reversing every time it tests the upper extreme levels.

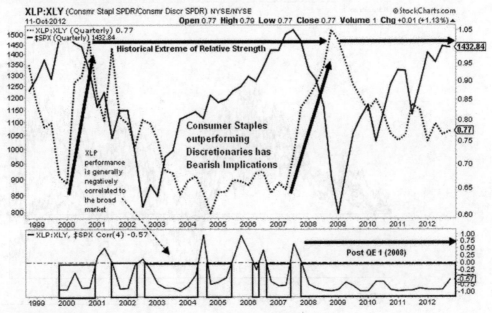

FIGURE 24.20 Correlation Study on RS Charts.
Source: StockCharts.com

FIGURE 24.21 Reveal the Effectiveness of a Fund by Tracking Its Underlying Instruments. Source: StockCharts.com

Figure 24.21 also illustrates a change in the behavior of the RS line of the U.S. Dollar Index/PowerShares DB US Dollar Index Bullish Fund ratio, after the start of 2008. The PowerShares DB US Dollar Index Bullish Fund underperforms the U.S. Dollar Index. Hence, RS charts are useful for helping to gauge the ability of various ETFs and funds to track underlying market effectively.

Figure 24.22 illustrates the ability of performance charts to track the percentage performance of multiple markets simultaneously, as measured from a single

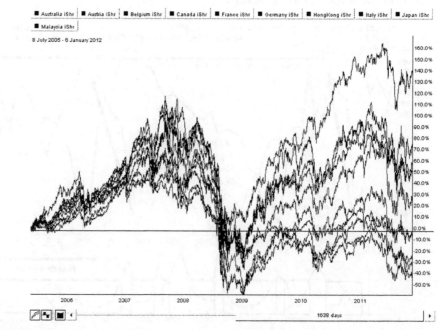

FIGURE 24.22 The Ability of Performance Charts to Display Multiple Percentage Performances.

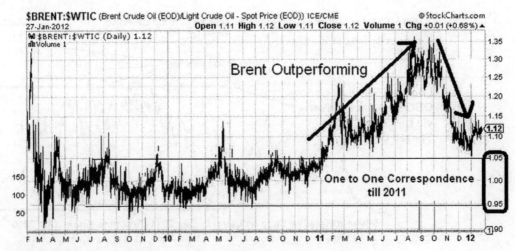

FIGURE 24.23 RS Charts Indicating Market Regime Change.
Source: StockCharts.com

point of reference. We observe the synchronicity that exists between all global markets. Unlike performance charts, RS charts can only track two markets at any one time.

Figure 24.23 shows how Brent Crude Oil left the average 1:1 correspondence with Light Crude Oil and outperformed Light Crude oil as the RS line rises from early 2011. Notice the RS line being contained within a horizontal range between 2009 to 2011.

Figure 24.24 shows the RS line of the Gold/TED Spread ratio testing the upper extreme level. Notice that the RS line tested the upper extreme level very accurately before Gold started to underperform the TED spread.

Figure 24.25 shows the RS line of Silver against the TED Spread testing the upper extreme level. Notice that the RS line exceeded the upper extreme level very decisively before Silver started to underperform.

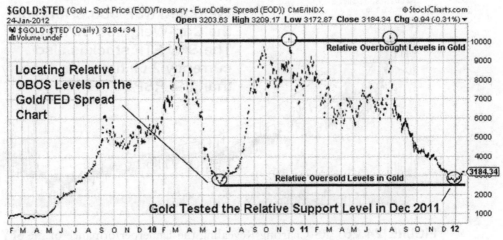

FIGURE 24.24 RS Charts Indicating Overextension in Gold.
Source: StockCharts.com

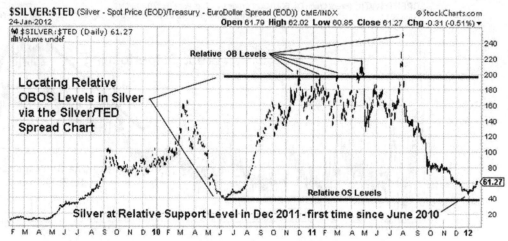

FIGURE 24.25 Charts Indicating Overextension in Silver.
Source: StockCharts.com

Figure 24.26 shows the equal-weighted RSP outperforming the capital-weighted SPY ETF. Again, RS lines are useful in revealing the effectiveness of funds with various weighting systems that track the same underlying component stocks.

Top-Down Approach Using RS Analysis for Equity Selection

RS charts may also be used to perform a *top-down* search for the strongest performing stocks. This is easily done by first identifying the strongest sectors and industries using RS analysis. Then a search for the top dozen outperforming stocks is

FIGURE 24.26 RS Charting Revealing the Underperformance of the SPY ETF to Its Equal-Weighted Counterpart.
Source: StockCharts.com

carried out. This process is repeated once the selected stocks exhibit deterioration in performance. Market participants then rotate out of the previous portfolio into a new set of better-performing stocks.

24.2 CHAPTER SUMMARY

Relative strength analysis affords the practitioner an added dimension to understanding how markets relate to and interact with each other. It provides a way of identifying weaker markets and forecasting potential trend changes based on intermarket behavior. It is also a vital tool and indispensible aid in the active process of managing the rotation of best performing stocks within a sector or industry.

CHAPTER 24 REVIEW QUESTIONS

1. Explain the meaning of relative strength.
2. List the number of ways one can study the relationship between two markets.
3. What is the difference between the ratio and difference methods of constructing RS charts?
4. What are the advantages of using RS charts?
5. Explain how two stocks can rally but have their RS line decline.
6. What technical tools would you employ to help identify RS trends?
7. How are performance charts better than RS charts?
8. Why would you need price confirmation when trading via the use of an RS line?

REFERENCES

Kirkpatrick, Charles, and Julie Dahlquist. 2007. *Technical Analysis: The Complete Resource for Financial Market Technicians*. Upper Saddle River, NJ: Pearson Education.

Murphy, John. 1999. *Technical Analysis of the Financial Markets*. New York: New York Institute of Finance (NYIF).

Pring, Martin J. 2002. *Technical Analysis Explained: The Successful Investor's Guide to Spotting Investment Trends and Turning Points*. 4th ed. New York: McGraw-Hill.

CHAPTER
25

Investor Psychology

The study of trader and investor psychology is critical to a full understanding of market action. In this chapter, we will look at the various behavioral elements and mechanisms that are responsible for the manifestation of trend action, consolidations, and market reversals.

25.1 GENERAL BEHAVIORAL ASPECTS

Psychology, Emotions, and Investment Decisions

It is a well-accepted fact that the market is driven by expectations. In other words, the market is driven by the expectation of future prices. Expectation itself is a consequence of various beliefs, biases, habits, knowledge, attitudes, and emotions. Fear, greed, and hope play a very large part in trading and investing. Peer pressure and other third-party influence may also affect investment decisions. Experiencing significant life events is another factor that may alter one's outlook and investment perspective. For every 20 good reasons, there are 20 other reasons why one should not invest in a certain market or stock. *The final decision is usually one based not so much on fact, but rather on psychological and emotional preference or pressure.*

As such the study of human behavior is a critical and necessary area of focus for any serious analyst or trader. Not only is it crucial to understand the underlying behavioral elements that drive the market, but it will also be important for the analyst or trader to understand and be aware of his or her own psychological and emotional quirks, biases, predilections, and unique responses when assessing market information.

The Conflicted Analytical Trader

It is very hard to adapt or be flexible when one has invested a significant amount of time, effort, and capital in promoting or supporting a particular view or analysis of the market. This makes it very difficult for directional traders to keep up with the constant flow of price action. When a trader or analyst begins to feel discomfort or anxiety when being confronted with contradictory evidence, we say that they are experiencing, or are in a state of, *cognitive dissonance*. The trader or analyst will attempt to reduce this uncomfortable state of dissonance by either selectively choosing only information that complements or conforms to his or her view of the market, or by attempting to rationalize away the problem. If the trader resorts to *selectively exposing* him- or herself only to information that agrees with the accepted view or analysis of the market, any opposing news, analysis, newsletter, or article is quickly dismissed or discarded. For example, once a trader is fully convinced that a particular market is bullish, there is a tendency to ignore signals that do not conform to this bullish view. The trader may also begin to *mentally compartmentalize information* in such a way that the overall impact of conflicting information is minimized, mentally confining and breaking it down into a less significant and meaningful threat. The trader may also resort to only focusing on the bullish aspects of the market in the face of overwhelming bearishness. The trader *selectively perceives* only what is in agreement with his or her view of the market and even misinterprets information so that it is in line with his or her current expectations.

In short, traders seldom trade based on what they actually perceive to be occurring in the market. They prefer to trade on what they *expect to see* occur in the markets. Hence, the market is driven primarily by trader and investor expectations.

Positive Feedback Loops and Market Trends

Positive feedback loops are usually responsible for creating spectacular market tops and bottoms. Positive feedback loops are self-promoting. They are responsible for trend action in the market. Unfortunately, positive feedback loops are not self-sustaining and are regarded as unstable. For example, a certain stock may be slightly undervalued. This attracts market participants to invest in the stock. As more investment flows into the stock, the demand drives the price up. As the price rises, this in turn attracts even more demand for the stock. The process repeats, driving the stock price higher and higher and eventually spiraling up into a frenzy of irrational buying. At some point, liquidity starts to dry up and prices cease to rise. The stock price then starts downward, forming a top in the stock. As prices fall, this influences more market participants to exit positions in the stock. As more participants start exiting, this oversupply causes the price to fall even further. And the process repeats, with prices now spiraling downward until all the sellers have liquidated most of their shares in the stock, forming a new potential bottom in the stock. Hence we have seen how positive feedback loops can cause the markets to boom or bust. George Soros's theory of reflexivity is based on positive feedback cycles.

Contrarianism, Herd Behavior, and the Under-Informed

The well-informed or smart participants are usually *contrarian* only at tops and bottoms. Being contrarian means buying when the under-informed public is selling and selling when the under-informed public is buying. They are not of a contrary opinion during a full-blown trend phase. In fact, many contrarians are trend followers during such a phase. It would spell financial suicide to adopt a contrary position in a strong and prolonged trend. It is the large combined capital of the under-informed public, or *herd*, that is usually responsible for driving a trend up or down. This, for example, allows the smart investors to accumulate shares at a lower and more advantageous price preceding an uptrend and distribute shares at a higher and more advantageous price preceding a downtrend.

25.2 BEHAVIORAL ELEMENTS ASSOCIATED WITH CHART PATTERNS

Price barriers and chart patterns exist because of behavioral phenomena. The building blocks of any chart pattern lie in the way traders place trade orders in the market. It is heuristic- or knowledge-based bias in action. See Figure 25.1. It is conventional to place buy orders above a barrier and sell orders below it. This is because it is a learned behavior or attitude. *This means that whenever price approaches a barrier, it will initially encounter an opposing force.* For example, as price descends toward a prior support level, it will initially encounter a concentration of buy orders, driving price back up. In similar fashion, as price ascends toward a prior resistance level, it will initially encounter a concentration of sell orders, driving price back down. As such, all price barriers are trend inhibiting.

This learned behavior explains why triangles and channels exist. Every time price tests the converging trendlines of a triangle or the parallel trendlines of a price channel, it will initially rebound or pull back from these trendlines. It also works fairly consistently because most traders react in the same manner to a price barrier, which in itself further reinforces the belief that prices will react in the expected manner. This is an example of the self-fulfilling prophecy in action. Figure 25.2 illustrates price reacting to the converging trendlines within a triangle formation. This learned behavior or knowledge-based attitude is also sometimes referred to as *magical thinking*. Although there is a behavioral basis for price reacting in such a manner, the trader soon forgets the original reason and tends to

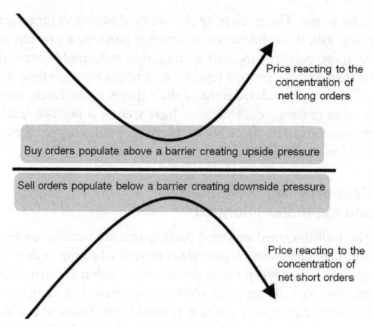

Price reacting to the concentration of net long orders

Buy orders populate above a barrier creating upside pressure

Sell orders populate below a barrier creating downside pressure

Price reacting to the concentration of net short orders

FIGURE 25.1 Behavioral Aspects of an Uptrend.

assume that every time price tests a trendline or price barrier it will magically and consistently rebound off it.

Unfortunately, professional traders and specialists are aware of this predictable learned behavior or knowledge-based attitude and as such may try to take advantage of the situation by orchestrating a profitable false breakout. For example, traders will short below a resistance barrier with a stoploss placed above it. The specialists will then drive price through the resistance and trigger the stoplosses, forcing the shorts

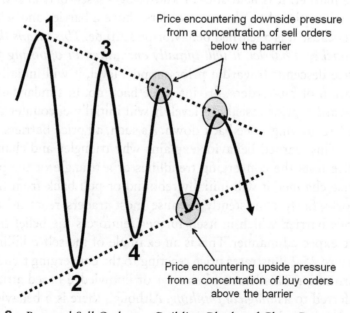

Price encountering downside pressure from a concentration of sell orders below the barrier

Price encountering upside pressure from a concentration of buy orders above the barrier

FIGURE 25.2 Buy and Sell Orders as Building Blocks of Chart Patterns.

to cover by buying to close their positions. The specialists will take the other side of the order by selling into the short-covering activity. As prices fall back below the resistance level, the specialists will then buy into the new shorts by selling to open new positions. Hence, the specialists continually bought low and sold high throughout the process. The trader, on the other hand, continually bought high and sold low. In short, it is a highly profitable venture for the specialist. Many advanced traders therefore resort to entering the market only after a failed breakout has occurred in order to avoid or reduce the instances of being put in a disadvantageous position. Victor Sperandeo's 2B approach is one example of entering on a failed breakout.

25.3 BEHAVIORAL ELEMENTS ASSOCIATED WITH MARKET TRENDS

There are numerous behavioral explanations for various trend-related price phenomena. We shall now look briefly at a few scenarios and their possible behavioral explanations.

Breakouts, Pullbacks, and Retests

Refer to Figure 25.3. Price breaches a resistance level at Point 1. Based on the assumption that price will persist in an upward direction after a breakout, traders go long at Point 1. This behavior is an example of a learned response or attitude. We find that in many situations, price does not in fact persist as expected but rather pulls back to the original breakout level, indicated at Point 1. This can be attributed to a behavioral bias where traders have a tendency to be *less willing to risk or gamble with profit than with losses*, in what is described by Kahneman and Tversky as *prospect theory*. This unwillingness to gamble with profit helps explain why prices frequently retrace back to the breakout level. This behavior is also sometimes referred to as *certainty bias*, where traders prefer the certainty of locking in a smaller profit rather than the uncertainty of securing a larger one.

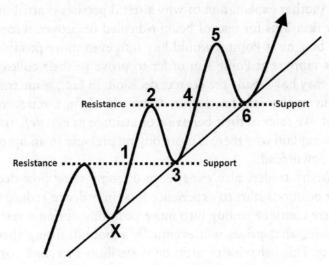

FIGURE 25.3 Behavioral Elements Associated with an Uptrend.

As price pulls back to Point 3, traders that failed to go long at the breakout level associated with Point 1 may now be regretting that they missed the opportunity to participate in what they believe is a reliable uptrend. Not wanting to miss out on another opportunity to get in, these traders now go long on the pullback to Point 3. Another group of traders may have gone long at Point X and liquidated their positions at the first resistance level. These traders may also be regretting exiting and re-enter on the pullback to the support level associated with Point 1. This behavior is referred to as *regret bias*. Both regret and prospect bias help explain why uptrends make higher peaks and troughs and downtrends make lower peaks and troughs. It also helps explain why resistance turns into support, and vice versa. The process repeats at Points 4, 5, 6, and so on, in an uptrend.

In Figure 25.3, a trendline was drawn based on Points X and 3. Traders have a tendency to buy at a trendline support in an uptrend (and at trendline resistance in a downtrend), as indicated at Point 6. This is a form of *heuristic* or knowledge-based bias. A heuristic represents a simple guideline or rule of thumb. As such, traders act on these rules of thumb without understanding the reasons behind them. In fact, many of these heuristics may not even have an underlying explanation. This may render the application of heuristics somewhat unreliable. Traders act on these simplistic preconceived notions and expect them to work consistently. This is also referred to as magical thinking. Magical thinking, which stems from heuristic bias, helps explain why traders tend to buy at barrier support and sell at barrier resistance.

As the trend persists, many traders are convinced that they would have bought the dips and sold at the highs in an uptrend. This overestimation in their ability to forecast or time the market is referred to as *hindsight bias*. Hindsight bias helps explain why a trend persists. Traders are more likely to recognize potential buy and sell signals retrospectively. Patterns and triggers are always clearer and more obvious after the fact. Traders tend to get even more frustrated and regretful for not participating in a trend if they can clearly identify it on hindsight. This regret further fuels the buying of upside breakouts and the subsequent buying at various rising support levels in an uptrend.

Another explanation of why a trend persists is attributed to traders defending their decisions for fear of being ridiculed or proven wrong. For example, traders that bought at Point 2 would buy into even more positions as price retraces and finds support at Point 3 in order to prove to their colleagues and acquaintances that they have made the correct decision. In fact, some traders may even continue to buy at the next few lower support levels in a retracement just to prove their point. We refer to their behavior or attitude as *ego defensive*. This behavioral bias helps explain why there is more buying pressure in an uptrend and selling pressure in a downtrend.

Many traders also experience discomfort or post-decision dissonance when their positions start to experience loss. In order to reduce this state of dissonance, traders continue to buy into more positions during a retracement in an uptrend, believing that prices will eventually rebound, lifting their portfolio into profitability. This behavior or attitude is attributed to *sunk cost bias*. It stems from an unwillingness to experience or face loss. As a consequence, traders sometimes make irrational decisions in order to remedy the situation. It is part of a larger classification of behavior referred to as *loss-aversion bias*.

Mental Framing and Anchors

As the trend unfolds, it starts to become obvious. This representation of a trend *frames* the mind, and all subsequent opinions, technical references, and thought patterns will tend to revolve around this mental frame. For example, traders tend to focus on buying at support, peaks, and higher prices in an uptrend. This mental frame is *anchored* by rising prices and the appearance of higher peaks and troughs. *Once a trader is influenced by this mental frame of a trend in effect, which is anchored by elements associated with the representation, all subsequent decisions and actions tend to be trend promoting.* There is a tendency to preserve the status quo. In short, the appearance of an uptrend will tend to cause more bullish-based or -biased decisions. The reverse is true for downtrends. We may refer to this effect of framing and anchoring as *representativeness bias*.

There are a couple more common behavioral biases that may account for trend persistence that are based on cognitive dissonance. As mentioned earlier, some traders resort to selectively exposing themselves only to information that conforms to their current expectations and opinions of the market. As a consequence, traders and investors tend to downplay and ignore bearish signals in an uptrend. Such behavior is trend promoting. Another common form of behavioral bias is the misinterpretation of data in such a way as to corroborate the trader's current view of the markets. One common example is the misinterpretation of a major reversal as a mere correction of the existing trend. We may refer to this form of bias as *misinterpretation bias*.

It is also human nature to be overly invested or influenced not only by our own decisions and beliefs, but also by those that conform to our view of the markets. Hence, once a decision is made, there is a tendency to maintain a certain view rather than change it. This form of bias is referred to as *confirmatory bias*. Hence once a trader has decided that the current uptrend is strong and reliable, he or she will be more likely to rely and maintain such a view rather than react to other views. As before, such behavior is trend promoting.

Many traders are also influenced by the behavior and attitude of others. In an uptrend, many traders go long not because of the conclusions reached by independent analysis or research, but rather because other traders and investors are going long. Trade decisions are based on the actions of others, rather than on analysis and information. Many traders also adopt the attitudes of other traders. Such behavior may explain the rapid movements in price during a trend.

Overconfidence is also responsible for trend persistence in the markets. It is not difficult for traders and investors to profit in an uptrend. But many traders and investors prefer to believe that it is their methodology that is responsible for their recent profitability. The more profit is made, the more likely that traders will be confident with their trading and investing methodology or approach. In many situations, it leads to a state of overconfidence. Such behavior or attitude is trend promoting, that is, it is bullish for uptrends and bearish for downtrends.

Hence we have seen how prospect theory–based bias, loss aversion bias, sunk cost bias, ego defensive bias, certainty bias, regret bias, magical thinking, hindsight bias, selective exposure bias, misinterpretation bias, confirmatory bias, overconfidence, and representativeness bias all help to explain why trends persist.

25.4 BEHAVIORAL ASPECTS OF MARKET CONSOLIDATIONS

The interplay between greed, hope, and fear helps explain market consolidations and their subsequent breakouts. Consolidations are essentially trend interruptions. As such, they involve a wide range of varying emotions.

In a ranging market, traders tend to employ limit entry orders rather than stop entry orders. This is because most trades are confined to a narrow price range, usually between an upper and lower price barrier.

The Effect of Trend Interruption

As a trend begins to decelerate, loss aversion bias starts to kick in, evinced by the tightening of stoplosses. The market then begins to range. Fear tends to build as the consolidation develops. This is because a consolidation usually represents a trend interruption and as such participants fear that a reversal may result in loss of unrealized profit or invested capital.

The upper resistance zone is created by traders placing sell limit orders, while the lower support zone is populated by buy limit orders. *As the market oscillates between the upper and lower barrier zones, traders buy low and sell high within the range via the execution of entry- and exit-based limit orders.* For example, a buy limit (entry) order is initiated at support, which is exited at the profit target located at the resistance zone. In similar fashion, a short position is initiated at the resistance zone that is exited at the profit target located at the support zone. In both scenarios, stoplosses are positioned just above the resistance zone for the sell limit entry orders and just below the support zone for the buy limit entry orders. This process repeats as long as price remains within the resistance and support zone. Buying and selling at the lower and upper barriers is the result of heuristic- or knowledge-based attitudes. See Figure 25.4.

There is another group of market participants who are more interested in accumulating long and short positions at the barriers. As price tests the lower and upper barrier zones, long and short positions are initiated. These positions are not exited at a profit target but are held in anticipation of a breakout move.

As time passes, the number of participants who want to accumulate long and short positions within the consolidation begins to decrease. This is because all the participants who wanted to accumulate long or short positions would have mostly done so after a sufficient amount of time has elapsed. Volume eventually diminishes to low levels. With the accumulation of long and short positions, stoplosses above and below the two barrier zones also accumulate. Once volume approaches very low levels, a potential breakout may be imminent.

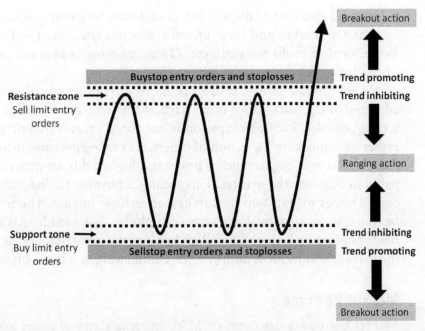

FIGURE 25.4   Behavioral Elements Associated with Ranging Action.

A third group of participants starts to appear. These chart pattern traders are more interested in trading breakouts from the consolidations. These participants place buystop entry orders above the resistance zone and sellstop entry orders below the support zone. In both cases, the stoplosses are usually positioned within the consolidation. As per most technical trading approaches, the trading of breakouts is the result of knowledge-based attitudes.

It should be noted that *limit orders are trend inhibiting in nature*, and as such, prices tend to remain within the barrier zones. But as the consolidation develops, the accumulation of stoploss orders above and below the two barrier zones creates an increasingly trend-promoting scenario. *This is because stoplosses are essentially stop orders, which are trend promoting in nature.*

It should also be noted that the longer it takes for a consolidation to unfold, the larger will be the number of potential buy stop orders that lie above the resistance zone and sell stop orders that populate just below the support zone. This explains why larger consolidations tend to produce stronger and more persistent breakouts.

25.5 BEHAVIORAL ASPECTS OF MARKET REVERSALS

No other price or market action elicits more emotion than the creation of a market top or bottom. This is evinced by the extreme volume action that normally accompanies such formations.

Market Tops

During the intermediate stages of an uptrend, confirmatory bias and representativeness bias will play a larger role in fueling the trend. Based on hindsight bias, traders will also start to display overconfidence, believing that the trend will never end. As the market and their unrealized profit rise, greed will begin to surface in the form of profit reinvestment. Overconfidence is also one of the underlying causes for increasing margin debt.

As the trend matures, traders begin to display irrationality by adopting and adapting to the behavior of other participants who are all caught up buying into a rising market. Such participation is not based on research or sound advice but rather on mimicking the action of others. As buying pressure increases, this forces price to rise even higher, and as prices rise higher, this attracts even more participants to buy into the market. This creates a positive feedback cycle or loop that causes prices to spiral up in a frenzy of reckless buying. The traders are said to be in a state of *irrational exuberance*, a phrase first used by Alan Greenspan and made popular by Robert J. Schiller's book of the same title. As the top approaches, the market is at its most bullish state, culminating in a blow-off or buying climax.

Market Bottoms

Market bottoms are accompanied by extreme states of panic and fear, with participants selling at any price available. The market will be at its most bearish and culminates in a selling climax. As the market starts to rebound to the upside, cognitive dissonance begins to build as most participants are still under the psychological and emotional influence of representativeness bias, believing that the market will decline further. They are still influenced by the recent decline, a view that is anchored by declining prices.

Cognitive Dissonance at Market Tops and Bottoms

Once the top is formed and price starts to exhibit bearishness, the amount of cognitive dissonance begins to build. *The greatest amount of dissonance is experienced during the early stages of a top or bottom reversal.* See Figure 25.5.

As we learned earlier, when traders experience dissonance, they will attempt to reduce their discomfort by:

- Ignoring or downplaying the problem (compartmentalization bias, loss aversion bias)
- Selectively exposing themselves only to information that conforms to or agrees with their current view of the markets (selective exposure bias)
- Misinterpreting the information in such a way so as to make it conform to their current view of the markets (misrepresentation bias)
- Being ego defensive and investing even more as the trend moves against their positions (sunk cost bias)
- Blaming the problem or loss on others

As such, when the market begins to turn, traders experiencing representativeness bias will attempt to maintain their view that the trend is still in effect in the face of contradictory information or evidence. They may react by either being ego defensive and sinking more capital into the market or rationalizing away the issues via

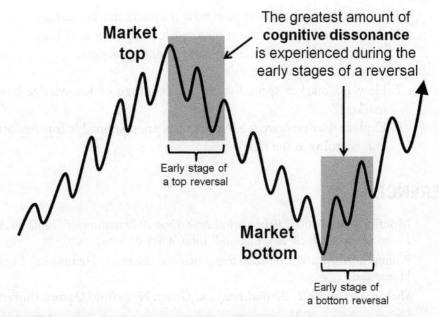

FIGURE 25.5 Behavioral Elements Associated with Market Tops and Bottoms.

misinterpretation and mental compartmentalization. The most common form of trying to resolve dissonance is to simply ignore the issues and hope that the market will rebound. Traders also choose to perceive only information that agrees with their view that the trend is still intact and any retracements are merely temporary or insignificant.

We have, in this chapter, seen how various behavioral biases affect trader and investor decisions with respect to trends, consolidations, and market reversals. Besides observing how trade and investment decisions are affected by such psychological and emotional biases in others, every analyst or trader should also strive to observe the degree that such biases affect their own view and decision making process. With a deeper understanding of oneself and the factors that influence one's actions and decisions, analysts will be able to offer a more objective view of market action and traders will be able to trade what they see instead of what they want or expect to see unfold in the markets.

25.6 CHAPTER SUMMARY

In this chapter, we learned that the market is essentially a consequence of human reaction to market action. Hence it behooves the practitioner to be familiar with the various human traits and biases that drive the market. We have seen how breakouts, retests, and various chart patterns are the result of human psychology and emotion in action.

CHAPTER 25 REVIEW QUESTIONS

1. What are the behavioral elements associated with market tops and bottoms?
2. What are the behavioral elements associated with consolidations?

3. Explain prospect theory and how it affects market action.
4. Explain how loss aversion bias can lead to sunk cost bias.
5. Describe how regret bias influences market action.
6. Why do chart patterns exist?
7. How do market specialists take advantage of knowledge-based bias in the markets?
8. Explain why positive feedback cycles are responsible for the formation of tops and bottoms in the market.

REFERENCES

Montier, James. 2007. *Behavioural Investing: A Practitioners Guide to Applying Behavioural Finance*. Chichester, England: John Wiley & Sons.

Plummer, Tony. 2009. *Forecasting Financial Markets*. Hampshire, England: Harriman House Ltd.

Shefrin, Hersh. 2002. *Beyond Fear and Greed*. New York: Oxford University Press.

Shiller, Robert J. 2005. *Irrational Exuberance*. Princeton, NJ: Princeton University.

Soros, Georgy. 2003. *The Alchemy of Finance*. Hoboken, NJ: Wiley Investment Classics.

CHAPTER
26

Trader Risk Profiling and Position Analysis

This chapter introduces the concept of risk capacity and how market participants align their trading and investment objectives in accordance with the level of risk that they can comfortably tolerate. The definition of risk capacity in trading is also discussed in terms of price, time, and risk size. The concept of whether a market participant is risk seeking and aggressive, or risk averse and conservative, is also covered in detail. Organizing, categorizing, and summarizing technical data is an important prerequisite for preparing the groundwork for effective and efficient technical analysis. Various charts are used to illustrate how this can be done methodically. The proper evaluation and application of signals and triggers is also demonstrated via chart examples of a popular stock and its relevant index.

26.1 FULFILLING CLIENT OBJECTIVES AND RISK CAPACITY

Before advising our clients as to whether they should further participate or exit the markets, we must first be familiar and understand the client's:

- Objectives
- Market and performance expectations
- Risk capacity

We may then proceed to advise the client in accordance with preferred trading and investment objectives and level of risk tolerance.

The client's objectives include:

- The client's preferred-term outlook, that is, the average length of time in the market that a client expects his or her investment or trading objectives to be met, profitably or otherwise, be it in the short, medium or longer term. Depending on the duration of the outlook, trading and investment styles may range from short-term speculation like day trading and scalping, to intermediate-term position or swing trading. Longer-term participation usually involves the conventional buy and hold approach but may also involve more active portfolio management approaches like sector rotation and investing in technically driven funds or exchange-traded funds (ETFs).
- The client's trading and investment intention, that is, the client's preferred mode of participation in the markets and style of trading or investment
- The client's market and performance expectation, which includes:
  - The client's personal beliefs, expectations, biases, and opinions about whether a market is currently bullish or bearish or will be so sometime in the future
  - The client's personal beliefs, expectations, biases, and opinions about current and future performance returns
- A client's risk capacity, which is the amount of risk that a client can handle or tolerate, and may be categorized as either:
  - Risk Seeking (aggressive)—more willing to take an *above average* level of risk
  - Risk Averse (conservative)—less willing to take an *above average* level of risk

Unfortunately, the determination as to whether risk is *above average* or otherwise is, at best, subjective.

Also note that risk-seeking behavior does not always imply a more aggressive market participant, nor does risk-averse behavior always imply a more conservative market participant. As you will shortly see, there are many ways to define aggressive and conservative behavior.

26.2 AGGRESSIVE AND CONSERVATIVE MARKET PARTICIPATION

There is much confusion when traders or investors refer to being aggressive or conservative when participating in the markets. As you will see, *in most cases* the participants are neither completely aggressive nor conservative in behavior, but are in most cases a *combination of both*.

Scenarios where the market participants are both risk seeking and risk averse with respect to price and time, occur in

- Long entries taken below resistance in an uptrend
- Short entries taken above support in a downtrend
- Long entries taken just below a failed support
- Short entries taken just above a failed resistance

Scenarios where the market participants are risk averse with respect to both price and time occur in:

- Very early short or long entries with respect to support or resistance

Scenarios where the market participants are risk seeking with respect to both price and time occur in:

- Very late short or long entries with respect to support or resistance
- Very early or premature long entries above support in a downtrend (both aggressive)
- Very early or premature short entries below resistance in an uptrend (both aggressive)

Behavior Profile for Entries

There are basically three elements to consider when trying to determine if a market participant is aggressive or conservative on entry:

1. Market participants can be aggressive or conservative in their *time of entry*
2. Market participants can be aggressive or conservative in their *price on entry*
3. Market participants can be aggressive or conservative in their *risk size at entry*

Behavior Profile for Exits

Similarly, there are three elements to consider when trying to determine if a market participant is aggressive or conservative on exit:

1. Market participants can be aggressive or conservative in their *time of exit*
2. Market participants can be aggressive or conservative in their *price on exit*
3. Market participants can be aggressive or conservative in their *risk size at exit*

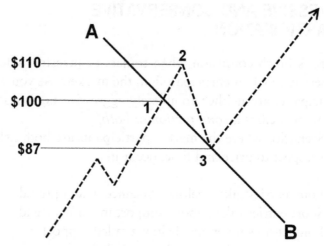

FIGURE 26.1 Risk Profile for Long Entries.

For all practical purposes, the phrase *risk seeking* may be used interchangeably with aggressive and the phrase *risk averse* may similarly be used interchangeably with conservative.

Therefore a trader or client may be risk seeking or aggressive with respect to the time of entry *by not requiring any price confirmation* of the expected move prior to entry. A trader or client may also be risk seeking or aggressive with respect to the price on entry by entering the market at a *less-favorable* price.

Refer to Figure 26.1. Let us assume that we intend to initiate a long position. We see price approaching the downtrend line AB from below.

If we bought into the market at Point 1 at $100, we have committed risk capital to the market before confirming whether price was able to penetrate the downtrend line AB. We say that our *time of entry* is aggressive, since we entered the market before the confirmation of a breakout. On the other hand, we would have bought into the market at a much cheaper price, making it less of a risk. We therefore say that we are *conservative with respect to the price* on entry. As you can see, the participant is both aggressive and conservative at the same time, with respect to time and price.

If we bought into the market at Point 2 instead, we say that we are *conservative with respect to the time* of entry, since we already have confirmation of the upside breakout, which represents less of a risk. One thing we need to remember is that *confirmation is not a guarantee* that price will continue to traverse in the expected direction of the breakout or reversal. It is merely proof that price has the ability to penetrate a certain technical barrier. At Point 2, we also say that we are *aggressive with respect to the price on entry*, as we are buying it at a higher price, which is less advantageous and represents a higher risk to a trading account.

Finally, if we had decided to buy in at Point 3, we would say that we were *aggressive with respect to the time of entry* as the market has not proven that it was capable of rebounding off the downtrend line AB. The pullback at Point 3 was not as yet confirmed by price action. We would also say that we were *conservative with respect to the price on entry* as we bought in at a lower price, resulting in a lower risk exposure.

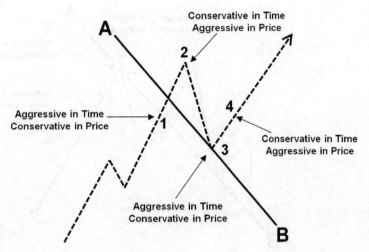

FIGURE 26.2 Risk Profile for Long Entries.

Now refer to Figure 26.2. We see that if we further decide to buy in at Point 4 after confirming the upside pullback from the downtrend line, our participation would be categorized simply as *conservative in time but aggressive in price*.

At this juncture, it is important to realize that the determination of whether a particular entry is risk seeking or risk averse is essentially a comparative measure. For example, an entry or exit is only considered risk seeking or risk averse when compared to another entry or exit, with respect to time and price. *It is strictly a relative measure.*

Let us now consider the case for short entries. Please refer to Figure 26.3. If we shorted at Point 1 at $110, we would be categorized as being risk seeking or aggressive *with respect to the time of entry* since we have no confirmation that price has reversed or been thrown back off the uptrend line AB. At the same time, we would also be regarded as risk averse or conservative *with respect to the price on entry* since we shorted at a much higher and therefore more favorable price. Entry at Point 2 at $100 would be regarded as risk averse or conservative with respect to

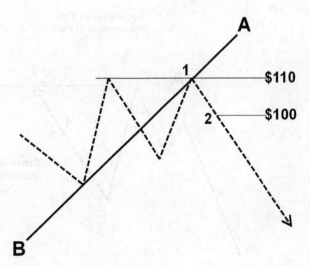

FIGURE 26.3 Risk Profile for Short Entries.

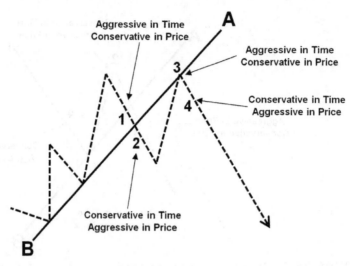

FIGURE 26.4 Risk Profile for Short Entries.

the time of entry since we have already received confirmation of a throwback off the uptrend line AB and prices are now headed downward. But the entry would also be regarded as risk seeking or aggressive with respect to the price on entry, since we are shorting at a less favorable price.

Refer to Figure 26.4. If we shorted at Point 1, before price breached the uptrend line AB, our entry would be regarded as risk seeking or aggressive with respect to time but conservative with respect to price. And if we shorted at Point 2, after confirmation of a price violation of uptrend line AB, our entry would be considered as aggressive in price.

We shall now turn our attention to exits. Refer to Figure 26.5. Assume that we bought in at a much lower price and are now considering exiting the market with a profit. Consider exiting at Point 1, which is below some significant resistance level AB. Exiting at this level would be considered conservative with respect to the time of exit, since we have obviated the possibility of any further loss.

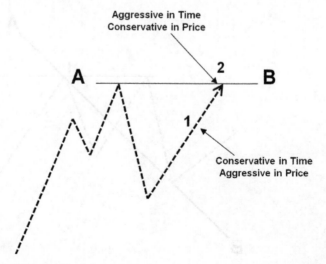

FIGURE 26.5 Risk Profile for Long Exits.

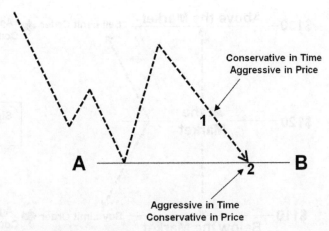

FIGURE 26.6 Risk Profile for Short Exits.

One important overriding principle in trading is the anticipation and application of the worst-case scenario outcome (WCS). This means that we always consider all situations with respect to the WCS outcome. We *never* plan for or expect the best-case scenario outcome to unfold. The WCS principle is the basis of many money-management applications. Reverting to best-case scenario expectations will eventually prove fatal in trading. Hence, in our example, applying the WCS principle implies that staying in the market increases the probability that the market may move adversely against a position. Therefore, exiting early is regarded as a conservative move, with respect to the time of exit. But at Point 1, our exit would be seen as aggressive with respect to the price of exit, as we exited at a less-favorable price. In similar fashion, exiting at point 2 would be regarded as aggressive with respect to the time of exit since we remained in the market for a much longer time, increasing the chances that price may unexpectedly move aversely against the long position. But the exit would also be seen as conservative in price on exit, since we exited at a more profitable price with respect to our long entry.

Refer now to Figure 26.6. Accordingly, we now understand why for a short exit, Point 1 would be regarded as risk averse or conservative with respect to time of entry but aggressive with respect to the price on exit, and for Point 2, it would be regarded as aggressive with respect to time but conservative with respect to the price on exit.

Effects of High Leverage on being Aggressive or Conservative with Respect to the Price on Entry

The main deciding factor for being regarded as either aggressive or conservative in the price on entry is the amount of capital at risk resulting from entering at a less or more favorable price. Entering long at a higher price, with all else being equal, demands more risk capital, hence it is deemed more aggressive.

But with higher leverage, traders need only to put up a small deposit or margin in order to participate in the market. The risk capital required is significantly less. The running profit and loss is of far greater relevance in such situations. Therefore, with higher leverage, the degree or level of aggressiveness or conservativeness that is attributed to entries with respect to the price on entry starts to lose its

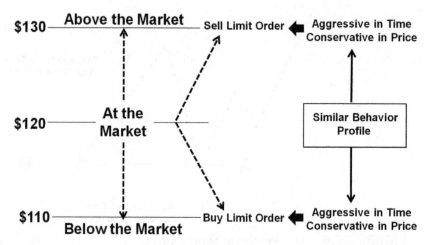

FIGURE 26.7 Risk Profile of a Counter-Trend Trader.

significance and relevance. At *extremely* high levels of leverage, the concept of aggressiveness and conservativeness with respect to the price on entry or exit diminishes rapidly, and may even be rendered somewhat redundant.

Consequently, with progressively higher leverage, the degree of aggressiveness and conservativeness associated with the time of entry becomes substantially more relevant and significant. This explains why *market timing* is seen as an essential feature in margin trading.

Behavioral Profile–Based Entry Orders

In a situation where a trader is concerned with being more risk averse or conservative with respect to the price on entry rather than time of entry, participation in the market via the use of buy or sell *limit orders* may be more appropriate and better suited to the behavioral profile of the trader. Conversely, for traders concerned with being more conservative in the time of entry rather than in the price on entry, participation in the market via the use of buy and sell *stop entry orders* may be more appropriate. See Figures 26.7 and 26.8.

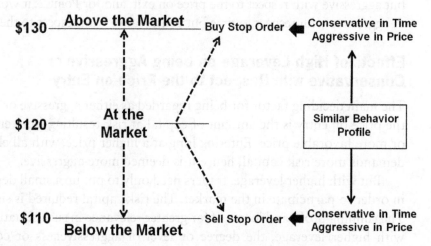

FIGURE 26.8 Risk Profile of a Breakout/Momentum Trader.

Summarizing Behavioral Profile According to Price and Time of Entry

Generally speaking, with the exclusion of late entries, the higher the price of a long entry, the more aggressive in price and conservative in time of entry it becomes. In similar fashion, with the exclusion of late entries, the lower the price of a short entry, the more aggressive in price and conservative in time of entry it becomes. But at high levels of leverage, the degree of aggressiveness and conservativeness with respect to the time of entry becomes increasingly more important than that of the price on entry.

On Risk Size

We must also consider the *risk size*, when trying to define aggressive or conservative behavior, be it in percentage of capital or simple absolute dollar terms.

Though we have already discussed how price and time affect the way we categorize aggressive and conservative behavior, we must also consider the amount of capital at risk during entries and exits.

To assess whether the risk size involved is aggressive or conservative, we need to *compare* the capital at risk between different entries and exits. As expected, it is a relative measure.

See Figure 26.9. Using A as our benchmark or baseline entry for risk size, we see clearly that entry B is comparatively more conservative in terms of risk size since the amount of risk capital exposed on entry is less than that in A. In B, the trader risked 80 shares at $100, making the total dollar risk $8,000, which is less than the $10,000 capital invested in A. Scenario C is considered more aggressive in risk size, when compared to A or B. But at entry D, though buying in at a very unfavorable price of $125, the maximum dollar risk exposed is identical to that in A. Hence we say that entry D is neutral in risk size on entry when compared to A.

When Do Conservative Entries Transform into Aggressive Ones?

Let us consider the following scenario depicted in Figure 26.10. Assume that we have a breakout of a prior resistance level at $100. As we now know, any long

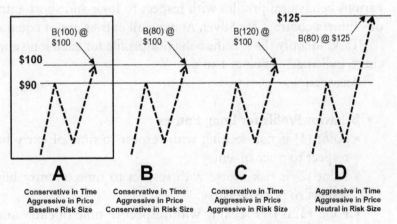

FIGURE 26.9 Risk Profile for Long Entries (Time, Price, and Risk Size).

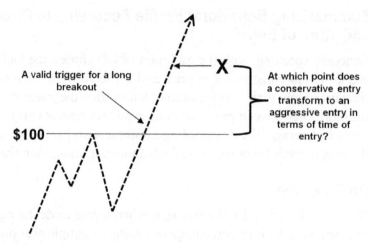

FIGURE 26.10 Risk Profile for Late Long Entries.

entry above that level is conservative in time but aggressive in price. But upon applying the WCS principle, we immediately realize that the longer we refrain from entering, the greater the probability that price may move *adversely* with respect to our intended long entry. Hence, the later the entry, the greater the chance of entering at a point highly unfavorable in price, where price may in fact be overextended or exhausted, with the market anticipating a correction. Therefore, overly late entries may be regarded as both aggressive with respect to the time *and* price on entry, in spite of having price confirmation. One way a trader can mitigate this risk is to enter with a more conservative risk size, thereby rebalancing the entire risk outlook.

On Behavioral Profile and Stoplosses

For stoplosses, we only refer to profiling risk with respect to risk size. As such, a large stopsize is better suited to traders who are risk seeking with respect to *risk size* on exit, whereas a smaller stopsize is more appropriate for traders who are more risk averse with respect to risk size.

Example: Refer to Figure 26.11. The following is an exercise in identifying the various behavioral profiles with respect to long and short entries on the continuous futures contract for Silver. Assume all entries are of equal risk size.

Task: Identify the specific behavior profile for each long and short entry on the chart, indicated at points 1 to 6.

Answers:

- **Behavior Profile for Long Entries**
  - Point (1) is risk seeking with respect to time of entry but risk averse with respect to price on entry
  - Point (2) is risk averse with respect to time of entry but risk seeking with respect to price on entry
  - Point (3) is risk seeking with respect to time of entry and risk seeking with respect to price on entry

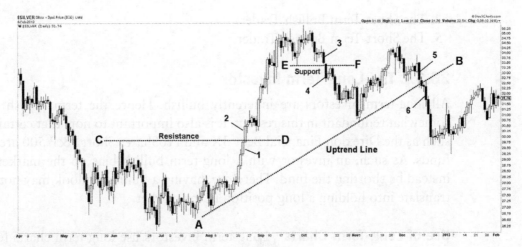

FIGURE 26.11 Risk Profile for Long and Short Entries.
Courtesy of Stockcharts.com

- ▪ Point (4) is risk seeking with respect to time of entry and risk seeking with respect to price on entry
- ▪ Point (5) is risk seeking with respect to time of entry and risk seeking with respect to price on entry
- ▪ Point (6) is risk seeking with respect to time of entry and risk seeking with respect to price on entry
- **Behavior Profile for Short Entries**
  - ▪ Point (1) is risk seeking with respect to time of entry and risk seeking with respect to price on entry
  - ▪ Point (2) is risk seeking with respect to time of entry but risk averse with respect to price on entry
  - ▪ Point (3) is risk seeking with respect to time of entry but risk averse with respect to price on entry
  - ▪ Point (4) is risk averse with respect to time of entry but risk seeking with respect to price on entry
  - ▪ Point (5) is risk seeking with respect to time of entry but risk averse with respect to price on entry
  - ▪ Point (6) is risk averse with respect to time of entry but risk seeking with respect to price on entry

26.3 CATEGORIZING CLIENTS ACCORDING TO TERM OUTLOOK AND SENTIMENT

The five main client categories, based on duration of a client's outlook and his or her sentiments on the market, are:

1. The Long-Term Investor
2. The Medium-Term Bullish Trader
3. The Medium-Term Bearish Trader

4. The Short-Term Bullish Trader
5. The Short-Term Bearish Trader

26.3.1 The Long-Term Investor

All long-term investors are inherently bullish. Hence the term bullish may be somewhat redundant in this respect. It is also important to note that certain funds such as the Direxion Financial Bear 3X and ProShares Short S&P 500 are *inverse* funds. As such, an investor with a long-term bullish bias on the market would instead be shorting the fund. Therefore, having a bullish outlook may not always translate into holding a long position in the market.

Use of Long-Term Charts Long-term investors use long-term charts for trend identification as well as for signaling potential setups for entries. They also use the long-term chart for locating important action points or *triggers* for initiating entries into the market as well as exits at predetermined price targets and stoploss levels, including price levels that would be expedient for the additional scaling in of new or out of current positions.

Use of Medium-Term Charts Long-term investors may also refer to important technical and actionable levels on medium-term charts to initiate new positions, add to or reduce positions by scaling in or out, or exit the market altogether. This allows for a *finer* level of participation in the markets, allowing for a lower-risk exposure, which is most advantageous. One perfect example is that of *buying the dips* in an uptrend, which is best identified and executed on the medium- or shorter-term charts.

On the contrary, long-term investors who have turned bearish may require:

- Technical levels whereby potentially lower-risk (cheaper) additions may be made to the existing portfolio, such as buying in at significant support levels during a correction or pullback, instead of buying in on upside breakouts, which is less cost-effective or favorable
- Technical levels whereby a reduction in positions could be made, in a defensive move, such as scaling out of some or all positions at the break of a significant support level

26.3.2 The Medium-Term Bullish or Bearish Trader

Unlike long-term investors, the medium-term traders are more inclined to resort to initiating both short and long positions in the market and normally tend to gravitate to higher leveraged instruments like Spot FOREX, Futures, or Options trading. Instead of marrying into a long-term view of the markets, the medium-term trader prefers to trade with the current *intermediate trend*, be it up or down.

The medium-term traders normally resort to short- or medium-term charts for a potentially finer and more precise technical entry and exit. These traders do not usually use the longer-term charts for entry, as most medium-term traders have limited trading capital that normally necessitates a much smaller stop size, which is best located on the medium- or short-term chart.

Use of Long-Term Charts Long-term charts are again used primarily to confirm if the medium-term entries are initiated in the direction of the prevailing or larger trend, as trading in the direction of the larger trend is regarded as a less risky and more advantageous venture.

Use of Short-Term Charts The medium-term trader may also prefer important technical levels on short-term charts to initiate new positions, add to or reduce positions by scaling in or out, or to exit the market altogether. This affords the medium-term trader a finer level of participation in the markets, allowing for a lower risk exposure when initiating breakout and reversal trades.

In summary, the medium-term trader therefore refers to the short- or medium-term charts for significant technical levels to enter, add, reduce, or exit the market, while referring to the long-term chart for trend identification purposes.

Medium-term traders may also look for:

- Technical levels whereby potentially lower-risk additions may be made to existing positions, such as buying at significant support levels during a correction or reversal instead of buying on upside breakouts, which is less cost effective
- Technical levels whereby a reduction in positions may be made, in a defensive move, such as scaling out of some or all positions at the break of any significant support, especially on the long-term charts
- Technical levels whereby shorting is advantageous, especially at the break of any significant support

26.3.3 The Short-Term Bullish or Bearish Trader

The shorter-term trader normally resorts to using the short-term charts for initiating trades as most short-term traders have very limited trading funds and therefore cannot typically afford to place large stoplosses. They identify and execute trades at the closest significant trigger levels, usually with fairly tight stops.

Use of Long- and Medium-Term Charts Long- and medium-term charts are used primarily to confirm if the short-term entries are initiated in the direction of the prevailing or larger trend. Short-term traders may also identify significant support and resistance levels on the long- and medium-term charts to alert them to any potential action points, for example, the breach of a *significantly clear and obvious* long-term trend line which was not visible on the short-term chart. Nonetheless, entries based on the breach of longer-term support and resistance is executed on the short-term charts.

Summarizing, the short-term trader therefore refers to the short-term charts for significant technical levels to enter, add, reduce, or exit the market, while referring to the medium- and long-term charts for technically significant price levels and trend identification.

Short-term traders may also look for:

- Technical levels whereby potentially lower-risk additions may be made to existing positions, such as buying at significant support levels and shorting at resistance, instead of trading breakouts which is less cost-effective
- Technical levels whereby a reduction in positions may be made, in a defensive move, such as scaling out of some or all positions at the break of any significant support
- Technical levels whereby shorting is advantageous, especially at the break of any significant support

26.4 THE SEVEN PARTICIPATORY OPTIONS

There are seven participatory options available to any market participant, namely:

1. To enter (i.e., to initiate) a new position
2. To add to (i.e., to scale into) a position
3. To reduce the size of (i.e., to scale out of) a position
4. To exit (i.e., to fully scale out of) a position
5. To re-enter a position in the same or opposite direction
6. To fully or partially hedge a position (i.e., to neutralize or diminish directional risk)
7. To remain in cash (i.e., to refrain from holding any positions)

It must be noted that the execution of all participatory options listed above, with the exception of being in cash, should be based on the penetration or violation of a *price trigger* on the traded instrument or stock, and not merely on a signal.

26.5 TRIGGERS, SIGNALS, PRICE TARGETS, AND STOPLOSSES

26.5.1 Triggers

A trigger is an event that causes a trade to be initiated, which for most practical purposes is simply an *entry filter* at work. Triggers can be classified as either price based or non-price based. Price based triggers are regarded as the most reliable type of trigger, and are most commonly used by traders, since price is the best indicator of directional change. Non-price based triggers are also sometimes employed, especially by robotic or automated trading programs, where entries and exits are executed when a specific trading condition is met, which may or may not be directly related to the penetration of some significant price level or overlay barrier.

Price based triggers are *price penetrations* of:

- Previous support and resistance levels
- Overlay indicators such as moving averages, trendlines, channels, fixed percentage and volatility bands, Fibonacci and Gann levels, fan lines, Ichimoku clouds, Floor Trader's Pivot Points, and so on
- Some form of algorithmically derived price level based on a particular sequence or counting of bars, candlesticks, boxes, lines, or bricks (e.g., Guppy's Count Back Lines, Two Bar Breakouts, Fibonacci and Lucas Bar Counts, etc.)

Though not usually recommended, *non-price* based events, penetrations, or violations are sometimes used as a trigger to initiate a trade, and these include:

- Oscillator signal line crossovers
- Oscillator zero level crossovers (for unbounded oscillators)
- Oscillator 50 percent level crossovers (for bounded oscillators)
- Oscillator chart pattern violations
- Oscillator overbought/oversold (OBOS) level tests or breaches
- Oscillator overlay tests or breaches (e.g., RSI breaching its own Bollinger Band)

Though some market participants actually use these non-price based events as *triggers*, they are usually regarded as merely *signals*.

One of the biggest disadvantages of using non-price based triggers is most evident when there is a *significant amount of divergence* between price and an oscillator or indicator, or between various oscillators and indicators. *Standard divergence* will usually misdirect the trader or automated trading programs into believing that the trend is reversing when it may actually still be intact. Conversely, *reverse divergence* may indicate that a trend is in continuation, when in reality it may already be reversing.

Therefore:

Directional change is best confirmed using *price* itself.

Finally, all price-based triggers are considered *confirmation* of a certain price trend or reaction, whereas signals only indicate potential future price action.

26.5.2 Signals

A signal merely indicates potential bullishness or bearishness in the market. It does not indicate whether price itself is actually reversing or otherwise. Signals represent a certain precondition or setup that alerts the market participants to a potential penetration of a specific price trigger, *in anticipation* of a reversal or breakout.

Signals may also be based on some form of *overextension or exhaustion* between price action, oscillators, and overlays.

Some examples of commonly used signals are:

- Divergences between price and overlays
- Divergences between price and oscillators
- Divergences in phase between similar oscillators
- Divergences between different oscillators
- Intermarket divergence
- Specific bullish or bearish price formations (such as shooting stars, head and shoulders, catapults, etc.)
- Oscillator signal line crossovers
- Oscillator zero and 50 percent level crossovers
- Oscillator chart pattern violations
- Oscillator overbought/oversold (OBOS) level tests or breaches
- Oscillator overlay tests or breaches (e.g., Bollinger Band on RSI)
- Specific algorithmic sequences and counts that set up a bullish or bearish condition or identify exhaustion in price (e.g., Tom DeMark's TD Sequential)
- Bullish or bearish indications derived from Sentiment, Market Breadth, Statistical, Seasonal, and Behavioral indicators, and similar
- Projected cycle lows and highs
- Bullish or bearish price triggers occurring in related or closely correlated markets

26.5.3 Price Objectives or Targets

Price objectives or targets are predetermined price levels at which a trader exits from long and short positions in the market. They are popularly referred to as a *take profit* level where a position is normally exited via a:

- Buy or sell limit order (upon triggering the take profit level)
- Buy or sell stop order (upon triggering the protective stoploss)

Price targets may be based on a simple test of support and resistance, or derived using various forms of price projection based on chart patterns, Fibonacci ratios, Gann levels, money management, or on important historical and psychological price levels. Even though market participants usually use price to trigger a profit exit, signals may also be used, especially in conjunction with a protective stop.

Some examples of price objectives or targets include:

- Chart-pattern based 1:1, 2:1, and 3:1 price target projections (typically based on the chart pattern's height)
- Reward to risk ratio (R/r ratio) based profit target projections
- Technically significant price levels such as previous support and resistance levels
- Technical barriers to price in the form of overlay targets such as moving averages, trend lines, channel tops and bottoms, Ichimoku clouds, Fibonacci and Gann levels, and fans

- Significantly clear and obvious *supportive and resistive confluences* or convergences
- Horizontal and vertical counts on the Point-and-Figure charts
- Any price-based triggers, which may also be used as potential price targets

26.5.4 Stoploss Levels

Stoploss levels represent the price levels at which positions are fully or partially exited, either for profit or loss. Stoploss levels are usually based on price. Some examples include the test or breach of:

- Support levels for longs and resistance levels for shorts
- Supportive confluences for longs and resistive confluence levels for shorts
- Overlay barriers

Not all stops are technical stops. Some stops are constructed on money management principles, and may therefore be based on a simple fixed-dollar risk or a percentage of current or initial capital.

26.6 CONFIRMING AND NON-CONFIRMING PRICE ACTION AND FILTERS

In order for a reversal or breakout to occur, the exact price of entry must be known to provide confirmation that a move has indeed occurred. As seen in an earlier chapter, the application of entry filters helps traders fine tune an entry, with the intention of *filtering out unwanted price action and noise* and in the process potentially reducing the probability of experiencing false breakouts or reversals that may interfere with an otherwise good entry.

There are two important caveats. First, no filter is foolproof. And second, the act of filtering *tends to attract* or encourage more filtering as the trader attempts use a second filter with the intention of correcting one or more defects in the original filter. This process may keep repeating, in a relentless feedback cycle, as the trader struggles to create the perfect filter with zero defects! The trader eventually realizes that his or her so-called perfect filter has in fact filtered out nearly all price action, making any potential entry most improbable.

Below are the four most commonly applied entry filters, which were covered in great detail in an earlier chapter:

1. Closing Filter
2. Price Filter
3. Time Filter
4. Algorithmic Filter

Refer to Figure 26.12. The point of entry into the market depends entirely on the type of filter and the parameter setting employed. It is also possible and sometimes preferable to apply one filter on another, but as mentioned previously, care must be taken to not overcomplicate the entry process. A valid breakout

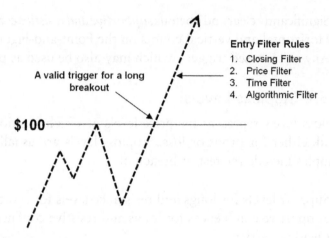

Entry Filter Rules
1. Closing Filter
2. Price Filter
3. Time Filter
4. Algorithmic Filter

A valid trigger for a long breakout

$100

FIGURE 26.12   Entry Filters.

or reversal is one where a selected filter condition is met. Depending on the filter setup, valid breakout and reversal entries could be initiated at different price levels.

It is important to note that a filter or combination of filters that a trader eventually elects must be in accordance with the type of market traded and the strategy used. It should also suit the trader's or investor's behavior profile, risk capacity, and trading objectives.

26.6.1 Reconciling Trader Profile with the Appropriate Entry Filter

Consider the behavior profile of the following four groups of market participants.

A. Risk averse with respect to time of entry but risk seeking with respect to price on entry.

These participants require confirmation of a breakout or reversal prior to initiating an entry. The entry filter is allowed to validate breakouts or reversals up to some distance beyond the initial price penetration or test, and therefore need not be too responsive. They do not mind paying a slightly less favorable price on entry.

B. Risk seeking with respect to time and price on entry.

These participants do not mind initiating an entry *prior* to an initial price penetration or test of a breakout or reversal, or very late thereafter. They do not mind paying a less favorable price on entry. In this case, should the participants elect to use an entry filter at all, it may be set to allow price the greatest possible freedom of movement before a late entry is validated, thus being more forgiving as it allows for greater noise exclusion. Should the participants anticipate entry prior to the breakout or test, the election of a pre-entry filter is more appropriate, although the actual pre-conditional settings may not be attributed with much weight.

C. Risk seeking with respect to time of entry but risk averse with respect to price on entry.

These participants do not require confirmation of a breakout or reversal prior to initiating an entry. But they do mind paying a less favorable price on entry. Therefore, should the participants anticipate an early entry prior to a breakout or test, the filtering or preconditions for that early entry will be critical and significantly more important to these participants. The pre-entry filter needs to be need fairly responsive.

D. Risk averse with respect to time and price on entry.

This risk profile reflects the behavioral characteristics of the majority of market participants. Generally speaking, for market participants who are mostly risk averse in *both* time and price, it is best to elect entry filters that are very responsive. The filter should be set to validate an entry fairly close to the initial price penetration or test of a breakout or reversal.

26.7 COLLECTING, CATEGORIZING, AND ORGANIZING TECHNICAL DATA

Before any serious analysis can be performed, the trader or analyst must first gather relevant technical data and subsequently categorize and organize it in some meaningful manner.

Assume that you were presented with a collection of charts for a certain stock. You were also provided with some charts for the index that reflected the climate or environment in which that stock was trading.

To collect and organize the data according to duration of outlook and sentiment:

1. Sort the charts for both the stock and index into *short, medium, and long term*. Short-term charts can be easily identified as they span from weeks to days, while medium-term charts span from months to weeks and long-term charts from years to months. Some traders and analysts refer to the periodicity or *timeframe* of a chart to gauge its term outlook. This can sometimes be very misleading, as an hourly chart can easily be constructed to span over a few months, tricking the analyst or trader into believing that it is a representation of medium-term market action. Regardless of the timeframe employed, it is best to observe the actual duration that the chart spans. Also, many charts like Point-and-Figure charts lack the time axis, making it sometimes quite difficult to determine which term outlook it represents. You may need to compare a Point-and-Figure chart with a few other time-based charts in order to accurately gauge whether it belongs to the short-, medium-, or long-term representation of market action.

2. Record all the bullish and bearish indications found on each chart, according to duration and bullish or bearish sentiment.

3. Arrange the information in the manner indicated in Figure 26.13.

	Long-Term Charts Major Trend (Years to Months) **(Investors)**	**Medium-Term Charts** Intermediate Trend (Months to Weeks) **(Traders)**	**Short-Term Charts** Minor Trend (Weeks to Days / Hours) **(Traders)**
Bullish Signals	1. Collect bullish technical signals & triggers for the stock 2. Collect bullish technical signals for the Index 3. Identify six participatory options for the stock	1. Collect bullish technical signals & triggers for the stock 2. Collect bullish technical signals for the Index 3. Identify six participatory options for the stock	1. Collect bullish technical signals & triggers for the stock 2. Collect bullish technical signals for the Index 3. Identify six participatory options for the stock
Bearish Signals	1. Collect bearish technical signals & triggers for the stock 2. Collect bearish technical signals for the Index 3. Identify six participatory options for the stock	1. Collect bearish technical signals & triggers for the stock 2. Collect bearish technical signals for the Index 3. Identify six participatory options for the stock	1. Collect bearish technical signals & triggers for the stock 2. Collect bearish technical signals for the Index 3. Identify six participatory options for the stock

FIGURE 26.13 Organizing Technical Data.

26.7.1 Collecting Bullish Indications

It is important to be cognizant of the fact that:

For every bullish or bearish signal or indication, there exists an equal and opposite interpretation of that signal or indication

For example, an overbought reading on the stochastic could mean that price is in a strong uptrend. It could also mean that price may be potentially overbought and as such may be due for a correction. Another scenario where this dualistic interpretation manifests itself is when there is a small breakout. It may be interpreted as price proving itself capable of penetrating the resistance level and hence be regarded as a bullish sign. Conversely, it could also be seen as a setup for potential exhaustion, with traders expecting a false breakout. Therefore, it is not difficult to see why technical analysis may sometimes prove challenging. We can never be privy to all information available, and therefore it is impossible to form an accurate or perfectly informed opinion of the markets. It is far more practical to formulate a simple working view of the markets with clearly defined risks and rewards, allowing us to limit our losses when we are wrong about the markets and letting us maximize our profit when we are right. After all, no one can truly foresee the future and we should expect, on applying the WCS principle, that many of our forecasts may be proven inaccurate.

So the next best thing to do once a market participant has formulated a certain outlook on the market is to gather all the relevant information that supports that view. From the information gathered, identify significant *key price levels* with which to define the maximum risk and minimum potential reward for maintaining that view.

Assume that we have a bullish outlook on the market. This next step is to identify all the bullish indications that will support that view, paying close attention to the key levels in that stock which we could use to manage our exposure in the market.

We collect all bullish and bearish indications from the short-, medium-, and long-term charts, in the form of bullish and bearish signals and triggers.

Below are a few examples that constitute bullish action on a chart:

- Higher highs and higher lows
- Bullish volume or open interest action
- New highs
- Swings low failures
- Upside breakouts of significant overlay indicators
- Price being contained and supported by a trendline or moving average
- Confirmation of bullishness in the broad market
- Bullish charts patterns
- No bearish divergence or overextension indicated between price and indicators
- Bullishness indicated on sentiment indicators that are not at extreme values

26.7.2 Collecting Bearish Indications

Below are a few examples that constitute bearish action on a chart:

- Lower highs and lower lows
- Bearish volume or open interest action
- New lows
- Downside breakouts of significant overlay indicators
- Swings high failures
- Price breaching a supporting trend line or moving average
- Non-confirmation of bullishness in the broad market
- Bearish charts patterns
- Bearish divergence or overextension indicated between price and indicators
- Bearishness indicated on sentiment indicators that are close to or at extreme values

26.8 MULTI-TIMEFRAME CONFIRMATION

It is very important to always refer to at least one higher and one lower *degree of trend* when considering participating in or analyzing the market. The longer-term market action (normally viewed through higher timeframe charts) is used to *identify the direction of the prevailing or larger trend* while the shorter-term price action (normally viewed through lower timeframe charts) is used to *time entries and exits* more effectively, and at the same time allowing for a lower-risk exposure as a result of trading with smaller stop sizes on the lower timeframe. Hence, in order to fully understand the current market sentiment or bias, and to effectively and efficiently participate or engage in the market, it is always wise to refer to all three degrees of trend.

Many traders employ multi-timeframe analysis (MTF) as a strategy for gauging higher-probability entries in the market. It is possible to set up the indicators and oscillators in a way that displays the values for the higher, current, and lower timeframes simultaneously on a single chart. Multi-timeframe setups were discussed in the earlier part of this handbook.

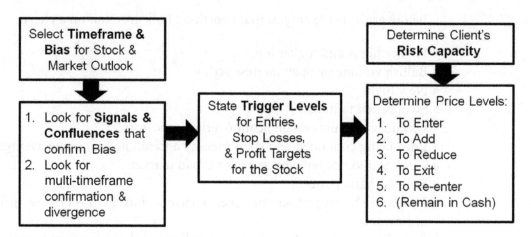

FIGURE 26.14 Decision Making Flow Chart.

26.9 RECONCILING TECHNICAL OUTLOOK WITH CLIENT INTEREST

After collecting and organizing the relevant technical data according to duration and sentiment, we proceed to apply the data in accordance with the client's objective, market, and performance expectations and risk capacity. See Figure 26.14.

The Process

1. Analyze the long-, medium-, and short-term charts of the stock in question, isolating all the bullish and bearish signals and price-based triggers

2. From the price-based triggers, identify potential price levels in the stock for the execution of the five participatory options, that is, price levels whereby we may enter a position, add to a position, reduce a position, exit the market, or initiate a hedge

3. Also identify suitable price levels for the placement of stop losses and profit targets in the stock (which are essentially the price-based trigger levels)

4. Then analyze the long- and medium-term charts of the index, isolating all the bullish and bearish signals

5. With the information from both the stock and index action, formulate an argument as to why the stock and index are both bullish or bearish

6. Provide technical reasons or evidence why a stock and its index are believed to be bullish and present that to the investors and medium-term and short-term bullish traders (repeat for the medium- and short-term bearish traders)

7. Present the clients with various scenarios for initiating, adding, reducing, hedging, and exiting the market at technically significant price levels

8. Finally, depending on the risk capacity of the client, you may have to *reconsider* certain trade recommendations. For example, you may advise against adding new positions in an upside breakout for a client who is especially risk averse with respect to the price on entry. Or you may, for another client who has an extremely bullish outlook, advise buying into a correction, especially since the client is also risk seeking with respect to price on entry. See Section 26.12 for a sample write-up.

26.10 HEDGING POSITIONS WITH DERIVATIVES

To *hedge* means to neutralize some or all directional risk associated with a position or portfolio. Traders and investors may mitigate or eliminate risk by *fully or partially* hedging a position or portfolio in the market.

Hedging can be done via the use of:

- Equal and opposite positions in the market for a fully hedged position (e.g., hedging one long position with an equally sized short position);
- Unequal opposite positions in the market for a partially hedged position (e.g., hedging two long positions with a single short position);
- Long and short call or put options based on the underlying stock or traded instrument;
- Long and short futures contracts based on the underlying stock or traded instrument; and
- Long and short a funds or ETFs/ETNs that track the underlying stock or traded instruments

When hedging with derivatives, it is very important to ensure that the tick values, contract limitations, and trading costs are fully accounted for in order for the hedge to work properly.

26.11 CHAPTER SUMMARY

As we have seen, we may categorize market partipants via their particular risk profiles. We also observed how these profiles relate to various choices with respect to order entry. In addition, we learned how a trader may be both conservative and aggressive at the same, with respect to time of entry and price on entry. There were situations where a trader could also be fully aggressive or conservative. It is always imperative that the practitioner understands his or her clients' risk and behavior profiles in order to better advise them with regard to appropriate investment recommendations and decisions.

CHAPTER 26 REVIEW QUESTIONS

1. Explain why client profiling is not merely about understanding their psychological makeup.
2. Describe why it may be difficult to exit all positions on behalf of your client.
3. Describe ways in which you would help your client understand that losses resulting from following a trading plan are justifiable.
4. Explain how you would use overreactions in the market to alter your overall capital exposure.
5. How much information about the daily management of a client's position should be made known to the client? Where would you draw the line?
6. "For every bullish or bearish signal or indication, there exists an equal and opposite interpretation of that signal or indication." Discuss with examples.

7. What is the behavior profile of a trader who goes long at support?

8. Under what conditions would you reconsider taking on a client?

REFERENCES

Bernstein, Jake. 1993. *The Investor's Quotient*. Hoboken, NJ: John Wiley & Sons.

Pompian, Michael. 2006. *Behavioral Finance and Wealth Management*. Hoboken, NJ: John Wiley & Sons.

Tvede, Lars. 2002. *The Psychology of Finance*. Hoboken, NJ: John Wiley & Sons.

CHAPTER 27

Integrated Technical Analysis

Technical analysis works best when it is applied in a timely and effective manner. Effective application consists of looking for areas of supportive and resistive confluences or clusters, which tend to provide the strongest and most reliable barriers to price. Such clustering may be purely in the price domain, but learning to identify clustering in both the time and price-time domains will greatly improve the accuracy and reliability of any forecast. In this chapter, we will discuss all three forms of clustering and apply technical analysis in the most efficacious manner, that is, via an integrated approach.

27.1 THE INTEGRATED COMPONENTS OF TECHNICAL ANALYSIS

Integrated technical analysis is the art and science of locating significantly clear and obvious price levels or zones comprising a concentration of supportive or resistive indications. Such concentrations are usually referred to as bullish or bearish *clusters*, *confluences*, *agreements*, or *convergences*.

Significantly Clear and Obvious Inflection Points

Clusters founded on significant inflection points tend to be more reliable. Inflection points are regarded as *significantly clear and obvious* if:

- They are separated by a reasonable distance.
- There is no significant intervening price action that either exceeds the prices between two inflection points or draws attention away from them.
- They are located at the end of an extended and aggressive trend.
- The price level at which they are situated has been tested multiple times.
- They coincide with projected cycle peaks and troughs.
- They coincide with projected chart pattern and money management–based price targets.
- They coincide with psychologically important numbers.
- They coincide with significant overbought and oversold levels on the window oscillators.
- They are supported by confirmatory volume and open interest action.
- They represent a very popular bar chart or Japanese candlestick pattern breakout or reaction level.
- They are part of a bullish or bearish cluster of indicator overlays.

Reliability of Clusters and Single Overlay Barriers

Before proceeding any further, it is important to define what is meant by the term *reliable*. Any single overlay or price cluster, including any prior support or resistance, is regarded as reliable if it acts as an effective barrier to price. The more it acts as a barrier to price, the more it is considered reliable. Note that only multiple overlays that are in proximity with each other will be regarded as a cluster. It is important to note that the point at which multiple overlays fail to represent a cluster is somewhat subjective and depends largely on the degree and type of filtering employed. (See Figure 27.1.)

Figure 27.1 shows price, as indicated on the left side of the illustration, having very little regard for the three overlay barriers, consisting of a Fibonacci 168.2 percent projection level, a prior support, and a Gann three-eighths support level. The price cluster on the right side of the illustration is potentially more reliable, as it provides a more effective barrier to price. The illustration on the left depicts price breaching the cluster with little respect for the individual barrier levels, and is therefore regarded as less reliable.

Figure 27.2 depicts two uptrend lines with the one on the left offering very little support (and resistance) to price and therefore considered a less-reliable uptrend line. Similarly, Figure 27.3 depicts two fixed-percentage moving average bands, with the band on the left offering very little support or resistance to price and therefore considered a less-reliable overlay.

Note that only single overlays and price clusters act as potential barriers to price. Single time overlays and clusters cannot act as barriers to price. They only indicate *potential activity* in price, often with little or no indication about the:

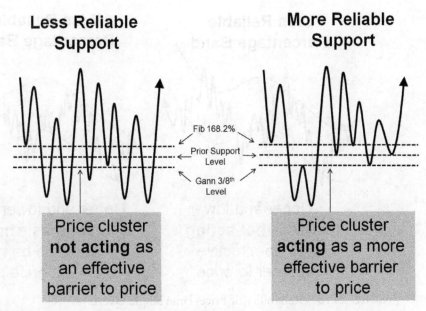

FIGURE 27.1 Reliability of Price Clusters (Multiple Barrier Overlays).

- Price level or zone at which such activity or price reaction may occur
- Type of activity, whether reversal or continuation
- Subsequent price or market direction resulting from such activity

However, an exception has to be made with respect to the projection of cycle peaks and troughs. Cycle analysis allows for the prediction of potential bullish and bearish cycle extremes, as well as, in some cases, the expected price level of these cycle extremes based on the projection of the cycle magnitude from the

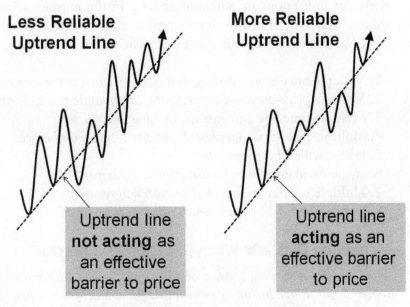

FIGURE 27.2 Reliability of a Single Dynamic Price Overlay.

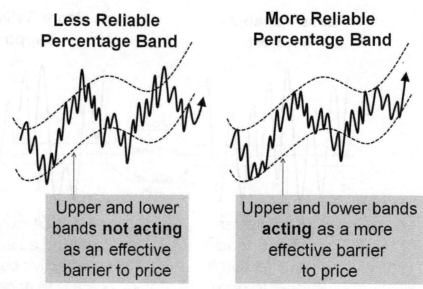

Less Reliable
Percentage Band

More Reliable
Percentage Band

Upper and lower
bands **not acting**
as an effective
barrier to price

Upper and lower bands
acting as a more
effective barrier
to price

FIGURE 27.3 Reliability of Price-Time Single Overlays.

immediately preceding peak or trough, especially in consistent and regular cycles. Refer to Chapter 20 for a detailed discussion on price and time projections via cycle analysis.

Bullish and Bearish Price Clusters

Clusters may be formed in price and time, or on a combination both elements, that is, in price-time clusters. Bullish and bearish indications are usually associated with price and price-time clusters. Bullish and bearish clustering are not usually associated with time-based projections, with the obvious exception of cycle-based projections. As mentioned earlier, most non-cycle-based time projections merely represent indications of potential activity in the market, with no indication or information about the direction or type of activity that may subsequently ensue.

Clusters may be identified in eight basic technical setups:

1. Multiple price-static level agreements, or *static price clusters*
2. Multiple price-dynamic agreements, or *dynamic price clusters*
3. Multiple time line agreements, or *time line clusters*
4. Multiple price-time agreements, or *price-time confluences*
5. Price-oscillator *agreements*
6. Single oscillators in MTF *directional agreement*
7. Multiple oscillators in STF *directional agreement*
8. Intermarket and broad market trend agreements

Identifying Clusters: When Is a Cluster a Cluster?

The task of identifying a price or time cluster may be somewhat challenging. *At which point do we include or exclude a price level from a price cluster?* Similarly, we may also ask, at which point do we include or exclude a projected time line

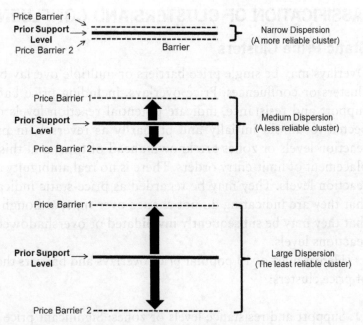

FIGURE 27.4 Dispersion of Price Cluster Levels.

from a time cluster? Figures 27.4 and 27.5 illustrate the various dispersions of price and time clusters. (TL in Figure 27.5 is short for time line).

One way to approach this is by analyzing the average dispersion of past clusters specific to a particular market. There is a fair amount of subjectivity as to what constitutes a past price cluster. Nevertheless, the practitioner should try to gain some familiarity with past cluster dispersion amounts as a basis for gauging the degree of reliability of a cluster. The strength and reliability of a cluster depends on the density of price barriers it is composed of within a range of prices. A cluster is regarded as more reliable if a greater number of barriers are concentrated within a narrower range of prices.

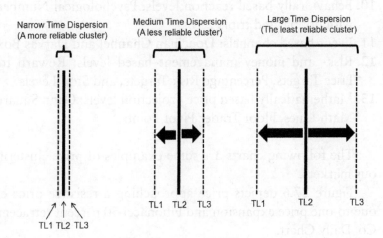

FIGURE 27.5 Dispersion of Time Cluster Levels.

27.2 CLASSIFICATION OF CLUSTERS AND CONFLUENCES

Static Price Clusters

Overlays may be single price barriers or multiple overlay barriers referred to as clusters or confluences. Price overlays, including price barrier levels like prior support and resistance, indicate potential reaction levels or zones and are expected to unfold initially and primarily as reversals in price. These potential reaction levels or zones are known ahead of time, and this allows for the early placement of limit-entry orders. There is no real ambiguity associated with these reaction levels. They may be regarded as price-static indicators since the prices that they are indicating do not change over time, although there is a possibility that they may be subsequently invalidated or overshadowed by more significant reactions levels.

Here is a list of 13 popular price overlays and barriers that may form the basis of price clusters:

1. Support and resistance levels or zones: Significant price inflection points and historical price extremes
2. Percentage-based retracement levels: Fibonacci Retracements, Gann's one-eighth, 50 percent, one-third, and one-fourth retracements
3. Percentage-based expansion levels: Fibonacci Expansions, Chart Pattern Minimum 1:1 Price Objectives
4. Percentage-based extension levels: Fibonacci Extensions
5. Percentage-based projection levels: Fibonacci Projections, The ABCD (Measured Move) Pattern
6. Retracement and projection levels: Gartley's Pattern
7. Volatility-based projection levels: Multiples of ATR and Standard Deviation Price Filters, Percentage of Price Filter
8. Algorithmically based reaction levels: DeMark's TD Sequential Bar Count, Guppy's Count Back Line
9. Pattern-based reaction levels: Japanese Candlestick and Bar Chart Based Trigger Levels
10. Behaviorally based reaction levels: Psychological Numbers (prices associated with double and triple zeros)
11. Event-based channels: Donchian Channel and Darvas Box Breakout Levels
12. Risk- and money management–based levels: Reward to Risk Ratio–Based Price Targets, Percentage Risk Targets, and Stop Levels
13. Mathematically based price projection levels: Gann Squaring of Price, Murray Math Lines, Floor Trader Pivot Points

The following charts are some examples of price clustering in action in various markets.

Figure 27.6 depicts price approaching a resistive price cluster comprising a one-to-one price expansion and Fibonacci 50 percent retracement level on the 3M Co. Daily Chart.

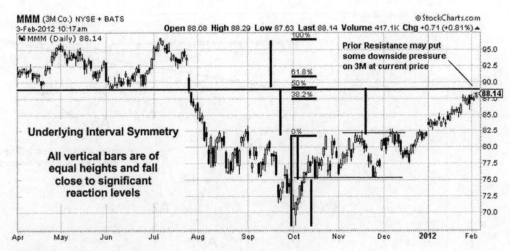

FIGURE 27.6 Price Clustering on the 3M Daily Chart.
Courtesy of Stockcharts.com

Figure 27.7 depicts price being rejected at a resistive price cluster comprising a Gann Level, prior resistance, and a 61.8 percent Fibonacci retracement level on the 4-hour Gold chart.

Figure 27.8 depicts price approaching a resistive price cluster comprising a double 61.8 percent Fibonacci projection level and prior resistance on the daily USDCHF chart. The Fibonacci projection levels are range projections of AB from C. (Three sets of projections on the charts are AB from C, A_2B from C, and A_3B_2 from C_2.)

Figure 27.9 depicts price approaching an intermarket price barrier confluence across the Daily AUDUSD, EURUSD, XAUUSD, and XAGUSD charts.

Figure 27.10 depicts price approaching a resistive price confluence at around the $36.40 price level, comprising various Fibonacci retracements, a prior support

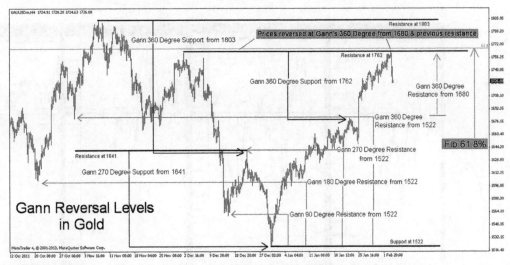

FIGURE 27.7 Price Clustering on the Four-Hour Gold Chart.
Source: MetaTrader 4

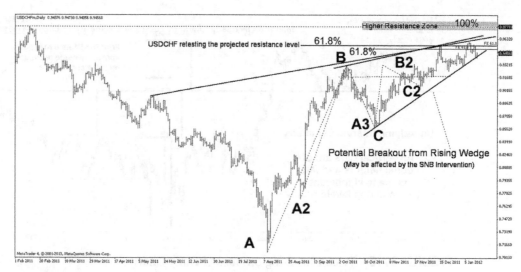

FIGURE 27.8 Price Clustering on the Daily USDCHF Chart.
Source: MetaTrader 4

(formed around 9 August 2011), and an uptrending internal line on the Daily Silver Chart. Notice also a couple more price confluences concentrated around the $40.80 and $49.95 price levels.

Figure 27.11 is a daily chart of the EURUSD. It depicts price approaching a resistive price cluster at Point 1, comprising a resistive channel top and a prior resistive price level (that is, support turned resistance) which formed around the 26th of March. Note that Point 1 also coincided with an overbought signal on the stochastics with above average volume. Notice that price declined after testing the resistive confluence at Point 1. Point 2 depicts another resistive confluence comprising a channel top and a prior resistance (Point 1). Point 2 also coincided

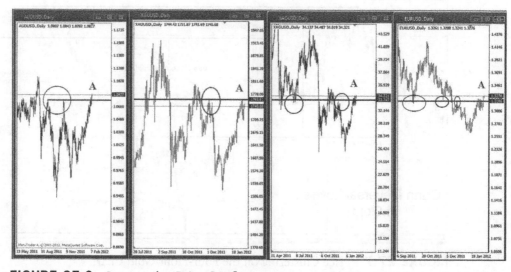

FIGURE 27.9 Intermarket Price Confluence.
Source: MetaTrader 4

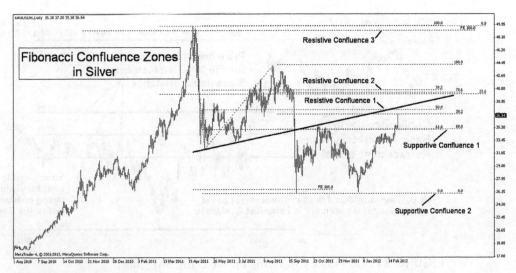

FIGURE 27.10 Fibonacci-Based Price Clusters on the Daily Silver Charts.
Source: MetaTrader 4

with an overbought signal on the stochastics with above average volume. Again, notice how price declined after testing the resistive confluence at Point 2. Points 3 and 4, comprising a test of a larger downtrending channel top and a two prior resistive price levels formed on the 29th of March and 2nd of April. Both points also coincided with overbought stochastics and above average volume.

Figure 27.12 depicts a price cluster comprising a multi-tested prior resistance level and a 50 percent Fibonacci retracement level on the daily chart of 3M Co. Note that the area of application for the Fibonacci retracement levels lies after the lowest price in October 2011. Notice how prices retested the resistive confluence level in November and again in December 2011.

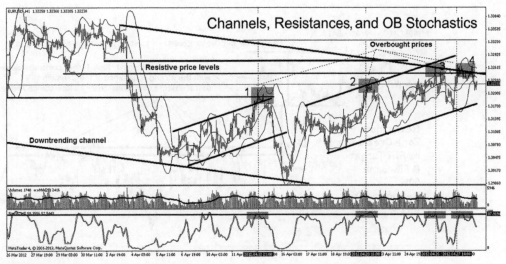

FIGURE 27.11 Price Confluence on the Daily EURUSD Chart.
Source: MetaTrader 4

FIGURE 27.12 Price Clustering on the Daily 3M Chart.
Courtesy of Stockcharts.com

Figure 27.13 depicts a price cluster comprising a one-to-one downside reward-to-risk ratio-based expansion, Fibonacci 50 percent retracement level, and a multi-tested resistance level around the $82 price level, on the Daily 3M Chart.

Figure 27.14 depicts price clustering around prior support levels at the right shoulder of an inverted head and shoulders formation on the daily 3M Co. chart, coinciding with the pivot point support levels.

Figure 27.15 depicts the use of a range filter to identify significant inflection points on the daily Gold chart. The threshold for the one-period ATR values is set at a level where only a small percentage of signals is allowed through, thereby providing the most significant overextended price activity as a guide to predicting potential reversals in price that frequently accompany these historically extreme values. It also provides the most significant inflection points upon which to apply Fibonacci and Gann analysis, draw trendlines and channels, and so on. Notice

FIGURE 27.13 Price Cluster on the Daily 3M Chart.
Courtesy of Stockcharts.com

FIGURE 27.14 Price Clustering around the Right Shoulder on the Daily 3M Chart.
Courtesy of Stockcharts.com

the confluence of various trendlines, channels, and prior support/resistance levels coinciding with the range spikes, providing for a potentially more reliable price reaction.

Figure 27.16 depicts bullish and bearish price confluences comprising prior support and resistance, a horizontal channel, and Bollinger bands on the hourly AUDUSD Chart. These confluences represent key support and resistance zones in price.

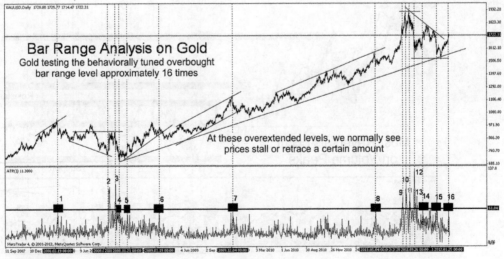

FIGURE 27.15 Range Filter on the Daily Gold Chart.
Source: MetaTrader 4

859

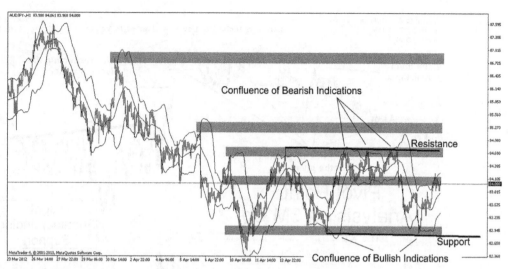

FIGURE 27.16 Price Confluences on the Hourly AUDUSD Chart.
Source: MetaTrader 4

Figure 27.17 depicts price on the same chart as Figure 27.16, but with the addition of volume spikes on the hourly AUDUSD chart. Reversals in price usually occur on volume spikes.

Dynamic Price Clusters

Single or multiple overlays that change their value with respect to time are also expected to unfold initially and primarily as reversals in price. There is no pre-knowledge of the precise levels or zones of potential future reversals until price actually tests or makes contact with these overlays. As such, there is some ambiguity associated with the final determination of these reaction levels. They may therefore be regarded as *price-dynamic* indicators, since the prices that they are indicating

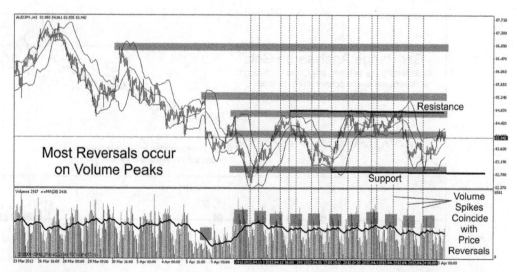

FIGURE 27.17 Price Confluences with Volume Action on the Hourly AUDUSD Chart.
Source: MetaTrader 4

change over time. These overlays are observed as traversing diagonally across the charts, unlike price overlays where all information about future price reaction levels are located horizontally, purely on the price axis. Note that although these price-dynamic overlays depend on time to ultimately determine the precise reaction levels, they are predicated or based on price information, mainly in the form of significant inflection points and average price.

Below is a list of popular price-dynamic overlays that form the basis of dynamic price clusters:

1. Trendlines and channels: Uptrending and Downtrending Lines and Channels, Linear Regression Lines
2. Event-based channels: Donchian Channels
3. Fixed percentage and price bands: Moving Average Fixed Percentage Bands, Fixed Price Bands
4. Volatility-based moving average bands: Starc and Keltner Bands, ATR Bands, Bollinger Bands
5. Price averaging: Moving Averages, Ichimoku Overlays
6. Geometric formations: Andrew's Pitchfork, Gann's Grid

The following charts are some examples of dynamic price clustering in action in various markets.

Figure 27.18 depicts dynamic price confluence at Point X, comprising prior support, a downtrending channel providing support at Point X, and a 100 percent Fibonacci downside projection of the range AB from Point C, on the Daily EURUSD Chart.

Figure 27.19 depicts price approaching a price-dynamic and price-static confluence comprising prior resistance, Andrew's Pitchfork median line, and Fibonacci 38.2 percent and 50 percent retracements on the daily Gold chart. Additional bearish evidence is signaled by the cycle-tuned stochastics being at the overbought level.

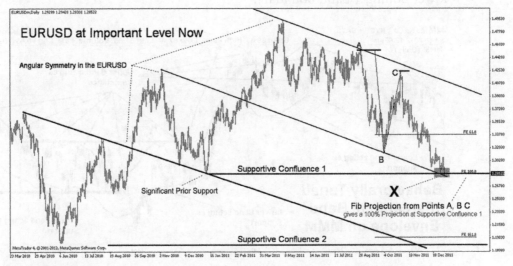

FIGURE 27.18 Dynamic Price Confluence on the Daily EURUSD Chart.
Source: MetaTrader 4

FIGURE 27.19 Dynamic and Static Price Confluence on the Daily Gold Chart.
Source: MetaTrader 4

Figure 27.20 depicts a price-dynamic and price-static confluence comprising prior support and resistance being contained by a fixed percentage band on the daily Gold chart.

Figure 27.21 depicts price currently finding resistance at a bearish dynamic price confluence comprising a resistive Gann's grid line coinciding with a downtrending channel on the daily Silver chart.

Figure 27.22 depicts dynamic and static price confluence comprising a fixed percentage envelope, prior support and resistance, channels, and trendlines on the daily Gold chart. The dynamic and static price confluence provided a high-probability short entry at the test of trendlines T1 and T2. Short entries at Point X at the test of the channel top and upper fixed percentage band also provided for a profitable trade. Point Y now represents a potential support at the channel bottom, comprising a supportive convergence of both the lower channel line and lower Bollinger band boundary.

FIGURE 27.20 Dynamic and Static Price Confluence the Daily Gold Chart.
Courtesy of Stockcharts.com

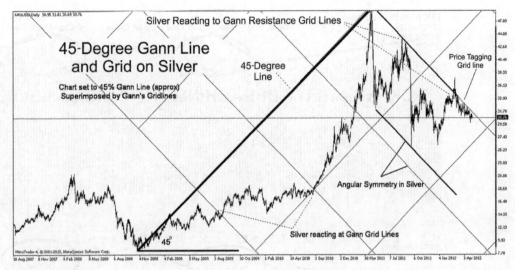

FIGURE 27.21 Dynamic Price Confluence the Daily Silver Chart.
Source: MetaTrader 4

Figure 27.23 depicts dynamic price filtering via a 2-sigma Bollinger band setting on the NYSE TICK Index chart. The market tends to bottom whenever the TICK level becomes overextended with respect to the 2-Sigma upper band level. Hence, the convergence of TICK values testing its historical extremes and the breaching the volatility range provides for a reasonable guide to predicting potential market bottoms.

Figure 27.24 depicts dynamic price filtering via a 5 percent band on the daily Silver intercontract price ratio. The intercontract price ratio is the price of the one futures contract month divided by the price of one futures contract from a different month. Every time the ratio exceeds the upper or lower bands, Silver tends to reverse in the markets, as can been at Points 1 to 9. The practitioner should therefore seek out any price barriers that may coincide with these volatility range breakouts as a means of pinpointing appropriate entries.

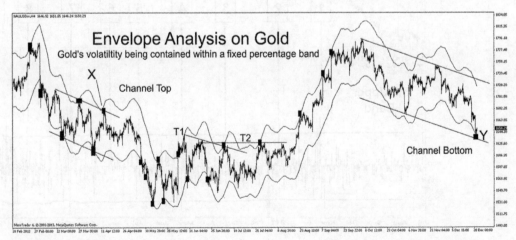

FIGURE 27.22 Dynamic and Static Price Confluence on the Daily Gold Chart.
Source: MetaTrader 4

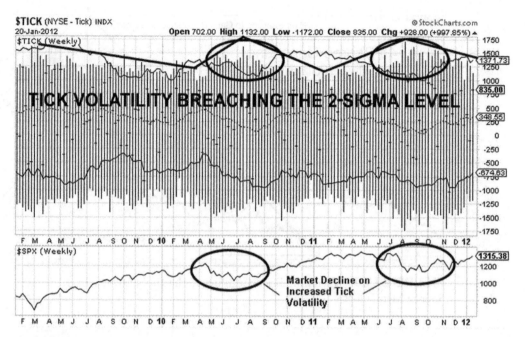

FIGURE 27.23 Dynamic Price Filtering on the NYSE TICK Index Chart.
Courtesy of Stockcharts.com

FIGURE 27.24 Dynamic Price Filtering the Daily Silver Intercontract Price Ratio.
Courtesy of Stockcharts.com

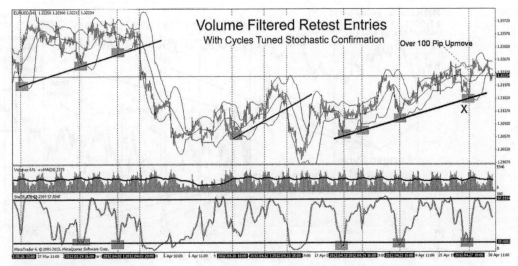

FIGURE 27.25 Dynamic Price Confluence on the Hourly EURUSD Chart.
Source: MetaTrader 4

Figure 27.25 depicts price approaching Point X, which represents a high-probability long entry. We see a bullish dynamic price confluence provided by the support of a lower Bollinger Band and uptrend line, accompanied by above average volume, and the stochastic oscillator being at the oversold (OS) level, on the hourly chart of the EURUSD. Notice how price rebounded to the upside upon testing the supportive confluence at Point X.

Time Clusters

Single time overlays and clusters indicate potential time lines of price activity. There is generally no information about the precise levels of potential reversals or reactions in price (with the exception of cycle-based projection). All information lies purely on the time axis. Just as for price-static and price-dynamic single overlays and clusters, time line predictions are predicated or based on significant inflection points in price. Forecasted time lines of potential activity are projected from significantly clear and obvious peaks and troughs.

Below is a list of popular time indicators that form the basis of time clusters:

- Period number counts: Fibonacci and Lucas Number Counts
- Varying ratio expansions of selected durations based on significant price ranges: Fibonacci Time Ratio Projections
- Number based ratio expansions of selected durations based on significant price ranges: Fibonacci Time Zone Projections
- Fixed one-to-one ratio expansions of selected durations based on significant price ranges: Cycle Projection of Peaks and Troughs
- Mathematically derived projections: Gann's Square of Nine Time Projections (Circle of Time)

FIGURE 27.26 Time Clusters on the Daily 3M Co. Chart.
Courtesy of Stockcharts.com

- Geometric formations: Apex Reaction Time Line Projections
- Recurring market behavior: Seasonal Cycles and Significant Recurring Dates

The following charts are some examples of time clustering in action in various markets.

Figure 27.26 depicts time clusters comprising both longer and shorter term cycle trough projections on the Daily 3M Co. chart. Notice the stock made a bottom in October 2011 on a time line cluster, which also happens to be the head of an inverted head and shoulders formation.

Figure 27.27 depicts apex reaction time line projections on the four-hour Gold chart. Notice the consistently accurate forecast of the next potential reversal or continuation in price at the projected time lines, indicated by the arrows situated at the tip of each apex.

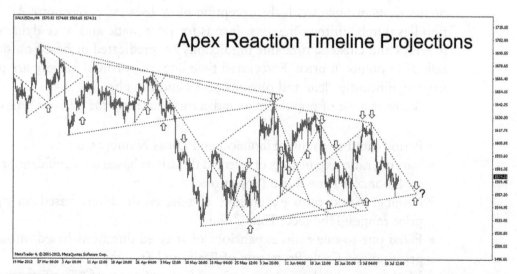

FIGURE 27.27 Apex Reaction Time Line Projections on the Four-Hour Gold Chart.
Source: MetaTrader 4

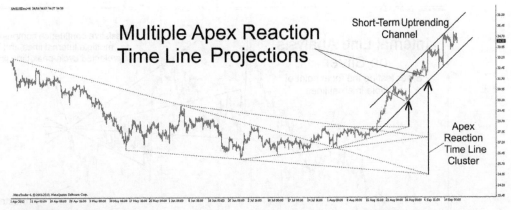

FIGURE 27.28 Apex Reaction Time Line Cluster on the Four-Hour Silver Chart.
Source: MetaTrader 4

Figure 27.28 depicts a time line cluster resulting from apex reaction projections, which tend to have a significant effect on price.

Price-Time Confluences

Price-time confluences comprise:

- Price-static single overlays and clusters
- Price-dynamic single overlays and clusters
- Time clusters

This represents the most potent form of technical analysis. It combines the highest probability reaction price levels and time lines. Such confluences are significant as they represent areas on the chart where the majority of market participants would potentially be acting upon many of the bullish or bearish signals within a very well-defined window of time. This has the potential for very strong reactions in the market, frequently precipitating rapid reversals or strong continuation of the existing trend should an unexpected violation of the confluent price zone occur.

The following charts are some examples of price-time clustering in action in various markets.

Figure 27.29 depicts a price-time confluence comprising an apex reaction time line and cycle-peak projection on the daily Silver chart.

Figure 27.30 depicts price-time confluence at Point X, comprising a cycle-peak projection and a channel top on the daily 10-Year U.S. Treasury Note chart. Notice that the Treasury note price corrected at that point.

Figure 27.31 depicts price approaching a price-time confluence comprising cycle peak projection and a resistive internal line on the daily PowerShares DB U.S. Dollar Index Bullish Fund chart.

Figure 27.32 depicts price-time confluence comprising cycle–trough projections, support from a lower regression band, and a central bank—backed support level on the daily EURCHF chart. Point X represents the best entry point for a potentially profitable long position.

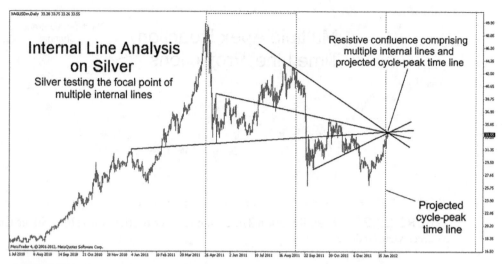

FIGURE 27.29   Price-Time Confluence on the Daily Silver Chart.
Source: MetaTrader 4

FIGURE 27.30   Price-Time Confluence on the Daily 10-Year U.S. Treasury Note Chart.
Courtesy of Stockcharts.com

FIGURE 27.31   Price-Time Confluence on the Daily PowerShares DB U.S. Dollar Index
Bullish Fund Chart.
Courtesy of Stockcharts.com

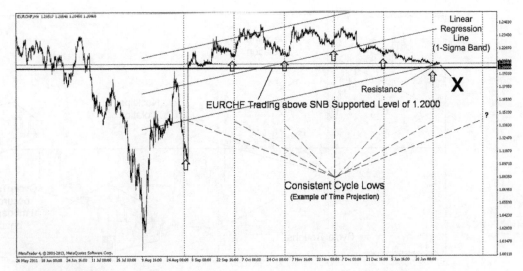

FIGURE 27.32   Price-Time Confluence on the Daily EURCHF Chart.
Source: MetaTrader 4

Figure 27.33 depicts a price-time confluence at Point X, comprising a cycle-peak projection and channel resistance on the daily AUDUSD chart.

Figure 27.34 depicts price-time confluences comprising cycle-trough projections and channel resistance on the four-hour EURUSD chart. Notice that the head-and-shoulders neckline violations all occurred as price was approaching the projected time line of a cycle trough, and that the bottom in the market occurred at a projected cycle trough.

Figure 27.35 depicts a price-time confluence at Point X, comprising an apex reaction time line projection, Bollinger Band upper band test, a 50 percent Fibonacci retracement, and a bearish double top on the daily U.S. Dollar Index chart. Notice how the index fell rapidly immediately after the price-time confluence.

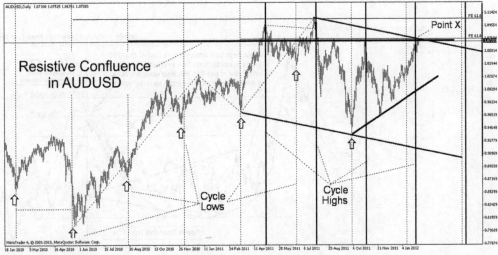

FIGURE 27.33   Price-Time Confluence the Daily AUDUSD Chart.
Source: MetaTrader 4

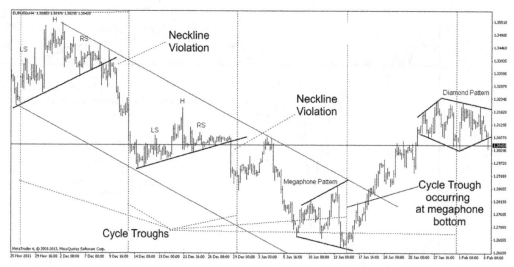

FIGURE 27.34 Price-Time Confluence on the Four-Hour EURUSD Chart.
Source: MetaTrader 4

Price-Oscillator Agreements

Market practitioners also look to agreements between price and oscillator action as a tentative confirmation of current market view. There are six basic ways of reading oscillator action, previously covered in more detail in Chapter 8, which are:

1. Overbought/oversold levels
2. Central Value Crossovers (also referred to as the zero line for unbounded oscillators and as the 50 percent level for bounded oscillators)
3. Signal line crossovers
4. Divergence between oscillator action and price action

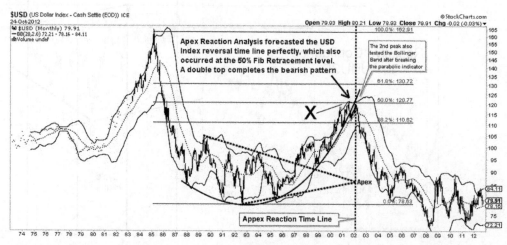

FIGURE 27.35 Price-Time Confluence on the Daily U.S. Dollar Index Chart.
Courtesy of Stockcharts.com

5. Chart pattern breakouts and pullbacks in oscillator action

6. Oscillator-on-oscillator analysis (e.g., Bollinger bands on RSI, moving average of volume, etc.)

The right choice of oscillator and lookback period is also important. Here is a very brief guide for choosing an oscillator:

- To identify current price relative to the last *n* periods: Stochastic oscillator with lookback values that are tuned to the dominant underlying cycles in the market
- To identify statistically overbought/oversold (OBOS) levels: CCI indicator
- To identify price changes between current and prices over the last *n* periods: Ratio and spread-type momentum indicators, that is, MOM and ROC indicators
- To identify volume changes over last *n* periods: Volume bars, accumulation/ distribution, OBV, money flow indicator, and so on
- To identify changes in average price over last *n* periods: RSI oscillator
- To identify changes in average bar range over last *n* periods: ATR indicator

The following charts are some examples of price-oscillator agreements in action in various markets.

Figure 27.36 depicts a price-oscillator agreement at Point X, comprising a channel top, a 161.8 percent Fibonacci projection, and overbought signals on the cycle-tuned stochastics on the four-hour USDCHF chart.

Figure 27.37 depicts price-oscillator agreements comprising prior support and oversold signals on the RSI and cycle-tuned stochastics on the daily Silver chart.

Figure 27.38 depicts a price-oscillator agreement at Point X, comprising trend-line barriers, a 38.2 percent Fibonacci retracement, and overbought signals on the cycle-tuned stochastics on the four-hour Gold chart.

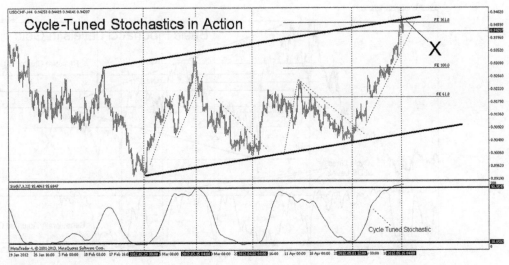

FIGURE 27.36 Price-Oscillator Agreements on the Four-Hour USDCHF Chart.
Source: MetaTrader 4

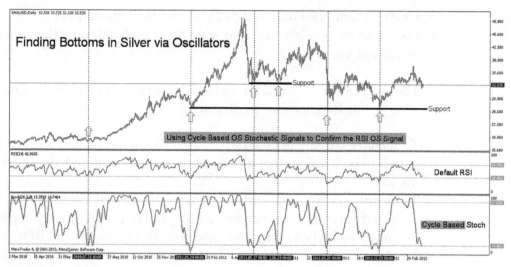

FIGURE 27.37 Price-Oscillator Agreements on the Daily Silver Chart.
Source: MetaTrader 4

Single Oscillator MTF Agreement

Single oscillators based on multiple timeframes (MTF) are sometimes found to be in *directional agreement*, providing additional evidence for the persistence of an existing trend. Single oscillator MTF agreement is a form of trend identification and confirmation. It is an extremely popular approach predominantly adopted by trend traders and trend-following systems. An oscillator is first selected based on its specific or desired properties. Its periodicity is then recalculated for all higher timeframes. Bullish and bearish signals are then identified by the degree of directional oscillator agreement between the various higher timeframes. Once a bullish or bearish signal is identified, a buy or sell trigger in the form of price confirmation is required, usually by way of a breach or penetration of a technical barrier.

FIGURE 27.38 Price-Oscillator Agreements on the Four-Hour Gold Chart.
Source: MetaTrader 4

872

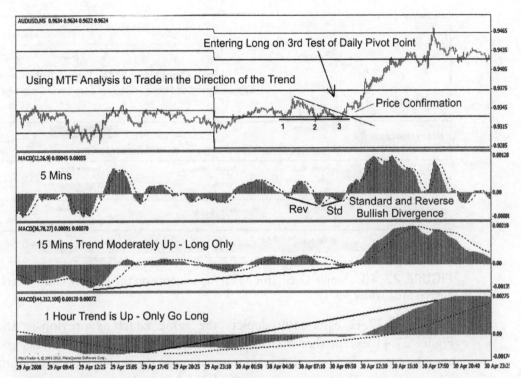

FIGURE 27.39 Single Oscillator MTF Agreements on the 5-Min AUDUSD Chart.
Source: MetaTrader 4

The following charts are some examples of single oscillator MTF agreements in action in various markets.

Figure 27.39 depicts single oscillator MTF agreements comprising the MACD 5-Min base period, pivot point support, and price confirmation on the 5-min AUDUSD chart. Once the 5-min, 15-min, and hourly moving average convergence-divergence (MACD) all turn bullish by crossing the zero line, any subsequent penetration of a trendline or significant overlay represents price confirmation. In our example, we observe a breach of a downtrend line just after price retested the daily pivot point for the third time. Note that some traders opt to enter long at the third pivot test instead of at the breakout of the downtrend line, that is, before price confirmation, as the distance between the two points is fairly close and entry at the pivot would afford traders a better reward/risk ratio (due to the smaller stopsize required to contain risk).

Figure 27.40 depicts single oscillator MTF agreements comprising the histogram hourly base period and its zero-level agreements on the hourly Gold chart. A bullish signal is issued once all the MACD histograms cross over the zero line. The reverse applies for bearish signals.

Figure 27.41 depicts single oscillator MTF agreements comprising the histogram hourly base period and its slope agreements on the hourly GBPUSD chart. In this case, a bullish signal is issued once all the slopes of the MACD histogram across all timeframes are sloping to the upside. The reverse applies for bearish signals.

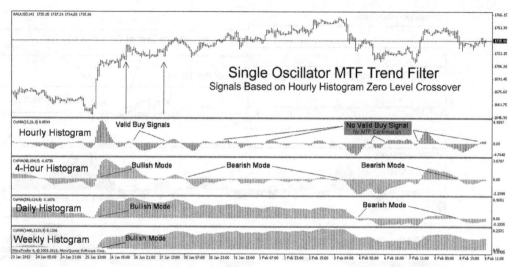

FIGURE 27.40 Single Oscillator MTF Agreements on the Hourly Gold Chart.
Source: MetaTrader 4

Figure 27.42 essentially depicts the same chart as previously shown in Figure 27.41 except that bullish signals are now issued once the faster-moving average crosses over the slower-moving average for the MACD histogram across all timeframes. The reverse applies for bearish signals.

Multiple Oscillator STF Agreement

Multiple oscillators, when applied on a single timeframe (STF), have a tendency to be in directional agreement, especially if they are constructed from the same technical data, that is, price. As such, evidence for the persistence of an existing trend is more reliable if the oscillators are constructed from data other than price itself, in order to avoid or mitigate the adverse effects of multicollinearity. Ideally, oscillators employed within a setup should be based on diverse technical data such as volume, open interest, and sentiment, apart from the basic price data.

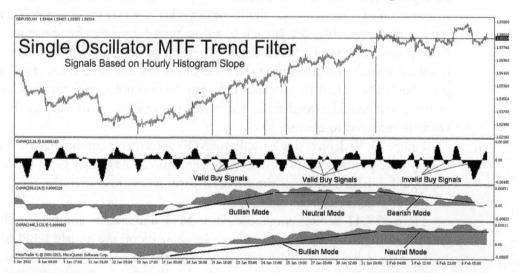

FIGURE 27.41 Single Oscillator MTF Agreements on the Hourly GBPUSD Chart.
Source: MetaTrader 4

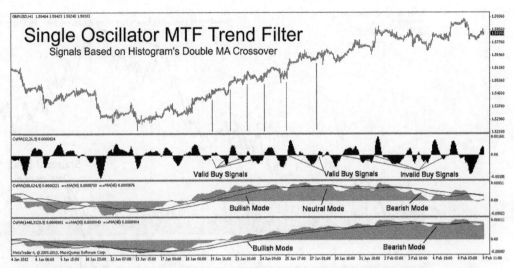

FIGURE 27.42 Single Oscillator MTF Agreements on the Hourly GBPUSD Chart.
Source: MetaTrader 4

Figure 27.43 depicts multiple oscillator STF agreements comprising RSI, MACD, and ROC on the daily Apple Inc. chart. Notice that all of the oscillators tend to give almost identical bullish and bearish signals. Notice that all three oscillators displayed standard bearish divergence simultaneously. To avoid multicollinearity, use oscillators constructed from data other than price alone.

Intermarket and Broad Market–Price Confluences

Exogenous information and data that may also be gleaned from other sources for additional evidence of an expected market top or bottom include:

- Broad Market and Market-Breadth Action
- Intermarket Action
- Sentiment and Flow of Funds

Commitment of Traders (COT) reports, polling sentiment (Market Vane, Investors Intelligence, etc.), CRB index, bond activity, VIX, Put-Call Ratios, Bullish Percent Index, diffusion index, and yield curve behavior are among the popular sources of market information.

Figure 27.44 shows the decline in the daily EURUSD when the Net Commercials and hedgers turned long in April 2012, accompanied by reverse bearish divergence between the Money Flow Index and exchange rate. Information on the Net Commercials was obtained from the COT weekly report.

Figure 27.45 depicts sentiment agreement comprising the S&P500 Bullish Percent Index and MACD on the daily S&P500 chart. Note that a bearish divergence signal arises from indicators that use very different data, which helps reduce the adverse effects of multicollinearity. Every time the Bullish Percent Index tests it historically overbought level, the market tends to correct or reverse.

875

FIGURE 27.43 Multiple Oscillator STF Agreements the Daily Apple Inc. Chart.
Courtesy of Stockcharts.com

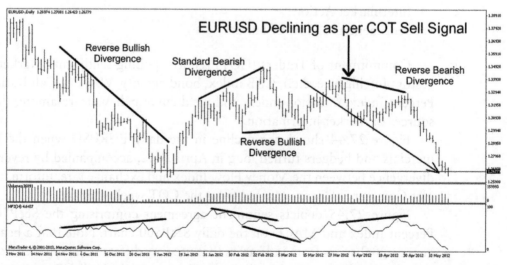

FIGURE 27.44 COT Data as Sentiment Agreement on the Hourly GBPUSD Chart.
Source: MetaTrader 4

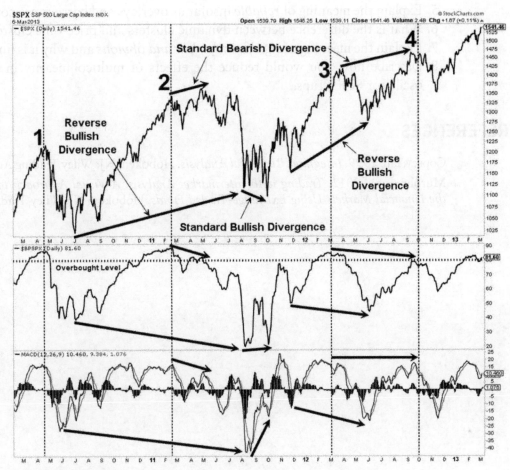

FIGURE 27.45 Sentiment Agreement the Daily S&P500 Chart.
Courtesy of Stockcharts.com

27.3 CHAPTER SUMMARY

In order to fully master the art and science of applying technical analysis effectively in the markets, an integrated approach is imperative. We have seen how, in basic terms, to combine various types of price and time based indicators to seek out key reaction price zones in the markets. It is at the convergence of a collection of bullish or bearish indications that practitioners find the most reliable action points for participation in the markets.

CHAPTER 27 REVIEW QUESTIONS

1. Explain what is meant by the term *integrated technical analysis*.
2. List the types of clusters that can be found in the markets.
3. Describe how you would integrate oscillators into your analysis of market cycles.
4. Explain why one-to-one, two-to-one, and three-to-one chart pattern height expansions are a significant part of risk management.

5. Explain the meaning of *reliable* insofar as overlays and barriers are concerned.
6. What is the difference between dynamic clusters and price-time clusters?
7. Explain the meaning of *significantly clear and obvious* and why it is important.
8. Describe how you would reduce the effects of multicollinearity in multiple oscillator STF setups.

REFERENCES

Copsey, Ian. 1999. *Integrated Technical Analysis*. Hoboken, NJ: Wiley Trading Advantage.

Murphy, John. 2012. *Trading with Intermarket Analysis: A Visual Approach to Beating the Financial Markets Using Exchange-Traded Funds*. Hoboken, NJ: Wiley Trading.

CHAPTER
28

Money Management

> **LEARNING OBJECTIVES**
>
> After studying this chapter, you should be able to:
>
> - Understand the significance of money management and its impact on trade performance
> - Describe the difference between fixed and dynamic sizing
> - Identify and differentiate between the passive and dynamic components of a money management system
> - Understand the effects of asymmetry on a trading system
> - Calculate the minimum winning percentage for both linear and non-linear sizing

Money management is critical to success and longer-term survivability in trading. Without the proper application of money management, the application of technical analysis to trading would be an exercise in futility. In this chapter, we will cover the various issues that plague traders and explain how they may be addressed via the proper and effective deployment of various sizing and capital-management techniques.

28.1 ELEMENTS OF MONEY MANAGEMENT

Let us begin by asking a few basic trade-related questions:

- Do you try to keep things simple and trade with only one lot or contract?
- Do you usually take a profit based reward to risk setup of 1:1 to 3:1?
- Do you usually place a fixed take profit order to exit?
- Do you usually risk around 2 to 5 percent per trade?
- Do you enjoy trading simultaneously on different timeframes?

- Will you risk more per trade if the system is guaranteed to make money?
- Imagine your trading system has a winning percentage of 34.6 percent and you are currently making money with a two-to-one reward-to-risk setup. To make more money, would you be willing to risk 2 to 5 percent, assuming that your system continues to perform consistently?
- Do you start re-optimizing your technical-based parameters once you suffer losses?

If your answers were affirmative for any of these questions, then there is a very high probability that your trading account may experience risk of ruin over the long term. The main problem is that the reasons for a trading account losing may not always be obvious to most traders and, as a consequence, they have no way to address issues that they are not even aware of within their trading systems. Traders in this situation resort instead to changing brokers, markets, timeframes, oscillators, and even trading strategies in the hope of finding a system that finally works. As you will see, the most effective solution is usually an adjustment based on money management parameters rather than on the never-ending re-optimization of oscillator and indicator settings.

We also need to ask the following question: *What is the main goal or objective of a directional trader or directional trading system?* The answer to this important question is simply to do whatever it takes to position oneself with the highest probability of profiting and lowest probability of losing over the longer term. Furthermore, there is no such thing as guaranteed outcome or success in an essentially semi-random and uncertain market environment. What a trader needs to do, and indeed the only thing that can be done, is to somehow severely *skew risk* in the trader's favor. This represents the only objective of any trader or trading system. The trader is not there to make a profit per se, but rather to control the risk associated with generating a profit. In fact, no directional trader can ever profit in the markets if the markets remain flat, regardless of how many orders are being placed in the markets (with the exception of collecting option premiums). To make money, the markets must move. Hence, it is actually the market's job to make money. All any trader can do is position him- or herself in the markets and wait. *All a trader can control is what he or she can control, which is risk.* Individual traders cannot control market action and, as a consequence, cannot exert any control over the amount of profit that can potentially be made. But losses can be controlled and contained. Money management is all about planning what to do should the worst-case scenario unfold. We shall refer to this as applying the worst-case scenario principle (WCSP).

In Figure 28.1, we see that a balanced trader requires mastery over three critical areas of management:

1. Money Management
2. Trade Management
3. Trader Management

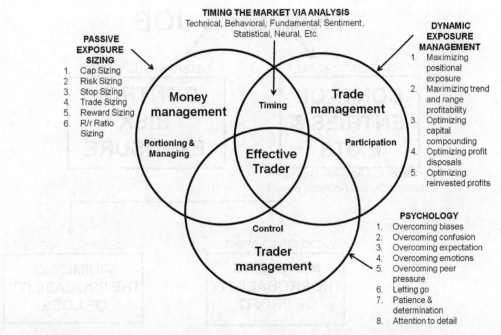

FIGURE 28.1 The Three Elements of a Balanced Trading Approach.

Money management involves the apportioning and management of capital, which involves:

- Passive Exposure Sizing:
  - Capital sizing
  - Risk sizing
  - Stop sizing
  - Trade sizing
  - Reward sizing
  - Reward-to-risk ratio (R/r) sizing
- Dynamic Exposure Sizing:
  - Maximizing positional exposure
  - Maximizing trend and range profitability
  - Compounding profits
  - Pyramiding positions
  - Managing profit disposals
  - Managing reinvested profits

A trader's job is two-fold, namely to:

1. Manage entries and exits
2. Manage risk exposure

The management of entries and exits is *probabilistic* in nature, whereas the management of risk is essentially *deterministic* in nature. This is because it is not

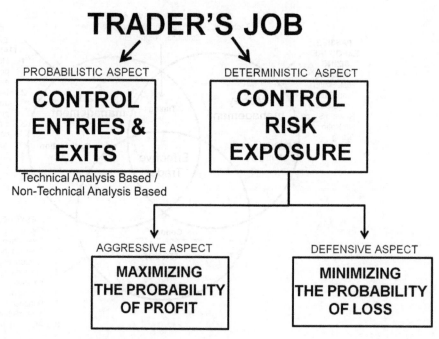

FIGURE 28.2 A Trader's Primary Functions.

possible to control the winning percentage of our trades, but it is possible to control risk and determine the worst-case scenario loss. Furthermore, maximizing the probability of profitability is a relatively more aggressive approach as compared to minimizing the probability of loss, which is essentially a more defensive approach to trading. See Figure 28.2.

The dual function of money management may be classified as:

1. Sizing an exposure
2. Managing an exposure

Sizing an exposure is a classified as a pre-entry activity, where its six passive components of sizing (i.e., capital, risk, stop, trade, reward, and R/r ratio) are all determined long before any trade is initiated. Managing an exposure is essentially a post-entry activity and is considered to be a dynamic activity. It is concerned with the management of a position via activities such as the rolling of stops and the scaling in and out of positions.

The passive components of money management have a definite sequence of determination:

1. **Capital Sizing:** The trader must first decide on how much *initial total capital to risk* in the markets.
2. **Risk Sizing:** The trader must then decide how much or what percentage of that initial *capital to risk per trade* in the markets. This is denoted as the dollar risk per trade, or $risk.

3. Stop Sizing: Once the risk per trade is determined, the trader must now determine the stopsize associated with an entry.

4. Trade Sizing: Once the stopsize is determined, the trader can calculate the size of the position per trade, which is normally found by dividing the dollar risk per trade ($risk) by the stopsize. In foreign exchange trading, the trade size is found by dividing the $risk by the stopsize and the dollar pip value ($pip):

$$\text{Trade size (Equity)} = \$risk\,/\,stopsize$$

$$\text{Trade size (FOREX)} = \$risk\,/(stopsize \times pip\ value)$$

5. Reward Sizing: Once the trade size is determined, the trader must now decide on how and where to take profit ($R).

6. Reward to risk Ratio (R/r Ratio) Sizing: The reward size and risk size chosen by the trader determine the final average R/r ratio per trade. This average R/r ratio will in turn determine the average minimum win percentage required for the strategy or system employed.

See Figure 28.3 for a flow chart of the sequence of sizing determination.

Dynamic money management has also a certain sequence for the determination of its parameters, namely:

1. Maximizing Positional Exposure: This involves the initiation of as many positions as possible in the market without the raising the overall level of risk across all open positions. This can only be done by risk-freeing each position via the use of any of the four stochastic exit mechanisms, *before* any new position is initiated.

2. Maximizing Trend and Range Profitability: This requires the trader to be flexible enough to employ the most effective entries, exits, pyramiding,

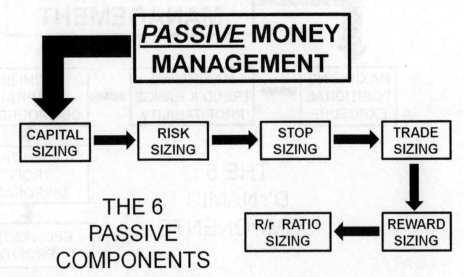

FIGURE 28.3 Sequence of Sizing determination during the Passive Money Management Stage.

and position scaling appropriate for the type of market behavior being observed.

3. Optimizing Capital Compounding: The trader must employ an appropriate level of compounding in order to maximize profit over the longer-term horizon.

4. Optimizing Profit Disposals: Being profitable over the shorter term is not sufficient to ensure longer-term survivability as a trader. One reason why so many accounts fail to succeed over the longer term is related to the spending of profits. The entire trading campaign is one based on the balance of probabilities. As such, all withdrawals of profit endanger the account by reducing its ability to withstand or buffer against futures loses.

5. Reinvesting Profits with Higher $risk Exposure: Once the account has accrued sufficient profit to withstand and buffer against the largest expected drawdown associated with a particular trading methodology or system, some profit may be reinvested with larger tradesizes, with the intention of making larger returns over shorter price excursions.

See Figure 28.4.

Maximizing Positional Exposure

In order to maximize positional exposure, we need to have as many simultaneous open orders in the market as possible. But this is not viable if each open position is still exposed to directional risk, as this would raise the total percentage or absolute dollar risk at any one moment in time to inordinate and unacceptable levels, exposing the trader to a very high probability of experiencing risk

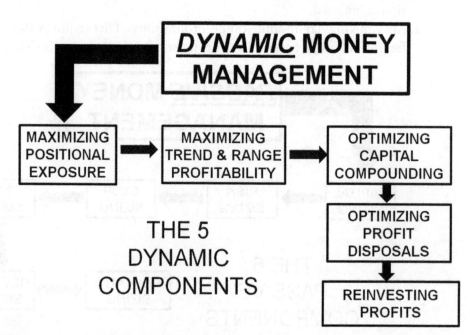

FIGURE 28.4 Sequence of Determination during the Dynamic Money Management Stage.

of ruin in the very immediate future. In order to safely establish such a setup, each open position needs to be risk-freed before a new position may be initiated. There are four main ways to achieve this state where each position experiences no directional risk, except for the most current position. We use the stochastic exit mechanisms or setups to establish risk-free positions. The term *stochastic* means random or arbitrary. Hence, stochastic exits means exits that are random in nature, with no predefined exit point. The stochastics mechanism has three main functions:

1. It frees an open position from directional risk.
2. It allows an open position to remain open safely without any predefined exit and hence able to ride a trend without risk.
3. It allows for the establishment of numerous open positions for the purposes of experiencing larger gains without the associated risk of having all positions exposed to directional risk.

Employing these stochastic exit setups transforms capital risk in trading into one of opportunity risk. It is more advantageous to trade with opportunity risk than with capital risk. With capital risk, a trader exposes him - or herself to the potential loss of capital. But with opportunity risk, a trader exposes him - or herself only to the loss of an opportunity to make more profit.

Therefore, we see that *most of the trader's work is actually done before even entering the market* via the setting up of the six passive components of money management. The remainder of the work is done after entry. Therefore trading begins even before the very first trade is initiated. Real traders do most of the work before entering the markets. Entries and exits alone are not the most important part of trading. See Figure 28.5.

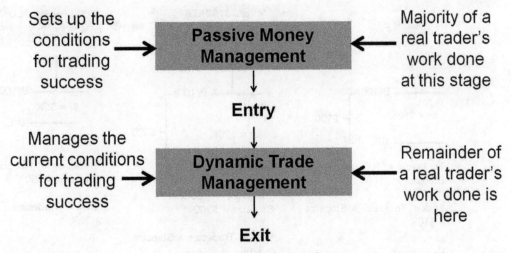

Trading is mainly about what a trader does BEFORE entry

FIGURE 28.5 Sequence of Determination during the Dynamic Money Management Stage.

The Conservation of Risk in Trading

Just like energy, risk cannot be removed, but it may be transformed into other states of risk, that is, risk is conserved. There are four types of risk in trading, namely:

- Percentage or Absolute Dollar Risk ($risk): This represents the risk of losing a certain specified amount of capital when the stoplosses are triggered.
- Positional Risk: This represents the risk of a stoploss being triggered by price. The closer a stop is to the entry, the higher the positional risk.
- Target Risk: This represents the risk of taking a lower profit due to smaller tradesizes.
- Opportunity Risk: This represents a position that has already been risk freed. Therefore, if its protective stop is taken out by price, the trader loses no capital except an opportunity to make more profit.

Consider the following example in Figure 28.6. Assume that we have a baseline setup for the purpose of comparison of risks. We now compare two setups where the stopsizes are different. Each setup longs 100 shares. Upon comparing risks in each setup with the baseline setup, we observe that setup A has a higher $risk but a lower positional risk, whereas setup B has a lower $risk and a higher positional risk. The target risk for both setups is identical with the baseline setup and hence both setups have an equal potential of making the same profit over the same amount of price excursion. We therefore see that setup B is no better than setup A in terms of risk. Risk has merely been transferred or converted from one form to another. There is no reduction is overall risk.

See Figure 28.7. We now increase the tradesize in setup B to 200 shares and we find that setup B has now an equal $risk when compared to the baseline setup, but now the target risk has decreased. Therefore, the overall risk is still the same.

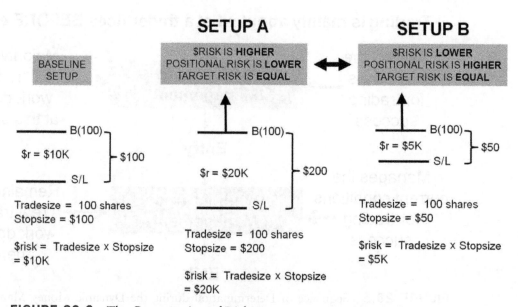

FIGURE 28.6 The Conservation of Risk.

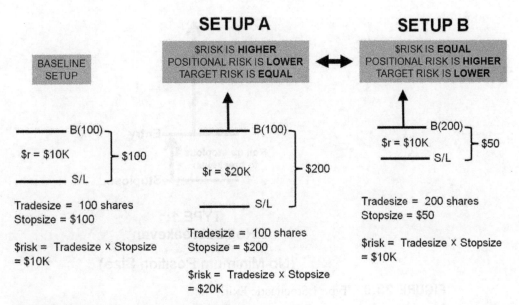

FIGURE 28.7 The Conservation of Risk.

Notice that no matter how a setup changes it parameters, there will always be one risk that increases, another that decreases, and one that remains unchanged. This indicates that risk is being conserved as a whole within the system.

But overall risk is not conserved when the stochastic exit mechanism is employed. *It transforms positional risk into opportunity risk and drastically diminishes the $risk component,* confining $risk to only the most recent trade entry. It exposes the system to large profit potentials with relatively low levels of accompanying $risk. This is the first step in skewing risk for greater profit potential. See Figure 28.8.

The Four Stochastic Exit Mechanisms/Setups

We shall refer to the four stochastic setups as Type 1, Type 2, Type 3, and Type 4. All four setups free an open position from $risk and transform positional risk into opportunity risk.

A Type 1 stochastic exit is simply rolling the stoploss to breakeven once price is a reasonable distance from the entry (in reality we need to roll the stoploss

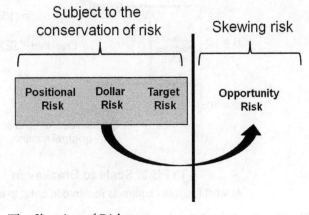

FIGURE 28.8 The Skewing of Risk.

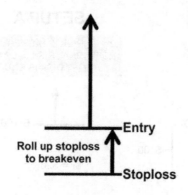

TYPE 1:
Roll to breakeven

(No Minimum Position Size)

FIGURE 28.9 Type 1 Stochastic Exit.

slightly farther out to account for slippage, trading costs, etc.). The initial stop is now functioning as a breakeven stop. As prices continue to advance, the stop may be made to trail price until it is taken out. In such a scenario, the breakeven stop is functioning as a protective trailing stop. See Figure 28.9.

A Type 2 stochastic exit is simply liquidating or covering (i.e., scaling out) enough positions to achieve a breakeven state, that is, to cover any potential losses that may arise if price reverses and takes out the stoploss, depending on whether the trader is long or short the initial position. The initial stop is not rolled to the entry level, but rather left in its original position. As prices continue to advance, the stoploss may be made to trail price until it is taken out. In Figure 28.10, we see that we are required to scale out 10 lots (or contracts) if we exited 90 points above the entry that had a stopsize of 10 points, using the formula on the next page:

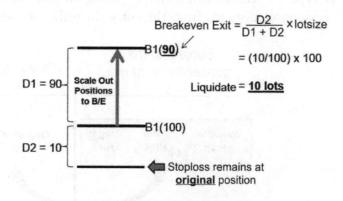

TYPE 2: Scale to Breakeven
At least two lots / contracts required in order to exit one

FIGURE 28.10 Type 2 Stochastic Exit.

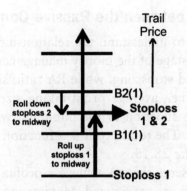

TYPE 3: Roll to B/Even
(No Minimum Position Size)

FIGURE 28.11   Type 3 Stochastic Exit.

[Stopsize /(Stopsize + Reward Size)] × total initial lotsize or contract size

A Type 3 stochastic exit is simply entering a new lot or contract anywhere beyond the entry level and rolling both the stoplosses to midway between the two entry levels. Hence, if price were to reverse and take out the both the stoplosses, the losses would be neutralized by an equal amount of profit made (in reality we need to roll the stoplosses slightly farther out to account for slippage, trading costs, etc.). As prices continue to advance, the stoploss may be made to trail price until it is taken out. See Figure 28.11.

A Type 4 stochastic exit is simply a combination of Types 1 and 2. Once price has moved a reasonable distance beyond the entry, the stoploss is rolled to breakeven, that is, the entry level. The trader then scales out some position to lock in a profit. Hence, if price were to reverse and take out the stoploss, a profit would be made (in reality we need to roll the stoploss slightly farther out to account for slippage, trading costs, etc.). As prices continue to advance, the stoploss may be made to trail price until it is taken out. The trader may also scale out first before rolling the stop to the entry level. See Figure 28.12.

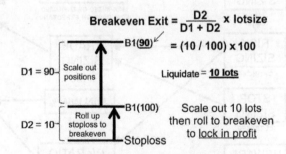

$$\text{Breakeven Exit} = \frac{D2}{D1 + D2} \times \text{lotsize}$$

$$= (10 / 100) \times 100$$

Liquidate = **10 lots**

Scale out 10 lots then roll to breakeven to _lock in profit_

TYPE 4: Scale & Roll to Breakeven
At least two lots / contracts required to exit one

FIGURE 28.12   Type 4 Stochastic Exit.

Relationship between the Passive Components

It is important to understand the relationship between passive components during the passive stage of the money management process. Tradesizing is a function of risksizing and stopsizing, while R/r ratio sizing is a function of risksizing and reward sizing (i.e., average profit-taking size). The average profit per trade, or *expectancy*, is a function of the minimum winning percentage, R/r ratio sizing, and tradesizing. The total profit is a function of expectancy and total number of trades. See Figure 28.13.

We also observe that to achieve a profitable trading system, not all the passive components are maximized. Maximizing some of these components may adversely affect the profitability of the system. Here is a list of actions allowed for each passive component:

- Capital Sizing: maximize capital
- Risk Sizing: minimize $risk
- Stop Sizing: optimize stopsize
- Trade Sizing: optimize tradesize
- Reward Sizing: maximize $Reward
- R/r Ratio Sizing: maximize R/r ratio

It is important to note that we should optimize the stopsize to account for the volatility of the price action. As for tradesizing, there exists a range of tradesizes whereby smaller or larger tradesizes above and below an optimal fraction of the invested capital will start to impact the system adversely. Hence tradesizes should be optimized around this optimal value.

Difference between Effective Trading and Gambling

There are four major differences between effective money management, real trading, and reckless gambling:

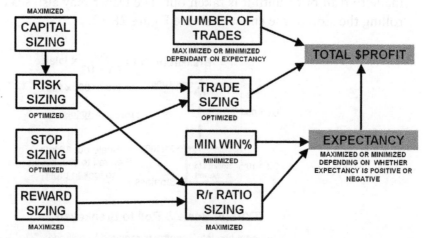

FIGURE 28.13 Sequence of Determination during the Dynamic Money Management Stage.

1. We can use stochastic exit mechanisms to reduce the uncontrollable and potentially adverse effects of the win percentage and win/loss distribution (applying the WCS Principle).
2. We can use unique risksizing techniques like *pseudo-martingales* (i.e., fixed-risk martingales) to derive the same earning power without increasing the percentage or absolute dollar risk.
3. We can use backtested data to statistically optimize our stopsizing so that we may attempt to maximize our profit potential.
4. We can use unique tradesizing techniques to optimize our exposure so that we can maximize our profit potential.

Money management can turn a winning system into an outperforming and extremely profitable system. In some cases, money management can even transform a losing system into a profitable system. In the worst-case scenario, money management helps reduce the rate of loss and thereby give the system a chance to recover to profitability. But money management cannot transform a losing system into a winning system when every trade is a losing trade.

The Minefield Analogy of Money Management

Let us assume that we are forced to traverse a minefield. It would therefore be in our best interests to avoid stepping on any mines as we move from one end to the other. One way to achieve this is to try to predict where the mines are located. This is akin to using technical analysis. But there are other decisions that we can make that will make a real difference and actually help reduce risk *without trying to predict* where the mines are buried. We could:

- Take the shortest path.
- Take the least number of steps.
- Take lighter steps.
- Take the path of a previous explosion.
- Refuse to take any steps.
- Wear protective gear to reduce potential damage.

We observe that these approaches each address the problem from a different perspective without trying to forecast where the mines may be located. This is akin to using money management in trading. Another factor that traders need to address is the number of *trade units* or trade opportunities afforded to them. A trader who risks 20 percent of his or her original capital per trade has only five trade opportunities to succeed, whereas a trader who risks 1 percent has 100 trade opportunities to succeed. Technical analysis plays a lesser role for systems that have fewer trade opportunities, as it is not provided with sufficient opportunities to allow any technical *edge*s or advantages to have a favorable impact on the system.

Risk of Ruin

Risk of ruin (ROR) is the probability that the account equity will decline to a level that the trader regards as catastrophic. This level of catastrophic loss is therefore arbitrary. There are many formulas available to calculate the risk of ruin based on R/r ratios, percent risk per trade (%risk), and average historical win percentage. Risk of ruin may be estimated using:

- Probabilistic formulas
- Hypothetical random tests via Monte Carlo simulations
- Empirical data from backtesting

Below are two important facts that are obvious from Monte Carlo simulation studies:

1. There is evidence that the probability of profitability increases as the number of trading units or trading opportunities increases in the system. This means that we should trade using a smaller percentage risk per trade.
2. It shows that greater asymmetric leverage within the system requires a higher number of trade units in order to remain profitable, that is, to maintain positive expectancy (which is not accounted for in most of the ROR formulas).

Although many risk of ruin formulas attempt to indicate the chance of experiencing catastrophic loss, it can be somewhat misleading. This is because such formulas do not account for many of the idiosyncrasies and anomalies associated with trading. Hypothetical trade simulation provides a more reliable gauge of the risk of ruin.

Capital Sizing

It is extremely important to be well capitalized in order to increase the probability of longer-term survivability in trading. Greater amounts of capital allow for more trade units or opportunities, giving the system a chance to recover to profitability. It also allows the trader to participate in certain markets or systems with the greatest chance of surviving large drawdowns.

Let us look at one simple example of how ineffective capital sizing may impact a trader adversely. In Figure 28.14, we are given a balance curve of some trading

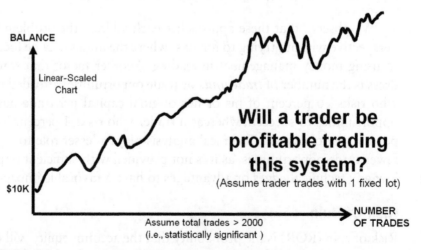

FIGURE 28.14   Balance Curve of a Hypothetical Trading System.

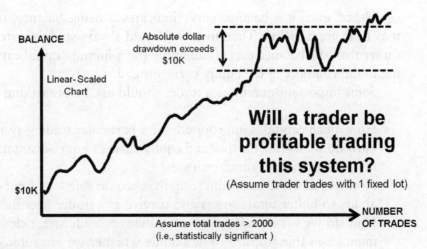

FIGURE 28.15 The Minimum Initial Capital Rule.

system. The system starts off with initial capital of $10,000. Assume that all trades were executed using single fixed lots without compounding profits and that the balance curve is plotted on a linearly scaled chart. Would a trader who starts off trading this system with an initial capital of $10,000 be profitable?

The trader would in fact be putting his capital at risk by trading such a system as the largest absolute dollar drawdown was significantly in excess of $10,000, as can be seen from the amount of decline in the balance curve as indicated in Figure 28.15. Therefore even though the system may prove to be consistently profitable over the long term, a trader may still lose all of his or her capital should the drawdown occur early on in the trades, where the trader has insufficient capital to withstand such volatility within a profitable and winning system. This is referred to as the *minimum initial capital rule*, where the minimum capital required must be at least equal to and preferably greater than the largest historical drawdown experienced by the system.

But there is another issue. Even if the minimum initial capital rule was satisfied, this balance curve does not account for the actual equity action in the system. Equity is simply the total balance and running profit and loss experienced by the system. Unfortunately, the balance only tracks the profitability of all closed trades. It does not account for the profitability of open positions. See Figure 28.16.

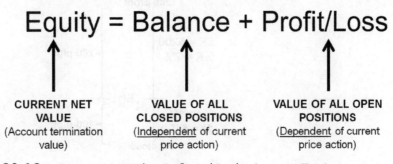

FIGURE 28.16 Current Net Value Reflected in the Account Equity.

Hence, even if a balance curve indicates a rising balance, the actual equity may be in great decline. Therefore, we should always study a system's equity curve rather than the balance curve, and apply the minimum initial capital rule according to the volatility in the equity curve instead.

Some important questions a trader should ask before risking capital are:

- How much capital is appropriate for a particular trading system?
- How do we use the balance and equity curves to our advantage when integrating passive and dynamic strategies?
- How do we withdraw profit from the account safely without endangering our ability to buffer future losses and survive as a trader over the longer term?
- How do we use margin, platform minimum trade size, tick values, and minimum allowable stopsize to determine whether we are sufficiently capitalized to trade a certain market?
- How do we use various broker facilities, including margin, to our advantage so that we can trade more effectively?

Reward-to-Risk Ratios

Let us now turn our attention to another passive component called the reward-to-risk ratio, that is, R/r ratio (little r is used to denote risk). Assume that our capital is $10,000 and that we intend to risk 1 percent per trade, that is, %risk = 1 percent. Therefore, our dollar risk, that is, $risk is simply:

$$\$risk = \$10,000 \times \% \ risk = \$10,000 \times 1\% = \$100$$

Now, assume that we are trading the minilots on the EURUSD exchange rate and that our stopsize is 100 pips. Our tradesize would therefore be:

$$\text{Trade size} = \$risk \, /(\text{stop size} \times \text{pip value})$$
$$= \$100 \, /(100 \times \$1 \, \text{per pip})$$
$$= 1 \, \text{minilot}$$

See Figure 28.17.

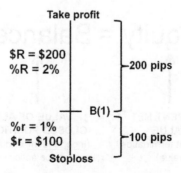

FIGURE 28.17 Reward and Risk.

Assume Take Profit (T/P) = 200 pips

$$\text{Our R /r ratio} = \$R\ /\ \$r = (200 \times 1\,\text{minilot})\ /\ (100 \times 1\,\text{minilot})$$
$$= 2$$

We may also say that the reward has a 2 to 1 ratio with risk, that is,

$$\text{R/r} \rightarrow 2{:}1$$

From the equation, we observe that the lotsize cancels out. *This means that the R/r ratio is independent of tradesize.* We can therefore visually gauge the R/r ratio of any setup just by measuring the distances of R and r on the charts.

The Term Structure Characteristics of Reward and Risk

The function of a stoploss and take profit varies with the time horizon. The stop-loss has six basic functions, namely:

1. It limits loss by exiting a position if price moves adversely by a specified amount.
2. It limits profit by exiting a position should price move adversely by a specified amount before reversing back in a favorable direction.
3. It limits profit by allowing a position to momentarily experience unrealized profit before reversing back and triggering or taking out the stoploss, hence exiting the position.
4. It acts as a trailing stop, locking in profit as price moves in a favorable direction until price reverses back and takes out the stoploss, forcing the exit of a position.
5. It acts as a buy and sell stop entry order, allowing traders to enter in the direction of the existing trend.
6. It acts as a buy and sell limit entry order, allowing traders to enter in the opposite direction of the existing trend.

As we can see, the stoploss acts as an exit mechanism for four out of six functions. We also see that three out of four exits function as a loss-exit mechanism, locking in short-term losses. It has only a single function that operates to lock in profit, that is, as a trailing stop. Therefore, all things being equal and assuming that the markets are somewhat random, the stoploss will function as a mechanism for locking in losses over the short term. Over the longer term a stoploss acts more like a stop profit mechanism, since *the majority of its exit functions act to limit the possibility of allowing a position to remain in the market long enough for profit to develop.* Hence, limiting the maximum losses allowable over the short term may well result in the accumulation of minimum profit over the longer term.

The take profit order has also differing characteristics over the short- and longer-term horizons. Taking the recommended minimum profit over the shorter term puts the system at risk over the longer term. This is because with fixed exit levels, positions are not allowed to experience profit beyond a profit target. This essentially shuts off any possibility of experiencing larger profits within the system

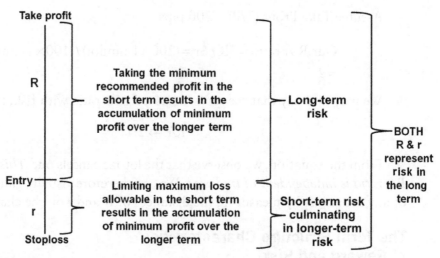

FIGURE 28.18 Term Structure Characteristics of Reward and Risk.

and hence puts more strain on the trader to consistently trade above the minimum winning percentage of the system. Unfortunately, winning percentage is largely an uncontrollable variable. Therefore, the term risk does not only refer to the loss experienced when a stop is triggered but it also refers to the reward characteristics over the longer term. Therefore both $reward and $risk represent risk over the longer term. This definition of risk also aligns itself with the general understanding that any injection of capital into the market is subject to risk. See Figure 28.18.

Figure 28.19 shows the various passive money management components and stochastic exit mechanisms and how they relate to the term structure of reward and risk. These passive components, together with the stochastic exit mechanisms, may be used to help diminish the effects of long-term risk on the system caused by the use of fixed take profit and stoploss orders.

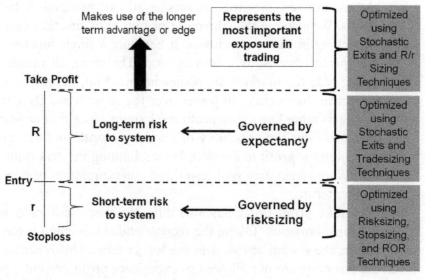

FIGURE 28.19 Techniques for Reducing Longer-Term Risk.

System Expectancy

The average profit and loss is also referred to as the *expectancy* of a trading system. Assume that we would like to gauge our trading performance by the number of wins and losses per every 10 trades. Assume that our system's winning percentage is 40 percent, that is, %win = 40 percent. Assume also that we set up our system with a R/r ratio of two to one, where all positions exit when $Reward = $2 and $risk = $1. Let the total trades be denoted by T. So the average profit and loss for every 10 trades is calculated as follows (ignoring trading costs, slippage, etc.):

$$\text{Average } \$P/L = (\$\text{Profit} - \$\text{Loss})/\text{Total Trades (T)}$$
$$= [(\$R \times \text{number of wins}) - (\$r \times \text{number of losses})]/T$$
$$= [(\$R \times (\text{number of wins}/T)) - (\$r \times (\text{number of losses})/T)]$$
$$= (\$R \times \text{win ratio}) - (\$r \times \text{loss ratio})$$
$$= (\$2 \times 0.4) - (\$1 \times 0.6)$$
$$= +\$0.20$$
$$= \text{Expectancy}$$

Assume now that we lost the first 10 trades:

$$\text{Expectancy} = (\$R \times \text{win ratio}) - (\$r \times \text{loss ratio})$$
$$= (\$2 \times 0.0) - (\$1 \times 1.0)$$
$$\text{Expectancy} = -\$1 \text{ per trade}$$

(We say that we have negative expectancy.)

How many trades do we need to recover from losing the first 10 trades? Because we make +$2 per every $10 trades, we need $Loss/$2 = $10/$2 = 5 windows = 50 trades to recover. How many trades do we need to recover if that happens again? Assuming our system becomes consistent again and begins performing at %win = 40 percent, we would need $50 \times 2 = 100$ trades. In fact, the more the trader tries to trade to get back to breakeven, the greater the chance that it will happen again. The trader would literally get drawn into a downward spiraling equity decline from which the trader may never escape. Also, imagine the trader's frustration after losing the last 10 trades after making money in the first 50 trades. The trader would be back to breakeven again. So what's the solution out of this dilemma? Well, one answer is money management, via the application of stochastic-based exit techniques and effective R/r ratio, capital, risk, stop, and trade sizing.

Non-Controllable Factors

Although there may parameters we can alter and amend, there are two critical variables that we have no real control of, and those are the %win and win/loss distribution. We have absolute control over the R/r ratio since we can place the stoploss and take profit at any price we so choose. This essentially renders expectancy as non-controllable, a performance metric of historical performance. See Figure 28.20.

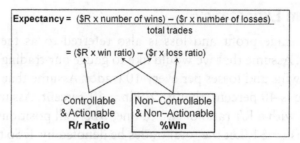

FIGURE 28.20 Techniques for Reducing Longer-Term Risk.

Expressing Reward in Terms of Risk

We can express R/r in various ways. We can express the R/r ratio as a multiple of $risk. This approach for expressing $Reward in terms of $risk was introduced by Dr. Van Tharp in his book entitled *Trade Your Way to Financial Freedom*. Here are some examples.

$$R/r \rightarrow 3:2 \text{ (divide both sides by \$risk to express \$reward in terms of \$risk)}$$
$$R/r \rightarrow (3/2):(2/2) \rightarrow 1.5:1$$

We can therefore represent the R/r ratio as *1.5r*. This means that $R is 1.5 times larger than $risk.

The Minimum Winning Percentage

For every R/r ratio setup, there is a corresponding *minimum %win or win ratio*. In ratio form, a %win of 40 percent becomes 40/100 = 0.4. So, a %win of 40 percent corresponds to a win ratio = 0.4 Let $Reward be R, $risk be r and win ratio be w. We already know that:

$$\%win = 100\% - \%loss$$
$$win\ ratio = 1 - loss\ ratio$$
$$Expectancy = (\$R \times win\ ratio) - (\$r \times loss\ ratio)$$
$$= (\$R \times w) - (\$r \times (1-w))$$

To get the min win%, we set Expectancy = 0. Expressing $R in terms of $r (i.e., dividing through by $r) we get (leaving out the $ sign):

$$(R \times w) - (1 \times (1-w)) = 0$$
$$Rw - 1 + w = 0$$
$$w(1+R) = 1$$
$$w = 1/(1+R)$$

This represents the *minimum win ratio required to break even*. From Figure 28.21, we see that this minimum win ratio is non-linear in nature.

See Figure 28.22 for more examples of calculating the minimum win ratio or percentage.

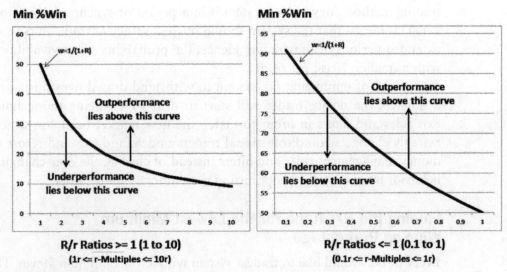

FIGURE 28.21 Techniques for Reducing Longer-Term Risk.

The Market-Methodology Mismatch

Can we guarantee that a system will maintain a minimum win ratio of $1/(1+R)$ indefinitely? Unfortunately, the answer is no. Although we have control over the win amount ($R), we have absolutely no control over the winning percentage. The situation is further exacerbated when the market changes behavior and we inevitably see our system fall below the minimum $1/(1+R)$ condition. Every trading system will have specific trading conditions with carefully tuned entry/exit rules and filters. The original methodology will inevitably experience mismatch with changing market behavior. The methodology will usually stay in mismatch over much longer periods as the market cycles through its infinite range of expressions. The system's specific conditions for profitability usually occupy only a small part of that spectrum of expressions and thus will stay profitable over smaller stretches of activity. That is why it is so important to be able to maximize profit when the

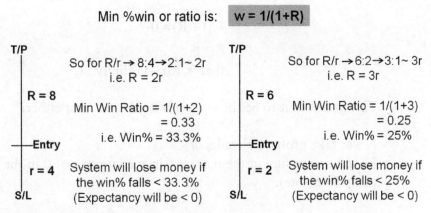

FIGURE 28.22 Calculating the Minimum Win Ratio or Percentage for a Fixed R/r Ratio.

trading methodology of the system is in a period of synchronicity with the market. This means that the system should possess sufficient trade units to withstand extended periods of drawdown. Hence, the probability of survivability increases with a smaller %risk per trade.

Instead of optimizing the system to withstand drawdowns during periods of mismatch, the novice trader will start to drift by changing the technical entry/exit rules and filters in order to match the new market behavior, which will inevitably change again. Professional traders understand this and resort to stricter money management rules and filters instead of chasing the ever-changing market behavior by constantly re-optimizing oscillators and indicators.

Finding the R/r Ratio for the Lowest Minimum Winning Percentage

Every trader would like to trade a system with a low minimum %win. This means that with only a low percentage of wining trades, the trader would still be profitable. So what R/r ratio setup would allow for the lowest %win? Let us look at few examples. What must R/r ratio be for a minimum win percentage of 50 percent?

$$1/(1+R) = 0.5$$
$$1+R = (1/0.5) = 2$$
$$R = 2-1 = 1$$

that is, $R/r \rightarrow 1:1$ (which is the minimum R/r ratio for a breakeven setup)

What if we reduce the %win so that we can win more easily, say to 20 percent?

$$1/(1+R) = 0.2$$
$$1+R = 1/0.2 = 5$$
$$R = 5-1 = 4$$

that is, $R/r \rightarrow 4:1$ (which is the minimum R/r ratio for a breakeven setup)

So, theoretically speaking, what is the lowest %win whereby it would be easiest and most effortless to be profitable? Answer: win% = 0 percent

$$1/(1+R) = 0$$
$$R = 8$$

that is, $R/r \rightarrow \text{infinity} : 1$

This means that to be the most profitable, we must either:

- Never take profit in a trade, or
- Have no exposure in the market (since a stopsize of 0 in the ratio R/r would make R infinite).

Unfortunately, not taking profit is not a viable option in the real world. It is interesting to note that the other option for achieving effortless wins in the market is to have no exposure in the market! (This means that in order to be profitable, we should not trade.) The best compromise is to design a stochastic R/r setup. This means that in order to allow a position to experience the greatest profit, the exit should be stochastic in nature. That would come closest to the *never taking a profit* condition. In the stochastic version, the exit would inevitably occur, although it is not known when the stoploss would be taken out.

Another Uncontrollable Factor: The Dreaded Win-Loss Distribution

Let's assume that a trader somehow has the ability control the %win and even guarantee that it will never fall below the minimum $1/(1+R)$ condition. Does this mean that the trader can now trade for a living and will then only be profitable? Unfortunately, it is not as straightforward as just satisfying the minimum $1/(1+R)$ condition. This is because the trader has still no control over the distribution or sequence of wins and losses. For example, assume that a trader sets up a trading system risking only 1 percent per trade, based on the original account equity. This would afford the trader 100 trade units (i.e., 100%/1% = 100). Refer to Figure 28.23.

We observe that if more losses appear first, the trader would have lost the ability to recover even though his overall minimum %win remains at 50 percent. This is because the trader has insufficient trade units to participate in the recovery of the losses. This implies that in order to ensure long-term survivability, a trader should trade a system with the greatest number of trade units available, that is, a system with the lowest %risk or $risk per trade. Again, it is interesting to note that according to this train of logic, the greatest chance of survivability would be to trade with a %risk or $risk of zero! Again, this would not be a viable option in the real world.

R/r Ratio and Its Statistical Edge in Random Systems

We learned earlier that a higher R/r is advantageous as it lowers the minimum %win and thus makes it easier for a trader to achieve trading success. But does a low R/r ratio have a statistical advantage or edge over a higher R/r with random price behavior? Statistically, a higher R/r ratio setup will experience more small losses with fewer larger wins, whereas a lower R/r ratio setup will experience more

Assume Minimum %win = 50%

Wins	Losses	Win%
1	1	= 50%
10	10	= 50%
50	50	= 50%
100	100	= 50%
1000	1000	= 50%

FIGURE 28.23 The Uncontrollable Win-Loss Distribution.

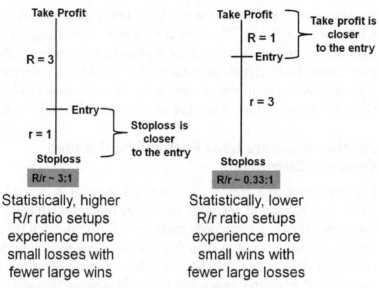

FIGURE 28.24 Comparing R/r Ratios in Random Systems.

small wins with fewer larger losses, in purely random markets. This is because with higher R/r ratios, the take profit is farther away from the entry as compared to the stoploss, rendering the stoploss with a higher probability of being taken out by price. With lower R/r ratios, the stoploss is farther away from the entry as compared to the take profit, rendering the take profit with a higher probability of being triggered. See Figure 28.24.

We have already learned that positional risk represents the risk of stoploss being taken out or hit. Let us now calculate the probability of a stoploss being taken out in a purely random market for a 1:1 R/r ratio setup. Since R/r is 1:1, this means that R= r. Therefore:

$$\text{Probability of the stoploss being hit} = R/(R + r) \times 100\%$$
$$= (r/2r) \times 100\%$$
$$= 50\%$$

Statistically, one out of every two entries will trigger the stoploss. Let us now calculate the probability of a stoploss being taken out in a purely random market for a two-to-one R/r ratio setup. In this case, R = 2r. See Figure 28.25.

$$\text{Probability of the stoploss being hit} = R/(R + r) \times 100\%$$
$$= (2r/2r + r) \times 100\%$$
$$= (2/3) \times 100\%$$
$$= 66.6\%$$

Take Profit————————|————————Stoploss
                 R=2r   Entry   r

FIGURE 28.25 2:1 R/r Ratio Setup.

Statistically, two out of every three trades will trigger the stoploss.

Let us now calculate the linear expectancy for a few R/r ratio setups *in purely random markets*. The probabilities of a stoploss being taken out for one-to-one, two-to-one, and three-to-one R/r ratio setups are one out of two (50%), two out of three (66.6%), and three out of four (75%), respectively.

   a. For R/r→1:1:
   Linear Exp = (R × win ratio) − (r × loss ratio)
   $(1 \times 0.5) - (\$1 \times 0.5) = 0$
   b. For R/r →2:1:
   Linear Exp = (R × win ratio) − (r × loss ratio)
   $= (2 \times 1/3) - (1 \times 2/3) = 0$
   c. For R/r →3:1:
   Linear Exp = ($R × w) − ($r × l)
   $= (\$3 \times 1/4) - (\$1 \times 3/4) = 0$

We therefore observe that irrespective of the R/r ratio setup being employed, there is no real edge in using a higher R/r ratio in purely random markets over the very long term. But R/r ratios react differently in real or semi-random markets. This is because there are fairly consistent underlying behavioral patterns that do not occur in random systems. One such behavioral pattern is the phenomenon of overextension in the markets. Conditions of being overbought or oversold exist because of human tendencies associated with emotions such as fear, greed, and hope. Such conditions are also the result of human biases and psychology with respect to risking capital and profit in the markets. Another such behavioral pattern is the phenomenon of persistent trends driven by irrational buying and selling. Therefore, the trader will need to be able to identify these behavioral patterns and participate at the most appropriate moment.

The Effect of Asymmetry in Risksizing

There are basically two ways to allocate capital to a trade, also called *risksizing*, namely:

   1. To allocate a fixed %risk per trade based on original or *initial* capital
   2. To allocate a fixed %risk per trade based on *current* capital

Allocating a fixed %risk per trade based on original or initial capital is referred to as *fixed sizing* while allocating a fixed %risk per trade based on initial capital is referred to as *dynamic sizing*. Let us now calculate the average profit and loss for a scenario with five wining trades and five losing trades based on the fixed-sizing approach. Average profit and loss based on fixed sizing is referred to as *linear expectancy*. Assume that we have a one-to-one R/r ratio setup with %win of 50 percent over 20 trades, that is, T = 20.

$$\text{Linear Exp} = (R \times \text{number of wins}) - (r \times \text{number of losses}) / T$$
$$= (R \times (\text{number of wins} / T)) - (r \times (\text{number of losses} / T))$$
$$= (R \times (10 / 20)) - (r \times (10 / 20))$$
$$= (R \times \text{win ratio}) - (r \times \text{loss ratio})$$
$$= (\$1 \times 0.5) - (\$1 \times 0.5)$$
$$= 0 \text{ (Breakeven)}$$

Therefore we see that five wins followed by five losses returns the capital to breakeven. The same result holds true regardless of the sequence of wins or losses. We say there is no asymmetry associated with fixed sizing since it took the same number of trades to neutralize an equal number of wins. See Figure 28.26.

Let us now turn our attention to dynamic sizing. Before that, it would be best to review some of the basic mathematics associated with compounding profit and loss.

To increase an amount M by a certain percentage P, we simply multiply M by the multiplication factor $[1 + (P/100)]$. For example, to make 10 percent on $100, we simply multiply $100 by $[1 + (10/100)] \times \$100 = 1.1 \times \$100 = \$110$. To make 10 percent on the new amount, we simply multiply the new amount by 1.1, or multiply the original $100 by 1.1 twice. To compound the original amount three times by 10 percent, we simply multiply the $100 by 1.1 three times. This can be shortened to multiplying the original amount by the multiplication factor raised to the power equal to the number of times an amount is compounded, that is, to compound $100 five times, we simply multiply $100 by $[1 + (P/100)]^5$. To compound a loss, we simply multiply an amount by $[1 - (P/100)]$, raised to the power equal to the number of times the amount is compounded. In dynamic sizing, $[1 + (P/100)]$ is called the *reward ratio* and $[1 - (P/100)]$ the *risk ratio*.

Assume now that we start off with a capital of $100 with a one-to-one R/r ratio setup where each win or loss is 10 percent, that is, %R = %r = 10 percent. Let us also assume that we experience five wining trades followed by five losing trades. The final capital will be:

$$\text{Capital after 10 trades} = \$100 \times (\text{Reward Ratio})^{\text{wins}} \times (\text{Risk Ratio})^{\text{losses}}$$
$$= \$100 \times [1 + (10 / 100)]^5 \times [1 - (10 / 100)]^5$$
$$= \$95$$

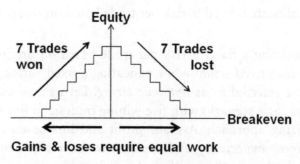

FIGURE 28.26 No Asymmetry via a Fixed-Sizing Approach.

We observe that we do not return to the original capital after the same number of wins and losses. To calculate the profit and loss, we first need to multiply the initial capital by the *return ratio,* which is simply:

$$\text{Return Ratio} = (\text{Reward Ratio})^{\text{wins}} \times (\text{Risk Ratio})^{\text{losses}}$$
$$= [1 + (10/100)]^5 \times [1 - (10/100)]^5$$
$$= 0.95099$$

It should be noted that the effects of asymmetry increase with the number of times an amount is compounded. For example, a return ratio of $1.2^5 \times 0.8^5$ gives 0.815, while $1.2^{10} \times 0.8^{10}$ gives 0.664. In this example, we see greater negative expectancies with more compounding, for an equal number of wins and losses.

The geometric profit and loss (P/L) is therefore:

$$\text{Geometric P/L} = (\text{Initial Capital} \times \text{Return Ratio}) - \text{Initial Capital}$$
$$= \text{Initial Capital} (\text{Return Ratio} - 1)$$
$$= \$100 \times (0.95099 - 1)$$
$$= -\$5 \,(\text{rounded to the closest integer})$$

The *geometric expectancy* may be calculated by finding the Tth root of the return ratio:

$$\text{Geometric Exp} = \text{Return Ratio} (1/T)$$
$$= [[1 + (10/100)]^5 \times [1 - (10/100)]^5]^{(1/10)}$$
$$= 0.99498$$

We may also use the geometric expectancy to calculate the geometric P/L accordingly:

$$\text{Geometric P/L} = \text{Initial Capital} \times \text{Geometric Exp}^T$$
$$= \$100 \times (0.99498)^{10}$$
$$= \$95$$

Assume now that we have seven winning trades where we risked 50 percent per trade. Assume that the R/r ratio is one to one. How many trades do we need to lose to fall back to breakeven? We therefore set the return ratio to 1.

$$(1.5)^7 \times (0.5)^N = 1$$
$$(0.5)^N = 1/(1.5)^7 = 0.0585$$
$$N = \ln(0.0585)/\ln(0.5)$$
$$= 4 \text{ trades}$$

We say there is *asymmetry* associated with dynamic sizing since it took a lesser number of trades to neutralize a larger number of wins. See Figure 28.27.

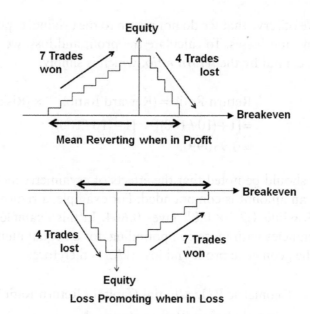

FIGURE 28.27 Asymmetry in the Dynamic-Sizing Approach.

This implies that the system, under dynamic sizing, has a *mean-reverting tendency or behavior when it is in profit*. Since the order or sequence of wins and losses has no effect on the outcome, this also means that it would take seven winning trades to return the capital to breakeven after losing only four trades, assuming that all trades were initiated with the same R/r ratio. This implies that dynamic sizing has a *loss-promoting tendency or behavior when the system is experiencing loss*. To reduce the effects of asymmetry (and thus reduce the impact of both the mean-reversion bias when in profit and loss-promoting bias when in loss) the trader may:

- Reduce the %risk per trade
- Reduce the number of trades being compounded

Monte Carlo simulations of fixed and dynamic sizing systems indicate the following with regard to asymmetry:

- When R/r →1:1, there is no asymmetry for small %r in fixed sizing systems
- When R/r →1:1, there is no asymmetry for large %r in fixed sizing systems, but the balance curve is more volatile
- When R/r →1:1, there is no discernible asymmetry for very small %r in dynamic sizing systems
- When R/r →1:1, there is significant asymmetry for large %r in dynamic sizing systems, but the balance curve is more volatile

It is also established via random simulations of hundreds of thousands of trades that any trading edge or advantage in the system kicks in and begins to impact the system favorably in the following manner:

- When R/r > 1, the favorable impact of edge kicks in earlier for small %r in fixed sizing systems
- When R/r > 1, the favorable impact of edge kicks in later for larger %r in fixed sizing systems
- When R/r > 1, the favorable impact of edge kicks in earlier for small %r in dynamic sizing systems
- When R/r > 1, the favorable impact of edge kicks in later for larger %r in dynamic sizing systems

It is also found that for a typical system with a two-to-one R/r ratio setup with a %risk of around 1%r and %win of 40 percent, a small edge can take anywhere from to 300 to 600 trades before it begins to impact the system favorably. From both these findings, the trader, in order to position him - or herself with the highest probability of being profitable over the longer term, should:

1. Trade with the smallest %risk per trade possible
2. Allow the system sufficient time and trades to allow any edge and trade advantage to kick in
3. Conduct backtests with at least 500 data points in order to see the effects of any edge in the system

Effect of Tradesizing on Linear and Geometric Expectancy

Let us now compare two setups with equal settings except for an increase in tradesize.

1. For Fixed-Sizing Systems:
   Lin Exp = (R × win ratio) − (r × loss ratio)
   a. For R/r →2:1 and %win = 50 percent:
      Lin Exp = ($2 × 0.5) − ($1 × 0.5) = $0.5 (positive expectancy)
   b. For R/r →2:1 and %win = 50 percent with Tradesize doubled:
      Lin Exp = ($4 × 0.5) − ($2 × 0.5) = $1 (positive expectancy)
   Therefore increasing tradesize actually increases expectancy if it is > $0
2. For Dynamic Sizing Systems:
   Return Ratio = (Reward Ratio)^{wins} × (Risk Ratio)^{losses}
   Geometric Expectancy = Return Ratio $^{(1/T)}$
   a. For R/r ~ 2:1, %win = 50 percent, %risk = 1 percent, wins = 26, losses = 49:
      Return Ratio = $(1.02)^{26} × (0.99)^{49} = 1.022$
      Geometric Expectancy = Return Ratio $^{(1/T)} = 1.022^{(1/75)}$
      = 1.00029 (i.e., >1)

   (We do not actually need to calculate the geometric expectancy to see if we have made or lost capital. If the Return Ratio is greater than one, then the geometric expectancy will also be greater than one. Values above one indicate positive expectancy and values below one indicate negative expectancy.)
   b. For R/r ~ 2:1, %win = 50 percent, %risk = 5 percent, wins = 26, losses = 49:
      Return Ratio = $(1.10)^{26} × (0.95)^{49} = 0.9653$

$$\text{Geometric Expectancy} = \text{Return Ratio}^{(1/T)} = 0.9653^{(1/75)}$$
$$= 0.99952 \text{ (i.e., } < 1)$$

Therefore, we see that increasing the tradesize actually decreases the geometric expectancy in this case and hence results in a loss. This is a very significant point. It tells us that we can turn a winning system into a losing system by just increasing the tradesize. It also tells us that there is a possibility that we may also be able to turn a losing system into a winning system by just decreasing the tradesize.

For dynamic sizing, there exists an optimal %risk for every R/r ratio setup. Crossing that threshold will cause a winning system to start losing money. The trader must therefore know what that tradesize is before embarking on a campaign of augmenting %risk and tradesizes in the hope of boosting profitability.

Minimum %Win for Dynamic Sizing Systems

Let wins equal W and losses equal L. To find the minimum wins required to return to breakeven, set the return ratio to equal 1. (R = Reward ratio, r = Risk ratio, W = number of wins, and L = number of losses)

$$\text{Return Ratio} = R^W \times r^L = 1$$
$$R^W = r^{-L}$$
$$W \ln R = -L \ln r$$
$$W = -L(\ln r / \ln R)$$

This represents the number of wins required to return to breakeven.

Effect of Risksizing on Dynamic Sizing Systems

Let us now calculate the minimum %win for dynamic sizing system.

a. Let R/r → 2:1, %r = 10 percent and L = 49 losing trades:
  W = −L (lnr/lnR)
  W = −49 (ln0.9/ln1.2) = 28.31 wins required to break even
  Minimum %win = (28.31/(28.31 + 49)) × 100% = 36.6%
b. Let R/r → 2:1, %r = 20 percent and L = 49 losing trades:
  W = −49 (ln0.8/ln1.4) = 32.49 wins required to break even
  Min %win = (32.49/(32.49 +49)) × 100% = 39.9%

We see that increasing the %risk actually increases the minimum %win, making it harder to maintain a positive expectancy over the longer term.

We learned from studying the relationships between risk, tradesize, number of trades, and R/r ratio sizing that:

- Increasing the number of trades when the geometric expectancy is less than one is detrimental to the trading account
- Increasing the number of trades when the geometric expectancy is greater than one is highly favorable to the trading account

- Larger tradesizes requires a higher minimum %win
- There is an optimal tradesize or %r, for every R/r and minimum %win

The Expectancy Box Problem

By taking profit and cutting loss based on predetermined *fixed exits* in R/r ratio setups, we inadvertently set up an *average* R/r ratio and consequently an average minimum %win condition. We must then constantly try to achieve the minimum %win to keep our expectancy positive. Unfortunately, the %win is an uncontrollable component of the system. One solution to significantly mitigate the damaging effects of the expectancy box problem is to employ stochastic exit mechanisms to allow for a greater variation in the R/r ratios within the system.

The Ease of Recovery (EOR)

Let us look at a multi-timeframe setup where trades are initiated over the short and longer term. Assume that the R/r ratios and $risk are identical. The shorter-term entries use five contracts while the longer-term entries use two contracts. For every loss over the shorter term, the longer-term trades need to extend five times the distance in order to neutralize the losses incurred over the shorter term. Statistically, the rate of shorter-term losses will occur more frequently than gains from the longer-term setups, raising the average rate of loss above the average rate of gain experienced by the system, eventually swamping the account permanently. This is one reason why multi-timeframe trading is very damaging to the account unless the trader knows how to counteract the imbalances. The best solution is to trade within a single timeframe. For more details on EOR, refer to the book *The Wiley Trading Guide (Volume II)* where the author discusses the median method as a test for the degree of EOR within the system.

Tradesizing

We shall now look at scenarios where making a profitable series of trades based on technical analysis is almost impossible without proper tradesizing. Let us employ a simple technical rule of entry. Breakout entries are triggered by a penetration of the previous swing point with the stoplosses placed at the most recent significant swing point before the breakout. See Figure 28.28.

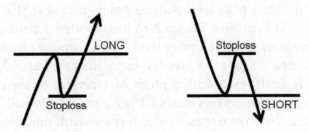

FIGURE 28.28 Simple Long and Short Breakout Entries.

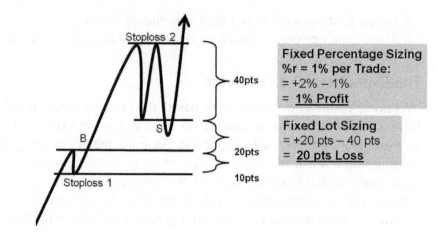

FIGURE 28.29 Comparing Percentage Sizing with Fixed-Lot Sizing.

Now assume that we have two traders, Trader A and Trader B. Trader A risks 1 percent per trade (fixed-percentage sizing) whereas Trader B trades with one fixed lot (fixed-lot sizing). Assume that Trader A is using fixed sizing, meaning that he is risking 1 percent of the initial capital and not of current capital.

Trader A enters at breakout Point B with a stoploss placed 10 points below the entry, that is, Stoploss 1 (SL1), as seen in Figure 28.29. Trader A exits at 20 points above the long entry where a new short is triggered. Since Trader A exited 20 points above entry, Trader A makes 2 percent (since the stopsize of 10 points represents a 1 percent risk). Unfortunately, Trader A lost 1 percent when the short exited at the stoplosses indicated at SL2. Overall, Trader A profited 1 percent from the two trades. Trader B also enters at the Point B breakout with one lot and a stoploss placed at exactly the same swing low, SL1. Trader B also exited 20 points above entry and makes $20 of profit (1 lot × 20 point move). Unfortunately Trader B lost $40 when the short exited at the stoplosses indicated at SL2. Overall, Trader B lost $20 from the two trades.

We see two traders trading the same entries and exits, yet the performance differs drastically! In this example, we also see that entries and exits have nothing much to do with profitability. Profit or loss depended on the type of tradesizing method employed. This is shocking news for technical traders. Let us now look at one more example.

Trader A enters at breakout Point B with a stoploss placed 10 points below the entry, that is, Stoploss 1 (SL1), as seen in Figure 28.30. Price moves up but reverses and takes out the SL1 stoploss, causing Trader A to lose 1 percent. A short is initiated at the same price level with a stoploss placed at SL2. Unfortunately, price also takes out SL2, causing Trader A to lose another 1 percent. Trader A enters a new long breakout at the SL2 price level with a stoploss placed at SL3 and a take profit (T/P) placed 50 points above the entry indicated at Take Profit in Figure 28.30. Trader A finally exits with a profit of 1 percent at the take profit (since the SL3 stopsize of 50 points represents a 1 percent risk). Overall Trader A now loses 1 percent from the three trades. Trader B enters with one fixed lot at breakout Point B with a stoploss placed 10 points below the entry, that is, at SL1. Price moves up

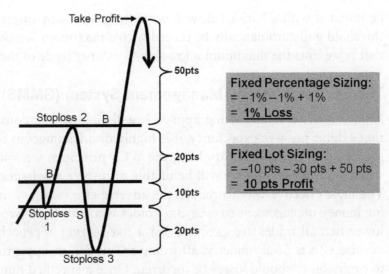

FIGURE 28.30 Comparing Percentage Sizing with Fixed-Lot Sizing.

but reverses and takes out the SL1 stoploss, causing Trader B to lose $10. A short is initiated at the same price level with a stoploss placed at SL2. Unfortunately, price also takes out SL2, causing Trader B to lose another $30. Trader B enters a new long breakout at the SL2 price level with a stoploss placed at SL3 and a take profit also placed 50 points above the entry at Take Profit. Trader B finally exits with a profit of $50 at the take profit. Overall, Trader B now makes $10 from the 3 trades.

Again, we see two traders trading the same entries and exits, yet the performance differs drastically! And again, we see that entries and exits have nothing much to do with profitability. Not only do we need to predict future price direction, which is hard enough, but we now also need to predict the correct tradesizing approach to use in order to be profitable. Our probability of winning has just been cut in half.

The solution to this is to use a tradesizing technique that the author has termed *proportional sizing*. Proportional sizing functions as fixed-lot sizing below a certain threshold and as percentage sizing above the same threshold. The trick is to make sure that at least 90 to 95 percent of all stopsizes fall below this threshold. The steps are as follows:

1. Perform a backtest to gauge the average stopsize for the strategy being employed
2. Find the 95 percent threshold level by locating the two standard deviation value for the average stopsize and adding this to the average stopsize (this amount represents the threshold value)
3. Find the average tradesize by dividing the $risk per trade by the new stopsize

For stoplosses that exceed the threshold value, revert to percentage sizing to determine the correct tradesize. This is easily done by dividing the $risk per trade by the stopsize. Assume that the $risk corresponds to the maximum 1 percent risk per trade for the system. With this technique, the majority of the trades will be initiated with a %risk below 1 percent. Trades with stopsizes that exceed the threshold will automatically be placed with a maximum %risk of 1 percent (since that represents the maximum allowable %risk per trade of the system).

The Geolinear Money Management System (GMMS)

Although the dynamic sizing approach will yield tremendous profit for systems that exhibit positive expectancy, it is highly disadvantageous for systems exhibiting negative expectancy. Applying the WCS principle, we must assume that the worst will happen and we will be unable to resolve any issues associated with it. The most effective way to reduce the adverse effects of asymmetry when applying money management to everyday trades is to employ a two-tier system. At the lower tier, all trades are executed via a fixed-sizing approach. This reduces the adverse effects of asymmetry, affording the trader an opportunity to trade back to profitability should losses be incurred. Once a specified number of trades have been executed, the new tradesize will now be recalculated based on the current equity in the account. This represents the second tier of risk management. In this way, traders can still access the power of compounding by applying it only after a certain number of trades have been made, while removing the effects of asymmetry from all the daily or individual trades. For more details of the GMMS approach, refer to the book *The Wiley Trading Guide (Volume II)* where the author discusses trading with a two-tiered money management approach.

CHAPTER 28 REVIEW QUESTIONS

1. List and explain the six passive components of a money management system.
2. Describe the relationship between the six passive components of a money management system.
3. How can traders reduce the effects of asymmetry in trading?
4. What is the difference between fixed and dynamic sizing?
5. Describe the two uncontrollable factors in trading and how they affect performance.
6. How would you use the R/r ratio setup effectively?
7. What are the advantages of using a stochastic exit?
8. Calculate the minimum %win for a system with an R/r ratio of 5:1.

REFERENCES

Balsara, Nauzer J. 1992. *Money Management Strategies for Futures Traders*. Hoboken, NJ: Wiley Finance.

Gehm, Fred. 1995. *Quantitative Trading and Money Management*. Scarborough, Canada: Irwin Professional Publishing.

Tharp, Van K. 2006. *Trade Your Way to Financial Freedom*. New York: McGraw-Hill.

The Wiley Trading Guide, Volume II. (Milton, Queensland: John Wiley & Sons Australia.

CHAPTER 29

Technical Trading Systems

LEARNING OBJECTIVES

After studying this chapter, you should be able to:

- Understand and identify the main components that make up a trading system
- Describe the use of in-sample and out-of-sample data during the backtesting and walk forward process
- Understand the difference between the various performance metrics
- Distinguish between passive and aggressive trading approaches with respect to chart patterns

---

There are various elements associated with designing and testing a trading system. This chapter introduces the practitioner to the basic components of a trading system and explains the importance of effective system testing. There is also a brief description of the various performance metrics related to trading systems.

29.1 CONCEPTUALIZING A TRADING SYSTEM

As we saw in chapter 28, an effective trader must account for three main areas of concern, namely:

1. Trade management: This involves the management of positions, which includes the timing of entries, profit targeting, stoploss placement, stopsizing, rolling of stops, scaling in and out of positions, reinvesting profits, and compounding profits.
2. Trader management: This involves the effectiveness of a trader in initiating, managing, and controlling the risk associated with open positions. The trader must be able to execute the trading plan effectively and efficiently, which may be adversely affected by various biases, expectations, emotions, confusion, and peer pressure.

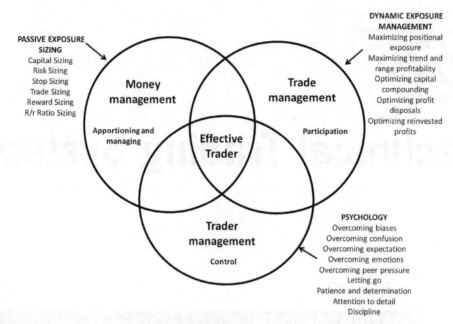

FIGURE 29.1 Components of a Trading System and the Effective Trader.

3. Money management: This involves the effective apportioning or sizing of risk and equity with respect to a trading system. It involves capital sizing, percentage risk sizing, stop sizing, trade sizing (size of the position), reward sizing (amount of take profit), and reward to risk ratio sizing (which determines the minimum average winning percentage of the system).

See Figure 29.1.

It is imperative that the trader decides on the trading approach and all its design implications before risking capital in the markets. A well-conceived trading system should take into account:

- The type of markets it will be used to trade in
- Whether it is a trend-following or counter-trend methodology
- The setup and filter specifications to be employed in order to determine entries and exits
- The frequency of trade signals expected for the setup and filters employed and the maximum rate of loss under the worst-case scenario
- The amount and type of risks associated with trading a particular market and the measures required to reduce such risks
- The minimum amount of capital required to trade a particular market
- The appropriate backtesting and forward walkthrough tests required to determine if a strategy is profitable (at least over the test period)
- The level of participation and commitment required of the trader to manage such an approach
- The trading platform limitations and how they affect the execution of the strategy

- The trading costs associated with such an approach and whether they significantly increase the minimum winning percentage required to maintain positive expectancy
- The kind of equity risk controls and money management style to be employed
- The type and degree of diversification intended and the amount of correlation between markets during a collapse
- The optimization method to be employed for such a system

All of the issues listed above should be addressed effectively. One of the most important elements to consider when designing trading systems is to account for the various worst-case scenarios that may unfold during a trade and the possible solutions to help mitigate the risks associated with such occurrences.

29.2 BASIC COMPONENTS OF A TRADING SYSTEM

A basic trading system consists primarily of:

- Entry and exit setup rules and filters: The rules for participation should be simple and straightforward to implement. Systems with too many complex rules for entry and exit will make subsequent system optimizations more challenging. It would be hard to pinpoint the issues causing a system to underperform when there are too many rules and price filters being employed. Also, with too many filters and rules of participation, there exists a real possibility of unintended curve fitting.
- Passive money management components: The trader should always backtest the system to identify the most appropriate capital, risk, stop, and trade sizing settings.
- Rules for dynamically managing a trade: The rules for managing open positions should also be objective and simple in order to allow for effective system optimization.
- Equity risk controls: The trader may also employ various risk controls when equity declines to specific levels within the system. For example, when equity declines by 30 percent, the trader may simultaneously halve the position size and double the stopsize of all subsequent trades. This will maintain the original maximum percentage risk associated with each trade and will also allow the trader to gauge if the system is being swamped by market noise. If equity continues to decline by more than 50 percent, the trader may opt to halve the position size and double the stopsize one more time. Should equity rise back above the threshold levels, these equity controls may be abandoned with the system resuming its original position size and stopsize. In addition, the use of equity curve management is critical to successful trade performance.

29.3 SYSTEM TESTING AND OPTIMIZATION

One of the main objectives of the test and development process is to *optimize* the trading system. Optimization simply means finding a set of conditions that maximizes the system's profit and minimizes its losses. Unfortunately, it is possible to over-optimize a system, producing unrealistic results that would not likely be replicated when tested using new data.

When testing a trading system, data is employed to develop the trading strategy and test for profitability and longer term positive expectancy. The original data set used to develop and test the strategy is called the *in-sample data*. The strategy is then back tested using past data that was not used during the development process. This data is referred to as *out-of-sample data*. Finally, the system is tested using live data. The process of testing the system with live data is referred to as forward testing or walkthrough. The data used during a forward test is also referred to as out-of-sample data since such data was not used during the development process. See Figure 29.2.

Generally speaking, the greater the amount of data used to back and forward test the system, the more reliable will be the results of the tests in gauging the expectancy and consistency of performance of the system. Although it is generally accepted that data corresponding to at least 30 trades is required for any test to be *statistically significant*, it is more realistic to employ data based on at least 300 to 500 trades to determine the true longer-term performance of a trading system. For example, the minimum 30 trades may consist of data that is entirely related to a series of trades that occurred during a very strong market rally. Such data may be biased and may not account for situations where the market was bearish or volatile. Hence testing a system under such limited market conditions will not produce a system that is flexible and robust enough to handle changing market conditions. Therefore, it is recommended that sufficient data be collected under a variety of market conditions, which should ideally include:

- Ranging markets
- Strong bullish and bearish markets
- Highly volatile markets
- Markets exhibiting gapping prices

The commonly held assumption that 30 trades is sufficient to yield statistically significant results is not true, and it varies with the stopsize. For example, a foreign exchange system that trades with a stop size of 50 pips cannot be compared with

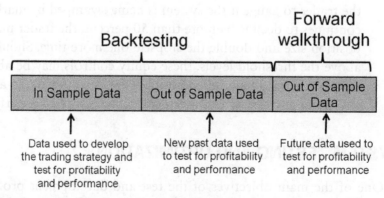

FIGURE 29.2 In-Sample and Out-of-Sample Data.

one that has an extremely tight stop of 2 pips. For very tight stops, the probability of being taken out by the market is significantly higher than with a system of with a stopsize of 50 pips. As such, it will experience many more losses on average, and this will introduce a statistical bias toward more degenerate results. Therefore, the smaller the stopsize, the less accurate will be the assumption that 30 trades would produce a statistically reliable result. In short, *statistical significance is a function of stopsize.*

It is possible during the development process to continue tweaking the system parameters until the system exhibits positive expectancy. In fact any trade methodology can be made to show positive expectancy with sufficient adjustment of the trade parameters. This is referred to as *curve fitting*. To avoid or reduce the effects of curve fitting, out-of-sample data is used to test the system. If the system fails to perform well using out-of-sample data, it will undergo additional re-optimization. Unfortunately, the out-of-sample data would now be used re-optimize the system. This process gradually reduces the amount of out-of-sample data available, which increases the likelihood of curve fitting with the system.

Another way to test for curve fitting is to *reorder* the data during the backtest. This simply means to shuffle the data around so that the order of the trades does not occur according to their original sequence. A robust and reliable trading system should continue to display the same level of positive performance under such randomization of trade sequences. Extreme underperformance during the randomization of trade sequences is an indication of potential curve fitting affecting the data.

One big mistake that many novice traders commit is to back test a system by looking for the parameter settings that produce the greatest profit, only to discover that the system fails to replicate its earlier performance when tested using out-of-sample data.

For example, let us assume that a trader is testing a moving average crossover strategy where the system goes long every time price crosses above a moving average and goes short when price crosses below it. Stoplosses are placed below the moving average when the system goes long and above it when it goes short. The trader is careful to ensure that enough trade data is tested across a variety of market conditions to ensure that the system is robust. A test is then conducted to identify the moving average with the lookback period that will produce the greatest profit. Occasionally this approach may work in producing a system that seems to display positive performance when tested with out-of-sample data. *But in most cases it will fail to maintain its positive performance.* The main reason has to do with the behavior of the equity curve. See Figure 29.3.

In Figure 29.3, we observe equity curves associated with moving averages with various lookback periods tested for returns over the in-sample test period. The moving average associated with equity curve B displays the greatest returns over the in-sample test period, indicated by the equity level at point 1. Most novice traders would therefore regard this moving average as the moving average with the optimum lookback period. Unfortunately they fail to realize that the equity curve associated with this moving average is in fact displaying diminishing returns over most of the in-sample testing period. Therefore, when they subsequently test the performance of the moving average using out-of-sample data,

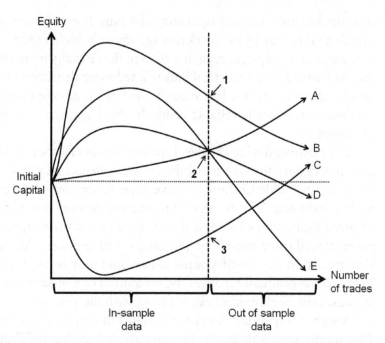

FIGURE 29.3 Equity Curve of Various Moving Average Returns during the In-Sample Test Period.

they are somewhat perplexed as to why the moving average is underperforming. We also see that the equity returns associated with point 2 may represent moving averages with varying equity curve behaviors. The best choice of moving averages would therefore be those associated with equity curves A and C. Both curves display increasing returns over the in-sample test period and we may assume that this behavior should persist at least for some duration before failing when tested with out-of-sample data. We also observe that although curve C displayed negative returns (below the initial capital level), the moving average associated with equity curve C is still a viable choice as it has a greater potential to be profitable during the out-of-sample test period than moving averages associated with curves B, D, and E.

This simple example shows that optimizing a system merely to produce the greatest returns is not the correct approach. It would be better to select the system associated with an up-sloping equity curve during the test period, regardless of the size of returns it produces over the test period.

Besides just testing for positive equity curve performance, the trader may also test the system for the largest percentage drawdown. It would be pointless to select a system with a positive equity curve performance that is accompanied by extreme and volatile drawdowns. See Figure 29.4.

In Figure 29.4, we now see that the moving average associated with equity curve A is displaying an extreme drawdown event, indicated at point X. This suggests the trader should in fact select a moving average associated with positive equity curve performance that is not overly volatile. It is interesting to note that the moving average associated with equity curve B displays the greatest return when compared to the equity curves associated with the other moving averages.

918

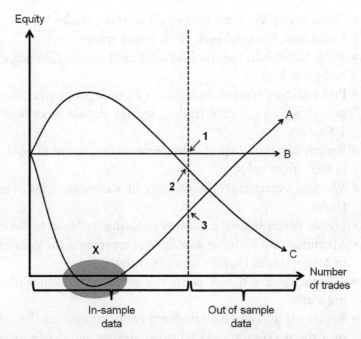

FIGURE 29.4 Equity Curve Displaying Extreme Drawdown During the In-Sample Test Period.

Unfortunately, it did not display any potential of being profitable during the in-sample test period. In this example, none of the moving averages associated with equity curves A, B, or C would represent wise choices for a moving average crossover system.

A trading system said to be *robust* if it has the ability to maintain consistent positive expectancy:

- Under all market conditions
- In a wide range of markets
- With variations in its parameter settings

Although it is universally agreed that a trading system should be robust under all market conditions, there is some debate as to whether a system has to also be robust in all markets, as there is nothing wrong or disadvantageous about designing a system to trade a specific market. Another common test of robustness is the ability of the system to perform consistently well with changes in its parameter settings. For example, if small adjustments in the lookback period of a moving average crossover system produce large volatility in the equity, we say that the system is less robust.

29.4 PERFORMANCE MEASUREMENT

It is important to be able to gauge the level of performance of a trading system in order to be able to analyze it and effect improvements. Below are a few performance- and trade-related metrics that help traders keep track of how the system is behaving:

- Gross profit: the total sum of all winning trades
- Gross loss: the total sum of all losing trades
- Total Net Profit: the total return based on the difference between gross profit and gross loss
- Profit factor: represents a ratio of gross profit over the absolute sum of the gross loss; an effective trading system should have profit factors at or above 1.5 to 2
- Return on initial equity: the percentage change in equity with respect to the initial equity value
- Winning percentage: the number of winning trades over the total number of trades
- Losing percentage: the number of losing trades over the total number of trades
- Maximum consecutive wins/losses: represents the greatest number of winning or losing trades that occurred in a row
- Average reward to risk ratio: the average winning trade over the average losing trade
- Return to maximum drawdown ratio: represents the return on initial equity over the maximum peak to valley drawdown experienced by the system

Other basic metrics include:

- Largest winning and losing trades
- Highest and lowest closed equity
- Maximum number of shares/contracts
- Length of drawdown
- Longest drawdown
- Average margin and leverage
- Average slippage
- Average monthly and annual compounded returns
- Sharpe ratio

29.5 CHAPTER SUMMARY

As we have seen, the choice of market and various trade parameters associated with risk, performance measurement, and equity management play a huge role in assessing the reliability, robustness, and effectiveness of a trading system. In most cases, professional fund managers use rather sophisticated management software to keep track of how these trade parameters vary with each other and how they perform under various market regimes.

CHAPTER 29 REVIEW QUESTIONS

1. Describe the various components of a trading system.
2. What constitutes an effective trader?
3. Explain what is meant by a robust system.

4. Categorize the trade-related metrics into return and risk metrics.
5. Is back testing for the largest return an effective strategy?
6. What is meant by curve fitting?
7. Explain how we can reduce the effects of curve fitting.
8. What is the difference between in-sample and out-of-sample data? Explain how you would use such data to test a trading system.

REFERENCES

Kaufman, Perry. 2005. *New Trading Systems and Methods*. Hoboken, NJ: John Wiley & Sons.

Kirkpatrick, Charles, and Julie Dahlquist. 2007. *Technical Analysis: The Complete Resource for Financial Market Technicians*. Upper Saddle River, NJ: Pearson Education.

Stridsman, Thomas. 2003. *Trading Systems and Money Management*. New York: McGraw-Hill.

Gehm, Fred. 1995. *Quantitative Trading and Money Management*. Scarborough, Canada: Irwin Professional.

Basic Investment Decision Making Based on Chart Analysis

A.1 USING TECHNICAL DATA TO SUPPORT CLIENT'S OBJECTIVE

[**Note:** Before reading this chapter, the reader should first be familiar with the concepts and content of Chapter 26.]

Once we have organized all our technical data according to duration, sentiment, and instrument, we may proceed to integrate all the available information, organizing it into a coherent presentation of facts and reasons for various trading decisions and recommendations.

One important point to keep in mind is that it does not really matter which outlook, be it bullish or bearish, that market participants are acting upon, as long as they have clearly defined the potential risks and rewards involved in maintaining a certain outlook on the market or on a stock. This is the most logical approach that any trader or investor can adopt in the markets, since no one possesses the ability to actually forecast future market or price action with any certainty.

The next section contains a sample analysis and basic participatory recommendations. It is by no means meant to be exhaustive or comprehensive. It will at least provide a basic idea of how technical data is used to support various market outlooks and trading objectives.

The format is as follows:

- Describe the climate or environment in which the stock is trading in bullish and bearish terms (i.e., an analysis of the index or broad market)
- Describe the outlook for the stock in bullish and bearish terms
- Describe the various participatory options available in the stock with respect to the risk capacity and expectation
- Clearly identify *actionable* price levels in the stock (i.e., entry points, take profits, and stoploss levels)

A.2 ADVICE FOR THE LONG-TERM INVESTOR (BULLISH OUTLOOK)

For the following section, refer to Figures A.1 to A.8. All charts will be referred to at various points in the following analysis. The duration and interval of each chart is indicated.

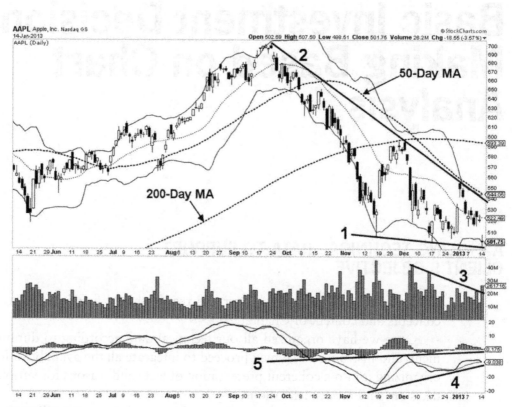

FIGURE A.1 Daily Chart of Apple Inc. (Medium Term).
Courtesy of Stockcharts.com

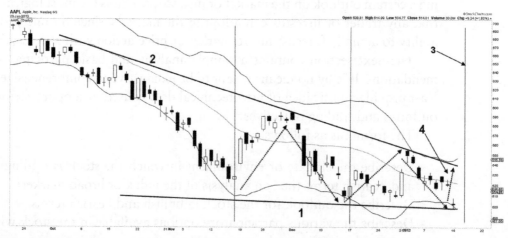

FIGURE A.2 Daily Chart of Apple Inc. (Medium Term).
Courtesy of Stockcharts.com

FIGURE A.3   60-Min Chart of Apple Inc. (Short Term).
Courtesy of Stockcharts.com

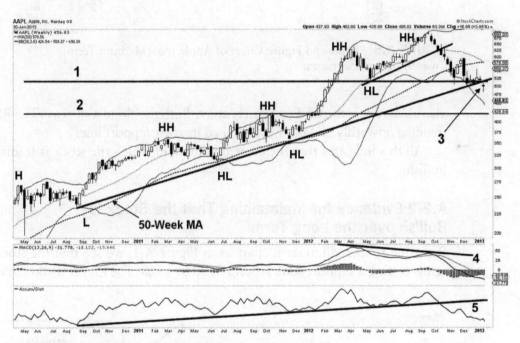

FIGURE A.4   Weekly Chart of Apple Inc. (Long Term).
Courtesy of Stockcharts.com

A.2.1 The Climate in Which the Stock Is Trading (the Index)

Referring to the long term chart in Figure A.7, we see that the Dow Jones is currently making higher highs and higher lows, indicating that the prevailing uptrend is still intact. We also see that the index is still being supported by two uptrend lines, 2 and 3, and that the index is currently above both the 50 and 200 week moving averages. Referring now to the medium term chart as seen in Figure A.8, we notice that the index is currently bullish with respect to the Ichimoku indicators. The index is currently above the cloud. It is also above both the Tenkan-sen and Kijun-sen. We

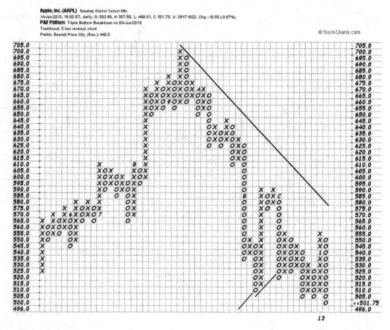

FIGURE A.5 Point and Figure Chart of Apple Inc. (Medium Term).
Courtesy of Stockcharts.com

also observe that the Chikou Span is above both the cloud and price. The RSI is also trending upwardly and has not breached its own support line.

All this indicates that the current climate in which the stock is trading is still bullish.

A.2.2 Evidence for Maintaining That the Stock Is Bullish over the Long Term

Referring to a medium term chart as in Figure A.1, we see that the stock is currently testing a support zone around $500 to $520. The longer it stays at or above

FIGURE A.6 Daily Chart of Apple Inc. (Medium Term).
Courtesy of Stockcharts.com

FIGURE A.7 Weekly Chart of Dow Jones Industrial Average (Long Term).
Courtesy of Stockcharts.com

this support zone, more bullishness is expected as it implies that the support is strong. We also notice bullish divergence in the volume action (3) and MACD (3) and (4). The stock price is also currently at the lower Bollinger Band, indicating potential support.

On the other medium term chart seen in Figure A.6, we observe that the stock is currently finding support at CD. As long as the stock stays above the support, our bullish view remains intact. In Figure A.2, we notice a five wave formation, suggesting a potential short-term move up to meet the downtrend line (2). We can clearly see the current spinning top, which is a bullish signal. We are also aware of a developing pattern of cycle lows with the new low expected around the current time (3). Again this is bullish.

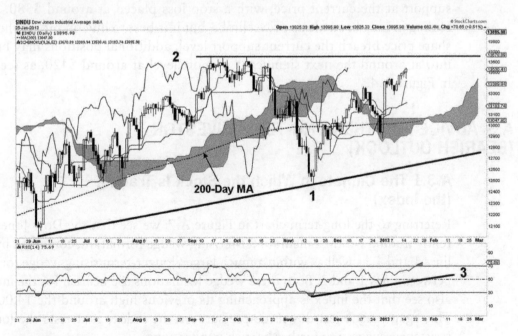

FIGURE A.8 Daily Chart of Dow Jones (Medium Term).
Courtesy of Stockcharts.com

A.2.3 Participatory Options for the Long-Term Investor

As a recap, here are the seven participatory options available to any market participant, namely:

1. To enter (i.e., to initiate) a new position
2. To add to (i.e., to scale into) a position
3. To reduce the size of (i.e., to scale out of) a position
4. To exit (i.e., to fully scale out of) a position
5. To re-enter a position in the same or opposite direction
6. To fully or partially hedge a position (i.e., to neutralize or diminish directional risk)
7. To remain in "cash" (i.e., to refrain from holding any positions)

For the more risk averse long-term investor who wants to initiate a new position in the stock, we would recommend buying into the stock at the current support level with a stop loss placed just below it at around $480. Once the stock proves that it can penetrate the medium-term downtrend line (2) as seen in Figure A.1, we recommend scaling in very small amounts with a stop placed just below the trend line. Should price pull back to the trendline (2), further scaling in of additional positions may be made, unless it falls back below the trendline. Also, some scaling in of additional positions is recommended should price break back above the long term trendline, as seen in Figure A.4. We also advise the client to roll up the stops for the position entered at the lower support. Finally, should the stock collapse below the current support, we advise the client to cut all losses by exiting at the stop that was placed below the support.

For the more risk seeking long term investor, we recommend buying into the support at the current price, with a stop loss placed at around $380. Further scaling in may be made as price climbs, but it is best to buy on profit. Should the share price breach the current support level, additional positions may be scaled into at around the next significant support level at around $420, as seen at (2) in Figure A.4.

A.3 ADVICE FOR THE LONG-TERM INVESTOR (BEARISH OUTLOOK)

A.3.1 The Climate in Which the Stock Is Trading (the Index)

Referring to the long-term chart in Figure A.7, we see that the Dow Jones is currently trading within a medium-term rising wedge formation, contained by trendlines 1 and 3, as well as within a much larger, longer-term rising wedge formation, between lines 1 and 2. Both these wedge formations are bearish for the index. We also see that the index is approaching its previous high around the 14,000 level. This again may exert downside pressure on the index, as it tests the long-term resistance, suggesting further bearish implications.

A.3.2 Evidence for Maintaining That the Stock Is Bearish over the Long Term

Referring to the medium-term chart in Figure A.1, we see that the stock is currently below its 20-, 50-, and 200-day moving averages, a bearish sign. We also see that price has been making lower highs over the last four months, forming a descending triangle of sorts. This is again a very bearish medium-term indication. We see in Figure A.4, a long-term chart for the stock, that price has finally breached the long-term uptrend line (3), as well as violated the previous support level (1). For the first time in many years, the stock has also finally made a lower low. The stock's MACD indicator also exhibits standard bearish divergence (4) and we also see that the accumulation/distribution indicator has also breached its own uptrend line. Finally, in Figure A.5, a medium-term Point and Figure chart, we observe a triple bottom breakout, adding to the evidence that the stock is currently overwhelmingly bearish.

A.3.3 Participatory Options for the Long-Term Investor Who Has Turned Bearish

For the more risk averse long-term investor we recommend staying in cash instead of participating in the stock.

For the more risk seeking long-term (bearish) investor, we recommend buying into the stock only after a significant decline in price and only beginning to consider participating in the stock once price starts to consolidate around a certain price range for at least a few months. We may then start to accumulate in small measures.

A.4 ADVICE FOR THE SHORT- AND MEDIUM-TERM BULLISH TRADER

A.4.1 The Climate in Which the Stock Is Trading (the Index)

We have already identified and covered the numerous bullish indications in the index as noted in Section 2.1 above and will apply them to the long-term chart in Figure A.7 and the medium-term chart in Figure A.8.

A.4.2 Evidence for Maintaining That the Stock Is Bullish over the Short to Medium Term

We have also already identified and covered the numerous bullish indications in the stock as noted in the previous paragraph in Section 2.1 with regard to Figures A.1, A.2, and A.6.

In Figure A.3, the short-term chart of the stock shows price finding support at D, the projected 1:1 minimum measuring objective based on the channel height. Price is also hovering above the previous support level (indicated by line 2). Again, as long as the stock remains above these supports, the bullish view of the stock remains intact.

A.4.3 Participatory Options for the Short- and Medium-Term Bullish Trader

For the more risk averse short- to medium-term trader who wants to initiate a new position in the stock, we would recommend buying into the stock at the current support level at around $500 with a stop loss placed at $490. Scaling into more positions may be possible should price rebound back above the lower Bollinger Band as in Figure A.3. Again, the client is advised to remain cautious in adding new positions and should only seriously consider doing so once price proves that it is able to break back up above the long-term trendline as seen in Figure A.4. Until then, that trendline represents a formidable resistance to price. Any profitable long positions should employ protective stops, trailing gradually closer to current price as the market approaches the resistance level. We may also calculate some basic downside price projections based on the Point and Figure vertical and horizontal counts seen in Figure A.5, providing important levels for potentially adding, reducing, or exiting positions. In addition, Fibonacci ratio projection based on the peaks and troughs, as well as the chart pattern projection based on the triangle formation found in Figure A.1, may help identify significant supportive confluences. At these supportive confluences, a trader who is risk adverse in the price on entry may elect to buy fewer shares whereas a trader who is risk seeking in the price on entry may add aggressively to his or her current portfolio. Violation of a supportive confluence may force risk averse traders to exit or reduce positions.

A.5 ADVICE FOR THE SHORT- AND MEDIUM-TERM BEARISH TRADER

A.5.1 The Climate in Which the Stock Is Trading (the Index)

We have, as before, already identified and covered the numerous bearish indications as noted in the previous paragraph in Section 3.1 with regard to the long-term chart in Figure A.7. As for the medium-term chart seen in Figure A.8, we see that price is rapidly approaching a significant resistance level as indicated at (2). This has the potential to exert downside pressure on the index. We also see that the RSI indicator is approaching the overbought level, possibly coinciding with price testing the resistance at (2). Also observed is the expanding divergence between price and the 200-day moving average, increasing the possibility of a short-term correction.

All this indicates that the current climate in which the stock is trading is still potentially bearish.

A.5.2 Evidence for Maintaining That the Stock Is Bearish over the Short and Medium Term

We have already identified and covered the numerous bearish indications as noted in the previous paragraph in Section 3.1 with regard to the long-term and medium-term charts as seen in Figures A.1, A.4, and A.5.

We further observe that the short-term chart seen in Figure A.3 depicts rather bearish price action, especially with price gapping down directly to level D, with the subsequent rebound being rejected at level C. All this is very bearish to the stock in the short term.

A.5.3 Participatory Options for the Short- and Medium-Term Bearish Trader

For the more risk seeking short- to medium-term bearish trader, we recommend shorting into the stock should it breach its current support level with a stop placed above at around $505 to $510, and continuing to scale in more short positions, preferably on profit, as price keeps declining. Another great shorting opportunity may well be the establishment of new short positions at the retest of the long-term uptrend line, as seen in Figure A.4.

Official IFTA CFTe, STA Diploma (UK), and MTA CMT Exam Reading Lists

Below are the official reading lists for the following examinations in financial technical analysis:

- IFTA CFTe Levels I and II
- MTA CMT Levels I, II, and III
- STA Diploma I and II Exam (UK)

For the latest recommended reading list and chapter reading requirement, please visit the official websites. Please note that for all the books listed below, refer to the current or latest versions.

1. IFTA CFTE OFFICIAL READING LIST

CFTe Level I: Recommended Reading List

Technical Analysis of the Financial Markets, by John Murphy (New York Institute of Finance/Prentice Hall)

Technical Analysis Explained, by Martin Pring (McGraw-Hill)

Technical Analysis of Stock Trends, by Robert D. Edwards and John Magee (AMACOM)

CFTe Level II: Recommended Reading List

Technical Analysis of the Financial Markets, by John Murphy (New York Institute of Finance/Prentice Hall)

Candlestick Charts, by Clive Lambert (Harriman House Ltd)

Technical Analysis: The Complete Resource for Financial Market Technicians, by Charles Kirkpatrick and Julie Dahlquist (FT Press)

The Definitive Guide to Point and Figure, by Jeremy du Plessis (Harriman House Ltd)

Forecasting Financial Markets, by Tony Plummer (Kogan Page)

R.N. Elliott's Masterworks, by R. N. Elliott (New Classics Library)

Ichimoku Charts: An Introduction to Ichimoku Kinko Clouds, by Nicole Elliott (Harriman House Ltd)

Cloud Charts: Trading Success with the Ichimoku Technique, by David Linton (Updata Plc)

2. STA (UK) DIPLOMA EXAM OFFICIAL READING LIST

Recommended / Core Reading List

Technical Analysis of the Financial Markets, by John Murphy (New York Institute of Finance/Prentice Hall)

Technical Analysis Explained, by Martin Pring (McGraw-Hill)

Technical Analysis: The Complete Resource for Financial Market Technicians, by Charles Kirkpatrick and Julie Dahlquist (FT Press)

Japanese Candlestick Charting Techniques, by Steve Nison (New York Institute of Finance)

Candlestick Charts, by Clive Lambert (Harriman House Ltd)

The Definitive Guide to Point and Figure, by Jeremy du Plessis (Harriman House Ltd)

Forecasting Financial Markets, by Tony Plummer (Kogan Page)

R.N. Elliott's Masterworks, by R. N. Elliott (New Classics Library)

Ichimoku Charts: An Introduction to Ichimoku Kinko Clouds, by Nicole Elliott (Harriman House Ltd)

Cloud Charts: Trading Success with the Ichimoku Technique, by David Linton (Updata Plc)

Breakthroughs in Technical Analysis, by David Keller (Bloomberg Financial)

Mastering Hurst Cycle Analysis, by Christopher Grafton (Harriman House Ltd)

Additional Reading

Trader Vic: Methods of a Wall Street Master, by Victor Sperandeo (John Wiley & Sons)

Against the Gods—The Remarkable Story of Risk, by Peter Bernstein (John Wiley & Sons)

Hedge Fund Market Wizards, by Jack Schwager and Ed Seykota (John Wiley & Sons)

3. MTA CMT OFFICIAL READING LIST

Note: At every level of the CMT examination, the candidates will be tested on the MTA Code of Ethics, which may be found at the MTA official website.

CMT Level I: Recommended Reading List

Technical Analysis of Stock Trends, by Robert D. Edwards and John Magee (AMACOM)

Technical Analysis Explained, by Martin Pring (McGraw-Hill)

Technical Analysis: The Complete Resource for Financial Market Technicians, by Charles Kirkpatrick and Julie Dahlquist (FT Press)

The Definitive Guide to Point and Figure, by Jeremy du Plessis (Harriman House Ltd)

CMT Level II: Recommended Reading List

Technical Analysis of Stock Trends, by Robert D. Edwards and John Magee (AMACOM)

Technical Analysis Explained, by Martin Pring (McGraw-Hill)

Technical Analysis: The Complete Resource for Financial Market Technicians, by Charles Kirkpatrick and Julie Dahlquist (FT Press)

Japanese Candlestick Charting Techniques, by Steve Nison (New York Institute of Finance)

The Definitive Guide to Point and Figure, by Jeremy du Plessis (Harriman House Ltd)

New Trading Systems and Methods, by Perry Kaufman (John Wiley & Sons)

Investment Psychology Explained, by Martin Pring (John Wiley & Sons)

Technically Speaking, by Chris Wilkinson (Traders Press Inc)

Evidence-Based Technical Analysis, by David Aronson (John Wiley & Sons)

CMT Level III: Recommended Reading List

Technical Analysis for the Trading Professional, by Constance Brown (McGraw-Hill)

The Definitive Guide to Point and Figure, by Jeremy du Plessis (Harriman House Ltd)

Behavioral Investing: A Practitioners Guide to Applying Behavioral Finance, by James Montier (John Wiley & Sons)

Elliott Wave Principle, by A. J. Frost and Robert Prechter (New Classics Library)

Trading with Intermarket Analysis: A Visual Approach to Beating the Financial Markets Using Exchange Traded Funds, by John Murphy (John Wiley & Sons)

Japanese Candlestick Charting Techniques, by Steve Nison (New York Institute of Finance)

About the Test Bank and Website

This book also includes access to ancillary materials. Visit www.wiley.com/go/wileytestsgetaccess to register your product and receive a code to access the following resources:

- An online test bank based on the topics outlined in the official syllabuses for both the MTA and IFTA professional examinations
- Answers to the end-of-chapter questions in the book
- Excel spreadsheets that help illustrate the mathematics underlying various technical and money management concepts within the handbook
- Updated charts
- Additional content on new topics added to the exams

Updated charts, Excel spreadsheets, and additional study material based on changes in the examination syllabus may be added to the website from time to time.

If you purchased the e-book, please go to www.wiley.com/go/wileytestsgetaccess and verify your purchase to obtain an access PIN.

Index